P9-DHQ-260

Frommer's®

Arizona

My Arizona

by Karl Samson

THINK ARIZONA AND THE GRAND CANYON IMMEDIATELY COMES TO MIND.

But there is more to this state than a breathtaking rent in the fabric of the earth's crust. Explore beyond the Grand Canyon and you'll discover countless otherworldly landscapes—the red rocks of Sedona, a massive meteorite crater, the sandstone "mittens" of Monument Valley, a natural bridge that resembles a rainbow turned to stone, Lake Powell's curious mix of water and cliff walls, and, perhaps strangest of all, the verdant golf courses of Phoenix and Tucson, surrounded by desert.

While many visitors rush through the state stopping only briefly at the highlights, my favorite Arizona experiences arise when I slow down and find an unconventional way to enjoy the scenery: Drifting over the desert in a hot-air balloon. Buzzing Sedona's Snoopy Rock in a bright-red biplane. Riding the range where John Wayne once rode into the sunset. Anchoring a houseboat on a remote Lake Powell beach. Rumbling down a natural red-rock staircase in a pink Jeep. Gazing into the depths of the Grand Canyon with the ears of a sure-footed mule to frame the view. Just remember: When you stop to smell the flowers in Arizona, watch out for cactus spines.

© Mitch Diamond/Alamy

© Dewitt Jones/Getty Images

Although astonishing views await everywhere you look in Sedona, few compare with the sight of **CATHEDRAL ROCK (left)** rising above the waters of Oak Creek at Coconino National Forest's Crescent Moon Recreation Area. Head out here at sunset (perhaps with a picnic dinner) to catch Cathedral Rock in the best light.

I'm a slow-lane kind of guy, and one of my favorite ways to experience the Arizona desert is from a **HOT-AIR BALLOON (above)** drifting above the cactus and mesquite. Phoenix is the state's hot spot for ballooning, with numerous companies offering rides, but Sedona is by far the most picturesque place to drift with the breezes.

First page: © Siegfried Tauqueur/eStock Photo

© Ginny Santora/Alamy

On one end of the spectrum, you've got the Grand Canyon. At the other end are Arizona's narrow slot canyons, some of which are barely wide enough to walk through. **ANTELOPE CANYON (left)**, outside Page, is the most accessible slot canyon, a photographer's dream come true.

Plan your trip through Northern Arizona so that you can be in **MONUMENT VALLEY (below)** at sunrise or sunset, and be sure to bring your camera.

© Wojtek Buss/AGE Fotostock

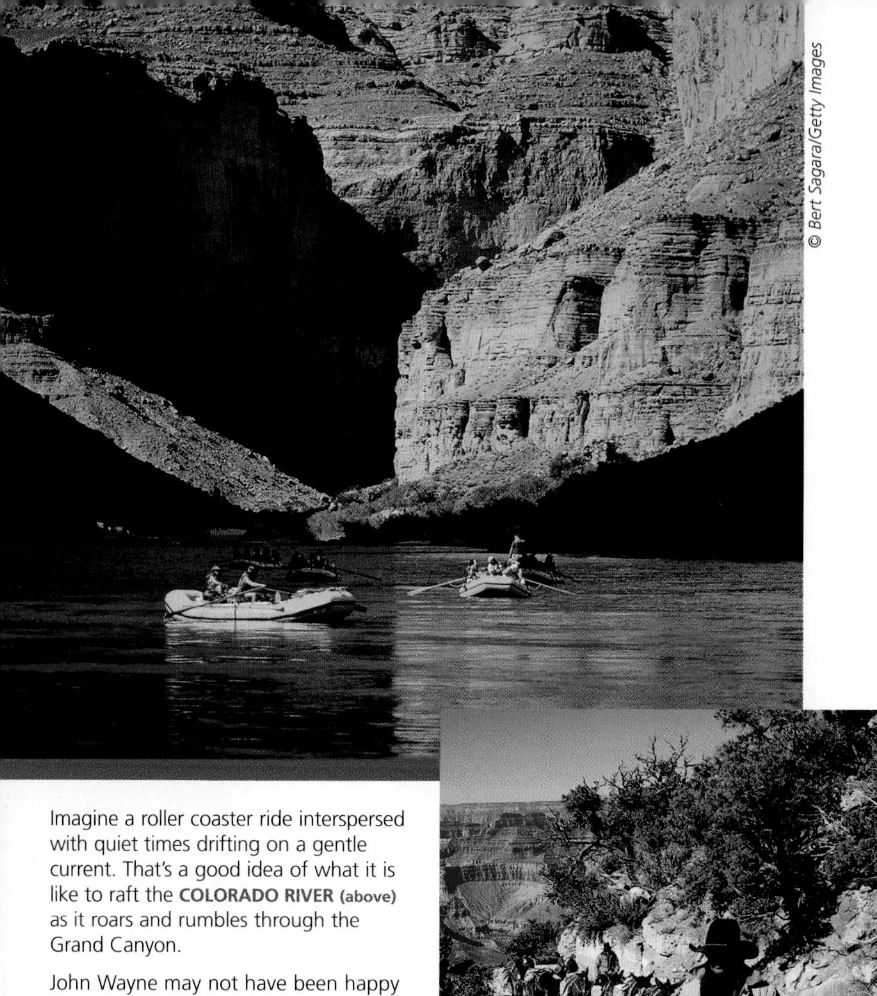

© Bert Sagara/Getty Images

Imagine a roller coaster ride interspersed with quiet times drifting on a gentle current. That's a good idea of what it is like to raft the **COLORADO RIVER (above)** as it roars and rumbles through the Grand Canyon.

John Wayne may not have been happy **RIDING A MULE (right)**, but these sure-footed beasts are a great way to explore the Grand Canyon without getting wet or working up a sweat. You can ride to the bottom of the canyon and overnight at Phantom Ranch, where all the supplies are brought in by pack trains such as this one.

© Doug Scott/AGE Fotostock

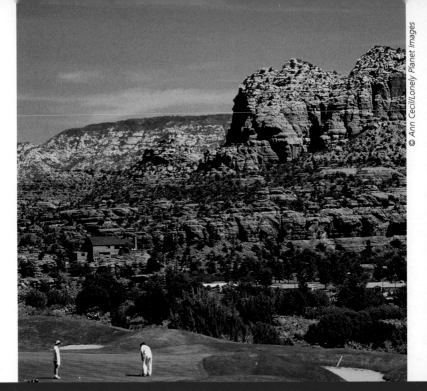

© Ann Cecil/Lonely Planet Images

Want to find out how well you handle distractions during your golf game? Book a tee time at a **SEDONA GOLF COURSE (above)**. I guarantee that the red-rock vistas will have an impact on your handicap. You'll find golf courses with breathtaking scenery all over Arizona.

Misbehaving children aren't the only ones who need a time out; sometimes adults do, too. That's why **SPAS (right)** were invented, and Arizona has plenty of them. A massage, a facial, a wrap. Ahhh!

© Chris Sanders/Getty Images

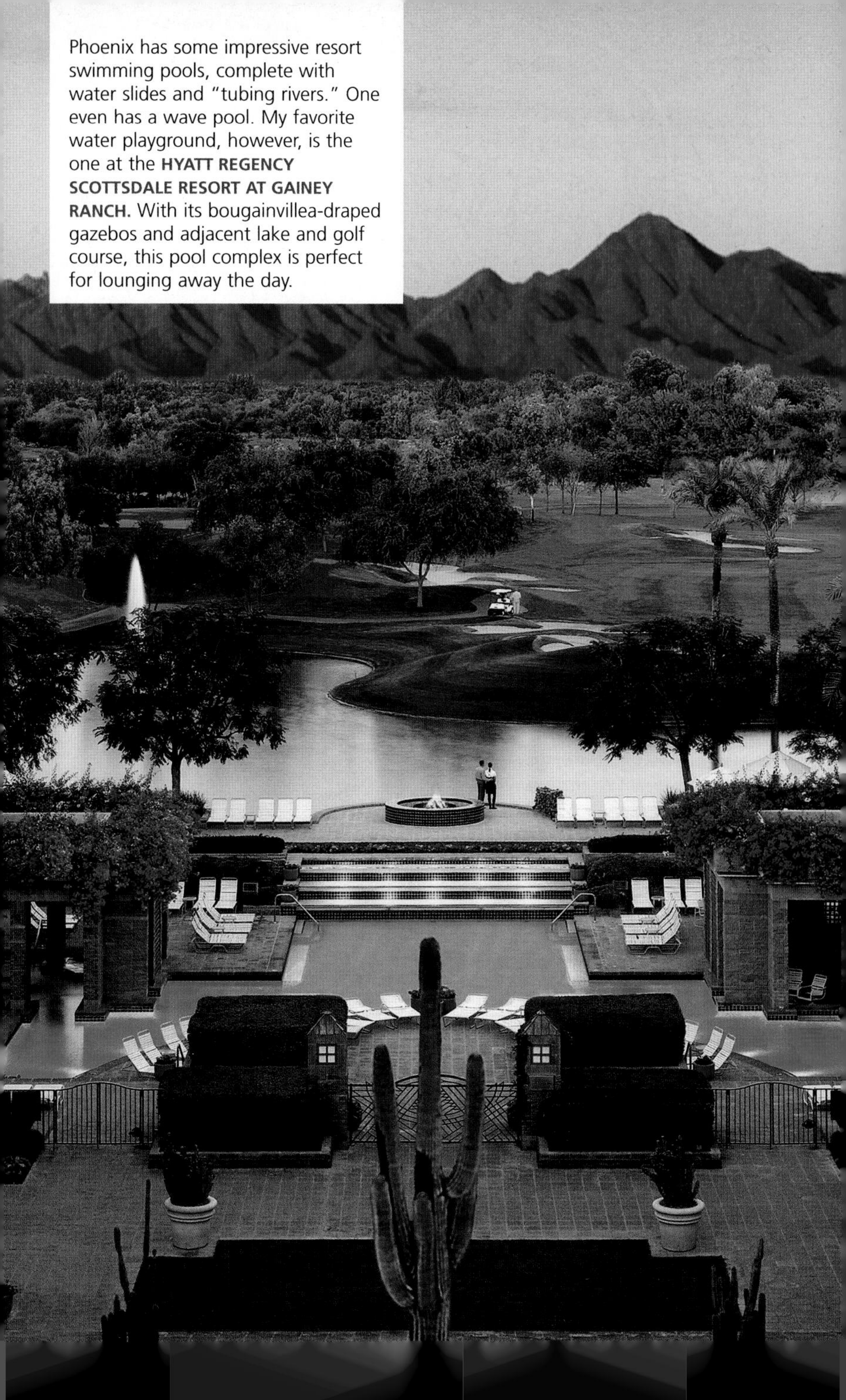

Phoenix has some impressive resort swimming pools, complete with water slides and "tubing rivers." One even has a wave pool. My favorite water playground, however, is the one at the **HYATT REGENCY SCOTTSDALE RESORT AT GAINEY RANCH.** With its bougainvillea-draped gazebos and adjacent lake and golf course, this pool complex is perfect for lounging away the day.

© T. Allofs/Masterfile

I wouldn't dream of driving through Kingman without stopping at **MR. D'Z (above)** for a cheeseburger and fries. This burger joint is right on the legendary Route 66 and conjures up the days of hot rods and sock hops.

TOMBSTONE (right) is Arizona's capital of kitsch, with faux cowboys and saloon girls on every corner, but this really is where Wyatt Earp and Doc Holiday shot their way into Wild West mythology. On the edge of town at Boot Hill Cemetery, wooden headstones serve as touristy reminders of the many cowboys and outlaws who met untimely deaths in the hometown of the OK Corral.

© Richard Cummins/Lonely Planet Images

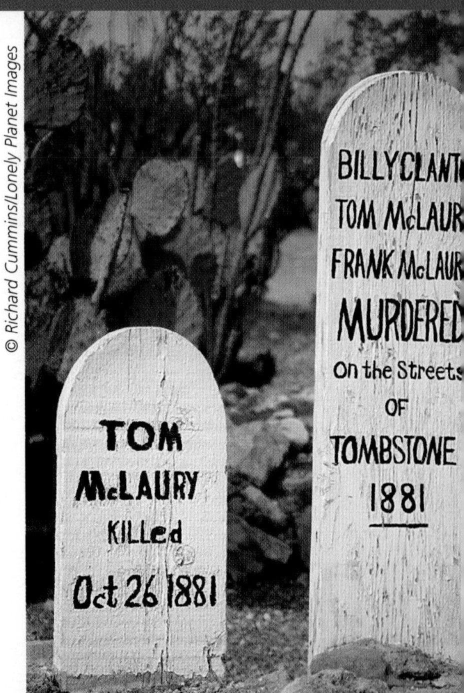

Ask a kid to draw a picture of a cactus, and you'll probably get a reasonable facsimile of a **SAGUARO (right)**. Along with cowboys and Indians, these giants of the desert, with their massive upraised arms, are the quintessential icons of Arizona.

Cacti of the Sonoran Desert are not just prickly plants that lie in wait to impale unwary hikers. They also provide food and shelter to many of the desert's wild residents. **GILA WOODPECKERS (below)** build their nests inside saguaro cacti, and often the nests are used by other bird species after the woodpeckers have moved on.

© Jeff Greenberg/eStock Photo

© John Canoalosi/AGE Fotostock

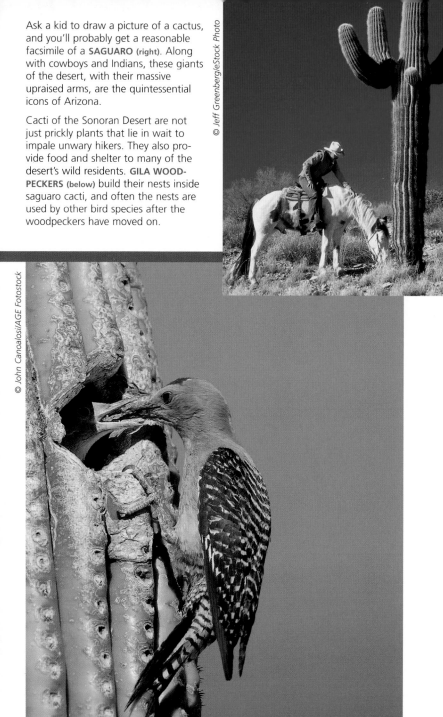

Phoenix, Scottsdale & the Valley of the Sun

- Biltmore District **11**
- Black Canyon Freeway **3**
- Central Avenue **4**
- Downtown Phoenix **7**
- Grand Avenue **2**
- Hohokam Expressway **15**
- Maricopa Freeway **6**
- Mill Avenue, Tempe **16**
- Papago Freeway **5**
- Paradise Valley **10**
- Pima Freeway **8**
- Red Mountain Freeway **13**
- Old Town Scottsdale **17**
- Piestewa Parkway **12**
- Scottsdale Road **9**
- Sky Harbor Airport **14**
- Superstition Freeway **18**
- Turf Paradise Racetrack **1**

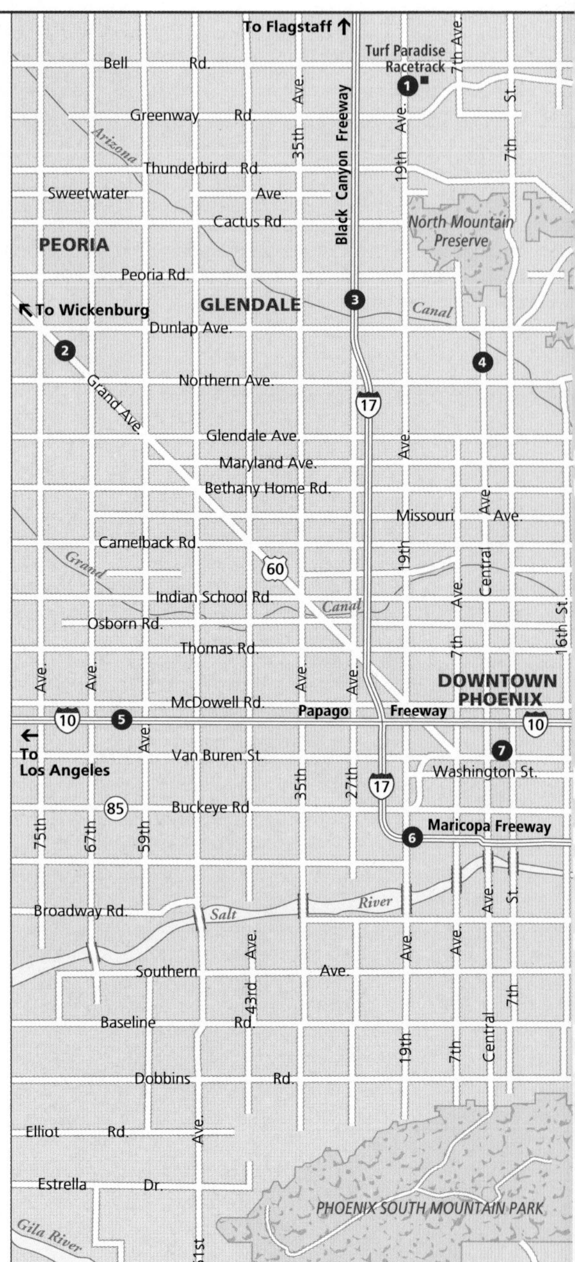

ARIZONA
Phoenix
0
3 mi
0
3 km
N
PARADISE VALLEY
SCOTTSDALE
TEMPE
MESA
Sky Harbor International Airport
Dreamy Draw Park
Phoenix Mountains Preserve
Piestewa Peak Park
Camelback Mountain/ Echo Canyon Recreation Area
Papago Park
Salt River
Bell Rd.
Frank Lloyd Wright Blvd.
Greenway Rd.
Thunderbird Rd.
Sweetwater Ave.
Cactus Rd.
Shea Blvd.
Doubletree Ranch Rd.
Indian Bend Rd.
Lincoln Dr.
McDonald Dr.
Camelback Rd.
Indian School Rd.
Osborn Rd.
Thomas Rd.
McDowell Rd.
Van Buren St.
McKellips Rd.
University Dr.
Apache Blvd.
Main St.
Broadway Rd.
Southern Ave.
Baseline Rd.
Guadalupe Rd.
Elliot Rd.
Warner Rd.
Ray Rd.
Cave Creek Rd.
Piestewa Pkwy.
Tatum Rd.
Invergordon Rd.
Scottsdale Rd.
Hayden Rd.
Pima Rd.
Pima Freeway
96th St.
104th St.
24th St.
32nd St.
40th St.
44th St.
48th St.
52nd St.
56th St.
64th St.
68th St.
Miller Rd.
Red Mountain Freeway
Hohokam Expy.
Priest Dr.
Mill Ave.
Dobson Rd.
Alma School Rd.
Country Club Dr.
Mesa Dr.
Stapley Dr.
Arizona Ave.
McQueen Rd.
Cooper Rd.
Gilbert Rd.
Rural Rd.
McClintock Dr.
Price Rd.
Pirice Freeway
Maricopa Freeway
Superstition Freeway
Beeline Hwy.
To Payson
To Tucson
101
51
202
143
10
87
60
8
9
10
11
12
13
14
15
16
17
18

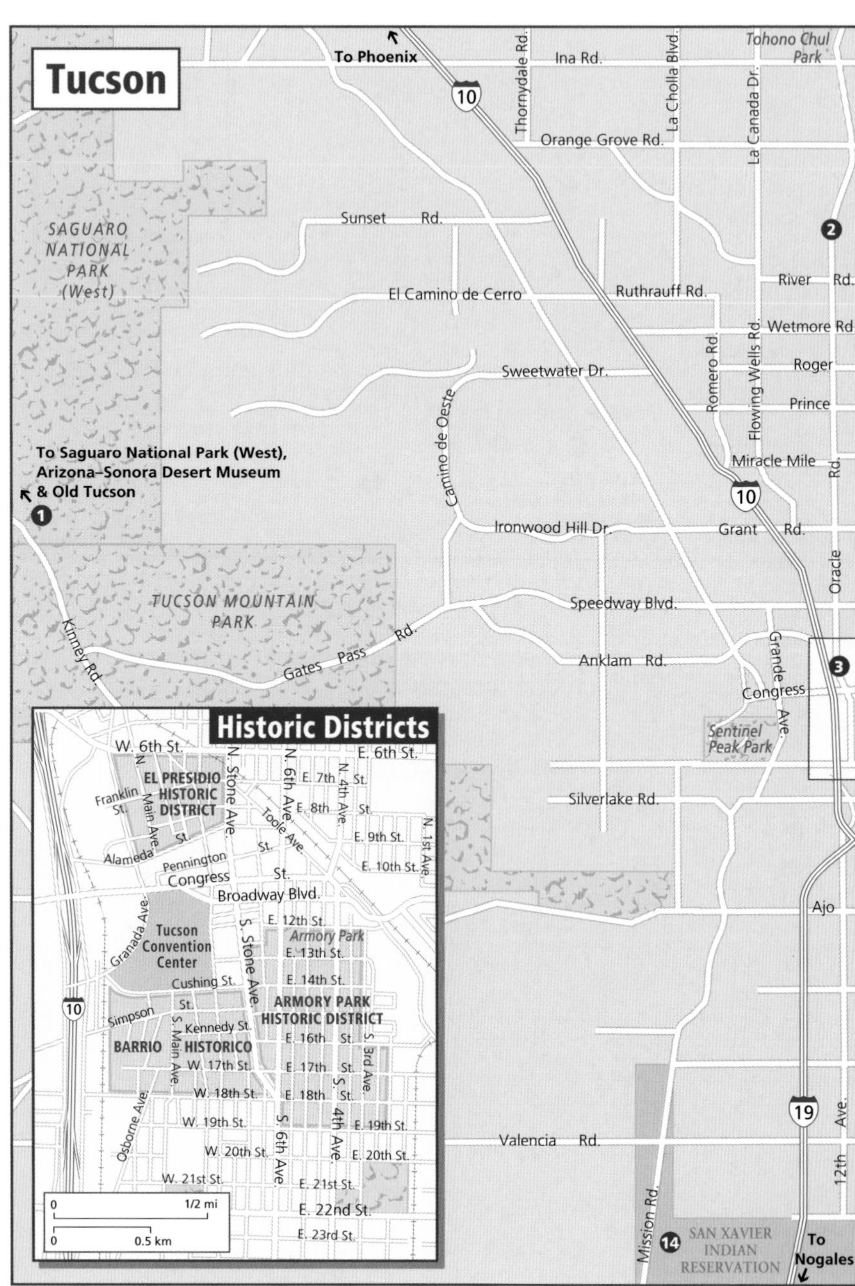

Tucson
To Phoenix
Ina Rd.
Thornydale Rd.
La Cholla Blvd.
Tohono Chul Park
La Canada Dr.
Orange Grove Rd.
10
Sunset Rd.
SAGUARO NATIONAL PARK (West)
River Rd.
El Camino de Cerro
Ruthrauff Rd.
Wetmore Rd.
Sweetwater Dr.
Romero Rd.
Flowing Wells Rd.
Roger
Prince
Camino de Oeste
Miracle Mile
To Saguaro National Park (West), Arizona–Sonora Desert Museum & Old Tucson
Ironwood Hill Dr.
Grant Rd.
Oracle Rd.
TUCSON MOUNTAIN PARK
Speedway Blvd.
Kinney Rd.
Gates Pass Rd.
Anklam Rd.
Grande Ave.
Congress
Sentinel Peak Park
Silverlake Rd.
Ajo
Valencia Rd.
19
12th Ave.
Mission Rd.
SAN XAVIER INDIAN RESERVATION
To Nogales
Historic Districts
W. 6th St.
E. 6th St.
N. Stone Ave.
N. 6th Ave.
N. 4th Ave.
EL PRESIDIO HISTORIC DISTRICT
E. 7th St.
Franklin St.
N. Main Ave.
E. 8th St.
Toole Ave.
E. 9th St.
N. 1st Ave.
Alameda St.
Pennington St.
E. 10th St.
Congress St.
Broadway Blvd.
E. 12th St.
Granada Ave.
Tucson Convention Center
S. Stone Ave.
Armory Park
E. 13th St.
Cushing St.
E. 14th St.
ARMORY PARK HISTORIC DISTRICT
Simpson St.
Kennedy St.
S. Main Ave.
BARRIO HISTORICO
E. 16th St.
S. 3rd Ave.
W. 17th St.
E. 17th St.
W. 18th St.
E. 18th St.
S. 4th Ave.
Osborne Ave.
W. 19th St.
S. 6th Ave.
E. 19th St.
W. 20th St.
E. 20th St.
W. 21st St.
E. 21st St.
E. 22nd St.
E. 23rd St.
0 1/2 mi
0 0.5 km

Ina Rd.
Orange Grove Rd.
Skyline Dr.
Kolb Rd.
Sabino Canyon Rd.
SABINO CANYON PARK
Sunrise Dr.
Hacienda del Sol Rd.
Swan Rd.
Craycroft Rd.
Snyder Rd.
Canyon Rd.
Rd.
Rd.
River Rd.
To Mount Lemmon
Stone Ave.
Euclid Ave.
Campbell Ave.
Tucson Blvd.
Ft. Lowell Rd.
Ft. Lowell Park
Bear
Catalina Hwy.
Tanque Verde Rd.
Country Club Rd.
Alvernon Way
Grant Rd.
See inset map for Historic Districts
Speedway Blvd.
6th St.
5th St.
Broadway Blvd.
Randolph Park
Reid Park
Wilmot Rd.
To Saguaro National Park (East)
22nd St.
210
Tucson Greyhound Park
36th St.
Golf Links Rd.
Pantano Rd.
Way
DAVIS MONTHAN AFB
Escalante Rd.
Irvington Rd.
Kino Blvd.
10
Drexel Rd.
Palo Verde Rd.
ARIZONA
Phoenix
Tucson
6th Ave.
Valencia Rd.
TUCSON INTERNATIONAL AIRPORT
0 2 mi
0 2 km
N
Broadway Blvd. 7
Campbell Ave. 6
Country Club Rd. 11
El Presidio Historic District 3
Grant Rd. 8
Mission San Xavier del Bac 14
Oracle Rd. 2
Saguaro National Park 1, 10
Speedway Blvd. 5, 9
Tucson Convention Center 4
Tucson Electric Park 12
Tucson International Airport 13

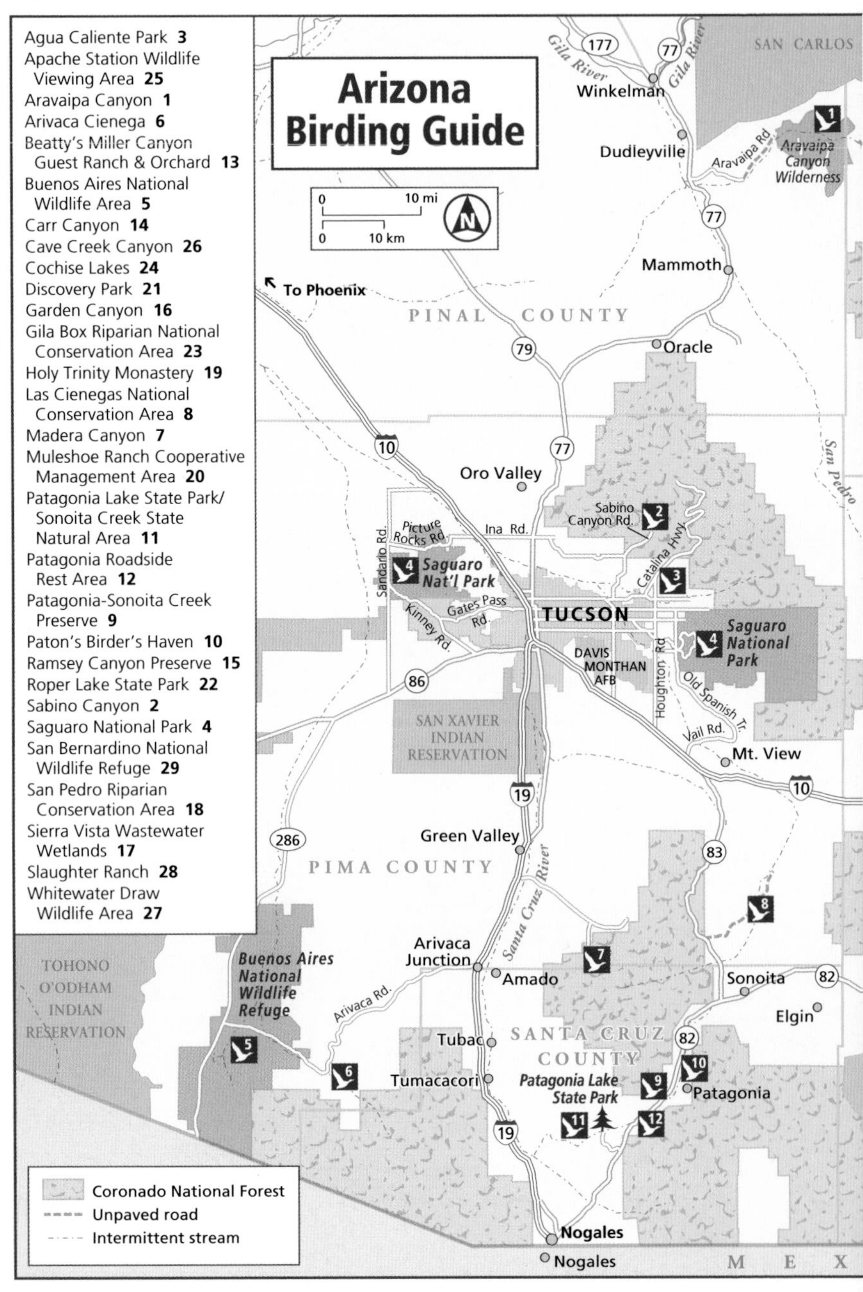

Arizona Birding Guide
Agua Caliente Park 3
Apache Station Wildlife Viewing Area 25
Aravaipa Canyon 1
Arivaca Cienega 6
Beatty's Miller Canyon Guest Ranch & Orchard 13
Buenos Aires National Wildlife Area 5
Carr Canyon 14
Cave Creek Canyon 26
Cochise Lakes 24
Discovery Park 21
Garden Canyon 16
Gila Box Riparian National Conservation Area 23
Holy Trinity Monastery 19
Las Cienegas National Conservation Area 8
Madera Canyon 7
Muleshoe Ranch Cooperative Management Area 20
Patagonia Lake State Park/ Sonoita Creek State Natural Area 11
Patagonia Roadside Rest Area 12
Patagonia-Sonoita Creek Preserve 9
Paton's Birder's Haven 10
Ramsey Canyon Preserve 15
Roper Lake State Park 22
Sabino Canyon 2
Saguaro National Park 4
San Bernardino National Wildlife Refuge 29
San Pedro Riparian Conservation Area 18
Sierra Vista Wastewater Wetlands 17
Slaughter Ranch 28
Whitewater Draw Wildlife Area 27
0 10 mi
0 10 km
N
To Phoenix
Gila River
177
77
Winkelman
SAN CARLOS
Dudleyville
Aravaipa Rd
Aravaipa Canyon Wilderness
Mammoth
PINAL COUNTY
79
Oracle
10
77
Oro Valley
San Pedro
Sabino Canyon Rd.
Picture Rocks Rd.
Ina Rd.
Sandario Rd.
Catalina Hwy.
Saguaro Nat'l Park
Gates Pass Rd.
Kinney Rd.
TUCSON
DAVIS MONTHAN AFB
Houghton Rd
Saguaro National Park
Old Spanish Tr.
86
SAN XAVIER INDIAN RESERVATION
Vail Rd.
Mt. View
10
19
Green Valley
286
PIMA COUNTY
Santa Cruz River
83
Arivaca Junction
Amado
TOHONO O'ODHAM INDIAN RESERVATION
Buenos Aires National Wildlife Refuge
Arivaca Rd.
Sonoita
82
Elgin
Tubac
SANTA CRUZ COUNTY
82
Tumacacori
Patagonia Lake State Park
Patagonia
19
Coronado National Forest
Unpaved road
Intermittent stream
Nogales
Nogales
MEX

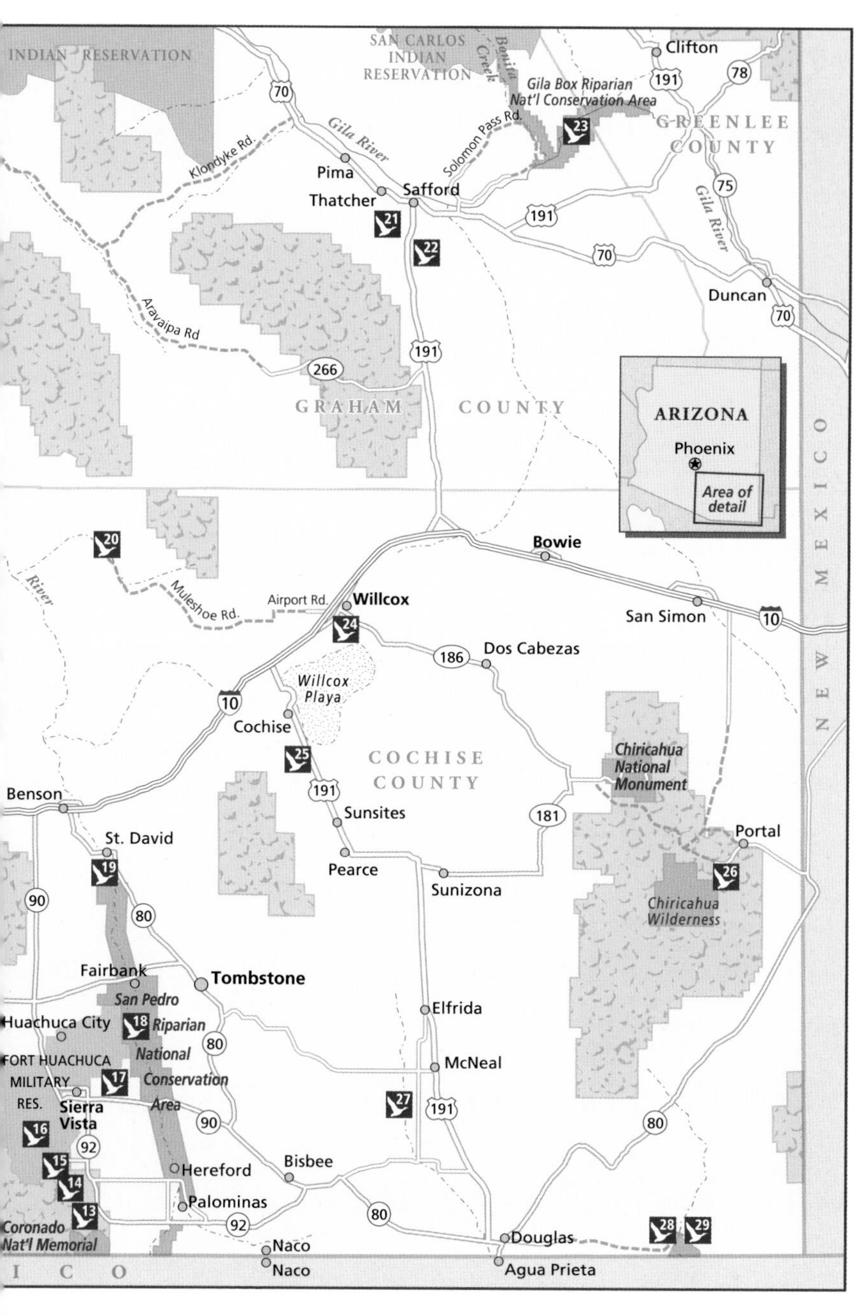

INDIAN RESERVATION
SAN CARLOS INDIAN RESERVATION
Bonita Creek
Clifton
Gila Box Riparian Nat'l Conservation Area
GREENLEE COUNTY
Klondyke Rd.
Gila River
Solomon Pass Rd.
Pima
Thatcher
Safford
Aravaipa Rd
Duncan
GRAHAM COUNTY
ARIZONA
Phoenix
Area of detail
NEW MEXICO
Bowie
River
Muleshoe Rd.
Airport Rd.
Willcox
San Simon
Dos Cabezas
Willcox Playa
Cochise
COCHISE COUNTY
Chiricahua National Monument
Benson
Sunsites
St. David
Pearce
Sunizona
Portal
Chiricahua Wilderness
Fairbank
Tombstone
San Pedro Riparian National Conservation Area
Huachuca City
Elfrida
FORT HUACHUCA MILITARY RES.
McNeal
Sierra Vista
Hereford
Bisbee
Palominas
Coronado Nat'l Memorial
Douglas
Naco
Naco
Agua Prieta
ICO

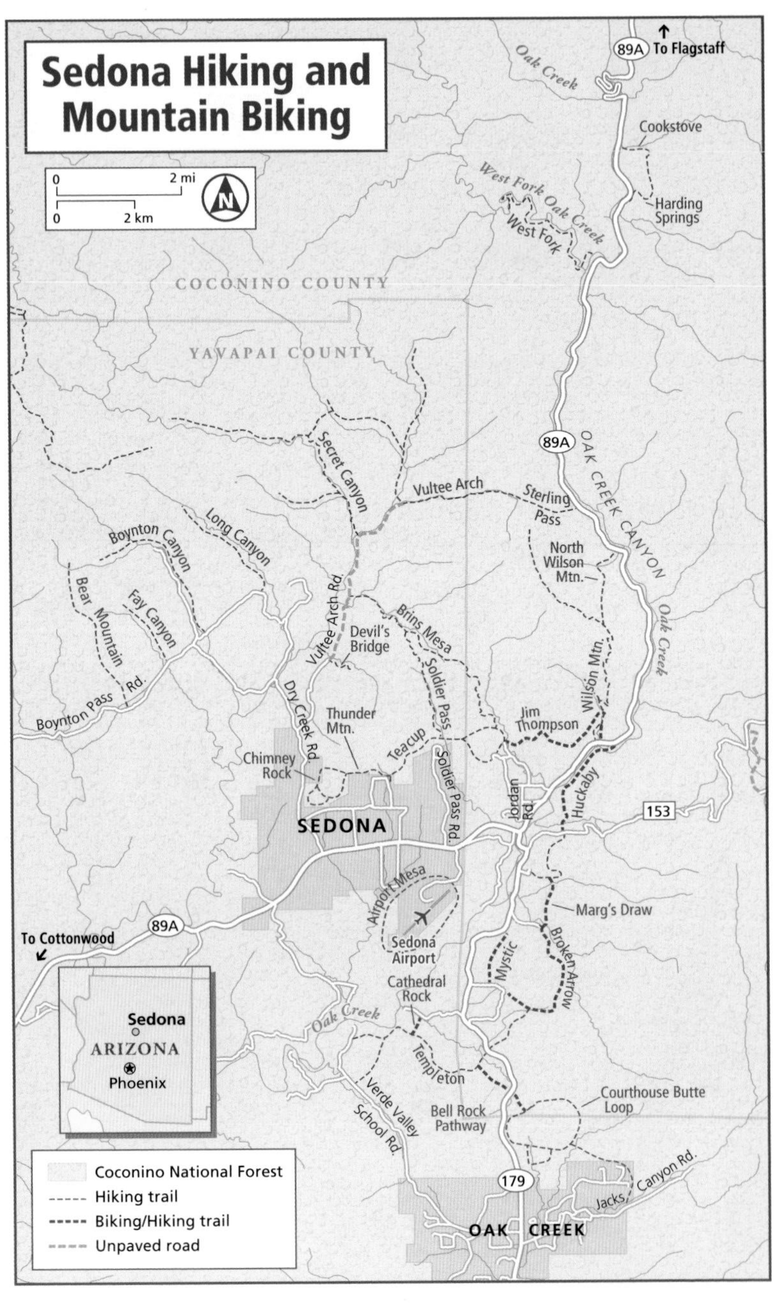

Sedona Hiking and Mountain Biking
0
2 mi
0
2 km
N
89A
To Flagstaff
Oak Creek
Cookstove
Harding Springs
West Fork Oak Creek
West Fork
COCONINO COUNTY
YAVAPAI COUNTY
89A
OAK CREEK CANYON
Oak Creek
Secret Canyon
Vultee Arch
Sterling Pass
North Wilson Mtn.
Long Canyon
Boynton Canyon
Bear Mountain
Fay Canyon
Boynton Pass Rd.
Vultee Arch Rd.
Devil's Bridge
Brins Mesa
Soldier Pass
Wilson Mtn.
Dry Creek Rd.
Thunder Mtn.
Jim Thompson
Chimney Rock
Teacup
Soldier Pass Rd.
Jordan Rd.
Huckaby
153
SEDONA
Airport Mesa
Marg's Draw
Sedona Airport
Mystic
Broken Arrow
89A
To Cottonwood
Sedona
ARIZONA
Phoenix
Cathedral Rock
Oak Creek
Templeton
Verde Valley School Rd.
Bell Rock Pathway
Courthouse Butte Loop
179
Jacks Canyon Rd.
OAK CREEK
Coconino National Forest
Hiking trail
Biking/Hiking trail
Unpaved road

Frommer's®

Arizona

2008

by Karl Samson

Here's what the critics say about Frommer's:

"Amazingly easy to use. Very portable, very complete."

—*Booklist*

"Detailed, accurate, and easy-to-read information for all price ranges."

—*Glamour Magazine*

"Hotel information is close to encyclopedic."

—*Des Moines Sunday Register*

"Frommer's Guides have a way of giving you a real feel for a place."

—*Knight Ridder Newspapers*

Wiley Publishing, Inc.

About the Author

Karl Samson lives in Oregon, where he spends his time juggling his obsessions with traveling, gardening, outdoor sports, and wine. Each winter, to dry out his webbed feet, he flees the soggy Northwest to update the *Frommer's Arizona* guide. Karl is also the author of *Frommer's Seattle* and *Frommer's Washington State.*

Published by:

Wiley Publishing, Inc.

111 River St.
Hoboken, NJ 07030-5774

Copyright © 2008 Wiley Publishing, Inc., Hoboken, New Jersey. All rights reserved. No part of this publication may be reproduced, stored in a retrieval system or transmitted in any form or by any means, electronic, mechanical, photocopying, recording, scanning or otherwise, except as permitted under Sections 107 or 108 of the 1976 United States Copyright Act, without either the prior written permission of the Publisher, or authorization through payment of the appropriate per-copy fee to the Copyright Clearance Center, 222 Rosewood Drive, Danvers, MA 01923, 978/750-8400, fax 978/646-8600. Requests to the Publisher for permission should be addressed to the Legal Department, Wiley Publishing, Inc., 10475 Crosspoint Blvd., Indianapolis, IN 46256, 317/572-3447, fax 317/572-4355, or online at http://www.wiley.com/go/permissions.

Wiley and the Wiley Publishing logo are trademarks or registered trademarks of John Wiley & Sons, Inc. and/or its affiliates. Frommer's is a trademark or registered trademark of Arthur Frommer. Used under license. All other trademarks are the property of their respective owners. Wiley Publishing, Inc. is not associated with any product or vendor mentioned in this book.

ISBN: 978-0-470-14570-8

Editor: Anuja Madar
Production Editor: M. Faunette Johnston
Cartographer: Andrew Murphy
Photo Editor: Richard Fox
Anniversary Logo Design: Richard Pacifico
Production by Wiley Indianapolis Composition Services

Front cover photo: Grand Canyon at sunset
Back cover photo: Pygmy Owl at home in saguaro cactus

For information on our other products and services or to obtain technical support, please contact our Customer Care Department within the U.S. at 800/762-2974, outside the U.S. at 317/572-3993 or fax 317/572-4002.

Wiley also publishes its books in a variety of electronic formats. Some content that appears in print may not be available in electronic formats.

Manufactured in the United States of America

5 4 3 2 1

Contents

List of Maps vi

What's New in Arizona 1

1 The Best of Arizona 5

1 The Best Places to Commune with Cactus 5
2 The Best Active Vacations 8
3 The Best Day Hikes & Nature Walks 8
4 The Best Scenic Drives 10
5 The Best Golf Courses 10
6 The Best Bird-Watching Spots 11
7 The Best Offbeat Travel Experiences 12
8 The Best Family Experiences 12
9 The Best Family Vacations 13
10 The Best Museums 13
11 The Best Places to Discover the Old West 14
12 The Best Places to See Indian Ruins 15
13 The Best Luxury Hotels & Resorts . . . 15
14 The Best Family Resorts 16
15 The Best Hotels for Old Arizona Character 17
16 The Best Bed & Breakfasts 18
17 The Best Swimming Pools 19
18 The Best Places to Savor Southwest Flavors 19

2 Planning Your Trip to Arizona 21

1 The Regions in Brief 21
2 Visitor Information & Maps 22
3 Entry Requirements 23
4 When to Go 24
Arizona Calendar of Events 25
5 Getting There 29
Getting Through the Airport 31
6 General Travel Resources 34
What Things Cost in Arizona 35
7 Specialized Travel Resources 39
8 Sustainable Tourism/Ecotourism 42
Frommers.com: The Complete Travel Resource 43
9 Staying Connected 44
Online Traveler's Toolbox 45
10 Packages for the Independent Traveler 45
Ask Before You Go 46
11 Escorted General-Interest Tours 46
12 Special-Interest Trips 47
13 The Active Vacation Planner 48
Hot Links 50
14 Getting Around Arizona 55
15 Tips on Accommodations 56
Fast Facts: Arizona 58

3 Suggested Arizona Itineraries 64

1 Arizona in 1 Week 64
2 Arizona in 2 Weeks 67
3 Arizona for Families 69
4 A Sojourn in Southeastern Arizona 70
5 Native Trails of Arizona 71
6 Arizona in the Winter 74

4 Phoenix, Scottsdale & the Valley of the Sun 76

1 Orientation .77
Neighborhoods in Brief 79
2 Getting Around 83
Fast Facts: Phoenix 84
3 Where to Stay 85
4 Where to Dine 102
5 Seeing the Sights 121
6 Organized Tours & Excursions 135
7 Outdoor Pursuits 136
8 Spectator Sports 143
9 Spas 145
10 Shopping .147
11 Phoenix & Scottsdale After Dark . . .154
12 A Side Trip from Phoenix: The Apache Trail 162
13 En Route to Tucson 164
14 En Route to Northern Arizona 165

5 Central Arizona 166

1 Wickenburg 167
2 Prescott 172
3 Jerome 180
4 The Verde Valley 183
5 Sedona & Oak Creek Canyon 187
Vortex Power 190
The High Cost of Red-Rock Views 192

6 The Grand Canyon & Northern Arizona 212

1 The Grand Canyon South Rim 213
Fast Facts: The Grand Canyon 217
2 The Grand Canyon North Rim 239
3 Flagstaff 244
4 Williams 255
5 Havasu Canyon & Grand Canyon West 258
6 Kingman .262
Get Your Kicks on Route 66 264

7 The Four Corners Region: Land of the Hopi & Navajo 268

1 Winslow 271
2 The Hopi Reservation 273
A Native American Crafts Primer . . .278
3 The Petrified Forest & Painted Desert 280
4 The Window Rock & Ganado Areas 284
5 Canyon de Chelly National Monument 287
Fred Harvey & His Girls 290

6 Navajo National Monument 292
7 Monument Valley Navajo Tribal Park 293
8 Lake Powell & Page 298

8 Eastern Arizona's High Country 306

1 Payson & the Mogollon Rim Country 306
2 Pinetop-Lakeside 310
3 Greer & Sunrise Park 313
4 Springerville & Eagar 316
5 The Coronado Trail 318

9 Tucson 321

1 Orientation 322
Neighborhoods in Brief 326
2 Getting Around 327
Fast Facts: Tucson 328
3 Where to Stay 329
4 Where to Dine 342
5 Seeing the Sights 356
Walking Tour: Downtown Historic Districts 368
6 Organized Tours 373
7 Outdoor Pursuits 373
8 Spectator Sports 377
9 Spas 378
10 Shopping 379
11 Tucson After Dark 385

10 Southern Arizona 391

1 Organ Pipe Cactus National Monument 392
2 Tubac & Buenos Aires National Wildlife Refuge 394
Starry, Starry Nights 399
3 Nogales 400
4 Patagonia & Sonoita 402
5 Sierra Vista & the San Pedro Valley 407
6 Tombstone 414
7 Bisbee 417
8 Exploring the Rest of Cochise County 422

11 Arizona's "West Coast" 430

1 Lake Mead National Recreation Area 432
2 Bullhead City & Laughlin, Nevada 435
3 Lake Havasu & the London Bridge 437
Canoeing the Colorado 440
4 Yuma 445

Appendix: Arizona in Depth 451

1 Arizona Today 452
2 History 101 454

Index 459

List of Maps

Arizona 6
Suggested Arizona Itineraries 65
More Suggested Arizona Itineraries 73
Phoenix, Scottsdale & the Valley of the Sun 80
Phoenix, Scottsdale & the Valley of the Sun Accommodations 86
Phoenix, Scottsdale & the Valley of the Sun Dining 104
Phoenix, Scottsdale & the Valley of the Sun Attractions 122
Central Arizona 169
Sedona & Vicinity 189
The Grand Canyon & Northern Arizona 215
Grand Canyon South Rim 221
Flagstaff 247
The Four Corners Region 269
Eastern Arizona's High Country 307
Tucson at a Glance 324
Tucson Accommodations 330
Tucson Dining 344
Tucson Attractions 358
Walking Tour: Downtown Historic Districts 371
Southern Arizona 393
Western Arizona 431

An Invitation to the Reader

In researching this book, we discovered many wonderful places—hotels, restaurants, shops, and more. We're sure you'll find others. Please tell us about them so we can share the information with your fellow travelers in upcoming editions. If you were disappointed with a recommendation, we'd love to know that, too. Please write to:

Frommer's Arizona 2008

Wiley Publishing, Inc. • 111 River St. • Hoboken, NJ 07030-5774

An Additional Note

Please be advised that travel information is subject to change at any time—and this is especially true of prices. We therefore suggest that you write or call ahead for confirmation when making your travel plans. The authors, editors, and publisher cannot be held responsible for the experiences of readers while traveling. Your safety is important to us, however, so we encourage you to stay alert and be aware of your surroundings. Keep a close eye on cameras, purses, and wallets, all favorite targets of thieves and pickpockets.

Other Great Guides for Your Trip:

Arizona For Dummies

Frommer's American Southwest

Frommer's National Parks of the American West

Frommer's Portable Phoenix & Scottsdale

Frommer's Grand Canyon National Park

Frommer's Star Ratings, Icons & Abbreviations

Every hotel, restaurant, and attraction listing in this guide has been ranked for quality, value, service, amenities, and special features using a **star-rating system.** In country, state, and regional guides, we also rate towns and regions to help you narrow down your choices and budget your time accordingly. Hotels and restaurants are rated on a scale of zero (recommended) to three stars (exceptional). Attractions, shopping, nightlife, towns, and regions are rated according to the following scale: zero stars (recommended), one star (highly recommended), two stars (very highly recommended), and three stars (must-see).

In addition to the star-rating system, we also use **seven feature icons** that point you to the great deals, in-the-know advice, and unique experiences that separate travelers from tourists. Throughout the book, look for:

Finds	Special finds—those places only insiders know about
Fun Fact	Fun facts—details that make travelers more informed and their trips more fun
Kids	Best bets for kids, and advice for the whole family
Moments	Special moments—those experiences that memories are made of
Overrated	Places or experiences not worth your time or money
Tips	Insider tips—great ways to save time and money
Value	Great values—where to get the best deals

The following **abbreviations** are used for credit cards:

AE American Express	DISC Discover	V Visa
DC Diners Club	MC MasterCard	

Frommers.com

Now that you have this guidebook to help you plan a great trip, visit our website at **www.frommers.com** for additional travel information on more than 3,600 destinations. We update features regularly to give you instant access to the most current trip-planning information available. At Frommers.com, you'll find scoops on the best airfares, lodging rates, and car rental bargains. You can even book your travel online through our reliable travel booking partners. Other popular features include:

- Online updates of our most popular guidebooks
- Vacation sweepstakes and contest giveaways
- Newsletters highlighting the hottest travel trends
- Online travel message boards with featured travel discussions

What's New in Arizona

Every year I scour the state of Arizona to track down what's new and noteworthy. There are always great new hotels and restaurants to be discovered, new tour companies that have started up, and museums that have opened or expanded. Occasionally there are even new parks or other natural areas to be explored. Inevitably, I also discover that a few old favorite restaurants, shops, and such have gone out of business. Worse still, I sometimes find that places I once liked no longer make the grade and have to be taken out of this guide. Following are some of my discoveries for this edition of *Frommer's Arizona.*

GENERAL If you're planning a trip to Grand Canyon National Park and also intend to visit a few other national parks or monuments within the year, consider buying an **America The Beautiful–The National Parks and Federal Recreational Lands Annual Pass.** This pass replaces the former National Parks and Gold Eagle passes. There are also passes for seniors and the disabled. For more information, go to www.nps.gov/fees_passes.htm, or call ✆ **888/467-2757.**

PHOENIX, SCOTTSDALE & THE VALLEY OF THE SUN Downtown Scottsdale has a couple of new hip business hotels this year, so if you're in town for the city's nightlife, the **Hyatt Place Scottsdale Old Town,** 7300 E. Third Ave., Scottsdale (✆ **888/492-8847** or 480/423-9944; www.hyattplace.com), and the **Hotel Indigo,** 4415 N. Civic Center Plaza, Scottsdale (✆ **866/2-INDIGO** or 480/941-9400; scottsdalehiphotel.com), are both good bets. On the other hand, if you're looking for a deal on a hotel with a big pool, green lawns, and tall palms, check out the **Best Western Dobson Ranch Inn & Resort,** 1666 S. Dobson Rd., Mesa (✆ **800/528-1356** or 480/831-7000; www.dobsonranchinn.com).

If you're going to be in Phoenix for a special occasion and want to splurge on dinner, I can think of no better place than **Kai,** 5594 W. Wild Horse Pass Blvd., Chandler (✆ **602/225-0100;** www.wildhorsepassresort.com), which is at the Sheraton Wild Horse Pass Resort & Spa. The sophisticated Southwestern-inspired menu relies on ingredients sourced from Native American tribes around the country.

In the same part of the southeastern valley, you'll find much more economical, yet still memorable, meals at **Guedo's,** 71 E. Chandler Blvd., Chandler (✆ **480/899-7841**), a Mexican restaurant; and at **Joe's Farm Grill,** 3000 E. Ray Rd., Gilbert (✆ **480/563-4745;** www.joesfarmgrill.com), a retro roadside diner.

If you're one of those people for whom hot dogs and sausages are guilty pleasures, you won't want to miss **Ted's Hot Dogs,** 1755 E. Broadway, Tempe (✆ **480/968-6678**); or **Stanley's Homemade Polish Sausage Co.,** 2201 E. McDowell Rd., Phoenix (✆ **602/275-8788;** www.stanleys-sausage.com).

For the best flour tortillas in Phoenix, join the crowds standing in line at

Carolina's, 1202 E. Mohave St., Phoenix (✆ **602/252-1503;** www.carolinasmex.com), which is located south of Chase Field.

It's a long way from north Scottsdale to the celebrated Heard Museum in downtown Phoenix, but you can get a taste for the museum at the new **Heard Museum North,** 32633 N. Scottsdale Rd., Scottsdale (✆ **480/488-9817;** www.heard.org), which is located just south of Carefree's el Pedregal Shops & Dining at The Boulders. If you do go to the main Heard Museum, be sure to also visit the recently expanded **Phoenix Art Museum,** 1625 N. Central Ave., Phoenix (✆ **602/257-1222;** www.phxart.org).

With suburban sprawl stretching for miles in every direction, it has become harder and harder to find any real desert in the Phoenix metropolitan area. For easy desert hikes, head to north Scottsdale's **McDowell Sonoran Preserve** (✆ **480/998-7971;** www.mcdowellsonoran.org), a large natural area with limited public access. Alternatively, head east to the Superstition Mountains and hike to the petroglyphs at **Hieroglyphic Canyon.** For information on this hike, contact Tonto National Forest's Cave Creek Ranger District, 40202 N. Cave Creek Rd., Scottsdale (✆ **480/595-3300;** www.fs.fed.us/r3/tonto).

CENTRAL ARIZONA If you're looking for something to do after dark in Prescott, be sure to check the schedule at the **Raven Café,** 142 N. Cortez St. (✆ **928/717-0009**). This arty cafe has an astonishing beer list. At night, the Raven offers live-music performances and shows vintage movies one night a week.

If you're heading to Sedona from Phoenix, you might want to avoid taking **Arizona 179,** which is the direct route from I-17 to Sedona. This narrow, winding, two-lane highway is being widened and improved, and construction is expected to last into 2009. To avoid the construction zone, take Arizona 260 from Camp Verde to Cottonwood and then Arizona 89A from Cottonwood to Sedona. Once you're in Sedona, you can avoid the traffic congestion and parking problems by hopping on the **Sedona Roadrunner,** a free shuttle bus that runs between uptown Sedona, Tlaquepaque, and the Hillside Shops.

You'd think that having some of the most awesome scenery in the world would be enough for Sedona, but no, this town is suffering from a case of pinot envy. It wants red rocks *and* red wine. Over the past few years, wineries have been sprouting along the banks of Oak Creek in the nearby community of Page Springs. Here you'll find **Page Springs Vineyards & Cellars,** 1500 N. Page Springs Rd. (✆ **928/639-3004;** www.pagespringscellars.com); and **Oak Creek Vineyards and Winery,** Page Springs Road (✆ **928/649-0290;** www.oakcreekvineyards.net), both of which produce decent wines and have tasting rooms open to the public on a regular basis. If you'd like to visit **Echo Canyon Vineyard & Winery,** which isn't usually open to the public, book a wine tour with **Sun Country Adventures** (✆ **877/783-6000;** www.scadventures.net), which is affiliated with El Portal, my favorite Sedona lodge. If you're more interested in the Big Dipper than big reds, sign up for a stargazing tour with **Evening Sky Tours** (✆ **866/701-0398** or 928/203-0006; www.eveningskytours.com).

The Sedona landscape has long brought out the spiritual side of people, and the latest manifestation of red-rock spirituality is the **Amitabha Stupa** (✆ **928/300-4435;** www.stupas.org), a Tibetan Buddhist shrine that has been erected on a hillside in west Sedona.

Sedona is a tourist town, and as such has loads of restaurants serving mediocre food at inflated prices. You can escape the tourist mediocrity and eat with the locals at west Sedona's **Casa Bonita,** 164 Coffee Pot Dr., Suite H (✆ **928/282-2728**).

THE GRAND CANYON & NORTHERN ARIZONA At **Grand Canyon National Park** (✆ **928/638-7888;** www.nps.gov/grca), there are additional lanes at the south entrance to the park, so, hopefully, the summertime wait to get into the park won't be as long as it has sometimes been in the past. Also, **Bright Angel Lodge & Cabins** (✆ **888/297-2757** or 303/297-2757; www.xanterra.com or www.grandcanyonlodges.com), one of the park's two historic lodges, underwent an extensive renovation in 2007. The Bright Angel's rooms are now both a great value and quite comfortable.

For up-to-the-minute creative cuisine in Flagstaff, search out **Brix,** 413 N. San Francisco St. (✆ **928/213-1021;** www.brixflagstaff.com), which is inside an old carriage house. Hip and casual, **Karma Sushi Bar Tapas,** 6 E. Rte. 66 (✆ **928/774-6100**), right across the street from the Flagstaff Visitor Center, is a fun place for a light meal. For a glass of wine at sunset, it's hard to beat **Cuveé 928,** 6 E. Aspen Ave., Suite 110 (✆ **928/214-9463**), which is located right on Heritage Square in downtown Flagstaff.

The biggest news in the region is the Hualapai Indian Reservation's opening of the much-publicized **SkyWalk** at Grand Canyon West. However, with a sky-high admission price and a long drive for a short walk on a horseshoe-shaped pier, the SkyWalk is a less than grand attraction. If you're interested, the SkyWalk is operated by **Destination Grand Canyon** (✆ **877/716-9378** or 702/878-9378; www.destinationgrandcanyon.com).

THE FOUR CORNERS REGION You can learn a bit about Navajo culture at the new **Explore Navajo Interactive Museum,** Main Street and Moenave Avenue, Tuba City (✆ **928/283-4545**). The museum is located behind the Tuba City Trading Post. If you happen to be in Window Rock at lunch time, you can try traditional Navajo fare at the **Chihootso Indian Marketplace** at the junction of Arizona 264 and Indian Route 12. The marketplace has several small restaurants serving fry bread, mutton stew, and other traditional Navajo dishes. On weekends, there's a flea market in the parking lot here.

EASTERN ARIZONA Up in Greer, in the high country of the White Mountains, there are a couple of lodges that I've added to the book this year. The **Amberian Peaks Lodge & Restaurant,** One Main St., Greer (✆ **800/556-9997** or 928/735-9977; www.thepeaksatgreer.com), is right in Greer and is set on a hillside overlooking the valley of the Little Colorado River. **Hidden Meadow Ranch** (✆ **866/333-4080** or 928/333-1000; www.hiddenmeadow.com), on the other hand, is off in the forest several miles from Greer and is a luxurious guest ranch.

TUCSON I've added a few new hotels to the Tucson chapter. These include the **Hyatt Place Tucson Airport,** 6885 S. Tucson Blvd. (✆ **800/492-8847** or 520/295-0405; www.hyattplace.com), which is a very pretty new business hotel near the airport. The **Varsity Clubs of America Tucson Chapter,** 3855 E. Speedway Blvd. (✆ **800/521-3131** or 520/318-3777; www.ilxresorts.com), is located in midtown Tucson and offers suites with full kitchens. If you're looking for basic, inexpensive accommodations, try the **Extended StayAmerica Tucson,** 5050 E. Grant Rd. (✆ **800/804-3724** or 520/795-9510; www.extendedstayamerica.com).

I know the desert may not seem the place for sushi, but **Sky Blue Wasabi,** 250 S. Craycroft Rd., no. 100 (✆ **520/747-0228**), is such a fun place and serves such great sushi that I think you should check it out. If you prefer your rolls with hot dogs rather than raw fish, be sure to eat at **El Guero Canelo,** 2480 N. Oracle Rd. (✆ **520/882-8977;** www.elguerocanelo.com), which is known for its Mexican-style hot dogs. For much more upscale south-of-the-border fare, dine at **Miguel's,** 5900 N. Oracle Rd. (✆ **520/887-3777;** www.miguelstucson.com), which is in La Posada hotel. If Mexican is too spicy for your, try **Le Delice,** 7245 E. Tanque Verde Rd. (✆ **520/290-9714;** www.le-delice.com), a casual little French place not far from Sabino Canyon.

SOUTHERN ARIZONA In Tubac, there's now a fine dining option in the form of **Nob Hill Gourmet Market and Fine Dining,** 10 Avenida Goya, Suite B (✆ **520/398-1010;** www.nobhilltubac.com), which is located in the Plaza de Anza shopping center and has both a restaurant and a gourmet grocery store.

If you're familiar with Mexico's curious Dia de los Muertos (Day of the Dead) celebrations, be sure to visit **La Galeria Dia de los Muertos,** 266 Naugle Ave. (✆ **520/394-2035**), which is a little cottage turned shrine to skeletons and skulls.

In Sonoita, be sure to stop in at **Dos Cabezas Wine Works** (✆ **602/622-0399;** www.doscabezaswinery.com), one of the area's newest wineries.

In Sierra Vista, **Adobe Southwestern Cuisine,** 5043 S. Hwy. 92, Sierra Vista (✆ **520/378-2762**), has become a hit with locals and should be on any birdwatcher's itinerary since Ramsey Canyon, the best-known birding spot in the area, is almost directly across the highway.

If you're looking for a pretty place to stay in Bisbee, check out the **Letson Loft Hotel,** 26 Main St., Bisbee (✆ **877/432-3210** or 520/432-3210; www.letsonlofthotel.com), which is filled with interesting Asian antiques. For big breakfasts with the locals, head to the **Bisbee Breakfast Club,** 75A Erie St. (✆ **520/432-5885;** www.bisbeebreakfastclub.com).

1

The Best of Arizona

Planning a trip to a state as large and diverse as Arizona involves a lot of decision making (other than which golf clubs to take), so in this chapter I've tried to give you some direction. Below I've chosen what I feel is the very best the state has to offer—the places and experiences you won't want to miss. Although sights and activities listed here are written up in more detail elsewhere in this book, this chapter should help you plan your trip.

1 The Best Places to Commune with Cactus

- **Desert Botanical Garden** (Phoenix): There's no better place in the state to learn about the plants of Arizona's Sonoran Desert and the many other deserts of the world. Displays at this Phoenix botanical garden explain plant adaptations and how indigenous tribes once used many of this region's wild plants. See p. 124
- **Boyce Thompson Arboretum** (east of Phoenix): Just outside the town of Superior, this was the nation's first botanical garden established in a desert environment. It's set in a small canyon framed by cliffs and has desert plantings from all over the world—a fascinating educational stroll in the desert. See p. 163
- **Arizona–Sonora Desert Museum** (Tucson): The name is misleading—this is actually more a zoo and botanical garden than a museum. Naturalistic settings house dozens of species of desert animals, including a number of critters you wouldn't want to meet in the wild (rattlesnakes, tarantulas, scorpions, black widows, and Gila monsters). See p. 357
- **Saguaro National Park** (Tucson): Lying both east and west of Tucson, this park preserves "forests" of saguaro cacti and is the very essence of the desert that so many imagine it to be. You can hike it, bike it, or drive it. See p. 360
- **Tohono Chul Park** (Tucson): Although this park is not that large, it packs a lot of desert scenery into its modest space. Impressive plantings of cacti are the star attractions, but there are also good wildflower displays in the spring. See p. 367
- **Organ Pipe Cactus National Monument** (west of Tucson): The organ pipe cactus is a smaller, multitrunked relative of the giant saguaro and lives only along the Mexican border about 100 miles west of Tucson. This remote national monument has hiking trails and a couple of scenic drives. See section 1 in chapter 10.

Arizona

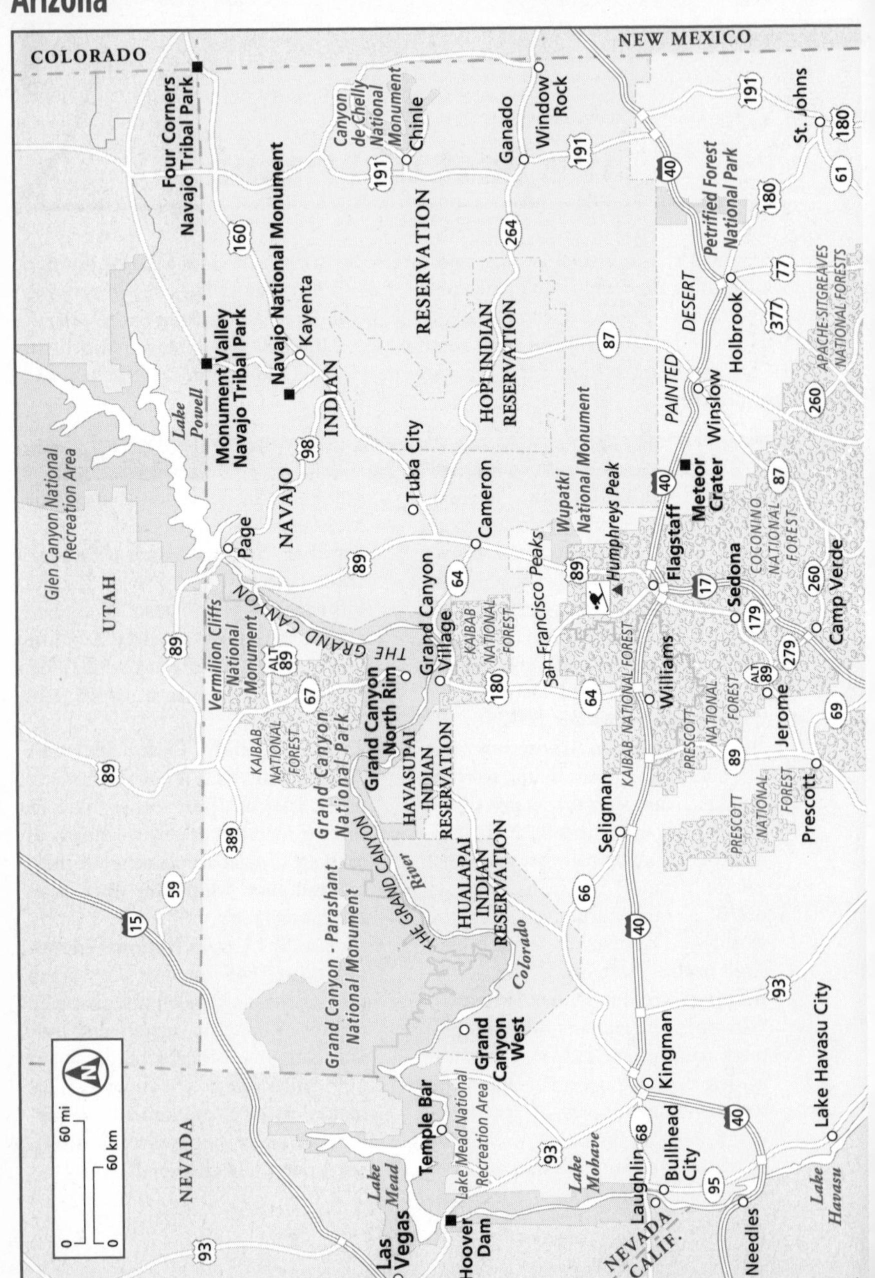

COLORADO
NEW MEXICO
UTAH
NEVADA
NEVADA
CALIF.
Four Corners Navajo Tribal Park
Monument Valley Navajo Tribal Park
Navajo National Monument
Kayenta
Canyon de Chelly National Monument
Chinle
Ganado
Window Rock
St. Johns
Petrified Forest National Park
Holbrook
PAINTED DESERT
Winslow
Meteor Crater
Flagstaff
Sedona
Camp Verde
COCONINO NATIONAL FOREST
APACHE-SITGREAVES NATIONAL FORESTS
NAVAJO INDIAN RESERVATION
HOPI INDIAN RESERVATION
Tuba City
Cameron
Wupatki National Monument
Humphreys Peak
San Francisco Peaks
Glen Canyon National Recreation Area
Lake Powell
Page
Vermilion Cliffs National Monument
THE GRAND CANYON
Grand Canyon North Rim
Grand Canyon Village
KAIBAB NATIONAL FOREST
Grand Canyon National Park
HAVASUPAI INDIAN RESERVATION
HUALAPAI INDIAN RESERVATION
Grand Canyon - Parashant National Monument
Colorado River
Grand Canyon West
Williams
Seligman
KAIBAB NATIONAL FOREST
PRESCOTT NATIONAL FOREST
Jerome
Prescott
Kingman
Lake Havasu City
Lake Havasu
Needles
Bullhead City
Laughlin
Lake Mohave
Lake Mead National Recreation Area
Temple Bar
Lake Mead
Las Vegas
Hoover Dam
0 60 mi
0 60 km
15 59 389 89 89 ALT 89 67 180 64 89 160 98 191 264 87 40 17 179 279 260 377 77 180 61 191 180 66 64 40 93 93 68 95 40 69 89 ALT 89 93

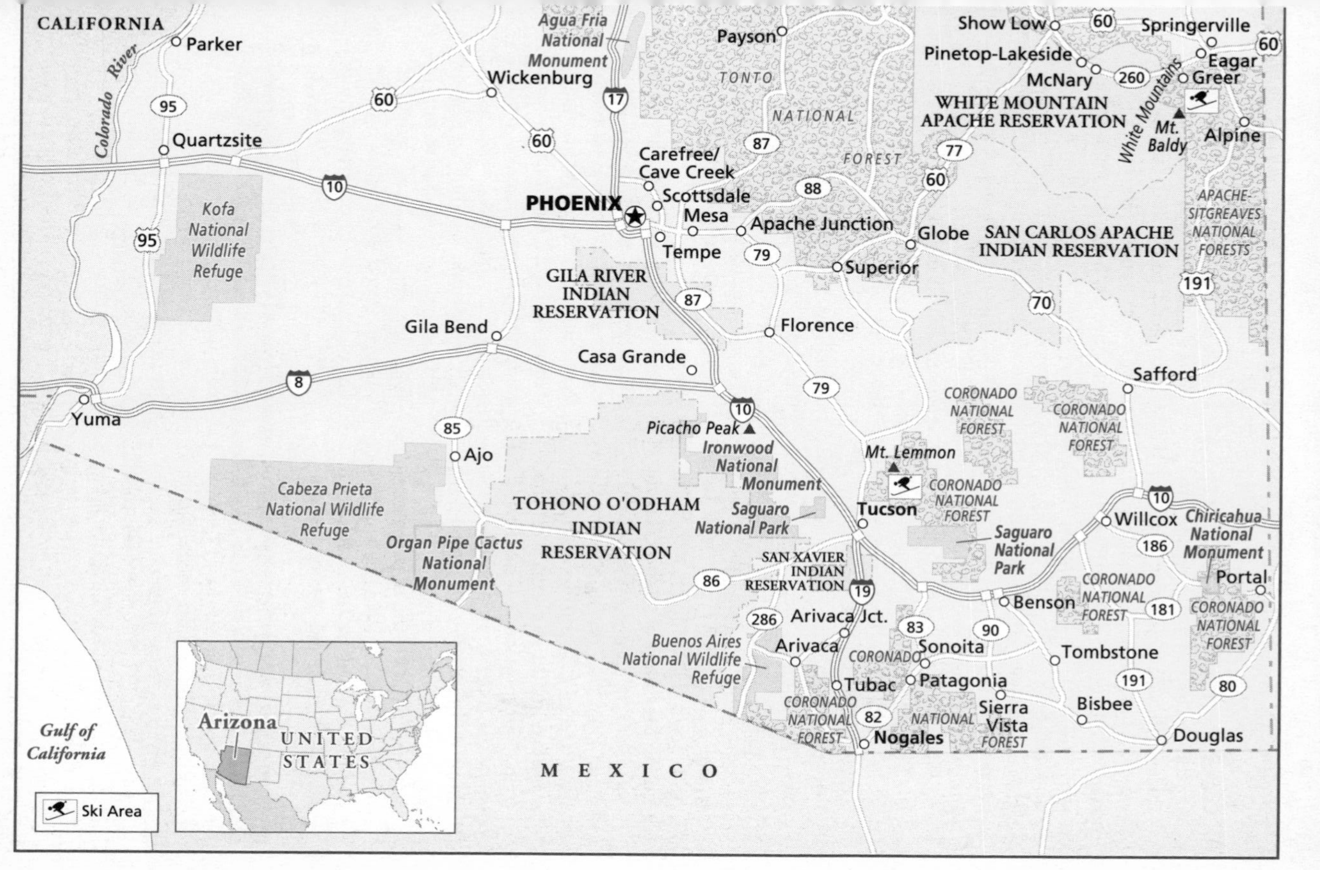
CALIFORNIA
Parker
Colorado River
95
Quartzsite
Kofa National Wildlife Refuge
Yuma
Gulf of California
Wickenburg
60
Agua Fria National Monument
17
10
PHOENIX
Carefree/ Cave Creek
Scottsdale
Mesa
Tempe
Apache Junction
GILA RIVER INDIAN RESERVATION
Gila Bend
Casa Grande
8
85
Ajo
Cabeza Prieta National Wildlife Refuge
Organ Pipe Cactus National Monument
TOHONO O'ODHAM INDIAN RESERVATION
Picacho Peak
Ironwood National Monument
Saguaro National Park
Payson
TONTO NATIONAL FOREST
87
88
79
77
Globe
Superior
Florence
SAN CARLOS APACHE INDIAN RESERVATION
70
Show Low
Pinetop-Lakeside
McNary
260
WHITE MOUNTAIN APACHE RESERVATION
Springerville
Eagar
Greer
White Mountains
Mt. Baldy
Alpine
APACHE-SITGREAVES NATIONAL FORESTS
191
Safford
CORONADO NATIONAL FOREST
Mt. Lemmon
Tucson
SAN XAVIER INDIAN RESERVATION
86
19
286
Arivaca Jct.
Arivaca
Buenos Aires National Wildlife Refuge
Tubac
82
Nogales
83
Sonoita
Patagonia
90
Sierra Vista
Benson
Willcox
186
Chiricahua National Monument
Portal
181
Tombstone
Bisbee
80
Douglas
MEXICO
Arizona
UNITED STATES
Ski Area

2 The Best Active Vacations

- **Rafting the Grand Canyon:** Whether you go for 3 days or 2 weeks, nothing comes even remotely close to matching the excitement of a rafting trip through the Grand Canyon. Sure, the river is crowded with groups in the summer, but the grandeur of the canyon is more than enough to make up for it. See p. 231
- **Hiking into the Grand Canyon or Havasu Canyon:** Not for the unfit or the faint of heart, a hike down into the Grand Canyon or Havasu Canyon is a journey through millions of years set in stone. This trip takes plenty of advance planning and requires some very strenuous hiking. With both a campground and a lodge at the bottom of each canyon, you can choose to make this trip with either a fully loaded backpack or just a light daypack. See p. 225 and 259.
- **Riding the Range at a Guest Ranch:** Yes, there are still cowboys in Arizona. They ride ranges all over the state, and so can you if you book a stay at one of the many guest ranches (once known as dude ranches). You might even get to drive some cattle down the trail. After a long or short day in the saddle, you can soak in a hot tub, go for a swim, or play a game of tennis before chowing down.
- **Staying at a Golf or Tennis Resort:** If horseback riding and cowboy cookouts aren't your thing, how about as much golf or tennis as you can play? The Phoenix/Scottsdale area has one of the nation's greatest concentrations of resorts, and Sedona and Tucson add many more options to the mix. There's something very satisfying about swinging a racket or club with the state's spectacular scenery in the background, and the climate means you can do it practically year-round. See chapters 4, 5, and 9.
- **Mountain Biking in Sedona:** Forget Moab—too many other hard-core mountain bikers. Among the red rocks of Sedona, you can pedal through awesome scenery on some of the most memorable single-track trails in the Southwest. There's even plenty of slickrock for that Canyonlands experience without the crowds. See p. 198.
- **Bird-Watching in Southeastern Arizona:** As an avid bird-watcher, I know that this isn't the most active of sports, but a birder can get in a bit of walking when it's necessary (like, to get to the nesting tree of an elegant trogon). The southeast corner of the state is one of the best birding regions in the entire country. See section 6, "The Best Bird-Watching Spots," of this chapter and the map on p. 14 of the color section at the front of this guide.

3 The Best Day Hikes & Nature Walks

- **Camelback Mountain** (Phoenix): For many Phoenicians, the trail to the top of Camelback Mountain is a ritual, a Phoenix institution. Sure, there are those who make this a casual but strenuous hike, but many more turn it into a serious workout by jogging to the top and back down. I prefer a more leisurely approach so I can enjoy the views. See p. 140.
- **Peralta Trail** (east of Phoenix in the Superstition Mountains): This moderately difficult trail through the rugged Superstition Mountains will lead you to one of the most astonishing views in the state. Hike the trail

on a weekday to avoid the crowds. See p. 141.

- **Picacho Peak State Park** (south of Casa Grande): The hike up this central Arizona landmark is short but strenuous, and from the top there are superb views out over the desert. The best time of year to make the hike is in spring, when the peak comes alive with wildflowers. Picacho Peak is between Casa Grande and Tucson just off I-10. See p. 164.
- **The West Fork of Oak Creek Trail** (outside Sedona): The West Fork of Oak Creek is a tiny stream that meanders for miles in a narrow steep-walled canyon. This is classic canyon country, and the hardest part of a hike here is having to turn back without seeing what's around the next bend. See p. 187.
- **The South Kaibab Trail** (Grand Canyon South Rim): Forget the popular Bright Angel Trail, which, near its start, is a human highway. The South Kaibab Trail offers better views to day hikers and is the preferred downhill route for anyone heading to Phantom Ranch for the night. This is a strenuous hike even if you go only a mile or so down the trail. Remember, the trip back is all uphill. See p. 226.
- **The White House Ruins Trail** (Canyon de Chelly National Monument): There's only one Canyon de Chelly hike that the general public can take without a Navajo guide, and that's the 2.5-mile trail to White House Ruins, a small site once inhabited by Ancestral Puebloans (formerly called Anasazi). The trail leads from the canyon rim across bare sandstone, through a tunnel, and down to the floor of the canyon. See p. 282.
- **The Wildcat Trail** (Monument Valley Navajo Tribal Park): As at Canyon de Chelly, there's only one trail at Monument Valley that you can hike without a guide. This easy 3.2-mile trail loops around West Mitten Butte, providing a close-up look at one of the most photographed rock formations in the West. Don't miss this hike. See p. 295.
- **Betatakin** (Navajo National Monument): Betatakin is one of the most impressive cliff dwellings in the Southwest, and while most people just marvel at it from a distance, it's possible to take a ranger-led 5-mile hike to the ruins. After hiking through remote Tsegi Canyon, you'll have a better understanding of the Ancestral Puebloan people who once lived here. See p. 293.
- **Antelope Canyon** (Page): More a slow walk of reverence than a hike, this short trail lets you see the amazing beauty that can result when water and rock battle each other in the Southwest. The trail leads through a picture-perfect sandstone slot canyon, which is only a few feet wide in some places. See p. 300.
- **The Seven Falls Trail** (Tucson): There is something irresistible about waterfalls in the desert, and on this trail you get more than enough falls to satisfy any craving to cool off on a hot desert day. This trail is in the Sabino Canyon Recreation Area in northeast Tucson. See p. 376.
- **The Heart of Rocks Trail** (Cochise County): While the national parks and monuments in northern Arizona get all the publicity, Chiricahua National Monument, down in the southeast corner of the state, quietly lays claim to some of the most spectacular scenery in Arizona. On this trail, you'll hike through a wonderland of rocks. See p. 424.

4 The Best Scenic Drives

- **The Apache Trail** (east of Phoenix): Much of this winding road, which passes just north of the Superstition Mountains, is unpaved and follows a rugged route once traveled by Apaches. Here is some of the most remote country in the Phoenix area, with far-reaching desert vistas and lots to see and do along the way. See section 12 in chapter 4.
- **Oak Creek Canyon** (Sedona): Slicing down from the pine country outside Flagstaff to the red rocks of Sedona, Oak Creek Canyon is a cool oasis. From the scenic overlook at the top of the canyon to the swimming holes and hiking trails at the bottom, this canyon road provides a rapid change in climate and landscape. See section 5 in chapter 5.
- **Canyon de Chelly National Monument** (Chinle): This fascinating complex of canyons on the Navajo Indian Reservation has limited public access because it is still home to numerous Navajo families. However, roads that parallel the north and south rims of the canyon provide lots of scenic overlooks. See section 5 in chapter 7.
- **Monument Valley Navajo Tribal Park** (north of Kayenta): This valley of sandstone buttes and mesas is one of the most photographed spots in America and is familiar to people all over the world from the countless movies, TV shows, and commercials that have been shot here. A 17-mile dirt road winds through the park, giving visitors close-up views of such landmarks as Elephant Butte, the Mittens, and Totem Pole. See section 7 in chapter 7.
- **Mount Lemmon** (Tucson): Sure, the views of Tucson from the city's northern foothills are great, but the vistas from Mount Lemmon are even better. This mountain rises up from the desert like an island rising from the sea, and the road up the mountain climbs from cactus country to cool pine forests. See p. 376.

5 The Best Golf Courses

- **The Boulders South Course** (Carefree, near Phoenix; ✆ **480/488-9028**): If you've ever seen a photo of someone teeing off beside a massive balancing rock and longed to play that same hole, then you've dreamed about playing The Boulders' South Course. Jay Morrish's desert-style design plays around and through the jumble of massive boulders for which the resort is named. See p. 137.
- **The Gold Course at The Wigwam Golf Club & Spa** (Litchfield Park, near Phoenix; ✆ **800/909-4224**): If you're a traditionalist who eschews those cactus- and rattlesnake-filled desert target courses, be sure to reserve a tee time on The Wigwam's Gold Course. This 7,100-yard resort course has long been an Arizona legend. See p. 137.
- **Gold Canyon Golf Resort** (Apache Junction, near Phoenix; ✆ **480/982-9449**): This resort east of Phoenix offers superb golf at the foot of the Superstition Mountains. The second, third, and fourth holes on the Dinosaur Mountain Course are truly memorable. They play across the foot of Dinosaur Mountain and are among the top holes in the state. See p. 138.
- **Troon North Golf Club** (Scottsdale; ✆ **480/585-7700**): Designed by Tom Weiskopf and Jay Morrish, this semiprivate, desert-style course is

named for the famous Scottish links that overlook the Firth of Forth and the Firth of Clyde—but that's where the similarities end. Troon North has two 18-hole courses, but the original, known as the Monument Course, is still the favorite. See p. 138.

- **Tournament Players Club (TPC) of Scottsdale** (Scottsdale; ✆ **888/400-4001**): If you've dreamed of playing where the pros play, then plan a visit to the Fairmont Scottsdale Princess. Book a tee time on the resort's Stadium Course, and you can play on the course that hosts the PGA Tour's FBR Open. See p. 138.
- **We-Ko-Pa Golf Club** (✆ **480/836-9000**): Located on the Yavapai Nation northeast of Scottsdale, this golf club includes two challenging 18-hole courses that are bounded by open desert and stupendous views. See p. 138.
- **Sedona Golf Resort** (Sedona; ✆ **877/733-9885**): It's easy to assume that all of Arizona's best courses are in the Phoenix and Tucson areas, but it just isn't so. Up in red-rock country, at the mouth of Oak Creek Canyon, the Sedona Golf Resort boasts a traditional course with terrific red-rock views. See p. 199.
- **Lake Powell National Golf Course** (Page; ✆ **928/645-2023**): Fairways wrap around the base of the red-sandstone bluff atop which sits the town of Page. This is one of the most scenic golf courses in the state. Walls of eroded sandstone come right down to the greens, and one tee box is up on top of the bluff. See p. 303.
- **Ventana Canyon Golf and Racquet Club** (Tucson; ✆ **520/577-4015**): Two Tom Fazio–designed courses, the Canyon and the Mountain, are shared by two of the city's finest resorts. Both desert-style courses play through some of the most stunning scenery in the state. If I had to choose between them, I'd go for the Canyon Course. See p. 375.
- **Omni Tucson National Golf Resort and Spa** (Tucson; ✆ **520/575-7540**): With its wide expanses of grass on 18 holes and its additional 9 holes of desert-style golf, this course, once the site of the PGA Tour's Tucson Open, is both challenging and forgiving. The 18th hole of the combined Orange and Gold courses was considered one of the toughest finishing holes on the tour. See p. 375.

6 The Best Bird-Watching Spots

- **Madera Canyon:** The mountain canyons of southern Arizona attract an amazing variety of bird life, from species common in lowland desert to those that prefer thick forest settings. Madera Canyon is a good place to experience this variety. See p. 374.
- **Buenos Aires National Wildlife Refuge:** Gray hawks and masked bobwhite quails are among the refuge's rarer birds, but a cienega (wetland), lake, and stream attract plenty of others. See section 2 in chapter 10.
- **Patagonia:** With a year-round stream and a Nature Conservancy preserve on the edge of town, Patagonia is one of the best spots in the state for sighting various flycatcher species. See section 4 in chapter 10.
- **Ramsey Canyon Preserve:** Nearly 200 species of birds, including 14 species of hummingbirds, frequent this canyon, one of the top birding spots in the country. See p. 411.
- **San Pedro Riparian National Conservation Area:** Water is a scarce

commodity in the desert, so it isn't surprising that the San Pedro River attracts a lot of animal life, including more than 300 bird species. This is a life-list bonanza spot. See p. 411.

- **Cave Creek Canyon:** Although other rare birds can be seen in this remote canyon, most people come in hopes of spotting the elegant trogon, which reaches the northernmost limit of its range here. See p. 425.
- **Cochise Lakes** (Willcox Ponds): Wading birds in the middle of the desert? You'll find them at the Willcox sewage-treatment ponds south of town. Avocets, sandhill cranes, and a variety of waterfowl all frequent these shallow bodies of water. See p. 426.

7 The Best Offbeat Travel Experiences

- **Taking a Vortex Tour in Sedona:** Crystals and pyramids are nothing compared to the power of the Sedona vortexes, which just happen to be in the middle of some very beautiful scenery. Organized tours shuttle believers from one vortex to the next. If you offer it, they will come. See p. 190.
- **Gazing at the Stars:** Insomniacs and stargazers will find plenty to keep them sleepless in the desert as they peer at the stars through telescopes at Lowell Observatory in Flagstaff or Kitt Peak National Observatory near Tucson. In the town of Benson, you can even stay at a B&B that doubles as an astronomical observatory. See p. 248.
- **Sleeping in a Wigwam:** Back in the heyday of Route 66, the Wigwam Motel in Holbrook lured passing motorists with its unusual architecture—concrete, wigwam-shape cabins. Today, this little motel is still a must for anyone on a Route 66 pilgrimage. See p. 283.
- **Touring Walpi Village:** Of the Hopi villages that stand atop the mesas of northeastern Arizona, only Walpi, one of the oldest, offers guided tours. Hopi guides share information on the history of the village and the Hopi culture. See p. 275.

8 The Best Family Experiences

- **Cowboy Steakhouses:** No family should visit Arizona without spending an evening at a "genuine" cowboy steakhouse. With false-fronted buildings, country bands, gunslingers, and gimmicks (one place cuts off your necktie, another has a slide from the bar to the dining room), these eateries are all entertainment and loads of fun.
- **Grand Canyon Railway:** Not only is this train excursion a fun way to get to the Grand Canyon, but it lets you avoid the parking problems and congestion that can be wearisome. Shootouts and train robberies are to be expected in this corner of the Wild West. See p. 229.
- **Arizona–Sonora Desert Museum** (Tucson): This is actually a zoo featuring the animals of the Sonoran Desert. Rooms are filled with snakes, a prairie-dog town, bighorn sheep, mountain lions, and an aviary full of hummingbirds. Kids and adults love this place. See p. 357.
- **Old Tucson Studios** (Tucson): Cowboy shootouts, cancan girls, wagon rides, and horseback rides make this old movie-studio set loads of fun for the family. You might even get to see a movie or commercial being filmed. See p. 361.
- **Shootouts at the O.K. Corral** (Tombstone): Tombstone may be "the town

too tough to die," but poor Ike Clanton and his buddies the McLaury boys have to die over and over again at the frequent reenactments of the famous gunfight. See p. 415.

- **Rawhide at Wild Horse Pass** (Phoenix): Your kids can climb atop a mechanical bull or a real camel, pan for gold, climb a rock wall, or ride in a stagecoach or a train. After all this activity, you'll want to head to Rawhide's steakhouse. See p. 99.
- **Goldfield Ghost Town** (Apache Junction): Although it may look a little too contrived these days, Goldfield really was a mining town at one time. Today, you can take a tour of the old mine, learn about the legend of the Lost Dutchman Mine, and otherwise have a thoroughly Wild West experience. See p. 132.

9 The Best Family Vacations

- **Saddling Up on a Dude Ranch:** Ride off into the sunset with your family at one of Arizona's many dude ranches (now called guest ranches). Most ranches have lots of special programs for kids. See p. 171, 341, and 427.
- **Floating on a Houseboat:** Renting a floating vacation home on Lakes Powell, Mead, or Mohave is a summer tradition for many Arizona families. With a houseboat, you aren't tied to one spot and can cruise from one scenic beach to the next. See p. 304 and 435.
- **Lounging by the Pool:** While most Arizona resorts are geared primarily toward adults, there are a handful in Phoenix and Tucson that have extensive pool complexes. The kids can play in the sand, shoot down a water slide, or even float down an artificial river in an inner tube. See "The Best Swimming Pools," later in this chapter.
- **Having a Grand Vacation:** You can spend the better part of a week exploring Grand Canyon National Park, with trails to hike, mules to ride down into the canyon (if your kids are old enough), air tours by plane or helicopter, rafting trips both wild and tame, and even a train to ride to and from the canyon. See chapter 6.

10 The Best Museums

- **Heard Museum** (Phoenix): This is one of the nation's premier museums devoted to Native American cultures. In addition to historical exhibits, a huge kachina collection, and an excellent museum store, there are annual exhibits of contemporary Native American art as well as dance performances and demonstrations of traditional skills. See p. 124.
- **Phoenix Art Museum** (Phoenix): This large art museum has acres of wall space and houses an outstanding collection of contemporary art as well as a fascinating exhibit of miniature rooms. See p. 126.
- **Scottsdale Museum of Contemporary Art** (Scottsdale): The Phoenix area's largest museum of contemporary art is noteworthy as much for its bold architecture as for its wide variety of exhibits. Unlike most art galleries here, this museum eschews cowboy art. See p. 127.
- **Desert Caballeros Western Museum** (Wickenburg): This little museum in the Wild West town of Wickenburg is a celebration of all things Western, including Western (or cowboy) art and the trappings of the American West. See p. 168.

- **Phippen Museum** (Prescott): This museum is devoted exclusively to Western art and features works by members of the prestigious Cowboy Artists of America. See p. 174.
- **Museum of Northern Arizona** (Flagstaff): The geology, ethnography, and archaeology of this region are all explored in fascinating detail at this Flagstaff museum. Throughout the year, excellent special exhibits and festivals focus on the region's tribes. See p. 248.
- **The University of Arizona Museum of Art** (Tucson): This collection ranges from the Renaissance to the present. Georgia O'Keeffe and Pablo Picasso are among the artists whose works are on display here. See p. 363.
- **Amerind Foundation Museum** (west of Willcox): Located in the remote southeastern corner of the state, this museum and research center houses a superb collection of Native American artifacts. Displays focus on tribes of the Southwest, but other tribes are also represented. See p. 424.

11 The Best Places to Discover the Old West

- **Rodeos:** Any rodeo, and this state has plenty, will give you a glimpse of the Old West, but the rodeos in Prescott and Payson both claim to be the oldest in the country. Whether you head for the one in Prescott or the one in Payson, you'll see plenty of bronco busting, bull riding, and beer drinking. See p. 173 and 307.
- **Guest Ranches:** The Old West lives on at guest ranches all over the state, where rugged wranglers lead city slickers on horseback rides through desert scrub and mountain meadows. Campfires, cookouts, and cattle are all part of the experience.
- **Monument Valley** (north of Kayenta): John Ford made it the hallmark of his Western movies, and no wonder: The starkly beautiful and fantastically shaped buttes and mesas of this valley are the quintessential Western landscape. You'll recognize Monument Valley the moment you see it. See section 7 in chapter 7.
- **Old Tucson Studios** (Tucson): Originally constructed as a movie set, this back lot and amusement park provides visitors with a glimpse of the most familiar Old West—the Hollywood West. Sure, the shootouts and cancan revues are silly, but it's all in good fun, and everyone gets a thrill out of seeing the occasional film crew in action. See p. 361.
- **Cowboy Poetry Contests:** From heroes on horseback to poets on the prairie, it's been a long lonesome ride for the American cowboy. At several events around the state, you can hear how some cowboys deal with the hardships and happiness of the cowboy life. See section 4 in chapter 2.
- **Tombstone:** This is the real Old West—Tombstone is a real town, unlike Old Tucson. However, "the town too tough to die" was reincarnated long ago as a major tourist attraction with gunslingers in the streets, stagecoach rides, and shootouts at the O.K. Corral. See section 6 in chapter 10.

12 The Best Places to See Indian Ruins

- **Tonto National Monument** (east of Phoenix): Located east of Phoenix and reached via the Apache Trail scenic road, this park has one of Arizona's few easily accessible cliff dwellings that still allows visitors to walk around inside the ruins; you don't have to observe from a distance. See p. 163.
- **Besh-Ba-Gowah Archaeological Park** (Globe): These reconstructed ruins have been set up to look the way they might have appeared 700 years ago. Consequently, this park provides a bit more cultural context than what you'll find at other ruins in the state. See p. 163.
- **Casa Grande Ruins National Monument** (west of Florence): Unlike most of Arizona's other ruins, which are constructed primarily of stone, this large and unusual structure is built of packed desert soil. Inscrutable and perplexing, Casa Grande seems to rise from nowhere. See p. 164.
- **Montezuma Castle National Monument** (north of Camp Verde): Located just off I-17, this is the most easily accessible cliff dwelling in Arizona, although it cannot be entered. Nearby Montezuma Well also has some small ruins. See p. 184.
- **Wupatki National Monument** (north of Flagstaff): Not nearly as well known as the region's Ancestral Puebloan cliff dwellings, these ruins are set on a wide plain. A ball court similar to those found in Central America, hints at cultural ties with the Aztecs. See p. 250.
- **Canyon de Chelly National Monument:** Small cliff dwellings up and down the length of Canyon de Chelly can be seen from overlooks, and a trip into the canyon itself offers a chance to see some of these ruins up close. See section 5 in chapter 7.
- **Navajo National Monument** (west of Kayenta): Both Keet Seel and Betatakin are some of the finest examples of Ancestral Puebloan cliff dwellings in the state. Although the ruins are at the end of long hikes, their size and state of preservation make them well worth the effort. See section 6 in chapter 7.

13 The Best Luxury Hotels & Resorts

- **Hyatt Regency Scottsdale Resort & Spa at Gainey Ranch** (Scottsdale; ✆ **800/55-HYATT;** www.scottsdale.hyatt.com): Contemporary desert architecture, dramatic landscaping, a water playground with its own beach, a staff that's always ready to assist you, good restaurants, and even gondola rides—it all adds up to a lot of fun at one of the most smoothly run resorts in Arizona. See p. 89.
- **Camelback Inn, A JW Marriott Resort & Spa** (Scottsdale; ✆ **800/24-CAMEL;** www.camelbackinn.com): The Camelback Inn opened in 1936 and today is one of the few Scottsdale resorts that retains an Old Arizona atmosphere while at the same time offering a wide range of modern amenities. A large, full-service spa caters to those who crave pampering, while two golf courses provide plenty of challenging fairways and greens. See p. 88.
- **The Phoenician** (Scottsdale; ✆ **800/888-8234;** http://thephoenician.com): This Xanadu of the resort world is brimming with marble, crystal, and works of art, and with staff seemingly around every corner, the

hotel offers guests impeccable service. Mary Elaine's, the resort's premier dining room, is one of the finest restaurants in the city, and the views are hard to beat. See p. 89.

- **The Boulders Resort & Golden Door Spa** (Carefree; ✆ **866/397-6520;** www.theboulders.com): Taking its name from the massive blocks of eroded granite scattered about the grounds, The Boulders is among the most exclusive and expensive resorts in the state. Pueblo architecture fits seamlessly with the landscape, and the golf course is the most breathtaking in Arizona. See p. 93.
- **The Fairmont Scottsdale Princess** (Scottsdale; ✆ **800/441-1414;** www.fairmont.com/scottsdale): The Moorish styling and numerous fountains and waterfalls of this resort create a setting made for romance. A beautiful spa, a challenging golf course, and a superb gourmet Mexican restaurant top it off. See p. 94.
- **Four Seasons Resort Scottsdale at Troon North** (Scottsdale; ✆ **888/207-9696;** www.fourseasons.com/scottsdale): Located in north Scottsdale not far from The Boulders, this is the most luxurious resort in Arizona. The setting is dramatic, the accommodations are spacious, and one of Arizona's top golf courses is just next door. See p. 94.
- **Arizona Biltmore Resort & Spa** (Phoenix; ✆ **800/950-0086;** www.arizonabiltmore.com): Combining discreet service and the architectural styling of Frank Lloyd Wright, the Biltmore has long been one of the most prestigious resorts in the state. This is a thoroughly old-money sort of place, though it continues to keep pace with the times. See p. 95.
- **Royal Palms Resort and Spa** (Phoenix; ✆ **800/672-6011;** www.royalpalmshotel.com): With Mediterranean styling and towering palm trees, this place seems far removed from the glitz that prevails at most area resorts. The Royal Palms is a classic, perfect for romantic getaways, and its 14 designer showcase rooms are among the most dramatic in the valley. See p. 96.
- **Enchantment Resort** (Sedona; ✆ **800/826-4180;** www.enchantment.com): A dramatic setting in a red-rock canyon makes this the most unforgettably situated resort in the state. If you want to feel as though you're vacationing in the desert, this place fits the bill. Guest rooms are constructed in a pueblo architectural style, and the spa is one of the finest in the state. See p. 201.
- **Loews Ventana Canyon Resort** (Tucson; ✆ **800/234-5117;** www.loewshotels.com): With the Santa Catalina Mountains rising in the backyard and an almost-natural waterfall steps away from the lobby, this is Tucson's most dramatic resort. Contemporary styling throughout makes constant reference to the desert setting. See p. 336.

14 The Best Family Resorts

- **Hyatt Regency Scottsdale Resort & Spa at Gainey Ranch** (Scottsdale; ✆ **800/55-HYATT;** www.scottsdale.hyatt.com): With children's programs; a "Lost Dutchman Mine" where children can dig for buried treasure; and a 10-pool, 2½-acre water playground complete with sand beach and waterfalls, this place is a kid's dream come true. See p. 89.
- **Pointe Hilton Squaw Peak Resort** (Phoenix; ✆ **800/876-4683;** www.pointehilton.com): A water slide, tubing river, and waterfall make the

water park here one of the most family-oriented at any resort in the valley. Throw in a miniature-golf course and a children's program, and you can be sure your kids will beg to come back. See p. 98.

- **Pointe South Mountain Resort** (Phoenix; ✆ **866/267-1321;** www.pointesouthmtn.com): Let's see . . . water slides that drop nearly 70 feet, a wave pool, a water play area for the youngest ones, a tubing river, horseback riding, even spa treatments for teens. Can you say fun for the whole family? See p. 99.
- **Loews Ventana Canyon Resort** (Tucson; ✆ **800/234-5117;** www.loewshotels.com): With a playground, a kids' club, and its own waterfall, this resort has plenty to keep the kids busy. A hiking trail starts from the edge of the property, and Sabino Canyon Recreation Area is nearby. See p. 336.
- **The Westin La Paloma Resort & Spa** (Tucson; ✆ **800/WESTIN-1;** www.westinlapalomaresort.com): Kids get their own lounge and game room, and the pool area has a great water slide. In summer and during holiday periods, special programs for the kids allow their parents a little free time. See p. 336.

15 The Best Hotels for Old Arizona Character

- **Hermosa Inn** (Phoenix; ✆ **800/241-1210;** www.hermosainn.com): The main building here dates from 1930 and was once the home of Western artist Lon Megargee. Today, the old adobe house is surrounded by beautiful gardens and has become a tranquil boutique hotel with luxurious Southwestern-style rooms and a beautiful restaurant terrace. See p. 95.
- **El Portal Sedona** (Sedona; ✆ **800/313-0017** or 928/203-9405; www.elportalsedona.com): Built of hand-cast adobe blocks and incorporating huge wooden beams salvaged from a railroad trestle, this inn is a work of art both inside and out. The mix of Arts and Crafts and Santa Fe styling conjures up haciendas of old. See p. 201.
- **El Tovar Hotel** (Grand Canyon Village; ✆ **888/297-2757;** www.grandcanyonlodges.com): This recently renovated classic log-and-stone mountain lodge stands in Grand Canyon Village only feet from the South Rim of the Grand Canyon. Although the lobby is small, it's decorated with the requisite trophy animal heads and has a stone fireplace. See p. 233.
- **Grand Canyon Lodge** (Grand Canyon North Rim; ✆ **888/297-2757;** www.grandcanyonnorthrim.com): This, the Grand Canyon's other grand lodge, sits right on the North Rim of the canyon. Rooms are primarily in cabins, which aren't quite as impressive as the main building, but guests tend to spend a lot of time sitting on the lodge's two viewing terraces or in the sunroom. See p. 242.
- **La Posada** (Winslow; ✆ **928/289-4366;** www.laposada.org): Designed by Mary Elizabeth Jane Colter, who also designed many of the buildings on the South Rim of the Grand Canyon, La Posada opened in 1930 and was the last of the great railroad hotels. Today, the hotel is again one of the finest in the West and has been restored to its former glory. See p. 272.
- **Arizona Inn** (Tucson; ✆ **800/933-1093** or 520/325-1541; www.arizonainn.com): With its pink-stucco walls

and colorful, fragrant gardens, this small Tucson resort dates from Arizona's earliest days as a vacation destination and epitomizes slower times, when guests came for the winter, not just a quick weekend getaway. See p. 332.

16 The Best Bed & Breakfasts

- **Rocamadour Bed & Breakfast for (Rock) Lovers** (Prescott; © **888/771-1933**): Set amid the rounded boulders of the Granite Dells just north of Prescott, this inn combines a spectacular setting with French antiques and very luxurious accommodations. You won't find a more memorable setting anywhere in the state. See p. 177.
- **Hacienda de la Mariposa** (Verde Valley; © **888/520-9095;** www.lamariposa-az.com): Set on the banks of Beaver Creek near Montezuma Castle National Monument, this inn was built in the Santa Fe style and blends beautifully with its surroundings. See p. 186.
- **Briar Patch Inn** (Sedona; © **888/809-3030;** www.briarpatchinn.com): This collection of luxurious cottages is located in tree-shaded Oak Creek Canyon, a few miles north of Sedona. Few experiences are more restorative than breakfast on the shady banks of the creek. See p. 202.
- **Adobe Village Graham Inn** (Sedona; © **866/846-1425;** www.sedonasfinest.com): With its "village" of luxury suites, this B&B is among the most elegant in the state. Everything is calculated to pamper you and put you in the mood for a romantic getaway. See p. 202.
- **The Inn at 410** (Flagstaff; © **800/774-2008;** www.inn410.com): This restored 1907 bungalow offers a convenient location in downtown Flagstaff, pleasant surroundings, comfortable rooms, and delicious breakfasts. Rooms all feature different, distinctive themes. See p. 251.
- **The Royal Elizabeth** (Tucson; © **877/670-9022;** www.royalelizabeth.com): In downtown Tucson just a block from the Temple of Music and Art, this territorial-style historic home is filled with beautiful Victorian antiques and architectural details. Guest rooms have lots of touches not often seen in historic B&Bs, including "vintage" phones, TVs, fridges, and safes. See p. 333.
- **La Zarzuela** (Tucson; © **888/848-8225;** www.zarzuela-az.com): Perched high on a hill on the west side of Tucson, this luxurious B&B boasts great views, colorful decor, and loads of outdoor spaces in which to relax in the warmth of the desert. See p. 338.
- **Across the Creek at Aravaipa Farms** (Winkelman; © **520/357-6901;** http://aravaipafarms.com): This is the quintessential desert B&B experience, though it isn't for everyone. To reach this inn, you have to drive *through* Aravaipa Creek (or have the innkeeper shuttle you across). Exploring the nearby wilderness area is the main activity in this remote area. See p. 339.
- **Cochise Stronghold B&B** (Cochise County; © **877/426-4141;** www.cochisestrongholdbb.com): Surrounded by the national forest and mountainsides strewn with giant boulders, this is another of the state's remote inns. The passive-solar building was constructed from straw bales and is not only energy-efficient, but also quite beautiful. See p. 426.

17 The Best Swimming Pools

- **Hyatt Regency Scottsdale Resort & Spa at Gainey Ranch** (Scottsdale; ✆ **800/55-HYATT**): This Scottsdale resort boasts a 10-pool, 2½-acre water playground complete with sand beach, sports pool, lap pool, adult pool, three-story water slide, giant whirlpool, and lots of waterfalls. See p. 89.
- **The Phoenician** (Scottsdale; ✆ **800/888-8234**): This resort's seven pools are as impressive as the Hyatt's, but they have a much more sophisticated air. Waterfalls, a water slide, play pools, a lap pool, and the crown jewel—a mother-of-pearl pool (actually, opalescent tile)—add up to plenty of aquatic fun. See p. 89.
- **Pointe Hilton Squaw Peak Resort** (Phoenix; ✆ **800/876-4683**): There's not just a pool here; there's a River Ranch, with an artificial tubing river, a water slide, and a waterfall pouring into the large free-form main pool. See p. 98.
- **Pointe Hilton Tapatio Cliffs Resort** (Phoenix; ✆ **800/876-4683**): The Falls, a slightly more adult-oriented pool complex than that at sister property Pointe Hilton Squaw Peak Resort, includes two lagoon pools, a 40-foot waterfall, a 138-foot water slide, and rental cabanas. See p. 98.
- **Pointe South Mountain Resort** (Phoenix; ✆ **866/267-1321**): The Oasis water park here leaves other area resort pools high and dry. The wave pool, tubing river, and two terrifyingly steep water slides are enough to make summer in the desert almost bearable. See p. 99.
- **The Buttes, A Marriott Resort** (Tempe; ✆ **888/867-7492**): A lush stream cascading over desert rocks seems to feed this free-form pool, a desert-oasis fantasy world you won't want to leave. A narrow canal connects the two halves of the pool, and tucked in among the rocks are several whirlpools. See p. 99.
- **The Westin La Paloma Resort & Spa** (Tucson; ✆ **800/WESTIN-1**): With a 177-foot-long water slide and enough poolside lounge chairs to put a cruise ship to shame, the pool at this Tucson foothills resort is a fabulous place to while away an afternoon. See p. 336.

18 The Best Places to Savor Southwest Flavors

- **Roaring Fork** (Scottsdale; ✆ **480/947-0795**): Roaring Fork has long been one of the most creative southwestern restaurants in the Phoenix area. The atmosphere is lively, and everything from the bread basket and bar snacks to the entrees and desserts shows an attention to detail. See p. 106.
- **Vincent's on Camelback** (Phoenix; ✆ **602/224-0225**): Chef Vincent Guerithault has made a career of merging classic French culinary techniques with the robust flavors of the Southwest. The results, for many years, have been absolutely unforgettable. See p. 113.
- **Fry Bread House** (Phoenix; ✆ **602/351-2345**): Unless you've traveled in the Southwest before, you've probably never had a fry-bread taco. This stick-to-your-ribs dish is a staple on Indian reservations throughout Arizona. The fry-bread tacos here are the best in the state. See p. 116.
- **Blue Adobe Grille** (Mesa; ✆ **480/962-1000**): This nondescript restaurant in an otherwise forgettable area

of Mesa serves some of the best Southwestern fare in the state. Meals are flavorful (without being too spicy), prices are great, and there's even a good wine list! See p. 117.

- **Cowboy Club Grille & Spirits** (Sedona; ✆ **928/282-4200**): This thoroughly Western restaurant is a great place to try such Arizona specialties as buffalo filet mignon, rattlesnake, and cactus fries. See p. 207.
- **The Turquoise Room** (Winslow; ✆ **928/289-2888**): This restaurant conjures up the days when the wealthy still traveled by railroad. Rarely will you find such superb meals in such an off-the-beaten-path locale. See p. 273.
- **Janos/J Bar** (Tucson; ✆ **520/615-6100**): Serving a combination of regional and Southwestern dishes, Janos has long been one of Tucson's premier restaurants. While Janos is as formal a place as you'll find in this city, J Bar is a more casual bar and grill. See p. 350 and 352.
- **Café Poca Cosa** (Tucson; ✆ **520/622-6400**): Forget the gloppy melted cheese and flavorless red sauces. This place treats south-of-the-border ingredients with the respect they deserve. It's Mexican food the likes of which you'll never find at your local Mexican joint. See p. 342.
- **The Gold Room** (Tucson; ✆ **520/917-2930**): The main dining room at Tucson's Westward Look Resort combines Southwestern-inspired flavors with a view that just won't quit. Although prices are quite high at dinner, there are reasonably priced lunches. See p. 349.
- **Terra Cotta** (Tucson; ✆ **520/577-8100**): Terra Cotta was one of Arizona's pioneers in the realm of Southwestern cuisine, and continues to serve creative and reasonably priced meals at its beautiful, art-filled restaurant in the Tucson foothills. See p. 352.

2

Planning Your Trip to Arizona

Whether you're headed to Arizona to raft the Grand Canyon or to golf in Scottsdale, you'll find all the advance-planning answers you need in this chapter—everything from when to go to how to get there.

1 The Regions in Brief

For a map of Arizona, see p. 6.

Phoenix, Scottsdale & the Valley of the Sun This region encompasses the sprawling metropolitan Phoenix area, which covers more than 400 square miles and includes more than 20 cities and communities surrounded by several distinct mountain ranges. It's the economic and population center of the state, and is Arizona's main winter and spring vacation destination. It is here that you'll find the greatest concentrations of resorts and golf courses. It is also where you'll find the worst traffic congestion and highest resort rates.

Central Arizona This region lies between Phoenix and the high country of northern Arizona and includes the red-rock country around the town of Sedona, which is one of the state's most popular tourist destinations. The rugged scenery around Sedona played many a role in old Western movies and has long attracted artists. Today, Sedona abounds in art galleries, recreational opportunities, and excellent lodging choices. Also within this region are historic Prescott (the former territorial capital of Arizona) and the old mining town of Jerome, now an artists' community. Several ancient Indian ruins and petroglyph sites can be found here as well.

The Grand Canyon & Northern Arizona Home to the Grand Canyon, one of the natural wonders of the world, northern Arizona is a vast and sparsely populated region comprised primarily of public lands and Indian reservations. Because Grand Canyon National Park attracts millions of visitors each year, the city of Flagstaff and the towns of Williams and Tusayan abound in accommodations and restaurants catering to canyon-bound travelers. North of the Grand Canyon and bordering on southern Utah lies the Arizona Strip, which is the most remote and untraveled region of the state. The Grand Canyon acts as a natural boundary between this region and the rest of the state, and the lack of paved roads and towns keeps away all but the most dedicated explorers. The inaccessible Grand Canyon–Parashant National Monument lies at the western end of the Arizona Strip.

The Four Corners The point where Arizona, Utah, Colorado, and New Mexico come together is the only place in the U.S. where four states share a common boundary. The region is also almost entirely composed of Hopi and Navajo reservation land. This region of spectacular canyons and towering mesas and buttes includes Canyon de Chelly, the

Painted Desert, the Petrified Forest, and Monument Valley.

Eastern Arizona's High Country This area, which comprises the Mogollon Rim region and the White Mountains, is a summertime escape for residents of the lowland desert areas, and abounds with mountain cabins and summer homes. Most of this high country is covered with ponderosa pine forests, laced with trout streams, and dotted with fishing lakes. Although this region comes into its own in summer, it also sees some winter visitation because it has the best ski area in the state: Sunrise Park Resort, on the White Mountain Apache Indian Reservation. Because the area lacks national parks, monuments, and other major geographical attractions, it is not much of a destination for out-of-state visitors.

Tucson Located a bit more than 100 miles south of Phoenix, Tucson is Arizona's second-most-populous metropolitan area and is home to numerous resorts and golf courses. The main attractions include Saguaro National Park and the Arizona–Sonora Desert Museum. With mountain ranges rising in all directions, this city seems more in touch with its natural surroundings than Phoenix, though traffic congestion and sprawl also plague Tucson. If you prefer Boston to New York, San Francisco to Los Angeles, or Portland to Seattle, you'll likely prefer Tucson to Phoenix.

Southern Arizona Southern Arizona is a region of great contrasts, from desert lowlands to mountain "islands" to vast grassy plains. Mile-high elevations also account for southeastern Arizona having one of the most temperate climates in the world. The mild climate has attracted lots of retirees, and it also brings in rare birds (and birders) and helps support a small wine industry. The western part of southern Arizona is one of the least-visited corners of the state, in part because much of this area is a U.S. Air Force bombing range. You will, however, find Organ Pipe Cactus National Monument out this way (wedged between the vast Cabeza Prieta National Wildlife Refuge and the Papago Indian Reservation). Tucson is at the northern edge of this region (and is not so temperate), but otherwise there are few communities of any size. However, a couple of interesting historic towns—Bisbee and Tubac—have become artists' communities.

Western Arizona Although Arizona is a landlocked state, its western region is bordered by hundreds of miles of lakeshore that were created by the damming of the Colorado River. Consequently, the area has come to be known as Arizona's West Coast. Despite the fact that the low-lying lands of this region are among the hottest places in the state during the summer (and the warmest in winter), Arizona's West Coast is a popular summer destination for budget-conscious desert denizens. College students and families come almost exclusively for the water-skiing, fishing, and other watersports.

2 Visitor Information & Maps

For statewide travel information, contact the **Arizona Office of Tourism,** 1110 W. Washington St., Suite 155, Phoenix, AZ 85007 (✆ **866/275-5816** or 602/364-3700; www.arizonaguide.com). Nearly every city and town in Arizona has a tourism office or a chamber of commerce that can also provide information. See the individual chapters for details on how to contact these sources. For some suggested driving tours along Arizona's scenic roads, also check out the Arizona Office of Tourism's **www.arizonascenicroads.com**.

For deals on vacation hotels and packages, check out **www.arizonavacation values.com**, a website operated by the

Arizona Office of Tourism and packed with all kinds of bargains and information.

Your best bet for a road map will be whatever you can pick up at a convenience store once you arrive. If you're a member of AAA, you can get a free map of the state that will be of some use. Other maps are available from tourist information offices in Phoenix and Tucson.

Blog-loving travelers can find out what other travelers are saying about Arizona at such sites as www.azreporter.com; www.gridskipper.com; www.travelblog.com; www.travelblog.org; and www.writtenroad.com.

3 Entry Requirements

ENTRY REQUIREMENTS

PASSPORTS

For information on how to get a passport, go to **"Passports"** in the **"Fast Facts"** section of this chapter—the websites listed provide downloadable passport applications as well as the current fees for processing passport applications. For an up-to-date, country-by-country listing of passport requirements around the world, go to the "Foreign Entry Requirement" Web page of the U.S. State Department at **http://travel.state.gov**. International visitors can obtain a visa application at the same website. ***Note:*** Children are required to present a passport when entering the U.S. at airports. More information on obtaining a passport for a minor can be found at http://travel.state.gov.

VISAS

For specifics on how to get a visa, go to **"Visas"** in the **"Fast Facts"** section of this chapter.

The U.S. State Department has a **Visa Waiver Program (VWP)** allowing citizens of the following countries (at press time) to enter the U.S. without a visa for stays of up to 90 days: Andorra, Australia, Austria, Belgium, Brunei, Denmark, Finland, France, Germany, Iceland, Ireland, Italy, Japan, Liechtenstein, Luxembourg, Monaco, the Netherlands, New Zealand, Norway, Portugal, San Marino, Singapore, Slovenia, Spain, Sweden, Switzerland, and the United Kingdom. Canadian citizens may enter the U.S. without visas; they will need to show passports and proof of residence, however. ***Note:*** Any passport issued on or after October 26, 2006 by a VWP country must be an **e-Passport** for VWP travelers to be eligible to enter the U.S. without a visa. Citizens of these nations also need to present a round-trip air or cruise ticket upon arrival. E-Passports contain computer chips capable of storing biometric information, such as the required digital photograph of the holder. (You can identify an e-Passport by the symbol on the bottom center cover of your passport.) If your passport doesn't have this feature,

U.S. Entry: Passport Required

New regulations issued by the Homeland Security Department now require virtually every air traveler entering the U.S. to show a passport—and future regulations will cover land and sea entry as well. As of January 23, 2007, all persons, including U.S. citizens, traveling by air between the United States and Canada, Mexico, Central and South America, the Caribbean, and Bermuda are required to present a valid passport. Similar regulations for those traveling by land or sea (including ferries) are expected as early as January 1, 2008.

you can still travel without a visa if it is a valid passport issued before October 26, 2005 and includes a machine-readable zone, or between October 26, 2005 and October 25, 2006 and includes a digital photograph. For more information, go to **www.travel.state.gov/visa**.

Citizens of all other countries must have (1) a valid passport that expires at least 6 months later than the scheduled end of their visit to the U.S.; and (2) a tourist visa, which may be obtained without charge from any U.S. consulate.

As of January 2004, many international visitors traveling on visas to the U.S. will be photographed and fingerprinted on arrival at Customs in airports and on cruise ships in a program created by the Department of Homeland Security called **US-VISIT.** Exempt from the extra scrutiny are visitors entering by land or those (mostly in Europe; see p. 23) who don't require a visa for short-term visits. For more information, go to the Homeland Security website at **www.dhs.gov/dhspublic**.

MEDICAL REQUIREMENTS

Unless you're arriving from an area known to be suffering from an epidemic (particularly cholera or yellow fever), inoculations or vaccinations are not required for entry into the U.S. If you have a medical condition that requires **syringe-administered medications,** carry a valid signed prescription from your physician; syringes in carry-on baggage will be inspected. Insulin in any form should have the proper pharmaceutical documentation. If you have a disease that requires treatment with **narcotics,** you should also carry documented proof with you—smuggling narcotics aboard a plane carries severe penalties in the U.S.

For **HIV-positive visitors,** requirements for entering the U.S. are somewhat vague and change frequently. For up-to-the-minute information, contact **AIDSinfo** (✆ **800/448-0440,** or 301/519-6616 outside the U.S.; www.aidsinfo.nih.gov) or the **Gay Men's Health Crisis** (✆ **212/367-1000;** www.gmhc.org).

CUSTOMS

WHAT YOU CAN BRING INTO ARIZONA

For information on what you can bring into and take out of Arizona, go to **"Customs"** in the **"Fast Facts"** section of this chapter.

4 When to Go

Arizona is a year-round destination, although people head to different parts of the state at different times of the year. In Phoenix, Tucson, and other parts of the desert, the high season runs from October to mid-May, with the highest hotel rates from January to April. At the Grand Canyon, summer is the busy season.

The all-around best times to visit are spring and autumn, when temperatures are cool in the mountains and warm in the desert, but without extremes (although you shouldn't be surprised to get a bit of snow as late as Memorial Day in the mountains and thunderstorms in the desert Aug–Sept). Late spring and early autumn (specifically May and Sept) are also good times to save money—low summer rates are still in effect at the desert resorts—and to see the Grand Canyon when it's not its most crowded. In spring, you might also catch great wildflower displays, which begin in mid-spring and last until May, when the tops of saguaro cacti are covered with waxy white blooms.

If for some reason you happen to be visiting the desert in July or August, be prepared for sudden thunderstorms. These storms often cause flash floods that make many roads briefly impassable. Signs warning motorists not to enter low areas when flooded should be taken very seriously.

Also, don't even think about venturing into narrow slot canyons, such as Antelope Canyon near Page or the West Fork of Oak Creek Canyon, if there's any chance of a storm anywhere in the region. Rain falling miles away can send flash floods roaring down narrow canyons with no warning. In 1997, several hikers died when they were caught in a flash flood in Antelope Canyon.

One more thing to keep in mind: Sedona is just high enough that it actually gets cold in the winter—sometimes it even snows. So if you're looking for sunshine and time by the pool, book your Sedona vacation for a time other than the winter.

CLIMATE

The first thing you should know is that the desert can be cold as well as hot. Although winter is the prime tourist season in Phoenix and Tucson, night temperatures can be below freezing and days can sometimes be too cold for sunning or swimming. However, although there can be several days in a row of cool, cloudy, and even rainy weather in January and February, on the whole, winters in Arizona are positively delightful.

In the winter, sun-seekers flock to the deserts, where temperatures average in the high 60s (low 20s Celsius) by day. In the summer, when desert temperatures top 110°F (43°C), the mountains of eastern and northern Arizona are pleasantly warm, with daytime averages in the low 80s (high 20s Celsius). Yuma is one of the desert communities where winter temperatures are the highest in the state, while Prescott and Sierra Vista, in the 4,000- to 6,000-foot elevation range, claim temperate climates that are just about ideal.

Phoenix's Average Temperatures & Days of Rain

	Jan	Feb	Mar	Apr	May	June	July	Aug	Sept	Oct	Nov	Dec
Avg. High (°F)	65	69	75	84	93	102	105	102	98	88	75	66
Avg. High (°C)	18	21	24	29	34	39	41	39	37	31	24	19
Avg. Low (°F)	38	41	45	52	60	68	78	76	69	57	45	39
Avg. Low (°C)	3	5	7	11	16	20	26	24	21	14	7	4
Days of Rain	4	4	3	2	1	1	4	5	3	3	2	4

Flagstaff's Average Temperatures & Days of Rain

	Jan	Feb	Mar	Apr	May	June	July	Aug	Sept	Oct	Nov	Dec
Avg. High (°F)	43	46	50	58	68	79	82	80	74	63	51	44
Avg. High (°C)	6	8	10	14	20	26	28	27	23	17	11	7
Avg. Low (°F)	17	19	23	27	34	41	50	49	42	31	22	17
Avg. Low (°C)	–8	–7	–5	–3	1	5	10	9	5	–1	–6	–8
Days of Rain	7	7	8	6	4	3	12	12	7	5	5	7

ARIZONA CALENDAR OF EVENTS

For an exhaustive list of events beyond those listed here, check http://events.frommers.com, where you'll find a searchable, up-to-the-minute roster of what's happening in cities all over the world.

January

Tostitos Fiesta Bowl Football Classic, University of Phoenix Stadium, Glendale. This college bowl game usually sells out nearly a year in advance. Call ✆ **800/635-5748** or 480/350-0911, or go to www.tostitosfiestabowl.com. January 1, 2008.

Wings over Willcox, Willcox. You can take part in birding tours, workshops, and, of course, watching the tens of thousands of sandhill cranes that gather in the Sulphur Springs Valley near Willcox. Call ✆ **800/200-2272,** or go to www.wingsoverwillcox.com. Mid-January.

Barrett-Jackson Collector Car Auction, Scottsdale. More than 1,000 immaculately restored classic cars are auctioned off in an event attended by more than 225,000 people. Call ✆ **480/421-6694,** or go to www.barrett-jackson.com. Mid-January.

FBR Open Golf Tournament, Scottsdale. Prestigious PGA golf tournament at the Tournament Players Club. Call ✆ **602/870-0163,** or go to www.fbropen.com. January 28 to February 3, 2008.

February

World Championship Hoop Dance Contest, Phoenix. Native American dancers from around the nation take part in this colorful competition held at the Heard Museum. Call ✆ **602/252-8848,** or go to www.heard.org. February 9 to 10, 2008.

Cochise Cowboy Poetry & Music Gathering, Sierra Vista. More than 50 cowboy poets, singers, and musicians gather in Sierra Vista for a weekend of Wild West poetry and music. Call ✆ **800/288-3861,** or go to www.cowboypoets.com. Early February.

Tubac Festival of the Arts, Tubac. Exhibits by North American artists and craftspeople. Call ✆ **520/398-2704,** or go to www.tubacaz.com/festival.asp. Early to mid-February.

Tucson Gem and Mineral Show, Tucson. This huge show at the Tucson Convention Center offers seminars, museum displays from around the world, and hundreds of dealers selling just about any kind of rock you can imagine. In addition, there are more than 40 other smaller shows in the weeks prior to the main show; for information on these smaller shows, visit www.tucsonshowguide.com. Call ✆ **520/322-5773,** or go to www.tgms.org. Mid-February.

Arizona Renaissance Festival, Apache Junction. Patterned after a 16th-century English country fair, this festival features costumed participants and tournament jousting. Call ✆ **520/463-2700,** or go to www.royalfaires.com. Weekends from early February to early April.

O'odham Tash, Casa Grande. This is one of the largest annual Native American festivals in the country, attracting dozens of tribes that participate in rodeos, arts-and-crafts exhibits, and dance performances. Call ✆ **520/836-4723.** Mid-February.

Scottsdale Arabian Horse Show, Scottsdale. A celebration of the Arabian horse. Call ✆ **480/515-1500,** or go to www.scottsdaleshow.com. Mid- to late February.

La Fiesta de los Vaqueros, Tucson. This cowboy festival and rodeo at the Tucson Rodeo Grounds includes the Tucson Rodeo Parade, which claims to be the world's largest nonmotorized parade. Call ✆ **800/964-5662** or 520/741-2233, or go to www.tucsonrodeo.com. Late February.

Sedona International Film Festival, Sedona. View various new indie features, documentaries, and animated films before they (it is hoped) get picked up for wider distribution. Call ✆ **928/282-1177,** or go to www.sedonafilmfestival.com. Late February to early March.

March

Heard Museum Guild Indian Fair and Market, Phoenix. Indian cultural and dance presentations and one of the greatest selections of Native American crafts in the Southwest make this a fascinating festival. Go early to avoid the crowds. Call ✆ **602/252-8848,** or go to www.heard.org. March 1 to 2, 2008.

Parada del Sol Parade and Rodeo, Scottsdale. The state's longest horse-drawn parade includes a street dance and rodeo. Call ✆ **480/990-3179,** or go to www.scottsdalejaycees.com. Early March.

Ostrich Festival, Chandler. Give the carnival a miss and head straight for the ostrich races. Although brief, these unusual races are something you ought to see at least once in your lifetime. Call ✆ **480/963-4571,** or go to www.ostrichfestival.com. Mid-March.

Scottsdale Arts Festival, Scottsdale Mall. This visual and performing-arts festival includes concerts, an art fair, and children's events. Call ✆ **480/874-4686,** or go to www.scottsdaleartsfestival.org. Second weekend in March.

Festival of the West, Chandler. A celebration of all things cowboy, from cowboy poetry to Western music and movies. There's a chuck-wagon cook-off, a mountain-man rendezvous, and horseback shooting contests. Call ✆ **602/996-4387,** or go to www.festivalofthewest.com. Mid-March.

Wa:k Pow Wow, Tucson. Tohono O'odham celebration at Mission San Xavier del Bac, featuring many Southwestern Native American groups. Call ✆ **520/294-5727.** Second weekend in March.

Ed Schieffelin Territorial Days, Tombstone. Tombstone's birthday celebration. Call ✆ **888/457-3929,** or go to www.tombstone.org. Mid-March.

Welcome Back Buzzards, Superior. A flock of turkey vultures (buzzards) arrives annually at the Boyce Thompson Arboretum to roost in the eucalyptus trees, and this festival celebrates their arrival. Call ✆ **520/689-2811,** or go to http://arboretum.ag.arizona.edu. Mid- to late March.

April

Tucson International Mariachi Conference. Mariachi bands from all over the world come to compete before standing-room-only crowds. Call ✆ **520/838-3908,** or go to www.tucsonmariachi.org. Mid- to late April.

May

Cinco de Mayo, Phoenix and other cities. Celebration of the Mexican victory over the French in a famous 1862 battle comes complete with food, music, and dancing. Check local newspapers for area festivities. Around May 5.

Route 66 Fun Run, Kingman area. Classic hot rods hit the road for 3 days of roaring up and down historic Route 66. Call ✆ **928/753-5001,** or go to www.azrt66.com. First weekend in May.

Waila Festival, Tucson. A festival celebrating the social dances of the Tohono O'odham nation, featuring "chicken scratch" music—a kind of polka—and native foods. Call ✆ **520/792-4806,** or go to www.tucsonfestival.org. Mid-May.

Wyatt Earp Days, Tombstone. Gunfights are reenacted in memory of the shootout at the O.K. Corral. Call ✆ **888/457-3929** or 520/457-3291, or go to www.tombstone.org. Late May.

Phippen Western Art Show and Sale, Prescott. This is the state's premier Western-art sale. Call ✆ **928/778-1385,** or go to www.phippenartmuseum.org. Memorial Day weekend.

July

Prescott Frontier Days/World's Oldest Rodeo, Prescott. This is one of the state's two rodeos that claim to be the nation's oldest. Call ✆ **800/358-1888** or 928/445-3103, or go to www.worldsoldestrodeo.com. Early July.

Hopi Festival of Arts and Culture, Flagstaff. This exhibition and sale are held at the Museum of Northern Arizona, and include cultural events. Call ✆ **928/774-5213,** or go to www.musnaz.org. Early July.

Sidewalk Egg-Frying Challenge, Oatman. In the ghost town of Oatman, located near one of the hottest places on earth, contestants use their own devices such as mirrors to fry an egg in 15 minutes. Call ✆ **928/768-6222.** July 4 at high noon.

Independence Day. For information on fireworks displays in Phoenix, call ✆ **602/534-FEST;** for Tucson, phone ✆ **520/624-1817.** For other areas, contact the local chamber of commerce. July 4.

Navajo Festival of Arts and Culture, Flagstaff. This exhibition and sale at the Museum of Northern Arizona includes cultural events. Call ✆ **928/774-5213,** or go to www.musnaz.org. Late July or early August.

August

Southwest Wings Birding and Nature Festival, Bisbee. Spotting hummingbirds and looking for owls and bats keep participants busy. Includes lectures and field trips throughout southeastern Arizona and Sonora, Mexico. Call ✆ **520/678-8237,** or go to www.swwings.org. Early August.

World's Oldest Continuous Rodeo, Payson. The second of Arizona's rodeos claiming to be the country's oldest. Call ✆ **800/672-9766** or 928/474-4515. Third weekend in August.

Arizona Cowboy Poets' Gathering, Prescott. Not just traditional and contemporary poetry are shared, but storytelling that focuses on the cowboy lifestyle. Call ✆ **928/445-3122,** or go to www.sharlot.org. Third weekend in August.

September

Navajo Nation Fair, Window Rock. The very large fair features traditional music and dancing, a fry bread contest, and more. Call ✆ **928/871-7055,** or go to www.navajonationfair.com. Early September.

Grand Canyon Music Festival, Grand Canyon Village. For more than 20 years, this festival has been bringing classical music to the South Rim of the Grand Canyon. Call ✆ **800/997-8285** or 928/638-9215, or go to www.grandcanyonmusicfest.org. Early to mid-September.

Sedona Jazz on the Rocks, Sedona. Jazz festival held amid the red rocks of Sedona. Call ✆ **928/282-1985,** or go to www.sedonajazz.com. Late September.

October

Sedona Arts Festival, Sedona. One of the better arts festivals in the state. Call ✆ **928/204-9456,** or go to www.sedonaartsfestival.org. Early to mid-October.

Arizona State Fair, Phoenix. Featured are rodeos, top-name entertainment, and ethnic food. Call ✆ **602/252-6771,** or go to www.azstatefair.com. Mid-October to early November.

Helldorado Days, Tombstone. Check out an 1880s fashion show, beard contest, reenactments, and street entertainment. Call ✆ **888/457-3929** or 520/457-3291, or go to www.tombstone.org. Third full weekend in October.

Goodyear Balloon & Air Spectacular, Litchfield Park. More than 150 hot-air balloons fill the Arizona sky. Call ✆ **623/882-9166,** or go to www.goodyearballoonandairspectacular.com. Late October.

Cowboy Artists of America Annual Sale & Exhibition, Phoenix. The Phoenix Art Museum hosts the most prestigious and best-known Western-art show in the region. Call ✆ **602/**

257-1222, or go to www.phxart.org. Late October to mid-November.

December

Festival of Lights, Sedona. Thousands of luminarias are lit at dusk at the Tlaquepaque Arts and Crafts Village. Call ✆ **928/282-4838,** or go to www.tlaq.com. Mid-December.

Pueblo Grande Museum Indian Market, Phoenix. This is the largest market of its kind in the state, with more than 450 Native American artisans. Call ✆ **877/706-4408** or 602/495-0901, or go to www.pueblogrande.com. Second full weekend in December.

Fiesta Bowl Parade, Phoenix area. The huge, nationally televised parade features floats and marching bands. Call ✆ **800/635-5748** or 480/350-0911, or go to www.tostitosfiestabowl.com. Late December.

5 Getting There

BY PLANE

Arizona is served by many airlines flying to both Phoenix (Code: PHX) and Tucson (Code: TUS) from cities around the U.S. and Canada. Phoenix is the more centrally located of the two airports and is closer to the Grand Canyon. However, if you plan to explore the southern part of the state or are going to visit both Phoenix and Tucson, I recommend flying into Tucson, which is a smaller airport and charges slightly lower taxes on its car rentals. The only drawback is that your plane will probably stop in Phoenix on its way to Tucson. If a trip to the Grand Canyon is your only reason for visiting Arizona, consider flying into Las Vegas, which sometimes has lower airfares and better car-rental rates.

In the past, I have usually flown America West Airlines, which was headquartered in Tempe, Arizona, and usually had the best rates to the state. However, in 2005 America West and US Airways merged, so this may no longer be the case. Alaska Airlines has also had reliably low fares to Arizona. Also be sure to check the fares at Southwest Airlines, which does not list its fares on big travel search engines.

Phoenix and Tucson are both served by the following airlines:

Alaska Airlines ✆ 800/252-7522; www.alaskaair.com
American ✆ 800/433-7300; www.aa.com
Continental ✆ 800/523-3273; www.continental.com
Delta ✆ 800/221-1212; www.delta.com
Frontier ✆ 800/432-1359; www.flyfrontier.com
JetBlue Airways ✆ 800/538-2583; www.jetblue.com
Northwest/KLM ✆ 800/225-2525; www.nwa.com
Southwest ✆ 800/435-9792; www.southwest.com
United ✆ 800/864-8331; www.ual.com

The following airlines serve Phoenix but not Tucson:

Air Canada ✆ 888/247-2262; www.aircanada.com
British Airways ✆ 800/247-9297; www.britishairways.com
Ted ✆ 800/225-5833; www.flyted.com
US Airways ✆ 800/428-4322; www.usairways.com
WestJet ✆ 888/937-8538; www.westjet.com

FLYING FOR LESS: TIPS FOR GETTING THE BEST AIRFARE

- Passengers who can book their ticket either **long in advance or at the last minute,** or who **fly midweek** or **at less-trafficked hours** may pay a fraction of the full fare. If your schedule is flexible, say so, and ask if you can secure a cheaper fare by changing your flight plans.
- Search **the Internet** for cheap fares. The most popular online travel agencies are **Travelocity.com** (www.travelocity.co.uk); **Expedia.com** (www.expedia.co.uk and www.expedia.ca); and **Orbitz.com**. In the U.K., go to **Travelsupermarket** (✆ **0845/345-5708;** www.travelsupermarket.com), a flight search engine that offers flight comparisons for the budget airlines whose seats often end up in bucket-shop sales. Other websites for booking airline tickets online include **Cheapflights.com**, **SmarterTravel.com**, **Priceline.com**, and **Opodo** (www.opodo.co.uk). Meta-search sites (which find and then direct you to airline and hotel websites for booking) include **Sidestep.com** and **Kayak.com**—the latter includes fares for budget carriers such as Jet Blue and Spirit as well as the major airlines. **Site59.com** is a great source for last-minute flights and getaways. In addition, most **airlines** offer online-only fares that even their phone agents know nothing about. British travelers should check **Flights International** (✆ **0800/0187050;** www.flights-international.com) for deals on flights all over the world.
- Watch local newspapers for **promotional specials** or **fare wars,** when airlines lower prices on their most popular routes. Also keep an eye on price fluctuations and deals at websites such as **Airfarewatchdog.com** and **Farecast.com**.
- Try to book a ticket **in its country of origin.** If you're planning a one-way flight from Johannesburg to New York, a South Africa–based travel agent will probably have the lowest fares. For foreign travelers on multi-leg trips, book in the country of the first leg; for example, book New York–Chicago–Montréal–New York in the U.S.
- **Consolidators,** also known as bucket shops, are wholesale brokers in the airline-ticket game. Consolidators buy deeply discounted tickets ("distressed" inventories of unsold seats) from airlines and sell them to online ticket agencies, travel agents, tour operators, corporations, and, to a lesser degree, the general public. Consolidators advertise in Sunday newspaper travel sections (often in small ads with tiny type), both in the U.S. and the U.K. They can be great sources of cheap international tickets. On the down side, bucket shop tickets are often rigged with restrictions, such as stiff cancellation penalties (as high as 50%–75% of the ticket price). And keep in mind that most of what you see advertised is of limited availability. Several reliable consolidators are worldwide and available online. **STA Travel** (www.statravel.com) has been the world's leading consolidator for students since purchasing Council Travel, but their fares are competitive for travelers of all ages. **Flights.com** (✆ **800/TRAV-800;** www.flights.com) has excellent fares worldwide, particularly to Europe. They also have "local" websites in 12 countries. **FlyCheap** (✆ **800/FLY-CHEAP;** www.1800flycheap.com) has especially good fares to sunny destinations. **Air Tickets Direct** (✆ **800/778-3447;** www.airticketsdirect.com) is based in Montreal and leverages the currently weak Canadian

Tips Getting Through the Airport

- Arrive at the airport at least 1 hour before a domestic flight and 2 hours before an international flight. You can check the average wait times at your airport by going to the TSA **Security Checkpoint Wait Times** site (waittime/tsa.dhs.gov).
- Know what you can carry on and what you can't. For the latest updates on items you are prohibited to bring inside carry-on luggage, go to **www.tsa.gov/travelers/airtravel**.
- Beat the ticket-counter lines by using the self-service electronic ticket kiosks at the airport or even printing out your boarding pass at home from the airline website. Using curbside check-in is also a smart way to avoid lines.
- Bring a current, government-issued photo ID such as a driver's license or passport. Children under 18 do not need government-issued photo IDs for flights within the U.S., but they do need passports for international flights to most countries.
- Help speed up security before you're screened. Remove jackets, shoes, belt buckles, heavy jewelry, and watches and place them either in your carryon luggage or the security bins provided. Place keys, coins, cell phones, and pagers in a security bin. If you have metallic body parts, carry a note from your doctor. When possible, pack liquids in checked baggage.
- Use a TSA-approved lock for your checked luggage. Look for Travel Sentry certified locks at luggage or travel shops and Brookstone stores (or online at www.brookstone.com).

dollar for low fares; they also book trips to places that U.S. travel agents won't touch, such as Cuba.

- Join **frequent-flier clubs.** Frequent-flier membership doesn't cost a cent, but it does entitle you to free tickets or upgrades when you amass the airline's required number of frequent-flier points. You don't even have to fly to earn points; **frequent-flier credit cards** can earn you thousands of miles for doing your everyday shopping. But keep in mind that award seats are limited, seats on popular routes are hard to snag, and more and more major airlines are cutting their expiration periods for mileage points—so check your airline's frequent-flier program so you don't lose your miles before you use them. ***Inside tip:*** Award seats are offered almost a year in advance, but seats also open up at the last minute, so if your travel plans are flexible, you may strike gold. To play the frequent-flier game to your best advantage, consult the community bulletin boards on **FlyerTalk** (www.flyertalk.com), or go to Randy Petersen's **Inside Flyer** (www.insideflyer.com). Petersen and friends review all the programs in detail and post regular updates on changes in policies and trends.

ARRIVING AT THE AIRPORT

IMMIGRATION & CUSTOMS CLEARANCE Foreign visitors arriving by air, no matter what the port of entry, should cultivate patience and resignation before setting foot on U.S. soil. U.S. airports

Tips Don't Stow It—Ship It

Though pricey, it's sometimes worthwhile to travel luggage-free, particularly if you're toting sports equipment, meetings materials, or baby equipment. Specialists in door-to-door luggage delivery include **Virtual Bellhop** (www.virtualbellhop.com); **SkyCap International** (www.skycapinternational.com); **Luggage Express** (www.usxpluggageexpress.com); and **Sports Express** (www.sportsexpress.com).

have considerably beefed up security clearances in the years since the terrorist attacks of 9/11, and clearing Customs and Immigration can take as long as 2 hours.

People traveling by air from Canada, Bermuda, and certain Caribbean countries can sometimes clear Customs and Immigration at the point of departure, which is much faster.

LONG-HAUL FLIGHTS: HOW TO STAY COMFORTABLE

- Your choice of airline and airplane will definitely affect your legroom. Find more details about U.S. airlines at **www.seatguru.com**. For international airlines, the research firm Skytrax has posted a list of average seat pitches at **www.airlinequality.com**.
- Emergency exit seats and bulkhead seats typically have the most legroom. Emergency exit seats are usually left unassigned until the day of a flight (to ensure that someone able-bodied fills the seats); it's worth getting to the ticket counter early to snag one of these spots for a long flight. Many passengers find that bulkhead seating (the row facing the wall at the front of the cabin) offers more legroom, but keep in mind that bulkhead seats have no storage space on the floor in front of you.
- To have two seats for yourself in a three-seat row, try for an aisle seat in a center section toward the back of coach. If you're traveling with a companion, book an aisle and a window seat. Middle seats are usually booked last, so chances are good you'll end up with three seats to yourselves. And in the event that a third passenger is assigned the middle seat, he or she will probably be more than happy to trade for a window or an aisle.
- Ask about entertainment options. Many airlines offer seatback video systems where you get to choose your movies or play video games—but only on some of their planes. (Boeing 777s are your best bet.)
- To sleep, avoid the last row of any section or the row in front of an emergency exit, as these seats are the least likely to recline. Avoid seats near highly trafficked toilet areas. Avoid seats in the back of many jets—these can be narrower than those in the rest of coach. Or reserve a window seat so you can rest your head and avoid being bumped in the aisle.
- Get up, walk around, and stretch every 60 to 90 minutes to keep your blood flowing. This helps avoid **deep vein thrombosis,** or "economy-class syndrome." See the box "Avoiding 'Economy Class Syndrome,'" p. 38.
- Drink water before, during, and after your flight to combat the lack of humidity in airplane cabins. Avoid caffeine and alcohol, which will dehydrate you.
- If you're flying with kids, don't forget to carry on toys, books, pacifiers, and snacks and chewing gum to help them relieve ear pressure buildup during ascent and descent.

GETTING THERE BY CAR

Because Phoenix and Tucson are major resort destinations, both have dozens of car-rental agencies. Prices at agencies elsewhere in the state tend to be higher, so if at all possible, try to rent your car in one or the other of these two major cities. However, because of high taxes at both airports, consider renting at a location outside the airport. If you stay at a hotel that offers a free airport shuttle, you can check in and then have an off-airport rental-car location pick you up and drive you to its office. However, if you have to pay for a shuttle or taxi to either your hotel or the off-airport rental-car office, you may wipe out any savings by renting away from the airport. Be sure to weigh all the costs carefully.

Major rental-car companies with offices in Arizona include:

Advantage © 800/777-5500; www.arac.com
Alamo © 800/462-5266; www.alamo.com
Avis © 800/331-1212; www.avis.com
Budget © 800/527-0700; www.budget.com
Dollar © 800/800-3665; www.dollar.com
Enterprise © 800/261-7331; www.enterprise.com
Fox Rent a Car © 800/225-4369; www.foxrentacar.com
Hertz © 800/654-3131; www.hertz.com
National © 800/227-7368; www.nationalcar.com
Thrifty © 800/847-4389; www.thrifty.com

Rates for rental cars vary considerably between companies and with the model you want to rent, the dates you rent, and your pickup and drop-off points. If you contact the same company three times and ask about renting the same model car, you may get three different quotes, depending on current availability of vehicles. It pays to shop early and ask lots of questions. At press time, Dollar was charging around $150 per week ($224 including taxes and surcharges) in Phoenix for a compact car with unlimited mileage during the winter high season.

At most rental-car agencies, you must be 25 years old to rent a car. However, some companies will rent to drivers between 21 and 24 if they pay an additional daily charge (usually $25–$35). Sometimes drivers as young as 18 can rent a car if they pay an even higher daily rate. In the U.S., virtually all rental cars have automatic transmissions. Of course, because Arizona is so sunny, convertibles are the preferred rental car. SUVs are also popular. Note that you cannot drive a rental car into Mexico.

If you're a member of a frequent-flier program, check to see which rental-car companies participate in your program. Also, when making a reservation, be sure to mention any discount you might be eligible for, such as corporate, military, or AAA. Beware of coupons offering discounts on rental-car rates—they often discount the highest rates only. It's always cheaper to rent by the week, so even if you don't need a car for 7 days, you might find that it's still more economical than renting for only 4 days.

Taxes on car rentals vary between around 12% and 50% and are always at the high end at the Phoenix and Tucson airports. You can save around 10% by renting your car at an office outside the airport, but many rental-car companies tend to raise the rates at these off-airport offices in order to negate any potential savings. Before making a reservation, be sure to ask about the tax and the loss-damage waiver (LDW) if you want to know what your total rental cost will be.

GETTING THERE BY TRAIN

Amtrak (© **800/872-7245;** www.amtrak.com) provides service aboard the

Southwest Chief between Flagstaff (for the Grand Canyon) and Los Angeles, Albuquerque, Kansas City, and Chicago. The *Sunset Limited* connects Tucson with Orlando, New Orleans, Houston, San Antonio, El Paso, and Los Angeles. At press time, the fare from Los Angeles to Flagstaff was as low as $58 one-way and $116 round-trip. There is no rail service to Phoenix, but Amtrak *will* sell you a ticket and then put you on a bus from either Tucson or Flagstaff to Phoenix. Book early for lower fares.

6 General Travel Resources

MONEY & COSTS

It's always advisable to bring money in a variety of forms on a vacation: a mix of cash, credit cards, and traveler's checks. You should also exchange enough petty cash to cover airport incidentals, tipping, and transportation to your hotel before you leave home, or withdraw money upon arrival at an airport ATM.

What will a vacation in Arizona cost? That depends on your comfort needs. If you drive an RV or carry a tent, you can get by very inexpensively and find a place to stay almost anywhere in the state. If you don't mind staying in motels that date from the Great Depression and can sleep just fine on a sagging mattress, you can stay for less money in Arizona than almost anyplace else in the U.S. (under $40 a night for a double in some places). On the other hand, you can easily spend several hundred dollars a day on a room at one of the state's world-class resorts. Expect to pay around $200 per day for a room at a midlevel resort in Phoenix or Tucson. Rooms in Sedona and at the Grand Canyon are also at a premium, so plan on spending between $150 and $200 for a midlevel room. If you're looking to stay in clean, modern motels at interstate highway off-ramps, expect to pay $45 to $65 a night for a double room in most places (a little bit more in Phoenix and Tucson).

ATMS

Nationwide, the easiest and best way to get cash away from home is from an ATM (automated teller machine), sometimes referred to as a "cash machine" or "cashpoint." The **Cirrus** (**© 800/424-7787;** www.mastercard.com) and **PLUS** (**© 800/843-7587;** www.visa.com) networks span the country; you can find them even in remote regions. Go to your bank card's website to find ATM locations at your destination. Be sure you know your daily withdrawal limit before you depart. Four-digit PINs work fine in Arizona.

Travel in the Age of Bankruptcy

Airlines go bankrupt, so protect yourself by **buying your tickets with a credit card.** The Fair Credit Billing Act guarantees that you can get your money back from the credit card company if a travel supplier goes under (and if you request the refund within 60 days of the bankruptcy). **Travel insurance** can also help, but make sure it covers against "carrier default" for your specific travel provider. And be aware that if a U.S. airline goes bust mid-trip, a 2001 federal law requires other carriers to take you to your destination (albeit on a space-available basis) for a fee of no more than $25, provided you rebook within 60 days of the cancellation.

What Things Cost in Arizona

	US$	British £
Weekly compact car rental (with taxes)	224.00	112.00
Local telephone call	.50	.25
Double room at Hyatt Resort, Scottsdale (high season)	419.00	209.50
Double room at El Tovar Hotel, Grand Canyon	142.00	71.00
Double room at Sky Ranch Lodge, Sedona	75.00	37.50
Dinner for one (without alcohol) at Roaring Fork, Scottsdale	35.00	17.50
Dinner for one (without alcohol) at Los Dos Molinos, Phoenix	20.00	10.00
Pint of beer in a restaurant	3.50	1.75
Double latte	3.00	1.50
Admission to the Heard Museum, Phoenix	10.00	5.00
Admission to the Grand Canyon	25.00	12.50
Sedona Pink Jeep "Broken Arrow" tour	72.00	36.00

Note: Many banks impose a fee every time you use a card at another bank's ATM, and that fee is often higher for international transactions (up to $5 or more) than for domestic ones (where they're rarely more than $2). In addition, the bank from which you withdraw cash may charge its own fee. To compare banks' ATM fees within the U.S., use **www.bankrate.com**. Visitors from outside the U.S. should also find out whether their bank assesses a 1–3% fee on charges incurred abroad.

In Arizona, you'll find ATMs at banks in even the smallest towns. You can also usually find them at gas station minimarts, although these machines usually charge a slightly higher fee than banks. You can sometimes avoid a fee by searching out a small community bank, a savings and loan, or a credit-union ATM. To avoid fees, you can also go into a grocery store, make a purchase, and ask for cash back on your debit card.

CREDIT CARDS & DEBIT CARDS

Credit cards are the most widely used form of payment in the U.S.: **Visa** (Barclaycard in Britain), **MasterCard** (EuroCard in Europe, Access in Britain, Chargex in Canada), **American Express, Diners Club,** and **Discover.** They also provide a convenient record of all your expenses, and offer relatively good exchange rates. You can withdraw cash advances from your credit cards at banks or ATMs, but high fees make credit-card cash advances a pricey way to get cash.

It's highly recommended that you travel with at least one major credit card. You must have a credit card to rent a car, and hotels and airlines usually require a credit card imprint as a deposit against expenses.

ATM cards with major credit card backing, known as **"debit cards,"** are now a commonly acceptable form of payment in most stores and restaurants. Debit cards draw money directly from your checking account. Some stores enable you to receive cash back on your debit-card purchases as well. The same is true at most U.S. post offices.

TRAVELER'S CHECKS

Though credit cards and debit cards are more often used, traveler's checks are still widely accepted in the U.S. Foreign visitors should make sure that traveler's checks are denominated in U.S. dollars; foreign-currency checks are often difficult to exchange.

You can buy traveler's checks at most banks. Most are offered in denominations of $20, $50, $100, $500, and sometimes $1,000. Generally, you'll pay a service charge ranging from 1% to 4%.

The most popular traveler's checks are offered by **American Express** (✆ **800/807-6233;** 800/221-7282 for card holders—this number accepts collect calls, offers service in several foreign languages, and exempts Amex gold and platinum cardholders from the 1% fee.); **Visa** (✆ **800/732-1322**)—AAA members can obtain Visa checks for a $9.95 fee (for checks up to $1,500) at most AAA offices or by calling ✆ **866/339-3378;** and **MasterCard** (✆ **800/223-9920**). Be sure to keep a copy of the traveler's checks serial numbers separate from your checks in the event that they are stolen or lost. You'll get a refund faster if you know the numbers.

Another option is the new **prepaid traveler's check cards,** reloadable cards that work much like debit cards but aren't linked to your checking account. The **American Express Travelers Cheque Card,** for example, requires a minimum deposit ($300), sets a maximum balance ($2,750), and has a one-time issuance fee of $15. You can withdraw money from an ATM ($2.50 per transaction, not including bank fees), and the funds can be purchased in dollars, euros, or pounds. If you lose the card, your available funds will be refunded within 24 hours.

TRAVEL INSURANCE

The cost of travel insurance varies widely, depending on the cost and length of your trip, your age and health, and the type of trip you're taking, but expect to pay between 5% and 8% of the vacation itself. You can get estimates from various providers through **InsureMyTrip.com.** Enter your trip cost and dates, your age, and other information for prices from more than a dozen companies.

For **U.K. citizens,** insurance is always advisable when traveling in the States. Travelers or families who make more than one trip abroad per year may find that an annual travel insurance policy works out cheaper. Check **www.moneysupermarket.com**, which compares prices across a wide range of providers for single- and multi-trip policies.

Most big travel agents offer their own insurance and will probably try to sell you their package when you book a holiday. Think before you sign. **Britain's Consumers' Association** recommends that you insist on seeing the policy and reading the fine print before buying travel insurance. **The Association of British Insurers** (✆ **020/7600-3333;** www.abi.org.uk) gives advice by phone and publishes *Holiday Insurance,* a free guide to policy provisions and prices. You might also shop around for better deals: Try **Columbus Direct** (✆ **0870/033-9988;** www.columbusdirect.net).

TRIP-CANCELLATION INSURANCE

Trip-cancellation insurance will help you retrieve your money if you have to back out of a trip or depart early, or if your travel supplier goes bankrupt. Trip cancellation traditionally covers such events as sickness, natural disasters, and State Department advisories. The latest news in trip-cancellation insurance is the availability of **expanded hurricane coverage** and the **"any-reason"** cancellation coverage—which costs more but covers cancellations made for any reason. You won't get back 100% of your prepaid trip cost, but you'll be refunded a substantial portion. **TravelSafe** (✆ **888/885-7233;** www.travelsafe.com) offers both types of coverage. Expedia also offers any-reason cancellation coverage for its air-hotel packages.

For details, contact one of the following recommended insurers: **Access America** (✆ 866/807-3982; www.accessamerica.com); **Travel Guard International** (✆ 800/826-4919; www.travelguard.com); **Travel Insured International** (✆ 800/243-3174; www.travelinsured.com); and **Travelex Insurance Services** (✆ 888/457-4602; www.travelex-insurance.com)

MEDICAL INSURANCE

Although it's not required of travelers, health insurance is highly recommended. Most health insurance policies cover you if you get sick away from home—but check your coverage before you leave.

International visitors should note that unlike many European countries, the U.S. does not usually offer free or low-cost medical care to its citizens or visitors. Doctors and hospitals are expensive, and in most cases will require advance payment or proof of coverage before they render their services. Good policies will cover the costs of an accident, repatriation, or death. Packages such as **Europ Assistance's "Worldwide Healthcare Plan"** are sold by European automobile clubs and travel agencies at attractive rates. **Worldwide Assistance Services, Inc.** (✆ **800/777-8710;** www.worldwideassistance.com) is the agent for Europ Assistance in the U.S.

Though lack of health insurance may prevent you from being admitted to a hospital in nonemergencies, don't worry about being left on a street corner to die: The American way is to fix you now and bill the living daylights out of you later.

If you're ever hospitalized more than 150 miles from home, **MedjetAssist** (✆ **800/527-7478;** www.medjetassistance.com) will pick you up and fly you to the hospital of your choice in a medically equipped and staffed aircraft 24 hours day, 7 days a week. Annual memberships are $225 individual, $350 family; you can also purchase short-term memberships.

Canadians should check with their provincial health plan offices or call **Health Canada** (✆ **866/225-0709;** www.hc-sc.gc.ca) to find out the extent of their coverage and what documentation and receipts they must take home in case they are treated in the U.S.

LOST-LUGGAGE INSURANCE

On flights within the U.S., checked baggage is covered up to $2,500 per ticketed passenger. On flights outside the U.S. (and on U.S. portions of international trips), baggage coverage is limited to approximately $9.07 per pound, up to approximately $635 per checked bag. If you plan to check items more valuable than what's covered by the standard liability, see if your homeowner's policy covers your valuables, get baggage insurance as part of your comprehensive travel-insurance package, or buy Travel Guard's "BagTrak" product.

If your luggage is lost, immediately file a lost-luggage claim at the airport, detailing the luggage contents. Most airlines require that you report delayed, damaged, or lost baggage within 4 hours of arrival. The airlines are required to deliver luggage, once found, directly to your house or destination free of charge.

HEALTH

STAYING HEALTHY

If you've never been to the desert, be sure to prepare yourself for this harsh environment. No matter what time of year it is, the desert sun is strong and bright. Use sunscreen when outdoors—particularly if you're up in the mountains, where the altitude makes sunburn more likely. The bright sun also makes sunglasses a necessity.

Even if you don't feel hot in the desert, the dry air steals moisture from your body, so drink plenty of fluids. You may want to use a body lotion as well; skin dries out quickly in the desert.

GENERAL AVAILABILITY OF HEALTH CARE

Contact the **International Association for Medical Assistance to Travelers (IAMAT; ✆ 716/754-4883,** or 416/652-0137 in Canada; **www.iamat.org**) for tips on travel and health concerns in the countries you're visiting, and for lists of local, English-speaking doctors. The United States **Centers for Disease Control and Prevention (✆ 800/311-3435;** www.cdc.gov) provides up-to-date information on health hazards by region or country and offers tips on food safety. The website **www.tripprep.com**, sponsored by a consortium of travel medicine practitioners, **Travel Health Online,** may also offer helpful advice on traveling abroad. You can find listings of reliable clinics overseas at the **International Society of Travel Medicine** (www.istm.org).

COMMON AILMENTS

DESERT ILLNESSES If you plan to do any camping or backcountry travel in the Four Corners region, which is where the Navajo and Hopi Indian reservations are located, you should be aware of hantavirus. This virus is spread by mice and is often fatal. Symptoms include fatigue, fever, and muscle aches; should you come down with any such symptoms within 1 to 5 weeks of traveling through the Four Corners area, see a doctor and mention that you have been in an area where hantavirus is known to occur.

BUGS, BITES & OTHER WILDLIFE CONCERNS It's not only the sun that makes the desert a harsh environment. Poisonous creatures are out there, too, but with a little common sense and some precautions you can avoid them. Rattlesnakes are common, but your chances of meeting one are slight—they tend not to come out in the heat of the day. However, never stick your hand into holes among the rocks in the desert, and look to see where you're going to step before putting your foot down.

Arizona is also home to a large poisonous lizard called the Gila monster. These black-and-orange lizards are far less common than rattlesnakes, and your chances of meeting one are very slight.

Although the tarantula has developed a nasty reputation, the tiny black widow is more likely to cause illness. Scorpions are another danger of the desert. Be extra careful when turning over rocks or logs that might harbor either black widows or scorpions.

RESPIRATORY ILLNESSES Valley fever, a fungal infection of the lungs, is common in the desert Southwest, although it generally affects only long-term residents

Avoiding "Economy Class Syndrome"

Deep vein thrombosis, or as it's know in the world of flying, "economy-class syndrome," is a blood clot that develops in a deep vein. It's a potentially deadly condition that can be caused by sitting in cramped conditions—such as an airplane cabin—for too long. During a flight (especially a long-haul flight), get up, walk around, and stretch your legs every 60 to 90 minutes to keep your blood flowing. Other preventative measures include frequent flexing of the legs while sitting, drinking lots of water, and avoiding alcohol and sleeping pills. If you have a history of deep vein thrombosis, heart disease, or another condition that puts you at high risk, some experts recommend wearing compression stockings or taking anticoagulants when you fly; always ask your physician about the best course for you. Symptoms of deep vein thrombosis include leg pain or swelling, or even shortness of breath.

Healthy Travels to You

The following government websites offer up-to-date health-related travel advice.

- **Australia:** www.dfat.gov.au/travel
- **Canada:** www.hc-sc.gc.ca/index_e.html
- **U.K.:** www.dh.gov.uk/PolicyAndGuidance/HealthAdviceForTravellers/fs/en
- **U.S.:** www.cdc.gov/travel

of the desert. The fungus is carried on dust particles, which are carried by dust storms and winds blowing across farms and construction sites. Symptoms include fever, chest pain, fatigue, headaches, and rashes. By the way, if you happen to be atop a mountain in Phoenix and can't see across the valley, blame it on the smog, which is as bad as that in Los Angeles.

WHAT TO DO IF YOU GET SICK AWAY FROM HOME

The best medical facilities in the state are in Phoenix, Scottsdale, and Tucson. I list **hospitals** and **emergency numbers** in chapters 4 and 9 under "Fast Facts," p. 84 and p. 328.

If you suffer from a chronic illness, consult your doctor before your departure. Pack **prescription medications** in your carry-on luggage, and carry them in their original containers, with pharmacy labels—otherwise they won't make it through airport security. Visitors from outside the U.S. should carry generic names of prescription drugs. For U.S. travelers, most reliable health-care plans provide coverage if you get sick away from home. Foreign visitors may have to pay all medical costs upfront and be reimbursed later. See "Medical Insurance," under "General Travel Resources," earlier in this chapter.

SAFETY

When driving long distances, always carry plenty of drinking water, and if you're heading off onto dirt roads, extra water for your car's radiator as well. When hiking or walking in the desert, keep an eye out for rattlesnakes; these poisonous snakes are not normally aggressive unless provoked, so give them a wide berth. Also be sure to give cactus a wide berth, especially cholla cactus, which have particularly painful spines that often break off in your skin and must be removed with tweezers.

Don't leave valuables, especially purses, wallets, or cameras, in view in your car when going for a hike or wandering off to take pictures at a scenic overlook in Canyon de Chelly National Monument, or anywhere for that matter.

7 Specialized Travel Resources

TRAVELERS WITH DISABILITIES

Most disabilities shouldn't stop anyone from traveling in the U.S. There are more options and resources out there than ever before.

If you have no intention of letting your disability prevent you from having the adventure of a lifetime, contact **Arizona River Runners,** P.O. Box 47788, Phoenix, AZ 85068 (© **800/477-7238;** www.arizonariverrunners.com), or **Arizona Raft Adventures,** 4050 E. Huntington Rd., Flagstaff, AZ 86004 (© **800/786-7238;** www.azraft.com), both of which offer Grand Canyon rafting trips for people with disabilities. **Wilderness Inquiry** (© **800/728-0719** or 612/676-9400; www.wildernessinquiry.org), which offers adventure-travel tours all over the country, operates Lake Powell sea-kayak trips for persons of all abilities. In the northwest corner of the state, **Stagecoach Trails Guest Ranch,** P.O. Box 580 Yucca, AZ 86438 (✆ **866/444-4471** or 928/727-8270; www.stagecoachtrails ranch.com), is a dude ranch that was designed with the needs of persons with disabilities in mind. All the ranch buildings are accessible, and there are horseback riding programs for persons with disabilities.

The **America the Beautiful—National Park and Federal Recreational Lands Pass—Access Pass** (formerly the **Golden Access Passport**) gives visually impaired or permanently disabled persons (regardless of age) free lifetime entrance to federal recreation sites administered by the National Park Service, including the Fish and Wildlife Service, the Forest Service, the Bureau of Land Management, and the Bureau of Reclamation. This may include national parks, monuments, historic sites, recreation areas, and national wildlife refuges.

The American the Beautiful Access Pass can only be obtained in person at any NPS facility that charges an entrance fee. You need to show proof of a medically determined disability. Besides free entry, the pass also offers a 50% discount on some federal-use fees charged for such facilities as camping, swimming, parking, boat launching, and tours. For more information, go to www.nps.gov/fees_passes.htm, or call ✆ **888/467-2757.**

Many travel agencies offer customized tours and itineraries for travelers with disabilities. Among them are **Flying Wheels Travel** (✆ **507/451-5005;** www.flying wheelstravel.com) and **Accessible Journeys** (✆ **800/846-4537** or 610/521-0339; www.disabilitytravel.com).

Flying with Disability (www.flying-with-disability.org) is a comprehensive information source on airplane travel. **Avis Rent a Car** (✆ **888/879-4273**) has an "Avis Access" program that offers services for customers with special travel needs. These include specially outfitted vehicles with swivel seats, spinner knobs, and hand controls; mobility scooter rentals; and accessible bus service. Be sure to reserve well in advance.

Organizations that offer a vast range of resources and assistance to disabled travelers include **MossRehab** (✆ **800/CALL-MOSS;** www.mossresourcenet.org); the **American Foundation for the Blind (AFB;** ✆ **800/232-5463;** www.afb.org); and **SATH (Society for Accessible Travel & Hospitality;** ✆ **212/447-7284;** www.sath.org). **AirAmbulanceCard.com** is now partnered with SATH and allows you to preselect top-notch hospitals in case of an emergency.

Also check out the quarterly magazine ***Emerging Horizons*** (www.emerging horizons.com), available by subscription ($17 per year U.S.; $22 outside U.S).

The "Accessible Travel" link at **Mobility-Advisor.com** (www.mobility-advisor.com) offers a variety of travel resources to disabled persons.

British travelers should contact **Holiday Care** (✆ **0845/124-9971** in U.K. only; www.holidaycare.org.uk) to access a wide range of travel information and resources for disabled and elderly people.

GAY & LESBIAN TRAVELERS

As elsewhere in the U.S., the major cities in Arizona (Phoenix and Tucson) are large enough to support businesses and organizations catering specifically to the gay and lesbian communities. On the Web, check out **www.visitgayarizona.com**, which has links to gay and lesbian organizations all over the state. At gay bars around Phoenix and Tucson, you can pick up various gay-oriented local publications, including **Echo Magazine** (✆ **602/266-0550;** www.echomag.com).

For information on gay- and lesbian-friendly businesses in the Phoenix metro area, contact the **Greater Phoenix Gay & Lesbian Chamber of Commerce** (© **888/4GPGLCC** or 602/266-5055; www.gpglcc.org). **Wingspan,** 425 E. Seventh St., Tucson (© **520/624-1779;** www.wingspan.org), is southern Arizona's lesbian, gay, bisexual, and transgender community center. *The Tucson Observer* (© **520/622-7176;** www.tucsonobserver.com) is a local Tucson gay newspaper available at both Wingspan and **Antigone Bookstore,** 411 N. Fourth Ave. (© **520/792-3715;** www.antigonebooks.com).

The International Gay and Lesbian Travel Association (**IGLTA;** © **800/448-8550** or 954/776-2626; www.iglta.org) is the trade association for the gay and lesbian travel industry, and offers an online directory of gay- and lesbian-friendly travel businesses and tour operators.

Many agencies offer tours and travel itineraries specifically for gay and lesbian travelers. **Above and Beyond Tours** (© **800/397-2681;** www.abovebeyondtours.com) are gay Australia tour specialists. San Francisco–based **Now, Voyager** (© **800/255-6951;** www.nowvoyager.com) offers worldwide trips and cruises, and **Olivia** (© **800/631-6277;** www.olivia.com) offers lesbian cruises and resort vacations.

Gay.com Travel (© **800/929-2268** or 415/644-8044; www.gay.com/travel or www.outandabout.com) is an excellent online successor to the popular ***Out & About*** print magazine. It provides regularly updated information about gay-owned, gay-oriented, and gay-friendly lodging, dining, sightseeing, nightlife, and shopping establishments in every important destination worldwide. British travelers should click on the "Travel" link at **www.uk.gay.com** for advice and gay-friendly trip ideas.

The Canadian website **GayTraveler (gaytraveler.ca)** offers ideas and advice for gay travel all over the world.

The following travel guides are available at many bookstores, or you can order them from any online bookseller: ***Spartacus International Gay Guide, 35th Edition*** (Bruno Gmünder Verlag; www.spartacusworld.com/gayguide), and ***Odysseus: The International Gay Travel Planner, 17th Edition*** (www.odyusa.com); and the ***Damron*** guides (www.damron.com), with separate, annual books for gay men and lesbians.

SENIOR TRAVEL

Mention the fact that you're a senior when you make your travel reservations. Many hotels offer discounts for seniors, and in most cities, people over the age of 60 qualify for reduced admission to theaters, museums, and other attractions, as well as discounted fares on public transportation.

Members of **AARP,** 601 E St. NW, Washington, DC 20049 (© **888/687-2277;** www.aarp.org), get discounts on hotels, airfares, and car rentals. AARP offers members a wide range of benefits, including *AARP: The Magazine* and a monthly newsletter. Anyone over 50 can join.

The U.S. National Park Service offers an **America the Beautiful—National Park and Federal Recreational Lands Pass—Senior Pass** (formerly the **Golden Age Passport**), which gives seniors 62 years or older lifetime entrance to all properties administered by the National Park Service—national parks, monuments, historic sites, recreation areas, and national wildlife refuges—for a one-time processing fee of $10. The pass must be purchased in person at any NPS facility that charges an entrance fee. Besides free entry, the American the Beautiful Senior Pass also offers a 50% discount on some federal-use fees charged for such facilities as camping, swimming, parking, boat launching, and tours. For more information, go to www.nps.gov/fees_passes.htm, or call © **888/467-2757.**

Many reliable agencies and organizations target the 50-plus market. **Elderhostel** (© **800/454-5768;** www.elderhostel.org) arranges worldwide study programs for those aged 55 and over. **ElderTreks** (© **800/741-7956** or 416/558-5000 outside North America; www.eldertreks.com) offers small-group tours to off-the-beaten-path or adventure-travel locations, restricted to travelers 50 and older.

Recommended publications offering travel resources and discounts for seniors include the quarterly magazine ***Travel 50 & Beyond*** (www.travel50andbeyond.com) and the best-selling paperback ***Unbelievably Good Deals and Great Adventures That You Absolutely Can't Get Unless You're Over 50 2005–2006, 16th Edition*** (McGraw-Hill), by Joann Rattner Heilman.

FAMILY TRAVEL

In summer, families flock to the Grand Canyon, often on a road trip that also takes in the canyon country of southern Utah. Remember, distances are great out here. Don't expect to find someplace to eat whenever the kids are hungry; pack food before heading out on a long drive. Also bring plenty to entertain the kids as you drive for hours through uninteresting scenery.

Be sure to check out "The Best Family Experiences," "The Best Family Vacations," and "The Best Family Resorts" sections in chapter 1. If you are planning to visit Phoenix or Tucson, see the "Especially for Kids" sections (p. 133 and 369) under "Seeing the Sights." To locate accommodations, restaurants, and attractions that are particularly kid-friendly, refer to the "Kids" icon throughout this guide.

Recommended family travel websites include **Family Travel Forum** (www.familytravelforum.com), a comprehensive site that offers customized trip planning; **Family Travel Network** (www.familytravelnetwork.com), an online magazine providing travel tips; and **TravelWithYourKids.com** (www.travelwithyourkids.com), a comprehensive site written by parents for parents offering sound advice for long-distance and international travel with children.

Frommer's Family Vacations in the National Parks (Wiley Publishing, Inc.) has tips for enjoying your trip to Grand Canyon National Park.

VEGETARIAN TRAVEL

Vegetarians may want to think twice about vacationing in Arizona. This is beef country, and cowboy steakhouses are a way of life in these parts. That said, there are actually plenty of options for meatless dining throughout the state. However, you'll find the greatest variety of vegetarian restaurants in Phoenix, Tucson, Sedona, and Flagstaff. Some of my favorite vegetarian places around the state include Tucson's Lovin' Spoonfuls (p. 348), Macy's European Coffee House & Bakery (p. 254), a cool college-town cafe in Flagstaff, and Sedona's modern little D'Lish (p. 210).

Happy Cow's Vegetarian Guide to Restaurants & Health Food Stores (www.happycow.net) has a restaurant guide with more than 6,000 restaurants in 100 countries. **VegDining.com** also lists vegetarian restaurants (with profiles) around the world. **Vegetarian Vacations** (www.vegetarian-vacations.com) offers vegetarian tours and itineraries.

8 Sustainable Tourism/Ecotourism

Each time you take a flight or drive a car, CO_2 is released into the atmosphere. You can help neutralize this danger to our planet through "carbon offsetting"—paying someone to reduce your CO_2 emissions by the same amount you've added.

Frommers.com: The Complete Travel Resource

It should go without saying, but we highly recommend **Frommers.com,** voted Best Travel Site by *PC Magazine.* We think you'll find our expert advice and tips; independent reviews of hotels, restaurants, attractions, and preferred shopping and nightlife venues; vacation giveaways; and an online booking tool indispensable before, during, and after your travels. We publish the complete contents of more than 128 travel guides in our **Destinations** section covering more than 3,600 places worldwide to help you plan your trip. Each weekday, we publish original articles reporting on **Deals and News** via our free **Frommers.com Newsletter** to help you save time and money and travel smarter. We're betting you'll find our new **Events** listings (http://events.frommers.com) an invaluable resource; it's an up-to-the-minute roster of what's happening in cities everywhere—including concerts, festivals, lectures and more. We've also added weekly **Podcasts, interactive maps,** and hundreds of new images across the site. Check out our **Travel Talk** area featuring **Message Boards** where you can join in conversations with thousands of fellow Frommer's travelers and post your trip report once you return.

Carbon offsets can be purchased in the U.S. from companies such as **Carbonfund.org** (www.carbonfund.org) and **TerraPass** (www.terrapass.org), and from **Climate Care** (www.climatecare.org) in the U.K.

Although you could argue that any vacation that includes an airplane flight can't be truly "green," you can go on holiday and still contribute positively to the environment. In addition to purchasing carbon offsets from the companies mentioned above, you can take other steps toward responsible travel. Choose forward-looking companies who embrace responsible development practices, helping preserve destinations for the future by working alongside local people. An increasing number of sustainable tourism initiatives can help you plan a family trip and leave as small a "footprint" as possible on the places you visit.

Responsible Travel (www.responsibletravel.com), run by a spokesperson for responsible tourism in the travel industry, contains a great source of sustainable travel ideas.

You can find eco-friendly travel tips, statistics, and touring companies and associations—listed by destination under "Travel Choice"—at the TIES website, **www.ecotourism.org**. Also check out **Conservation International** (www.conservation.org)—which, with *National Geographic Traveler,* annually presents **World Legacy Awards** (www.wlaward.org) to those travel tour operators, businesses, organizations, and places that have made a significant contribution to sustainable tourism. **Ecotravel.com** is part online magazine and part ecodirectory that lets you search for touring companies in several categories (water-based, land-based, spiritually oriented, and so on).

9 Staying Connected

TELEPHONES

Generally, hotel surcharges on long-distance and local calls are astronomical, so you're better off using your **cellphone** or a **public pay telephone.** Many convenience and grocery stores and packaging services sell **prepaid calling cards** in denominations up to $50; for international visitors these can be the least expensive way to call home. Many public pay phones at airports now accept American Express, MasterCard, and Visa credit cards. **Local calls** made from pay phones in most locales cost either 25¢ or 35¢ (no pennies, please).

Most long-distance and international calls can be dialed directly from any phone. **For calls within the U.S. and to Canada,** dial 1 followed by the area code and the seven-digit number. **For other international calls,** dial 011 followed by the country code, city code, and the number you are calling.

Calls to area codes **800, 888, 877,** and **866** are toll-free. However, calls to area codes **700** and **900** (chat lines, bulletin boards, "dating" services, and so on) can be very expensive—usually a charge of 95¢ to $3 or more per minute, and they sometimes have minimum charges that can run as high as $15 or more.

For **reversed-charge or collect calls,** and for person-to-person calls, dial the number 0 then the area code and number; an operator will come on the line, and you should specify whether you are calling collect, person-to-person, or both. If your operator-assisted call is international, ask for the overseas operator.

For **local directory assistance** ("information"), dial 411; for long-distance information, dial 1, then the appropriate area code and 555-1212.

CELLPHONES

Just because your cellphone works at home doesn't mean it'll work everywhere in the U.S. (thanks to our nation's fragmented cellphone system). It's a good bet that your phone will work in major cities, but take a look at your wireless company's coverage map on its website before heading out; T-Mobile, Sprint, and Nextel are particularly weak in rural areas. If you need to stay in touch in a destination where you know your phone won't work, **rent** a phone that does from **InTouch USA** (✆ **800/872-7626;** www.intouchglobal.com) or a rental car location, but beware that you'll pay $1 a minute or more for airtime.

If you're not from the U.S., you'll be appalled at the poor reach of our **GSM (Global System for Mobile Communications) wireless network,** which is used by much of the rest of the world. Your phone will probably work in most major U.S. cities; it definitely won't work in many rural areas. To see where GSM phones work in the U.S., check out www.t-mobile.com/coverage/national_popup.asp. And you may or may not be able to send SMS (text messaging) home.

You can rent a cellphone from **Dollar rent-a-phone** (✆ **800/964-2468** or 212/734-6344; www.dollar-rent-a-phone.com). If you're heading down into the Grand Canyon and want to rent a satellite phone, contact **Professional River Outfitters** (✆ **800/648-3236** or 928/779-1512; www.proriver.com).

VOICE-OVER INERNET PROTOCOL (VOIP)

If you have Web access while traveling, you might consider a broadband-based telephone service (in technical terms, **Voice over Internet protocol,** or **VoIP**) such as Skype (www.skype.com) or Vonage (www.vonage.com), which allows you to make free international calls if you use their services from your laptop or in a cybercafe. The people you're calling must

Online Traveler's Toolbox

Veteran travelers usually carry some essential items to make their trips easier. Following is a selection of handy online tools to bookmark and use.

- **Official state tourism website** (www.arizonaguide.com)
- **Official Phoenix visitors bureau** (www.visitphoenix.com)
- **Official Tucson visitors bureau** (www.visittucson.org)
- **Phoenix events and nightlife listings** (www.phoenixnewtimes.com)
- **Tucson events and nightlife listings** (www.tucsonweekly.com)
- **Arizona state parks information** (www.pr.state.az.us)
- **Maps** (www.mapquest.com)
- **Visa ATM Locator** (www.visa.com), **MasterCard ATM Locator** (www.mastercard.com)
- **The Weather Underground** (www.wunderground.com) and **Weather.com** (www.weather.com) provide weather forecasts.

also use the service for it to work; check the sites for details.

INTERNET/E-MAIL WITHOUT YOUR OWN COMPUTER

To find cybercafes in your destination, check **www.cybercaptive.com** and **www.cybercafe.com**.

Most major airports have **Internet kiosks** that provide basic Web access for a per-minute fee that's usually higher than cybercafe prices. Check out copy shops such as **Kinko's** (FedEx Kinkos), which offer computer stations with fully loaded software (as well as Wi-Fi).

WITH YOUR OWN COMPUTER

More and more hotels, resorts, airports, cafes, and retailers are going Wi-Fi (wireless fidelity), becoming "hotspots" that offer free high-speed Wi-Fi access or charge a small fee for usage. Wi-Fi is even found in campgrounds, RV parks, and entire towns. Most laptops sold today have built-in wireless capability. To find public Wi-Fi hotspots at your destination, go to **www.jiwire.com**; its Hotspot Finder holds the world's largest directory of public wireless hotspots.

For dial-up access, most business-class hotels in the U.S. offer dataports for laptop modems, and a few thousand hotels in the U.S. and Europe now offer free high-speed Internet access.

Wherever you go, bring a **connection kit** of the right power and phone adapters, a spare phone cord, and a spare Ethernet network cable—or find out whether your hotel supplies them to guests.

For information on electrical currency conversions, see "Electricity," in the "Fast Facts" section at the end of this chapter.

10 Packages for the Independent Traveler

Package tours are simply a way to buy the airfare, accommodations, and other elements of your trip (such as car rentals, airport transfers, and sometimes even activities) at the same time and often at discounted prices.

One good source of package deals is the airlines themselves. Most major airlines

Tips Ask Before You Go

Before you invest in a package deal or an escorted tour:

- Always ask about the **cancellation policy.** Can you get your money back? Is a deposit required?
- Ask about the **accommodations choices and prices** for each. Then look up the hotels' reviews in a Frommer's guide and check their rates online for your specific dates of travel. Also find out what types of rooms are offered.
- Request a complete **schedule.** (Escorted tours only)
- Ask about the **size** and demographics of the group. (Escorted tours only)
- Discuss what is included in the **price** (transportation, meals, tips, airport transfers, and so on.). (Escorted tours only)
- Finally, look for **hidden expenses.** Ask whether airport departure fees and taxes, for example, are included in the total cost—they rarely are.

offer air/land packages, including **American Airlines Vacations** (© 800/321-2121; www.aavacations.com), **Continental Airlines Vacations** (© 800/301-3800; www.covacations.com), **Delta Vacations** (© 800/654-6559; www.deltavacations.com), **United Vacations** (© 888/854-3899; www.unitedvacations.com), and **US Airways Vacations** (© 800/455-0123; www.usairwaysvacations.com). Several big **online travel agencies**—Expedia, Travelocity, Orbitz, Site59, and Lastminute.com—also do a brisk business in packages.

One great place to shop for Arizona vacation packages is at **www.arizonavacationvalues.com**, a website sponsored by the Arizona Office of Tourism (© **866/275-5816** or 602/364-3700; www.arizonaguide.com). This website is a clearinghouse for a wide variety of packages. Want a package that's geared toward bringing your pooch? A girlfriends' getaway or a couples' spa package? You'll find it here.

If you're coming to Arizona specifically to play golf, you might want to let a golf packager arrange your trip for you. For vacations in Scottsdale, contact **Arizona Golf Packages** (© **800/426-6148** or 623/215-2124; www.arizonagolfpackages.com). For vacations in Tucson, contact **Tucson Golf Travel** (© **800/426-6148;** www.tucsongolftravel.com).

Travel packages are also listed in the travel section of your local Sunday newspaper. Or check ads in the national travel magazines such as *Budget Travel Magazine, Travel + Leisure, National Geographic Traveler,* and *Condé Nast Traveler.*

11 Escorted General-Interest Tours

Escorted tours are structured group tours with a group leader. The price usually includes everything from airfare to hotels, meals, tours, admission costs, and local transportation.

Despite the fact that escorted tours require big deposits and predetermine hotels, restaurants, and itineraries, many people derive security and peace of mind from the structure they offer. Escorted tours—whether they're navigated by bus, motorcoach, train, or boat—let travelers sit back and enjoy the trip without having to drive or worry about details. They take you to the maximum number of sights in the minimum amount of time with the least amount of hassle. They're particularly convenient for people with limited mobility and they can be a great way to make new friends.

On the downside, you'll have little opportunity for serendipitous interactions with locals. The tours can be jam-packed with activities, leaving little room for individual sightseeing, whim, or adventure—plus, they often focus on the heavily touristed sites, so you miss out on many a lesser-known gem.

Gray Line Tours Phoenix (✆ **800/777-3484** or 602/437-3484; www.graylinearizona.com) offers a 3-day tour to the Grand Canyon by way of Sedona and Oak Creek Canyon.

Maupintour (✆ **800/255-4266;** www.maupintour.com), one of the largest tour operators in the world, offers an 8-day Arizona itinerary that covers the Grand Canyon, the Four Corners region, Phoenix, and Scottsdale.

Open Road Tours (✆ **800/766-7117;** www.openroadtours.com) offers a variety of 2- to 5-day tours around the state. Most of these focus on the Grand Canyon.

Detours (✆ **866/438-6877;** www.detoursaz.com) specializes in small-group tours throughout Arizona and other parts of the Southwest. One of its tours, **Hillerman Country,** is a 5-day journey through northern Arizona with a focus on spots that have been mentioned in Tony Hillerman novels about Navajo Tribal Police officers Jim Chee and Joe Leaphorn.

The British tour company **Trek America** (✆ **800/221-0596,** or 973/983-1144 outside the U.S.; www.trekamerica.com) specializes in off-the-beaten-path small-group adventure travel and offers lots of tours of the American Southwest; most include stops at the Grand Canyon and other scenic locations in Arizona.

12 Special-Interest Trips

If you'd like to turn a trip to the Grand Canyon into an educational experience, the **Grand Canyon Field Institute,** P.O. Box 399, Grand Canyon, AZ 86023 (✆ **866/471-4435** or 928/638-2485; www.grandcanyon.org/fieldinstitute), offers a variety of programs from early spring to late fall. Examples include day hikes, photography and painting classes, backpacking trips for women, mule-assisted treks, archaeology trips, and guided hikes and backpacking trips with a natural-history or ecological slant.

Once a year, **Canyon Calling Tours,** 200 Carol Canyon Dr., Sedona, AZ 86336 (✆ **928/282-0916;** www.canyoncalling.com), offers a weeklong women-only tour that visits Canyon de Chelly, Lake Powell, the Grand Canyon, and Havasu Canyon. The cost is $1,750 per person.

Learning Expeditions, a program run by the **Arizona State Museum,** occasionally offers scholar-led archaeological tours, including a trip to Navajo and Hopi country. For information, contact the marketing department at the **Arizona State Museum,** P.O. Box 210026, Tucson, AZ 85721-0026 (✆ **520/626-8381;** www.statemuseum.arizona.edu). The **Museum of Northern Arizona,** 3101 N. Fort Valley Rd., Flagstaff, AZ 86001 (✆ **928/774-5213;** www.musnaz.org), offers educational backpacking, river-rafting, and van tours primarily in the Colorado Plateau region of northern Arizona in a program called Ventures. Trips range in length from 1 to 6 days.

Old Pueblo Archaeology Center, P.O. Box 40577, Tucson, AZ 85717-0577 (✆ **520/798-1201;** www.oldpueblo.org), is a nonprofit educational and scientific organization that throughout the years has led numerous archaeology-oriented trips around Arizona.

If you have an interest in the Native American cultures of Arizona, contact **Crossing Worlds Journeys & Retreats,** P.O. Box 623, Sedona, AZ 86339 (✆ **800/350-2693** or 928/203-0024; www.crossingworlds.com), which offers tours throughout the Four Corners region, visiting the Hopi mesas as well as backcountry ruins on the Navajo Reservation. Journeys of self-discovery are a specialty of this company.

If you enjoy the wilderness and want to get more involved in its preservation, consider a Sierra Club service trip. These trips are for building, restoring, and maintaining hiking trails in wilderness areas. Contact the **Sierra Club Outings Department,** 85 Second St., Second Floor, San Francisco, CA 94105 (✆ **415/977-5522;** www.sierraclub.org). The Sierra Club also offers hiking, camping, and other adventure trips to various destinations in Arizona.

You can also join a work crew organized by the **Arizona Trail Association,** P.O. Box 36736, Phoenix, AZ 85067-6736 (✆ **602/252-4794;** www.aztrail.org). These crews spend 1 to 2 days building and maintaining various portions of the Arizona Trail, which will eventually stretch from the Utah state line to the Mexico border.

Another sort of service trip is offered by the National Park Service. It accepts volunteers to pick up garbage left by thoughtless visitors to Glen Canyon National Recreation Area. In exchange for picking up trash, you'll get to spend 5 days on a houseboat called the Trash Tracker, cruising through the gorgeous canyonlands of Lake Powell. Volunteers must be at least 18 years old and in good physical condition, and must provide their own food, sleeping bag, and transportation to the marina. For information, contact **Glen Canyon National Recreation Area,** Attn: GLCA Interpretation Tracker, P.O. Box 1507, Page, AZ 86040 (✆ **928/608-6350;** www.nps.gov/glca/tracker/tthome.htm).

Finally, if you're interested in architecture or the ecology of urban design, you may want to help out on the continued construction of **Arcosanti,** the slow realization of Paolo Soleri's dream of a city that merges architecture and ecology. Located 70 miles north of Phoenix, Arcosanti offers 4-week learning-by-doing workshops ($1,125 per person) and 1-week seminars ($475 per person). Contact Arcosanti, Attn: Workshop Coordinator, H.C. 74, Box 4136, Mayer, AZ 86333 (✆ **928/632-6233** or 928/632-6217; www.arcosanti.org).

In addition to these specialty-tour companies, you'll find outdoor-oriented tour companies mentioned below in "The Active Vacation Planner."

13 The Active Vacation Planner

Because Arizona is home to the Grand Canyon—the most widely known white-water-rafting spot in the world and also one of the world's premier backpacking destinations—the state is known for active, adventure-oriented vacations. For others, Arizona is synonymous with winter golf and tennis. Whichever category of active vacationer you fall into, you'll find information below to help you plan your trip.

BICYCLING With its wide range of climates, Arizona offers good biking somewhere in the state every month of the year. In winter, there's good road biking around Phoenix and Tucson, while from spring to fall, the southeastern corner of the state offers good routes. In summer, the White Mountains (in the eastern part of the state) and Kaibab National Forest (between Flagstaff and Grand Canyon National Park) offer good mountain biking. There's also excellent mountain biking at several Phoenix parks, and Tucson is one of the most bicycle-friendly cities in the country.

Backroads, 801 Cedar St., Berkeley, CA 94710-1800 (✆ **800/462-2848** or 510/527-1555; www.backroads.com), offers 7-day multisport trips through southern Utah and the Grand Canyon for $1,898 to $2,698. **Western Spirit Cycling Adventures,** 478 Mill Creek Dr., Moab, UT 84532 (✆ **800/845-2453** or 435/259-8732; www.westernspirit.com), has a number of interesting mountain-bike tours, including trips to both the North and South rims of the Grand Canyon and through the desert south of Tucson. Each trip lasts 5 days and costs $945 to $975.

Arizona Outback Adventures, 16447 N. 91st St., Suite 101, Scottsdale, AZ 85260 (✆ **866/455-1601** or 480/945-2881; www.azoutbackadventures.com), does 5-day Sonoran Desert single-track mountain-bike tours for $999.

WomanTours, 2340 Elmwood Ave., Rochester, NY 14618 (✆ **800/247-1444;** www.womantours.com), offers a couple of different Arizona bike tours that are exclusively for women. You'll pay $1,390 for a 7-night tour.

For information on mountain-bike tours and recommended rides in Phoenix and Tucson, see "Outdoor Pursuits" in chapters 4 and 9. You'll also find recommended rides in the Sedona and Prescott sections of chapter 5. If you plan to do much mountain biking around the state, pick up a copy of *Fat Tire Tales and Trails,* by Cosmic Ray. This little book of rides is both fun to read and fun to use; it's available in bike shops around the state.

BIRD-WATCHING Arizona is a birder's bonanza. In the southeastern corner of the state, many species found primarily south of the border reach the northern limits of their ranges. Combine this with several mountains that rise like islands from the desert and provide an appropriate habitat for hundreds of species, and you have some of the best bird-watching in the country.

Birding hot spots include Ramsey Canyon Preserve (known for its many species of hummingbirds); Cave Creek Canyon (nesting site for elegant trogons); Patagonia–Sonoita Creek Sanctuary (home to 22 species of flycatchers, kingbirds, and phoebes, as well as Montezuma quails); Madera Canyon (another "mountain island" that attracts many of the same species seen at Ramsey Canyon and Sonoita Creek); Buenos Aires National Wildlife Refuge (home to masked bobwhite quails and gray hawks); and the sewage ponds outside the town of Willcox (known for avocets and sandhill cranes). For further information on these birding spots, see chapter 10. To find out which birds have been spotted lately, call the **Tucson Audubon Society's Bird Report** (✆ **520/798-1005**).

Serious birders eager to add lots of rare birds to their life lists may want to visit southeastern Arizona on a guided tour. These are available through **High Lonesome Ecotours,** 570 S. Little Bear Trail, Sierra Vista, AZ 85635 (✆ **800/743-2668** or 520/458-9446; www.hilonesome.com), which charges $975 per person for a 5-day trip and $1,750 per person for an 8-day trip.

CANOEING/KAYAKING Okay, so maybe these sports don't jump to mind when you think of the desert, but there are indeed rivers and lakes here (and they happen to be some of the best places to see wildlife). By far the most memorable place for a flat-water kayak tour is Lake Powell. **Wilderness Inquiry,** 808 14th Ave. SE, Minneapolis, MN 55414-1516 (✆ **800/728-0719** or 612/676-9400; www.wildernessinquiry.org), offers several 6-day trips on the lake each spring and fall. The cost is $795. Multiday kayak tours are also offered by **Hidden Canyon Kayak** (✆ **800/343-3121** or

Hot Links

You don't have to be a hotshot golfer to get all heated up over the prospect of a few rounds of golf in Arizona. Combine near-perfect golf weather most of the year with great views and some unique challenges, and you've got all the makings of a great game. Phoenix and Tucson are known as winter golf destinations, but the state also offers golf throughout the year at higher-altitude courses in such places as Prescott, Flagstaff, and the White Mountains.

State water-conservation legislation limits the acreage that new Arizona golf courses can irrigate, which has given the state some of the most distinctive and difficult courses in the country. These desert or "target" courses are characterized by minimal fairways surrounded by natural desert landscapes. You might find yourself teeing off over the tops of cacti or searching for your ball amid boulders and mesquite. If your ball comes to rest in the desert, you can play the ball where it lies or, with a one-stroke penalty, drop it within two club lengths of the nearest point of grass (but no nearer the hole).

Keep in mind that resort courses and daily-fee public courses are not cheap. For most of the year, greens fees, which include golf-cart rentals, range from around $100 to $200 or more. Municipal courses usually have greens fees of around $40 for 18 holes, with golf-cart rentals costing extra (usually under $20).

It might not seem so initially, but summer is really a good time to visit many of Arizona's golf resorts. No, they don't have indoor courses or air-conditioned golf carts (at least not at most courses), but in summer, greens fees can be less than half what they are in winter. How does $64 for a round on the famous Gold Course at The Wigwam Golf Club sound?

With more than 200 golf courses, the Phoenix metropolitan area has the greatest concentration of fairways in the state. Whether you're looking to play one of the area's challenging top-rated resort courses or an economical-but-fun municipal course, you'll find plenty of choices.

For spectacular scenery at a resort course, it's just plain impossible to beat **The Boulders** (✆ **480/488-9028**), located north of Scottsdale in the town of Carefree. Elevated tee boxes beside giant balanced boulders are enough to distract anyone's concentration. Way over on the east side of the valley in Apache Junction, the **Gold Canyon Golf Resort** (✆ **480/982-9449**) has what have been rated as 3 of the best holes in the state: the 2nd, 3rd, and 4th holes on the Dinosaur Mountain course. Jumping over to Litchfield Park, on the far west side of the valley, you'll find **The Wigwam Golf Club & Spa** (✆ **800/909-4224** or 623/935-9414) and its three 18-hole courses; the Gold Course here is legendary. The **Phoenician Golf Club** (✆ **800/888-8234** or 480/423-2450) is another noteworthy resort course in the area. It has a mix of traditional and desert-style holes. The semiprivate **Troon North Golf Club (✆ 480/585-7700)**, a course that seems only barely carved out of raw desert, garners the most local accolades (and charges some of the highest greens fees in the state). If you want to swing where the pros do, beg, borrow, or steal a tee time on the Stadium Course at the **Tournament Players Club (TPC) of Scottsdale** (✆ **888/400-4001** or 480/585-4334). The area's favorite municipal course is Phoenix's **Papago Golf Course** (✆ **602/275-8428**), which has a killer 17th hole.

Tucson may not have as many golf courses as the Valley of the Sun, but the courses here are every bit as challenging and memorable. Among the city's resort courses, the Mountain Course at the **Ventana Canyon Golf and Racquet Club** (✆ **520/577-4015**) is legendary, especially the spectacular 107-yard, par-3 hole 3. Likewise, the 8th hole on the Sunrise Course at **El Conquistador Country Club** (✆ **520/544-1800**) is among the most memorable par-3 holes in the area. If you want to play where the pros have played, reserve a tee time at the **Omni Tucson National Golf Resort and Spa** (✆ **520/575-7540**), which for many years was home to the Tucson Open. **Randolph North** (✆ **520/791-4161**), Tucson's best municipal course, has been the site of the city's annual LPGA tournament. The **Silverbell Municipal Course** (✆ **520/791-5235**) boasts a bear of a par-5 17th hole,; and at **Fred Enke Municipal Course** (✆ **520/791-2539**), you'll find the city's only desert-style municipal golf course.

Courses worth trying in other parts of the state include **Los Caballeros Golf Club** (✆ **928/684-2704**), which is part of a luxury guest ranch outside Wickenburg. *Golf Digest* has rated this course one of Arizona's top 10. For concentration-taxing scenery, few courses compare with the **Sedona Golf Resort** (✆ **877/733-9885** or 928/284-9355), which has good views of the red rocks; try to get a sunrise or twilight tee time. Way up in the Four Corners region, in the town of Page, you'll find the 27-hole **Lake Powell National Golf Course** (✆ **928/645-2023**), which is one of the most spectacular in the state. The fairways here wrap around the base of the red-sandstone bluff atop which sits the town of Page. South of Tucson, the **Tubac Golf Resort** (✆ **520/398-2211**) has cows grazing along its fairways for a classic Wild West feel. Along the Colorado River, there are a couple of memorable courses. Lake Havasu City's **London Bridge Golf Club** (✆ **928/855-2719**) offers a view of, you guessed it, the London Bridge. For more dramatic views, check out the **Emerald Canyon Golf Course** (✆ **928/667-3366**), a municipal course in Parker that plays up and down small canyons and offers the sort of scenery usually associated only with the most expensive desert resort courses.

928/645-8866; www.diamondriver.com/kayak), which charges $760 to $1,000 for 4- to 6-day trips.

There are also a couple of companies that rent canoes and offer trips on the Colorado River south of Lake Mead. See chapter 11 for details.

FISHING The fishing scene in Arizona is as diverse as the landscape. Large and small lakes around the state offer excellent fishing for warm-water game fish such as largemouth, smallmouth, and striped bass. Good trout fishing can be found up on the Mogollon Rim and in the White Mountains, as well as in the easily accessible section of the free-running Colorado River between Glen Canyon Dam and Lees Ferry just upstream from the Grand Canyon. In fact, this latter area is among the country's most fabled stretches of trout water.

Fishing licenses for nonresidents are available for 1 day, 5 days, 4 months, and 1 year. Various special stamps and licenses may also apply. Nonresident fees range from $17 for a 1-day license (valid for trout) to $70 for a 1-year license ($58 additional for a trout stamp). Keep in mind that if you're heading for an Indian reservation, you'll have to get a special permit for that reservation. For information on Arizona state fishing licenses, contact the **Arizona Game and Fish Department,** 2221 W. Greenway Rd., Phoenix, AZ 85023-4399 (© **800/705-4165** or 602/942-3000; www.azgfd.com).

GOLF For many of Arizona's winter visitors, golf is the main attraction. The state's hundreds of golf courses range from easy public courses to PGA championship links that have challenged the best.

In Phoenix and Tucson, greens fees, like room rates, are seasonal. In the popular winter months, greens fees at resort courses generally range from about $100 to $250 for 18 holes, although this usually includes a mandatory golf-cart rental. In summer, fees often drop to less than half this amount. Almost all resorts offer special golf packages as well.

For information on some of the state's top courses, see "Hot Links," below. For more information on golfing in Arizona, contact the **Arizona Golf Association,** 7226 N. 16th St., Suite 200, Phoenix, AZ 85020 (© **800/458-8484** in Arizona, or 602/944-3035; www.azgolf.org), which publishes a directory listing all the courses in the state. You can also access the directory online. In addition, you can pick up the *Phoenix Golf Guide* and the *Tucson Golf Guide* (www.azgolfguides.com) at visitor centers, golf courses, and many hotels and resorts.

HIKING/BACKPACKING Arizona offers some of the most fascinating and challenging hiking in the country. All across the state's lowland deserts, parks and other public lands are laced with trails that lead past saguaro cacti, to the tops of desert peaks, and deep into rugged canyons. The state also has vast forests, many of which are protected in wilderness areas, which have many more miles of hiking trails. In northern Arizona, there are good day hikes in Grand Canyon National Park, in the San Francisco Peaks north of Flagstaff, near Page and Lake Powell, and in Navajo National Monument. In the Phoenix area, popular day hikes include the trails up Camelback Mountain and Piestewa (Squaw) Peak, and the many trails in South Mountain Park. In the Tucson area, there are hikes on Mount Lemmon and in Saguaro National Park, Sabino Canyon, and Catalina State Park. In the southern part of the state, there are good day hikes in Chiricahua National Monument, Coronado National Forest, Cochise Stronghold, Organ Pipe Cactus National Monument, and the Nature Conservancy's Ramsey Canyon Preserve and Patagonia–Sonoita Creek Sanctuary.

The state's two most unforgettable overnight backpack trips are the hike down to Phantom Ranch at the bottom of the Grand Canyon, and the hike into Havasu Canyon, a side canyon of the Grand Canyon. A third popular backpacking trip is through Paria Canyon, a narrow slot canyon that originates in Utah and terminates in Arizona at Lees Ferry. There are also many overnight opportunities in the San Francisco Peaks north of Flagstaff and in the White Mountains of eastern Arizona.

Guided backpacking trips of different durations and difficulty levels are offered by the **Grand Canyon Field Institute,** P.O. Box 399, Grand Canyon, AZ 86023 (✆ **866/471-4435** or 928/638-2485; www.grandcanyon.org/fieldinstitute); and by **Discovery Treks,** 28248 N. Tatum Blvd., Suite B1, no. 414, Cave Creek, AZ 85331 (✆ **888/256-8731;** www.discoverytreks.com).

Backroads, 801 Cedar St., Berkeley, CA 94710 (✆ **800/462-2848** or 510/527-1555; www.backroads.com), better known for its bike trips, also offers a couple of 7-day hiking/biking trips to Grand Canyon, Bryce Canyon, and Zion national parks for between $1,900 and $2,700.

Vermont-based **Country Walkers** (✆ **800/464-9255** or 802/244-1387; www.countrywalkers.com) has a hiking-oriented trip that takes in the Grand Canyon and Sedona.

HORSEBACK RIDING/WESTERN ADVENTURES Saddle up that palomino, pardner, and let's ride. Arizona is a city slicker's dream come true. All over Arizona there are stables where you climb into the saddle of a sure-footed trail horse and ride off into the sunset. Among the more scenic spots for riding are Grand Canyon National Park, Monument Valley Navajo Tribal Park, Canyon de Chelly National Monument, the red-rock country around Sedona, Phoenix's South Mountain Park, the foot of the Superstition Mountains east of Phoenix, and the foot of the Santa Catalina Mountains outside Tucson. See the individual chapters that follow for listings of riding stables; see below for information on overnight guided horseback rides.

Among the most popular guided adventures in Arizona are the mule rides down into the Grand Canyon. These trips vary in length from 1 to 2 days; for reservations and more information, contact **Grand Canyon National Park Lodges/Xanterra Parks & Resorts** (✆ **888/297-2757,** 303/297-2757, or for last-minute reservations, 928/638-2631; www.grandcanyonlodges.com). Be advised, however, that you'll need to make mule-ride reservations many months in advance. If at the last minute (1 or 2 days before you want to ride) you decide you want to go on a mule trip into the Grand Canyon, contact Grand Canyon National Park Lodges at its last-minute reservations phone number (see above), or stop by the **Bright Angel Transportation Desk,** in Grand Canyon Village, on the chance there might be space available.

It's also possible to do overnight horseback rides in various locations around the state. For information on overnight rides into the Superstition Mountains east of Phoenix, contact **Don Donnelly Horseback Adventures** (✆ **602/810-7029;** www.dondonnelly.com).

Want to kick it up a notch? At the **Arizona Cowboy College,** Lorill Equestrian Center, 30208 N. 152nd St., Scottsdale, AZ 85262 (✆ **888/330-8070** or 480/471-3151; www.cowboycollege.com), you can literally learn the ropes and the brands and how to say, "Git along little doggie" like you really mean it. This is no city slicker's staged roundup; this is the real thing. You actually learn how to be a real cowboy. Six-day programs cost $2,250.

HOT-AIR BALLOONING For much of the year, the desert has the perfect environment for hot-air ballooning—cool, still air and wide-open spaces. Consequently, dozens of ballooning companies operate across the state. Most are in Phoenix and Tucson, but several others operate near Sedona, which is by far the most picturesque spot in the state for a balloon ride. See the individual chapters for specific information.

HOUSEBOATING With the Colorado River turned into a string of long lakes, houseboat vacations are a natural in Arizona. Although this doesn't have to be an active vacation, fishing, hiking, and swimming are usually part of a houseboat stay. Rentals are available on Lake Powell, Lake Mead, and Lake Mohave; however, the canyon scenery of Lake Powell makes it the hands-down best spot for a houseboat vacation. Make reservations well in advance for a summer trip. No prior experience (or license) is necessary, and plenty of hands-on instruction is provided before you leave the marina. See chapters 7 and 11 for more information on houseboat rentals.

SKIING Although Arizona is better known as a desert state, it does have plenty of mountains and even a few ski areas. The two biggest and best ski areas are **Arizona Snowbowl** (**© 928/779-1951;** www.arizonasnowbowl.com), outside Flagstaff, and **Sunrise Park Resort** (**© 800/772-7669** or 928/735-7669; www.sunriseskipark.com), on the Apache Reservation outside the town of McNary in the White Mountains. Snowbowl is more popular because of the ease of the drive from Phoenix and the proximity to good lodging and dining options in Flagstaff. However, despite the convenience and the fact that Snowbowl has more vertical feet of skiing, Sunrise is my favorite Arizona ski area because it offers almost twice as many runs. Both ski areas offer rentals and lessons.

When it's a good snow year, Tucsonans head up to **Mount Lemmon Ski Valley** (**© 520/576-1400**), the southernmost ski area in the U.S. Snows here aren't as reliable as they are farther north, so be sure to call first to make sure the ski area is operating.

During snow-blessed winters, cross-country skiers can find plenty of snow-covered forest roads outside Flagstaff, at Sunrise Park outside the town of McNary, at the South Rim of the Grand Canyon, in the White Mountains around Greer and Alpine, outside Payson on the Mogollon Rim, and on Mount Lemmon outside Flagstaff.

TENNIS After golf, tennis is probably the most popular winter sport in the desert, and resorts all over Arizona have tennis courts. Many resorts require you to wear traditional tennis attire and don't include court time in the room rates. No courts anywhere in the state can match the views you'll have from those at Enchantment Resort, outside Sedona. Other noteworthy tennis-oriented resorts include, in the Phoenix/Scottsdale area, The Phoenician, Copperwynd Resort & Club, The Fairmont Scottsdale Princess, the Pointe South Mountain Resort, and the Pointe Hilton Tapatio Cliffs Resort; and, in Tucson, The Lodge at Ventana Canyon, the Hilton Tucson El Conquistador Golf & Tennis Resort, The Westin La Paloma Resort & Spa, the Westward Look Resort, and the Omni Tucson National Golf Resort & Spa.

WHITE-WATER RAFTING The desert doesn't support a lot of roaring rivers, but with the white water in the Grand Canyon, you don't need too many other choices. Rafting the Grand Canyon is the dream of nearly every white-water enthusiast—if it's one of yours as well, plan well ahead. Companies and trips are limited, and they tend to fill up early. For a discussion and list of companies that run trips down the canyon, see chapter 6.

For 1-day rafting trips on the Colorado below the main section of the Grand

Canyon, contact **Hualapai River Runners** (✆ **928/769-2219;** www.grandcanyon resort.com). For a half-day float on the Colorado above the Grand Canyon, contact **Colorado River Discovery** (✆ **888/522-6644;** www.raftthecanyon.com), which runs trips between Glen Canyon Dam and Lees Ferry.

Rafting trips are also available on the upper Salt River east of Phoenix. **Wilderness Aware Rafting** (✆ **800/462-7238;** www.inaraft.com), **Canyon Rio Rafting** (✆ **800/272-3353;** www.canyonrio.com), and **Mild to Wild Rafting** (✆ **800/567-6745;** www.mild2wildrafting.com) all run trips of varying lengths down this river (conditions permitting).

14 Getting Around Arizona

BY PLANE

Overseas visitors can take advantage of the APEX (Advance Purchase Excursion) reductions offered by all major U.S. and European carriers. In addition, some large airlines offer transatlantic or transpacific passengers special discount tickets under the name **Visit USA,** which allows mostly one-way travel from one U.S. destination to another at very low prices. Unavailable in the U.S., these discount tickets must be purchased abroad in conjunction with your international fare. This system is the easiest, fastest, and cheapest way to see the country.

Arizona is a big state (the 6th largest), so if your time is short, you may want to consider flying between cities. **US Airways** (✆ **800/428-4322;** www.us airways.com) serves Phoenix, Tucson, Flagstaff, Lake Havasu City, and Yuma. **Scenic Airlines** (✆ **800/634-6801;** www.scenic.com) flies between Las Vegas and the Grand Canyon.

BY CAR

For detailed information on renting a car in Arizona, see "Getting There" earlier in this chapter.

Unless you plan to spend the bulk of your vacation in a city where walking is the best way to get around (read: New York City), the most cost-effective way to travel is by car.

If you're visiting from abroad and plan to rent a car in the U.S., keep in mind that foreign driver's licenses are usually recognized in the U.S., but you should get an international one if your home license is not in English.

Check out **Breezenet.com,** which offers domestic car-rental discounts with some of the most competitive rates around.

In Arizona, a right turn on a red light is permitted after a complete stop. Seat belts are required for the driver and for all passengers. Children 4 and under, or who weigh 40 pounds or less, must be in a child's car seat. General speed limits are 25 to 35 mph in towns and cities, 15 mph in school zones, and 55 to 65 mph on two-lane highways. On rural interstate highways, the speed limit ranges from 65 to 75 mph.

Always be sure to keep your gas tank topped off. In many parts of Arizona, it's not unusual to drive 60 miles without seeing a gas station. ***Note:*** A breakdown in the desert can be more than just an inconvenience—it can be dangerous. Always carry drinking water with you while driving through the desert, and if you plan to head off on back roads, carry extra water for the car's radiator as well.

BY TRAIN

International visitors can buy a **USA Rail Pass,** good for 5, 15, or 30 days of unlimited travel on **Amtrak** (✆ **800/USA-RAIL;** www.amtrak.com). The pass is available online or through many overseas travel agents. See Amtrak's website for the cost of travel within the western, eastern, or northwestern United States. Reservations are generally required and should be made as early as possible. Regional rail passes are also available.

The train is not really a viable way of getting around much of Arizona because there is no north-south Amtrak service between Grand Canyon/Flagstaff and Phoenix or between Tucson and Phoenix. However, Amtrak will sell you a ticket to Phoenix, which includes a shuttle-bus ride from Flagstaff or Tucson. You can also get to the town of Williams, 30 miles west of Flagstaff, on Amtrak, and in Williams transfer to the Grand Canyon Railway excursion train, which runs to Grand Canyon Village at the South Rim of the Grand Canyon (see chapter 6 for details). Be aware, however, that the Williams stop is on the outskirts of town; you'll have to arrange in advance to be picked up.

15 Tips on Accommodations

When making hotel reservations for late spring or early fall, find out when hotel rates drop for the summer or go up for the fall so that you can schedule your trip for right after the rates go down (or just before they go back up). Many resorts also have a short discounted season right before Christmas (just think, you can do your holiday shopping in Arizona).

As if winter resort rates in Arizona aren't high enough, you can expect to also pay a resort fee at most resorts around the state. These fees, which are generally around $15 to $20, cover such things as local calls and toll-free phone number access, daily newspaper delivery, and exercise room use. Of course, if you're like me, you think all those things should be included in the regular room rates.

Remember, if you don't absolutely need all the amenities of a big resort, there are dozens of chain-motel options in the Phoenix and Tucson areas. Alternatively, you can get a bit more for your money if you head to such smaller towns as Wickenburg, Bullhead City, Lake Havasu City, and Yuma. If you must stay in the Phoenix or Tucson area, head for the suburbs. The farther you drive from the resort areas, the more you can save.

If you like to stay at B&Bs, there are a few helpful resources you should know about. **Mi Casa Su Casa** (✆ **800/456-0682** or 480/990-0682; www.azres.com) can book you into hundreds of homes across the state, as can **Arizona Trails Travel Services** (✆ **888/799-4284** or 480/837-4284; www.arizonatrails.com), which also books tour and hotel reservations. For a list of some of the best B&Bs in the state, contact the **Arizona Association of Bed & Breakfast Inns** (www.arizona-bed-breakfast.com).

SURFING FOR HOTELS

In addition to the online travel booking sites **Travelocity, Expedia, Orbitz, Priceline,** and **Hotwire,** you can book hotels through **Hotels.com**; **Quikbook** (www.quikbook.com); and **Travelaxe** (www.travelaxe.net).

HotelChatter.com is a daily webzine offering smart coverage and critiques of hotels worldwide. Go to **TripAdvisor.com** or **HotelShark.com** for helpful independent consumer reviews of hotels and resort properties.

It's a good idea to **get a confirmation number** and **make a printout** of any online booking transaction.

SAVING ON YOUR HOTEL ROOM

The **rack rate** is the maximum rate that a hotel charges for a room. Hardly anybody pays this price, however, except in high season or on holidays. To lower the cost of your room:

- **Ask about special rates or other discounts.** You may qualify for corporate, student, military, senior, frequent flier, trade union, or other discounts.

- **Dial direct.** When booking a room in a chain hotel, you'll often get a better deal by calling the individual hotel's reservation desk rather than the chain's main number.
- **Book online.** Many hotels offer Internet-only discounts, or supply rooms to Priceline, Hotwire, or Expedia at rates much lower than the ones you can get through the hotel itself.
- **Remember the law of supply and demand.** Resort hotels are most crowded and therefore most expensive on weekends, so discounts are usually available for midweek stays. Business hotels in downtown locations are busiest during the week, so you can expect big discounts over the weekend.
- **Look into group or long-stay discounts.** If you come as part of a large group, you should be able to negotiate a bargain rate. Likewise, if you're planning a long stay (at least 5 days), you might qualify for a discount. As a general rule, expect 1 night free after a 7-night stay.
- **Sidestep excess surcharges and hidden costs.** Many hotels have the unpleasant practice of nickel-and-diming its guests with opaque surcharges. When you book a room, ask what is included in the room rate and what is extra. Avoid dialing direct from hotel phones, which can have exorbitant rates. And don't be tempted by the room's minibar offerings: Most hotels charge through the nose for water, soda, and snacks. Finally, ask about local taxes and service charges, which can increase the cost of a room by 15% or more.
- **Consider enrolling in hotel "frequent-stay" programs,** which are upping the ante lately to win the loyalty of repeat customers. Frequent guests can now accumulate points or credits to earn free hotel nights, airline miles, in-room amenities, merchandise, tickets to concerts and events, discounts on sporting facilities—and even credit toward stock in the participating hotel, in the case of the Jameson Inn hotel group. Perks are awarded not only by many chain hotels and motels (Hilton HHonors, Marriott Rewards, Wyndham ByRequest, to name a few), but individual inns and B&Bs. Many chain hotels partner with other hotel chains, car-rental firms, airlines, and credit-card companies to give consumers additional incentive to do repeat business.

LANDING THE BEST ROOM

Somebody has to get the best room in the house. It might as well be you. You can start by joining the hotel's frequent-guest program, which may make you eligible for upgrades. A hotel-branded credit card usually gives its owner "silver" or "gold" status in frequent-guest programs for free. Always ask about a corner room. They're often larger and quieter, with more windows and light, and they often cost the same as standard rooms. When you make your reservation, ask if the hotel is renovating; if it is, request a room away from the construction. If you're a light sleeper, request a quiet room away from vending or ice machines, elevators, restaurants, bars, and discos. Ask for a room that has most recently been renovated or redecorated.

If you aren't happy with your room when you arrive, ask for another one. Most lodgings will be willing to accommodate you.

In resort areas, particularly in warm climates such as Arizona, ask the following questions before you book a room:

- What's the view like? Cost-conscious travelers may be willing to pay less for a back room facing the parking lot, especially if they don't plan to spend much time in their room.

- Does the room have air-conditioning or ceiling fans? Do the windows open? If they do and the nighttime entertainment takes place alfresco, you may want to find out when showtime is over.

FAST FACTS: Arizona

American Express There are offices or representatives in Phoenix and Scottsdale. For information, call © **800/528-4800.**

Area Codes The area code in Phoenix is 602. In Scottsdale, Tempe, Mesa, and the east valley, it's 480. In Glendale and the west valley, it's 623. The area code for Tucson and southeastern Arizona is 520. The rest of the state is area code 928.

ATM Networks See "ATMs," p. 34.

Automobile Organizations Auto clubs will supply maps, suggested routes, guidebooks, accident and bail-bond insurance, and emergency road service. The **American Automobile Association (AAA)** is the major auto club in the U.S. If you belong to an auto club in your home country, inquire about AAA reciprocity before you leave. You may be able to join AAA even if you're not a member of a reciprocal club; to inquire, call AAA (© **800/222-4357**). AAA is actually an organization of regional auto clubs, so look under "AAA Automobile Club" in the White Pages of the telephone directory. AAA has a nationwide emergency road service telephone number (© 800/AAA-HELP).

Business Hours The following are general hours; specific establishments' hours may vary. Banks are open Monday through Friday from 9am to 5pm (some also Sat 9am–noon). Stores are open Monday through Saturday from 10am to 6pm, and Sunday from noon to 5pm (malls usually stay open until 9pm Mon–Sat). Bars are legally allowed to be open until 2am.

Car Rentals See "Getting There by Car," p. 33.

Cashpoints See "ATMs," p. 34.

Currency The most common bills are the $1 (a "buck"), $5, $10, and $20 denominations. There are also $2 bills (seldom encountered), $50 bills, and $100 bills (the last two are usually not welcome as payment for small purchases).

Coins come in eight denominations: 1¢ (1 cent, or a penny); 5¢ (5 cents, or a nickel); 10¢ (10 cents, or a dime); 25¢ (25 cents, or a quarter); 50¢ (50 cents, or a half dollar); the gold-colored Sacagawea coin, worth $1; Presidential $1 coin; and the rare silver dollar.

For additional information see "Money & Costs," p. 34.

Customs **What You Can Bring Into Arizona** Every visitor older than 21 may bring in, free of duty, the following: 1 liter of wine or hard liquor; 200 cigarettes, 100 cigars (but not from Cuba), or 3 pounds of smoking tobacco; and $100 worth of gifts. These exemptions are offered to travelers who spend at least 72 hours in the U.S. and who have not claimed them within the preceding 6 months. It is altogether forbidden to bring into the country foodstuffs (particularly fruit, cooked meats, and canned goods) and plants (vegetables, seeds, tropical plants, and the like). Foreign tourists may carry in or out up to

$10,000 in U.S. or foreign currency with no formalities; larger sums must be declared to U.S. Customs on entering or leaving, which includes filing form CM 4790. For details regarding U.S. Customs and Border Protection, consult your nearest U.S. embassy or consulate, or **U.S. Customs** (✆ **202/927-1770;** www.customs.ustreas.gov).

What You Can Take Home from Arizona:

Canadian Citizens: For a clear summary of Canadian rules, write for the booklet *I Declare,* issued by the **Canada Border Services Agency** (✆ **800/461-9999** in Canada, or 204/983-3500; **www.cbsa-asfc.gc.ca**).

U.K. Citizens: For information, contact **HM Customs & Excise** at ✆ **0845/010-9000** (from outside the U.K., 020/8929-0152), or consult their website at **www.hmce.gov.uk**.

Australian Citizens: A helpful brochure available from Australian consulates or Customs offices is *Know Before You Go.* For more information, call the **Australian Customs Service** at ✆ **1300/363-263,** or log on to **www.customs.gov.au**.

New Zealand Citizens: Most questions are answered in a free pamphlet available at New Zealand consulates and Customs offices: *New Zealand Customs Guide for Travellers, Notice no. 4.* For more information, contact **New Zealand Customs,** The Customhouse, 17–21 Whitmore St., Box 2218, Wellington (✆ **04/473-6099** or 0800/428-786; **www.customs.govt.nz**).

Drinking Laws The legal age for purchase and consumption of alcoholic beverages is 21; proof of age is required and often requested at bars, nightclubs, and restaurants, so it's always a good idea to bring ID when you go out. Beer and wine can often be purchased in supermarkets, but liquor laws vary from state to state. In Arizona, liquor is sold at supermarkets.

Do not carry open containers of alcohol in your car or any public area that isn't zoned for alcohol consumption. The police can fine you on the spot. And nothing will ruin your trip faster than getting a citation for DUI ("driving under the influence"), so don't even think about driving while intoxicated.

Driving Rules See "Getting Around Arizona," p. 55.

Electricity Like Canada, the U.S. uses 110–120 volts AC (60 cycles), compared to 220–240 volts AC (50 cycles) in most of Europe, Australia, and New Zealand. Downward converters that change 220–240 volts to 110–120 volts are difficult to find in the U.S., so bring one with you.

Embassies & Consulates All embassies are located in the nation's capital, Washington, D.C. Some consulates are located in major U.S. cities, and most nations have a mission to the United Nations in New York City. If your country isn't listed below, call for directory information in Washington, D.C. (✆ **202/555-1212**), or log on to **www.embassy.org/embassies**.

The embassy of **Australia** is at 1601 Massachusetts Ave. NW, Washington, DC 20036 (✆ **202/797-3000;** www.austemb.org). There are consulates in New York, Honolulu, Houston, Los Angeles, and San Francisco.

The embassy of **Canada** is at 501 Pennsylvania Ave. NW, Washington, DC 20001 (✆ **202/682-1740;** www.canadianembassy.org). Other Canadian consulates are in Buffalo (New York), Detroit, Los Angeles, New York, and Seattle.

The embassy of **Ireland** is at 2234 Massachusetts Ave. NW, Washington, DC 20008 (✆ **202/462-3939;** www.irelandemb.org). Irish consulates are in Boston, Chicago, New York, San Francisco, and other cities. See website for complete listing.

The embassy of **New Zealand** is at 37 Observatory Circle NW, Washington, DC 20008 (✆ **202/328-4800;** www.nzemb.org). New Zealand consulates are in Los Angeles, Salt Lake City, San Francisco, and Seattle.

The embassy of the **United Kingdom** is at 3100 Massachusetts Ave. NW, Washington, DC 20008 (✆ **202/588-7800;** www.britainusa.com). Other British consulates are in Atlanta, Boston, Chicago, Cleveland, Houston, Los Angeles, New York, San Francisco, and Seattle.

Emergencies Call ✆ **911** to report a fire, call the police, or get an ambulance anywhere in the U.S. This is a toll-free call. (No coins are required at public telephones.)

Gasoline (Petrol) At press time, in the U.S., the cost of gasoline (also known as gas, but never petrol), is abnormally high. Taxes are already included in the printed price. One U.S. gallon equals 3.8 liters or .85 imperial gallons. Fill-up locations are known as gas or service stations.

Holidays Banks, government offices, post offices, and many stores, restaurants, and museums are closed on the following legal national holidays: January 1 (New Year's Day), the third Monday in January (Martin Luther King, Jr., Day), the third Monday in February (Presidents' Day), the last Monday in May (Memorial Day), July 4 (Independence Day), the first Monday in September (Labor Day), the second Monday in October (Columbus Day), November 11 (Veterans' Day/Armistice Day), the fourth Thursday in November (Thanksgiving Day), and December 25 (Christmas). The Tuesday after the first Monday in November is Election Day, a federal government holiday in presidential-election years (held every 4 years, and next in 2008).

For more information on holidays, see "Arizona Calendar of Events," earlier in this chapter.

Hospitals The state's top hospitals are in Phoenix and Tucson. See "Fast Facts" in chapters 4 (p. 84) and 9 (p. 328) for recommendations.

Legal Aid If you are "pulled over" for a minor infraction (such as speeding), never attempt to pay the fine directly to a police officer; this could be construed as attempted bribery, a much more serious crime. Pay fines by mail, or directly into the hands of the clerk of the court. If accused of a more serious offense, say and do nothing before consulting a lawyer. Here the burden is on the state to prove a person's guilt beyond a reasonable doubt, and everyone has the right to remain silent, whether he or she is suspected of a crime or actually arrested. Once arrested, a person can make one telephone call to a party of his or her choice. International visitors should call your embassy or consulate.

Lost & Found Be sure to tell all of your credit card companies the minute you discover your wallet has been lost or stolen, and file a report at the nearest police precinct. Your credit card company or insurer may require a police report number or record of the loss. Most credit card companies have an emergency toll-free number to call if your card is lost or stolen; they may be able to wire you a cash advance immediately or deliver an emergency credit card in a day or two. Visa's U.S. emergency number is © **800/847-2911** or 410/581-9994. American Express cardholders and traveler's check holders should call © **800/221-7282.** MasterCard holders should call © **800/307-7309** or 636/722-7111. For other credit cards, call the toll-free number directory at © **800/555-1212.**

If you need emergency cash over the weekend when all banks and American Express offices are closed, you can have money wired to you via **Western Union** (© **800/325-6000;** www.westernunion.com).

Mail At press time, domestic postage rates were 26¢ for a postcard and 41¢ for a letter. For international mail, a first-class letter of up to 1 ounce costs 90¢ (69¢ to Canada and Mexico), and a first-class postcard costs 90¢ (69¢ to Canada and Mexico). For more information go to **www.usps.com** and click on "Calculate Postage."

If you aren't sure what your address will be in the U.S., mail can be sent to you, in your name, c/o General Delivery at the main post office of the city or region where you expect to be. (Call © **800/275-8777** for information on the nearest post office.) The addressee must pick up mail in person and must produce proof of identity (driver's license, passport, and so on.). Most post offices will hold your mail for up to 1 month. They are open Monday to Friday from 8am to 6pm, and Saturday from 9am to 3pm.

Always include zip codes when mailing items in the U.S. If you don't know your zip code, visit www.usps.com/zip4.

Newspapers & Magazines The *Arizona Republic* is Arizona's largest daily newspaper and can be found throughout central and northern Arizona. In the southern part of the state, you are more likely to find Tucson's *Arizona Daily Star,* a morning daily. *Arizona Highways* is a beautiful and informative photo-driven monthly magazine published by the Arizona Department of Transportation. Both Phoenix and Tucson have a number of glossy monthly lifestyle magazines that are worth picking up for their monthly events listings.

Passports **For Residents of Australia:** You can pick up an application from your local post office or any branch of Passports Australia, but you must schedule an interview at the passport office to present your application materials. Call the **Australian Passport Information Service** at © **131-232,** or visit the government website at www.passports.gov.au.

For Residents of Canada: Passport applications are available at travel agencies throughout Canada or from the central **Passport Office,** Department of Foreign Affairs and International Trade, Ottawa, ON K1A 0G3 (© **800/567-6868;** www.ppt.gc.ca). ***Note:*** Canadian children who travel must have their own passports. However, if you hold a valid Canadian passport issued before December 11, 2001 that bears the name of your child, the passport remains valid for you and your child until it expires.

For Residents of Ireland: You can apply for a 10-year passport at the **Passport Office,** Setanta Centre, Molesworth Street, Dublin 2 (© **01/671-1633;** www.irl gov.ie/iveagh). Those under age 18 and over 65 must apply for a 3-year passport. You can also apply at 1A South Mall, Cork (© **021/272-525**) or at most main post offices.

For Residents of New Zealand: You can pick up a passport application at any New Zealand Passports Office or download it from their website. Contact the

Passports Office at ✆ **0800/225-050** in New Zealand or 04/474-8100, or log on to www.passports.govt.nz.

For Residents of the United Kingdom: To pick up an application for a standard 10-year passport (5-yr. passport for children under 16), visit your nearest passport office, major post office, or travel agency, or contact the **United Kingdom Passport Service** (✆ **0870/521-0410;** www.ukpa.gov.uk).

Police In most places in Arizona, phone ✆ **911** for emergencies. A few small towns have not adopted this emergency phone number, so if 911 doesn't work, dial 0 (zero) for the operator and state your reason for calling.

Safety See "Safety," earlier in this chapter.

Taxes The U.S. has no value-added tax (VAT) or other indirect tax at the national level. Every state, county, and city may levy its own local tax on all purchases, including hotel and restaurant checks and airline tickets. These taxes will not appear on price tags.

In Arizona, the state sales tax is 5.6%, but communities can add local sales tax on top of this. You'll pay 8% or more at most places in Arizona. Expect to pay around 30% tax on car rentals at the Tucson airport and around 50% in taxes and surcharges at the Phoenix airport (around 10% less if you rent outside the airports). Hotel room taxes range from around 6% to 17%.

Telegraph, Telex & Fax **Telegraph and telex services** are provided primarily by Western Union. You can telegraph money, or have it telegraphed to you, very quickly over the Western Union system, but this service can cost as much as 15% to 20% of the amount sent.

Most hotels have **fax machines** available for guest use (be sure to ask about the charge to use it). Many hotel rooms are even wired for guests' fax machines. A less expensive way to send and receive faxes may be at stores such as **The UPS Store** (formerly Mail Boxes Etc.).

Time The continental U.S. is divided into **four time zones:** Eastern Standard Time (EST), Central Standard Time (CST), Mountain Standard Time (MST), and Pacific Standard Time (PST). Alaska and Hawaii have their own zones. For example, when it's 9am in Los Angeles (PST), it's 7am in Honolulu (HST),10am in Denver (MST), 11am in Chicago (CST), noon in New York City (EST), 5pm in London (GMT), and 2am the next day in Sydney.

Daylight saving time is in effect from 1am on the second Sunday in March to 1am on the first Sunday in November, except in Arizona, Hawaii, the U.S. Virgin Islands, and Puerto Rico. Daylight saving time moves the clock 1 hour ahead of standard time.

Arizona is in the Mountain Time zone, but it does *not* observe daylight saving time. From the second Sunday in March until the first Sunday in November, there is no time difference between Arizona and California and other states on the West Coast. There is an exception, though—the Navajo Reservation observes daylight saving time. However, the Hopi Reservation does not.

Tipping Tips are a very important part of certain workers' income, and gratuities are the standard way of showing appreciation for services provided. (Tipping is certainly not compulsory if the service is poor!) In hotels, tip **bellhops** at least $1 per bag ($2–$3 if you have a lot of luggage) and tip the **chamber staff**

$1 to $2 per day (more if you've left a disaster area for him or her to clean up). Tip the **doorman** or **concierge** only if he or she has provided you with some specific service (for example, calling a cab for you or obtaining difficult-to-get theater tickets). Tip the **valet-parking attendant** $1 every time you get your car.

In restaurants, bars, and nightclubs, tip **service staff** 15% to 20% of the check, tip **bartenders** 10% to 15%, tip **checkroom attendants** $1 per garment, and tip **valet-parking attendants** $1 per vehicle.

As for other service personnel, tip **cab drivers** 15% of the fare; tip **skycaps** at airports at least $1 per bag ($2–$3 if you have a lot of luggage); and tip **hairdressers** and **barbers** 15% to 20%.

Toilets You won't find public toilets or "restrooms" on the streets in most U.S. cities, but they can be found in hotel lobbies, bars, restaurants, museums, department stores, railway and bus stations, and service stations. Large hotels and fast-food restaurants are often the best bet for clean facilities. If possible, avoid the toilets at parks, which tend to be dirty; some may be unsafe. Restaurants and bars in resorts or heavily visited areas may reserve their restrooms for patrons.

Useful Phone Numbers Arizona Office of Tourism ✆ 866/275-5816 or 602/364-3700; Greater Phoenix Convention & Visitors Bureau ✆ 877/225-5749 or 602/452-6282; Metropolitan Tucson Convention & Visitors Bureau ✆ 800/638-8350 or 520/624-1817; road conditions ✆ 888/411-7623 or 928/638-7888; U.S. Passport Agency ✆ 877/487-2778.

Visas For information about U.S. Visas, go to **http://travel.state.gov**, and click on "Visas." Or go to one of the following websites:

Australian citizens can obtain up-to-date visa information from the **U.S. Embassy Canberra,** Moonah Place, Yarralumla, ACT 2600 (✆ **02/6214-5600**), or by checking the U.S. Diplomatic Mission's website at **http://usembassy-australia.state.gov/consular**.

British subjects can obtain up-to-date visa information by calling the **U.S. Embassy Visa Information Line** (✆ **0891/200-290**) or by visiting the "Visas to the U.S." section of the American Embassy London's website at **www.usembassy.org.uk**.

Irish citizens can obtain up-to-date visa information through the **Embassy of the USA Dublin,** 42 Elgin Rd., Dublin 4, Ireland (✆ **353/1-668-8777;** or by checking the "Consular Services" section of the website at **http://dublin.usembassy.gov**).

Citizens of **New Zealand** can obtain up-to-date visa information by contacting the **U.S. Embassy New Zealand,** 29 Fitzherbert Terrace, Thorndon, Wellington (✆ **644/472-2068**), or get the information directly from the website at **http://wellington.usembassy.gov**.

3

Suggested Arizona Itineraries

You could spend a lifetime exploring Arizona—an important fact to keep in mind when planning a trip to this incredibly diverse region of the American Southwest. A map just isn't going to give you a clear picture of how big this state is. It's roughly 400 miles from north to south (about as far as New York City to Raleigh, North Carolina) and 300 miles from east to west (think New York to Richmond, Virginia). It could easily take you 9 hours to drive from one end of the state to the other, and if you want to see it all, you'll be doing just that—driving for hours and hours. Even if you just want to hit the highlights, reconcile yourself to doing a lot of driving. Luckily, the speed limit on interstate highways here can be as high as 75 mph.

Where should you go? What should you see? What's the best route? How do you maximize your time? I know all these questions well. I've asked them myself when I've been planning vacations, and I've been asked them by other people planning trips to Arizona. This chapter helps you answer those questions. I'm not going to get down to the nitty-gritty details such as where to get gas (just keep that tank topped up; it can be 60 miles to the next gas station), but I do mention the occasional not-to-be-missed or out-of-the-way restaurant.

If you read through all these itineraries, you'll notice a bit of overlap. There are some attractions that just should not be missed on any visit to the state. Also, try to think of these as general ideas. Because Phoenix and Tucson are less than 2 hours apart, you could easily swap days I mention for Phoenix for time spent in Tucson (or vice versa) and not add too much extra driving to your vacation. Personally, I prefer Tucson's more low-key character to the congested streets of Phoenix and Scottsdale. However, because these two cities have the state's two main airports, you'll likely end up starting and ending your trip at one or the other.

1 Arizona in 1 Week

Arizona is a big state, so don't expect to see it *all* in 7 days. If you want to take in some of my favorite spots in just a week, you'll need to do a lot of driving and get up early most mornings. (As an added incentive for early rising, let me tell you that sunrises at most of the destinations listed in this itinerary are absolutely awe-inspiring.) This itinerary is best from fall through spring. During the summer, Phoenix is just too hot for hanging out or playing golf (unless you do your swimming at night and your golfing very early in the morning). In the hot months, you may want to head straight to Sedona after touching down in Phoenix, and, if your return flight isn't too early, it's possible to spend your last night in Sedona or Prescott and still have not too long a drive to the airport in Phoenix.

Suggested Arizona Itineraries

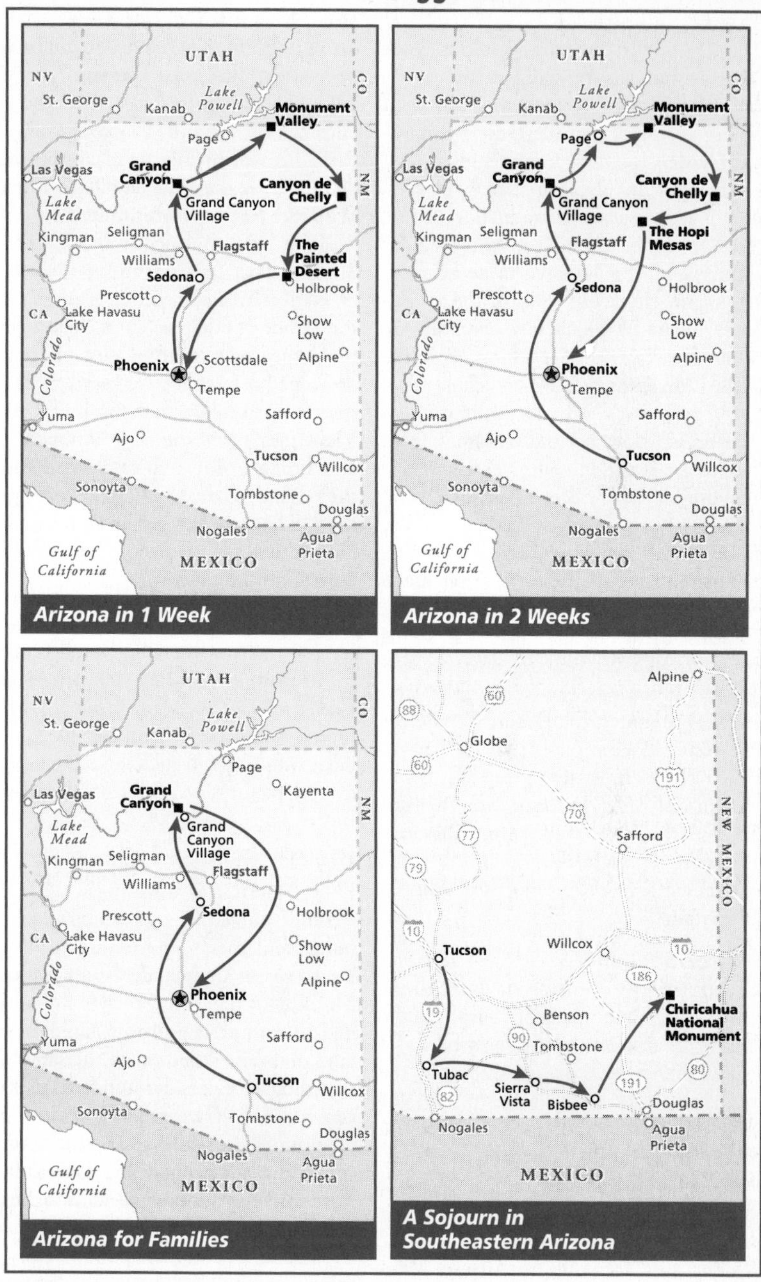

Day 1: Phoenix ★★

Head straight for the pool at your resort—after all, lounging in the sun is one of the main reasons to be here. If you've got time, visit the **Desert Botanical Garden** (p. 124) around sunset. This garden has an amazing variety of cacti and is an excellent introduction to the Arizona desert. Head to Scottsdale for dinner, and, if it happens to be a Thursday night, check out some of the art galleries, many of which stay open late on Thursday. The next morning, visit the **Heard Museum** (p. 124), which is one of the Southwest's premier museums of Native American art and culture. Grab a bite to eat at the museum's excellent cafe or nearby at the **Fry Bread House** (p. 116), where you can try a fry-bread taco. These filling meals are a standard on Indian reservations across the state. After lunch head north to Sedona, and, if you leave Phoenix early enough, take the scenic route through Wickenburg, Prescott, and Jerome. If you take the scenic route, stop in Wickenburg at the **Desert Caballeros Western Museum** (p. 168) or in Prescott at the **Phippen Museum** (p. 174). If you time it just right, you can catch the sunset over the Verde Valley from the artsy historic town of **Jerome** (p. 180), which is perched high on the slopes of Mingus Mountain.

Day 2: Sedona ★★★

Sedona may be touristy, but the red-rock cliffs, buttes, and mesas that surround the city make this one of the most beautiful places in America. To get out amid the red rocks, take a **jeep tour** (p. 196) or hike the 4- to 5-mile loop trail around **Bell Rock** and **Courthouse Rock.** Although this trail sees a lot of hikers, it is just about the best introduction to the amazing hiking that can be done in the Sedona area. Head up on **Airport Mesa** for the sunset. If you don't do a jeep tour this day, plan to do one the next morning.

Day 3: Grand Canyon ★★★

Drive north to the Grand Canyon by way of scenic **Oak Creek Canyon** (p. 193). Take U.S. 89 from Flagstaff to the east entrance of Grand Canyon National Park. It's worthwhile to make the short detour to see the Sinagua pueblo ruins at **Wupatki National Monument** (p. 250). Also be sure to stop at the **Cameron Trading Post** (p. 232) to see the gallery of Native American artifacts in the historic stone building across the parking lot from the main trading post. If you've developed a taste for fry-bread tacos, be sure to have lunch here. Stop at **Desert View,** just inside the park entrance, and also **Lipan Point,** and catch sunset over the Grand Canyon. Check into your hotel. The next day, get up early to catch the sunrise, and then do a half-day hike down into the canyon.

Day 4: Monument Valley ★★★

It's a long drive from the Grand Canyon to **Monument Valley Navajo Tribal Park** (p. 293), but it's worth it. Arrive in time to take an afternoon jeep tour of the valley with a Navajo guide, and stick around to take pictures of sunset on the Mitten Buttes.

Day 5: Canyon de Chelly ★★★

Even if you're not an early riser, I highly recommend getting up for sunrise on the buttes and mesas of Monument Valley. Next, drive to **Canyon de Chelly National Monument** (p. 287), which is still inhabited in summer by Navajo families who farm and raise sheep much the same way that their ancestors did hundreds of years ago. Make reservations in advance for one of the **"shake-and-bake" truck tours** (p. 291) of the canyon. If you don't have reservations, you may be able to hire a Navajo guide to take you into the canyon by jeep or on horseback. Alternatively, drive one of the rim drives. I recommend the **South Rim Drive** (p. 289) because it provides the opportunity to hike down into the canyon on the **White House Ruins Trail** (p. 289).

Day ❻: The Painted Desert & Petrified Forest ★★

The next day, head west across the Hopi Reservation and stop in the village of **Walpi** (p. 275), where you can do a guided tour of this ancient mesa-top pueblo. Also be sure to stop at **Tsakurshovi** (p. 277), a tiny crafts shop that specializes in traditional Hopi kachina dolls. Have lunch at the **Hopi Cultural Center** (p. 275). Continue south to Holbrook and **Petrified Forest National Park** (p. 280), which preserves both the petrified forest and parts of the Painted Desert. End your day in Winslow at historic **La Posada** hotel (p. 272).

Day ❼: Phoenix ★★

On the way back to Phoenix, stop to see the cliff dwellings at **Montezuma Castle National Monument** (p. 184) near Camp Verde. Stop at the **Rock Springs Café** (p. 165) for some of the best pie in the state. After this whirlwind tour of Arizona's highlights, you'll probably want to park yourself by the pool for a while.

2 Arizona in 2 Weeks

Plan on spending 2 weeks in Arizona, and you'll get a much better sense of this state's diverse landscapes. You can spend more time at the Grand Canyon, marvel at massive saguaro cacti in the desert lowlands, spend a bit more time lounging at a resort, and visit one or more of the state's picturesque artists' communities. Just remember that Arizona's size makes occasional long drives a necessity. Sometimes it's just too far between towns or destinations.

Days ❶, ❷ & ❸: Tucson ★★

To get yourself in vacation mode, head straight for the pool at your resort. If you're a hiker, try one of the trails in the foothills of the Santa Catalina Mountains. **Sabino Canyon** (p. 360), with its trams and network of trails, is just about the best place in the city for a quick hike. The next day, go west to the **Arizona–Sonora Desert Museum** (p. 357), the state's single-best introduction to the Sonoran Desert. Despite the name, this is more zoo than museum. By the way, there's a great cafe here. After you've hung out with the hummingbirds and communed with the coatis, drive a few miles farther west to **Saguaro National Park** (p. 360). This park has units on both the east and west sides of Tucson, but this western unit has the most impressive stands of the saguaro cacti for which the park is named. Be sure to check out the petroglyphs at Signal Hill. On your third day, drive south to the historic arts community of **Tubac** (p. 394). En route, stop at **Mission San Xavier del Bac** (p. 361), a Spanish mission church that is known as the "White Dove of the Desert." In Tubac, check out the galleries, **Tubac Center of the Arts,** and **Tubac Presidio State Historic Park** (p. 395), and then head a few miles south to **Tumacácori National Historical Park** (p. 395), which preserves the ruins of another Spanish mission church. Since you're so close, you may want to continue south to Nogales and cross the border to Mexico for a bit of border-town shopping.

Days ❹ & ❺: Sedona ★★★

En route north to Sedona from Tucson, be sure to stop in Phoenix to visit the **Heard Museum** (p. 124). This is the state's best introduction to the Native American cultures of the region. After lunch, take the scenic route to Sedona via Wickenburg and Prescott. This will allow you to stop at Wickenburg's **Desert Caballeros Western Museum** (p. 168) for the cowboy perspective on the Wild West. Alternatively, you could stop at Prescott's **Phippen Museum** (p. 174), which showcases artworks by members of the Cowboy Artists of America. If you time things right, you should be in the historic artists' community of Jerome just in time to catch the sunset on Sedona's distant red rocks.

To get out amid the red rocks of Sedona, take a **jeep tour** (p. 196) or hike the 4- to 5-mile loop trail around **Bell Rock** and **Courthouse Butte** (p. 191). In the afternoon, visit either the **V Bar V petroglyph site** (p. 193) or **Palatki Ruins** (p. 191). When the sun sets, be sure you're either at the **Crescent Moon Recreation Area** (p. 192) or atop **Airport Mesa.**

Days 6 & 7: Grand Canyon ★★★

For Day 6, follow my suggestions for Day 3 in the "Arizona in 1 Week" itinerary above.

The next day, get up early to catch the sunrise, and then do a day hike or mule ride down into the canyon. If you plan ahead, you can even spend the night down in the canyon at Phantom Ranch. If you're not a hiker, spend the day exploring along Hermit Drive, where there are numerous overlooks. I always spend time sitting by the fire at **Hermit's Rest,** a fascinating little building designed by Mary Elizabeth Jane Colter, who designed several buildings on the South Rim.

Days 8 & 9: Page & Lake Powell ★★

From the Grand Canyon, go northeast to the town of Page. En route, you may want to make a short detour to Tuba City, where you can see **dinosaur tracks** (p. 280) in sedimentary stone east of town. Page sits atop a mesa overlooking **Glen Canyon National Recreation Area** (p. 299) and **Lake Powell,** the reservoir created by Glen Canyon Dam. This reservoir is the most astonishing body of water in the West. The vast miragelike lake is flanked by red-rock canyon walls similar to those of the Grand Canyon. You can tour the massive dam and rent a variety of boats for exploring the lake. The morning after you arrive, take the boat tour up the lake to **Rainbow Bridge National Monument** (p. 300).

Day 10: Monument Valley ★★★

From Page, head to **Monument Valley Navajo Tribal Park** (p. 293). On the way, be sure to visit **Antelope Canyon** (p. 300), which is one of the most accessible slot canyons in the Southwest. If you get an early enough start, you should also have time to visit **Navajo National Monument** (p. 292) and take a look at the Betatakin cliff dwellings. Just be sure you arrive at Monument Valley early enough in the afternoon to do a jeep tour of the valley with a Navajo guide. Stick around to take pictures of sunset on the Mitten Buttes. Also, the unforgettable landscape here makes Monument Valley the best place in Arizona to go for a horseback ride.

Days 11 & 12: Canyon de Chelly ★★★

The next day, perhaps after a horseback ride or jeep tour, drive to **Canyon de Chelly National Monument** (p. 287). The following day, do one of the **"shake-and-bake" truck tours** (p. 291) of the canyon, or hire a Navajo guide to take you into the canyon by jeep or on horseback. Alternatively, drive the rim drives. The **South Rim Drive** (p. 289) is my favorite of the two because it provides the opportunity to hike down into the canyon on the **White House Ruins Trail** (p. 289).

Day 13: The Hopi Mesas

After leaving Canyon de Chelly, drive south to Ganado and visit the historic **Hubbell Trading Post National Historic Site** (p. 284). Then head west across the Hopi Reservation and stop in the village of **Walpi** (p. 275), where you can take a guided tour of this ancient mesa-top pueblo. Be sure to stop at **Tsakurshovi** (p. 277), a tiny crafts shop that specializes in traditional Hopi kachina dolls. Continue south to Winslow and stay at the historic **La Posada** hotel (p. 272).

Day ⓮: Phoenix ★★

On your way back to Phoenix to catch a plane home, stop at **Meteor Crater** (p. 271), which is 20 miles east of Winslow. You may want to have lunch in Flagstaff. Once you get back to Phoenix, lie by the pool and chill out for a few hours.

3 Arizona for Families

With the exception of the Grand Canyon and a few other mountainous areas of the state, Arizona is just too darn hot in the summer for an enjoyable family vacation. Arizonans all head for the hills or San Diego when the temperatures hit triple digits, so you'd have to be crazy to want to spend summer vacation in the middle of the desert. However, spring break is a completely different matter. The weather is usually just warm enough in Tucson and Phoenix, and not too cold or snowy at the Grand Canyon. So, if you're looking for a fun family vacation for the kids' annual spring break, consider the following itinerary. A bit of time by the pool, a little culture, the grandest of canyons—this one should keep everyone happy.

Days ❶, ❷ & ❸: Tucson ★★

In Tucson you can learn about the desert and the kids can pet snakes and tarantulas at the **Arizona–Sonora Desert Museum** (p. 357). Spend the morning at this amazing place, which is actually more of a zoo than a museum. After lunch, head to **Old Tucson Studios** (p. 361), a one-time movie set that is now a sort of Wild West amusement park—albeit without any Disneyesque thrill rides—with plenty to keep kids and adults entertained. On one of your nights in town, have dinner at a cowboy steakhouse. Alternatively, spend a couple of days at a dude ranch, of which there are three in the Tucson area. On your third day in Tucson, do a day trip to **Tombstone** (p. 414). Yes, there is a Tombstone, and it's where Wyatt Earp and Doc Holliday once shot it out with the bad guys at the O.K. Corral. On the way down to or from Tombstone, you should be sure to head underground at **Kartchner Caverns State Park** (p. 408). The caverns here are second only to Carlsbad Caverns for impressiveness.

Day ❹: Sedona ★★★

From Tucson, drive north to Sedona. It's a long drive, so get an early start. Stop for lunch (and great pie) at the **Rock Springs Café** (p. 165), north of Phoenix in the town of Rock Springs. If you get to Sedona early enough, take the kids on the **Pink Jeep Tours'** (p. 196) gnarly "Broken Arrow" tour. This is four-wheeling at its most rugged. If you arrive too late, schedule the tour for the next morning. At sunset, head to **Crescent Moon Recreation Area** (p. 192), where the kids can splash in Oak Creek while you marvel at the sunset light show on Cathedral Rock.

Days ❺ & ❻: Grand Canyon ★★★

Leave Sedona and head up scenic **Oak Creek Canyon** (p. 193) to Flagstaff, and then continue north on U.S. 89 to the east entrance of **Grand Canyon National Park** (p. 213). Check out the views from the many overlooks as you make your way west to Grand Canyon Village and its many hotels. You can dawdle along the way, perhaps stopping at **Wupatki National Monument** (p. 250), but just be sure you make it to the Grand Canyon in time for sunset. Spend the next day hiking into the canyon a little way, riding a mule down into the canyon, or exploring along Hermit Road. The historic little Hermit's Rest is a good place to get cocoa and hang out by a fire.

Days 7 & 8: Phoenix ★★

From the Grand Canyon, head back south to **Phoenix** and spend a couple of days chilling out at one of the city's big resorts. Many resorts in the area have water parks with slides and other features aimed specifically at keeping kids happy. If you can pry the kids away from the pool area, take them to the **Heard Museum** (p. 124) to expose them to a little Native American culture. If you haven't yet had enough of Wild West towns, head east of the city to **Goldfield Ghost Town** (p. 132), which is a bit lively to really be a ghost town but is loads of fun.

4 A Sojourn in Southeastern Arizona

Tombstone, Wyatt Earp, Doc Holliday, Geronimo, Cochise, the O.K. Corral. The names are familiar, but what you might not know is that these are all names from southeastern Arizona. This corner of the state may not have the major natural attractions that northern Arizona has, but it does have loads of Wild West history; plenty of natural beauty; and great resorts, restaurants, and museums in and around Tucson. With the exception of the Tucson area, the climate here is mild year-round, so you'll be comfortable whether you visit in summer or winter. Southeastern Arizona is also one of the best bird-watching regions in the country. Many bird species reach the northern limits of their ranges in this area.

Days 1, 2 & 3: Tucson ★★

Spend your first few days exploring Tucson and, if the weather is warm, lounging by the pool. On your first full day in town, head first to the **Arizona–Sonora Desert Museum** (p. 357), which is more zoo than museum and is the state's best introduction to the flora and fauna of the Sonoran Desert. The museum is just a few miles down the road from the west unit of **Saguaro National Park** (p. 360), so once you've gotten familiar with life in the desert, strike out on the trail or on a scenic drive to get up close and personal with some gigantic saguaro cacti. If you're in good shape, I recommend hiking the **Hugh Morris Trail** to the summit of **Wasson Peak,** which has superb views across miles of desert. Try to stick around until sunset so that you can watch the sunset light on the petroglyphs at **Signal Hill,** which is within the national park. The next day, wander around downtown Tucson's historic neighborhoods to get a feel for the city's mix of Spanish, Mexican, and Anglo history. If your timing is right, do one of the guided historical walking tours offered by the **Sosa-Carillo-Frémont House Museum** (p. 364). In the afternoon, visit Tohono Chul Park and Sabino Canyon.

Day 4: Tubac ★★

After you've gotten a feel for Tucson, head south toward Mexico. Just south of Tucson, you'll come to **Mission San Xavier del Bac** (p. 361), a historic Spanish mission church that is known as the "White Dove of the Desert." If you're hungry, this is a good place to try Indian fry-bread tacos; there's a little walk-up food window in the plaza across the parking lot from the church, and Native Americans often set up grills and sell food from stalls in the parking lot. Continue south to the historic town of **Tubac,** which was founded by the Spanish and is now filled with art galleries. Just south of Tubac is **Tumacácori National Historical Park**

(p. 395), where you can see the ruins of another mission church.

Days ❺ & ❻: Bisbee or Sierra Vista ★★

From Tubac, drive down to the border town of **Nogales** and cross into Mexico to shop for inexpensive crafts, tequila, and, if you brought your prescriptions, cut-price pharmaceuticals. From here continue east through **Patagonia,** a small town best known for its great bird-watching, and Sonoita, which is wide-open ranch country with a few vineyards and wineries thrown in to keep things interesting (Callaghan Vineyards is my favorite). Birders should be sure to stop at **Patagonia Lake State Park** (p. 404), the Nature Conservancy's **Patagonia–Sonoita Creek Preserve** (p. 403), and **Paton's Birder's Haven** (p. 404). Try to time things so that you can have lunch at Patagonia's **Velvet Elvis Pizza Company** (p. 406). If you're a birder, you'll want to stay a couple of nights at one of the inns south of Sierra Vista. Several inns cater specifically to the birders who flock to the area to see hummingbirds at **Ramsey Canyon Preserve** (p. 411) and a wide variety of other birds at area birding hot spots such as the **San Pedro Riparian National Conservation Area** (p. 411). If you're not a birder, continue to the funky historic town of Bisbee, which is full of counter-cultural types who have turned this former copper-mining town into the most interesting small town in Arizona. Be sure to eat dinner at **Cafe Roka** (p. 421) and breakfast or lunch at **Dot's Diner** (p. 422). While you're in the area, visit **Coronado National Memorial** (p. 410) to learn about the Spanish explorer who passed through this region between 1540 and 1542. And, of course, you can't miss **Tombstone** (p. 414), home of the famous shootout at the O.K. Corral.

Days ❼ & ❽: The Chiricahuas ★★

From Bisbee or Sierra Vista, head northeast to **Chiricahua National Monument** (p. 424) and **Cochise Stronghold** (p. 423). At the former, hike part or all of the **Heart of Rocks Trail,** which is one of the most memorable hikes in the state. If you have an interest in Western history, save time for the 3-mile round-trip hike to **Fort Bowie National Historic Site** (p. 425). You'll be hiking with the ghosts of Apaches, soldiers, and stagecoach travelers. On your last day in the area, visit the remote **Amerind Foundation Museum** (p. 424), which has an outstanding collection of Native American artifacts and is set amid huge granite boulders in Texas Canyon. On your way back to Tucson, be sure to detour south from Benson to **Kartchner Caverns State Park** (p. 408). The caverns here are among the most spectacular in the country.

5 Native Trails of Arizona

You may think you're venturing off into the great unknown when you take off across Arizona, but believe me, others have been here before you. Down in the southeastern part of the state near the present-day San Pedro River, archaeologists discovered a mammoth kill site that proves humans were living in and exploring Arizona more than 10,000 years ago. All across Arizona you'll find signs of those who have come before. Cliff dwellings, pueblo ruins, and petroglyphs abound in the desert. This itinerary will help you search out the outstanding remains of Arizona's Native American cultures both past and present. Along the way, you can also learn about the state's native cultures at museums that focus on Native American art, artifacts, and culture. Of course, you'll also have plenty of opportunities to meet today's Navajos, Hopis, and Apaches, as well as members of other tribes.

Days ❶, ❷ & ❸: Phoenix ★★

The best "trail head" for an exploration of Arizona's native trails is Phoenix. Here you should visit the superb **Heard Museum** (p. 124) to learn all about the tribes of the region and see samples of their traditional arts and crafts. Right in Phoenix, at **Pueblo Grande Museum and Archaeological Park** (p. 125), you can visit the remains of a Hohokam village and learn about the people who once built an extensive network of canals here in the middle of the desert. If you fly into Phoenix, you may want to visit this museum as soon as you get to town, since it's near the airport. When you visit the Heard Museum, be sure to have lunch at the nearby **Fry Bread House** (p. 116), where you can try Indian fry-bread tacos, which are a staple on reservations across the state. Visit the **Deer Valley Rock Art Center** (p. 124) to see a dense concentration of petroglyphs and then, late in the day, go to the **Desert Botanical Garden** (p. 124). In addition to having lots of cacti on display, this attraction has an ethnobotanical garden where you can learn about the desert plants traditionally utilized by the native inhabitants of the Sonoran Desert. On your third day, do a day trip out of the city. If you head south to Coolidge, you can visit **Casa Grande Ruins National Monument** (p. 164), and then drive northeast to Globe to see the reconstructed **Besh-Ba-Gowah Archaeological Park** (p. 163). After lunch, continue to **Tonto National Monument** (p. 163), which is the southernmost cliff dwelling in the state. Return to Phoenix on the winding, gravel Apache Trail route.

Days ❹ & ❺: Sedona ★★★

From Phoenix, journey north to Sedona. En route, there are three stops you should make. At Camp Verde, detour to Cottonwood to visit the reconstructed hilltop ruins of **Tuzigoot National Monument** (p. 185). Head back to I-17 and continue north to **Montezuma Castle National Monument** (p. 184), another well-preserved cliff dwelling. At the Arizona 179 exit for Sedona, get off I-17, but turn away from Sedona, not toward it. A few miles down this road is the **V Bar V Ranch** (p. 193), which is on the Coconino National Forest and preserves one of the most impressive petroglyph sites in the state. The next day, after you've spent some time ogling the red rocks, head west of town to **Palatki Ruins** (p. 191), another site protected on national forest land. While you're out this way, hike up Boynton Canyon, where you may spot some of the canyon's small ruin sites.

Day ❻: Flagstaff ★★

It's barely an hour's drive from Sedona to Flagstaff, and the first place to visit is the **Museum of Northern Arizona** (p. 248). This museum has outstanding exhibits on the native cultures of the Colorado Plateau. Outside of town, you'll find two national monuments that preserve old ruin sites. **Wupatki National Monument** (p. 250) is, in my opinion, the more impressive of the two. Not only can you wander around several Sinagua pueblo sites, but at the main pueblo of Wupatki, you'll find both a ball court similar to those found in Mexico and a fascinating "blow hole" that either blows or sucks air, depending on temperature and barometric pressure. Closer to Flagstaff, you can explore small cliff dwellings at **Walnut Canyon National Monument** (p. 250). The small rooms wedged into the cliffs at this monument were also built by the Sinagua. Be sure to stop in at **Jonathan Day's Indian Arts** (p. 246) before you leave town. This shop specializes in traditional Hopi kachinas and old Indian trade blankets.

Day ❼: The Hopi Mesas ★★

From Flagstaff, head east to the villages of the Hopi mesas. Along the way, you'll pass numerous shops selling Hopi silver overlay jewelry, as well as kachina dolls,

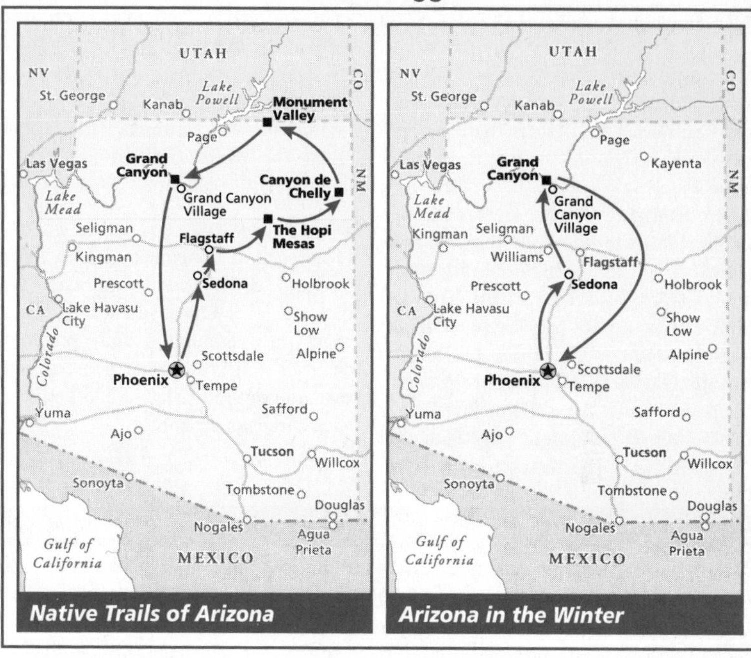

pottery, and baskets. Stop at the **Hopi Cultural Center** (p. 275) to tour the small museum and have a lunch of traditional Hopi stew and paper-thin piki bread. At First Mesa, you can take a guided tour of the ancient cliff-top village of **Walpi** (p. 275). Continue east to the Navajo community of Ganado, where you can tour the historic **Hubbell Trading Post** (p. 284), and then backtrack a few miles to head north to **Canyon de Chelly National Monument** (p. 287).

Day 8: Canyon de Chelly National Monument ★★★

Do a "shake-and-bake" tour of Canyon de Chelly. These tours, which are in rugged military surplus trucks outfitted with bench seats, head deep into the canyon to places you're not allowed to visit without a Navajo guide. You'll stop at numerous ruin sites and see well-preserved pictographs. You may even encounter Navajo farmers and shepherds who still live in the canyon during the summer months. See p. 291.

Day 9: Monument Valley Navajo Tribal Park ★★★

Monument Valley Navajo Tribal Park (p. 293) is really a landscape attraction and not a cultural attraction, but you can't visit this park without meeting a few Navajos. Local families operate jeep tours, horseback tours, and hiking tours. Take a **jeep tour** (p. 294), and you'll probably stop at someone's grandmother's hogan (traditional Navajo home) for a photo op (yes, you'll have to pay, but you'll probably get a great photo), or maybe you'll encounter a Navajo gazing off into the distance as he sits astride his noble steed (I'm not kidding, there really is someone who poses on horseback for photos at a place called John Ford's Point).

Days 10 & 11: Grand Canyon

Okay, so the **Grand Canyon** (p. 213) isn't primarily known for its cultural heritage, but it's out there. You just can't see it. All through the canyon there are caves, cliff dwellings, and pueblo sites. However, most of them are way off the beaten track and hard to get to. Besides that, the park service doesn't even want you to know most of these sites exist, for fear you might vandalize them. That said, you should be sure to visit the **Tusayan Museum** (p. 220), which is built on the site of an Ancestral Puebloan (Anasazi) ruin. En route to the Grand Canyon from Monument Valley, be sure to visit **Navajo National Monument** (p. 292), where you can take a 1-mile walk to a viewpoint overlooking the large Betatakin cliff dwelling. If you have an extra day to spare and can be here at the monument early in the morning, you can try to get a space on one of the guided hikes to the Betatakin ruins. Spend a second day in Grand Canyon National Park exploring along the park's rim drives or hiking down into the canyon.

Day ⓬: Phoenix

Head back to Phoenix by taking Arizona 64 S to U.S. 180 to Flagstaff, where you'll pick up I-17. Once you reach Phoenix, check into your hotel, pull up a lounge chair by the pool, and meditate on all that you've seen as you've followed the native trails of Arizona.

6 Arizona in the Winter

Arizona in the winter means golf, desert explorations, and enough sunshine to help you forget all about shoveling the snow out of your driveway. Sure, you can go to the Grand Canyon (and even avoid the crowds), but it will be very cold, and snow often makes the area's roads impassable. So think of this as an escape from the cold up north, not just as a once-in-a-lifetime trip to see the Grand Canyon. Although I have written this itinerary with the emphasis on Phoenix, you could just as easily spend the bulk of your week in Tucson. You'd just have a longer drive north to Sedona.

Days ❶, ❷ & ❸: Phoenix ★★

I know I've said it before, but when my wife and I get to the sunshine and warmth of the desert, we always make the resort pool our very first stop. Order a froufrou cocktail, grab a lounge chair, and say "Aaaahhh." Repeat when necessary for the next 3 days. Once you've relaxed for a bit, it's time to get to know this city, and the best way I can think of is a bit strenuous but, for anyone in good shape, exhilarating. What I'm talking about is a little peak bagging. If you've got lots of energy, hike up **Camelback Mountain** (p. 140) or **Piestewa Peak** (p. 140) for incomparable views of the valley. While you're up here with all the other buff hikers, get your bearings. After a shower (you'll need it), head to Scottsdale for dinner and check out some of the great nightlife. On your second day, play a round of golf or some tennis in the morning, or, if you're more interested in culture, visit the **Heard Museum** (p. 124) and the **Phoenix Art Museum** (p. 126). In the afternoon, get in another swim, and then, around sunset, visit the **Desert Botanical Garden** (p. 124). Phoenix is a huge metropolitan area, so to see what the desert is really like, drive the **Apache Trail** (p. 162), east of the city, on Day 3. This drive will take all day, so get an early start.

Days ❹ & ❺: Sedona ★★★

Maybe you've never heard of Sedona before, but once you see the red-rock cliffs, buttes, and mesas that frame this wealthy community, you'll probably start scheming ways to move here. Sedona quite simply has the most beautiful setting of any town in the West. On your way north from Phoenix, be sure to stop at **Montezuma Castle National Monument** (p. 184). Once in Sedona, your best introduction to the area is a **jeep tour** (p. 196). Just make sure that by sunset you're atop **Airport Mesa** (p. 191) to take in the natural light show. The next day, in the morning, visit the **V Bar V Ranch petroglyph site** (p. 193), which is one of the most impressive such sites in the state and is at its photogenic best before the sun hits the rocks in the early afternoon. After you've marveled at these ancient symbols, do some hiking or mountain biking. Sedona is surrounded by national forest, and there are dozens of miles of easily accessed trails. I recommend any of the trails to the west of the city. Hiking the **Boynton Canyon Trail** (p.191) or the **Vultee Arch Trail** (p. 197) will put you close to **Palatki Ruins** (p. 191), a small cliff dwelling site that is open to the public. You'll also end the day not far from **Crescent Moon Recreation Area** (p. 192), where you can watch the sunset light up Cathedral Rock as the waters of Oak Creek flow by in the foreground. If you're a golfer, be sure to get in a round amid the red rocks while you're in town.

Day 6: Grand Canyon ★★★

This is a tough one; if you plan this day in advance, you may be disappointed. The road to the **Grand Canyon** (p. 213) is sometimes closed by snow in winter, though usually only for a short time. Still, you came to Arizona to get away from snow, right? So, who wants to head back into subfreezing temperatures? But, as long as you're this close, you might as well try to see the canyon, so, if the weather is good, make a mad dash up to the canyon and snap some photos before your fingers freeze. Either spend the night at the canyon or drive back to Sedona the same day. Your best route for this quick visit is to drive north to Flagstaff and then take U.S. 89 N to Arizona 64 W, which leads to the east entrance of Grand Canyon National Park. Return via U.S. 180 to Flagstaff.

Day 7: Phoenix ★★

Head back to Phoenix by way of **Jerome** (p. 180), a former mining town that is now an artists' community. Peruse the galleries, visit the state park, and tour the ghost town and mine on the edge of town. If you have time, schedule a ride on the **Verde Canyon Railroad** (p.183). Try to get in one last swim when you get back to your resort in Phoenix. Or come straight back to Phoenix from Sedona and get in some more golf.

4

Phoenix, Scottsdale & the Valley of the Sun

Forget the stately cacti and cowboys riding off into the sunset; think Los Angeles without the Pacific. While the nation has carefully nurtured its image of Phoenix as a desert cow town, this city in the Sonoran Desert has rocketed into the 21st century and become the fifth-largest city in the country. Sprawling across more than 500 square miles of what once was cactus and creosote bushes, the greater Phoenix metropolitan area, also known as the Valley of the Sun (or, more commonly, just the Valley), is now a major metropolitan area replete with dozens of resort hotels, fabulous restaurants, excellent museums, hundreds of golf courses, world-class shopping, four pro sports teams, and a red-hot nightlife scene.

Sure, it also has traffic jams and smog, but at the end of the day, it can usually claim to have had beautiful sunny weather. Sunshine and blue skies, day after day after day, have made this one of the most popular winter destinations in the country. When Chicago weather forecasts call for snow and subzero temperatures, you can have a hard time getting a tee time on a Phoenix-area golf course. Phoenicians may get the summertime blues when temperatures hit the triple digits, but from September to May, the climate here can verge on perfect—warm enough in the daytime for lounging by the pool, cool enough at night to require a jacket.

With green lawns, orange groves, swimming pools, and palm trees, it's easy to forget that Phoenix is in the middle of the desert. Water channeled in from distant reservoirs has allowed this city to flourish like a desert oasis. However, if you find yourself wondering where the desert is, you need only lift your eyes to one of the many mountains that rise amid the suburban sprawl. South Mountain, Camelback Mountain, Mummy Mountain, Piestewa Peak, Papago Buttes, Pinnacle Peak—these rugged, rocky summits have been preserved in their natural states, and it is to these cactus-covered uplands that the city's citizens retreat when they've had enough asphalt and air-conditioning. From almost anywhere in the Valley, you're no more than a 15- or 20-minute drive from a natural area where you can commune with cacti while gazing out across a bustling, modern city.

Best of all, at the end of the day, you can retreat to a comfortable bed at one of the country's top resorts.

1 Orientation

ARRIVING

BY PLANE Centrally located 3 miles east of downtown Phoenix, **Sky Harbor International Airport,** 3400 E. Sky Harbor Blvd. (✆ **602/273-3300;** www.phxsky harbor.com), has three terminals, with a free 24-hour shuttle bus offering frequent service between them. For lost and found, call ✆ **602/273-3307.** For information on airlines serving Phoenix, see chapter 2.

There are two entrances to the airport. The west entrance can be accessed from either the Papago Freeway (I-10) or 24th Street, while the east entrance can be accessed from the Hohokam Expressway (Ariz. 143) or the Sky Harbor Expressway (Ariz. 153), which is an extension of 44th Street. If you're headed to downtown Phoenix, leave by way of the 24th Street exit and continue west on Washington Street. If you're headed to Scottsdale, Tempe, or Mesa, head east out of the airport and follow signs for Arizona 202 Loop.

SuperShuttle (✆ **800/BLUE-VAN** or 602/244-9000; www.supershuttle.com) offers 24-hour door-to-door van service between Sky Harbor Airport and resorts, hotels, and homes throughout the Valley. Per-person fares average $7 to $12 to the downtown and Tempe area, $16 to downtown Scottsdale, and $30 to $35 to north Scottsdale.

Taxis can be found outside all three terminals and cost only slightly more than shuttle vans. You can also call **AAA Cab** (✆ **602/437-4000**), **Discount Cab** (✆ **602/200-2000**), or **Allstate Cab** (✆ **602/275-8888**). A taxi from the airport to downtown Phoenix will cost around $16; to Scottsdale, between $20 and $35.

Valley Metro (✆ **602/253-5000;** www.valleymetro.org) provides public bus service throughout the Valley, with the Red Line operating between the airport and downtown Phoenix, Tempe, and Mesa. The Red Line runs daily starting between 3:30 and 5:30am and continues operating until between 10:30pm and 1am, depending on the day of the week and whether you are traveling east or west. The ride from the airport to downtown takes about 20 minutes and costs $1.25. There is no direct bus to Scottsdale, so you would first need to go to Tempe and then transfer to a northbound bus. You can pick up a copy of the *Bus Book,* a guide and route map for the Valley Metro bus system, at airport information desks or at Central Station, which is at the corner of Central Avenue and Van Buren Street.

BY CAR Phoenix is connected to Los Angeles and Tucson by I-10 and to Flagstaff via I-17. If you're headed to Scottsdale, the easiest route is to take the Red Mountain Freeway (Ariz. 202) east to U.S. 101 N. U.S. 101 loops all the way around the east, north, and west sides of the Valley. The Superstition Freeway (U.S. 60) leads to Tempe, Mesa, and Chandler.

Tips **A Name Change**

In 2003, the official name of Phoenix's Squaw Peak was changed to Piestewa Peak (pronounced Pie-*ess*-too-uh) to honor Pfc. Lori Ann Piestewa, a member of the Hopi tribe and the first female soldier killed in the Iraq War. The peak in north Phoenix has long been a popular hiking destination. If you hear people referring to both Squaw Peak and Piestewa Peak, it's one and the same place. Ditto for the Squaw Peak Parkway, which is now Piestewa Freeway.

BY TRAIN There is no passenger rail service to Phoenix. **Amtrak** (✆ **800/872-7245;** www.amtrak.com) will sell you a ticket to Phoenix, but you'll have to take a shuttle bus from either Flagstaff or Tucson. The scheduling is so horrible on these routes that you'd have to be a total masochist to opt for Amtrak service to Phoenix.

VISITOR INFORMATION

You'll find **tourist information desks** in all three terminals at Sky Harbor Airport. The city's main visitor center is the **Greater Phoenix Convention & Visitors Bureau,** 50 N. Second St. (✆ **877/225-5749** or 602/452-6282; www.visitphoenix.com), on the corner of Adams Street in downtown Phoenix. There's also a small visitor information center at the Biltmore Fashion Park shopping center, at Camelback Road and 24th Street (✆ **602/957-0380**).

The **Visitor Information Line** (✆ **602/252-5588**) has recorded information about current events in Phoenix and is updated weekly.

If you're staying in Scottsdale, you can get information at the **Scottsdale Convention & Visitors Bureau Visitor Center,** Galleria Corporate Center, 4343 N. Scottsdale Rd., Suite 170 (✆ **800/782-1117** or 480/421-1004; www.scottsdalecvb.com).

CITY LAYOUT

MAIN ARTERIES & STREETS **U.S. Loop 101** forms a loop around the east, north, and west sides of the Valley, providing freeway access to Scottsdale from I-17 on the north side of Phoenix and from U.S. 60 in Tempe.

I-17 (Black Canyon Fwy.), which connects Phoenix with Flagstaff, is the city's main north-south freeway. This freeway curves to the east just south of downtown (where it is renamed the **Maricopa Fwy.** and merges with I-10). **I-10,** which connects Phoenix with Los Angeles and Tucson, is called the **Papago Freeway** on the west side of the Valley and as it passes north of downtown; as it curves around to pass to the west and south of the airport, it merges with I-17 and is renamed the Maricopa Freeway. At Tempe, this freeway curves to the south and heads out of the Valley.

North of the airport, **Arizona 202 (Red Mountain Fwy.)** heads east from I-10 and passes along the north side of Tempe, providing access to downtown Tempe, Arizona State University, Mesa, and Scottsdale (via U.S. Loop 101). On the east side of the airport, **Arizona 143 (Hohokam Expwy.)** connects Arizona 202 with I-10.

At the interchange of I-10 and Arizona 202, northwest of Sky Harbor Airport, **Arizona 51 (Piestewa Fwy.)** heads north through the center of Phoenix to U.S. Loop 101 and is the best north-south route in the city.

South of the airport off I-10, **U.S. 60 (Superstition Fwy.)** heads east to Tempe, Chandler, Mesa, and Gilbert. **U.S. Loop 101** leads north from U.S. 60 (and Ariz. 202) through Scottsdale and across the north side of Phoenix to connect with I-17. U.S. 60 and U.S. 101 provide the best route from the airport to the Scottsdale resorts. U.S. Loop 101 also heads south through Chandler to connect with I-10. This section is called the Price Freeway. The section of this freeway north through Scottsdale is called the Pima Freeway.

Secondary highways in the Valley include the **Beeline Highway (Ariz. 87),** which starts at the east end of Arizona 202 (Red Mountain Fwy.) in Mesa and leads to Payson, and **Grand Avenue (U.S. 60),** which starts downtown and leads west to Sun City and Wickenburg.

Phoenix and the surrounding cities of Mesa, Tempe, Scottsdale, and Chandler, and even those cities farther out in the Valley, are laid out in a grid pattern with major avenues and roads about every mile. For traveling east to west across Phoenix, your best choices (other than the above-mentioned freeways) are Camelback Road, Indian School Road, and McDowell Road. For traveling north and south, 44th Street, 24th Street, and Central Avenue are good choices. Hayden Road is a north-south alternative to Scottsdale Road, which gets jammed at rush hours.

FINDING AN ADDRESS **Central Avenue,** which runs north to south through downtown Phoenix, is the starting point for all east-and-west street numbering. **Washington Street** is the starting point for north and south numbering. North-to-south numbered *streets* are to be found on the east side of the city, while north-to-south numbered *avenues* will be found on the west. For the most part, street numbers advance by 100 with each block. Odd-numbered addresses are on the south and east sides of streets, while even-numbered addresses are on the north and west sides of streets.

For example, if you're looking for 4454 E. Camelback Rd., you'll find it 44 blocks east of Central Avenue between 44th and 45th streets on the north side of the street. If you're looking for 2905 N. 35th Ave., you'll find it 35 blocks west of Central Avenue and 29 blocks north of Washington Street on the east side of the street. Just for general reference, Camelback Road marks the 5000 block north. Also, whenever you're getting directions, ask for the cross street closest to where you're going. Street numbers can be hard to spot when you're driving past at 45 mph.

STREET MAPS The street maps handed out by rental-car companies may be good for general navigation around the city, but they are almost useless for finding a particular address if it is not on a major arterial, so as soon as you can, stop at a minimart and buy a Phoenix map. Unfortunately, you'll probably also have to buy a separate Scottsdale map. Alternatively, if you are a member of AAA, you can get a good Phoenix map before you leave home. You can also get a simple map at the airport tourist information desks or at the downtown visitor center.

NEIGHBORHOODS IN BRIEF

Because of urban sprawl, Phoenix has yielded its importance to an area known as the Valley of the Sun (or just "the Valley"), an area encompassing Phoenix and its metropolitan area of more than 20 cities. Consequently, as outlying cities have taken on regional importance, neighborhoods per se have lost much of their significance. Think of the Valley's many cities as automobile-oriented neighborhoods. That said, there are some actual neighborhoods worth noting.

Downtown Phoenix Roughly bordered by Thomas Road on the north, Buckeye Road on the south, 19th Avenue on the west, and Seventh Street on the east, downtown is primarily a business, financial, and government district, where both the city hall and the state capitol are located. Downtown Phoenix is also the Valley's prime sports, entertainment, and museum district. The Arizona Diamondbacks play big-league baseball at **Chase Field,** while the Phoenix Suns shoot hoops at the **US Airways Center.** Of course, there are also lots of sports bars in the area. There are three major performing-arts venues—the historic **Orpheum Theatre, Symphony Hall,** and the **Herberger Theater Center.** Downtown museums include the **Phoenix Museum of History** and the **Arizona Science Center,** both located in Heritage and Science Park. Other area attractions include **Heritage Square** (historic homes), the **Arizona Capitol Museum,** and the **Arizona Mining & Mineral Museum.** On the northern edge of downtown are the

Phoenix, Scottsdale & the Valley of the Sun

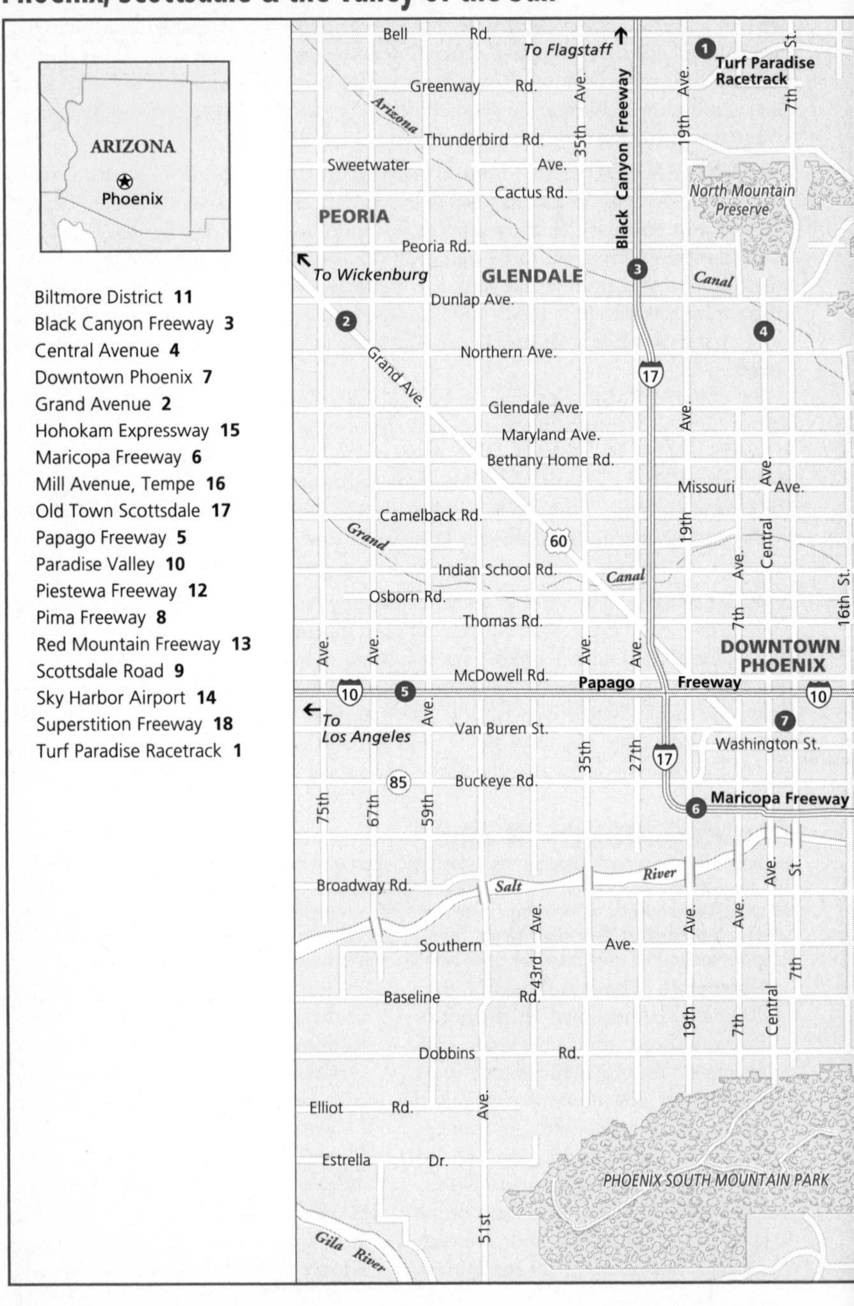
ARIZONA
Phoenix
Biltmore District 11
Black Canyon Freeway 3
Central Avenue 4
Downtown Phoenix 7
Grand Avenue 2
Hohokam Expressway 15
Maricopa Freeway 6
Mill Avenue, Tempe 16
Old Town Scottsdale 17
Papago Freeway 5
Paradise Valley 10
Piestewa Freeway 12
Pima Freeway 8
Red Mountain Freeway 13
Scottsdale Road 9
Sky Harbor Airport 14
Superstition Freeway 18
Turf Paradise Racetrack 1
Bell Rd.
To Flagstaff
Turf Paradise Racetrack
Greenway Rd.
Arizona
Thunderbird Rd.
Sweetwater Ave.
Cactus Rd.
North Mountain Preserve
PEORIA
Black Canyon Freeway
Peoria Rd.
To Wickenburg
GLENDALE
Canal
Dunlap Ave.
Northern Ave.
Grand Ave.
Glendale Ave.
Maryland Ave.
Bethany Home Rd.
Missouri Ave.
Camelback Rd.
Grand
Indian School Rd.
Canal
Osborn Rd.
Thomas Rd.
DOWNTOWN PHOENIX
McDowell Rd.
Papago Freeway
To Los Angeles
Van Buren St.
Washington St.
Buckeye Rd.
Maricopa Freeway
75th Ave.
67th Ave.
59th Ave.
35th Ave.
27th Ave.
19th Ave.
7th Ave.
Central Ave.
7th St.
16th St.
Broadway Rd.
Salt River
Southern Ave.
43rd Ave.
Baseline Rd.
Dobbins Rd.
Elliot Rd.
Estrella Dr.
51st Ave.
PHOENIX SOUTH MOUNTAIN PARK
Gila River

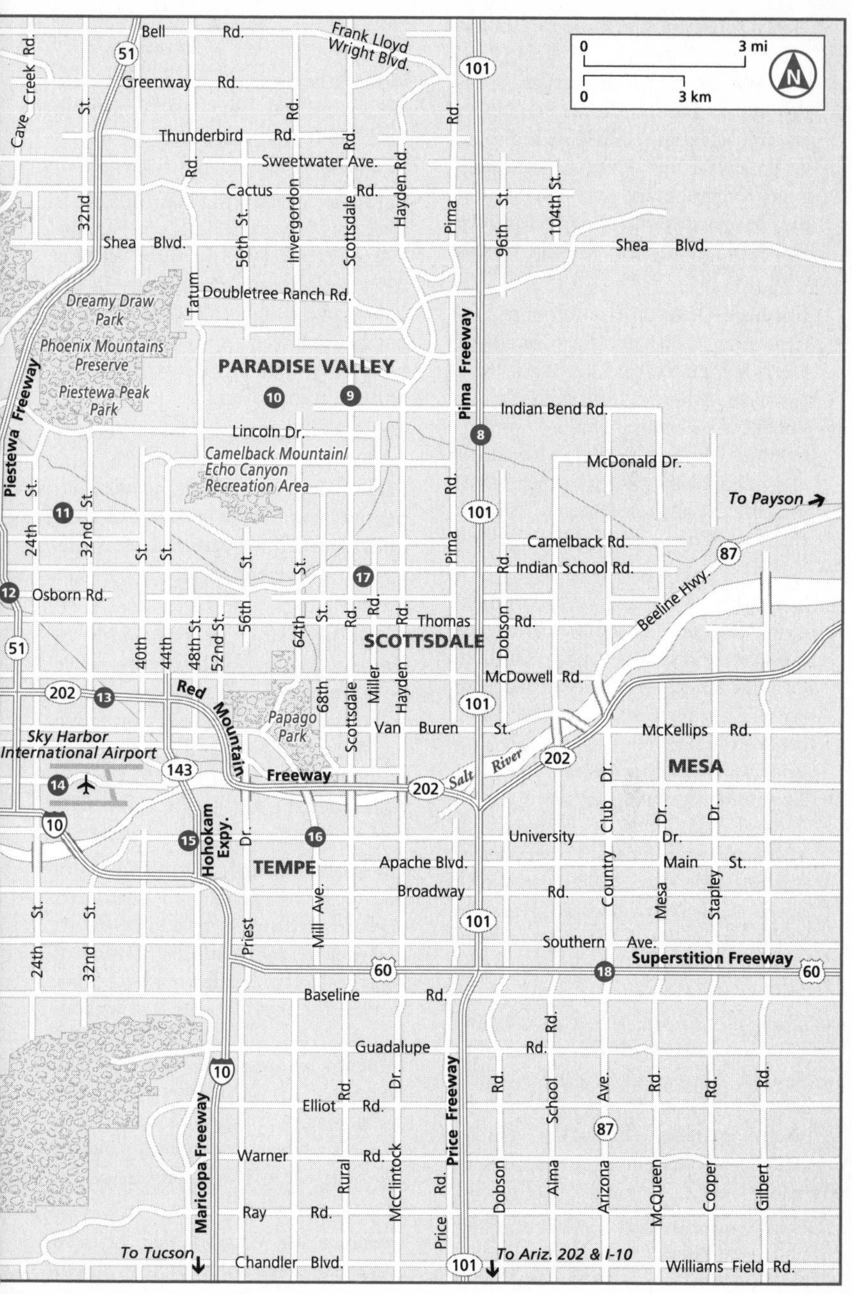

PARADISE VALLEY
SCOTTSDALE
TEMPE
MESA
Sky Harbor International Airport
Dreamy Draw Park
Phoenix Mountains Preserve
Piestewa Peak Park
Camelback Mountain/ Echo Canyon Recreation Area
Papago Park
Salt River
Piestewa Freeway
Pima Freeway
Red Mountain Freeway
Hohokam Expy.
Maricopa Freeway
Price Freeway
Superstition Freeway
Beeline Hwy.
To Payson
To Tucson
To Ariz. 202 & I-10
Bell Rd.
Greenway Rd.
Thunderbird Rd.
Sweetwater Ave.
Cactus Rd.
Shea Blvd.
Doubletree Ranch Rd.
Lincoln Dr.
Indian Bend Rd.
McDonald Dr.
Camelback Rd.
Indian School Rd.
Osborn Rd.
Thomas Rd.
McDowell Rd.
Van Buren St.
McKellips Rd.
University Dr.
Apache Blvd.
Main St.
Broadway Rd.
Southern Ave.
Baseline Rd.
Guadalupe Rd.
Elliot Rd.
Warner Rd.
Ray Rd.
Chandler Blvd.
Williams Field Rd.
Frank Lloyd Wright Blvd.
Cave Creek Rd.
0 3 mi
0 3 km
N

Heard Museum, the **Phoenix Central Library** (an architectural gem), and the **Phoenix Art Museum.** The core of downtown goes by the name Copper Square. Downtown Phoenix is also an art-gallery district featuring cutting-edge contemporary art. Condominiums have been proliferating downtown as well in recent years, infusing the area with new life.

Biltmore District The Biltmore District, also known as the **Camelback Corridor,** centers on Camelback Road between 24th and 44th streets and is Phoenix's upscale shopping, residential, and business district. The area is characterized by modern office buildings and is anchored by the Arizona Biltmore Hotel and Biltmore Fashion Park shopping mall.

Scottsdale A separate city of more than 200,000 people, Scottsdale extends from Tempe in the south to Carefree in the north, a distance of more than 20 miles. Scottsdale Road between Indian School Road and Shea Boulevard was once known as **Resort Row** and was home to more than a dozen major resorts. However, as Scottsdale has sprawled ever northward, so, too, have the resorts. North Scottsdale has now become the center of the resort, shopping, and restaurant scene. Downtown Scottsdale—Old Town, the Main Street Arts and Antiques District, the Marshall Way Contemporary Arts District, the Fifth Avenue Shops, and the Scottsdale Waterfront—is filled with tourist shops, galleries, boutiques, Native American crafts stores, and restaurants.

Tempe Tempe is the home of Arizona State University and has lots of nightclubs and bars as well as all the other trappings of a university town. **Mill Avenue,** which has dozens of interesting shops along a stretch of about 4 blocks, is the center of activity both day and night. This is one of the few areas in the Valley where locals actually walk the streets and hang out at sidewalk cafes. (Old Town Scottsdale always has people on its streets, but few are locals.)

Paradise Valley If Scottsdale is Phoenix's Beverly Hills, then Paradise Valley is its Bel-Air. Paradise Valley is the most exclusive community in the Valley and is almost entirely residential, but you won't see too many of the more lavish homes because they're set on large tracts of land.

Mesa This eastern suburb of Phoenix is the Valley's main high-tech area. Large shopping malls, numerous inexpensive chain motels, a couple of small museums, and the beautiful Mesa Arts Center attract both locals and visitors to Mesa.

Chandler Lying to the south of Tempe, this city has been booming over the past decade. New restaurants have opened and the old downtown has had a bit of a face-lift. This area is of interest primarily to east Valley residents, but there is an attractive older resort right in downtown Chandler.

Glendale Located northwest of downtown Phoenix, Glendale has numerous historic buildings in its downtown, and with its dozens of antiques and collectibles stores, it has become the antiques capital of the Valley. The city is home to the Bead Museum, an interesting little specialty museum. This is also where you'll find the Jobing.com Arena, home of the Phoenix Coyotes hockey team; and the Arizona Cardinals' University of Phoenix Stadium.

Carefree & Cave Creek Located about 20 miles north of Old Scottsdale, these two communities represent the Old West and the New West.

Carefree is a planned community and home to the prestigious Boulders resort and el Pedregal shopping center. Neighboring Cave Creek, on the other hand, plays up its Western heritage with contemporary cow-town architecture and a preponderance of saloons, steakhouses, and shops selling Western crafts and other gifts.

2 Getting Around

BY CAR

Phoenix and the surrounding cities that together make up the Valley of the Sun sprawl across more than 400 square miles, so if you want to make the best use of your time, it's essential to have a car. Outside downtown Phoenix, there's almost always plenty of free parking wherever you go (although finding a parking space can be time-consuming in Old Scottsdale and at some of the more popular malls and shopping plazas). If you want to feel like a local, opt for the ubiquitous valet parking (just be sure to keep plenty of small bills on hand for tipping the parking attendants).

Because Phoenix is a major tourist destination, good car-rental rates are often available. However, taxes and surcharges on rentals at Sky Harbor Airport now run 50% or more, which pretty much negates any deal you might get on your rate. Expect to pay anywhere from $160 to $250 per week ($225–$370 with taxes) for a compact car in the high season. See chapter 2 for general tips on car rentals.

All major rental-car companies have desks at Sky Harbor Airport's Rental Car Center, which is separate from the airport terminals and is served by a free shuttle bus. Be sure to leave time in your schedule to get from the Rental Car Center to the correct terminal for your flight. There are also plenty of other car-rental offices in Phoenix and Scottsdale. Rental-car companies at the airport include the following: **Advantage** (✆ 800/777-5500 or 602/244-0450), **Alamo** (✆ 800/462-5266 or 602/244-0897), **Avis** (✆ 800/331-1212 or 602/261-5900), **Budget** (✆ 800/527-0700 or 602/261-5950), **Dollar** (✆ 800/800-3665 or 866/434-2226), **Enterprise** (✆ 800/261-7331 or 602/225-0588), **Hertz** (✆ 800/654-3131 or 602/267-8822), **National** (✆ 800/227-7368 or 602/275-4771), **Payless** (✆ 800/729-5377 or 602/681-9589), and **Thrifty** (✆ 800/847-4389 or 877/283-0898).

For a bit more style while you cruise from resort to golf course to nightclub, **Rent-a-Vette,** 1215 N. Scottsdale Rd., Scottsdale (✆ **888/308-5995** or 480/941-3001; www.exoticcarrentalsphoenix.com), charges $229 to $349 per day for a Corvette. It also rents Porsche Boxsters, Porsche 911s, Hummers, and a variety of Mercedes.

BY PUBLIC TRANSPORTATION

Unfortunately, **Valley Metro** (✆ **602/253-5000;** www.valleymetro.org), the Phoenix public bus system, is not very useful to tourists. It's primarily meant to be used by commuters. However, if you decide you want to take the bus, pick up a copy of the *Bus Book* at one of the tourist information desks in the airport (where it's sometimes available), at Central Station at the corner of Central Avenue and Van Buren Street, or at any Fry's supermarket. Local bus fare is $1.25; express bus fare is $1.75. A 10-ride ticket book, an all-day pass, and a monthly pass are also available.

Of slightly more value to visitors is the free **Downtown Area Shuttle (DASH),** which provides bus service within the downtown area Monday through Friday from 6:30am to 11pm. These buses serve regular stops every 6 to 18 minutes; they're primarily for downtown workers, but attractions along the route include the state capitol and

Heritage and Science Park. In Tempe, **Free Local Area Shuttle (FLASH)** buses provide a similar service on a loop around Arizona State University. The route includes Mill Avenue and Sun Devil Stadium. For information on both DASH and FLASH, call ✆ **602/253-5000.**

In Scottsdale, you can ride the **Scottsdale Trolley** (✆ **480/421-1004;** www.valley metro.org) shuttle buses between Scottsdale Fashion Square, the Fifth Avenue shops, the Main Street Arts district, and the Old Town district. These buses run Monday through Saturday from 11am to 9pm. Between mid-January and mid-April, free shuttles serve many of the area's resorts, including, among others, Camelback Inn, Sanctuary on Camelback, Hyatt Regency Scottsdale Resort and Spa at Gainey Ranch, and Renaissance Scottsdale Resort. These trolleys operate Tuesday through Sunday and will take you to Scottsdale Fashion Square. From there you can take the Scottsdale Trolley to other shopping districts.

BY TAXI

Because distances in Phoenix are so great, the price of an average taxi ride can be quite high. However, if you don't have your own wheels or had too much to drink and the bus isn't running because it's late at night or the weekend, you won't have any choice but to call a cab. **Yellow Cab** (✆ **602/252-5252**) charges $2.50 for the first mile and $1.80 per mile thereafter. **Discount Cab** (✆ **602/200-2000**) charges $1.80 for the first mile and $2.95 per mile after that.

FAST FACTS: Phoenix

American Express There's an American Express office in Biltmore Fashion Park, 2508 E. Camelback Rd. (✆ **602/468-1199**), open Monday through Saturday from 10am to 6pm.

Babysitters If you need a babysitter, check with the concierge or front desk at your hotel.

Car Rentals See "Getting Around," above.

Dentist Call the Dental Referral Service (✆ **800/428-8774;** www.dentalreferral.com).

Doctor Call the Banner Health Physician & Resource Line (✆ **602/230-2273**) for doctor referrals.

Emergencies For police, fire, or medical emergencies, phone ✆ **911.**

Eyeglass Repair The **Nationwide Vision Center** (www.nationwidevision.com) has nearly 30 locations around the Valley, including 7904 E. Chaparral Rd., Suite A-108, Scottsdale (✆ **480/874-2543**); 3202 E. Greenway, Suite 1631, Phoenix (✆ **602/788-8413**); 4280 E. Indian School Rd., Suite 107, Phoenix (✆ **602/952-8667**); and 933 E. University Dr., Suite 106, Tempe (✆ **480/966-4992**).

Hospitals The **Banner Good Samaritan Medical Center,** 1111 E. McDowell Rd., Phoenix (✆ **602/239-2000**), is one of the largest hospitals in the Valley.

Hot Lines The **Visitor Information Line** (✆ **602/252-5588**) has recorded tourist information on events in Phoenix and the Valley of the Sun.

Information See "Visitor Information," earlier in this chapter.

Internet Access If your hotel doesn't provide Internet access, your next best bet is to visit one of the **FedEx Kinko's** in the area. There are locations in downtown Phoenix at 201 E. Washington St. (✆ **602/252-4055**); off the Camelback Corridor at 3801 N. Central Ave. (✆ **602/241-9440**); and in Scottsdale just off Indian School Road at 4150 N. Drinkwater Blvd. (✆ **480/946-0500**).

Lost Property If you lose something at the airport, call ✆ **602/273-3307;** on a bus, call ✆ **602/253-5000.**

Newspapers & Magazines The *Arizona Republic* is Phoenix's daily newspaper. The Thursday edition has a special section ("Calendar") with schedules of the upcoming week's movie, music, and cultural performances. *New Times* is a free weekly journal with comprehensive listings of cultural events, films, clubs, and concert schedules. The best place to find *New Times* is at corner newspaper boxes in downtown Phoenix, Scottsdale, or Tempe.

Pharmacies Call ✆ **800/WALGREENS** for the Walgreens pharmacy that's nearest you; some are open 24 hours a day.

Police For police emergencies, phone ✆ **911.**

Post Office The Phoenix Downtown Station, 522 N. Central Ave. (✆ **800/275-8777** or 602/253-9648), is open Monday through Friday from 9am to 6pm. In Scottsdale, the Scottsdale Hopi Station, 8790 E. Via de Ventura (✆ **800/275-8777** or 480/998-9356), is open Monday through Friday from 8am to 5pm and on Saturday from 9am to 4pm.

Safety Don't leave valuables in view in your car, especially when parking in downtown Phoenix. Put anything of value in the trunk or, if you're driving a hatchback or station wagon, under the seat. Take extra precautions after dark in the south central Phoenix area and downtown. Violent acts of road rage have been all too common in Phoenix in the past, so it's a good idea to be polite when driving. Aggressive drivers should be given plenty of room.

Taxes State sales tax is 5.6% (plus variable local taxes, so expect to pay around 8%). Hotel room taxes vary considerably by city but are mostly between 10% and 11%. It's in renting a car that you really get pounded. The total taxes and surcharges when renting a car at Sky Harbor Airport add up to more than 50%.

Taxis See "Getting Around," above.

Weather For weather information, call ✆ **800/555-8355,** and say "weather."

3 Where to Stay

Because the Phoenix area has long been popular as a winter refuge from cold and snow, it now has the greatest concentration of resorts in the continental United States. However, even with all the hotel rooms here, sunshine and baseball's spring training combine to make it hard to find a room on short notice between February and April. If you plan to visit during these months, make your reservations as far in advance as possible. Also keep in mind that in late winter and early spring, the Phoenix metro area has some of the highest room rates in the country.

Most resorts offer a variety of weekend, golf, and tennis packages, as well as off-season discounts and corporate rates (which you can often get just by asking). I've given

Phoenix, Scottsdale & the Valley of the Sun Accommodations

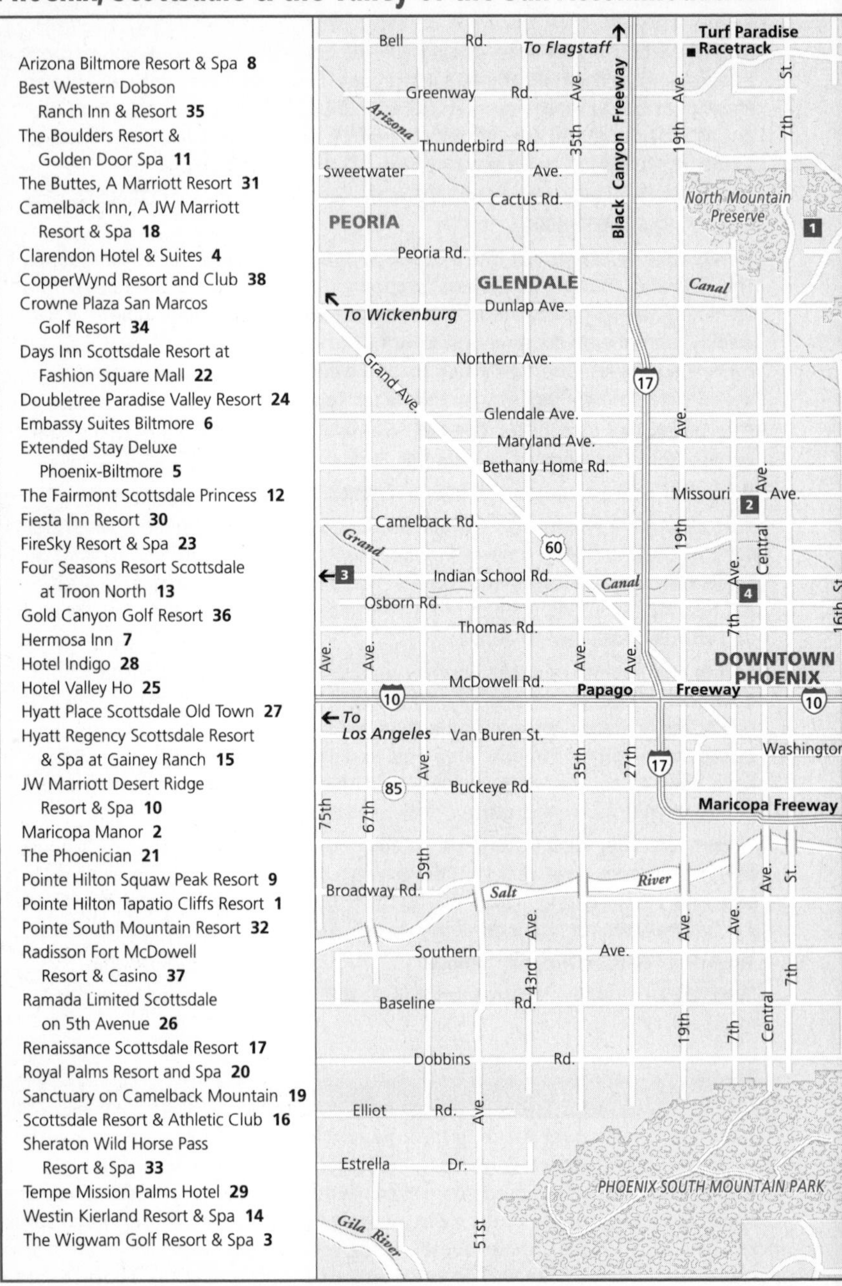

Arizona Biltmore Resort & Spa 8
Best Western Dobson Ranch Inn & Resort 35
The Boulders Resort & Golden Door Spa 11
The Buttes, A Marriott Resort 31
Camelback Inn, A JW Marriott Resort & Spa 18
Clarendon Hotel & Suites 4
CopperWynd Resort and Club 38
Crowne Plaza San Marcos Golf Resort 34
Days Inn Scottsdale Resort at Fashion Square Mall 22
Doubletree Paradise Valley Resort 24
Embassy Suites Biltmore 6
Extended Stay Deluxe Phoenix-Biltmore 5
The Fairmont Scottsdale Princess 12
Fiesta Inn Resort 30
FireSky Resort & Spa 23
Four Seasons Resort Scottsdale at Troon North 13
Gold Canyon Golf Resort 36
Hermosa Inn 7
Hotel Indigo 28
Hotel Valley Ho 25
Hyatt Place Scottsdale Old Town 27
Hyatt Regency Scottsdale Resort & Spa at Gainey Ranch 15
JW Marriott Desert Ridge Resort & Spa 10
Maricopa Manor 2
The Phoenician 21
Pointe Hilton Squaw Peak Resort 9
Pointe Hilton Tapatio Cliffs Resort 1
Pointe South Mountain Resort 32
Radisson Fort McDowell Resort & Casino 37
Ramada Limited Scottsdale on 5th Avenue 26
Renaissance Scottsdale Resort 17
Royal Palms Resort and Spa 20
Sanctuary on Camelback Mountain 19
Scottsdale Resort & Athletic Club 16
Sheraton Wild Horse Pass Resort & Spa 33
Tempe Mission Palms Hotel 29
Westin Kierland Resort & Spa 14
The Wigwam Golf Resort & Spa 3
Bell Rd.
To Flagstaff
Turf Paradise Racetrack
Greenway Rd.
Arizona
Thunderbird Rd.
Sweetwater Ave.
Cactus Rd.
35th Ave.
Black Canyon Freeway
19th Ave.
7th St.
North Mountain Preserve
PEORIA
Peoria Rd.
GLENDALE
Canal
To Wickenburg
Dunlap Ave.
Northern Ave.
Grand Ave.
17
Glendale Ave.
Maryland Ave.
Bethany Home Rd.
Missouri Ave.
Camelback Rd.
Grand
60
Central Ave.
Indian School Rd.
Canal
Osborn Rd.
Thomas Rd.
16th St.
DOWNTOWN PHOENIX
McDowell Rd.
Papago Freeway
10
To Los Angeles
Van Buren St.
Washington
75th Ave.
67th Ave.
59th Ave.
35th Ave.
27th Ave.
85
Buckeye Rd.
Maricopa Freeway
Broadway Rd.
Salt River
Southern Ave.
43rd Ave.
Baseline Rd.
Dobbins Rd.
Elliot Rd.
51st Ave.
Estrella Dr.
PHOENIX SOUTH MOUNTAIN PARK
Gila River

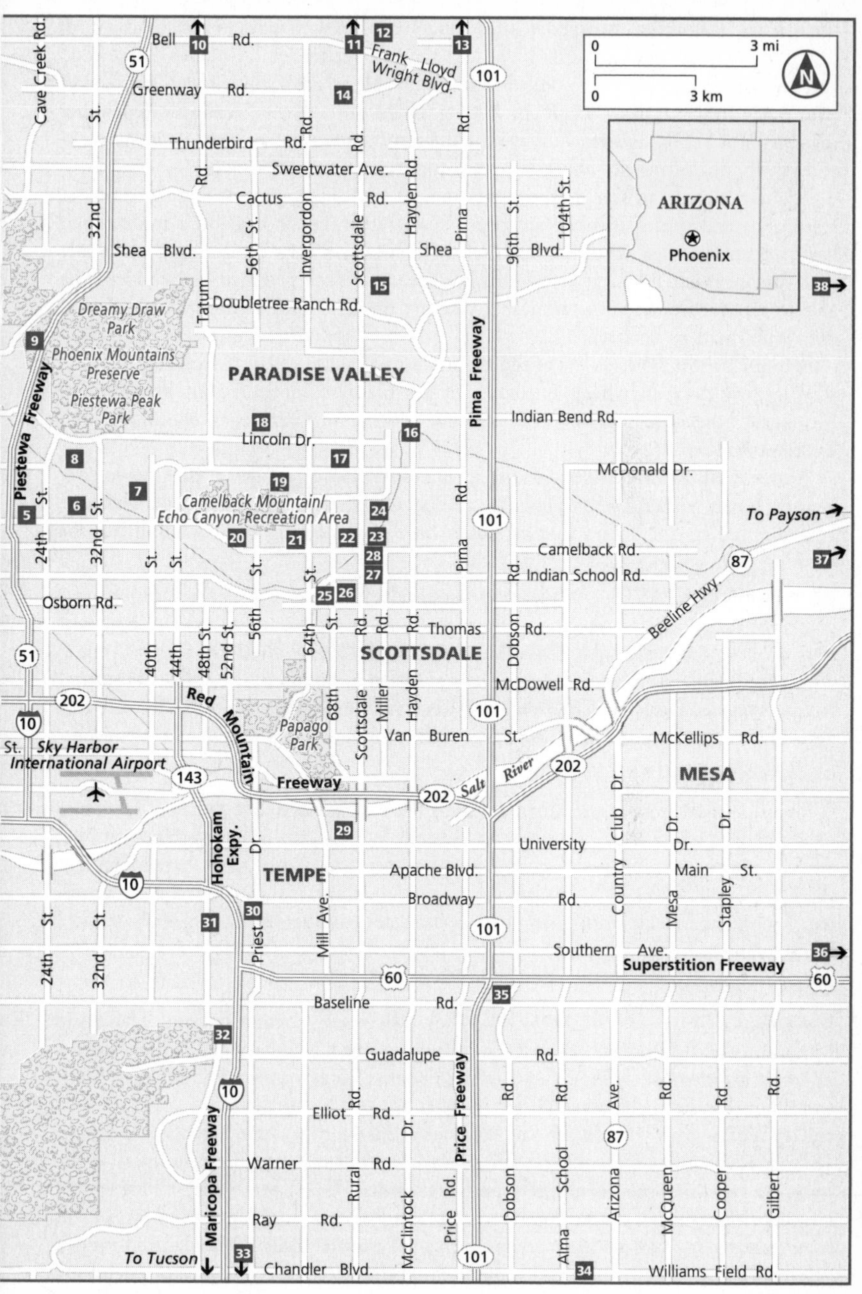

0
3 mi
0
3 km
N
ARIZONA
Phoenix
Cave Creek Rd.
Bell Rd.
Greenway Rd.
Frank Lloyd Wright Blvd.
Thunderbird Rd.
Sweetwater Ave.
Cactus Rd.
Shea Blvd.
Shea Blvd.
Doubletree Ranch Rd.
Dreamy Draw Park
Phoenix Mountains Preserve
Piestewa Peak Park
Piestewa Freeway
PARADISE VALLEY
Pima Freeway
Indian Bend Rd.
McDonald Dr.
Lincoln Dr.
Camelback Mountain/ Echo Canyon Recreation Area
To Payson
Camelback Rd.
Indian School Rd.
Beeline Hwy.
Osborn Rd.
Thomas Rd.
SCOTTSDALE
McDowell Rd.
Red Mountain Freeway
Papago Park
Van Buren St.
McKellips Rd.
Sky Harbor International Airport
Salt River
MESA
Freeway
University Dr.
Hohokam Expy.
TEMPE
Apache Blvd.
Main St.
Broadway Rd.
Southern Ave.
Superstition Freeway
Baseline Rd.
Guadalupe Rd.
Elliot Rd.
Warner Rd.
Ray Rd.
Chandler Blvd.
Williams Field Rd.
To Tucson
Maricopa Freeway
Price Freeway
24th St.
32nd St.
40th St.
44th St.
48th St.
52nd St.
56th St.
64th St.
68th St.
Tatum Rd.
Invergordon Rd.
Scottsdale Rd.
Hayden Rd.
Miller Rd.
Pima Rd.
96th St.
104th St.
Dobson Rd.
Priest Dr.
Mill Ave.
Rural Rd.
McClintock Dr.
Price Rd.
Alma School Rd.
Arizona Ave.
McQueen Rd.
Cooper Rd.
Gilbert Rd.
Country Club Dr.
Mesa Dr.
Stapley Dr.
51
101
202
10
143
60
87
1
5
6
7
8
9
10
11
12
13
14
15
16
17
18
19
20
21
22
23
24
25
26
27
28
29
30
31
32
33
34
35
36
37
38

the official "rack rates," or walk-in rates, below, but it always pays to ask about special discounts or packages. Sometimes you can get a lower rate just by asking. If a hotel isn't full and isn't expected to be, you should be able to get a lower rate. Don't forget your AAA or AARP discounts if you belong to one of these organizations. Remember that business hotels downtown and near the airport often lower their rates on weekends. Also, don't forget to check hotel websites for special deals.

If you're looking to save even more money, consider traveling during the shoulder seasons of late spring and late summer. Temperatures are not at their midsummer highs and room rates are often only slightly higher than they are during the summer slow season. If you'll be traveling with children, always ask whether your child will be able to stay for free in your room, and whether there's a limit to the number of children who can stay for free.

Request a room with a view of the mountains whenever possible. You can overlook a swimming pool anywhere, but some of the main selling points of Phoenix and Scottsdale hotels are the views of Mummy Mountain, Camelback Mountain, and Piestewa Peak.

With the exception of valet-parking services and parking garages at downtown convention hotels, parking is free at almost all Phoenix hotels. If there is a parking charge, I have noted it. You'll find that all hotels have nonsmoking rooms and all but the cheapest have wheelchair-accessible rooms.

BED & BREAKFASTS While most people dreaming of a Phoenix vacation have visions of luxury resorts dancing in their heads, there are plenty of bed-and-breakfast inns around the Valley. **Mi Casa Su Casa** (✆ **800/456-0682** or 480/990-0682; www.azres.com) can book you into dozens of different homes in the Valley of the Sun, as can **Arizona Trails Bed & Breakfast Reservation Service** (✆ **888/799-4284** or 480/837-4284; www.arizonatrails.com), which also books tour and hotel reservations.

SCOTTSDALE

With a dozen or more resorts lined up along Scottsdale Road, Scottsdale is the center of the Valley's resort scene. And because Scottsdale is also the Valley's prime shopping and dining district, this is the most convenient place to stay if you're here to eat and shop. However, traffic in Scottsdale is bad, the landscape at most resorts is flat (compared with the hillside settings in north Scottsdale), and you don't get much of a feel for the desert.

VERY EXPENSIVE

Camelback Inn, A JW Marriott Resort & Spa ★★★ Set at the foot of Mummy Mountain and overlooking Camelback Mountain, the Camelback Inn, which opened in 1936, is one of the grande dames of the Phoenix hotel scene and abounds in traditional Southwestern character. Forget the glitz of The Phoenician (see below); this legendary retreat gives you old-school luxury with 21st-century enhancements. The two 18-hole golf courses are a magnet for golfers, and the spa is among the finest in the state. An extensive pool complex appeals to families. Guest rooms, which are spread over the sloping grounds, are decorated with Southwestern furnishings and art, and all have balconies or patios. Some rooms even have private pools. This is an old-money getaway that seamlessly melds tradition with modern amenities. The Camelback Inn's $50-million renovation is expected to be done by March 2008, but because the lobby has been moved and rooms in construction areas closed, the work is hard to notice, and noise and dust should be minimal.

5402 E. Lincoln Dr., Scottsdale, AZ 85253. ✆ **800/24-CAMEL** or 480/948-1700. Fax 480/951-8469. www.camelback inn.com. 453 units. Jan to early June $299–$549 double, $570–$2,500 suite; early June to early Sept $179–$199 double, $260–$900 suite; early Sept to Dec $349–$459 double, $595–$1,700 suite. Children under 18 stay free in parent's room. AE, DC, DISC, MC, V. Small pets accepted. **Amenities:** 7 restaurants (American, Mexican, healthy); 2 lounges; 3 pools; 2 outstanding 18-hole golf courses; 6 tennis courts; exercise room; full-service spa; 6 Jacuzzis; bike rentals; children's programs and playground; concierge; car-rental desk; seasonal courtesy shopping shuttle; business center; 24-hr. room service; massage; babysitting; guest laundry and laundry service; dry cleaning. *In room:* A/C, TV, dataport, minibar, coffeemaker, hair dryer, iron, safe, high-speed Internet access.

Hotel Valley Ho ★★ This Scottsdale grande dame dates back to the 1950s, but in 2005, the hotel got a complete face-lift. What a looker she is now. The Valley Ho has become one of my favorite Scottsdale hotels; it's hip and convenient, and has loads of outdoor space for soaking up the sun. I just love the big rooms, which are done in a bold contemporary style. The studio rooms are my favorites; they have curtains to partition off the vanity area and an ultracool free-standing tub. Big balconies and patios provide plenty of space for lounging outdoors. When it's time to get even more relaxed, grab one of the plush, circular lounge chairs at the pool. Back in the day when midcentury modern was fresh and not retro, this hotel was a favorite hangout of Hollywood stars. I've got a feeling the Valley Ho will be seeing celebs again now that it looks like one of the prettiest young things in town. For that totally retro experience, there's even a Trader Vic's here.

6850 E. Main St., Scottsdale, AZ 85251. ✆ **866/882-4484** or 480/248-2000. Fax 480/248-2002. www.hotelvalley ho.com. 194 units. Jan–Apr $319–$359 double, $419–$569 suite; May and Sept $199–$259 double, $299–$449 suite; June–Aug $149–$179 double, $249–$399 suite; Oct–Dec $259–$299 double, $359–$509 suite. Children under 18 stay free in parent's room. AE, DC, DISC, MC, V. Valet parking $12. Pets accepted. **Amenities:** 2 restaurants (American, Polynesian); 3 lounges; pool; exercise room; access to nearby health club; full-service spa; 2 Jacuzzis; bike rental; children's programs; concierge; business center; 24-hr. room service; massage; babysitting; laundry service; dry cleaning. *In room:* A/C, TV, dataport, minibar, coffeemaker/espresso maker, hair dryer, iron, safe, high-speed Internet access, Wi-Fi.

Hyatt Regency Scottsdale Resort & Spa at Gainey Ranch ★★★ *Kids* From the colonnades of palm trees to the lobby walls that slide away, this luxurious resort is designed to impress and continues to be my favorite Scottsdale resort. It's relatively close to downtown Scottsdale and has interesting architecture, beautiful grounds, and a large spa. What's not to love? A 2½-acre water playground serves as the resort's focal point, and the extravagant complex of 10 swimming pools includes a water slide and a huge whirlpool spa. Guest rooms are luxurious and are designed to reflect the desert location. The resort's Ristorante Sandolo features after-dinner gondola rides. The resort's Native American and Environmental Learning Center provides a glimpse into Sonoran Desert culture and ecology. Children's programs make this a super choice for families.

7500 E. Doubletree Ranch Rd., Scottsdale, AZ 85258. ✆ **800/55-HYATT** or 480/444-1234. Fax 480/483-5550. www. scottsdale.hyatt.com. 490 units. Jan to late May $419 double, from $629 suite and casita; late May to early Sept $195 double, from $289 suite and casita; early Sept to Dec $315 double, from $479 suite and casita. Children under 18 stay free in parent's room. AE, DC, DISC, MC, V. Valet parking $20. **Amenities:** 3 restaurants (American, Italian); snack bar; lounge; coffee bar; juice bar; 10 pools; 27-hole golf course (w/lots of water hazards); 4 tennis courts; access to nearby health club; health club; full-service spa; 3 Jacuzzis; bikes; children's programs; concierge; car-rental desk; business center; room service; massage; babysitting; laundry service; dry cleaning; concierge-level rooms. *In room:* A/C, TV, dataport, minibar, coffeemaker, hair dryer, iron, safe, free local calls, high-speed Internet access, Wi-Fi.

The Phoenician ★★★ *Kids* Situated on 250 acres at the foot of Camelback Mountain, this palatial resort is one of the finest resorts in the world. So, if you must stay at the very best, this is it. Polished marble and sparkling crystal abound in the lobby, but the valley view through a long wall of glass is what commands most guests' attention when they first arrive. Service here is second to none, and the character is very international. The pool complex, which has a water slide for the kids, is irresistibly seductive, and the resort's Centre for Well Being offers all the spa pampering anyone could ever want. There are also 27 challenging holes of golf. Mary Elaine's (p. 111) is Phoenix's ultimate special-occasion restaurant. The luxurious guest rooms have large patios and sunken tubs for two.

6000 E. Camelback Rd., Scottsdale, AZ 85251. ✆ **800/888-8234** or 480/941-8200. Fax 480/947-4311. www.thephoenician.com. 654 units. Jan–May $625 double, from $1,550 suite; June to mid-Sept $295 double, from $995 suite; mid-Sept to Dec $525 double, from $1,450 suite. Children under 12 stay free in parent's room. AE, DC, DISC, MC, V. Valet parking $26. Pets under 40 lb. accepted. **Amenities:** 3 restaurants (Modern French, Southwestern, American); 4 snack bars/cafes; lounge; 9 pools; 27-hole golf course; putting green; 12 tennis courts; health club and spa; Jacuzzi; bike rentals; children's programs; concierge; car-rental desk; business center; shopping arcade; salon; 24-hr. room service; massage; babysitting; laundry service; dry cleaning; executive-level rooms; lawn games. *In room:* A/C, TV, dataport, minibar, hair dryer, iron, safe, high-speed Internet access.

Sanctuary on Camelback Mountain ★★★ The Mondrian Scottsdale may be the hippest hotel in Scottsdale, but this visually breathtaking place did the W Hotel thing first, and I still like the contemporary rooms here better than those at the Mondrian. Located high on the northern flanks of Camelback Mountain, the lushly landscaped property has unforgettable views across the valley, especially from the restaurant and lounge. The extremely spacious guest rooms are divided between the more conservative deluxe casitas and the boldly contemporary spa casitas. With their dyed-cement floors, kidney-shape daybeds, and streamline-moderne cabinetry, these latter units are absolutely stunning. Bathrooms are huge, and some have private outdoor soaking tubs. The resort's spa is gorgeous!

5700 E. McDonald Dr., Paradise Valley, AZ 85253. ✆ **800/245-2051** or 480/948-2100. Fax 480/483-7314. www.sanctuaryoncamelback.com. 98 units. Jan to late May and late Dec $495–$690 double, $620–$1,505 suite; late May to mid-Sept and mid-Dec $225–$395 double, $325–$890 suite; mid-Sept to mid-Dec $395–$590 double, $520–$1,305 suite. Children under 17 stay free in parent's room. AE, DC, DISC, MC, V. Pets accepted. **Amenities:** Restaurant (New American); lounge; 4 pools; 5 tennis courts; fitness center; full-service spa; 2 Jacuzzis; bike rentals; concierge; business center; 24-hr. room service; massage; babysitting; laundry service; dry cleaning. *In room:* A/C, TV/DVD, dataport, minibar, coffeemaker, hair dryer, iron, safe, high-speed Internet access.

Westin Kierland Resort & Spa ★★★ *Kids* A convenient location and distinct sense of place make this one of my favorite Phoenix-area resorts. Located just off Scottsdale Road adjacent to the Kierland Commons shopping center, the resort features artwork by Arizona artists, numerous interpretive plaques, and historical photos that provide insight into Arizona's cultural and natural history. Guest rooms all have balconies or patios, and although the bathrooms aren't all that large, this minor inconvenience is compensated for by Westin's Heavenly Beds, which are incredibly comfortable pillow-top beds. Excellent Nuevo Latino cuisine is served at deseo, and there's a great cowboy-style bar as well. The main pool area includes a long tubing river, a water slide, and a beach area.

6902 E. Greenway Pkwy., Scottsdale, AZ 85254. ✆ **800/WESTIN-1** or 480/624-1000. Fax 480/624-1001. www.kierlandresort.com. 735 units. Jan–Apr $279–$529 double; May–June $189–$369 double; July to mid-Sept $149–$269 double; mid-Sept to Dec $189–$489 double. Children under 16 stay free in parent's room. AE, DC, DISC, MC, V. Valet parking $21. Pets accepted ($100 refundable deposit). **Amenities:** 5 restaurants (Nuevo Latino, American, Southwestern); poolside snack bar; espresso bar/ice-cream parlor; 4 lounges; 4 pools; 3 9-hole golf courses; 2 tennis courts; health club; full-service spa; 3 Jacuzzis; children's programs; concierge; car-rental desk; courtesy shopping shuttle; business center; 24-hr. room service; massage; babysitting; laundry service; dry cleaning; executive-level rooms. *In room:* A/C, TV, dataport, minibar, coffeemaker, hair dryer, iron, safe, high-speed Internet access, Wi-Fi, free local calls.

EXPENSIVE

Doubletree Paradise Valley Resort ★★ *Value* With its distinctive styling and convenient location, this is an excellent choice. Its low-rise design and textured-block construction gives a bow to the pioneering architectural style of Frank Lloyd Wright and thus stands out from comparable resorts in the area. Built around several courtyards containing swimming pools, bubbling fountains, palm trees, and gardens with desert landscaping, the property has much the look and feel of the nearby Hyatt Regency Scottsdale (although on a less grandiose scale and at more bearable room rates). Accommodations have a very contemporary feel, with lots of blond wood and, in some cases, high ceilings that make the rooms feel particularly spacious.

5401 N. Scottsdale Rd., Scottsdale, AZ 85250. ✆ **877/445-6677** or 480/947-5400. Fax 480/946-1524. www.paradisevalley.doubletree.com. 387 units. Jan–Mar $329–$359 double; Apr–May and Sept $139–$199 double; Oct–Dec $249–$289 double; June–Aug $119–$159 double. Children under 18 stay free in parent's room. AE, DC, DISC, MC, V. Pets accepted ($50 fee). **Amenities:** Restaurant (Southwestern); lounge; poolside snack bar; 2 outdoor pools; putting green; 2 tennis courts; 2 racquetball courts; health club; 2 Jacuzzis; seasonal children's programs; concierge; car-rental desk; business center; room service; massage; laundry service; dry cleaning. *In room:* A/C, TV, dataport, minibar, coffeemaker, hair dryer, iron, high-speed Internet access.

FireSky Resort & Spa ★★ An exceptional location in the heart of the Scottsdale shopping district, a dramatic Southwestern/Moroccan styling (the focal point of the lobby is a massive sandstone fireplace), and a small but well-designed pool area are the main reasons I like this little resort. Set in a lushly planted courtyard are a small lagoon-style pool, complete with sand beach and short water slide, and a second pool with flame-topped columnar waterfalls. An artificial stream and faux sandstone ruins all add up to a fun desert fantasy landscape (although not on the grand scale to be found at some area resorts). The guest rooms are quite comfortable, and there's a pretty little spa on the premises.

4925 N. Scottsdale Rd., Scottsdale, AZ 85251. ✆ **800/528-7867** or 480/945-7666. Fax 480/946-4056. www.fireskyresort.com. 204 units. Jan to late May $289 double, $599 suite; late May to early Sept $149 double, $299 suite; early Sept to Dec $239 double, $549 suite. Children under 18 stay free in parent's room. AE, DISC, MC, V. Pets accepted. **Amenities:** Restaurant (Italian); lounge; snack bar; 2 pools; exercise room; access to nearby health club; full-service spa; Jacuzzi; concierge; courtesy shopping shuttle; business center; room service; massage; laundry service; dry cleaning. *In room:* A/C, TV, dataport, minibar, coffeemaker, hair dryer, iron, safe, high-speed Internet access, Wi-Fi.

Hotel Indigo ★★ Located in the heart of downtown Scottsdale's nightlife district, this stylish hotel is a great choice for anyone in town to party. Guest rooms are distinctively different from most hotels in that they have wood floors and area rugs. The rooms are designed in a Scandinavian-modern aesthetic and have absolutely gorgeous bathrooms. Clock radios have MP3 jacks, and the beds have halogen reading lamps. Seasonal fragrances scent the air; and photo-murals of, among other things, northern Arizona's famous sandstone formation "The Wave," make the Indigo a feast for the senses.

4415 N. Civic Center Plaza, Scottsdale, AZ 85251. ✆ **866/2-INDIGO** or 480/941-9400. Fax 480/675-5240. http://scottsdalehiphotel.com. 126 units. Jan–Apr $259–$279 double; May and Oct–Dec $174–$199 double; June–Sept $79–$105 double. Children under 18 stay free in parent's room. AE, DC, DISC, MC, V. **Amenities:** Restaurant (American); lounge; small outdoor pool; exercise room; concierge; courtesy shopping shuttle; business center; room service; laundry service; dry cleaning. *In room:* A/C, TV, dataport, hair dryer, iron, safe, Wi-Fi.

Hyatt Place Scottsdale Old Town ★★ With a great location in the heart of downtown Scottsdale, this hip business hotel is well worth choosing even if you're in town on vacation. The guest rooms are all spacious suites done in a homey, contemporary style with separate sitting and sleeping areas and 42-inch wall-hung flat-panel

TVs that can be angled to either area. Unusual features include electronic self-service check-in kiosks, continental (free) or hot (charge) breakfasts, and a tiny lounge area to one side of the lobby. You can even get a light meal here if you don't feel like going out to a restaurant for dinner.

7300 E. Third Ave., Scottsdale, AZ 85251. ✆ **888/492-8847** or 480/423-9944. Fax 480/423-2991. www.hyattplace.com. 127 units. $159–$229 double. Rates include continental breakfast. Children under 18 stay free in parent's room. AE, DC, DISC, MC, V. **Amenities:** Restaurant (American); lounge; outdoor pool; exercise room; courtesy shopping shuttle; business center. *In room:* A/C, TV, dataport, fridge, coffeemaker, hair dryer, iron, high-speed Internet access, Wi-Fi.

Renaissance Scottsdale Resort ★★ *Value* If I were coming to Scottsdale for a romantic getaway, I would stay here. Located adjacent to the upscale Borgata shopping center (which is designed to resemble Tuscany's San Gimignano), this casual yet luxurious boutique resort feels like an isolated hideaway and is designed to resemble a Spanish oasis. Set amid shady lawns, the Renaissance Scottsdale consists of spacious, comfortable casita-style rooms and suites that are done in a Southwestern style. More than 100 of the suites have their own private outdoor hot tubs (very romantic). Several excellent restaurants are within walking distance.

6160 N. Scottsdale Rd., Scottsdale, AZ 85253. ✆ **800/309-8138** or 480/991-1414. Fax 480/951-3350. www.renaissancescottsdale.com. 171 units. Jan–May $259–$319 double, $279–$369 suite; June to early Sept $129 double, $149–$159 suite; early Sept to Dec $219 double, $269–$319 suite. Children under 16 stay free in parent's room. AE, DC, DISC, MC, V. Pets accepted ($50 deposit). **Amenities:** 3 restaurants (Mediterranean, Spanish, American); lounge; 2 pools; putting green; 4 tennis courts; croquet court; access to nearby health club; 2 Jacuzzis; bike rentals; concierge; courtesy shopping shuttle; business center; room service; massage; babysitting; laundry service; dry cleaning. *In room:* A/C, TV, dataport, minibar, coffeemaker, hair dryer, iron, safe, high-speed Internet access, Wi-Fi.

Scottsdale Resort & Athletic Club ★★ Fitness fanatics rejoice; this club's for you. If you can't stand the thought of giving up your workout just because you're on vacation, book a stay at this little boutique hotel (and timeshare resort) just off busy Scottsdale Road and adjacent to the Silverado Golf Course. With standard rooms and huge one- and two-bedroom "villas," this place is plenty comfortable, but the main reason I like this hotel is that it's affiliated with the Scottsdale Athletic Club, a large workout facility that emphasizes its tennis program. The basic rooms are a real steal for Scottsdale, and while the villas are quite a bit more expensive, they're gigantic and have fireplaces, DVD players, full kitchens, and washers and dryers. On top of all this, you get a view of Camelback Mountain.

8235 E. Indian Bend Rd., Scottsdale, AZ 85250. ✆ **877/343-0033** or 480/344-0600. Fax 480/344-0650. www.scottsdaleresortandathleticclub.com. 85 units. Late Dec to Apr $249 double, $359–$1,100 suite or villa; May–Sept $119 double, $179–$549 suite or villa; Oct–Dec $149 double, $219–$669 suite or villa. Rates include continental breakfast. Children under 12 stay free in parent's room. AE, DISC, MC, V. **Amenities:** Restaurant (American); lounge; 3 pools; 11 tennis courts; health club; full-service spa; Jacuzzi; sauna; children's programs; concierge; car-rental desk; business center; room service; massage; babysitting; coin-op laundry. *In room:* A/C, TV/DVD, dataport, fridge, coffeemaker, hair dryer, iron, high-speed Internet access, free local calls.

MODERATE

Days Inn Scottsdale Resort at Fashion Square Mall ★ *Kids* *Value* This is one of the last economical hotels in the Old Town Scottsdale area, and its location adjacent to the Scottsdale Fashion Square mall makes it a great choice for shopaholics. This may be just an aging chain motel, but green lawns, tall palm trees, and a convenient location all make it worth recommending.

4710 N. Scottsdale Rd., Scottsdale, AZ 85251. ✆ **800/DAYS-INN** or 480/947-5411. Fax 480/946-1324. www.scottsdaledaysinn.com. 167 units. Jan–Mar $101–$199 double; Apr–Dec $59–$199 double. Rates include continental breakfast. Children under 18 stay free in parent's room. AE, DC, DISC, MC, V. **Amenities:** Seasonal poolside bar; small outdoor pool; tennis court; Jacuzzi; car-rental desk; courtesy shopping shuttle; coin-op laundry; dry cleaning service. *In room:* A/C, TV, dataport, fridge, coffeemaker, hair dryer, iron.

Ramada Limited Scottsdale on 5th Avenue *Value* For convenience and price, this motel can't be beat. Located at the west end of the Fifth Avenue shopping district, the Ramada Limited is within walking distance of some of the best shopping and dining in Scottsdale. The three-story building is arranged around a central courtyard, where you'll find the small pool. Guest rooms are large.

6935 Fifth Ave., Scottsdale, AZ 85251. ✆ **800/528-7396** or 480/994-9461. Fax 480/947-1695. www.ramadascottsdale.com. 92 units. Jan–Apr $89–$159 double; Oct–Dec $79–$89 double; May–Sept $59 double. Rates include continental breakfast. Children 18 and under stay free in parent's room. AE, DISC, MC, V. Small pets accepted ($15 fee). **Amenities:** Small outdoor pool; exercise room; coin-op laundry; laundry service. *In room:* A/C, TV, dataport, fridge, coffeemaker, hair dryer, iron, free local calls.

INEXPENSIVE

Despite the high-priced real estate, Scottsdale does have a few relatively inexpensive chain motels, although during the winter season, prices are higher than you might expect. For location alone, your best choice would be the **Motel 6–Scottsdale,** 6848 E. Camelback Rd. (✆ **480/946-2280**), which has doubles for $76 to $86 during the high season.

NORTH SCOTTSDALE, CAREFREE & CAVE CREEK

North Scottsdale is the brave new world for Valley of the Sun resorts. Situated at least a 30-minute drive from downtown Scottsdale, this area boasts the newest resorts, the most spectacular hillside settings, and the best golf courses.

VERY EXPENSIVE

The Boulders Resort & Golden Door Spa ★★★ Set amid a jumble of giant boulders 45 minutes north of Old Town Scottsdale, this was the first luxury golf resort in the north Valley's rugged foothills. The adobe buildings blend unobtrusively into the desert, and the two golf courses epitomize the desert golf course experience. When not golfing, you can lounge around the small pool, play tennis, relax at the resort's Golden Door Spa, or try your hand at rock climbing. The lobby is in a Santa Fe–style building with tree-trunk pillars and a flagstone floor, and the guest rooms continue the pueblo styling with stucco walls, beehive fireplaces, and beamed ceilings. For the best views, ask for one of the second-floor units. Bathrooms are large and luxuriously appointed, with tubs for two and separate showers. In addition to the resort's restaurants, there are several other dining options at adjacent el Pedregal, Shops & Dining. A complete renovation of the rooms here is scheduled to be finished in early 2008.

34631 N. Tom Darlington Dr. (P.O. Box 2090), Carefree, AZ 85377. ✆ **866/397-6520** or 480/488-9009. Fax 480/488-4118. www.theboulders.com. 215 units. Late Dec to May $599 double, from $1,099 villa; May to early Sept $199 double, from $499 villa; early Sept to early Dec $349 double, from $799 villa; early to late Dec $299 double, from $699 villa. (For all rates there is an additional $29–$33 nightly service charge.) Children under 17 stay free in parent's room. AE, DC, DISC, MC, V. Pets accepted ($100). **Amenities:** 6 restaurants (regional American, Southwestern, Mexican, spa cuisine, bakery/deli); lounge; 4 pools; 2 18-hole golf courses; 8 tennis courts; exercise room; full-service spa; 3 Jacuzzis; bike rentals; concierge; business center; shopping arcade; room service; massage; babysitting; laundry service; dry cleaning; rock climbing. *In room:* A/C, TV, dataport, minibar, coffeemaker, hair dryer, iron, safe, high-speed Internet access, Wi-Fi.

CopperWynd Resort and Club ★★ *Value* Tucked away on a ridge top on the northeastern edge of the Valley, this little boutique resort overlooking the town of Fountain Hills is one of the most luxurious resorts in the area. The resort boasts some of the most picturesque mountain vistas in the Valley, which is one of the reasons I like it so much. CopperWynd has a fabulous tennis facility, an impressive health club, and a spa, and although there is no golf course on the premises, there are four highly regarded courses nearby. The resort's Jacuzzi, tucked into a rocky hillside, is as romantic as they come. All guest rooms have great views and feature European deluxe decor. Balconies provide plenty of room for taking in the vista. There's an excellent restaurant on the premises.

13225 N. Eagle Ridge Dr., Fountain Hills, AZ 85268. ✆ **877/707-7760** or 480/333-1900. Fax 480/333-1901. www.copperwynd.com. 40 units. Late Dec to late Apr $379–$425 double, $825–$925 villa; late Apr to mid-May and late Sept to late Dec $229–$269 double, $750–$900 villa; mid-May to late Sept $129–$189 double, $550–$650 villa. Children under 18 stay free in parent's room. AE, DC, DISC, MC, V. **Amenities:** 2 restaurants (New American, American); 2 lounges; 2 pools; 9 tennis courts; health club and full-service spa; 3 Jacuzzis; saunas; children's game room; concierge; business center; room service; massage; babysitting; laundry service; dry cleaning. *In room:* A/C, TV, dataport, fridge, coffeemaker, hair dryer, iron, safe, high-speed Internet access, Wi-Fi, free local calls.

Four Seasons Resort Scottsdale at Troon North ★★★ Located in the foothills of north Scottsdale adjacent to (and with privileges at) the legendary Troon North golf course, the Four Seasons is even more impressive than the nearby Boulders resort. This superluxurious resort may not feel as expansive as the Boulders, but in every other aspect it is superior. With casita accommodations scattered across a boulder-strewn hillside, the Four Seasons boasts one of the Valley's most dramatic settings, and with a hiking trail to nearby Pinnacle Peak Park, the resort is a good choice for anyone who wants to explore the desert on foot. Guest rooms and suites are among the most lavish you'll find in Arizona. If you can afford it, opt for one with a private plunge pool and an outdoor shower—a luxury usually found only in tropical resorts.

10600 E. Crescent Moon Dr., Scottsdale, AZ 85262. ✆ **888/207-9696** or 480/515-5700. Fax 480/515-5599. www.fourseasons.com/scottsdale. 210 units. Jan–May $525–$725 double, $845–$5,000 suite; June–Aug $195–$270 double, $450–$2,650 suite; Sept–Dec $475–$715 double, $845–$5,000 suite. Children under 18 stay free in parent's room. AE, DC, DISC, MC, V. Small pets accepted. **Amenities:** 4 restaurants (Southwest, contemporary steakhouse, American); lounge; 2 pools (including large 2-level pool); 2 18-hole golf courses; 2 tennis courts; large exercise room; health club; spa; Jacuzzi; children's programs; concierge; car-rental desk; business center; 24-hr. room service; massage; laundry service; dry cleaning. *In room:* A/C, TV/DVD, dataport, minibar, coffeemaker, hair dryer, iron, safe, high-speed Internet access.

EXPENSIVE

The Fairmont Scottsdale Princess ★★★ I know this faux Moorish palace belongs in Spain, not Arizona, but I still love it. With its royal palms, tiled fountains, and waterfalls, the Princess offers an exotic atmosphere unmatched in the area and will delight anyone in search of a romantic hideaway. A water playground (with two water slides) and a kids' fishing pond also make this resort a hit with families. The resort is located a 20-minute drive from Old Town Scottsdale and is home to the FBR Open golf tournament (a stop on the PGA Tour), which means the fairways here are top-notch. There's also the Willow Stream spa. Guest rooms, which have just been renovated, are done in an elegant Southwestern style, and bathrooms have double vanities and separate showers and tubs. All units have private balconies.

7575 E. Princess Dr., Scottsdale, AZ 85255. ✆ **800/441-1414** or 480/585-4848. Fax 480/585-0091. www.fairmont.com/scottsdale. 651 units. $159–$589 double; $319–$3,800 suite. Children 12 and under stay free in parent's room. AE, DC, DISC, MC, V. Pets accepted ($25 per night). **Amenities:** 3 restaurants (Mexican, steakhouse, American); 3 lounges; 5 pools; 2 18-hole golf courses; 7 tennis courts; exercise room; full-service spa; Jacuzzi; concierge; car-rental desk; business center; golf and tennis pro shops; shopping arcade; salon; 24-hr. room service; massage; babysitting; laundry service; dry cleaning. *In room:* A/C, TV, dataport, minibar, coffeemaker, hair dryer, iron, safe.

Radisson Fort McDowell Resort & Casino ★★★ In the Scottsdale area, you just can't stay any closer to the desert than at this beautiful new resort northeast of Fountain Hills. Although the Radisson is a 30-minute drive from downtown Scottsdale, the location is hard to beat if you've come to the area to experience the desert. The resort is on the Fort McDowell Yavapai Nation and, consequently, the tribe's Fort McDowell Casino is a big draw for many guests. However, the two 18-hole courses at the adjacent We-Ko-Pa Golf Club are also a major draw here. Personally, I like the resort best for its creative Native American styling and its great desert and mountain views. For families, there's a children's water-play area, and, in summer, float trips down the nearby Verde River. For a good night's sleep, there are Sleep Number beds.

10438 N. Fort McDowell Rd., Scottsdale/Fountain Hills, AZ 85264. ✆ **800/333-3333** or 480/789-5300. Fax 480/789-5333. www.radisson.com/ftmcdowellaz. 246 units. Jan–Mar $269–$299 double; Apr $199–$210 double; May, Sept, and Dec $169–$189 double; June–Aug $109–$139 double; Oct–Nov $219–$239 double. Children under 12 stay free in parent's room. AE, DC, DISC, MC, V. Pets accepted. **Amenities:** 2 restaurants (Southwestern, American); 2 lounges; 2 outdoor pools; 2 18-hole golf courses; exercise room; full-service spa; 2 Jacuzzis; concierge; car-rental desk; courtesy shopping shuttle; business center; room service; massage; babysitting; dry cleaning; executive-level rooms; casino; horseback riding. *In room:* A/C, TV, dataport, minibar, coffeemaker, hair dryer, safe, high-speed Internet access, Wi-Fi.

CENTRAL PHOENIX & THE CAMELBACK CORRIDOR

This area is the heart of the upscale Phoenix shopping and restaurant scene and is home to the prestigious Arizona Biltmore resort. Old money and new money rub shoulders along the avenues here, and valet parking is de rigueur. Located roughly midway between Old Scottsdale and downtown Phoenix, this area is a good bet for those intending to split their time between the downtown Phoenix cultural and sports district and the world-class shopping and dining in Scottsdale.

VERY EXPENSIVE

Arizona Biltmore Resort & Spa ★★★ For decades this resort has been the favored Phoenix address of celebrities, politicians, and old money, and the distinctive cast-cement blocks inspired by a Frank Lloyd Wright design make it a unique architectural gem. It's the historical character and timeless elegance that really set this place apart. With wide lawns, colorful flower gardens, and views of Piestewa Peak, this is a resort for outdoor lounging. While the two golf courses and expansive spa are the main draws, the children's activities center also makes this a popular choice for families. Of the several different styles of accommodations, the "resort rooms" are quite comfortable and come with balconies or patios. Those rooms in the Arizona Wing are also good choices. Afternoon tea is served in the lobby.

2400 E. Missouri Ave., Phoenix, AZ 85016. ✆ **800/950-0086** or 602/955-6600. Fax 602/381-7600. www.arizonabiltmore.com. 738 units. Jan to mid-May $465–$675 double, from $730 suite; mid-May to early Sept $205–$310 double, from $340 suite; early Sept to Dec $394–$604 double, from $709 suite. Rates do not include the $25 daily service fee. Children under 18 stay free in parent's room. AE, DC, DISC, MC, V. Pets under 50 lb. accepted in cottage rooms ($100 deposit, $50 nonrefundable). **Amenities:** 4 restaurants (American, Southwestern); lounge; 8 pools; 2 18-hole golf courses; 7 tennis courts; health club and full-service spa; 2 Jacuzzis; saunas; bike rentals; lawn games children's programs; concierge; car-rental desk; courtesy shopping shuttle; business center; 24-hr. room service; massage; laundry service; dry cleaning. *In room:* A/C, TV, dataport, minibar, hair dryer, iron, safe, high-speed Internet access, free local calls.

Hermosa Inn ★★ *Finds* This luxurious boutique hotel, once a guest ranch, is one of the few hotels in the Valley to offer any Old Arizona atmosphere, and because the Hermosa Inn is all about getting a little peace and quiet, I breathe a big sigh of relief every time I arrive here. Built in the 1930s by cowboy artist Lon Megargee, the inn is situated on more than 6 acres of attractive gardens in an upscale residential neighborhood.

The inn provides luxury, yet is completely removed from Scottsdale's hectic pace. The only other nearby place this tranquil is the Royal Palms (see below), which is more service oriented. Rooms vary from cozy to spacious and are decorated in contemporary Western decor. The largest suites have much more Southwestern flavor than suites at other area resorts. The dining room, located in the original adobe home, serves excellent food in a rustic, upscale setting (see LON's, in "Where to Dine," later in this chapter).

5532 N. Palo Cristi Rd., Paradise Valley, AZ 85253. ✆ **800/241-1210** or 602/955-8614. Fax 602/955-8299. www.hermosainn.com. 35 units. Jan–May $299–$369 double, $399–$709 suite; June–Aug $159–$189 double, $159–$469 suite; Sept–Dec $219–$349 double, $219–$639 suite. Rates do not include daily hospitality fee of $12. Rates include full breakfast. AE, DC, DISC, MC, V. Take 32nd St. north from Camelback Rd., turn right on Stanford Rd., and turn left on N. Palo Cristi Rd. From Lincoln Dr., turn south on N. Palo Cristi Rd. (east of 32nd St.). Pets accepted ($50 fee). **Amenities:** Restaurant (New American); lounge; outdoor pool; tennis court; access to nearby health club; 2 Jacuzzis; concierge; room service; massage; babysitting; laundry service; dry cleaning. *In room:* A/C, TV, dataport, minibar, coffeemaker, hair dryer, iron, safe, high-speed Internet access, Wi-Fi, free local calls.

Royal Palms Resort and Spa ★★ This gorgeous little hideaway has the feel of a Spanish villa that was transported to Arizona and is so romantic and beautiful that the moment you set foot in the first cloistered garden, you might imagine you hear flamenco guitar. Located midway between Old Town Scottsdale and Biltmore Fashion Park, the Royal Palms was constructed more than 50 years ago by Cunard Steamship executive Delos Cooke and is done in Spanish mission style. Giving the resort the tranquil feel of a Mediterranean monastery are lush walled gardens where antique water fountains splash. The most memorable guest rooms are the designer casitas, each with a distinctive decor ranging from opulent contemporary to classic European. However, all the rooms are beautiful and have superplush beds. T. Cook's restaurant is one of the city's most romantic restaurants (see "Where to Dine," later in this chapter). The Alvadora Spa provides a place to be pampered and expects to offer an updated services menu in early 2008.

5200 E. Camelback Rd., Phoenix, AZ 85018. ✆ **800/672-6011** or 602/840-3610. Fax 602/840-6927. www.royalpalmsresortandspa.com. 119 units. Jan–May $429–$609 double, $459–$2,600 suite; June to mid-Sept $199–$329 double, $229–$1,600 suite; mid-Sept to Dec $389–$559 double, $429–$2,400 suite. Rates do not include daily service fee of $22. Children under 18 stay free in parent's room. AE, DC, DISC, MC, V. Pets accepted ($300 deposit, $100 nonrefundable). **Amenities:** Restaurant (Mediterranean); poolside grill; lounge; outdoor pool w/cabanas; exercise room; full-service spa; Jacuzzi; bike rentals; concierge; business center; 24-hr. room service; massage; babysitting; laundry service; dry cleaning. *In room:* A/C, TV, dataport, minibar, coffeemaker, hair dryer, iron, safe, Wi-Fi.

EXPENSIVE

Embassy Suites Biltmore ★★ Located across the parking lot from the Biltmore Fashion Park shopping center, this hotel makes a great base if you want to be within walking distance of half a dozen good restaurants. The atrium is filled with interesting tile work, tropical greenery, waterfalls, and ponds filled with koi (colorful Japanese carp). In the atrium, you'll also find a romantic lounge with huge banquettes shaded by palm trees. With a major renovation planned at press time, this place should look better than ever in 2008. All in all, this hotel is a good value, especially when you consider that rates include both breakfast and afternoon drinks.

2630 E. Camelback Rd., Phoenix, AZ 85016. ✆ **800/EMBASSY** or 602/955-3992. Fax 602/955-6479. www.phoenixbiltmore.embassysuites.com. 232 units. Jan to late May $239–$409 double; late May to early Sept $109–$219 double; early Sept to Dec $239–$329 double. Rates include full breakfast and afternoon drinks. Children under 18 stay free in parent's room. AE, DC, DISC, MC, V. Valet parking $8. Pets accepted ($25). **Amenities:** Restaurant (steakhouse); lounge; outdoor pool; exercise room; access to nearby health club; Jacuzzi; concierge; courtesy shopping shuttle; business center;

room service; massage; coin-op laundry; laundry service; dry cleaning; executive-level rooms. *In room:* A/C, TV, dataport, fridge, microwave, coffeemaker, hair dryer, iron, high-speed Internet access, Wi-Fi.

Maricopa Manor Centrally located between downtown Phoenix and Scottsdale, Maricopa Manor is just a block off busy Camelback Road and has long been Phoenix's best B&B. The inn's main building, designed to resemble a Spanish manor house, was built in 1928, and the orange trees, palms, and large yard all lend an Old Phoenix atmosphere. All guest rooms are large, comfortable suites, many with Arts and Crafts touches. One suite has a sunroom and kitchen, while another has two separate sleeping areas. You can eat your breakfast, which is delivered to your door, at tables in the garden.

15 W. Pasadena Ave., Phoenix, AZ 85013. ✆ **800/292-6403** or 602/274-6302. Fax 602/266-3904. www.maricopamanor.com. 7 units. Late Dec to Apr $179–$229 double; May–June and Nov to late Dec $139–$179 double; mid-Sept to Oct $129–$169 double; July to mid-Sept $99–$129 double. Rates include extended continental breakfast. Children under 13 stay free in parent's room. AE, DC, DISC, MC, V. **Amenities:** Outdoor pool; access to nearby health club; Jacuzzi; massage. *In room:* A/C, TV/VCR/DVD, dataport, fridge, coffeemaker, hair dryer, iron, high-speed Internet access, Wi-Fi, free local calls.

INEXPENSIVE

Extended Stay Deluxe Phoenix-Biltmore ★ Billing itself as a temporary residence and offering discounts for stays of 7 days or more, this hotel consists of studio-style apartments located just north of Camelback Road and not far from Biltmore Fashion Park. Although designed primarily for corporate business travelers on temporary assignment in the area, this lodging makes a good choice for families as well. All units have full kitchens, big bathrooms, and separate sitting areas.

5235 N. 16th St., Phoenix, AZ 85016. ✆ **800/804-3724** or 602/265-6800. Fax 602/265-4111. www.extendedstaydeluxe.com. 112 units. $55–$130 double. Children under 17 stay free in parent's room. AE, DC, DISC, MC, V. Pets accepted ($25 per night, $75 maximum). **Amenities:** Small outdoor pool; exercise room; Jacuzzi; coin-op laundry; dry cleaning. *In room:* A/C, TV, dataport, kitchen, coffeemaker, hair dryer, iron, high-speed Internet access.

NORTH PHOENIX

Some of the Valley's best scenery is in north Phoenix, where several small mountains have been protected as parks and preserves; the two Pointe Hilton resorts claim great locations close to these parks. So, if you're looking for quick access to desert trails, the resorts here are good choices. However, the Valley's best shopping and dining, as well as most major attractions, are all at least a 30-minute drive away.

VERY EXPENSIVE

JW Marriott Desert Ridge Resort & Spa ★★★ This is the largest resort in the state and stays crowded with conference and convention groups. Because it is miles from any other resorts, high-end shopping areas, or concentrations of good restaurants, Desert Ridge is primarily a place to stay put and spend your days sitting in the sun drinking margaritas by the pool. To this end, there are 4 acres of water features and pools (including a tubing "river"). The Revive Spa, where the focus is on indigenous ingredients such as turquoise, has its own lap pool and plans to unveil a new services menu this year. At the resort's grand entrance, desert landscaping and rows of palm trees give the resort a sense of place, and the lobby's roll-up walls let plenty of balmy desert air in during the cooler months. Guest rooms have balconies and hints of Mediterranean styling. Be sure to ask for a room with a view to the south; these rooms look out to several of Phoenix's mountain preserves.

5350 E. Marriott Blvd., Phoenix, AZ 85054. ✆ **800/835-6206** or 480/293-5000. Fax 480/293-3600. www.jwdesertridgeresort.com. 950 units. Jan to early May $449–$569 double; early May to mid-June and early Sept to Dec

$349–$489 double; mid-June to early Sept $169–$249 double; $319–$1,999 suite year-round. Children under 18 stay free in parent's room. AE, DC, DISC, MC, V. **Amenities:** 5 restaurants (Southwestern, Hawaiian fusion, Italian, steakhouse, healthful); 2 snack bars/cafes; 3 lounges; 5 pools; 2 18-hole golf courses; 8 tennis courts; health club; full-service spa; 3 Jacuzzis; children's programs; concierge; car-rental desk; business center; 24-hr. room service; massage; babysitting; guest laundry; laundry service; dry cleaning. *In room:* A/C, TV, dataport, minibar, coffeemaker, hair dryer, iron, safe, high-speed Internet access.

EXPENSIVE

Pointe Hilton Squaw Peak Resort ★★★ *Kids* At the foot of the Phoenix Mountains, this lushly landscaped resort makes a big splash with its 4-acre Hole-in-the-Wall River Ranch aquatic playground, which features a tubing "river," water slide, waterfall, sports pool, and lagoon pool. An 18-hole putting course and shopping arcade also help make it a great family vacation spot. The resort is done in the Spanish villa style, and most of the guest rooms are large suites. For a family vacation, this place is hard to beat. However, I prefer the nearby Pointe Hilton Tapatio Cliffs Resort for its dramatic hillside setting and location adjacent to the hiking trails of the North Mountain Recreation Area.

7677 N. 16th St., Phoenix, AZ 85020. ✆ **800/876-4683** or 602/997-2626. Fax 602/997-2391. www.pointehilton.com. 563 units. Jan to mid-May $159–$379 double; mid-May to mid-Sept $89–$199 double; mid-Sept to Dec $99–$299 double, year-round $1,500 grande suite. Rates do not include daily resort fee of $9. Children under 18 stay free in parent's room. AE, DC, DISC, MC, V. Pets accepted ($75–$100 deposit). **Amenities:** 3 restaurants (American, Southwestern, Western); 2 snack bars; 5 lounges; 8 pools; 18-hole golf course (4 miles away by shuttle); 4 tennis courts; health club (extra charge) and small spa; 6 Jacuzzis; saunas; children's programs; concierge; car-rental desk; business center; shopping arcade; room service; massage; babysitting; coin-op laundry; laundry service; dry cleaning. *In room:* A/C, TV, dataport, minibar, coffeemaker, hair dryer, iron, high-speed Internet access.

Pointe Hilton Tapatio Cliffs Resort ★★★ *Value* If you love to lounge by the pool, then this resort is a great choice. The Falls, a 3½-acre water playground, includes two pools, a 138-foot water slide, 40-foot cascades, a whirlpool tucked into an artificial grotto, and rental cabanas. If you're a hiker, you can head out on the trails of the adjacent North Mountain Recreation Area. All rooms are spacious suites with Southwest-inspired furnishings; corner units are particularly bright. This resort has steep walkways, so you need to be in good shape to stay here. At the top of the property is Different Pointe of View, a restaurant with one of the finest views in the city. This resort is more adult-oriented than the Pointe Hilton Squaw Peak Resort, but is similar.

11111 N. Seventh St., Phoenix, AZ 85020. ✆ **800/876-4683** or 602/866-7500. Fax 602/993-0276. www.pointehilton.com. 585 units. Jan to mid-May $159–$379 double; mid-May to mid-Sept $89–$199 double; mid-Sept to Dec $99–$299 double; year-round $1,500 grande suite. Rates do not include $9 daily resort fee. Children under 18 stay free in parent's room. AE, DC, DISC, MC, V. Pets accepted ($75–$100 deposit). **Amenities:** 5 restaurants (Continental, Tuscan, American, Mexican); 2 poolside cafes; 5 lounges; 8 pools; golf course; 2 tennis courts; fitness center (extra charge); small full-service spa; 8 Jacuzzis; sauna; steam room; seasonal children's programs; concierge; business center; shopping arcade; room service; massage; babysitting; coin-op laundry; laundry service; dry cleaning. *In room:* A/C, TV, dataport, minibar, coffeemaker, hair dryer, iron, high-speed Internet access.

MODERATE/INEXPENSIVE

Among the better moderately priced chain motels in north Phoenix are the **Best Western Inn Suites Hotel Phoenix,** 1615 E. Northern Ave., at 16th Street (✆ **800/752-2204** or 602/997-6285; www.bestwestern.com), charging high-season rates of $99 to $199 double; and the **Best Western Bell Hotel,** 17211 N. Black Canyon Hwy. (✆ **877/263-1290** or 602/993-8300; www.bestwestern.com), charging $89 to $149 in the high season.

DOWNTOWN, SOUTH PHOENIX & THE AIRPORT AREA

Unless you're a sports fan or are in town for a convention, there's not much to recommend downtown Phoenix. This 9-to-5 area can feel like a ghost town at night. For the most part, south Phoenix is one of the poorest parts of the city. However, it does have a couple of wealthy enclaves that are home to exceptional resorts, and Phoenix South Mountain Park is one of the best places in the city to experience the desert.

VERY EXPENSIVE

Pointe South Mountain Resort ★★★ *Kids* This sprawling resort abuts the 17,000-acre South Mountain Park and is one of the best choices in the Valley for families. If I were a 12-year-old, I would beg my parents to stay here and spend every day playing in the wave pool, tubing "river," twisty water slide, and two free-fall-style water slides. Stables at the resort allow you and the kids to ride into the sunset on South Mountain, and there are numerous children's programs. The guest rooms, all suites, feature contemporary Southwestern furnishings and lots of space. A complete renovation scheduled for 2007 and early 2008 should have these rooms looking great by the time you visit. Rustler's Rooste, the resort's fun cowboy steakhouse, serves rattlesnake appetizers (see "Where to Dine," below) and is a favorite with families. At the resort's spa, both adults and kids can avail themselves of a wide range of treatments.

7777 S. Pointe Pkwy., Phoenix, AZ 85044. ✆ **866/267-1321** or 602/438-9000. Fax 602/431-6535. www.pointesouthmtn.com. 640 units. Jan–Apr from $279 double; May to early Sept from $139 double; early Sept to Dec from $159 double. Rates do not include $16 daily resort fee. Children under 18 stay free in parent's room. AE, DC, DISC, MC, V. **Amenities:** 6 restaurants (steakhouse, Mexican, Southwestern, international); 3 lounges; 11 outdoor pools (including 6-acre water park); 18-hole golf course; 5 tennis courts; racquetball court; health club; full-service spa; 9 Jacuzzis; bike rentals; children's programs; concierge; business center; room service; massage; babysitting; coin-op laundry; laundry service; dry cleaning; executive-level rooms; horseback riding. *In room:* A/C, TV, dataport, minibar, coffeemaker, hair dryer, iron, high-speed Internet access, Wi-Fi, free local calls.

Sheraton Wild Horse Pass Resort & Spa ★★★ Named for the area's wild horses, this resort is located 20 minutes south of Phoenix Sky Harbor International Airport on the Gila River Indian Reservation, and because the resort looks out across miles of desert, it has a pleasantly remote feel. Throw in horseback riding, a full-service spa featuring desert-inspired treatments, two golf courses, a nature trail along a 2½-mile-long artificial river, a pool with a water slide, the Rawhide wild-west theme park, and a nearby casino, and you'll find plenty to keep you busy. The resort is owned by the Maricopa and Pima tribes, who go out of their way to share their culture with resort guests. Guest rooms have great beds, small patios, and large bathrooms with separate tubs and showers. The menu in Kai, the main dining room, focuses on indigenous Southwestern flavors.

5594 W. Wild Horse Pass Blvd., Chandler, AZ 85226. ✆ **888/218-8989** or 602/225-0100. Fax 602/225-0300. www.wildhorsepassresort.com. 500 units. Early Jan to late May $329–$495 double, $650–$1,400 suite; late May to mid-Sept $189–$289 double, $600–$950 suite; mid-Sept to early Jan $289–$495 double, $650–$1,400 suite. Children stay free in parent's room. AE, DC, DISC, MC, V. Pets accepted. **Amenities:** 5 restaurants (Native American, Southwestern, American); 3 lounges; 4 outdoor pools; 2 18-hole golf courses; 2 tennis courts; health club; full-service spa; 6 Jacuzzis; bike rentals; concierge; car-rental desk; business center; shopping arcade; 24-hr. room service; massage; babysitting; laundry service; dry cleaning; horseback riding. *In room:* A/C, TV, dataport, minibar, coffeemaker, hair dryer, iron, safe, high-speed Internet access.

EXPENSIVE

The Buttes, A Marriott Resort ★★ Just 3 miles from Sky Harbor Airport, this resort makes the most of its craggy hilltop location, and although some people complain that the nearby freeway ruins the view, the rocky setting is quintessentially Southwestern. The only other resorts in the area with as much desert character are the far more expensive Boulders and Four Seasons. From the cactus garden and waterfall *inside* the lobby to the circular restaurant and free-form swimming pools, this resort is calculated to take your breath away. Guest rooms are stylishly elegant. The city-view rooms are a bit larger than the hillside-view rooms, but second-floor hillside-view rooms have patios. Unfortunately, most bathrooms have only three-quarter-size tubs. The Top of the Rock restaurant has great views.

2000 Westcourt Way, Tempe, AZ 85282. © **888/867-7492** or 602/225-9000. Fax 602/438-8622. www.marriott.com/phxtm. 353 units. Jan to mid-Apr $199–$329 double, from $475 suite; mid-Apr to mid-May $189–$289 double, from $475 suite; mid-May to early Sept $99–$199 double, from $375 suite; early Sept to Dec $159–$279 double, from $475 suite. Children 18 and under stay free in parent's room. AE, DC, DISC, MC, V. **Amenities:** 3 restaurants (New American/Southwestern, American, bar and grill); 3 lounges; 2 pools; 4 tennis courts; volleyball courts; exercise room; health club; full-service spa; 4 Jacuzzis; sauna; bike rentals; concierge; business center; room service; massage; babysitting; dry cleaning; executive-level rooms. *In room:* A/C, TV, dataport, minibar, coffeemaker, hair dryer, iron, high-speed Internet access.

Clarendon Hotel & Suites ★ *Finds* If you're young and hip and looking for a stylish yet casual place in downtown Phoenix, the Clarendon is a great choice. The Clarendon recently got an extreme makeover that has turned it into a hip hangout for young, style-conscious travelers. Guest rooms are fitted with contemporary furniture, including red microsuede headboards and bedside stands and desks that are topped with cool-blue glass tops. The coolest features, though, are the window "blinds," which are actually wood panels painted with abstract art. The paintings slide on industrial-grade pipes. In the hotel's central courtyard, a hot tub and small pool are surrounded by a patio deck that has been painted cobalt blue. The restaurant and cocktail bar are designed to appeal to young nightclubbers and fashionistas.

401 W. Clarendon Ave., Phoenix, AZ 85013. © **602/252-7363.** Fax 602/296-0469. www.theclarendon.net. 104 units. Oct–May $189–$229 double; June–Sept $109–$129 double. Children under 12 stay free in parent's room. AE, DC, DISC, MC, V. Pets accepted ($50 fee). **Amenities:** Restaurant (American); lounge; outdoor pool; access to nearby health club; Jacuzzi; concierge; business center; room service; massage; laundry service; dry cleaning. *In room:* A/C, TV, minibar, fridge, hair dryer, iron, high-speed Internet access, Wi-Fi, free local and long-distance calls.

TEMPE, MESA & THE EAST VALLEY

Tempe, which lies just a few miles east of the airport, is home to Arizona State University and consequently supports a lively nightlife scene. Along Tempe's Mill Avenue, you'll find one of the only neighborhoods in the Valley where locals actually get out of their cars and walk the streets. Tempe is also convenient to Papago Park, which is home to the Phoenix Zoo, the Desert Botanical Garden, a municipal golf course, and hiking and mountain-biking trails.

EXPENSIVE

Gold Canyon Golf Resort ★★ *Value* Golfers willing to stay way out on the eastern outskirts of the Valley of the Sun (a 30- to 45-min. drive from the airport) should be thrilled by the economical room rates and great golf at this resort. Located at the foot of the Superstition Mountains, Gold Canyon is a favorite of golfers for its exceedingly scenic holes. The spacious guest rooms are housed in blindingly white pueblo-inspired buildings; some have fireplaces, while others have whirlpools. The deluxe golf-course rooms are definitely worth the higher rates. If you're here primarily to play golf and don't have a fortune to spend, this is *the* place to stay.

6100 S. Kings Ranch Rd., Gold Canyon, AZ 85218. ✆ **800/624-6445** or 480/982-9090. Fax 480/983-9554. www.gcgr.com. 101 units. $135–$260 double. Children under 16 stay free in parent's room. AE, DISC, MC, V. Pets accepted ($75 fee). **Amenities:** 2 restaurants (American); lounge; pool; 2 18-hole golf courses; exercise room; small full-service spa; Jacuzzi; bike rentals; concierge; room service; massage; laundry service; dry cleaning. *In room:* A/C, TV, dataport, minibar, coffeemaker, hair dryer, iron, free local calls.

Tempe Mission Palms Hotel ★★ With a great location on Tempe's lively Mill Avenue and guest rooms decorated in a wild combination of bold colors and modern geometric patterns, this is the perfect choice for a fun-filled weekend in Tempe. Sure, this is a business hotel (ergonomic desk chairs), but with a rooftop pool, tennis court, and Mill Avenue's nightlife right out the front door, it's also a great choice for active travelers. Come in the spring and you won't want to leave the courtyard, which is scented by the flowers of citrus trees.

60 E. Fifth St., Tempe, AZ 85281. ✆ **800/547-8705** or 480/894-1400. Fax 480/968-7677. www.missionpalms.com. 303 units. Jan–Apr $189–$259 double, $359 suite; May–June $129–$179 double, $279 suite; July–Aug $99–$169 double, $269 suite; Sept–Dec $149–$209 double, $309 suite. Rates do not include $9.75 daily hospitality fee. Children under 18 stay free in parent's room. AE, DC, DISC, MC, V. Pets accepted ($100 deposit, $25 nonrefundable). **Amenities:** 2 restaurants (Southwestern); 2 lounges; outdoor pool; tennis court; exercise room; access to nearby health club; 2 Jacuzzis; bike rentals; concierge; car-rental desk; courtesy airport shuttle; business center; room service; massage; laundry service; dry cleaning. *In room:* A/C, TV, dataport, coffeemaker, hair dryer, iron, high-speed Internet access, Wi-Fi, free local calls.

MODERATE

Best Western Dobson Ranch Inn & Resort ★ This aging budget resort may not be very luxurious, but it has just about everything a sun-starved winter visitor could ask for—green lawns, flower gardens, palm trees, and a big pool surrounded by lounge chairs. The location right off U.S. 60 at the junction with U.S. 101 also makes this resort relatively convenient for exploring the valley. Guest rooms are functional, not fancy, and are certainly dated, but the grounds more than make up for the unremarkable rooms. Oh, and by the way, this is the spring training home of the Chicago Cubs.

1666 S. Dobson Rd., Mesa, AZ 85202. ✆ **800/528-1356** or 480/831-7000. Fax 480/831-7000. www.dobsonranchinn.com. 213 units. Mid-Sept to Feb and Apr $105–$185 double; Mar $160–$200 double; May to mid-Sept $80–$130 double. Rates include full breakfast. Children 12 and under stay free in parent's room. AE, DC, DISC, MC, V. Pets accepted. **Amenities:** Restaurant (American); lounge; large outdoor pool; exercise room; 2 Jacuzzis; business center; room service; massage; free self-service laundry; laundry service; dry cleaning. *In room:* A/C, TV, dataport, fridge, coffeemaker, hair dryer, iron, free local calls, high-speed Internet access.

Crowne Plaza San Marcos Golf Resort ★★ Built in 1912, the San Marcos is the oldest golf resort in Arizona and has a classic mission-revival styling. I love the timeless feel of this resort's palm-shaded courtyards, and I'm sure you will, too. Downtown Chandler, where the San Marcos is located, has been undergoing something of a renaissance in recent years. There are now art galleries and some decent restaurants on the plaza just outside the resort's front door. Guest rooms are simply furnished, nothing special, but they have been kept up-to-date. You'll want to spend your time splashing around in the pool when you aren't playing tennis or golf. Although the San Marcos is out of the tourist mainstream, the rates make it a real bargain.

One San Marcos Place, Chandler, AZ 85225. ✆ **800/528-8071** or 480/812-0900. Fax 480/963-6777. www.sanmarcosresort.com. 295 units. $124–$250 double; $176–$300 suite (lower rates in summer). Children under 18 stay free in parent's room. AE, DC, DISC, MC, V. Pets accepted ($50 nonrefundable deposit). **Amenities:** 2 restaurants (American); 2 lounges; outdoor pool; 18-hole golf course; 2 tennis courts; exercise room; Jacuzzi; concierge; business center; salon; room service; laundry service; dry cleaning. *In room:* A/C, TV, dataport, coffeemaker, hair dryer, high-speed Internet access, free local calls.

Fiesta Inn Resort ★ *Value* Reasonable rates, green lawns, palm- and eucalyptus-shaded grounds, and a location close to the airport, ASU, and Tempe's Mill Avenue make this older, casual resort one of the best deals in the Valley. Okay, so it doesn't have the desert character of The Buttes resort across the freeway, and it isn't as stylish as the resorts in Scottsdale, but you can't argue with the rates. The large guest rooms, although a bit dark, have an appealing retro mission styling. You may not feel like you're in the desert when you stay here (due to the lawns and shade trees), but you'll certainly get a lot more for your money than at other area hotels in this price range.

2100 S. Priest Dr., Tempe, AZ 85282. ✆ **800/528-6481** or 480/967-1441. Fax 480/967-0224. www.fiestainnresort.com. 270 units. Nov to late May $109–$250 double; late May to Oct $100–$124 double. Children under 15 stay free in parent's room. AE, DC, DISC, MC, V. **Amenities:** 2 restaurants (American/Southwestern); lounge; pool; exercise room; Jacuzzi; concierge; courtesy airport shuttle; business center; room service; laundry service; dry cleaning. *In room:* A/C, TV, dataport, fridge, coffeemaker, hair dryer, iron, high-speed Internet access, free local calls.

INEXPENSIVE

Apache Boulevard in Tempe becomes Main Street in Mesa, and along this stretch of road there are numerous old motels charging some of the lowest rates in the Valley. However, these motels are very hit-or-miss. If you're used to staying at nonchain motels, you might want to cruise this strip and check out a few places. Otherwise, try the chain motels in the area (which tend to charge $20–$40 more per night than nonchain motels).

WEST VALLEY

VERY EXPENSIVE

The Wigwam Golf Resort & Spa ★★ Located 20 minutes west of downtown Phoenix, this property opened its doors to the public in 1929 and remains one of the nation's premier golf resorts. It's a classic, with old-school gentility, but when the money all headed to Scottsdale, this place became an elegant oasis surrounded by tract houses. Like the Arizona Biltmore and the Camelback Inn, The Wigwam Golf Resort & Spa is an old-money sort of place, and the traditional-style golf courses are the main attraction. Most of the guest rooms are in adobe-style buildings, surrounded by green lawns and colorful gardens, and all of the spacious units feature contemporary Southwestern furniture, plush new beds, and flatscreen TVs. Some units have fireplaces, but the rooms to request are those along the golf course. A large Red Door Spa opened in 2006, and two of the golf courses were renovated in 2005. There's also a golf school here.

300 Wigwam Blvd., Litchfield Park, AZ 85340. ✆ **800/327-0396** or 623/935-3811. Fax 623/935-3737. www.wigwamresort.com. 331 units. Early Jan to mid-May $269–$799 double, from $329 suite; mid-May to early Sept $119–$259 double, from $159 suite; early Sept to early Jan $199–$449 double, from $249 suite. Children under 17 stay free in parent's room. AE, DC, DISC, MC, V. Pets accepted ($50 deposit, $25 nonrefundable). **Amenities:** 3 restaurants (Southwestern, American, steakhouse); 3 lounges; 2 pools; 3 18-hole golf courses; 9 tennis courts; croquet court; health club; full-service spa; 2 Jacuzzis; bikes; children's programs; concierge; car-rental desk; business center; 24-hr. room service; massage; babysitting; laundry service; dry cleaning; executive-level rooms. *In room:* A/C, TV, dataport, minibar, coffeemaker, hair dryer, iron, safe, high-speed Internet access.

4 Where to Dine

The Valley of the Sun boasts hundreds of excellent restaurants, with most of the best dining options concentrated in the Scottsdale Road, north Scottsdale, and Biltmore Corridor areas. If you want to splurge on only one expensive meal while you're here, consider a resort restaurant that offers a view of the city lights. Other meals not to be missed are the cowboy dinners served amid Wild West decor at the area's "cowboy" steakhouses.

Good places to go trolling for a place to eat include the trendy Biltmore Fashion Park shopping center, at Camelback Road and 24th Street (© **602/955-1963**), and Old Town Scottsdale. At the former, you'll find nearly a dozen restaurants. In downtown Scottsdale, within an area of roughly 4 square blocks, you'll also find about a dozen good restaurants. A few of my favorites in both places are listed in the following pages.

Phoenix is a sprawling city, and it can be a real pain to have to drive around in search of a good lunch spot. If you happen to be visiting the Phoenix Art Museum, the Heard Museum, or the Desert Botanical Garden anytime around lunch, stay put for your noon meal. All three of these attractions have cafes serving decent, if limited, menus.

SCOTTSDALE

EXPENSIVE

Bloom ★★ *Value* NEW AMERICAN Located in the upscale Shops at Gainey Village, Bloom is part of a regional chain that includes several great Phoenix area restaurants and a couple of my favorite Tucson restaurants—Wildflower and Bistro Zin. The minimalist decor emphasizes flowers, an elegant wine bar serves a wide range of flights (tasting assortments), and the bistro-style menu has lots of great dishes in a wide range of prices. Opt for one of the wonderfully creative salads, such as fresh artichoke hearts with shaved Parmesan and white-truffle oil; there are also enough interesting appetizers to create a very satisfying dinner. The roast duck with drunken cherry sauce is excellent. This place is big and always buzzing with energy.

8877 N. Scottsdale Rd. © **480/922-5666.** Reservations recommended. Main courses $9–$15 lunch, $15–$29 dinner. AE, DC, DISC, MC, V. Mon–Thurs 11am–3pm and 5–10pm; Fri–Sat 11am–3pm and 5–10:30pm; Sun 5–9pm.

Cowboy Ciao ★ SOUTHWESTERN/FUSION Yee-ha, bambino, the food at this place is great! A fun, "cowboy chic" atmosphere and delicious food with a global influence make a meal here unforgettable. You absolutely have to start your meal with the Stetson chopped salad; it's both a work of art and an explosion of flavors and textures once it passes your lips. Other not-to-be-missed dishes include the exotic mushroom pan-fry and the daily soup. Whatever you decide on for an entree, think small; you want to save room for one of pastry chef Tracy Dempsey's legendary desserts. Cowboy Ciao is also notable for its wine list and bar. Located in downtown Scottsdale, the restaurant attracts a diverse crowd.

7133 E. Stetson Dr. (at Sixth Ave.). © **480/WINE-111.** www.cowboyciao.com. Reservations recommended. Main courses $8–$32 lunch, $22–$32 dinner. AE, DC, DISC, MC, V. Sun–Thurs 11:30am–2:30pm and 5–10pm; Fri–Sat 11:30am–2:30pm and 5–11pm.

deseo ★★★ NUEVO LATINO Jaded palates and sleepy taste buds will thank you profusely when you introduce them to the vibrant flavors on this restaurant's *ceviche* menu. Don't bother trying to decide between rainbow *ceviche* (tuna, *hamachi,* and salmon with white soy sauce, citrus juices, sesame seeds, and pickled jalapeños), lobster *ceviche* (with horseradish, coconut, mint, chives, and garlic chips), and *hamachi ceviche* (with mango, ginger, and lime); order all three. If you're more in the mood for a hot appetizer, try the goat cheese empanadas, the Kobe-beef meatballs, or the bacon-wrapped dates with almonds and *cabrales* cheese. If you're like me, you'll never make it past the appetizers list, but if you do, the grilled beef dishes are well worth trying.

Phoenix, Scottsdale & the Valley of the Sun Dining

Alice Cooper'stown 9
Arcadia Farms 33
Bandera 37
Bloom 25
Blue Adobe Grille 39
Carlsbad Tavern 36
Carolina's 7
Chelsea's Kitchen 16
The Counter 23
Coup des Tartes 3
Cowboy Ciao Wine Bar & Grill 30
Delux 12
deseo 22
El Chorro Lodge 17
elements 18
El Molino Mexican Café 34
El Paso Barbeque Company 26
The Farm at South Mountain/ Morning Glory Café & Bakery 45
5 & Diner 2
Fry Bread House 5
Grazie 31
House of Tricks 42
La Grande Orange Pizzeria 13
La Hacienda 21
Lon's 14
Los Dos Molinos 10
Los Olivos 38
Los Sombreros 35
MacAlpine's Restaurant and Soda Fountain 6
Mary Elaine's 20
Monti's La Casa Vieja 43
Old Town Tortilla Factory 32
Organ Stop Pizza 40
Pane Bianco 4
Pizzeria Bianco 8
Quiessence 45
Rancho Pinot 27
Razz's Restaurant 24
Roaring Fork 29
Rustler's Rooste 44
Sea Saw 30
Sierra Bonita Grill 1
Stanley's Polish Sausage Co. 11
T. Cook's 19
Ted's Hot Dogs 41
Thaifoon 25
Veneto Trattoria Italiana 28
Vincent Guerithault on Camelback 15
Vincent's Market Bistro 15
Zinc Bistro 23
To Flagstaff
Turf Paradise Racetrack
Bell Rd.
Greenway Rd.
Arizona
Thunderbird Rd.
Sweetwater Ave.
Cactus Rd.
PEORIA
Peoria Rd.
GLENDALE
Dunlap Ave.
To Wickenburg
Northern Ave.
Grand Ave.
Glendale Ave.
Maryland Ave.
Bethany Home Rd.
Missouri Ave.
Camelback Rd.
Grand
Indian School Rd.
Canal
Osborn Rd.
Thomas Rd.
McDowell Rd.
Papago Freeway
DOWNTOWN PHOENIX
To Los Angeles
Van Buren St.
Washington St.
Buckeye Rd.
Maricopa Fwy.
Broadway Rd.
Salt River
Southern Ave.
Baseline Rd.
Dobbins Rd.
Elliot Rd.
PHOENIX SOUTH MOUNTAIN PARK
North Mountain Preserve
Canal
Black Canyon Freeway
35th Ave.
19th Ave.
7th Ave.
7th St.
Central Ave.
16th St.
67th Ave.
59th Ave.
27th Ave.
43rd Ave.
51st Ave.
17
10
60
85

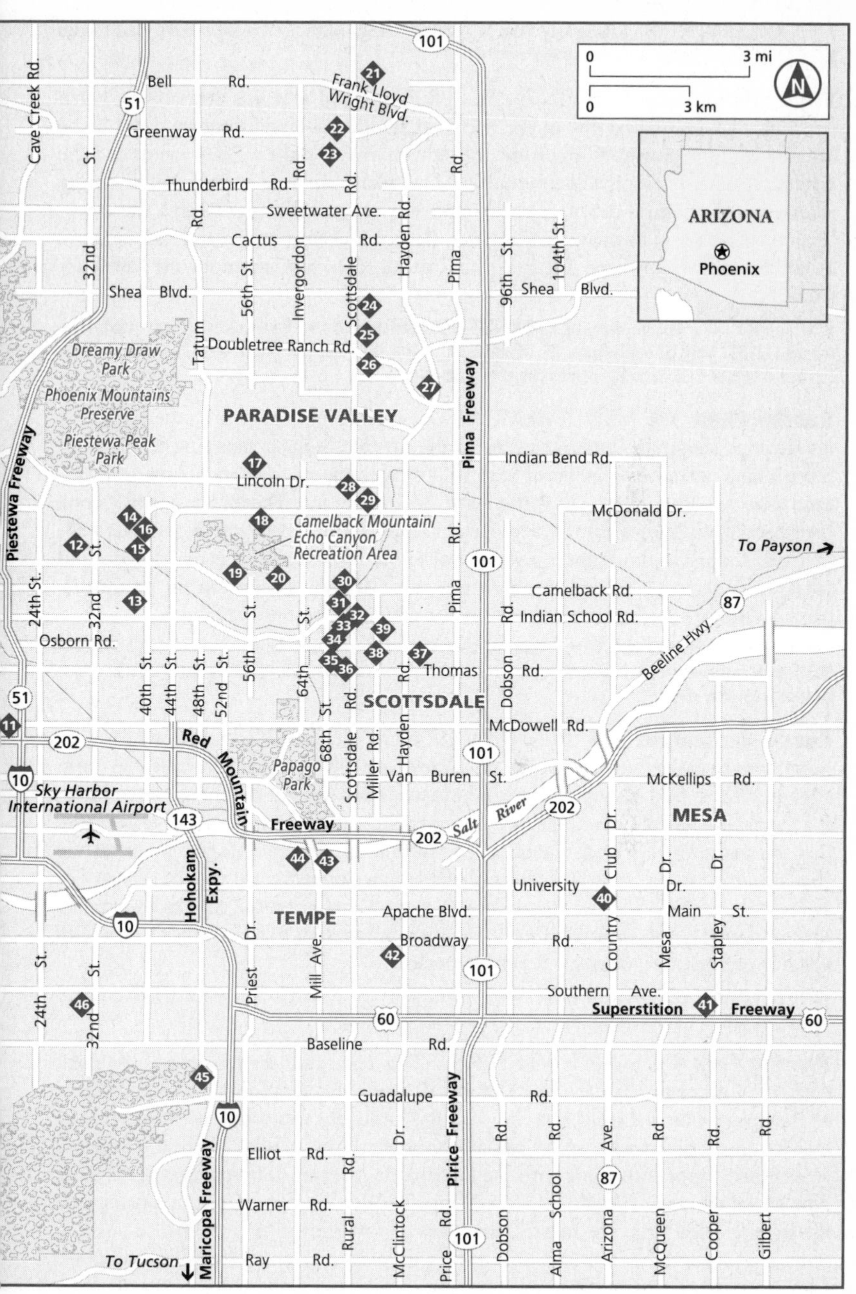

0
3 mi
0
3 km
N
ARIZONA
Phoenix
Bell Rd.
Greenway Rd.
Thunderbird Rd.
Sweetwater Ave.
Cactus Rd.
Shea Blvd.
Doubletree Ranch Rd.
Frank Lloyd Wright Blvd.
Cave Creek Rd.
32nd St.
Tatum Rd.
56th St.
Invergordon Rd.
Scottsdale Rd.
Hayden Rd.
Pima Rd.
96th St.
104th St.
Dreamy Draw Park
Phoenix Mountains Preserve
Piestewa Peak Park
PARADISE VALLEY
Pima Freeway
Piestewa Freeway
Indian Bend Rd.
Lincoln Dr.
McDonald Dr.
Camelback Mountain/ Echo Canyon Recreation Area
To Payson
Camelback Rd.
Indian School Rd.
24th St.
32nd St.
56th St.
64th St.
68th St.
Osborn Rd.
Thomas Rd.
40th St.
44th St.
48th St.
52nd St.
Scottsdale Rd.
Miller Rd.
Hayden Rd.
Dobson Rd.
SCOTTSDALE
Beeline Hwy.
McDowell Rd.
Red Mountain Freeway
Papago Park
Van Buren St.
McKellips Rd.
Sky Harbor International Airport
Salt River
MESA
Hohokam Expy.
University Dr.
Country Club Dr.
Mesa Dr.
Stapley Dr.
TEMPE
Apache Blvd.
Main St.
Broadway Rd.
Priest Dr.
Mill Ave.
Southern Ave.
Superstition Freeway
24th St.
32nd St.
Baseline Rd.
Guadalupe Rd.
Elliot Rd.
Warner Rd.
Ray Rd.
Rural Rd.
McClintock Dr.
Price Rd.
Pirice Freeway
Dobson Rd.
Alma School Rd.
Arizona Ave.
McQueen Rd.
Cooper Rd.
Gilbert Rd.
To Tucson
Maricopa Freeway
101
51
202
10
143
87
60
11
12
13
14
15
16
17
18
19
20
21
22
23
24
25
26
27
28
29
30
31
32
33
34
35
36
37
38
39
40
41
42
43
44
45
46

Westin Kierland Resort, 6902 E. Greenway Pkwy. ✆ **480/624-1030.** Reservations recommended. Main courses $20–$29. AE, DC, DISC, MC, V. Daily 6–10pm.

El Chorro Lodge ★ CONTINENTAL Built in 1934 as a girls' school, El Chorro is a Valley landmark and one of the area's last traditional establishments. Even if the interior is a little dowdy, at nighttime the lights twinkle on the saguaro cactus and the restaurant takes on a timeless tranquility. The adobe building houses several dining rooms, but the patio is the place to be, especially on cool evenings when a fire crackles in the fireplace. The menu features such classics as chateaubriand and rack of lamb, as well as such seldom-seen dishes as shad roe on toast. Save room for the legendary sticky buns.

5550 E. Lincoln Dr., Paradise Valley. ✆ **480/948-5170.** www.elchorro.com. Reservations recommended. Main courses $12–$21 lunch, $15–$65 dinner. AE, DC, DISC, MC, V. Mon–Fri 11am–2pm and 5:30–10pm; Sat 5:30–10pm; Sun 9am–2pm and 5:30–9pm. Sun brunch served only Oct–May.

Rancho Pinot ★★ NEW AMERICAN Rancho Pinot, hidden at the back of a nondescript shopping center adjacent to the upscale Borgata shopping plaza, combines a homey cowboy-chic decor with nonthreatening contemporary American cuisine, and has long been a favorite with Scottsdale and Phoenix residents. Look elsewhere if you crave wildly creative flavor combinations, but if you like simple, well-prepared food, Rancho Pinot is a great choice. My favorite starter is the grilled squid salad with preserved lemon; for an entree, you can always count on the handmade pasta or Nonni's chicken, braised with white wine, mushrooms, and herbs.

6208 N. Scottsdale Rd., in Lincoln Village Shops (southwest corner of Scottsdale Rd. and Lincoln Dr.). ✆ **480/367-8030.** www.ranchopinot.com. Reservations recommended. Main courses $18–$29. AE, MC, V. Mon–Sat 5:30–10pm. Summer hours may vary.

Razz's Restaurant ★★ SOUTHWESTERN/ECLECTIC Chef/owner Razz Kamnitzer has long been one of the most creative chefs in Scottsdale, so it may seem a bit unusual to find his superb restaurant in a nondescript old shopping center. However, step through the door, and you'll immediately be immersed in the conviviality that characterizes this locals' favorite. For the full-on experience, take a seat at the chef's counter where you can order a chef's sampler dinner consisting of as many or as few courses ($13–$17 per course) as you want. Razz makes the choices and you sit back and enjoy. You may wind up with spicy Indonesian noodles, duck cakes with *nopalito* cactus sauce, or crispy veal sweetbreads.

10315 N. Scottsdale Rd. ✆ **480/905-1308.** www.razzsrestaurant.com. Reservations recommended. Main courses $21–$31. AE, DC, DISC, MC, V. Tues–Sat 5–10pm. Closed June to mid-Sept.

Roaring Fork ★★ SOUTHWESTERN This restaurant serves some of the most creative Southwestern fare in the Valley. While no meal here is complete without a side of the green-chile macaroni and cheese, you'll probably also want an entree. Try the excellent duck breast with onion jam and sour-cherry mustard or the beef tenderloin (which just happens to come with the green-chile macaroni). If you can't get a table, dine in the saloon or the saloon patio. Happy hour (Mon–Sat 4–7pm) is a good time for an early meal from the saloon menu, actually worth eating from just so you can order the "big ass burger," a 12-ounce patty with roasted green chiles. Wash it all down with a huckleberry margarita.

4800 N. Scottsdale Rd. (in the Finova Building at the corner of Chaparral Rd.). ✆ **480/947-0795.** www.roaringfork.com. Reservations highly recommended. Main courses $17–$35. AE, DISC, MC, V. Mon–Sat 5–10pm; Sun 5–9pm.

Sea Saw ★★ JAPANESE You'd never guess that this unpretentious hole-in the-wall with seating for only 28 people is home to chef Nobuo Fukuda, considered one of the best chefs in the country. The menu lists barely more than a dozen dishes, so it's almost impossible to go wrong here. Not one of these dishes can really be considered sushi, so don't expect items such as California rolls. Instead, consider the seared tuna *tataki* or warm white-fish carpaccio. For the full treatment from Nobuo, order the multicourse *omakase* dinner. The restaurant is affiliated with the adjacent Cowboy Ciao and has an overwhelmingly long wine list that includes lots of premium sakes. By press time, Sea Saw will have moved to its new location at Scottsdale's South Waterfront (call for address), and this space will be home to pastry chef Tracey Dempsey's French tea room.

7133 E. Stetson Dr. ✆ **480/481-9463.** www.seasaw.net. Reservations not accepted. All plates $6–$16; tasting menu $90 ($125 w/wine). AE, DC, DISC, MC, V. Sun–Thurs 5:30–10pm; Fri–Sat 5:30–11pm.

MODERATE

Arcadia Farms ★ NEW AMERICAN Long a favorite of the Scottsdale ladies-who-lunch crowd, this Old Town restaurant features a romantic setting and well-prepared contemporary fare. Try the delicious raspberry goat cheese salad with jicama and candied pecans. The warm mushroom, spinach, and goat cheese tart is another winner. Try to get a seat on the shady patio. This restaurant also operates cafes at the Heard Museum, the new Heard Museum North, and the Phoenix Art Museum.

7014 E. First Ave. ✆ **480/941-5665.** www.arcadiafarmscafe.com. Reservations recommended. Main courses $12–$15. MC, V. Daily 11am–3pm.

Bandera ★ *Value* AMERICAN Once you've gotten a whiff of the wood-roasted chickens turning on the rotisseries in Bandera's back-of-the-building, open-air stone oven, you'll know exactly what to order when you finally get seated at this perennially popular spot in Old Town. What an aroma! The succulent spit-roasted chicken is the meal to have here, and make sure you get it with some of Bandera's great mashed potatoes or cornbread. Sure, you could order prime rib or clams, but you'd be a fool if you did. Stick with the chicken or maybe the barbecued ribs, and you won't go wrong.

3821 N. Scottsdale Rd. ✆ **480/994-3524.** Reservations recommended. Main courses $14–$29. AE, DC, DISC, MC, V. Sun–Thurs 4:30–10pm; Fri–Sat 4:30–11pm.

Carlsbad Tavern ★ NEW MEXICAN Carlsbad Tavern blends the fiery tastes of New Mexican cuisine with a hip and humorous bat-theme atmosphere (a reference to Carlsbad Caverns). The menu lists traditional New Mexican dishes such as *carne adovada* (pork simmered in a fiery red-chile sauce), as well as contemporary Southwestern specialties such as poblano chiles stuffed with crab and pasta with an unusual chipotle stroganoff. Cool off your taste buds with a prickly-pear margarita. A lagoon makes this place feel like a beach bar, while the patio fireplace is cozy on a cold night.

3313 N. Hayden Rd. (south of Osborn). ✆ **480/970-8164.** www.carlsbadtavern.com. Reservations accepted for 5 or more. Main courses $9–$23. AE, DISC, MC, V. Daily 11am–2am (limited menu daily 10 or 11pm–2am).

Old Town Tortilla Factory ★ MEXICAN Located in an old house surrounded by attractive patios and citrus trees that bloom in winter and spring, this moderately priced Mexican restaurant has a great atmosphere, great food, and a lively bar scene (more than 80 premium tequilas). As you enter the restaurant grounds, you might even see someone making fresh tortillas, which come in a dozen different flavors. The rich tortilla soup and the tequila-lime salad make good starters. For an entree, try the pork chops crusted with ancho chile powder and raspberry sauce.

6910 E. Main St. ✆ **480/945-4567**. www.oldtowntortillafactory.com. Reservations accepted only for parties of 6 or more. Main courses $9.25–$33. AE, DC, DISC, MC, V. Sun–Thurs 4:30–9:30pm; Fri–Sat 4:30–10:30pm.

Thaifoon ★★ THAI This may not be traditional Thai food, but it sure is good. Thaifoon merges a hip upscale setting with flavorful food at economical prices. In fact, the dishes here are so good you'll likely find yourself coming back repeatedly to try others. The *tom kha gai* (Thai-style coconut-mushroom soup) is the best I've ever had, and the many shrimp dishes are packed with lively flavors. Don't miss the great tropical cocktails.

At The Shops at Gainey Village, 8777 N. Scottsdale Rd. ✆ **480/998-0011**. www.thaifoon.com. Reservations recommended. Main courses $8–$16. AE, DISC, MC, V. Mon–Fri 11am–10pm; Sat noon–10pm; Sun 1–10pm.

Veneto Trattoria Italiana ★ VENETIAN ITALIAN This pleasantly low-key bistro, specializing in the cuisine of Venice, serves satisfying "peasant food," including traditional pork-and-garlic sausages served with grilled polenta and braised savoy cabbage. *Baccala mantecato* (creamy fish mousse on grilled polenta, made with dried salt cod soaked overnight in milk) may sound unusual, but it's absolutely heavenly. Other good bets include the salad of thinly sliced smoked beef, shaved Parmesan, and arugula. For a finale, try the *semifreddo con frutta secca,* a partially frozen meringue with dried fruits in a pool of raspberry sauce. There's a welcoming bistro ambience and outdoor seating on the patio.

6137 N. Scottsdale Rd., in Hilton Village. ✆ **480/948-9928**. www.venetotrattoria.com. Reservations recommended. Main courses $8.50–$20 lunch, $14–$25 dinner. AE, DC, DISC, MC, V. Mon–Sat 11:30am–2:30pm and 5–10pm.

Zinc Bistro ★★ *Finds* FRENCH It may seem incongruous to find a French bistro in sunny Scottsdale, and in a modern outdoor shopping center at that, but here it is. This place is a perfect reproduction of the sort of bistro you may have loved on your last trip to Paris. Everything is authentic, from the zinc bar to the sidewalk cafe seating to the hooks under the bar for ladies' purses. Try the Provençal-style ahi tuna, the omelet piled high with shoestring potatoes, or anything that comes with the fabulous bistro fries. For dessert, try the Zinc chocolate soufflé.

In Kierland Commons, 15034 N. Scottsdale Rd. ✆ **480/603-0922**. www.zincbistroaz.com. Reservations accepted only for parties of 6 or more. Main courses $12–$15 lunch, $8–$43 dinner. AE, DC, MC, V. Daily 11am–10pm.

INEXPENSIVE

The Counter ★ AMERICAN When was the last time you had a 25¢ cup of coffee? Well, you can still get one at this 21st-century lunch counter in the sprawling Kierland Commons new-urban shopping center. Soups and sandwiches are the mainstays on the Counter's very limited menu. However, there's bound to be something you'll like, and it's so fun to sit at the counter with the local lunch crowd that you probably won't mind the brevity of the menu. This isn't just a lunch counter, though; it's also an upscale minimart that sells everything from estate-bottled olive oil to Italian sparkling wine. There's even designer jewelry. It may sound a little strange, but it's a whole lot of fun. Check it out.

In Kierland Commons, 15215 N. Kierland Blvd. ✆ **480/998-0202**. www.foxrc.com. Main dishes $4–$7. AE, DISC, MC, V. Mon–Sat 8am–8pm; Sun 10am–6pm.

El Molino Mexican Café ★ *Finds* MEXICAN Located a bit out of the Old Town Scottsdale mainstream, this small Mexican joint is little more than a fast-food place, but it serves the best chimichangas in town. If you're among the few people in this country still not familiar with what a chimichanga is, it's a deep-fried burrito. That said, the chimis here have crispy, light shells and are packed with tasty fillings. Try one with *machaca* (shredded and spiced beef) or green chile, and I'm sure you'll become a convert. If fried food just doesn't do it for you, opt for a couple of green corn tamales, an Arizona specialty.

3554 N. Goldwater Blvd. ✆ **480/994-3566.** www.elmolinocafe.com. Reservations not accepted. Main courses $2–$9.50. DISC, MC, V. Mon–Sat 9am–8pm.

El Paso Barbeque Company ★ BARBECUE This is Scottsdale-style barbecue, which means you'll be licking your fingers amid upscale cowboy decor. If you're in the mood for raucous good times, this place is worth the trip. The barbecue runs the gamut from ribs to smoked chicken to more uptown dishes such as barbecued salmon and prime rib. The pulled pork with a smoky sauce and fresh coleslaw is scrumptious. There's also a wide variety of sandwiches, making this a good lunch or takeout spot. The roll of paper towels on your table should give you an idea of how messy a meal here will be.

8220 N. Hayden Rd. ✆ **480/998-2626.** www.elpasobarbeque.com. Reservations accepted for parties of 8 or more. Main courses $8–$24. AE, DISC, MC, V. Sun–Thurs 11am–10pm; Fri–Sat 11am–11pm.

Grazie ★ *Finds* PIZZA This little neighborhood pizzeria and wine bar is in downtown Scottsdale at the west end of Main Street near the Valley Ho resort and is a little gem of a place—sophisticated and full of contemporary art. It's also very popular on weekends, and the noise level can be deafening. Come on a weeknight or for lunch if you want to carry on a conversation without shouting. The weekend buzz aside, this is a great place to sip Italian wines and share a couple of designer pizzas from the wood-fired oven. Start your meal with the carpaccio, which is served with arugula, parmigiano-reggiano cheese, and a lemon vinaigrette; or a salad made with arugula, baby greens, parmigiano-reggiano, red onions, red bell peppers, and pine nuts. The pizzas here have paper-thin crusts, so don't worry about filling up before it's time to order the signature ice cream calzone.

6952 E. Main St. ✆ **480/663-9797.** www.grazie.us. Reservations recommended Fri–Sat nights. Main courses $9–$15. AE, MC, V. Mon–Sat 11am–2pm and 5–10pm; Sun 5–10pm.

Los Olivos ★ MEXICAN Los Olivos is a Scottsdale institution, one of the last restaurants in Old Town that dates to the days when cowboys tied up their horses on Main Street. Although the food is just standard Mexican fare, the building is a fascinating folk-art construction. The entrance is a bit like a cement cave, with strange figures rising from the roof. Amazingly, this throwback to slower times is only steps away from the Scottsdale Museum of Contemporary Art. On Friday and Saturday nights, there's Latin dancing from 9pm until 1am.

There's another Los Olivos up in north Scottsdale at 15544 N. Pima Rd. (✆ **480/596-9787**).

7328 Second St. ✆ **480/946-2256.** www.losolivosrestaurant.com. Reservations recommended. Main courses $6.50–$16. AE, DISC, MC, V. Sun–Thurs 11am–10pm; Fri–Sat 11am–11pm.

Los Sombreros ★ *Finds* MEXICAN Although this casual Mexican restaurant is in an attractive old house, it doesn't look all that special from the outside. However, the menu is surprisingly creative and veers from the standard dishes served at most Mexican restaurants. Start with the chunky homemade guacamole, which is some of the best in the city. Be sure to order the *puerco en chipotle,* succulent, slow-roasted pork in tomatillo-chipotle sauce. Finish it all off with the flan, which will spoil you for flan anywhere else. For a real treat, get it with almond-flavored tequila.

2534 N. Scottsdale Rd. (at McKellips Rd.), Scottsdale. ✆ **480/994-1799.** www.lossombreros.com. Reservations accepted for 5 or more. Main courses $14–$17. AE, DC, MC, V. Sun and Tues–Thurs 5–9pm; Fri–Sat 5–10pm.

NORTH SCOTTSDALE, CAREFREE & CAVE CREEK

VERY EXPENSIVE

Sassi ★★ ITALIAN If you've had to forego this year's vacation in Italy, then don't miss an opportunity to have a meal at this Tuscan villa transplanted to the Arizona desert. Every room in this beautiful, sprawling building is gorgeous and has a distinctive character of its own. You just might have to eat here a few times before you decide which room you like the best. The menu is not your standard southern Italian menu, so don't go looking for spaghetti and meatballs (although you might find an excellent spaghetti primavera). Instead, try the wood-oven shrimp with asparagus, lemon, roasted garlic, and prosciutto broth, or a dish with the house-made sausage or house-made mortadella. In fact, the best thing to do here is order a bunch of dishes and then share everything, as any good Italian family would.

10455 E. Pinnacle Peak Pkwy., Scottsdale. ✆ **480/502-9095.** www.sassi.biz. Reservations highly recommended. Primi $12–$20; secondi $18–$38. AE, DC, DISC, MC, V. Tues–Sun 5:30–9 or 10pm.

EXPENSIVE

La Hacienda ★★ GOURMET MEXICAN As you may guess from the price range below, this is not your average taco joint. La Hacienda serves gourmet Mexican cuisine in an upscale, glamorous, but rustic setting reminiscent of an early 1900s hacienda (stone-tiled floor, Mexican glassware and crockery, a beehive fireplace). Be sure to start with the *antojitos* (appetizers) platter, which might include pork flautas (a rolled-up fried tortilla), baked shrimp, crabmeat enchiladas, and a red-corn quesadilla made with squash blossoms, wild mushrooms, and goat cheese. Roasted whole suckling pig carved tableside is the house specialty and should not be missed. However, the rack of lamb crusted with pumpkin seeds has long been a local favorite. Live music lends a party atmosphere.

At The Fairmont Scottsdale Princess, 7575 E. Princess Dr. (about 12 miles north of downtown Scottsdale). ✆ **480/585-4848.** Reservations recommended. Main courses $25–$42. AE, DC, DISC, MC, V. Thurs–Tues 5:30–10pm.

Michael's ★★ NEW AMERICAN/INTERNATIONAL Located in the classy little Citadel shopping/business plaza in north Scottsdale, this restaurant is one of the Valley's best. The setting is simple yet elegant, which allows the drama of food presentation to come to the fore. To start things off, do not miss the "silver spoons" hors d'oeuvres—tablespoons each containing three or four ingredients that burst with flavor. From there, it's on to main courses such as duck and foie gras with a sweet-potato raviolo in sage-balsamic butter. For drinks with or without a light meal, head upstairs to the bar.

8700 E. Pinnacle Peak Rd., N. Scottsdale. ✆ **480/515-2575.** www.michaelsrestaurant.com. Reservations recommended. Main courses $8–$18 lunch, $25–$36 dinner; prix-fixe menu $55 ($90–$100 w/wine). AE, DC, DISC, MC, V. Mon–Fri 11am–2pm and 6–10pm; Sat 6–10pm; Sun 10am–2pm (brunch) and 6–10pm.

Mosaic ★★★ *Finds* NEW AMERICAN The Pinnacle Peak area of north Scottsdale boasts one of the Valley's greatest concentrations of excellent, high-end restaurants, and this just may be the best of a very good bunch. Okay, so dinner here is going to set you back quite a bit, but the food is superb, and if you come before the sun goes down, you can soak up some of the best desert views in the Valley. Chef/owner Deborah Knight is one of the best chefs around and likes to show off her culinary creativity with a menu that changes regularly and is always provocative and daring. How about Sri Lankan–spiced prime rib or crispy duck in Tanzanian peanut curry to start things out? For an entree, you might order a lamb rack crusted with almonds and walnuts or pork loin dusted with four peppercorns. You get the picture; this is a foodie's nirvana.

10600 E. Jomax Rd., N. Scottsdale. ✆ **480/563-9600.** www.mosaic-restaurant.com. Reservations recommended. Main courses $26–$40; tasting menu $65–$85 ($100–$120 w/wine). AE, DC, DISC, MC, V. Tues–Sat 5:30–9 or 10pm. Closed mid-Aug to mid-Sept.

MODERATE

Bodega Bistro & Tapas Bar ★★ SPANISH This tiny Spanish tapas restaurant, tucked away in a courtyard in downtown Carefree's Spanish Village shopping center, is well worth searching out. Not only will you find the best tapas in the Phoenix area, but an excellent wine list (try some of the Argentine wine). The friendly owner and staff make this a fun, casual place for a light meal after cowboying up in adjacent Cave Creek. Try the Catalan flatbread (sort of like pizza), the *banderillas* (skewers of meat, olives, and red and yellow peppers), or paella.

In Spanish Village, 7208 Ho Rd., Carefree. ✆ **480/488-4166.** www.bodegabistroaz.com. Reservations recommended. Main courses $8–$38. AE, MC, V. Sun–Thurs 5–9pm; Fri–Sat 5–10pm.

The Original Crazy Ed's Satisfied Frog Saloon & Restaurant *Finds* AMERICAN/BARBECUE Cave Creek is the Phoenix area's favorite cow-town hangout and is filled with Wild West–themed saloons and restaurants. Crazy Ed's—affiliated with the Black Mountain Brewing Company, which produces Cave Creek Chili Beer—is my favorite. This place is just plain fun, with big covered porches and sawdust on the floor. Stick to steaks and barbecue. You'll find Crazy Ed's in the tourist-trap Frontier Town.

At Frontier Town, 6245 E. Cave Creek Rd., Cave Creek. ✆ **480/488-3317.** www.satisfiedfrog.com. Reservations recommended on weekends. Main courses $9–$29. AE, DC, DISC, MC, V. Daily 11am–10pm.

INEXPENSIVE

Greasewood Flat ★ *Finds* AMERICAN Burgers and beer are the mainstays at this rustic open-air restaurant in the Pinnacle Peak area of north Scottsdale. Located down a potholed gravel road behind Reata Pass steakhouse, Greasewood Flat is a desert party spot where families, motorcycle clubs, cyclists, and horseback riders all rub shoulders. Place your order at the window and grab a seat at one of the picnic tables. While you wait for your meal, you can check out the old farm equipment. This place is the antithesis of Scottsdale posh, and that's exactly why I love it. Only in Arizona could you find a place like this.

27375 N. Alma School Pkwy. ✆ **480/585-9430.** www.greasewoodflat.net. Main courses $3.75–$8. No credit cards. Daily 11am–1am.

CENTRAL PHOENIX & THE CAMELBACK CORRIDOR

VERY EXPENSIVE

Mary Elaine's ★★★ FRENCH There quite simply is no place else in Arizona to compare with Mary Elaine's, and if you happen to be in town for a major wedding anniversary or milestone birthday, this is the place to celebrate. At least once in your life you should splurge on the sort of dining experience provided here. Situated atop the posh Phoenician resort, this elegant restaurant is the pinnacle of Arizona dining not only for its haute cuisine, but also for its award-winning wine list (and master sommelier), exemplary service, and superb table settings. The menu focuses on classic French cuisine with an emphasis on impeccably fresh ingredients; foie gras, truffles, lobster, and caviar all make frequent appearances. Menus change seasonally, and there are also themed tasting menus. Try to make a reservation that allows you to take in the sunset.

At The Phoenician, 6000 E. Camelback Rd. ✆ **480/423-2530.** Reservations highly recommended. Jackets suggested for men. Main courses $45–$48; 7-course tasting menu $125 (plus $85 for matched wines). AE, DC, DISC, MC, V. Tues–Thurs 5:30–9:30pm; Fri–Sat 5:30–10pm.

EXPENSIVE

Chelsea's Kitchen ★ NEW AMERICAN Although this restaurant can seem a bit expensive for what you get, the setting, on the banks of a canal just a block off Camelback Road, is gorgeous. The patio, with a wood-burning fireplace, is nearly as large as the dining room and is where you should try to get a table. The sunsets can be absolutely unforgettable. Separating the dining room and patio is a fun indoor-outdoor bar. Under the same ownership as the nearby La Grande Orange Pizzeria and Postino wine bar, Chelsea's Kitchen features a menu of familiar comfort foods with a few more creative dishes thrown into the mix. The seasonal salads are usually a good choice, as are the ahi tuna tacos. Be sure to try the fried chicken and the short-rib hash.

5040 N. 40th St. ✆ **602/957-2555.** www.chelseaskitchenaz.com. Main courses $10–$27. AE, MC, V. Mon–Fri 11am–10pm; Sat–Sun 4–10pm.

Coup des Tartes ★ *Finds* COUNTRY FRENCH Chain restaurants, theme restaurants, restaurants that are all style and little substance: Sometimes in Phoenix it seems impossible to find a genuinely homey little hole-in-the-wall that serves good food. Don't despair; Coup des Tartes is just the ticket. With barely a dozen tables and no liquor license (bring your own wine; $8 corkage fee), it's about as removed from the standard Phoenix glitz as you can get without boarding a plane and leaving town. Start your meal with pâté de campagne or the scrumptious brie brûlée, which is covered with caramelized apples. The entree menu changes regularly, but the Moroccan lamb shank with couscous is so good that it's always available. The filet mignon, with the sauce of the moment, is another good choice. Of course, for dessert, you absolutely must have a tart.

4626 N. 16th St. (a couple blocks south of Camelback Rd.). ✆ **602/212-1082.** www.nicetartes.com. Reservations recommended. Main courses $18–$36. AE, MC, V. Wed–Sat 5:30–10pm.

LON'S at the hermosa ★★ NEW AMERICAN Located in a beautiful old adobe hacienda built by cowboy artist Lon Megargee and surrounded by colorful gardens, this restaurant is one of the most classically Arizonan places in the Phoenix area, and the patio, with its views of Camelback Mountain, is blissfully tranquil. Lunch on the patio is the meal to have here. Entrees are reliable, and if you peruse the menu closely, you'll turn up some interesting Southwestern ingredients, including prickly pear and Arizona-farmed shrimp. Basically, you eat here more for the atmosphere than for gustatory epiphanies. The bar has a cozy and romantic Wild West feel.

At the Hermosa Inn, 5532 N. Palo Cristi Rd. ✆ **602/955-7878.** www.lons.com. Reservations recommended. Main courses $11–$15 lunch, $23–$34 dinner. AE, DC, DISC, MC, V. Mon–Fri 11:30am–2pm and 6–10pm; Sat 6–10pm; Sun 10am–2pm (brunch) and 6–10pm.

T. Cook's ★★★ MEDITERRANEAN Ready to pop the question? On your honeymoon? Celebrating an anniversary? This is the place for you. There just isn't a more romantic restaurant in the Valley. Located within the walls of the Mediterranean-inspired Royal Palms Resort and Spa, it's surrounded by decades-old gardens and even has palm trees growing right through the roof of the dining room. The focal point of the open kitchen is a wood-fired oven that turns out a fabulous spit-roasted chicken as well as an impressive platter of paella. T. Cook's continues to make big impressions right through to the dessert course.

At the Royal Palms Resort and Spa, 5200 E. Camelback Rd. ✆ **866/579-3636** or 602/808-0766. www.royalpalmshotel.com. Reservations highly recommended. Main courses $11–$16 lunch, $25–$36 dinner. AE, DC, DISC, MC, V. Mon–Sat 6–10am, 11am–2pm, and 5:30–10pm; Sun 6–10am, 10am–2pm (brunch), and 5:30–10pm.

Vincent's on Camelback ★★ SOUTHWESTERN Vincent's is a Phoenix bastion of Southwestern cuisine and has long enjoyed a devoted local following. The menu blends Southwestern influences with classic European dishes. You could order a delicious lobster salad or sautéed beef tenderloins with pinot noir glaze, but if you're from outside the region, you should try the Southwestern dishes. Don't miss the duck tamale or the tequila soufflé, and for an entree, the veal sweetbreads with blue cornmeal are an enduring favorite. For a casual breakfast or lunch, try the attached Vincent's Market Bistro (see below), which is affiliated with the restaurant's Saturday farmers' market.

3930 E. Camelback Rd. ✆ **602/224-0225.** www.vincentsoncamelback.com. Reservations highly recommended. Main courses $11–$16 lunch, $29–$32 dinner. AE, DC, DISC, MC, V. Mon–Fri 11:30am–2pm and 5–10pm; Sat 5–10pm.

MODERATE

Delux ★ BURGERS With a sleek and stylish decor, a very limited menu (you'd better like burgers), and one of the best selections of draft beers in the Valley, this is the ultimate ultra-hip burger-and-beer joint. The burgers get my vote for best burgers in the city, but it's the cute Barbie-size shopping carts full of crispy french fries that are the real reason to dine here. Talk about your guilty pleasures—it just doesn't get much better than a cart of fries and a pint of Old Rasputin imperial stout. If you're not a burger-meister, don't despair; there are great salads and a few nonbeef sandwiches.

In the Biltmore Plaza, 3146 E. Camelback Rd. ✆ **602/522-2288.** www.deluxburger.com. Reservations not accepted. Main courses $6–$10. AE, DC, DISC, MC, V. Daily 11am–2am.

La Grande Orange Pizzeria ★ PIZZA Good pizza and an off-the-beaten-tourist-path neighborhood location make this casual restaurant a good place to feel like a local. Best of all, La Grande Orange is convenient to both downtown Scottsdale and the pricey Camelback corridor. Gourmet pizzas are what this place is all about, but you should start with the orange-fennel salad or one of the other great salads. While you're here, check out the adjacent La Grande Orange gourmet grocery (great for stocking a picnic) and gelateria (delightful on a hot day).

4410 N. 40th St. (at Campbell St.). ✆ **602/840-7777.** www.lagrandeorangepizzeria.com. Reservations not accepted. Main courses $10–$14. AE, MC, V. Daily 4–10pm.

Sierra Bonita ★ SOUTHWESTERN This neighborhood restaurant is the sort of place you dream about finding—flavorful food, big portions, moderate prices. What's not to like? Well, it is a bit out-of-the-way if you're just visiting Phoenix, but don't let that scare you off. Start with the guacamole and the bacon-wrapped shrimp, and then maybe order the same thing again. Next, order whatever's being served with the mashed sweet potatoes (they're heavenly). If you're really hungry, opt for the pork *osso buco* (pork shank) with green chile sauce. Did somebody say Oaxacan chocolate soufflé for dessert?

6933 N. Seventh St. ✆ **602/264-0700.** www.sierrabonitagrill.com. Reservations recommended. Main courses $8–$26. AE, MC, V. Sun–Thurs 11am–10pm; Fri–Sat 11am–11pm.

Vincent's Market Bistro ★★ FRENCH Located in back of the ever-popular Vincent's restaurant, this casual place does a respectable job of conjuring up a casual backstreet bistro in Paris. It's utterly quaint without being froufrou. Tables have cast-iron bases, and chairs have woven-reed seats. You can sit down and have a meal here (try the coq au vin), or get some gourmet food to go. This place stays packed on Saturday mornings when Vincent's farmers' market attracts crowds of shoppers in search of gourmet snacks and fresh produce.

3930 E. Camelback Rd. ✆ **602/224-3727.** www.vincentsoncamelback.com. Main courses $7–$13. AE, DC, DISC, MC, V. Mon–Fri 7am–8pm; Sat–Sun 7am–2pm.

INEXPENSIVE

5 & Diner AMERICAN If it's 2am and you just have to have a big, greasy burger and a side of fries, head for the 24-hour 5 & Diner. You can't miss it—it's the classic streamliner diner that looks as if it just materialized from New Jersey.

Other locations are in Paradise Valley, 12802 N. Tatum Blvd. (✆ **602/996-0033**); and in Scottsdale at Scottsdale Pavilions, 9069 E. Indian Bend Rd. (✆ **480/949-1957**).

5220 N. 16th St. ✆ **602/264-5220.** www.5anddiner.com. Reservations not accepted. Sandwiches/plates $5.50–$15. AE, DC, DISC, MC, V. Daily 24 hr.

Pane Bianco ★ *Finds* BAKERY/SANDWICHES Chris Bianco, owner of downtown's immensely popular Pizzeria Bianco (see below), has another winner on his hands with this casual counter-service bakery and sandwich shop not far from the Heard Museum. The menu consists of only four sandwiches and a couple of salads, but all the breads are baked on the premises in a wood-fired oven. The house-made mozzarella is exquisitely fresh and is served both as a caprese salad with tomatoes and basil and in a focaccia sandwich with the same ingredients. And that focaccia? The best in Phoenix.

4404 N. Central Ave. ✆ **602/234-2100.** Reservations not accepted. Main courses $8. AE, MC, V. Tues–Sat 11am–3pm.

Stanley's Homemade Polish Sausage Co. *Finds* DELI Located on a rundown stretch of McDowell Road just off Arizona 51, Stanley's has been in business since 1963 and is the oldest Polish deli in Phoenix. This place doesn't look like much from the outside, but inside you'll find walls hung with dozens of different types of sausages and smoked meats. You can order your meat by the pound and take it with you on a picnic, or get a huge submarine made with homemade cold cuts or sausage and eat at one of the deli's handful of tables.

2201 E. McDowell Rd. ✆ **602/275-8788.** www.stanleys-sausage.com. Sandwiches $4.75–$6.75. AE, DISC, MC, V. Tues–Fri 9am–6pm; Sat 9am–5pm.

DOWNTOWN, SOUTH PHOENIX & THE AIRPORT AREA

EXPENSIVE

Quiessence ★★ *Finds* NEW AMERICAN This place is as far from a typical Phoenix/Scottsdale dining experience as you can get without going to the airport and getting on a plane, and that's exactly why I love it. Set at the back of a shady pecan

Forbidden City in the Desert

So you're driving along the Loop 202 freeway near Sky Harbor Airport and this strange mirage materializes. You think you're seeing a mall-size complex of classical Chinese buildings. Don't worry, it's not a heat-induced hallucination—it's the **COFCO Chinese Cultural Center,** 668 N. 44th St. (✆ **602/275-8578;** www.phxchinatown.com). This fascinating complex includes several Chinese restaurants, gift shops, and an Asian supermarket. There's also a Chinese garden with numerous traditional viewing pavilions.

grove not far from South Mountain Park, Quiessence is surrounded by organic vegetable gardens. It is these gardens, and the freshness of the ingredients they provide, that makes the food here so wonderful, but it is the delightfully rural setting that makes Quiessence truly special. The herbed chicken here is so good you'll forget that it's actually good for you. Don't pass it up if it's on the menu. Oh, and by the way, the desserts are outrageous!

6106 S. 32nd St. ✆ **602/276-0601.** www.quiessencerestaurant.com. Reservations recommended. Main courses $19–$24. AE, DC, MC, V. Tues–Sat 5–9pm.

MODERATE

Alice Cooper'stown ★ BARBECUE Owned by Alice Cooper himself, this sports-and-rock-themed restaurant/bar is downtown's premier eat-o-tainment center. Sixteen video screens (usually showing sporting events) are the centerpiece, but there's also an abundance of memorabilia, including guitars once used by the likes of Fleetwood Mac and Eric Clapton. The waitstaff even wears Alice Cooper makeup. Barbecue is served in various permutations, including a huge barbecue sandwich. If you're an Alice Cooper fan, or hope to spot some local pro athletes, this place is a must.

101 E. Jackson St. ✆ **602/253-7337.** www.alicecooperstown.com. Reservations accepted for only parties of 7 or more. Sandwiches/barbecue $8–$19. AE, MC, V. Sun–Thurs 11am–8 or 9pm; Fri–Sat 11am–9 or 10pm.

Pizzeria Bianco ★ PIZZA Even though this historic brick building is in the heart of downtown Phoenix, the atmosphere is so cozy it feels like your neighborhood local, and the wood-burning oven turns out delicious rustic pizzas. One of my favorites is made with red onion, Parmesan, rosemary, and crushed pistachios. Don't miss the fresh mozzarella, either: Pizzeria Bianco makes its own, and it can be ordered as an appetizer or on a pizza.

At Heritage Sq., 623 E. Adams St. ✆ **602/258-8300.** www.pizzeriabianco.com. Reservations accepted for 6–10 people. Pizzas $10–$14. AE, MC, V. Tues–Sat 5–10pm.

INEXPENSIVE

Carolina's *Finds* MEXICAN Located in a somewhat run-down neighborhood south of the US Airways Center and Chase Field, Carolina's is a Phoenix institution. As such you'll find everyone from Hispanic construction workers to downtown corporate-types (men in suits, women in high heels and pearls). Everyone enjoys the down-home Mexican cooking here, but Carolina's flour tortillas are what really set this place apart. Order a burrito, perhaps with shredded beef in a spicy green sauce, and you'll be handed what feels like a down-filled pillow, so soft you'll want to lay your head on it. Or get the tortillas to go and use them as the basis for a fun Phoenician picnic.

There's a second Carolina's in north Phoenix at 2126 E. Cactus Rd. (✆ **602/275-8231**).

1202 E. Mohave St. ✆ **602/252-1503.** www.carolinasmex.com. Main dishes $3–$5.75. AE, DISC, MC, V. Mon–Fri 7am–7:30pm; Sat 7am–6pm.

The Farm at South Mountain/The Farm Kitchen & Morning Glory Café ★ *Finds* *Kids* SANDWICHES/SALADS If being in the desert has you dreaming of shady trees and green grass, you'll enjoy The Farm Kitchen, an oasis reminiscent of a Deep South pecan orchard. A rustic outbuilding has been converted to a counter-service lunch restaurant where you can order a filling sandwich or a delicious pecan turkey Waldorf salad. Breakfast means baked goods such as muffins and scones. The grassy lawn, shaded by pecan trees, is ideal for a picnic. And you can let the kids run all over while you enjoy your salad or sandwich. At the back of the farm, you'll find the **Morning Glory Café** (✆ **602/276-8804**), a cozy little breakfast place.

6106 S. 32nd St. ✆ **602/276-7288.** www.thefarmatsouthmountain.com. Sandwiches and salads $9.95. AE, DC, MC, V. Mid-Sept to May Tues–Sun 8am–4pm. (If weather is inclement, call to be sure it's open.) Closed June to mid-Sept. Take Exit 151A off I-10 and go south on 32nd St.

Fry Bread House *Finds* NATIVE AMERICAN Fry bread is just what it sounds like—fried bread—and it's a mainstay on Indian reservations throughout the West. Although you can eat these thick, chewy slabs of fried bread plain, salted, or with honey, they also serve as the wrappers for Indian tacos, which are made with meat, beans, and lettuce. If you've already visited the Four Corners region of Arizona, then you've probably had an Indian taco. Forget them—the ones here are the best in the state. Try one with green chile. If you still have room for dessert, do not miss the fry bread with chocolate and butter.

4140 N. Seventh Ave. ✆ **602/351-2345.** Reservations not accepted. Main courses $3–$6.50. DISC, MC, V. Mon–Thurs 10am–7pm; Fri–Sat 10am–8pm.

Los Dos Molinos ★ MEXICAN I hope you travel with a fire extinguisher, because you're gonna need it if you eat at this legendary hot spot in south Phoenix. The food here is New Mexican–style, which means that everything, with the exception of the margaritas, is incendiary. Actually, there are a few dishes for the timid, but people who don't like their food fiery know enough to stay away from this place. So popular is the food at Los Dos Molinos that there's even one in New York. Here in the Phoenix area, there's another at 260 S. Alma School Rd., Mesa (✆ **480/969-7475**). Expect a 2- to 3-hour wait for a table on weekends.

8646 S. Central Ave. ✆ **602/243-9113.** Reservations not accepted. Main courses $3.50–$13. AE, DC, DISC, MC, V. Tues–Fri 11am–2:30pm and 5–9pm; Sat 11am–9pm.

MacAlpine's Restaurant and Soda Fountain *Finds* AMERICAN This is the oldest operating soda fountain in the Southwest, and it hasn't changed much since its opening in 1928. Wooden booths and worn countertops show the patina of age. Big burgers and sandwiches make up the lunch offerings and should be washed down with a root beer float, chocolate malted, or egg cream.

2303 N. Seventh St. ✆ **602/262-5545.** Reservations not accepted. Sandwiches/specials $4–$6.75. AE, DISC, MC, V. Sun–Thurs 11am–7pm; Fri–Sat 11am–8pm.

TEMPE & MESA

MODERATE

Blue Adobe Grille ★★ *Finds* MEXICAN This restaurant looks like the sort of place you should drive right past. Don't! Despite appearances, this New Mexican–style restaurant serves deliciously creative Southwestern fare at very economical prices. To get an idea of what the food here is all about, order the Tres Santa Fe combination plate and request a tenderloin burrito, a shrimp enchilada, and *carne adovada.* Of course, there are great margaritas, but there's also a surprisingly good wine list. This place is a hangout for Chicago Cubs fans and makes a good dinner stop on the way back from driving the Apache Trail. There's a second Blue Adobe at 10885 N. Frank Lloyd Wright Blvd., Scottsdale (✆ **480/314-0550**).

144 N. Country Club Dr., Mesa. ✆ **480/962-1000.** www.blueadobegrille.com. Reservations recommended. Main courses $9–$24. AE, DC, DISC, MC, V. Sun–Thurs 11am–9pm; Fri–Sat 11am–10pm.

House of Tricks ★★ NEW AMERICAN Despite the name, you'll find far more treats here than tricks. Housed in a pair of old Craftsman bungalows surrounded by a garden of shady trees, this restaurant seems a world away from the bustle on nearby Mill Avenue. This is a nice spot for a romantic evening and a good place to try some innovative cuisine. The garlicky Caesar salad and house-smoked salmon with avocado, capers, and lemon cream are good bets for starters. Among the entrees, the seared ahi tuna is a good choice. Try to get a seat on the grape-arbor–covered patio.

114 E. Seventh St., Tempe. ✆ **480/968-1114.** www.houseoftricks.com. Reservations recommended. Main courses $7.25–$12 lunch, $22–$34 dinner. AE, DISC, MC, V. Mon–Sat 11am–10pm.

Monti's La Casa Vieja ★ AMERICAN If you're tired of the Scottsdale glitz and are looking for Old Arizona, try this place. The adobe building was constructed in 1873 (*casa vieja* means "old house" in Spanish) on the site of the Salt River ferry, which operated in the days when the river flowed year-round. Today, local families know Monti's well and rely on the restaurant for solid meals and low prices—you can get a filet mignon for as little as $12. The dark dining rooms are filled with memorabilia of the Old West.

100 S. Mill Ave. (at Rio Salado Pkwy.), Tempe. ✆ **480/967-7594.** www.montis.com. Reservations recommended for dinner. Main courses $10–$33. AE, DC, DISC, MC, V. Sun–Thurs 11am–10pm; Fri–Sat 11am–11pm.

INEXPENSIVE

Organ Stop Pizza ★ *Kids* PIZZA The pizza here may not be the best in town, but the mighty Wurlitzer theater organ, the largest in the world, sure is memorable. This massive instrument, which contains more than 5,500 pipes, has four turbine blowers to provide the wind to create the sound, and with 40-foot ceilings in the restaurant, the acoustics are great. As you marvel at the skill of the organist, who performs songs ranging from the latest pop tunes to *The Phantom of the Opera,* you can enjoy simple pizzas, pastas, or snacks.

1149 E. Southern Ave. (at Stapley Dr.), Mesa. ✆ **480/813-5700.** www.organstoppizza.com. Reservations for large groups only. Pizzas and pastas $5–$17. No credit cards. Thanksgiving to mid-Apr Sun–Thurs 4–9pm, Fri–Sat 4–10pm; mid-Apr to Thanksgiving Sun–Thurs 5–9pm, Fri–Sat 5–10pm.

Ted's Hot Dogs *Finds* AMERICAN Would you stand in line 30 minutes for a hot dog? No? You might want to reconsider and drop by Ted's Hot Dogs at the corner of Broadway and McClintock Drive in Tempe. At this, the only Arizona outpost of a small chain of hot dog stands in western New York state, there always seems to be a line, but no one seems to mind the wait. The dogs are all charcoal-broiled, and you get to pick what toppings you want (I always get the special hot sauce). Sure it's going to take you less time to eat your dog than to order it, but these pups are so tasty they're well worth the wait.

1755 E. Broadway, Tempe. ✆ **480/968-6678.** Main dishes $2–$5. No credit cards. Mon–Thurs 10am–9pm; Fri–Sat 10am–10pm; Sun 10:30am–9pm.

CHANDLER & GILBERT

EXPENSIVE

Kai ★★★ NEW AMERICAN With a menu overseen by Tucson's celebrated Janos Wilder and ingredients that are frequently sourced from Native American tribes around the country, the food at Kai is as adventurous and alluring as any you'll find in Arizona. Whether you order buffalo tenderloin with saguaro-blossom syrup and cholla-cactus flower buds, or scallops dusted with dried mango and sandalwood, you'll savor some of the most exotic flavors in the Southwest. Add service that is second to none in the state and, if you're lucky, a big-sky sunset for an unforgettable meal, and there just isn't another restaurant in the state to compare with Kai.

5594 W. Wild Horse Pass Blvd., Chandler. ✆ **602/225-0100.** Reservations highly recommended. Main courses $34–$50; tasting menu $100–$165 ($140–$225 w/wine). AE, DC, DISC, MC, V. Tues–Thurs 5:30–9:30pm; Fri–Sat 5:30–10pm. Closed first 3 weeks in Aug.

INEXPENSIVE

Guedo's ★ *Finds* MEXICAN Taco stands are a peso a dozen around the greater Phoenix metro area, but few have the cult following of Guedo's Taco Shop in downtown Chandler. Located at the corner of Chandler Boulevard and Arizona Avenue, this colorful place looks as if it were transported from a Mexican beach town. The patios even have sand floors and palm-thatched shade umbrellas. The food is simple yet fresh and bursting with flavor. Order two or three tacos (I like the fish and shrimp tacos), and then load them with toppings from the salsa bar. Accompany your meal with a cold beer or a margarita, and you just might forget you're still in the States.

71 E. Chandler Blvd., Chandler. ✆ **480/899-7841.** Main dishes $2–$6.50. No credit cards. Tues–Sat 11am–9pm.

Joe's Farm Grill ★★ *Kids* AMERICAN Gilbert is a booming suburb southeast of Phoenix; before I ate at Joe's, I hardly knew where Gilbert was. However, now that you can get from Scottsdale to Gilbert entirely on freeways (and in as little as 30 minutes if it isn't rush hour), there's no reason not to search out this unique eatery. Designed to resemble a 1950s burger stand and set in the middle of a farm that's part of a new housing development, Joe's serves creative comfort food and is a huge hit with families. There are big salads with a various toppings, barbecued ribs, chicken sandwiches, pizzas, and, best of all, burgers that just might be the best in the valley.

3000 E. Ray Rd., Gilbert. ✆ **480/563-4745.** www.joesfarmgrill.com. Main dishes $5.50–$20. AE, DISC, MC, V. Sun–Thurs 11am–9pm; Fri–Sat 11am–11pm.

DINING WITH A VIEW

elements ★★ NEW AMERICAN When you've got one of the best views around and some of the best patio dining, do you really have to serve good food? Probably not, but luckily, elements, the stylish restaurant at the Sanctuary on Camelback Mountain resort, doesn't try to slide by on looks alone; it also serves great food. That said, the view is a big part of dinner here, so try to make a reservation so that you can catch the sunset light on Mummy Mountain. The menu changes regularly and includes influences from around the world. On the appetizer menu, expect the likes of crab-and-spinach fondue; Japanese-style escargot; and tuna tartare on crisp cucumbers. Entrees are equally wide ranging in their culinary influences; the seasonal menu might include spiced venison loin or ginger-cured pork tenderloin. If you'll be eating inside, try to get one of the lower-level booths.

At Sanctuary on Camelback, 5700 E. McDonald Dr., Paradise Valley. ✆ **800/298-9766** or 480/607-2300. www.elementsrestaurant.com. Reservations highly recommended. Main courses $12–$21 lunch, $27–$36 dinner. AE, DC, DISC, MC, V. Mon–Thurs 7–10:30am, 11:30am–2pm, and 6–9:30pm; Fri–Sat 7–10:30am, 11:30am–2pm, and 6–10pm; Sun 7am–2pm (brunch) and 6–9:30pm.

COWBOY STEAKHOUSES

Cowboy steakhouses are family restaurants that generally provide big portions of grilled steaks and barbecued ribs, outdoor and "saloon" dining, live country music, and various other sorts of entertainment.

Rawhide Steakhouse ★★ *Kids* STEAK Of the many cowboy steakhouses around the valley, this is by far your best bet for a family dinner. Not only are the steaks some of the best you'll find at a family steakhouse, but there's an entire Western town mock-up surrounding the restaurant, so there's plenty to keep you and your kids entertained before and after dinner. If you feel adventurous, start your meal with some rattlesnake or "Rocky Mountain oysters" (bull's testicles). Cowboy bands keep the crowds entertained during dinner. From February to June, there are also sundown cookouts ($45 adults, $19 children) that include a hayride, chuck-wagon dinner, live country music, and lots of other traditional Wild West entertainment.

5700 W. North Loop Rd., Chandler. ✆ **480/502-5600.** www.rawhide.com. Reservations accepted only for parties of 9 or more. Main courses $17–$30. AE, DC, DISC, MC, V. Early Oct to late May Mon–Thurs 5–10pm, Fri–Sun 11:30am–3pm and 5–10pm; late May to early Oct daily 4–9pm.

Reata Pass ★ STEAK This is by far the most authentic cowboy steakhouse in the Phoenix area. Part of the large restaurant is even housed in an old stagecoach stop, and the building incorporates an adobe building that dates back to 1862. With live music and a huge patio set with picnic tables, this place is a nonstop party. In the warmer months, have your steak out under the stars or the clear blue Sonoran Desert sky. In business since the 1950s, this rustic roadhouse, its bar ceiling plastered with dollar bills, is a local favorite, a place to see what Phoenix was like before it began to sprawl. Check the website for discount coupons.

27500 N. Alma School Pkwy. ✆ **480/585-7277.** www.reatapass.com. Reservations recommended. Main courses $7–$35. AE, DC, DISC, MC, V. Sun–Thurs 11am–10pm; Fri–Sat 11am–11pm.

Rustler's Rooste ★ *Kids* STEAKHOUSE This location, in the middle of a sprawling golf resort, doesn't exactly seem like cowboy country. However, up at the top of the hill, you'll find a fun Western-themed restaurant where you can start your evening by scooting down a big slide from the bar to the main dining room. There's a good view over the city, and cowboy bands play for those who like to kick up their heels. Daring diners always start with the rattlesnake appetizer and follow up with the enormous cowboy "stuff" platter, which includes steak and seafood kabobs, barbecued pork ribs, fried shrimp, barbecued chicken, and cowboy beans.

At the Pointe South Mountain Resort, 8383 S. 48th St., Phoenix. ✆ **602/431-6474.** www.rustlersrooste.com. Reservations accepted for 8 or more, but there's a call-ahead waiting list. Main courses $15–$30. AE, DC, DISC, MC, V. Daily 5–10pm.

ESPRESSO BARS, BAKERIES & ICE CREAM PARLORS

Perhaps it's the heat or the sunshine, but espresso is not the ubiquitous drink in Phoenix that it is in many other parts of the country. However, there are still plenty of places to get a good latte or cappuccino. In Scottsdale, try **The Village Coffee Roastery,** 8120 N. Hayden Rd., Suite E-104 (✆ **480/905-0881;** www.villagecoffee.com), which roasts its own beans and makes what just might be the best lattes in Scottsdale. Alternatively, try **The Coffee Bean & Tea Leaf,** which has locations in the Shops at Gainey Village, 8877 N. Scottsdale Rd. (✆ **480/315-9335;** www.coffeebean.com); and at 4513 N. Scottsdale Rd. (✆ **480/946-1581**), which is at the corner of Scottsdale and Camelback roads.

Up on the north side of the Valley, I always get my latte at **Cave Creek Coffee Company,** 6033 E. Cave Creek Rd., Cave Creek (✆ **480/488-0603;** www.cavecreekcoffee.com), which doubles as a wine bar and the Valley's best live-music venue.

Along the Camelback Corridor, there's **Hava Java,** 3166 E. Camelback Rd. (✆ **602/954-9080**), in the Safeway Shopping Center. Not far from the Heard Museum, **Lux,** 4404 N. Central Ave. (✆ **602/266-6469**), serves the best espresso in Phoenix. It's also the hippest espresso bar in town. Right next door there's a great little bakery run by the owners of Pizzeria Bianco.

If ever there were a place where ice cream is a necessity, it is Arizona. In the desert heat, ice cream is a survival food, a means to cool off when the temperatures soar. When the heat gets to be too much for you, head to some of these great chill-out spots. Scottsdale's **Sugar Bowl,** 4005 N. Scottsdale Rd. (✆ **480/946-0051**), in the heart of Old Town, is a longtime locals' favorite that has been immortalized in "Family Circus" cartoons. If you find yourself dying from the heat as you motor through central Phoenix on a toasty afternoon, there's no better antidote than **Mary Coyle,** 5521 N. Seventh Ave. (✆ **602/265-0405;** www.marycoyle.net), which makes its own ice cream and has been in business for more than 50 years. However, the absolute cream of the crop is The Phoenician resort's **Café & Ice Cream Parlour,** 6000 E. Camelback Rd. (✆ **480/941-8200**). Not only can you cool off with house-made ice cream, but the pastries here are positively divine. To top it all off, you get to hang out at this posh resort for as long as you can make your ice cream last. If old-fashioned ice cream just doesn't do it for you, and you absolutely have to have gelato, check out **The Gelato Spot,** 3164 E. Camelback Rd. (✆ **602/957-8040;** www.gelatospot.com), which is right next door to Hava Java in the Safeway shopping plaza.

If you've just spent half the day at the Heard Museum and suddenly find yourself craving a cupcake or an almond-peach tart, head down Central Avenue to **Tammie Coe Cakes,** 610 E. Roosevelt St., no. 145 (✆ **602/253-0829;** www.tammiecoecakes.com), a tiny pastry shop in downtown Phoenix. The cases here are filled with irresistibly tempting goodies. There's a second Tammie Coe Cakes at 4410 N. 40th St. (✆ **602/840-3644**). For equally tasty treats in an artistic setting, head south of downtown Phoenix to **City Bakery at Bentley Projects,** 215 E. Grant St. (✆ **602/253-7200;** www.citybakeryaz.com), which is located in the same building that houses the impressive Bentley Projects art gallery. The bakery is affiliated with Arcadia Farms (earlier in this chapter), a local restaurant chain with cafes at the Phoenix Art Museum and the Heard Museum.

BREAKFAST, BRUNCH & QUICK BITES

Most of Phoenix's best Sunday brunches are to be had at restaurants in major hotels and resorts. Among the finest are those served at **Marquesa** (at the Scottsdale Princess,

CLOSED
due to
accidental demolition

WEGEN BISSIGEN
EICHHÖRNCHEN GESCHLOSSEN

CERRADO
CABRAS

Κλειστό
Μετεωρίτες

POOL CLOSED
プールも
閉鎖中
ELECTRIC EELS

FECHADO!
POR CAUSA DE
ATAQUES DOS CROCODILOS

Hotel
closed for
facelifting

FERMÉ POUR
RAISON
DE GRÈVE
DES BONNES
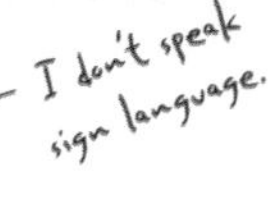
I don't speak
sign language.

A hotel can close for all kinds of reasons.

Our Guarantee ensures that if your hotel's undergoing construction, we'll let you know in advance. In fact, we cover your entire travel experience. See www.travelocity.com/guarantee for details.

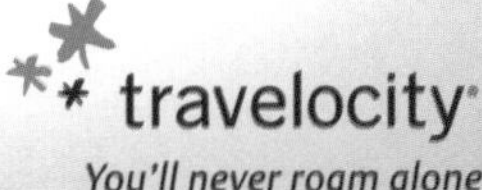
travelocity
You'll never roam alone.

©2007 Travelocity.com LP. CST# 2056372-50.

Frommers.com

So many places, so little time?

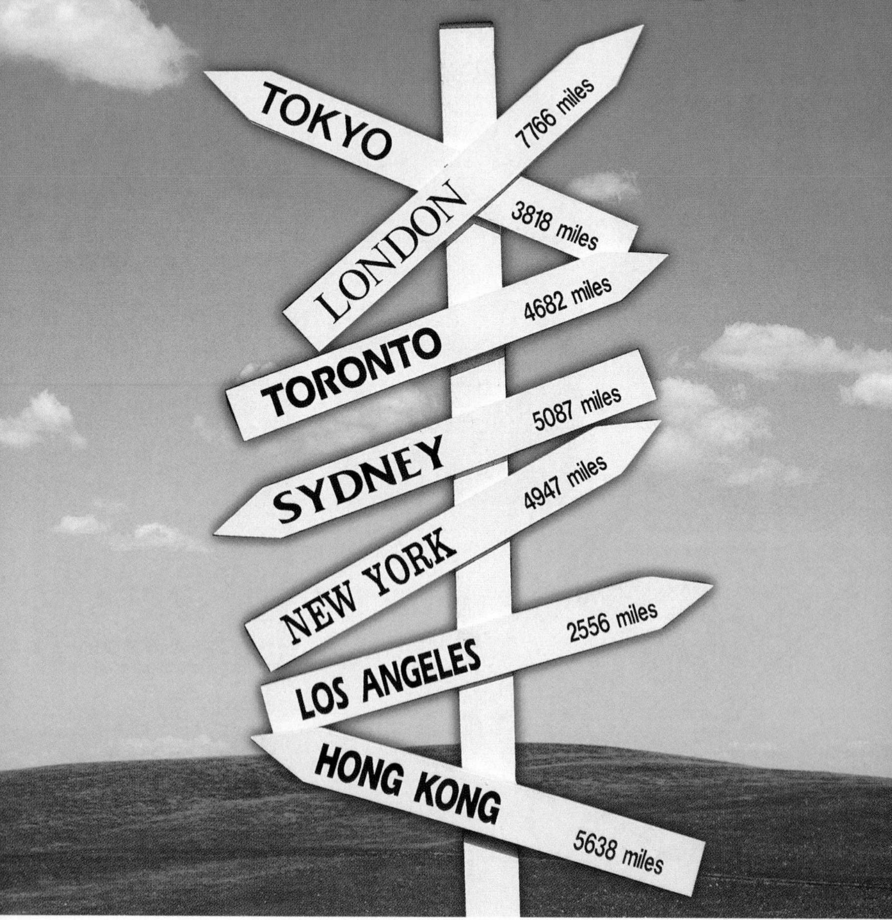

Frommers.com makes the going fast and easy.

Find a destination. ✓ Buy a guidebook. ✓ Book a trip. ✓ Get hot travel deals.
Enter to win vacations. ✓ Check out the latest travel news.
Share trip photos and memories. ✓ Download podcasts. ✓ And much more.

Frommers.com

Rated #1 Travel Web Site by *PC Magazine*®

p. 94), **LON's** (at the Hermosa Inn, p. 112), **T. Cook's** (at the Royal Palms Resort and Spa, p. 113), the **Terrace Dining Room** (at The Phoenician, p. 89), and **Top of the Rock** (at The Buttes, A Marriott Resort, p. 99). However, for a unique experience, make a brunch reservation at **Geordie's at the Wrigley Mansion Club,** 2501 E. Telawa Trail (© **602/955-4079**). The meal is served in the historic mansion built by chewing gum. Brunch here is served Sunday from 10:30am to 2pm and costs $42 ($21 for children 12 and under).

The **Desert Botanical Garden,** 1201 N. Galvin Pkwy., in Papago Park (© **480/941-1225;** www.dbg.org), has picnic lunches available during its Music in the Garden concerts held on Sundays from September to March. Concert tickets are $16 and include admission to the gardens, but meals cost extra.

If your idea of the perfect breakfast is a buttery croissant and a good cup of coffee, try **La Madeleine,** 3102 E. Camelback Rd. (© **602/952-0349;** www.lamadeleine.com), *the* place for a leisurely French breakfast amid antique farm implements.

For smoothies, muffins, and healthful things, try **Wild Oats Natural Marketplace,** which has stores at 3933 E. Camelback Rd. at 40th Street (© **602/954-0584;** www.wildoats.com); and at 8688 E. Raintree Dr., Scottsdale (© **480/368-1279**).

5 Seeing the Sights

THE DESERT & ITS NATIVE CULTURES

Although the **Sears-Kay Ruins** 15 miles northeast of Cave Creek have never been restored and are, in fact, in ruins, they are close enough to north Scottsdale to be well worth searching out. They're also just far enough away to feel like a real discovery. It's an easy 1-mile round-trip hike to this hilltop Hohokam pueblo ruin, and along the way, interpretive plaques explain aspects of Hohokam culture. The pueblo, which dates to between 1050 and 1500, consisted of 40 rooms in four compounds. To find the ruins, head northeast from Carefree on Cave Creek Road, which becomes first Seven Springs Road and then Forest Service Road 24. For more information, contact the Tonto National Forest's Cave Creek Ranger District, 40202 N. Cave Creek Rd., Scottsdale (© **480/595-3300;** www.fs.fed.us/r3/tonto/home).

On the south side of the Superstition Mountains, near the Gold Canyon Resort, a relatively short hike will lead you to a small canyon where ancient petroglyphs cover a rock wall beside several pools of water. Known as **Hieroglyphic Canyon,** this rock-art site is reached via a 1.1-mile trail up a gentle slope through dense stands of cactus. To reach the trail head, drive east from Phoenix on U.S. 60 to Gold Canyon. Turn

---

Tips **Show Up Now for Savings**

If your Phoenix vacation plans include museum-hopping and you're good at planning a day's sightseeing, you should consider buying a **Show Up Now Pass** (© **602/971-2223;** www.showupnowpass.com). These passes provide discounts on admissions to numerous attractions around the Valley of the Sun and come in 1-day ($18 adults, $10 children ages 3–12), 2-day ($34 adults, $12 children) and 5-day ($49 adults, $16 children) passes, While the 1-day pass provides admission to up to 15 attractions and is a great deal, you'll have to do a lot of running around to get your money's worth.

Phoenix, Scottsdale & the Valley of the Sun Attractions

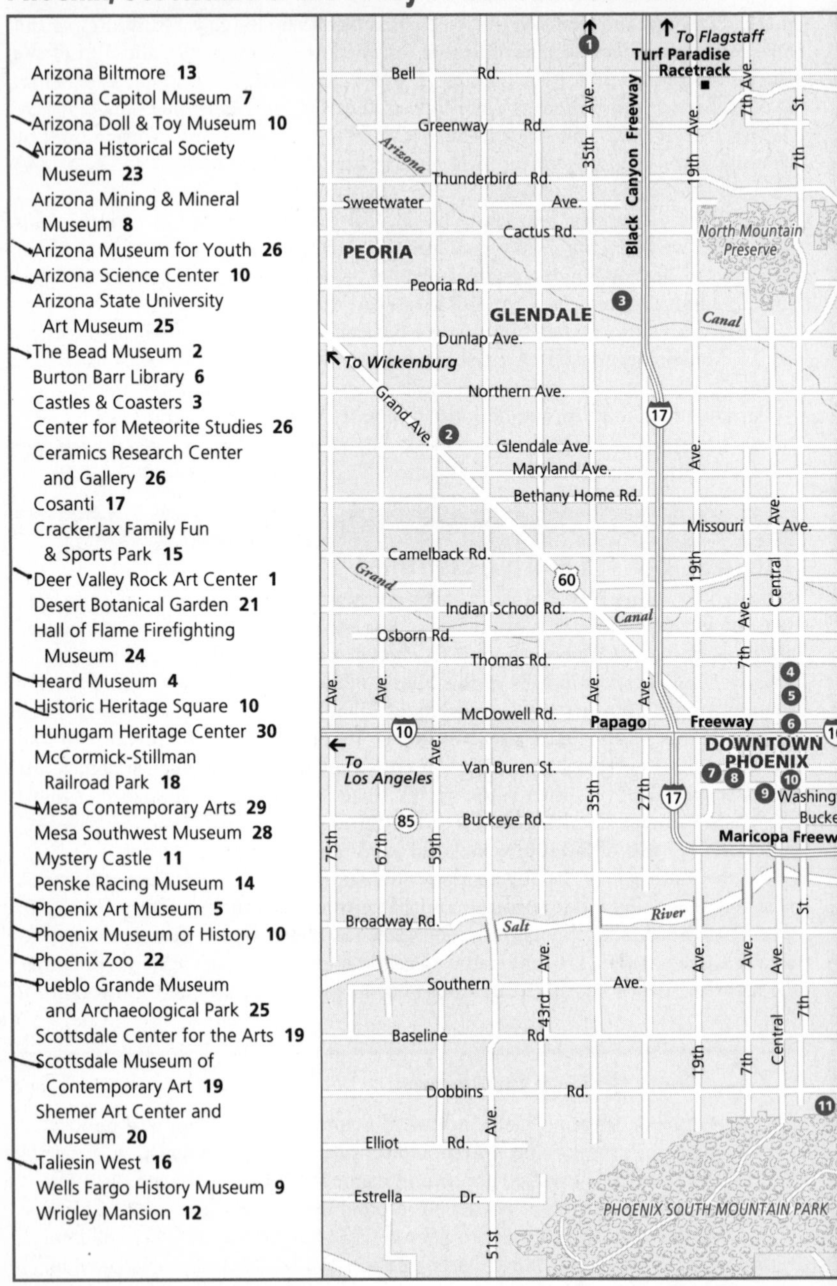
Arizona Biltmore 13
Arizona Capitol Museum 7
Arizona Doll & Toy Museum 10
Arizona Historical Society Museum 23
Arizona Mining & Mineral Museum 8
Arizona Museum for Youth 26
Arizona Science Center 10
Arizona State University Art Museum 25
The Bead Museum 2
Burton Barr Library 6
Castles & Coasters 3
Center for Meteorite Studies 26
Ceramics Research Center and Gallery 26
Cosanti 17
CrackerJax Family Fun & Sports Park 15
Deer Valley Rock Art Center 1
Desert Botanical Garden 21
Hall of Flame Firefighting Museum 24
Heard Museum 4
Historic Heritage Square 10
Huhugam Heritage Center 30
McCormick-Stillman Railroad Park 18
Mesa Contemporary Arts 29
Mesa Southwest Museum 28
Mystery Castle 11
Penske Racing Museum 14
Phoenix Art Museum 5
Phoenix Museum of History 10
Phoenix Zoo 22
Pueblo Grande Museum and Archaeological Park 25
Scottsdale Center for the Arts 19
Scottsdale Museum of Contemporary Art 19
Shemer Art Center and Museum 20
Taliesin West 16
Wells Fargo History Museum 9
Wrigley Mansion 12
To Flagstaff
Turf Paradise Racetrack
Bell Rd.
Greenway Rd.
Arizona
Thunderbird Rd.
Sweetwater Ave.
Cactus Rd.
Black Canyon Freeway
North Mountain Preserve
PEORIA
Peoria Rd.
GLENDALE
Canal
Dunlap Ave.
To Wickenburg
Northern Ave.
Grand Ave.
Glendale Ave.
Maryland Ave.
Bethany Home Rd.
Missouri Ave.
Camelback Rd.
Grand
Indian School Rd.
Canal
Osborn Rd.
Thomas Rd.
McDowell Rd.
Papago Freeway
DOWNTOWN PHOENIX
To Los Angeles
Van Buren St.
Washingt
Buckeye Rd.
Buckey
Maricopa Freewa
Broadway Rd.
Salt River
Southern Ave.
Baseline Rd.
Dobbins Rd.
Elliot Rd.
Estrella Dr.
PHOENIX SOUTH MOUNTAIN PARK
75th Ave.
67th Ave.
59th Ave.
51st Ave.
43rd Ave.
35th Ave.
27th Ave.
19th Ave.
7th Ave.
Central Ave.
7th St.

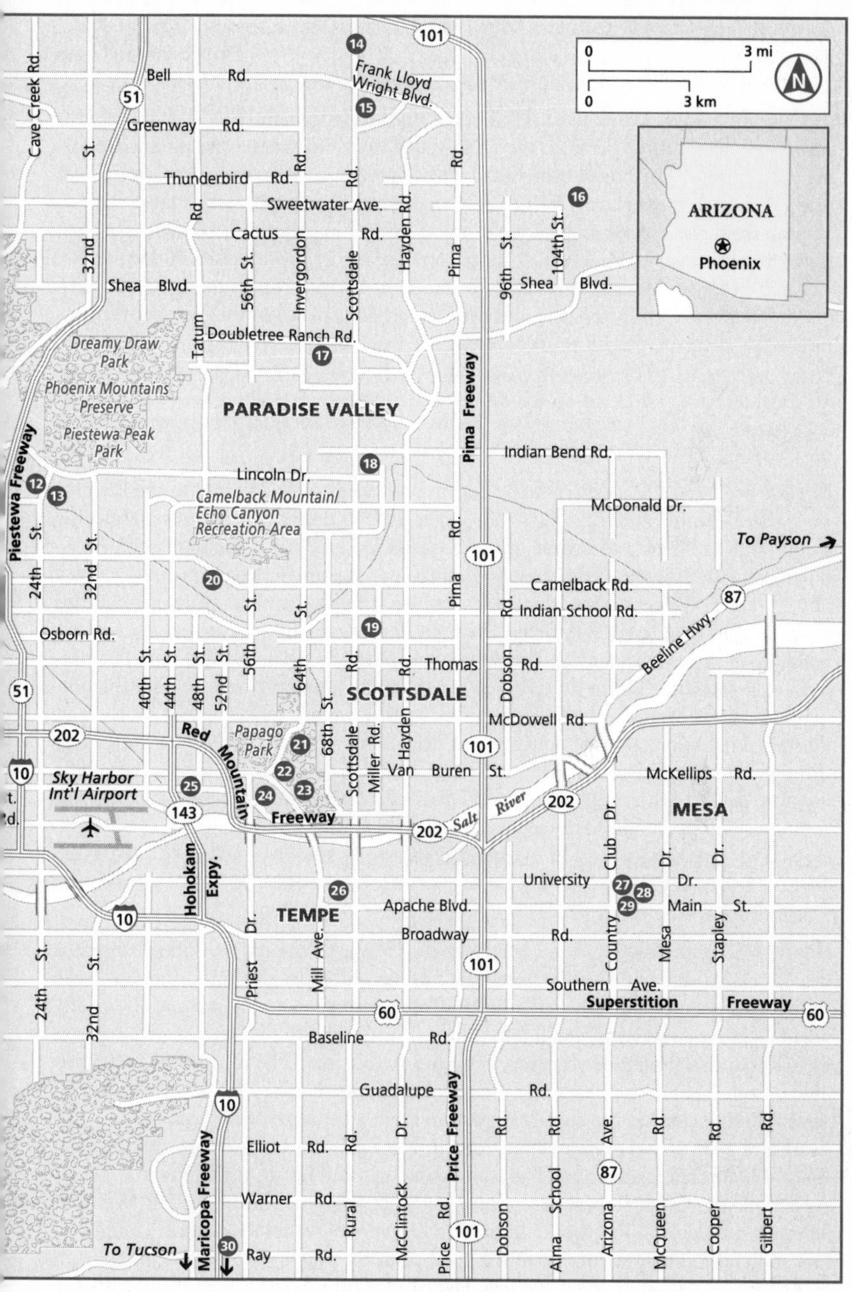

PARADISE VALLEY
SCOTTSDALE
TEMPE
MESA
ARIZONA
Phoenix
Sky Harbor Int'l Airport
Dreamy Draw Park
Phoenix Mountains Preserve
Piestewa Peak Park
Camelback Mountain/ Echo Canyon Recreation Area
Papago Park
Salt River
Pima Freeway
Piestewa Freeway
Red Mountain Freeway
Hohokam Expy.
Superstition Freeway
Price Freeway
Maricopa Freeway
Beeline Hwy.
Frank Lloyd Wright Blvd.
To Payson
To Tucson
3 mi
3 km

north on King's Ranch Road and follow this road to a right turn onto Baseline Road. Then turn left on Mohican Road, left again on Valley View Drive, and right on Cloudview Avenue, which leads into the trail head parking lot.

Deer Valley Rock Art Center ★ Located in the Hedgepeth Hills in the northwest corner of the Valley of the Sun, the Deer Valley Rock Art Center preserves an amazing concentration of Native American petroglyphs, some of which date back 5,000 years. Although these petroglyphs may not at first seem as impressive as those at more famous sites, the sheer numbers make this a fascinating spot. The drawings, which range from simple spirals to much more complex renderings of herds of deer, are on volcanic boulders along a quarter-mile trail. An interpretive center provides background information on this site and on rock art in general. From October through early May, there are guided tours Saturday at 10am.

3711 W. Deer Valley Rd. ✆ **623/582-8007.** www.asu.edu/clas/anthropology/dvrac. Admission $5 adults, $3 seniors and students, $2 children 6–12. Oct–Apr Tues–Sat 9am–5pm, Sun noon–5pm; May–Sept Tues–Fri 8am–2pm, Sat 9am–5pm, Sun noon–5pm. Closed major holidays. Take the Loop 101 highway west to 27th Ave., go north to Deer Valley Rd., and go west 2½ miles to just past 35th Ave.

Desert Botanical Garden ★★★ Located in Papago Park adjacent to the Phoenix Zoo, this botanic garden displays more than 20,000 desert plants from around the world, and its Plants and People of the Sonoran Desert Trail is the state's best introduction to Southwestern ethnobotany (human use of plants). Along this trail you can make your own yucca-fiber brush and practice grinding corn as Native Americans once did. On the Desert Wildflower Trail, you'll find colorful wildflowers throughout much of the year. Each spring, there's usually a butterfly pavilion filled with live butterflies. If you come late in the day, you can stay until after dark and see night-blooming flowers and dramatically lit cacti. A cafe on the grounds makes a great lunch spot. During the cooler months, concerts are held in the garden. From late November through late December, during *Las Noches de las Luminarias,* the gardens are lit at night by *luminarias* (candles inside small bags). By early 2008, the garden's cactus and succulent houses should have reopened after an extensive renovation.

In Papago Park, 1201 N. Galvin Pkwy. ✆ **480/941-1225.** www.dbg.org. Admission $10 adults, $9 seniors, $5 students 13–18, $4 children 3–12. Oct–Apr daily 8am–8pm; May–Sept daily 7am–8pm. Closed July 4th, Thanksgiving, and Christmas. Bus: 3.

Heard Museum ★★★ The Heard Museum is one of the nation's finest museums dealing exclusively with Native American cultures and is an ideal introduction to the indigenous peoples of Arizona. From pre-Columbian to contemporary, if it's art created by Native Americans, you'll find it here. If you're interested in the native cultures of Arizona, this should be your very first stop in the state. The museum is an invaluable introduction to the state's many tribes. The **Home: Native Peoples of the Southwest** exhibit examines the culture of each of the major tribes of the region and is the heart and soul of the museum. Included in this exhibit are more than 500 kachina dolls. In another gallery, you'll find fascinating exhibits of contemporary Native American art. Guided tours are offered daily. The annual **Guild Indian Fair and Market,** held on the first weekend in March, includes traditional dances along with arts and crafts. The museum's cafe is a good place for lunch.

The museum also operates the new **Heard Museum North,** 32633 N. Scottsdale Rd. (✆ **480/488-9817**), in Carefree. This gallery features changing exhibits and is open Monday through Saturday from 10am to 5:30pm, and Sunday from noon to

Moments **Native Trails in Scottsdale**

The sound of drumming coming from the Scottsdale Mall is insistent and irresistible, and if you happen to be shopping in Old Town Scottsdale and hear that drumming, be sure to follow the sound to its source. On a stage in front of the Scottsdale Center for the Arts, you'll find members of several Native American tribes performing traditional songs and dances. The show is a cross-cultural journey and is a great way to learn a bit about a few native cultures. The free programs, called **Native Trails,** are held January through mid-April on most Tuesdays, Thursdays, and Saturdays between noon and 1:30pm, and are part of the **Culture Quest Scottsdale** (✆ **480/421-1004;** www.culturequestscottsdale.com) program, which includes a variety of seasonal programming geared toward tourists.

5pm. Admission is $3 for adults and is free for children under 6. A third museum—**Heard Museum West**—is located in the city of Surprise at 16126 N. Civic Center Plaza (✆ **623/344-2200**). This museum is open Tuesday through Sunday from 9:30am to 5pm. Admission is $5 for adults, $4 for seniors, $2 for students, and free for children under 6. Both of these satellite museums are free for all on the second Sunday of each month.

2301 N. Central Ave. ✆ **602/252-8848.** www.heard.org. Admission $10 adults, $9 seniors, $5 students, $3 children 6–12. Daily 9:30am–5pm. Closed major holidays. Bus: Blue (B), Red (R), or O.

Huhugam Heritage Center ★ This architectural gem adjacent to the Sheraton Wild Horse Pass Resort is operated by the Pima and Maricopa tribes and offers a glimpse into the cultural heritage of the two tribes. Although the center has only a few small exhibits, it is well worth a visit for its architecture and ethnobotanical garden. The center complex is built within a huge berm that was designed to resemble a giant pot buried in the ground. Exhibits include an outstanding display of Pima and Maricopa baskets dating back to the 1920s.

4759 N. Maricopa Rd., Chandler. ✆ **520/796-3500.** www.huhugam.com. Admission $5 adults, $3 seniors and students, $2 children 6–12. Thurs–Sat 10am–4pm. Take Exit 164 (Queen Creek Rd.) off I-10 and continue 1 mile west.

Pueblo Grande Museum and Archaeological Park Located near Sky Harbor Airport and downtown Phoenix, the Pueblo Grande Museum and Archaeological Park houses the ruins of an ancient Hohokam village that was one of several villages along the Salt River between A.D. 300 and 1400. Sometime around 1450, this and other villages were mysteriously abandoned. Some speculate that drought and a buildup of salts from irrigation water reduced the fertility of the soil and forced the people to seek more fertile lands. The small museum here displays many of the artifacts that have been dug up on the site. Although these exhibits are actually more interesting than the ruins themselves, some furnished replicas of Hohokam-style houses give a good idea of how the Hohokam lived. The museum sponsors interesting workshops (some just for kids), demonstrations, and tours (including petroglyph hikes). The **Pueblo Grande Museum Indian Market,** held in mid-December at Steele Indian School Park, which is on the northeast corner of Indian School Road and Central Avenue, is the largest of its kind in the state and features more than 450 Native American artisans.

4619 E. Washington St. (between 44th and 48th sts.). ✆ **877/706-4408** or 602/495-0901. www.pueblogrande.com. Admission $2 adults, $1.50 seniors, $1 children 6–17; free on Sun. Mon–Sat 9am–4:45pm; Sun 1–4:45pm. Closed major holidays. Bus: 1.

ART MUSEUMS

Arizona State University Art Museum at Nelson Fine Arts Center ★ Although it isn't very large, this museum is memorable for its innovative architecture and excellent temporary exhibitions. With its purplish-gray stucco facade and pyramidal shape, the stark, angular building conjures up images of sunsets on desert mountains. The entrance is down a flight of stairs that leads to a cool underground garden area. Inside are galleries for crafts, prints, contemporary art, and Latin American art, along with outdoor sculpture courts and a gift shop. The collection of American art includes works by Georgia O'Keeffe, Edward Hopper, and John James Audubon. Definitely a must for both art and architecture fans. Across the street is the **Ceramics Research Center,** 10th Street and Mill Avenue (✆ **480/965-2787**), a gallery that showcases the university's extensive collection of fine-art ceramics. The latter gallery is open Tuesday through Saturday from 10am to 5pm and is another place not to miss. You just won't believe the amazing creativity on display.

10th St. and Mill Ave., Tempe. ✆ **480/965-2787.** http://asuartmuseum.asu.edu. Free admission. Tues 10am–9pm (10am–5pm in summer); Wed–Sat 10am–5pm. Closed major holidays. Bus: Red (R), 1, 66, or 72.

Mesa Contemporary Arts ★ Although this contemporary arts museum is not very large, it is the newest art museum in the Valley and is located in the Mesa Arts Center, which is one of the valley's architectural gems. You'll find the art museum down in a sunken courtyard beneath the arts center's sail-like canopies. Exhibits change regularly in the five small galleries, and there are occasional sculpture installations in the courtyard.

1 E. Main St., Mesa. ✆ **480/644-6500.** www.mesaartscenter.com. Admission $3.50, free for children 7 and under; free on Thurs. Tues–Wed 10am–5pm; Thurs–Sat 10am–8pm; Sun noon–5pm. Bus: Red (R) or 30.

Phoenix Art Museum ★★ This is one of the largest art museums in the Southwest, and within its labyrinth of halls and galleries is a respectable collection that spans the major artistic movements from the Renaissance to the present. Exhibits cover decorative arts, historical fashions, Spanish colonial furnishings and religious art, and, of course, works by members of the Cowboy Artists of America. The collection of modern and contemporary art is particularly good, with works by Diego Rivera, Frida Kahlo, Pablo Picasso, Alexander Calder, Henry Moore, Georgia O'Keeffe, Henri Rousseau, and Auguste Rodin. The popular Thorne Miniature Collection consists of tiny rooms on a scale of 1 inch to 1 foot. Because this museum is so large, it frequently mounts traveling blockbuster exhibits. The cafe here is a good spot for lunch.

Moments Love Story

Take a walk around the Scottsdale Mall, a refuge of green lawns and shade trees in downtown Scottsdale, and you just might fall in love—make that on *Love.* Robert Indiana's famous pop art *Love* image, the one with the skewed letter *O*—yes, the one that became a postage stamp—has been installed as a 12-foot-tall sculpture on the lawn outside the Scottsdale Center for the Arts.

1625 N. Central Ave. (at McDowell Rd.). ✆ **602/257-1222.** www.phxart.org. Admission $10 adults, $8 seniors and students, $4 children 6–17; free on Tues 3–9pm. Tues 10am–9pm; Wed–Sun 10am–5pm. Closed major holidays. Bus: Blue (B), Red (R), or O.

Scottsdale Museum of Contemporary Art ★★ Scottsdale may be obsessed with art featuring lonesome cowboys and solemn Indians, but this boldly designed museum makes it clear that patrons of contemporary art are also welcome here. Cutting-edge art, from the abstract to the absurd, fills the galleries, with exhibits rotating every few months. In addition to the main building, there are several galleries in the adjacent Scottsdale Center for the Arts. Don't miss James Turrell's skyspace *Knight Rise,* which is accessed from a patio off the museum shop and can be visited for free. By the way, the museum shop is full of beautiful items that will fit in your suitcase.

7374 E. Second St., Scottsdale. ✆ **480/994-ARTS.** www.smoca.org. Admission $7 adults, $5 students, free for children under 15; free on Thurs. Early Sept to early June Tues–Wed and Fri–Sat 10am–5pm, Thurs 10am–8pm, Sun noon–5pm; early June to early Sept Wed noon–5pm, Thurs 10am–8pm, Fri–Sat 10am–5pm, Sun noon–5pm. Closed major holidays. Bus: 41, 50, or 72. Also accessible via Scottsdale Trolley shuttle bus.

Shemer Art Center and Museum ★ This art center may be small, but it mounts some of the more interesting little shows in the Valley. Exhibits change monthly and showcase Arizona artists. You might catch an exhibit of ceramic art, jewelry, or photography. The art center, which is housed in a 1920s Santa Fe mission-style home in the Arcadia neighborhood, also offers a variety of art classes. It's easy to miss as you're speeding along Camelback Road, so keep your eyes peeled.

5005 E. Camelback Rd. ✆ **602/262-4727.** www.phoenix.gov/shemer. Free admission. Mon and Wed–Fri 10am–5pm; Tues 10am–9pm; Sat 9am–1pm. Closed Veteran's Day, Thanksgiving (Thurs–Sat), Christmas. Bus: 50.

HISTORY MUSEUMS & HISTORIC LANDMARKS

Arizona Capitol Museum ★ In the years before Arizona became a state, the territorial capital moved from Prescott to Tucson, then back to Prescott, before finally settling in Phoenix. In 1898, a stately territorial capitol building was erected (with a copper roof to remind the local citizenry of the importance of that metal in the Arizona economy). Atop this copper roof was placed the statue *Winged Victory,* which still graces the old capitol building today. This building no longer serves as the actual state capitol, but has been restored to the way it appeared in 1912, the year Arizona became a state. Among the rooms on view are the senate and house chambers, as well as the governor's office. Excellent exhibits provide interesting perspectives on early Arizona events and lifestyles. There are free guided tours at 10am and 2pm.

1700 W. Washington St. ✆ **602/542-4675.** www.lib.az.us/museum. Free admission. Mon–Fri 8am–5pm. Closed state holidays. Bus: 1 or DASH downtown shuttle.

Arizona Historical Society Museum in Papago Park ★ This museum, at the headquarters of the Arizona Historical Society, focuses its well-designed exhibits on the history of central Arizona. Temporary exhibits on the lives and works of the people who helped shape this region are always the highlights of a visit. An interesting permanent exhibit features life-size statues of everyday people from Arizona's past (a Mexican miner, a Chinese laborer, and so on). Quotes relate their individual stories, while props reveal what items they might have traveled with during their days in the desert.

1300 N. College Ave. (just off Curry Rd.), Tempe. ✆ **480/929-0292.** www.arizonahistoricalsociety.org. Admission $5 adults, $4 seniors and students 12–18, free for children under 12; free on 1st Sat of each month. Tues–Sat 10am–4pm; Sun noon–4pm. Bus: 66.

Historic Heritage Square The city of Phoenix was founded in 1870, but today few of the city's early homes remain. However, if you have an appreciation for old houses and want a glimpse of how Phoenix once looked, stroll around this collection of historic homes, which stand on the original town site. All of the buildings are listed on the National Register of Historic Places, and although most are modest buildings from the early 20th century, one impressive Victorian home was built in 1895. Today, the buildings house museums, restaurants, and gift shops. The Eastlake Victorian Rosson House, furnished with period antiques, is open for tours. The Stevens House features the Arizona Doll & Toy Museum (see later in this chapter). The Teeter House (© **602/252-4682;** www.theteeterhouse.com) now serves as a Victorian tearoom (with cocktails and live jazz in the evening), the old Baird Machine Shop contains Pizzeria Bianco (see "Where to Dine," earlier in this chapter), and the Thomas House is home to Bar Bianco (see "Phoenix & Scottsdale After Dark," later in this chapter).

115 N. Sixth St., at Monroe. © **602/262-5029.** www.rossonhousemuseum.org. Rosson House tours $5 adults, $4 seniors and students, $2 children 6–12. Wed–Sat 10am–4pm; Sun noon–4pm. Hours vary for other buildings; call for information. Closed Easter, Thanksgiving, Christmas Eve, Christmas, and New Year's. Bus: Red (R), 0, 1, or DASH downtown shuttle.

Phoenix Museum of History ★ Located in the Heritage and Science Park in downtown Phoenix, this modern museum presents an interesting look at the history of a city that, to the casual visitor, might not seem to *have* any history. The modern design and interactive exhibits make this place much more interesting than your average local history museum. One unusual exhibit explores how "lungers" (tuberculosis sufferers) inadvertently helped originate the tourism industry in Arizona, while another exhibit looks at the once-popular occupation of ostrich farming.

105 N. Fifth St. © **602/253-2734.** www.pmoh.org. Admission $6 adults, $4 seniors and students, $3 children 7–12, free for children 6 and under. Tues–Sat 10am–5pm. Closed major holidays. Bus: Red (R), 0, 1, or DASH downtown shuttle.

Wells Fargo History Museum ★ *Finds* Yes, this museum is small, and, yes, it's run by the Wells Fargo Bank, but the collection of artifacts here goes a long way toward conjuring up the Wild West so familiar from Hollywood movies. Not only is there an original Wells Fargo stagecoach on display, but there are also gold nuggets to ogle, old photos from the *real* Wild West, and plenty of artifacts and memorabilia from the days of stagecoach travel. There are also original paintings by N. C. Wyeth and bronze sculptures by Frederic Remington and Charles Russell.

100 W. Washington St. © **602/378-1852.** www.wellsfargohistory.com. Free admission. Mon–Fri 9am–5pm. Closed major holidays. Bus: Red (R), 0, 1, or DASH downtown shuttle.

SCIENCE & INDUSTRY MUSEUMS

Arizona Science Center ★ *Kids* So, the kids weren't impressed with the botanical garden or the Native American artifacts at the Heard Museum. Bring 'em here. They can spend the afternoon pushing buttons, turning knobs, and interacting with all kinds of cool science exhibits. In the end, they might even learn something in spite of all the fun they have. The science center also includes a planetarium and a large-screen theater, both of which carry additional charges.

600 E. Washington St. © **602/716-2000.** www.azscience.org. Admission $9 adults, $7 seniors and children 3–12. Planetarium and film combination tickets also available. Daily 10am–5pm. Closed Thanksgiving and Christmas. Bus: Red (R), 0, 1, or DASH downtown shuttle.

Finds **Out-of-This-World Rocks**

On October 9, 1992, a meteorite slammed into a car in Peekskill, New York. It was a nightmare for the car's owner, but a dream come true for the tabloids. Here was a reminder of just how dangerous out-of-this-world rocks can be. You can see a piece of the Peekskill meteorite and dozens of other otherworldly rocks at Arizona State University's **Center for Meteorite Studies,** Bateman Physical Sciences Center, C wing, Room 139, Palm Walk and University Drive (✆ **480/965-6511;** http://meteorites.asu.edu), on the ASU campus. The center, which is just a single small room, is open Monday through Friday from 9am to 5pm, and admission is free.

Mesa Southwest Museum ★★ *Kids* This is one of the best museums in the Valley, and its wide variety of exhibits appeals to people with a range of interests. For the kids, there are animated dinosaurs on an indoor "cliff" with a roaring waterfall. Of course, there are also plenty of dinosaur skeletons. Also of interest are an exhibit on movies that have been filmed in the state, a display on Arizona mammoth kill sites, some old jail cells, and a walk-through mine mock-up with exhibits on the Lost Dutchman Mine. There's also a mock-up of a Hohokam village and an artificial cave filled with beautiful mineral specimens.

53 N. MacDonald St. (at First St.), Mesa. ✆ **480/644-2230.** www.mesasouthwestmuseum.com. Admission $8 adults, $7 seniors and students, $4 children 3–12. Tues–Fri 10am–3pm; Sat 11am–5pm; Sun 1–5pm. Closed major holidays. Bus: Red (R) or 30.

A MUSEUM MISCELLANY: PLANES, FLAMES, CARS & MORE

Arizona Mining & Mineral Museum Arizonans have been romancing the stones for more than a century at colorfully named mines such as the Copper Queen, Sleeping Beauty, and Lucky Boy. Out of such mines have come countless tons of copper, silver, and gold, as well as beautiful minerals with tongue-twisting names. Chalcanthite, chalcoaluminate, and chrysocolla are just some of the richly colored minerals on display at this small downtown museum. Rather than playing up the historical or profit-making side of the industry, exhibits focus on the amazing variety of Arizona minerals. Displays have a dated feel, but the beauty of the minerals themselves makes this an interesting stop.

1502 W. Washington St. ✆ **602/255-3795.** www.admmr.state.az.us. Admission $2 adults. Mon–Fri 8am–5pm; Sat 11am–4pm. Closed state holidays. Bus: 1 or DASH downtown shuttle.

The Bead Museum You'll see beads and body adornments from around the world at this interesting little museum in the Glendale antiques district. Beads both ancient and modern are on display, and exhibits often focus on such subjects as beaded bags, prayer beads, or natural beads.

5754 W. Glenn Dr., Glendale. ✆ **623/931-2737.** www.beadmuseumaz.org. Admission $4 adults, $2 children under 12 (free Thurs 5–8pm). Mon–Sat 10am–5pm (Thurs until 8pm); Sun 11am–4pm. Bus: 24.

Hall of Flame Firefighting Museum ★ *Kids* The world's largest firefighting museum houses a fascinating collection of vintage fire trucks. The displays date from a 1725 English hand pumper to several classic engines from the 20th century. All are beautifully restored and, mostly, fire-engine red. In all, more than 90 vehicles are on display.

At Papago Park, 6101 E. Van Buren St. ✆ **602/275-3473.** www.hallofflame.org. Admission $6 adults, $5 seniors, $4 students 6–17, $1.50 children 3–5, free for children under 3. Mon–Sat 9am–5pm; Sun noon–4pm. Closed New Year's Day, Thanksgiving, and Christmas. Bus: 3.

Penske Racing Museum ★ *Finds* At first you may think I've sent you to the local Jaguar dealer, but tucked inside the car dealerships here is the coolest little museum in Scottsdale. Inside this museum, you'll find the personal collection of Roger Penske, which includes more than a dozen immaculately maintained race cars, many of them Indianapolis 500 winners. If you follow Indy car racing, you know that the Penske team is the winningest team in the business, and the cars in here are why.

7125 E. Chauncey Lane, Scottsdale. ✆ **480/538-4444.** www.penskeracingmuseum.com. Free admission. Tues–Sat 8am–4pm; Sun noon–4pm.

ARCHITECTURAL HIGHLIGHTS

Arizona Biltmore This resort hotel, although not designed by Frank Lloyd Wright, shows the famed architect's hand in its distinctive cast-cement blocks. It also displays sculptures, furniture, and stained glass designed by Wright. The best way to soak up the ambience of this exclusive resort (if you aren't staying here) is over dinner, a cocktail, or tea. To learn more about the building, however, take a tour, given Tuesday, Thursday, and Saturday at 10am.

2400 E. Missouri Ave. ✆ **602/955-6600.** Tours $10 (free for resort guests).

Burton Barr Library This library is among the most daring pieces of public architecture in the city, and no fan of futuristic art or science fiction should miss it. The five-story cube is partially clad in enough ribbed copper sheeting to produce roughly 17.5 million pennies. The building's design makes use of the desert's plentiful sunshine to provide light for reading, but also incorporates computer-controlled louvers and shade sails to reduce heat and glare.

1221 N. Central Ave. ✆ **602/262-4636.** www.phoenixpubliclibrary.org. Free admission. Mon–Thurs 10am–9pm; Fri–Sat 10am–6pm; Sun noon–6pm. Bus: Red (R), Blue (B), or 0.

Cosanti This complex of cast-concrete structures served as a prototype and learning project for architect Paolo Soleri's much grander Arcosanti project, currently under construction north of Phoenix (see "En Route to Northern Arizona," later in this chapter). It's here at Cosanti that Soleri's famous bells are cast, and most weekday mornings you can see the foundry in action. Visit between 10am and noon Monday through Friday for the best chance of seeing bronze bells being poured.

6433 E. Doubletree Ranch Rd., Paradise Valley. ✆ **480/948-6145.** www.arcosanti.org. Free admission. Mon–Sat 9am–5pm; Sun 11am–5pm. Closed major holidays. Drive 1 mile west of Scottsdale Rd. on Doubletree Ranch Rd.

Mystery Castle ★ *Finds* Built for a daughter who longed for a castle more permanent than those built in the sand at the beach, Mystery Castle is a wondrous work of folk-art architecture. Boyce Luther Gulley, who had come to Arizona in hopes of curing his tuberculosis, constructed the castle during the 1930s and early 1940s using stones from the property. The resulting 18-room fantasy has 13 fireplaces, parapets, and many other unusual touches.

800 E. Mineral Rd. ✆ **602/268-1581.** Admission $5 adults, $3 children 5–15. Thurs–Sun 11am–4pm. Closed June–Sept. Take Seventh St. south to Mineral Rd. (2 miles south of Baseline Rd.).

Taliesin West ★★★ Frank Lloyd Wright loved the Arizona desert and, in 1937, built Taliesin West as a winter camp that served as his home, office, and school. Today

Hunt's Tomb: The Great Pyramid of Phoeni

If you're driving through Papago Park, perhaps on y Botanical Garden, and see a shimmering white pyramid o at first imagine that you're having a heat-induced halluc pyramid is real. However, it was *not* built by wandering Azte tians. It is the tomb of Gov. George W. P. Hunt, who was the f sixth, seventh, eighth, and tenth governor of Arizona. No ot in any state has served as many terms in office as Hunt, who was b 1859 and died in 1934. The tomb is accessible from a parking area near the zoo.

the buildings of Taliesin West are the headquarters of the Frank Lloyd Wright Foundation and School of Architecture.

Tours include a general introduction to Wright and his theories of architecture, and also explain the campus buildings. Wright believed in using local materials in his designs, and this is much in evidence at Taliesin West, where local stone was used for building foundations. With its open-walled buildings and patio areas, Taliesin West also showcases Wright's ability to integrate indoor and outdoor spaces.

For a brief introduction to Wright and his theories of architecture, take a basic introductory tour (listed below) or an Insights Tour ($19–$23), which will take you inside Wright's personal living area. There are also behind-the-scenes tours ($35–$45), guided desert walks ($25), apprentice shelter tours ($30), and night hikes ($25–$30). These latter tours are available only at certain times of year. Call ahead for schedule information.

12621 Frank Lloyd Wright Blvd. (at Cactus/114th St.), Scottsdale. © **480/860-8810** for information or 480/860-2700, ext. 494 or 495, for reservations. www.franklloydwright.org. Basic tours: Nov–Apr $18 adults, $16 seniors and students, $5 children 4–12; May–Oct $19 adults, $16 students and seniors, $10 children 4–12. Nov–Apr daily 9am–4:15pm; May–Oct daily 9am–4pm. Closed Tues–Wed July–Aug, Easter, Thanksgiving, Christmas, New Year's Day, and occasional special events. From Scottsdale Rd., go east on Shea Blvd. to 114th St., then north 1 mile to the entrance road.

Wrigley Mansion Situated on a hilltop adjacent to the Arizona Biltmore, this elegant mansion was built by chewing-gum magnate William Wrigley, Jr., between 1929 and 1931 as a present for his wife, Ada. Designed with Italianate styling, the mansion has so many levels and red-tile roofs that it looks like an entire village. The mansion is now a National Historic Landmark, with the interior restored to its original elegance. Tours of the mansion are offered 4 days a week and offer a fascinating glimpse into the lives of the Wrigleys.

2501 E. Telawa Trail. © **602/955-4079.** www.wrigleymansionclub.com. Tours $11; Wed–Sat 10am and 3pm.

WILD WEST THEME TOWNS

Despite a population running to the millions, Phoenix and Scottsdale occasionally like to present themselves as grown-up Wild West cow towns. But since there are more Ford Mustangs than wild mustangs around these parts, you'll have to get out of town way before sundown if you want a taste of the Old West. At the outer edges of the Valley, you'll find a couple of Hollywood-style cow towns that are basically tourist traps, but, hey, if you've got the kids along, you owe it to them to visit at least one of these places.

ek, founded as a gold-mining camp in the 1870s, is the last of the Valley at still has some semblance of Wild West character, but this is rapidly fading area real-estate prices skyrocket and Scottsdale's population center moves ever northward. Still, you'll see several steakhouses, saloons, and shops selling Western and Native American crafts and antiques. The main family attraction is a place called **Frontier Town,** which is right on Cave Creek Road in the center of town. It's a sort of mock cow town that also happens to be home to the Black Mountain Brewing Company, which brews Cave Creek Chili Beer. You can try this fiery beer at **The Original Crazy Ed's Satisfied Frog Saloon & Restaurant** (p. 111), located here in Frontier Town. Another popular local watering hole goes by the name of **The Horny Toad.** To learn more about the history of this area, stop in at the **Cave Creek Museum,** at Skyline Drive and Basin Road (© **480/488-2764;** www.cavecreekmuseum.org). It's open from October through May Wednesday, Thursday, Saturday, and Sunday from 1 to 4:30pm and Friday from 10am to 4:30pm. Admission is $3 for adults and $2 for seniors and students.

Goldfield Ghost Town ★ *Kids* Over on the east side of the Valley, just 4 miles northeast of Apache Junction, you'll find a reconstructed 1890s gold-mining town. Although it's a bit of a tourist trap—gift shops, an ice-cream parlor, and the like—it's also home to the **Goldfield Superstition Museum** (© **480/677-6463**), which has interesting exhibits on the history of the area. Of particular note is the exhibit on the Lost Dutchman gold mine, perhaps the most famous mine in the country, despite the fact that no one knows where it is. Goldfield Mine Tours provides guided tours of the gold mine beneath the town. The Superstition Scenic Narrow Gauge Railroad circles the town, and the **Goldfield Livery** (© **480/982-0133**) offers horseback riding and carriage rides. If you're here at lunchtime, you can get a meal at the steakhouse/saloon.

Ariz. 88, 4 miles northeast of Apache Junction. © **480/983-0333.** www.goldfieldghosttown.com. Museum admission $4 adults, $3 seniors, $1 children ages 5–12; train rides $5 adults, $4 seniors, $3 children 5–12; mine tours $6 adults, $5 seniors, $3 children 6–12; horseback rides $30 for 1 hr., $50 for 2 hr. Town daily 10am–5pm; museum, tour, and ride hours vary. Closed Christmas.

Rawhide at Wild Horse Pass *Kids* Sure, it's a tourist trap, but this fake cow town, originally located in north Scottsdale, is so much fun and such a quintessentially Phoenician experience that no family should get out of town without first moseying

---

Carefree Living

Carefree, a planned community established in the 1950s and popular with retirees, is much more subdued than its neighbor Cave Creek, which effects a sort of Wild West character. Ho Hum Road and Easy Street are just two local street names that reflect the sedate nature of Carefree, which is home to **The Boulders Resort & Golden Door Spa.** This resort boasts a spectacular setting, a 33,000-square-foot spa, and a couple of excellent restaurants. On Easy Street, in what passes for Carefree's downtown, you'll find one of the world's largest sundials. The dial is 90 feet across, and the gnomon (the part that casts the shadow) is 35 feet tall. In the middle of the dial are a pool of water and a fountain. Also downtown is a sort of reproduction Spanish-village shopping area, and just south of town, adjacent to The Boulders, is the upscale **el Pedregal** shopping center, with interesting boutiques, galleries, and a few restaurants.

---

down the dusty streets of Rawhide. Those streets are lined with lots of tourist shops and plenty of places for refreshments, including a steakhouse. Rawhide is run like other amusement parks in that you buy a bunch of $1 tickets and then trade various numbers of those tickets for performances (stunt shows, gunfights, trick-roping demonstrations) and activities and attractions (stagecoach, camel, and train rides; a mechanical bull; gold panning). There are also Saturday-night sundown cookouts ($45 adults, $19 children) with hayrides, live music, and storytellers. Throughout the year, lots of special events include rodeos.

5700 W. North Loop Rd., Chandler. ✆ **480/502-5600**. www.rawhide.com. Free admission (individual shows and rides priced separately). Hours vary with the seasons; call for details.

PARKS & ZOOS

Perhaps the most unusual park in the Phoenix metro area centers on **Tempe Town Lake,** 620 N. Mill Ave., Tempe (✆ **480/350-8625;** www.tempe.gov/rio), which was created in 1999 by damming the Salt River with inflatable dams. Tempe's 2-mile-long lake is lined with parks and bike baths on both the north and south shores. The best lake access is at Tempe Town Beach, at the foot of the Mill Avenue Bridge. Here you can rent kayaks and other small boats. Tempe Town Lake is the focus of a grand development plan that includes the new Tempe Center for the Arts.

Among the city's most popular parks are its natural areas and preserves. These include Phoenix South Mountain Park, Papago Park, Phoenix Mountains Preserve (site of Piestewa Peak), North Mountain Preserve, North Mountain Recreation Area, and Camelback Mountain–Echo Canyon Recreation Area. For more information on these parks, see "Hiking," "Bicycling," and "Horseback Riding" under "Outdoor Pursuits," below.

Not far from downtown Phoenix, you can wander around the **Steele Indian School Park,** at Third Street and Indian School Road (✆ **602/495-0739;** www.phoenix.gov/PARKS/sisp.html). This park, as its name implies, was once an Indian school. Several of the old buildings are still standing, but it's the many new fountains, gardens, and interpretive displays that make this park such a fascinating place. A stop here can easily be combined with a visit to the nearby Heard Museum.

Phoenix Zoo ★ *Kids* Forget about polar bears and other cold-climate creatures; this zoo focuses its attention primarily on animals that come from climates similar to that of the Phoenix area (the rainforest exhibit is an exception). Most impressive of the displays are the African savanna and the baboon colony. The Southwestern exhibits are also of interest, as are the giant Galápagos tortoises and the exhibit featuring monkeys from Central and South America. All animals are kept in naturalistic enclosures, and what with all the palm trees and tropical vegetation, the zoo sometimes manages to make you forget you're in the desert. Families will enjoy *Zoolights,* an after-hours holiday light display held late November to early January.

At Papago Park, 455 N. Galvin Pkwy. ✆ **602/273-1341**. www.phoenixzoo.org. Admission $14 adults, $9 seniors, $6 children 3–12. Oct to early Nov and early Jan to May daily 8am–5pm; early Nov to early Jan daily 8am–4pm; June–Sept Mon–Fri 7am–2pm, Sat–Sun 7am–4pm. Closed Christmas. Bus: 3.

ESPECIALLY FOR KIDS

In addition to the following suggestions, kids are likely to enjoy the Arizona Science Center, the Mesa Southwest Museum, the Hall of Flame Firefighting Museum, and the Phoenix Zoo—all described in detail earlier in this chapter.

Now *That's* a Fountain

Arizona loves its water features. Reservoirs, canals, pools, fountains—they're everywhere in the desert. You'd never think that water is in short supply around these parts. One of the most unusual water features is the Fountain Hills fountain, less than 20 miles northeast of Scottsdale. This fountain, for which the town is named, is the second-tallest fountain in the world. Using three 600-horsepower pumps, it can shoot water 560 feet into the air. However, the fountain usually operates on only two pumps, with the plume reaching a mere 330 feet on average. The fountain operates daily from 10am to 9pm every hour on the hour for 10 minutes. To find the fountain, take Shea Boulevard east from Scottsdale Road or U.S. 101. By the way, the tallest fountain (627 ft.) is the Gateway Geyser in East St. Louis, Illinois.

Arizona Doll & Toy Museum This small museum is located in the historic Stevens House on Heritage Square in downtown Phoenix. The miniature classroom peopled by doll students is a favorite exhibit. With dolls dating from the 19th century, this is a definite must for doll collectors.

At Heritage Sq., 602 E. Adams St. ✆ **602/253-9337.** Admission $3 adults, $1 children. Tues–Sat 10am–4pm; Sun noon–4pm. Closed Aug. Bus: Red (R), 0, 1, or DASH downtown shuttle.

Arizona Museum for Youth Using both traditional displays and participatory activities, this museum allows children to explore the fine arts and their own creativity. It's housed in a refurbished grocery store, and the highlight is Artville, an arts-driven kid-size town. Exhibits are geared mainly to toddlers through 12-year-olds, but all ages can work together to experience the activities.

35 N. Robson St. (between Main and First sts.), Mesa. ✆ **480/644-2467.** www.arizonamuseumforyouth.com. Admission $5, free for children under 1. Tues–Sat 10am–4pm; Sun noon–4pm. Closed all government holidays. Bus: Red (R) or 30.

Castles & Coasters Located adjacent to Metrocenter, one of Arizona's largest shopping malls, this small amusement park boasts an impressive double-loop roller coaster, plenty of tamer rides, four 18-hole miniature-golf courses, and a huge pavilion full of video games.

9445 N. Metro Pkwy. E. ✆ **602/997-7575.** www.castlesncoasters.com. Ride and game prices vary; all-day passes $23–$27. Daily (hours change seasonally; call ahead). Bus: Red (R) or 27.

CrackerJax Family Fun & Sports Park Two miniature-golf courses are the main attraction here, but you'll also find a driving range, a professional putting course for grown-up golfers, batting cages, go-cart tracks, a bumper-boat lagoon, and a video-game arcade.

16001 N. Scottsdale Rd. (¼ mile south of Bell Rd.), Scottsdale. ✆ **480/998-2800.** www.crackerjax.com. Activity prices vary; multiple-activity pass $21–$40. Sun–Thurs 10am–10pm; Fri–Sat 10am–midnight (driving range opens at 8am). Bus: 72.

McCormick-Stillman Railroad Park If you or your kids happen to like trains, you won't want to miss this park. On the grounds are restored railroad cars and engines, two old railway depots, model railroad layouts, and, best of all, a 5⁄12-scale model railroad that takes visitors around the park. There's also a 1929 carousel and a general store.

7301 E. Indian Bend Rd. (at Scottsdale Rd.), Scottsdale. ✆ **480/312-2312.** www.therailroadpark.com. Train and carousel rides $1; museum admission $1 adults, free for children 12 and under. Hours vary with the season; call for schedule. Closed Thanksgiving and Christmas. Bus: 72.

6 Organized Tours & Excursions

The Valley of the Sun is a sprawling, often congested place, and if you're unfamiliar with the area, you may be surprised at how great the distances are. If map reading and urban navigation are not your strong points, consider taking a guided tour. Numerous companies offer tours of both the Valley of the Sun and the rest of Arizona. However, tours of the Valley tend to include only brief stops at highlights.

BUS TOURS **Gray Line Tours Phoenix** (✆ **800/777-3484** or 602/437-3484; www.graylinearizona.com) is one of the largest tour companies in the Valley. It offers a 4-hour tour of Phoenix and the Valley of the Sun for $52; reservations are necessary. The tour points out such local landmarks as the state capitol, Heritage Square, Arizona State University, and Old Town Scottsdale.

GLIDER RIDES The thermals that form above the mountains in the Phoenix area make this an ideal place for flying sailplanes (gliders). On the south side of the Valley at the Estrella Sailport, **Arizona Soaring,** 22548 N. Sailport Way, Maricopa (✆ **520/568-2318;** www.azsoaring.com), offers sailplane rides as well as instruction. A basic 20-minute flight is $100; for $150, you can take an aerobatic flight with loops, rolls, and inverted flying. To reach the airstrip, take I-10 E to Exit 164 (Queen Creek Rd.), go west on Queen Creek Road (which becomes Maricopa Rd. [Ariz. 347]) for 15 miles, turn right on Arizona 238, and continue 6½ miles. On the north side of the Valley, there's **Turf Soaring School,** 8700 W. Carefree Hwy., Peoria (✆ **602/439-3621;** www.turfsoaring.com), which charges $95 for a basic flight and $175 for a deluxe aerobatic flight. Turf Soaring School also offers flights for two people ($160–$220), although your combined weight can't exceed 300 pounds. Reservations are a good idea at either place.

HOT-AIR BALLOON RIDES The still morning air of the Valley of the Sun is perfect for hot-air ballooning, and because of the stiff competition, prices are among the lowest in the country—between $135 and $195 per person for a 1- to 1½-hour ride. Companies to try include **Over the Rainbow** (✆ **602/225-5666;** www.letsgoballooning.com) and **Adventures Out West** (✆ **800/755-0935** or 480/991-3666; www.adventuresoutwest.com).

Tips Top Gun

Ever wanted to be a fighter pilot? Well, at **Fighter Combat International** (✆ **866/FLY-HARD** or 480/279-1881; www.fightercombat.com) you can find out if you've got the right stuff. This company, which operates out of the Williams Gateway Airport in Mesa, offers a variety of exciting aerobatic flights, including mock dogfights. Best of all, on some flights, you get to fly the plane up to 75% of the time and learn how to do loops, rolls, spins, and other aerobatic moves. Flights start at $445; for a mock air combat mission, you'll have to shell out $695.

JEEP TOURS After spending a few days in Scottsdale, you'll likely start wondering where the desert is. Well, it's out there, and the easiest way to explore it is to book a jeep tour. Most hotels and resorts work with particular companies, so start by asking your concierge. Alternatively, you can contact one of the following companies. Most will pick you up at your hotel, take you off through the desert, and maybe even let you pan for gold or shoot a six-gun. Depending on how many people there are in your party and where you're staying, rates range from $65 to $100 for a 3-hour tour. Companies include **Arizona Desert Mountain Jeep Tours** (✆ **800/567-3619;** www.azdesertmountain.com) and **Arizona Bound Tours** (✆ **480/962-6620;** www.arizonabound.com).

If you want to really impress your friends when you get home, you'll need to try something a little different. How about a Hummer tour? Sure, a Hummer is nothing but a jeep on steroids, but these military-issue off-road vehicles still turn heads. Contact **Desert Storm Hummer Tours** (✆ **866/374-8637** or 480/922-0020; www.dshummer.com), which charges $95 for a 4-hour tour; or **Stellar Adventures** (✆ **877/878-3552** or 602/402-0584; www.stellaradventures.com), which charges $125 for a basic 4-hour tour and $155 for its extreme tour. Both companies also offer night tours ($125–$130) that let you spot wildlife with night-vision equipment.

SCENIC FLIGHTS If you're short on time but want to at least see the Grand Canyon, book an air tour in a small plane. **Westwind Scenic Air Tours,** 732 W. Deer Valley Rd., Phoenix (✆ **888/869-0866** or 480/991-5557; www.westwindaviation.com), charges $320 to $525 for its Grand Canyon tours, $225 to $305 for its Sedona tours, and $525 for its Monument Valley tour. This company flies out of the Deer Valley Airport in the northwest part of the Valley.

7 Outdoor Pursuits

BICYCLING Although the Valley of the Sun is a sprawling place, it's mostly flat and has numerous paved bike paths, which makes bicycling a breeze as long as it isn't windy or, in the summer, too hot. In Scottsdale, **Arizona Outback Adventures,** 16447 N. 91st St. (✆ **866/455-1601** or 480/945-2881; www.azoutbackadventures.com), rents road bikes for $50 to $85 per day, hybrid bikes for $35 per day, and mountain bikes for $35 to $85 per day. Mountain-biking trail maps are also available. This company also does half-day and full-day guided mountain-bike tours.

Among the best mountain-biking spots in the city are Papago Park (at Van Buren St. and Galvin Pkwy.), Phoenix South Mountain Park (use the entrance off Baseline Rd. on 48th St.), and North Mountain Preserve (off Seventh St. between Dunlap Ave. and Thunderbird Rd.). With its rolling topography and wide dirt trails, Papago Park is the best place for novice mountain-bikers to get in some desert riding (and the scenery here is great). For hard-core pedalers, Phoenix South Mountain Park is the place to go. The National Trail is the ultimate death-defying ride here, but there are lots of trails for intermediate riders, including the Desert Classic Trail and the short loop trails just north of the parking area at the 48th Street entrance. North Mountain is another good place for intermediate riders.

There's also plenty of good road biking and mountain biking up in the Cave Creek area, where you can rent a bike for $40 to $45 a day at **Flat Tire Bike Shop,** 6149 E. Cave Creek Rd. (✆ **480/488-5261;** www.flattirebikes.com). If you'd like a guide for some of the best biking in the desert, contact **Desert Biking Adventures** (✆ **888/249-BIKE** or 602/320-4602; www.desertbikingadventures.com), which leads 2-, 3-, and 4-hour tours (and specializes in downhill rides). Prices range from $75 to $97.

If you'd rather confine your cycling to a paved surface, there's no better route than Scottsdale's **Indian Bend Wash greenbelt,** a paved path that extends for more than 10 miles along Hayden Road (from north of Shea Blvd. to Tempe). The Indian Bend Wash pathway can be accessed at many points along Hayden Road. At the south end, the path connects to paved paths on the shores of Tempe Town Lake and provides easy access to Tempe's Mill Avenue shopping district.

GOLF With roughly 200 courses in the Valley of the Sun, golf is just about the most popular sport in Phoenix and one of the main reasons people flock here in winter. Sunshine, spectacular views, and the company of coyotes, quails, and doves make playing a round of golf here a truly memorable experience.

However, despite the number of courses, it can be difficult to get a tee time on any of the more popular courses (especially during the months of Feb, Mar, and Apr). If you're staying at a resort with a course, be sure to make your tee-time reservations at the same time you make your room reservations. If you aren't staying at a resort, you might still be able to play a round on a resort course if you can get a last-minute tee time. Try one of the tee-time reservations services below.

The only thing harder than getting a winter or spring tee time in the Valley is facing the bill at the end of your 18 holes. Greens fees at most public and resort courses range from $90 to $170, with the top courses often charging $200 to $250 or more. Municipal courses, on the other hand, charge less than $50. You can save money on many courses by opting for twilight play, which usually begins between 1 and 3pm.

You can get more information on Valley of the Sun golf courses from the **Greater Phoenix Convention & Visitors Bureau,** 50 N. Second St. (© **877/225-5749** or 602/452-6282; www.visitphoenix.com).

It's a good idea to make reservations well in advance. You can avoid the hassle of booking tee times yourself by contacting **Golf Xpress** (© **888/679-8246** or 602/404-GOLF; www.azgolfxpress.com), which can make reservations farther in advance than you could if you called the golf course directly, and can sometimes get you lower greens fees as well. This company also makes hotel reservations, rents golf clubs, and provides other assistance to golfers visiting the Valley. For last-minute reservations, call **Stand-by Golf** (© **800/655-5345;** www.discountteetimes.com).

The many resort courses are the favored fairways of Valley visitors, and for spectacular scenery, the two Jay Morrish–designed 18-hole courses at **The Boulders** ★★, 34631 N. Tom Darlington Dr., Carefree (© **480/488-9028;** www.thebouldersclub.com), just can't be beat. Given the option, play the South Course, and watch out as you approach the tee box on the 7th hole—it's a real heart-stopper. Tee times for non-resort guests are very limited in winter and spring (try making reservations a month in advance if you aren't staying at the resort). You'll pay $165 to $285 for a round in winter if you aren't staying at the resort.

Jumping over to Litchfield Park, on the far west side of the Valley, there's **The Wigwam Golf Resort & Spa** ★, 300 Wigwam Blvd. (© **800/909-4224** or 623/935-9414; www.wigwamresort.com), which has, count 'em, three championship 18-hole courses. The Gold Course is legendary, but even the Blue and Red courses are worth playing. These are traditional courses for purists who want vast expanses of green rather than cacti and boulders, and all three courses have been renovated in recent years. In high season, greens fees are $162 for any of the three courses. Reservations for nonguests can be made no more than 7 days in advance.

Way over on the east side of the Valley at the foot of the Superstition Mountains is the **Gold Canyon Golf Resort** ★, 6100 S. Kings Ranch Rd., Gold Canyon (✆ **480/982-9449;** www.gcgr.com), which has been rated the best public course in the state and has three of the state's best holes—the 2nd, 3rd, and 4th on the visually breathtaking, desert-style Dinosaur Mountain course. Greens fees on this course range from $164 to $189 in winter. The Sidewinder course is more traditional and less dramatic, but much more economical. Greens fees are $89 to $104 in winter. You can make tee-time reservations 10 days in advance over the phone or 60 days in advance online. It's well worth the drive.

If you want a traditional course that has been played by presidents and celebrities alike, try to get a tee time at one of the two 18-hole courses at the **Arizona Biltmore Golf & Country Club,** 24th Street and Missouri Avenue (✆ **602/955-9655;** www.arizonabiltmore.com). The courses here are more relaxing than challenging, good to play if you're not yet up to par. Greens fees are $105 to $175 in winter and spring. Reservations can be made one month in advance. There's also a championship 18-hole putting course.

Of the two courses at the **Camelback Golf Club,** 7847 N. Mockingbird Lane (✆ **480/596-7050;** www.camelbackinn.com), the tree-shaded Padre Course is more challenging. The Indian Bend Course is a links-style course with great mountain views and lots of water hazards. Padre Course greens fees are $139 to $179 in winter; Indian Bend Course fees are $109 to $139 in winter. Reservations can be made up to 60 days in advance.

Set at the base of Camelback Mountain, the **Phoenician Golf Club,** 6000 E. Camelback Rd. (✆ **800/888-8234** or 480/423-2450; www.thephoenician.com), at the Valley's most glamorous resort, has 27 holes that mix traditional and desert styles. Greens fees for those not staying at the resort are $139 to $199 in winter and spring and can be made up to 30 days in advance.

Of the Valley's many daily-fee courses, it's the two 18-hole courses at **Troon North Golf Club** ★★★, 10320 E. Dynamite Blvd., Scottsdale (✆ **480/585-7700;** www.troonnorthgolf.com), seemingly carved out of raw desert, that garner the most local accolades. This is the finest example of a desert course that you'll find anywhere in the state, and with five tee boxes on each hole, golfers of all levels can enjoy this course. Greens fees are $195 to $295 in winter and spring.

If you want to swing where the pros do, beg, borrow, or steal a tee time on the Tom Weiskopf and Jay Morrish–designed Stadium Course at the **Tournament Players Club (TPC) of Scottsdale** ★★, 17020 N. Hayden Rd. (✆ **888/400-4001** or 480/585-4334; www.playatpc.com), which hosts the Phoenix Open. The 18th hole has standing room for 40,000 spectators, but hopefully there won't be that many around the day you double-bogey on this hole. The TPC's second 18, the Desert Course, is actually a municipal course, thanks to an agreement with the landowner, the Bureau of Land Management, and was completely renovated in 2007. Stadium course fees top out at $249 in winter and spring, while Desert Course fees are a reasonable $63 in winter and spring.

We-Ko-Pa Golf Club, 18200 E. Toh Vee Circle, Fort McDowell (✆ **480/836-9000;** www.wekopa.com), is located off the Beeline Highway (Ariz. 87) on the Fort McDowell Yavapai Nation in the northeast corner of the Valley, and gets rave reviews. The course name is Yavapai for "Four Peaks," which is the mountain range you'll be marveling at as you play. Unlike at other area courses, fairways at the two 18-hole courses here are bounded by desert, not luxury homes, so make sure you keep your ball on the grass. The Saguaro Course here opened in late 2006 and was immediately voted one of the best new courses in the country. Greens fees are $170 to $195 in winter. Reservations are taken up to 90 days in advance.

The **Kierland Golf Club,** 15636 Clubgate Dr., Scottsdale (✆ **480/922-9283;** www.kierlandgolf.com), which was designed by Scott Miller and consists of three 9-hole courses that can be played in combination, is another much-talked-about local daily-fee course. It's affiliated with the Westin Kierland Resort and is conveniently located adjacent to the Kierland Commons shopping center. Greens fees are $169 to $199 in winter.

The Pete Dye–designed **ASU Karsten Golf Course,** 1125 E. Rio Salado Pkwy., Tempe (✆ **480/921-8070;** www.asukarsten.com), part of Arizona State University, is also highly praised and a very challenging training ground for top collegiate golfers. Greens fees are $92 to $105 in winter. Phone reservations are taken up to 14 days in advance; online reservations are taken up to 30 days in advance.

If you're looking for good value in traditional or links-style courses, try the Legacy Golf Resort, Stonecreek Golf Club, or Ocotillo Golf Resort. The **Legacy Golf Resort,** 6808 S. 32nd St. (✆ **888/828-FORE** or 602/305-5555; www.legacygolfresort.com), is a fairly forgiving course on the south side of the Valley. Greens fees are $89 to $149 in winter. **Stonecreek Golf Club,** 4435 E. Paradise Village Pkwy. (✆ **602/953-9111;** www.americangolf.com), conveniently located in Paradise Valley close to downtown Scottsdale, is named for the artificial stream that meanders through the course. Greens fees are $125 in winter. **Ocotillo Golf Club,** 3751 S. Clubhouse Dr., Chandler (✆ **888/624-8899** or 480/917-6660; www.ocotillogolf.com), in the southeast part of the Valley, has three 9-hole courses centered on 95 acres of man-made lakes, and that means a lot of challenge. Greens fees are $130 to $175 in winter.

If you want to take a crack at a desert-style course or two but don't want to take out a second mortgage, try Dove Valley Ranch Golf Club or Rancho Mañana Golf Club. **Dove Valley Ranch Golf Club,** 33750 N. Dove Lakes Dr., Cave Creek (✆ **480/488-0009;** www.dovevalleyranch.com), designed by Robert Trent Jones, Jr., was voted Arizona's best new public course when it opened back in 1998. It's something of a merger of desert and traditional styles. Greens fees are $120 to $140 in winter.

Rancho Mañana Golf Club, 5734 E. Rancho Mañana Blvd., Cave Creek (✆ **480/488-0398;** www.ranchomanana.com), on the north side of the Valley near The Boulders Resort, makes a good introduction to desert-style courses, as it's not as challenging as some other options in the area. Greens fees are $89 to $139 in winter.

Of the municipal courses in Phoenix, **Papago Golf Course,** 5595 E. Moreland St. (✆ **602/275-8428**), at the foot of the red sandstone Papago Buttes, offers fine views and a killer 17th hole. This is such a great course that it's used for Phoenix Open qualifying. **Encanto Golf Course,** 2775 N. 15th Ave. (✆ **602/253-3963**), is the third-oldest course in Arizona and, with its wide fairways and lack of hazards, is very forgiving. **Cave Creek Golf Course,** 15202 N. 19th Ave. (✆ **602/866-8076**), in north Phoenix, is another good, economical choice. In winter, greens fees at these three municipal courses are $18 to $38 to walk ($12 extra for a golf cart). For details on these courses, go to www.ci.phoenix.az.us/SPORTS/golf.html.

Tempe's **Rolling Hills Golf Course,** 1415 N. Mill Ave., Tempe (✆ **480/350-5275;** www.tempe.gov/pkrec/golf), on the south side of Papago Park, is another good little municipal course with economical rates. There are two executive 9-hole courses here, and greens fees are a very reasonable $24 for 18 holes. A golf cart will cost you another $21. Reservations can be made a week in advance.

HIKING Several mountains around Phoenix, including Camelback Mountain and Piestewa Peak, have been set aside as parks and nature preserves, and these natural areas are among the city's most popular hiking spots. The city's largest nature preserve, **South Mountain Park/Preserve** (✆ **602/534-6324;** www.phoenix.gov/PARKS/southmnt.html), covers 16,000 acres and is one of the largest city parks in the world. This park contains around 50 miles of hiking, mountain-biking, and horseback-riding trails, and the views of Phoenix (whether from along the National Trail or from the parking lot at the Buena Vista Lookout) are spectacular, especially at sunset. To reach the park's main entrance, drive south on Central Avenue, which leads right into the park. Once inside the park, turn left on Summit Road and follow it to the Buena Vista Lookout, which provides a great view of the city and is the trail head for the National Trail. If you hike east on this trail for 2 miles, you'll come to an unusual little tunnel that makes a good turnaround point.

Another place to get in some relatively easy and convenient hiking is **Papago Park,** Galvin Parkway and Van Buren Street (✆ **602/256-3220**), home to the Desert Botanical Garden, the Phoenix Zoo, and the fascinating Hole in the Rock (a red-rock butte with a large natural opening in it). There are both paved and dirt trails within the park; the most popular hikes are around the Papago Buttes (park on W. Park Dr.) and up onto the rocks at Hole in the Rock (park past the zoo at the information center). During World War II, there was a German POW camp here.

Perhaps the most popular hike in the city is the trail to the top of **Camelback Mountain,** in the **Echo Canyon Recreation Area** (✆ **602/262-6862;** www.phoenix.gov/PARKS/hikecmlb.html), near the boundary between Phoenix and Scottsdale. At 2,704 feet high, this is the highest mountain in Phoenix and boasts the finest mountaintop views in the city. The 1.2-mile Summit Trail that leads to the top of Camelback Mountain is outrageously steep and gains 1,200 feet from trail head to summit. Yet on any given day there will be ironmen and ironwomen nonchalantly jogging up and down to stay fit. At times, it almost feels like a health-club singles scene. To reach the trail head, drive up 44th Street until it becomes McDonald Drive, turn right on East Echo Canyon Drive, and continue up the hill until the road ends at a parking lot, which is often full. Don't attempt this one in the heat of the day, and bring at least a quart of water.

At the east end of Camelback Mountain is the Cholla Trail, which, at 1.75 miles in length, isn't as steep as the Summit Trail (at least, not until you get close to the summit, where the route gets steep, rocky, and quite difficult). The only parking for this trail is along Invergordon Road at Chaparral Road, just north of Camelback Road (along the east boundary of The Phoenician resort). Be sure to park in a legal parking space and watch the hours that parking is allowed. There's a good turnaround point about 1.5 miles up the trail, and great views down onto the fairways of the golf course at The Phoenician.

The 2,608-foot-tall **Piestewa Peak,** in the **Phoenix Mountains Park and Recreation Area/Dreamy Draw Park** (✆ **602/262-7901;** www.phoenix.gov/PARKS/hikephx.html), offers another aerobic workout of a hike and has views almost as spectacular as those from Camelback Mountain. The round-trip to the summit is 2.4 miles and gains almost 1,200 feet. Piestewa Peak is reached from Squaw Peak Drive off Lincoln Drive between 22nd and 23rd streets. Another section of this park, with much easier trails, can be reached by taking the Northern Avenue exit of Arizona 51 and then driving east into Dreamy Draw Park.

Of all the popular mountain trails in the Phoenix area, the trail through **Pinnacle Peak Park,** 26802 N. 102nd Way (✆ **480/312-0990;** www.scottsdaleaz.gov/parks/pinnacle), in north Scottsdale, is my favorite. The trail through the park is a 3.5-mile round-trip hike and is immensely popular with the local fitness crowd. Forget about stopping to smell the desert penstemon; if you don't keep up the pace, someone's liable to knock you off the trail into a prickly pear. If you can find a parking space (arrive before 9am on weekends) and can ignore the crowds, you'll be treated to views of rugged desert mountains (and posh desert suburbs). November through April, there are guided hikes Tuesday through Sunday at 10am. There are also wildflower walks, full-moon hikes, and astronomy evenings here. To find the park from central Scottsdale, go north on Pima Road, east on Happy Valley Road, and north on Alma School Parkway, and turn left at the sign for Pinnacle Peak Patio restaurant.

For much less vigorous hiking (without the crowds), try **North Mountain Park** (✆ **602/262-7901;** www.phoenix.gov/PARKS/nmvc.html), in North Mountain Preserve. This natural area, located on either side of Seventh Street between Dunlap Avenue and Thunderbird Road, has more flat hiking than Camelback Mountain or Piestewa Peak. To orient yourself and get trail maps, stop by the **North Mountain Visitor Center,** 12950 N. Seventh St. (✆ **602/495-5540**).

The **Peralta Trail** in the impossibly steep and jagged Superstition Mountains just might be my favorite hike in the entire state. Unfortunately, a lot of other people feel the same way, and on weekends, the trail is almost always packed with people. However, if you come early on a weekday, you can have this trail almost all to yourself. The route climbs steadily, though not too steeply, past huge old saguaros to a saddle with a view that will take your breath away (or was it the hike up from the trail head that's left you gasping?). The view is an in-your-face look at Weaver's Needle, the Superstition Mountains' most famous pinnacle. The hike to the view at Fremont Saddle is a 4.6-mile round-trip hike. To reach the trail head, drive east from Phoenix on U.S. 60 past Apache Junction to Peralta Road, and then drive 8 miles north, mostly on gravel road, to the trail head. For information, contact the **Tonto National Forest's Mesa Ranger District,** 5140 E. Ingram St., Mesa (✆ **480/610-3300;** www.fs.fed.us/r3/tonto).

Way out on the west side of the Valley, where suburban sprawl bumps up against the rugged mountains, you'll find **White Tank Mountain Regional Park,** 13025 N. White Tank Mountain Rd., Waddell (✆ **623/935-2505;** www.Maricopa.gov/parks/white_tank), and the popular but very rewarding **Waterfall Trail.** This 1.8-mile round-trip hike leads past Indian petroglyphs to, you guessed it, a waterfall. Well, sometimes. Most of the year, the waterfall isn't running, but after a rainstorm, water cascades over the rocks here. Whether the creek is running or not, this is a pretty spot. You can also escape the crowds by heading out on some of the park's more remote and rugged trails.

Another great place to go for a hike in the desert is north Scottsdale's **McDowell Sonoran Preserve** (✆ **480/998-7971;** www.mcdowellsonoran.org), where you'll find miles of relatively easy and uncrowded trails. The best place to access these trails is at the Lost Dog Trailhead at 124th Street north of Via Linda. To reach this trail head, drive east on Shea Boulevard, turn north on 124th Street, and watch for the parking lot after you pass Via Linda. The 2.5-mile Ringtail Loop Trail is a good choice for an hour's hike.

HORSEBACK RIDING Even in the urban confines of the Phoenix metro area, people like to play at being cowboys, and there are plenty of places around the Valley to saddle up your palomino. Because any guided ride is going to lead you through interesting desert scenery, your best bet is to pick a stable close to where you're staying. Keep in mind that most stables require or prefer reservations.

On the south side of the city, try **Ponderosa Stables,** 10215 S. Central Ave. (✆ **602/268-1261;** www.arizona-horses.com), which leads rides into South Mountain Park and charges $25 for a 1-hour ride or $45 for a 2-hour ride. These stables also offer fun dinner rides ($34) to the T-Bone Steakhouse, where you buy your own dinner before riding back under the stars. If you have time for only one horseback ride while you're in Phoenix, make it this latter ride.

On the north side of the Valley, **Cave Creek Outfitters,** off Dynamite Boulevard at 31313 N. 144th St. (✆ **888/921-0040** or 480/471-4635; www.cavecreekoutfitters.com), offers 2-hour rides for $65 to $80.

On the east side of the Valley, on the southern slopes of the Superstitions, you'll find **D-Spur Ranch/Preservation of the Cowboy Way Society,** 15371 Ojo Rd. (off Peralta Rd.), Apache Junction (✆ **602/810-7029;** www.cowboywaysociety.org), which charges $26 for a 1-hour ride, $50 for a 2-hour ride, and $190 per person for an overnight trip.

TENNIS Most major hotels in the area have tennis courts, and there are several tennis resorts around the Valley. If you're staying someplace without a court, try the **Scottsdale Ranch Park & Tennis Center,** 10400 E. Via Linda, Scottsdale (✆ **480/312-7774**). Court fees range from $4 to $10 for 1½ hours.

WATER PARKS At **Phoenix Waterworld Safari,** 4243 W. Pinnacle Peak Rd. (✆ **623/581-8446;** www.golfland.com), you can free-fall down the Kilimanjaro speed slide or catch a gnarly wave in the wave pool. **Mesa Golfland Sunsplash,** 155 W. Hampton Ave., Mesa (✆ **480/834-8319;** www.golfland.com), has a wave pool and a water roller coaster. **Big Surf,** 1500 N. McClintock Rd., Tempe (✆ **480/947-2477;** www.golfland.com), has the country's original wave pool and all kinds of wild water slides.

All three of these parks charge $24 for anyone taller than 48 inches, $20 for seniors and anyone under 48 inches, and $3 for children 2 and under. Phoenix Waterworld Safari is open from Memorial Day weekend to Labor Day weekend Monday through Saturday from 10am to 8pm and Sunday from 11am to 7pm. Mesa Golfland/Sunsplash is open from Memorial Day weekend to Labor Day weekend Monday through Saturday from 10am to 8pm and Sunday from noon to 8pm. Big Surf is open from around Memorial Day to Labor Day Monday through Saturday from 10am to 6pm and Sunday from 11am to 7pm. Mesa Golfland also has three slides that open at the start of spring break and are open Saturday and Sunday from noon to 6pm. After Memorial Day, these slides are open the same hours as Sunsplash.

WHITE-WATER RAFTING & TUBING The desert may not seem like the place for white-water rafting, but up in the mountains to the northeast of Phoenix, the **Upper Salt River** still flows wild and free and offers some exciting rafting. Most years from about late February to late May, snowmelt from the White Mountains floods the river and fills it with exciting Class III and IV rapids (sometimes, however, there just isn't enough water). Companies operating full-day, overnight, and multiday rafting trips on the Upper Salt River (conditions permitting) include **Wilderness Aware Rafting** (✆ **800/462-7238;** www.inaraft.com), **Canyon Rio Rafting** (✆ **800/272-3353;**

www.canyonrio.com), and **Mild to Wild Rafting** (✆ **800/567-6745;** www.mild2wild rafting.com). Prices range from $99 to $115 for a day trip.

Tamer river trips can be had from **Salt River Tubing & Recreation** (✆ **480/984-3305;** www.saltrivertubing.com), which has its headquarters 20 miles northeast of Phoenix on Power Road at the intersection of Usery Pass Road in Tonto National Forest. For $13, the company will rent you a large inner tube and shuttle you by bus upriver for the float down. The inner-tubing season runs from mid-May to September.

8 Spectator Sports

Phoenix is nuts for pro sports and is one of the few cities in the country with teams for all four of the major sports (baseball, basketball, football, and hockey). Add to this baseball's spring training, professional women's basketball, golf and tennis tournaments, the annual Fiesta Bowl college football classic, and ASU football, basketball, and baseball, and you have enough action to keep even the most rabid sports fans happy. The all-around best month to visit is March, when you could feasibly catch baseball's spring training, the Suns, the Coyotes, and ASU basketball and baseball, as well as the Safeway International LPGA Tournament.

Call **Ticketmaster** (✆ **480/784-4444;** www.ticketmaster.com) for tickets to most of the events below. For sold-out events, try **Tickets Unlimited** (✆ **800/289-8497** or 602/840-2340; www.ticketsunlimitedinc.com) or **Ticket Exchange** (✆ **800/800-9811;** ticketexchangeusa.com).

AUTO RACING At the **Phoenix International Raceway,** 7602 S. Avondale Blvd. at Baseline Road, Avondale (✆ **602/252-2227;** www.phoenixintlraceway.com), there's NASCAR and IndyCar racing on the world's fastest 1-mile oval. Tickets generally range from around $10 to $100.

BASEBALL Although the **Arizona Diamondbacks** (✆ **888/777-4664** or 602/514-8400; www.diamondbacks.com) haven't put in as impressive a showing in the years since they won the 2001 World Series, they still have a devoted fan base and regularly pack downtown Phoenix's impressive Chase Field. The ballpark's retractable roof allows for comfortable play during the blistering summers and makes this one of only a few enclosed baseball stadiums with natural grass. Tickets to ballgames are available through the Chase Field ticket office and cost between $5 and $185. The best seats are in sections J and Q. If you'd like to get a behind-the-scenes look at Chase Field, you can take a guided tour. Tours cost $6 for adults, $4 for seniors and children ages 7 to 12, and $2 for children ages 4 to 6.

For decades, baseball's spring-training season has been immensely popular, especially with fans from northern teams, and don't think that the Cactus League's preseason exhibition games are any less popular just because the Diamondbacks play all summer. **Spring-training games** may rank second only to golf in popularity with winter visitors to the Valley. Nine major-league baseball teams have spring-training camps around the Valley in the month of March, and exhibition games are scheduled at seven different stadiums. Tickets cost $5 to $24. Get a schedule from a visitor center, check the *Arizona Republic* while you're in town, check the website of the Cactus League (www.cactusleague.com), or visit www.cactusleagueinfo.com. Games often sell out, especially on weekends, so be sure to order tickets in advance. The spring-training schedule for 2008 should be out by November 2007.

Teams training in the Valley include the **Los Angeles Angels of Anaheim,** Tempe Diablo Stadium, 2200 W. Alameda Dr. (48th St. and Broadway Rd.), Tempe (✆ 480/350-5205 or 480/784-4444 for tickets; www.angelsbaseball.com); the **Chicago Cubs,** HoHoKam Park, 1235 N. Center St., Mesa (✆ 800/905-3315 for tickets or 480/964-4467; www.chicagocubs.com); the **Kansas City Royals,** Surprise Stadium, 15754 N. Bullard Ave., Surprise (✆ 623/594-5600 or 480/784-4444 for tickets; www.kcroyals.com); the **Milwaukee Brewers,** Maryvale Baseball Park, 3600 N. 51st Ave., Phoenix (✆ 623/245-5500; www.milwaukeebrewers.com); the **Oakland Athletics,** Phoenix Municipal Stadium, 5999 E. Van Buren St., Phoenix (✆ 602/392-0217 or 877/493-BALL for tickets; www.oaklandathletics.com); the **San Diego Padres,** Peoria Sports Complex, 16101 N. 83rd Ave., Peoria (✆ 800/409-1511, 623/878-4337, or 480/784-4444 for tickets; www.padres.com); the **San Francisco Giants,** Scottsdale Stadium, 7408 E. Osborn Rd., Scottsdale (✆ 480/312-2586 or 800/225-2277 for tickets; www.sfgiants.com); the **Seattle Mariners,** Peoria Sports Complex, 16101 N. 83rd Ave., Peoria (✆ 800/409-1511, 623/878-4337, or 480/784-4444 for tickets; www.seattlemariners.com); and the **Texas Rangers,** Surprise Stadium, 15850 N. Bullard Ave., Surprise (✆ 623/594-5600 or 480/784-4444 for tickets; www.texasrangers.com).

BASKETBALL The NBA's **Phoenix Suns** play at the US Airways Center, 201 E. Jefferson St. (✆ **800/4-NBA-TIX** or 602/379-SUNS; www.suns.com). Most tickets cost between $10 and $200. Suns tickets are hard to come by; if you haven't planned ahead, try contacting the box office the day before or the day of a game to see if tickets have been returned. Otherwise, you'll have to try a ticket agency and pay a premium.

Phoenix also has a WNBA team, the **Phoenix Mercury** (✆ **602/252-9622** or 602/514-8333; www.phoenixmercury.com), which plays at the US Airways Center between late May and mid-August. Tickets cost $10 to $146.

FOOTBALL The **Arizona Cardinals** (✆ **800/999-1402** or 602/379-0102; www.azcardinals.com) play at the $450-million state-of-the-art University of Phoenix Stadium in the west valley city of Glendale. This stadium has a retractable roof made of translucent fabric that lets lots of light in when the roof is closed. However, the stadium's most distinctive feature is its moveable playing field, which is rolled out into the sun outside the stadium until a game is scheduled. This 2-acre, grass-covered tray is the first of its kind in North America. Most tickets cost $15 to $67, and single-game tickets for the entire season go on sale around mid-July. Of course, if you're a football fan, you know that the 2008 Superbowl is being played here.

GOLF TOURNAMENTS It's not surprising that, with more than 200 golf courses and ideal golfing weather throughout the fall, winter, and spring, the Valley of the Sun hosts some major golf tournaments. Late January's **FBR Open Golf Tournament** (✆ **602/870-0163;** www.fbropen.com) is by far the biggest. Held at the Tournament Players Club (TPC) of Scottsdale, it attracts more spectators than any other golf tournament in the world (more than 500,000 each year). The 18th hole has standing room for 40,000. Tickets start at $25 and are available through Ticketmaster (see above).

Each March, the **Safeway International LPGA Tournament** (✆ **877/983-3300** or 602/495-4653; www.safewaygolf.com), held at the Superstition Mountain Golf & Country Club, 800 E. Club Village Dr., lures nearly 100 of the top women golfers from around the world. Daily tickets are $20; weekly tickets are $50.

HOCKEY Ice hockey in the desert? It may not make sense, but even Phoenicians are crazy about ice hockey (maybe it's all those northern transplants). In fact, the NHL's **Phoenix Coyotes** (✆ **480/563-PUCK;** www.phoenixcoyotes.com) have a state-of-the-art arena in Glendale (northwest of downtown Phoenix). Tickets cost $15 to $300.

HORSE/GREYHOUND RACING **Turf Paradise,** 1501 W. Bell Rd. (✆ **602/942-1101;** www.turfparadise.com), is Phoenix's horse-racing track. The season runs from early October to early May. Admission ranges from free to $5.

The **Phoenix Greyhound Park,** 3801 E. Washington St. (✆ **602/273-7181;** www.phoenixgreyhoundpark.com), is a fully enclosed, air-conditioned facility offering seating in various grandstands, lounges, and restaurants. There's racing throughout the year; tickets are free to $3.

RODEOS, POLO & HORSE SHOWS Cowboys, cowgirls, and other horsey types will find plenty of the four-legged critters going through their paces most weeks at **WestWorld of Scottsdale,** 16601 N. Pima Rd., Scottsdale (✆ **480/312-6802;** www.scottsdaleaz.gov/westworld). With its hundreds of stables, numerous equestrian arenas, and a polo field, this complex provides an amazing variety of entertainment and sporting events. There are rodeos, polo matches, horse shows, horseback rides, and horseback-riding instruction.

9 Spas

Ever since the first "lungers" showed up in the Phoenix area hoping to cure their tuberculosis, the desert has been a magnet for those looking to get healthy. In the first half of the 20th century, health spas were all the rage in Phoenix, and today spas are still immensely popular in the Valley of the Sun. Over the past decade, most of the area's top resorts have added new full-service spas or expanded existing ones to cater to guests' increasing requests for services such as massages, body wraps, mud masks, and salt glows.

If you can't or don't want to spend the money to stay at a top resort and avail yourself of the spa, you may still be able to indulge. Most resorts open their spas to the public, and for the cost of a body treatment or massage, you can spend the day at the spa taking classes, working out in an exercise room, or lounging by the pool. Barring this indulgence, you can slip into one of the Valley's many day spas and take a stress-reduction break the way other people take a latte break.

If you want truly spectacular surroundings and bragging rights, head north to **The Boulders Resort & Golden Door Spa,** 34631 N. Tom Darlington Dr., Carefree (✆ **480/595-3500;** www.goldendoorspas.com). Although this spa has the best name recognition of any spa in the Valley, it is not the most impressive. However, at 33,000 square feet and with 24 treatment spaces, it is certainly large. Also, the list of services is one of the most extensive in the Valley and includes both ayurvedic and Native American–inspired treatments. The turquoise wrap, the spa's signature treatment, is a real desert experience. Most 50-minute treatments cost around $145 to $165. Packages are $320 to $1,600.

Willow Stream–The Spa at the Fairmont Scottsdale Princess, 7575 E. Princess Dr. (✆ **800/908-9540** or 480/585-2732; www.fairmont.com), is my favorite Valley spa. Designed to conjure up images of the journey to Havasu Canyon, it includes a rooftop swimming pool and a large hot tub in a grotto below the pool. Because this is one of the largest spas in the Valley, you stand a better chance of getting last-minute reservations. Most 60-minute treatments cost $169 to $179. Packages range from $219 to $799; there are also several package options for couples.

At **Revive,** JW Marriott Desert Ridge Resort & Spa, 5350 E. Marriott Blvd., Phoenix (✆ **866-REVIVE-4U** or 480/293-3700; www.jwdesertridgeresort.com), indigenous materials—turquoise, wildflowers, desert sage—are used in treatments, while a small herb garden contributes to the spa bistro menu. The spa boasts its own pool, and at press time, finishing touches were being put on a co-ed spa loft. Treatments range from $45 to $195, while packages run from $250 to $520. Try the Desert Foothills Firming Body Wrap or the Turquoise Blue Sage Body Ritual.

Spa Avania, Hyatt Regency Scottsdale Resort and Spa at Gainey Ranch, 7500 E. Doubletree Ranch Rd., Scottsdale (✆ **480/444-1234;** www.spaavania.com), which takes its name from the Greek work for "tranquil," is one of the newest major resort spas in Scottsdale. Spa treatments here are designed to stimulate all the senses and also take into consideration the time of day and the body's natural rhythms. One-hour treatments run $130 to $150, while packages cost anywhere from $270 to $468.

The **Spa at Gainey Village,** 7477 E. Doubletree Ranch Rd., Scottsdale (✆ **480/609-6980;** www.thespaatgaineyvillage.com), is a spa and health club near the Hyatt Regency Scottsdale. Although the health club, which is popular with the Scottsdale Mercedes set, seems to be the main draw, the spa offers a wide range of specialized treatments, including hot stone massages, desert-clay body masks, and just about anything else you can think of. With any 1-hour treatment (average price $100), you can use the extensive exercise facilities or take a class. Packages range from $100 to $385.

Located high on the flanks of Mummy Mountain, the **Spa at Camelback Inn,** 5402 E. Lincoln Dr., Scottsdale (✆ **800/922-2635** or 480/596-7040; www.camelbackspa.com), has long been one of the Valley's premier spas and gets my vote for all-around best spa in the Valley. The location is convenient, the views are fabulous, the setting is tranquil, and there's a long menu of relaxing spa services. For the cost of a single 1-hour treatment—between $110 and $155—you can use all the facilities, which include a fitness center and pool. Among the treatments available are the Para-Joba Body Moisturizer, which will leave your skin feeling like silk, and the Sonoran Rose Facial, perfect for making sure you come back from vacation looking like you were actually on one. Packages run from $185 to $320.

The **Centre for Well Being** at The Phoenician, 6000 E. Camelback Rd., Scottsdale (✆ **800/843-2392** or 480/423-2452; www.centreforwellbeing.com), is one of the Valley's most prestigious spas. For $140 to $165, you can get a 50-minute spa treatment (anything from a botanical hydrating wrap to an aromatherapy tranquility scrub) and then spend the day using the many facilities. Packages range from $210 to $590.

Romance and relaxation take center stage **Alvadora,** the Spa at Royal Palms, 5200 E. Camelback Rd. (✆ **602/840-3610;** www.royalpalmshotel.com), where the Mediterranean finds its way into everything from the Mimosa & Fig Pedicure to the Vino Therapy Facial. Treatments range from $125 to $390. Unlike many other spas, no facial equipment is used here, so the only thing that stands between you and a clear complexion is a soothingly hot towel.

The historic setting and convenient location of the **Arizona Biltmore Spa,** 2400 E. Missouri Ave. (✆ **602/381-7632;** www.arizonabiltmore.com), make this facility an excellent choice if you're spending time along the Camelback Corridor. The spa menu includes dozens of different treatments, including massages with lavender and a saguaro-flower salt glow (body scrub). If you have just one 50-minute treatment (priced between $130 and $165), you can use all of the spa's facilities for the rest of the day. Packages cost $375 to $775.

10 Shopping

For the most part, shopping in the Phoenix area means malls. They're everywhere, and they're air-conditioned, which, I'm sure you'll agree, makes shopping in the desert far more enjoyable when it's 110°F (43°C) outside.

Scottsdale and the Biltmore District of Phoenix (along Camelback Rd.) are the Valley's main upscale shopping areas, with several high-end shopping centers and malls. The various distinct shopping districts of downtown Scottsdale are among the few outdoor shopping areas in the Valley and are home to hundreds of boutiques, galleries, jewelry stores, Native American crafts stores, and souvenir shops. The Western atmosphere of Old Town Scottsdale is partly real and partly a figment of the local merchants' imaginations, but nevertheless it's the most popular tourist shopping area in the Valley. With dozens of galleries in the Main Street Arts and Antiques District and the nearby Marshall Way Contemporary Arts District, it also happens to be the heart of the Valley's art market.

For locals, Scottsdale's shopping scene has been moving steadily northward over the past decade. Kierland Commons and the Shops at Gainey Village are both north of Old Town Scottsdale on North Scottsdale Road and are packed with women's fashion boutiques.

Shopping hours are usually Monday through Saturday from 10am to 6pm and Sunday from noon to 5pm; malls usually stay open until 9pm Monday through Saturday.

ANTIQUES & COLLECTIBLES

With more than 80 antiques shops and specialty stores, downtown Glendale (northwest of downtown Phoenix) is the Valley's main antiques district. You'll find the greatest concentration of antiques stores just off Grand Avenue between 56th and 59th avenues. A half dozen times each year, the **Arizona Antique Shows** (© **602/717-7337**; www.azantiqueshow.com), Arizona's largest collectors' shows, are held at the Arizona State Fairgrounds, 19th Avenue and McDowell Road.

Antique Trove If you love browsing through packed antiques malls searching for your favorite collectibles, then this should be your first stop in the Valley. With more than 100 dealers, it's one of the biggest antiques malls in the area. 2020 N. Scottsdale Rd., Scottsdale. © **480/947-6074.** www.antiquetrove.com.

Arizona West Galleries ★★ Nowhere else in Scottsdale will you find such an amazing collection of cowboy collectibles and Western antiques. There are antique saddles and chaps, old rifles and six-shooters, sheriffs' badges, spurs, and the like. 7149 E. Main St., Scottsdale. © **480/994-3752.**

Bishop Gallery for Art & Antiques ★ This cramped shop is wonderfully eclectic, featuring everything from Asian antiques to unusual original art. Definitely worth a browse. 7164 Main St., Scottsdale. © **480/949-9062.**

ART

In the Southwest, only Santa Fe is a more important art market than Scottsdale, and along the streets of Scottsdale's Main Street Arts and Antiques District and the Marshall Way Contemporary Arts District, you'll see dozens of galleries selling everything from monumental bronzes to contemporary art created from found objects. On Main Street, you'll find primarily cowboy art, both traditional and contemporary, while on North Marshall Way, you'll discover much more imaginative and daring contemporary art.

In addition to the galleries listed here, you'll usually find a huge tent full of art along Scottsdale Road in north Scottsdale. The annual **Celebration of Fine Art** (© **480/443-7695**; www.celebrateart.com) takes place each year between mid-January and late March. Not only will you get to see the work of 100 artists, but on any given day, you'll also find dozens of the artists at work on the premises. Admission is $8 for adults and $7 for seniors. Call or check the website for this year's location and hours of operation.

Art One This gallery specializes in works by art students and other area cutting-edge artists. The works here can be surprisingly good, and prices are very reasonable. There's a second Art One in downtown Phoenix at 1504 NW Grand Ave. (© **602/462-1106**). 4120 N. Marshall Way, Scottsdale. © **480/946-5076.** www.artonegalleryinc.com.

Bentley Projects Housed in a huge old warehouse south of Chase Field in downtown Phoenix, this massive gallery is one the city's most cutting-edge contemporary-art spaces. You probably aren't in the market for a 12-foot-tall Jim Dine bronze statue of Venus, but if you'd like to see one, stop by this gallery. There's a second gallery in Scottsdale at 4161 N. Marshall Way (© **480/946-6060**). 215 E. Grant St., Phoenix. © **602/340-9200.** www.bentleygallery.com.

Cervini Haas Gallery This is Scottsdale's premier gallery of fine contemporary crafts, including furniture, ceramics, and jewelry. The works on display here often push the envelope of what's possible in any given medium. 4222 N. Marshall Way, Scottsdale. © **480/429-6116.** www.cervinihaas.com.

Chiaroscuro With two other galleries in Santa Fe, this is one of the Southwest's premier contemporary art galleries. 7160 Main St., Scottsdale. © **480/429-0711.** www.chiaroscuroaz.com.

Lisa Sette Gallery If you aren't a fan of cowboy or Native American art, don't despair. Instead, drop by this gallery, which always mounts eclectic and fascinating shows, often melding 19th- and 21st-century aesthetics. 4142 N. Marshall Way, Scottsdale. © **480/990-7342.** www.lisasettegallery.com.

Overland Gallery of Fine Art ★★ Traditional Western and Russian Impressionist paintings form the backbone of this gallery's fine collection. These are museum-quality works (prices sometimes approach $100,000) definitely worth a look. The gallery also shows the angular Southwest landscapes of Ed Mell, one of my favorite Southwest artists. 7155 Main St., Scottsdale. © **800/920-0220** or 480/947-1934. www.overlandgallery.com.

Riva Yares Gallery This is one of Scottsdale's largest and most respected contemporary-art galleries, and has a second location in Santa Fe. You may not have room in your car for the monumental sculptures sold here, but I'm sure they'll deliver for you. If you're lucky, you might stumble on a show by the likes of George Segal, Milton Avery, or Fritz Scholder. 3625 Bishop Lane, Scottsdale. © **480/947-3251.** www.rivayaresgallery.com.

Roberts Gallery The feathered masks and sculptures of Virgil Walker are highlights, and if you have an appreciation for fine detail work, you'll likely be fascinated by these pieces. Walker's annual show is held on Thanksgiving weekend. el Pedregal Festival Marketplace, 34505 N. Scottsdale Rd., Carefree. © **480/488-1088.**

Wilde Meyer Gallery Brightly colored and playful are the norm at this gallery, which represents Linda Carter-Holman, a Southwestern favorite who does cowgirl-inspired paintings. There are also Wilde Meyer galleries at 7100 E. Main St., Scottsdale (✆ **480/947-1489**) and in the Shops at Gainey Village, 8777 N. Scottsdale Rd. (✆ **480/488-3200**). 4142 N. Marshall Way, Scottsdale. ✆ **480/945-2323.** www.wildemeyer.com.

BOOKS

Major chain bookstores in the area include **Borders,** at Biltmore Fashion Park, 2402 E. Camelback Rd., Phoenix (✆ **602/957-6660**), 699 S. Mill Ave., Tempe (✆ **480/921-8659**), and 4555 E. Cactus Rd., Phoenix (✆ **602/953-9699**); and **Barnes & Noble,** 10235 N. Metro Parkway E., Phoenix (✆ **602/678-0088**), in Kierland Commons, N. Scottsdale Rd. and Greenway Rd., Scottsdale (✆ **480/948-8551**), and 10500 N. 90th St., Scottsdale (✆ **480/391-0048**).

Guidon Books Whether you're already a student of Western and Civil War history or have only recently developed an interest in the past, this cramped little bookshop in Old Town Scottsdale should not be missed. Rare and out-of-print books are a specialty, but there are plenty of new books as well. Western Americana and the Civil War are the main focus here. 7117 W. Main St., Scottsdale. ✆ **480/945-8811.** www.guidon.com.

The Poisoned Pen The store name should give you a clue as to what sort of bookstore this is: It specializes in mysteries. There's a second Poisoned Pen in Phoenix at 215 E. Grant St. (✆ **602/252-0663**). 4014 N. Goldwater Blvd., Suite 101, Scottsdale. ✆ **888/560-9919** or 480/947-2974. www.poisonedpen.com.

CHOCOLATE

Cerreta Candy Company Want to feel like a kid in Willy Wonka's candy factory? Head west to Glendale and Cerreta's candy factory, which is open for tours Monday through Friday at 10am and 1pm. The store here is packed with all kinds of sweet treats and is open Monday through Saturday from 8am to 6pm. 5345 W. Glendale Ave., Glendale. ✆ **623/930-1000.** www.cerreta.com.

Chatham's Fine Chocolate Ever since I discovered Belgian chocolates on a trip to Brussels, I have had a weakness for fine chocolates, so when I discovered this shop in Scottsdale, I was like a, well, like a kid in a candy shop. I'll have one of those and one of those and one of those. The chocolates are from 13 chocolatiers around the world and they are absolutely exquisite. At Hilton Village, 6107 N. Scottsdale Rd., Scottsdale. ✆ **480/443-7752.** www.chathamsfinechocolates.com.

FASHION

In addition to the options mentioned below, there are lots of great shops in malls all over the city. Favorite destinations for upscale fashions include Biltmore Fashion Park, The Borgata of Scottsdale, el Pedregal Festival Marketplace, and Scottsdale Fashion Square. See "Malls & Shopping Centers," below, for details.

For cowboy and cowgirl attire, see "Western Wear," below.

Barbwire Western Couture If you, or perhaps your daughter, are looking for the latest in over-the-top cowgirl chic fashions, look no further. Barbwire is, well, cutting edge when it comes to clothes and accessories inspired by both the Wild West and rock 'n' roll. 15425 N. Scottsdale Rd., Suite 230, Scottsdale. ✆ **866/929-9473** or 480/443-9473. www.barbwire.com.

Conrad Leather Boutique It may be hot when you visit Arizona, but remember, you have to go home where it's probably a whole lot cooler. If you need a new leather jacket or belt, there's no better place in the Valley to look than this north Scottsdale boutique. Beautiful leather jackets for both men and women fill the shop. In el Pedregal, 34505 N. Scottsdale Rd., Suite E-7, Scottsdale. ✆ **480/488-2190.**

Electric Ladyland With its way-over-the-top supercluttered decor, this shop feels a bit like a cross between a drag queen's boutique and a bordello supply store. Got you curious? The clothes are sexy, that's for sure, and you have to be young and shapely to look good in anything they sell here. It's just such a fun shop, though—check it out even if you have no intention of buying. Also be sure to check out Electric Ladyland Denim, 3925 E. Camelback Rd., Phoenix (✆ **602/954-8438**). 15435 N. Scottsdale Rd., Suite 100, Scottsdale. ✆ **480/948-9341.** www.electricladyland.com.

Objects This eclectic shop carries hand-painted, wearable art—both casual and dressy—along with unique artist-made jewelry, contemporary furnishings, and all kinds of delightful and unusual items for the home. In The Shops at Gainey Village, 8787 N. Scottsdale Rd., Scottsdale. ✆ **480/994-4720.** www.objectsgallery.com.

Stefan Mann Purses, purses, purses. Gorgeous leather purses, wallets, and luggage are to be had here at Stefan Mann, which has been in business for more than 25 years. If you're constantly on the prowl for a standout handbag, you'll certainly find something here. In el Pedregal, 34505 N. Scottsdale Rd., Suite J-6, Scottsdale. ✆ **480/488-3371.** www.stefanmann.com.

Scottsdale Jean Company If you're searching for the latest high-fashion jeans, don't leave town without dropping by this shop in north Scottsdale. It has the biggest and best selection of jeans in the city. 14747 N. Northsight Blvd. (at Raintree Dr., on the NE corner), Scottsdale. ✆ **480/905-9300.** www.scottsdalejc.com.

GIFTS & SOUVENIRS

Bischoff's Shades of the West This is a one-stop shop for all things Southwestern. From T-shirts to regional foodstuffs, this sprawling store has it all, with good selections of candles, Mexican crafts, and wrought-iron cabinet hardware that can give your kitchen a Western look. 7247 Main St., Scottsdale. ✆ **480/945-3289.** www.shadesofthewest.com.

Sphinx Date Ranch Dates—love 'em or hate 'em, there's no denying the connection these super-sweet little palm fruits have to the desert. At this old-fashioned shop just south of Old Town Scottsdale, you can buy all kinds of dates and date products. 3039 N. Scottsdale Rd., Scottsdale. ✆ **800/482-3283** or 480/941-2261. www.sphinxdateranch.com.

The Store @ Scottsdale Center for the Performing Arts ★ This gift shop on the downtown Scottsdale mall has a wonderful selection of fun, contemporary, and artistic gifts, including lots of jewelry. There's another gift shop next door at the Scottsdale Museum of Contemporary Art. 7380 E. Second St., Scottsdale. ✆ **480/874-4644.** www.scottsdaleperformingarts.com.

Two Plates Full I love wandering through this shop just to marvel at all the bright colors and fun designs. Featuring functional art and crafts, home accessories, and jewelry, this is a great place to shop for unique gifts. In The Borgata, 6166 N. Scottsdale Rd., Suite 402, Scottsdale. ✆ **480/443-3241.** www.twoplatesfull.com.

GOLF

In Celebration of Golf ★★ Sort of a supermarket for golfers (wi [illegible] neyland thrown in), this amazing store sells everything from clubs a [illegible] art and golf antiques. A golf-simulation room allows you to test out n [illegible] there are even unique golf cars on display in case you want to take to th [illegible] s in a custom car. An old club-maker's workbench, complete with talking mannequin, makes a visit to this shop educational as well as fun. Also at Kierland Commons, 15220 N. Scottsdale Rd. (✆ **480/948-1766**). At Scottsdale Seville, 7001 N. Scottsdale Rd., Suite 172, Scottsdale. ✆ **800/310-9459** or 480/951-4444. www.incelebrationofgolf.com.

JEWELRY

Cornelis Hollander Although this shop is much smaller and not nearly as dramatic as the nearby Jewelry by Gauthier store (see below), the designs are just as cutting edge. Whether you're looking for classic chic or trendy modern designs, you'll find plenty to interest you here. There's a second store in north Scottsdale at 36207 N. Scottsdale Rd. (✆ **480/575-5583**). 4151 N. Marshall Way, Scottsdale. ✆ **480/423-5000.** www.cornelishollander.com.

Jewelry by Gauthier This elegant store sells the designs of the phenomenally talented Scott Gauthier. The stylishly modern pieces use precious stones and are miniature works of art. There's a second, much smaller shop in Kierland Commons, 15034 N. Scottsdale Rd., Suite 120 (✆ **480/443-4030**). 4211 N. Marshall Way, Scottsdale. ✆ **888/411-3232** or 480/941-1707. www.jewelrybygauthier.com.

Molina Boutique If you can spend as much on a necklace as you can on a Mercedes, then this is *the* place to shop for your baubles. Although you don't need an appointment, it's highly recommended. You'll then get personalized service as you peruse the classically styled jewelry. 3134 E. Camelback Rd. ✆ **800/257-2695** or 602/955-2055. www.molinafinejewelers.com.

Sami This little jewelry store northeast of Scottsdale in the town of Fountain Hills specializes in amethyst from a mine in the nearby Four Peaks Mountains. The mine has been producing gemstones since Spanish colonial times, and the very best of the stones wind up at this shop. You'll also find Arizona peridot and "anthill" garnet jewelry here. 16704 Avenue of the Fountains, Suite 100, Fountain Hills. ✆ **877/376-6323** or 480/837-8168. www.arizonagems.com.

MALLS & SHOPPING CENTERS

While locals don't want to call it a shopping center, the **Scottsdale Waterfront,** an ambitious mixed-use development along a canal at the corner of Camelback and Scottsdale roads, is essentially just that. There are shops, most of which are either national chains or satellites of popular local boutiques, restaurants (once again national and local chains), and high-rise residential towers. The only real difference between the Scottsdale Waterfront and the attached Scottsdale Fashion Square is that at the waterfront you actually have to (get to?) walk around outside. Now, when I say this development is along a canal, don't start thinking Venice-style canals. Scottsdale's canal, a cement-lined trough, is not exactly a romantic water course. Still, the Scottsdale Waterfront and its sister development, the **South Waterfront,** are the prettiest new shopping and dining destinations in town and are worth a visit.

Biltmore Fashion Park ★ This open-air shopping plaza with garden courtyards is one of the most pleasant places to shop in Phoenix. Saks Fifth Avenue and Macy's are e two anchors, while smaller storefronts bear familiar names including Tommy Bahama, Victoria's Secret, Ralph Lauren, and The Sharper Image. There are also nearly a dozen moderately priced restaurants here. 2502 E. Camelback Rd. (at 24th St.). ✆ **602/955-8400** or 602/955-1963. www.shopbiltmore.com.

The Borgata of Scottsdale ★★ Designed to resemble the medieval Italian village of San Gimignano, complete with turrets, stone walls, and ramparts, The Borgata is far and away the most architecturally interesting mall in the Valley. Within its walls, you'll find about 50 upscale boutiques, galleries, and restaurants. On Friday evenings, there's live jazz. This shopping center has just undergone an extensive remodeling and is looking better than ever. 6166 N. Scottsdale Rd. ✆ **602/953-6311.** www.borgata.com.

el Pedregal Shops & Dining at The Boulders ★★ Adjacent to The Boulders resort 30 minutes north of Old Scottsdale, el Pedregal is the most self-consciously Southwestern shopping center in the Valley, and it's worth the long drive out just to see the neo–Santa Fe/Moroccan architecture. The shops offer high-end merchandise, fashions, and art. The Heard Museum also has a branch here. 34505 N. Scottsdale Rd., Carefree. ✆ **480/488-1072.** www.elpedregal.com.

Kierland Commons ★★ The urban-village concept of a shopping center—narrow streets, sidewalks, and residences mixed in with retail space—has taken off all over the country, and here in Scottsdale, the concept has taken on Texas-size proportions. However, despite the grand scale of this shopping center, it has a great feel. You'll find Tommy Bahama, Ann Taylor Loft, Crate & Barrel, and even a few local boutiques, including favorites Mahsa and 42 Saint, which stock fashions not found elsewhere. North Scottsdale and Greenway Rds. ✆ **480/348-1577.** www.kierlandcommons.com.

Scottsdale Fashion Square Scottsdale has long been the Valley's shopping mecca, and for years this huge mall has been the reason why. It now houses four major department stores—Nordstrom, Dillard's, Neiman Marcus, and Macy's—and smaller stores such as Coach, Eddie Bauer, J. Crew, and Louis Vuitton. 7014–590 E. Camelback Rd. (at Scottsdale Rd.), Scottsdale. ✆ **480/949-0202.** www.westcor.com.

The Shops Gainey Village This upscale shopping center is much smaller than Kierland Commons farther up Scottsdale Road, but is no less impressive, especially after dark when lights illuminate the tall palm trees. There may not be a more impressive concentration of women's clothing stores anywhere in Scottsdale. 8777–8989 N. Scottsdale Rd. (at Doubletree Ranch Rd.). ✆ **858/622-0858.** www.theshopsgaineyvillage.com.

NATIVE AMERICAN ARTS, CRAFTS & JEWELRY

Bischoff's at the Park ★★ This museum-like store and gallery is affiliated with another Bischoff's right across the street (see "Gifts & Souvenirs," above). However, this outpost carries higher-end jewelry, Western-style home furnishings, and clothing, ceramics, sculptures, contemporary paintings, and books and music with a regional theme. 3925 N. Brown Ave., Scottsdale. ✆ **480/946-6155.**

Blue Sage Gallery Collectors of old Navajo rugs should be sure to make the drive north to the town of Carefree to visit this little shop. It has one of the best selections of antique Navajo rugs in the state. There are also great old Native American baskets from around the West. el Pedregal Shops & Dining at The Boulders, 34505 N. Scottsdale Rd., Suite E-4, Scottsdale. ✆ **480/945-3385.**

Faust Gallery ★ Old Native American baskets and pottery, as well as old and new Navajo rugs, are the specialties at this interesting shop. It also sells Native American and Southwestern art, including ceramics, paintings, bronzes, and unusual sculptures. 7103 E. Main St., Scottsdale. ✆ **480/946-6345.** www.faustgallery.com.

Gilbert Ortega Gallery & Museum You'll find Gilbert Ortega shops all over the Valley, but this is the biggest and best. As the name implies, there are museum displays throughout the store. Jewelry is the main attraction, but there are also baskets, sculptures, pottery, rugs, paintings, and kachina dolls. 3925 N. Scottsdale Rd. ✆ **480/990-1808.** www.gilbertortega.com.

Heard Museum Gift Shop The Heard Museum (see "Seeing the Sights," earlier in this chapter) has an astonishing collection of well-crafted and very Native American jewelry, art, and crafts of all kinds. This is the best place in the Valley to shop for Native American arts and crafts; you can be absolutely assured of the quality. Because the store doesn't have to charge sales tax, you'll save a bit of money. At the Heard Museum, 2301 N. Central Ave. ✆ **602/252-8344.** www.heard.org.

John C. Hill Antique Indian Art ★★ While shops selling Native American art and artifacts abound in Scottsdale, few offer the high quality available in this tiny shop. Not only does the store have one of the finest selections of Navajo rugs in the Valley, including quite a few older rugs, but there are kachina dolls, superb pieces of Navajo and Zuni silver-and-turquoise jewelry, baskets, and pottery. 6962 E. First Ave., Suite 104, Scottsdale. ✆ **480/946-2910.** www.johnhillgallery.com.

Old Territorial Shop ★★ Owned and operated by Alston and Deborah Neal, this is the oldest Indian arts-and-crafts store on Main Street and offers good values on jewelry, concho belts, kachina dolls, fetishes, pottery, and Navajo rugs. 7077 E. Main St., Suite 7, Scottsdale. ✆ **480/945-5432.** www.oldterritorialshop.com.

River Trading Post If you are interested in getting into collecting Native American art or artifacts, this is a good place to get in on the ground floor. Quality is high and prices are relatively low. Not only are there high-quality Navajo rugs, but there are also museum-quality pieces of ancient Southwestern pottery. 7140 E. First Ave., Scottsdale. ✆ **866/426-6901** or 480/444-0001. www.rivertradingpost.com.

OUTLET MALLS & DISCOUNT SHOPPING

Arizona Mills This huge mall in Tempe is a temple of budget consumerism that attracts primarily young, cash-strapped shoppers. You'll find lots of name-brand outlets, a multiplex theater, and an IMAX theater. 5000 Arizona Mills Circle, Tempe. ✆ **480/491-7300.** www.arizonamills.com. From I-10, take the Baseline Rd. east exit. From U.S. 60, exit Priest Dr. south.

My Sister's Closet This is where the crème de la crème of Scottsdale's used clothing comes to be resold. You'll find reasonable prices on such labels as Armani, Donna Karan, and Calvin Klein. Also at Town & Country shopping plaza, 2033 E. Camelback Rd., Phoenix (✆ **602/954-6080**), and Desert Village, 23435 N. Pima Rd., Suite 171 (✆ **480/419-6242**). At Lincoln Village, 6204 N. Scottsdale Rd. (near Trader Joe's), Scottsdale. ✆ **480/443-4575.** www.mysisterscloset.com.

WESTERN WEAR

Az-Tex Hat Company If you're looking to bring home a cowboy hat, this is the best place in Scottsdale to do your shopping. The small shop in Old Scottsdale offers custom shaping and fitting of both felt and woven hats. 3903 N. Scottsdale Rd., Scottsdale. ✆ **800/972-2116** or 480/481-9900. www.aztexhats.com.

Out West ★ If the revival of 1950s cowboy fashions and interior decor has hit your nostalgia button, then you'll want to high-tail it up to this eclectic shop. All things Western are available, and the fashions are both beautiful and fun (although fancy and pricey). 7003 E. Cave Creek Rd., Cave Creek. ✆ **480/488-0180.** www.outwestmercantile.com.

Saba's Western Stores Since 1927, this store has been outfitting Scottsdale's cowboys and cowgirls, visiting dude ranchers, and anyone else who wants to adopt the look of the Wild West. Call or check the website for other locations around Phoenix. 7254 Main St., Scottsdale. ✆ **877/342-1835** or 480/949-7404. www.sabaswesternwear.com.

Sheplers Western Wear Although it isn't the largest Western-wear store in the Valley, Sheplers is still sort of a department store of cowboy duds. If you can't find it here, it just ain't available in these parts. Other locations include 8999 E. Indian Bend Rd., Scottsdale (✆ **480/948-1933**), and 2643 E. Broadway Rd., Mesa (✆ **480/827-8244**). 9201 N. 29th Ave., Suite 39. ✆ **602/870-8085.** www.sheplers.com.

Stockman's Cowboy & Southwestern Wear This is one of the oldest Western-wear businesses in the Valley, although the store is now housed in a modern shopping plaza. You'll find denim jackets, suede coats, and flashy cowboy shirts. Prices are reasonable and quality is high. 23587 N. Scottsdale Rd. (at Pinnacle Peak Rd.), Scottsdale. ✆ **480/585-6142.**

11 Phoenix & Scottsdale After Dark

If you're looking for nightlife in the Valley of the Sun, you won't have to look hard, but you may have to drive quite a ways. Although much of the nightlife scene is centered on Old Town Scottsdale, Tempe's Mill Avenue, and downtown Phoenix, you'll find things going on all over.

The weekly *Phoenix New Times* tends to have the most comprehensive listings for clubs and concert halls. "Calendar" in the Thursday edition of the *Arizona Republic* also lists upcoming events and performances. *Get Out,* published by the *Tribune,* is another tabloid-format arts-and-entertainment publication that is available free around Scottsdale, Phoenix, and Tempe. Other publications to check for abbreviated listings are *Valley Guide, Arizona Key,* and *Where Phoenix/Scottsdale,* all of which are free and can usually be found at hotels and resorts.

Tickets to many concerts, theater performances, and sporting events are available through **Ticketmaster** (✆ **480/784-4444;** www.ticketmaster.com), which has outlets at Macy's department stores and Fry's Marketplace grocery stores.

THE CLUB & MUSIC SCENE

Even if it were not in the middle of the desert, the Scottsdale club scene would be red hot. Packed into a few dozen blocks surrounding Old Town Scottsdale, near the corner of Camelback and Scottsdale roads, there are dozens of trendy dance clubs and chic bars. This is where the wealthy fashionistas (and the wannabes) come to party. The crowd is young, affluent, and attractive, and with all the beautiful people cruising around in Porsches and limousines, it's easy to think you're in L.A. Cruise along **Stetson Drive,** which is divided into two sections (east and west of Scottsdale Rd.), to find the latest hot spots.

While Scottsdale is the nexus of nightclubbing for the fashion conscious, the Valley has plenty of clubs and bars for those who don't wear Prada. Other nightlife districts include Tempe's Mill Avenue and downtown Phoenix. This latter area comes into its own after basketball and baseball games and concerts at the US Airways Center.

Mill Avenue in Tempe is a good place to wander around in search of your favorite type of music. The bars and clubs here are mostly within walking distance of one another. Because Tempe is a college town, the crowd tends to be young and rowdy.

Downtown Phoenix is home to Symphony Hall, the Herberger Theater Center, and several sports bars. However, much of the action revolves around sports events and concerts at US Airways Center and Chase Field.

As most denizens of any urban nightlife scene know, clubs come and go. To find out what's hot, get a copy of the *New Times.* Many dance clubs in the Phoenix area are open only on weekends, so be sure to check what night the doors will be open. Bars and clubs are allowed to serve alcohol until 2am.

COUNTRY

Buffalo Chip Saloon & Steakhouse Cave Creek is the Valley's last Wild West town and is full of cowboy bars. This barnlike place is a local favorite, especially with fans of the Green Bay Packers. There's live country music Thursday through Sunday nights, all-you-can-eat fish fries featuring walleye, and s'mores on the dessert menu. Currently, on the first Sunday of each month, there's cowboy-comedy dinner theater. 6811 E. Cave Creek Rd., Cave Creek. ✆ **480/488-9118.** www.buffalochipsaloon.com.

Handlebar-J This Scottsdale landmark is about as genuine a cowboy bar as you'll find in Phoenix, and cowpokes often stop by when they come in from the ranch. You'll hear live git-down two-steppin' nightly; free dance lessons are given Wednesday, Thursday, and Sunday at 7pm. 7116 Becker Lane (1 block N of the NW corner of Scottsdale Rd. and Shea Blvd.), Scottsdale. ✆ **480/948-0110.** www.handlebarj.com. No cover to $5.

Rusty Spur Saloon A small, rowdy, drinkin'-and-dancin' place frequented by tourists, this bar is loads of fun, with peanut shells all over the floor, dollar bills stapled to the walls, and live country music afternoons and evenings. If you're a cowboy or cowgirl at heart, this is the place to party when you're in Scottsdale. 7245 E. Main St., Old Scottsdale. ✆ **480/425-7787.** www.rustyspursaloon.com.

DANCE CLUBS & DISCOS

Axis/Radius If you're looking to do a bit of celebrity-spotting, Axis is one of the best places in town to keep your eye on. For several years now, this has been one of Scottsdale's hottest dance clubs and liveliest singles scenes. The two-story glass box is a bold contemporary space with an awesome sound system. These twin clubs are open Wednesday through Saturday. 7340 E. Indian Plaza (2 blocks east of Scottsdale Rd. and 1 block south of Camelback Rd.), Scottsdale. ✆ **480/970-1112.** www.axis-radius.com. No cover to $10.

Barcelona It's big, it's beautiful, and it's busy. This is Scottsdale's premier supper club, and after the dinner crowd gives up its tables Thursday through Saturday nights, Barcelona becomes one of the city's top dance spots. The well-heeled crowd ranges primarily from their 30s to 50s. 15440 Greenway-Hayden Loop. ✆ **480/603-0370.** www.barcelonadining.com. No cover to $10.

e4 Taking its design theme from the four elements—earth, air, fire, and water—this stylish nightclub provides the four coolest club spaces in Scottsdale. There's the sexy red light and dance floor of the fire room, the cool blue and bubbly liquid room (another dance space), the space-age air patio, and the subterranean earth lounge for chilling out. You could spend the whole night just seeing it all. 4282 N. Drinkwater Blvd., Scottsdale. ✆ **480/970-3325.** www.e4-az.com. No cover to $10.

Myst Always packed to the walls with the Valley's beautiful people, Myst is currently *the* place to see and be seen. The atmosphere is lavishly ostentatious, with various themed rooms. There's even a pool room called the Ballroom. The club is usually open Wednesday, Friday, and Saturday. 7340 E. Shoeman Lane, Scottsdale. © **480/970-5000.** www.mystaz.com. Cover $5–$20.

Pepin Friday and Saturday starting at 10pm and Sunday beginning at 9pm, a DJ plays Latin dance music at this small Spanish restaurant located in the Scottsdale Mall. Friday and Saturday evenings, there are also live flamenco performances. 7363 Scottsdale Mall, Scottsdale. © **480/990-9026.** www.pepinrestaurant.com. Cover $8.

ROCK, BLUES & JAZZ

Geordie's at the Wrigley Mansion Open only on Friday and Saturday nights, this lounge is inside the historic Wrigley Mansion, which was built between 1929 and 1931 by chewing gum magnate William Wrigley, Jr. The sprawling mansion is located on a hilltop adjacent to the Arizona Biltmore resort. 2501 E. Telawa Trail. © **602/955-4079.** www.wrigleymansionclub.com. No cover.

Char's Has the Blues You wouldn't think to look at this little cottage, but it really does have those mean-and-dirty, low-down blues. All of the best blues brothers and sisters from around the city and around the country make the scene here. 4631 N. Seventh Ave., 4 blocks south of Camelback Rd. © **602/230-0205.** www.charshastheblues.com. No cover to $10.

The Rhythm Room This blues club, long the Valley's most popular, books quite a few national acts as well as the best of the local scene, and has a dance floor if you want to move to the beat. 1019 E. Indian School Rd. © **602/265-4842.** www.rhythmroom.com. No cover to $25.

Sugar Daddy's You're probably used to cheap drinks and appetizers at happy hour, but how about live music? This place has rock and blues bands for happy hour and for Sunday brunch, and it features live music most nights at 9:30pm. There's a huge patio as well. The crowd tends to be college age or slightly older. 3102 N. Scottsdale Rd. © **480/970-6556.** www.sugardaddysaz.com. Cover $3.

THE BAR, LOUNGE & PUB SCENE

AZ88 Located across the park from the Scottsdale Center for the Arts, this sophisticated bar/restaurant has a cool, contemporary ambience that's just right for a cocktail (try a martini) or a basket of waffle fries before or after a performance. There's also a great patio area. 7353 Scottsdale Mall, Scottsdale. © **480/994-5576.** www.az88.com.

Bar Bianco ★ Located downtown on Heritage Square, this little wine bar is in a restored historic home and is affiliated with Pizzeria Bianco, the tiny and ever-popular designer pizza place right next door. This is a very romantic place for a drink. 609 E. Adams St. © **602/528-3699.**

camus Located just a couple of blocks west of Central Avenue, camus is another stylish midtown bar/restaurant for fashionably dressed young professionals. The minimalist decor has a retro feel, and the blue lights give the place a modern, romantic feel. At the Clarendon Hotel, 401 W. Clarendon Ave. © **602/21-CAMUS.**

Dos Gringos For young partiers who don't feel like getting dressed up to go out on the town, this is a great choice. With its open-air bar, Dos Gringos is patterned after Mexican beach bars and can be loads of fun on a Saturday night. The Tempe location, 1001 E. Eighth St. (© **480/968-7879**), is frequented by ASU students. 4209 N. Craftsman Court, Scottsdale. © **480/423-3800.** www.dosgringosaz.com.

Durant's In business for decades, Durant's has long been downtown Phoenix's favorite after-work watering hole. Although especially popular with the old guard, this classic bar has caught on with the young martini-drinking crowd as well. 2611 N. Central Ave. ✆ **602/264-5967.** www.durantsfinefoods.com.

Fez If you happen to be in downtown Phoenix and are looking for a stylish place for a cocktail, drop by this hip bar/restaurant on Central Avenue. Although the name sounds like this might be some exotic Moroccan place, nothing is further from the truth. About the only thing remotely North African here is the pomegranate juice used in the cocktails. 3815 N. Central Ave. ✆ **602/287-8700.** www.fezoncentral.com.

Four Peaks Brewing Company Consistently voted the best brewpub in Phoenix, this Tempe establishment, housed in a former creamery, brews good beers and serves decent pub grub. It's a favorite of ASU students. You'll find this pub south of East University Drive between South Rural Road and South McClintock Drive. There's a second brewpub in north Scottsdale at the corner of Hayden Road and Frank Lloyd Wright Boulevard (✆ 480/991-1795). 1340 E. Eighth St., Tempe. ✆ **480/303-9967.** www.fourpeaks.com.

Hyatt Regency Scottsdale Lobby Bar ★★ The open-air lounge just below the main lobby of this posh Scottsdale resort sets a romantic stage for nightly live music (often flamenco or Caribbean steel drum music). Wood fires burn in patio fire pits, and the terraced gardens offer plenty of dark spots for a bit of romance. 7500 E. Doubletree Ranch Rd., Scottsdale. ✆ **480/444-1234.** www.scottsdale.hyatt.com.

Rula Bula ★ The middle of the desert may seem like an odd place for an Irish pub, but Rula Bula has such an authentic feel that it's easy to imagine that it's damp and dreary outside. 401 S. Mill Ave., Tempe. ✆ **480/929-9500.** www.rulabula.com.

Six ★ There are those who frequent this posh bar just to see the look on newcomers' faces when they see the high-tech unisex bathrooms—the glass is transparent until you go inside! Regardless of why you come, you'll find one of the coolest and most stylish drinking establishments in the state. Popular with visiting celebrities. 7316 E. Stetson Dr., Scottsdale. ✆ **480/663-6620.** www.6az.com.

T. Cook's ★★ If you aren't planning on having dinner at this opulent Mediterranean restaurant, at least stop by for a cocktail in the bar. With its mix of Spanish colonial and 1950s tropical furnishings, this is as romantic a lounge as you'll find anywhere in the Valley. You can also snuggle with your sweetie out on the patio by the fireplace. At the Royal Palms Resort & Spa, 5200 E. Camelback Rd. ✆ **602/840-3610.** www.royalpalmshotel.com.

WINE BARS

Cave Creek Coffee Co. & Wine Purveyors Located way up north in the cow town of Cave Creek, this hip coffeehouse doubles as a lively wine bar that also happens to book some great music. Past performers have included Kelly Joe Phelps, Michelle Shocked, Richie Havens, and Leo Kottke. 6033 E. Cave Creek Rd., Cave Creek. ✆ **480/488-0603.** www.cavecreekcoffee.com. Cover $15–$38.

Kazimierz World Wine Bar ★ Sort of a spacious speak-easy crossed with a wine cellar, this place, which is associated with the nearby Cowboy Ciao restaurant, offers the same wide selection of wines available at the restaurant. There are dozens of wines by the glass and live jazz ($5 cover after 8pm) several nights each week. The entrance is hard to find (look for the big wood door with a sign that says THE TRUTH IS INSIDE), but it's worth seeking out. 7137 E. Stetson Dr., Scottsdale. ✆ **480/946-3004.** www.kazbar.net.

Postino ★★ This immensely popular wine bar is in the heart of the Arcadia neighborhood, south of Camelback Road, and is housed in a former post office. Casual yet stylish, the bar has garage-style doors that roll up to expose the restaurant to the outdoors. Choose from a great selection of wines by the glass and a limited menu of European-inspired appetizers. 3939 E. Campbell Ave. ✆ **602/852-3939.** www.postinowinecafe.com.

Uncorked: The Unpretentious Wine Bar ★ This unpretentious little north Scottsdale wine bar is a challenge to locate, but that's what makes it such an enjoyable spot. You'll find Uncorked in the courtyard of the Promenade Corporate Center at the intersection of Scottsdale Road and Frank Lloyd Wright Boulevard in the same shopping center that houses the big blue Frank Lloyd Wright spire. 16427 N. Scottsdale Rd., Suite 130. ✆ **480/699-9230.** www.uncorkedwinebar.com.

COCKTAILS WITH A VIEW

The Valley of the Sun has more than its fair share of spectacular views. Unfortunately, most of them are from expensive restaurants. All these restaurants have lounges, though, where, for the price of a drink (and perhaps valet parking), you can sit back and ogle a crimson sunset and the purple mountains' majesty. Among the best choices are **Different Pointe of View,** at the Pointe Hilton Tapatio Cliffs Resort; **Rustler's Rooste,** at the Pointe South Mountain Resort; and **jade bar,** at The Sanctuary on Camelback Mountain.

Wright Bar & Squaw Peak Terrace Can't afford the lifestyles of the rich and famous? For the cost of a couple of drinks, you can sink into a seat here at the Biltmore's main lounge and watch the sunset test its color palette on Piestewa Peak. Alternatively, you can slide into a seat near the piano and let the waves of mellow jazz wash over you. At the Arizona Biltmore Resort & Spa, 2400 E. Missouri Ave. ✆ **602/381-7632.** www.arizonabiltmore.com.

Thirsty Camel Whether you've already made your millions or are still working your way up the corporate ladder, you owe it to yourself to spend a little time in the lap of luxury. You may never drink in more ostentatious surroundings than here at Arizona's most luxurious resort. The view is one of the best in the city. At The Phoenician, 6000 E. Camelback Rd. ✆ **480/941-8200.**

SPORTS BARS

Alice Cooper'stown Sports and rock mix it up at this downtown restaurant/bar run by, you guessed it, Alice Cooper. Chase Field, where the Arizona Diamondbacks play ball, is only a block away. See p. 143 for more information. 101 E. Jackson St. ✆ **602/253-7337.** www.alicecooperstown.com.

Don & Charlie's Although this is primarily a steakhouse, it also has the best sports bar in Scottsdale. What makes Don & Charlie's such a great sports bar is not the size or number of its TVs, but rather all the sports memorabilia on the walls. 7501 E. Camelback Rd. ✆ **480/990-0900.** www.donandcharlies.com.

Majerle's Sports Grill If you're a Phoenix Suns fan, you won't want to miss this sports bar located only a couple of blocks from US Airways Center, where the Suns play. Suns memorabilia covers the walls, and who knows, you just might bump into a team member or two while you're here. 24 N. Second St. ✆ **602/253-0118.** www.majerles.com.

GAY & LESBIAN BARS & CLUBS

Ain't Nobody's Bizness Located in a small shopping plaza, this is the city's most popular lesbian bar. The music here is primarily hip-hop, and on weekends, the dance floor is usually packed. 3031 E. Indian School Rd., Suite 7. ✆ **602/224-9977.** www.aintnobodysbizness-az.com.

Amsterdam/Club Miami/Malibu Beach Bar This downtown Phoenix nightclub complex may not look like much from the outside, but through the doors, you'll find a classy spot that's known across the Valley for its great martinis. There's usually a female impersonator one night of the week, and other nights, there's live music or DJ dance music. 718 N. Central Ave. ✆ **602/258-6122.** www.amsterdambar.com.

THE PERFORMING ARTS

Although downtown Phoenix claims the Valley's greatest concentration of performance halls, including Symphony Hall, the Orpheum Theatre, and the Herberger Theater Center, there are major performing arts venues scattered across the Valley. No matter where you happen to be staying, you're likely to find performances being held somewhere nearby.

Calling these many Valley venues home are such major companies as the Phoenix Symphony, Arizona Opera Company, Ballet Arizona, Center Dance Ensemble, Actors Theatre of Phoenix, and Arizona Theatre Company. Adding to the performances held by these companies are the wide variety of touring companies that make stops here throughout the year.

While you'll find box-office phone numbers listed below, you can also purchase most performing-arts tickets through **Ticketmaster** (✆ **480/784-4444;** www.ticketmaster.com). For sold-out shows, check with your hotel concierge, or try **Tickets Unlimited** (✆ **800/289-8497** or 602/840-2340; www.ticketsunlimitedinc.com).

MAJOR PERFORMING-ARTS CENTERS

Symphony Hall, 225 E. Adams St. (✆ **602/262-7272;** www.ci.phoenix.az.us/CIVPLAZA/stages.html#SYMPH), which underwent an extensive renovation and remodeling in 2005, is Phoenix's premier performance venue and is home to the Phoenix Symphony, Ballet Arizona, and the Arizona Opera Company. It also hosts touring Broadway shows and various other concerts and theatrical productions. The hall's Grand Drape is the world's largest piece of machine-made embroidery.

The **Orpheum Theatre,** 203 W. Adams St. (✆ **602/262-7272;** www.ci.phoenix.az.us/STAGES/orpheum.html), is the most elegant hall in the Valley. The historic Spanish colonial baroque-revival theater was built in 1929 and at the time was considered the most luxurious theater west of the Mississippi. Today, its ornately carved sandstone facade stands in striking contrast to the glass-and-steel City Hall building, with which the theater shares a common wall.

Although not the largest performance venue in town, the **Celebrity Theatre,** 440 N. 32nd St. (✆ **602/267-1600;** www.celebritytheatre.com), books some of the best shows. With its revolving stage and no seat farther than 75 feet from the performers, this is a great place to catch the likes of Carole King, Chris Isaak, or Joe Satriani.

The **Dodge Theatre,** 400 W. Washington St. (✆ **602/379-2888;** www.dodgetheatre.com), is another of Phoenix's major downtown performance halls and seats from 2,000 to 5,000 people. It books many top names in entertainment, as well as the occasional Broadway show or international touring company.

The Frank Lloyd Wright–designed **Grady Gammage Auditorium,** Mill Avenue and Apache Boulevard, Tempe (✆ **480/965-3434;** www.asugammage.com), on the Arizona State University campus, is at once massive and graceful. This 3,000-seat hall hosts everything from barbershop quartets to touring Broadway shows.

The **Scottsdale Center for the Arts,** 7380 E. Second St., Scottsdale (© **480/994-2787;** www.scottsdaleperformingarts.org), hosts a variety of performances and series, ranging from alternative dance to classical music. This center seems to get the best of the touring performers who come through the Valley.

In Scottsdale, near The Borgata shopping center, ASU's **Kerr Cultural Center,** 6110 N. Scottsdale Rd. (© **480/596-2660;** www.asukerr.com), a tiny venue in a historic home, offers up an eclectic season that includes music from around the world. The Kerr Cultural Center sponsors a couple of different free concert series, so be sure to check the calendar as you plan your Phoenix vacation.

With its sail-like shade canopies, sunken sculpture courtyard, numerous water features, and colorful architecture, the **Mesa Arts Center,** 1 E. Main St. (© **480/644-6500;** www.mesaartscenter.com), which opened in 2005, is the prettiest performing arts center in the valley. Check out the performance schedule when planning your visit. In the cooler months, there are weekly free lunchtime concerts.

OUTDOOR VENUES & SERIES

Given the weather, it should come as no surprise that Phoenicians like to attend performances under the sun and stars.

The **Cricket Pavilion,** 2121 N. 83rd Ave., Phoenix (© **602/254-7200;** www.cricket-pavilion.com), west of downtown and ½-mile north of I-10 between 75th and 83rd avenues, is the city's top outdoor venue. This 20,000-seat amphitheater is open year-round and hosts everything from Broadway musicals to rock concerts.

The **Mesa Amphitheater,** at University Drive and Center Street, Mesa (© **480/644-2560;** www.mesaamp.com), is a much smaller amphitheater that holds a wide variety of concerts in spring and summer, and occasionally other times of year as well.

Throughout the year, the **Scottsdale Center for the Arts,** 7380 E. Second St., Scottsdale (© **480/994-2787;** www.scottsdaleperformingarts.org), stages outdoor performances in the adjacent Scottsdale Amphitheater on the Scottsdale Civic Center Mall. The Sunday A'fair series runs from October to April, with free concerts from noon to 4:30pm on selected Sundays of each month. Performances range from acoustic blues to zydeco.

Two perennial favorites of Valley residents take place in particularly attractive surroundings. The Music in the Garden concerts at the **Desert Botanical Garden,** 1201 N. Galvin Pkwy. in Papago Park (© **480/941-1225;** www.dbg.org), are held on Sundays between January and March. The season always includes an eclectic array of musical styles. Tickets are $16 and include admission to the gardens. Sunday brunch is served for an additional charge. Between late March and late June, there are also Friday-night jazz concerts. Up on the north side of the Valley, just outside Carefree,

---

Moments Lunch & a Show

At downtown Phoenix's **Herberger Theater Center,** 222 E. Monroe St. (© **602/254-7399;** www.herbergertheater.org), lunch break means the actors hit the stage while the audience grabs sandwiches for Lunch Time Theater. Throughout much of the year, 30- to 45-minute plays are staged at noon on Tuesday, Wednesday, and Thursday. Tickets are only $6, and inexpensive boxed salads, sandwiches, and pasta salads can be ordered in advance.

---

el Pedregal Shops & Dining at The Boulders, 34505 N. Scottsdale Rd., Scottsdale (✆ **480/488-1072;** www.elpedregal.com), stages occasional jazz, blues, and rock concerts, and sometimes has free live music on weekends.

Outdoor concerts are also held at various parks and plazas around the Valley during the warmer months. Check local papers for listings.

CLASSICAL MUSIC, OPERA & DANCE

The **Phoenix Symphony** (✆ **800/776-9080** or 602/495-1999; www.phoenixsymphony.org), the Southwest's leading symphony orchestra, performs at Symphony Hall (tickets mostly run $18–$67).

Opera buffs will want to see what the **Arizona Opera Company** (✆ **602/266-7464;** www.azopera.org) has scheduled. Each season, this company stages up to five operas, both familiar and more obscure, and splits its time between Phoenix and Tucson. Tickets cost $30 to $125. Performances are held at Symphony Hall.

Ballet Arizona (✆ **888/3-BALLET** or 602/381-1096; www.balletaz.org) performs at both the Orpheum Theatre and Symphony Hall and stages both classical and contemporary ballets; tickets run $10 to $104. The **Center Dance Ensemble** (✆ **602/252-8497;** www.centerdance.com), the city's contemporary dance company, stages several productions a year at the Herberger Theater Center. Tickets cost $21. Between September and April, **Southwest Arts & Entertainment** (✆ **602/482-6410;** www.southwestae.com) brings acclaimed dance companies and music acts from around the world to Phoenix, with performances staged primarily at the Orpheum. Tickets are usually around $30.

THEATER

With nearly a dozen professional companies and the same number of nonprofessional companies taking to the boards throughout the year, a play is always being staged somewhere in the Valley.

The **Herberger Theater Center,** 222 E. Monroe St. (✆ **602/254-7399** or 602/252-8497; www.herbergertheater.org), which is located downtown and vaguely resembles a Spanish colonial church, is the city's main venue for live theater. Its two Broadway-style theaters together host hundreds of performances each year, including productions by the **Actors Theatre** and the **Arizona Theatre Company (ATC).** Actors Theatre (✆ **602/253-6701;** www.atphx.org) tends to stage smaller, lesser-known off-Broadway-type works, with musicals, dramas, and comedies equally represented; tickets go for $24 to $49. The annual production of *A Christmas Carol* is always a big hit. ATC (✆ **602/256-6995;** www.aztheatreco.org) is the state theater company and splits its performances between Phoenix and Tucson. Founded in 1967, it's the major force on the Arizona thespian scene. Productions range from world premieres to recent Tony award-winners to classics. Tickets run $21 to $62.

The **Phoenix Theatre,** 100 E. McDowell Rd. (✆ **602/254-2151;** www.phxtheatre.org), is in the Phoenix Art Museum building and has been around for more than 85 years. Musicals are the mainstays here; tickets are $24 to $39. If your interest lies in Broadway plays, see what **Broadway in Arizona** (✆ **480/965-3434;** www.broadwayacrossamerica.com/tempe) has scheduled. The series, focusing mostly on comedies and musicals, is held at the Gammage Auditorium in Tempe; tickets cost between $20 to $70, with the occasional higher-price ticket for a real blockbuster show. The **Theater League** (✆ **800/776-7469** or 602/262-7272; www.theaterleague.com) is another series that brings in Broadway musicals. Performances are held in the Orpheum Theatre, and tickets range from $45 to $49.

Scottsdale's small **Stagebrush Theatre,** 7020 E. Second St. (✆ **480/990-7405;** www.stagebrush.org), is the home of the Scottsdale Community Players and stages tried-and-true comedies and musicals, with the occasional drama thrown in. Tickets are $20. The **Arizona Jewish Theatre Co.** (✆ **602/264-0402;** www.azjewishtheatre.org), which stages plays by Jewish playwrights and with Jewish themes, performs at Playhouse on the Park, in the Viad Corporate Center, 1850 N. Central Ave. (at Palm Lane). Tickets range from $30 to $32. If you're staying in Scottsdale and are looking for something to do with the whole family, the **Scottsdale Desert Stages Theatre,** 4720 N. Scottsdale Rd. (✆ **480/483-1664;** www.desertstages.com), stages primarily musicals and children's theater productions. Tickets range from $12 to $25.

CASINOS

Casino Arizona at Salt River Operated by the Salt River Pima-Maricopa Indian Community, this is actually two separate operations that together comprise the most conveniently located casinos in the area. They're both just off U.S. 101 on the east side of Scottsdale and offer plenty of slot machines, cards, and other games of chance. Of course, they've got a free shuttle, too. U.S. 101 and Indian Bend Rd., and U.S. 101 and McKellips Rd. ✆ **480/850-7777.** www.casinoaz.com.

Fort McDowell Casino Located about 45 minutes northeast of downtown Scottsdale, this Indian casino is the oldest in the state, offering slot machines, poker, keno, bingo, and free shuttles from hotels around the Valley. There's also a very attractive resort hotel here. On Fort McDowell Rd. off Ariz. 87, 2 miles northeast of Shea Blvd., Fountain Hills. ✆ **800/THE-FORT.** www.fortmcdowellcasino.com.

12 A Side Trip from Phoenix: The Apache Trail ★★

There isn't a whole lot of desert or history left in Phoenix, but only an hour's drive to the east you'll find quite a bit of both. The **Apache Trail,** a narrow, winding, partially gravel road that snakes its way around the north side of the Superstition Mountains, offers some of the most scenic desert driving in central Arizona. Along the way are ghost towns and ancient ruins, saguaros and century plants, reservoirs and hiking trails. You could easily spend a couple days traveling this route, though most people make it a day trip. Pick and choose the stops that appeal to you, and be sure to get an early start. The gravel section of the road is well graded and is passable for regular passenger cars.

If you'd rather leave the driving to someone else, **Apache Trail Tours** (✆ **480/982-7661;** www.apachetrailtours.com) offers guided half-day and full-day tours along the Apache Trail. This company also offers off-road adventures in the Superstition Mountains and Four Peaks area. Tours range in price from $70 to $145.

To start this drive, head east on U.S. 60 to the town of Apache Junction, and then go north on Arizona 88. About 4 miles out of town is **Goldfield Ghost Town,** a reconstructed gold-mining town (see "Wild West Theme Towns" under "Seeing the Sights," earlier in this chapter). Allow plenty of time if you plan to stop here.

Not far from Goldfield is **Lost Dutchman State Park,** 6109 N. Apache Trail (✆ **480/982-4485**), where you can hike into the rugged Superstition Mountains and see what the region's gold seekers were up against. Springtime wildflower displays here can be absolutely gorgeous. Park admission is $5 per vehicle ($3 during the summer); a campground charges $12 to $25 per site.

Continuing northeast, you'll reach **Canyon Lake,** set in a deep canyon flanked by colorful cliffs and rugged rock formations. It's the first of three reservoirs you'll pass on this drive. The lakes provide much of Phoenix's drinking water, without which the city would never have been able to grow as large as it is today. At Canyon Lake, you can swim at the Acacia Picnic Area or the nearby Boulder Picnic Area, which is in a pretty side cove. You can also take a cruise on the ***Dolly* steamboat** (**© 480/827-9144;** www.dollysteamboat.com). A 90-minute jaunt on this reproduction paddle-wheeler costs $18 for adults and $10 for children 5 to 12. Lunch and dinner cruises ($34–$52) are also available, and there's a lakeside restaurant at the boat landing. But if you're at all hungry, try to hold out for nearby **Tortilla Flat** (**© 480/984-1776;** www.tortillaflataz.com), an old stagecoach stop with a restaurant, saloon, and general store. The ceiling and interior walls of this funky old place are plastered with thousands of dollar bills that have been left by previous customers. If it's hot out, be sure to stop in at the general store for some prickly-pear ice cream (guaranteed spineless).

A few miles past Tortilla Flat, the pavement ends and the truly spectacular desert scenery begins. Among the rocky ridges, arroyos, and canyons of this stretch of road, you'll see saguaro cacti and century plants (a type of agave that dies after sending up its flower stalk, which can reach heights of 15 ft.). Next you'll come to **Apache Lake,** which is not nearly as spectacular a setting as Canyon Lake, though it does have the **Apache Lake Marina and Resort** (**© 928/467-2511;** www.apachelake.com), with a motel, restaurant, general store, and campground. If you're inclined to turn this drive into an overnight trip, this would be a good place to spend the night. Room rates are $75 to $100; boat rentals are available.

Shortly before reaching pavement again, you'll see **Theodore Roosevelt Dam.** This dam, built in 1911, forms Roosevelt Lake and, despite its concrete face, is the largest masonry dam in the world.

Continuing on Arizona 88, you'll next come to **Tonto National Monument** ★ (**© 928/467-2241;** www.nps.gov/tont), which preserves some of the southernmost cliff dwellings in Arizona. These pueblos were occupied between about 1300 and 1450 by the Salado people and are some of the few remaining traces of this tribe, which once cultivated lands now flooded by Roosevelt Lake. The lower ruins are a half-mile up a steep trail from the visitor center, and the upper ruins are a 3-mile round-trip hike. The lower ruins are open daily year-round; the upper ruins are open November through April on guided tours. Tour reservations are required (reserve at least 2 weeks in advance). The park is open daily (except Christmas) from 8am to 5pm (you must begin the lower ruin trail by 4pm); admission is $3.

Keep going on Arizona 88 to the copper-mining town of **Globe.** Although you can't see the mines themselves, the tailings (remains of rock removed from the copper ore) can be seen piled high all around the town. Be sure to visit **Besh-Ba-Gowah Archaeological Park** ★ (**© 928/425-0320**), on the eastern outskirts of town. This Salado Indian pueblo site has been partially reconstructed, and several rooms are set up to reflect the way they might have looked when they were first occupied about 700 years ago. For this reason, they're among the most fascinating ruins in the state. Besh-Ba-Gowah is open daily from 9am to 5pm; admission is $3 for adults, $2 for seniors, and free for children 12 and under. To get here, head out of Globe on South Broad Street to Jesse Hayes Road.

From Globe, head west on U.S. 60. Three miles west of Superior, you'll come to **Boyce Thompson Arboretum** ★★, 37615 U.S. 60 (**© 520/689-2811;** arboretum.ag.arizona.

edu), dedicated to researching and propagating desert plants. This was the nation's first botanical garden established in the desert and is set in two small, rugged canyons. From the impressive cactus gardens, you can gaze up at sun-baked cliffs before ducking into a forest of eucalyptus trees along the stream that runs through the arboretum. As you hike the nature trails of this 320-acre garden, watch for the two bizarre boojum trees. September through April, the arboretum is open daily from 8am to 5pm, and May through August, it's open 6am to 3pm. Admission is $7.50 for adults and $3 for children 5 to 12. There are guided tours of the garden daily at 1pm.

If after a long day on the road you're looking for a place to eat, stop in at **Gold Canyon Golf Resort,** 6100 S. Kings Ranch Rd., Gold Canyon (✆ **800/624-6445** or 480/982-9090; www.gcgr.com), which has a good formal dining room and a more casual bar and grill.

13 En Route to Tucson

Driving southeast from Phoenix for about 60 miles will bring you to the Casa Grande and Coolidge area, where you can learn about the Hohokam people who once inhabited this region. If you're continuing south toward Tucson and you're not in a big hurry, I suggest taking the scenic **Pinal Pioneer Parkway** (Ariz. 79), which was the old highway between Phoenix and Tucson before the interstate was built.

ATTRACTIONS ALONG THE WAY

Attention discount shoppers! In the town of Casa Grande you can shop 'til you drop at the **Outlets at Casa Grande,** 2300 E. Tanger Dr. (✆ **800/405-5016** or 520/836-9663; www.outletsatcasagrande.com). You'll find this collection of discount outlet stores at exit 198 off I-10.

Casa Grande Ruins National Monument ★★ Located outside the town of Coolidge, this national monument preserves one of the most unusual Indian ruins in the state. In Spanish, *Casa Grande* means "Big House," and that's exactly what you'll find. In this instance, the big house is the ruin of an earth-walled structure built 650 years ago by the Hohokam people. It is speculated that the building was once some sort of astronomical observatory, but this is not known for certain. Whatever the original purpose of the building, today it provides a glimpse of a style of ancient architecture rarely seen. Instead of using adobe bricks or stones, the people who built this structure used layers of hard-packed soil, which have survived the ravages of the weather and still stand in silent testament to the Hohokam's long-ago architectural endeavors. The Hohokam began farming the valleys of the Gila and Salt rivers about 1,500 years ago, and eventually built an extensive network of irrigation canals for watering their fields. By the middle of the 15th century, the Hohokam had abandoned both their canals and their villages and disappeared without a trace.

1100 W. Ruins Dr., Coolidge (Ariz. 87, 1 mile north of Coolidge). ✆ **520/723-3172.** www.nps.gov/cagr. Admission $5. Daily 8am–5pm. Closed Christmas.

Picacho Peak State Park ★★ If you're heading to Tucson by way of I-10, consider a stop at this state park, 35 miles northwest of Tucson at Exit 219. Picacho Peak, a wizard's cap of rock rising 1,500 feet above the desert, is a visual landmark for miles around. Hiking trails lead around the lower slopes of the peak and up to the summit; these trails are especially popular in spring, when the wildflowers bloom (the park is known as one of the best places in Arizona to see spring wildflowers). In addition to its natural beauty, Picacho Peak was the site of the only Civil War battle to take place in the state. Each March, Civil War reenactments are staged here. Campsites in the park cost $10 to $22.

Exit 219 off I-10. ✆ **520/466-3183.** www.pr.state.az.us. Admission $6 per car ($3 in summer). Daily 8am–10pm.

14 En Route to Northern Arizona

If you enjoy searching out deals at factory-outlet stores, then you'll be in heaven at the **Outlets at Anthem,** 4250 W. Anthem Way (✆ **623/465-9500;** www.outletsanthem.com). Among the offerings are Ann Taylor, Geoffrey Beene, Polo Ralph Lauren, and Levi's. Take Exit 229 (Anthem Way) off I-17.

Some 13 miles farther north is the town of Rock Springs, which is barely a wide spot in the road and is easily missed by drivers roaring up and down I-17. However, if you're a fan of pies, then do *not* miss Exit 242. Here you'll find the **Rock Springs Café,** 35769 S. Old Black Canyon Hwy., Rock Springs (✆ **623/374-5794;** www.rockspringscafe.com), in business since 1918. Although this aging, nondescript building looks like the sort of place that would best be avoided, the packed parking lot says different. Why so popular? It's not the "hogs in heat" barbecue or the Bradshaw Mountain oysters. No, what keeps this place packed are the pies, the most famous in Arizona. Every year, this place sells upwards of 45,000 pies. If one slice isn't enough, order a whole pie to go.

If you appreciate innovative architecture, don't miss the Cordes Junction exit (Exit 262) off I-17. Here you'll find **Arcosanti** (✆ **928/632-6217;** www.arcosanti.org), Italian architect Paolo Soleri's vision of the future—a "city" that merges architecture and ecology. Soleri, who came to Arizona to study with Frank Lloyd Wright at Taliesin West, envisions a compact, energy-efficient city that disturbs the natural landscape as little as possible—and that's just what's rising out of the desert here at Arcosanti. The organic design built of cast concrete will fascinate both students of architecture and those with only a passing interest in the discipline. Arcosanti has been built primarily with the help of students and volunteers who live here for various lengths of time. To help finance the construction, Soleri designs and sells wind bells cast in bronze or made of ceramic. These distinctive bells are available at the gift shop. Arcosanti is open daily from 9am to 5pm, and tours are held hourly between 10am and 4pm ($8 suggested donation). If you'd like to stay overnight, basic accommodations ($25–$75 double) are available by reservation. There's also a cafe that serves buffet meals to overnight guests.

East of I-17 between Black Canyon City and Cordes Junction lies **Agua Fria National Monument,** which is administered by the Bureau of Land Management, Phoenix Field Office, 21605 N. Seventh Ave., Phoenix (✆ **623/580-5500;** www.az.blm.gov/aguafria/pmesa.htm). The monument protects the region's numerous prehistoric Native American ruin sites, which date between 1250 and 1450 (at least 450 prehistoric sites are known to exist in this area). There is very limited access to the monument, and there are no facilities for visitors.

5

Central Arizona

Let's say you're planning a trip to Arizona. You're going to fly in to Phoenix, rent a car, and head north to the Grand Canyon. Glancing at a map of the state, you might easily imagine that there's nothing to see or do between Phoenix and the Grand Canyon. This is the desert, right? Miles of desolate wasteland, that sort of thing. Wrong!

Between Phoenix and the Grand Canyon lies one of the most beautiful landscapes on earth, the red-rock country of Sedona. But don't get the idea that Sedona is some sort of pristine wilderness waiting to be discovered. Decades ago, Hollywood came to Sedona to shoot Westerns; then came the artists and the retirees and the New Agers. Now it seems Hollywood is back, but this time the stars aren't shooting Westerns; they're building huge homes on the range.

Central Arizona isn't just red rock and retirees, though. It also has the former territorial capital of Prescott, historic sites, ancient Indian ruins, an old mining town turned artists' community, even a few good old-fashioned dude ranches out Wickenburg way. There are, of course, thousands of acres of cactus-studded desert, but there are also high mountains, cool pine forests, and a fertile river valley, appropriately named the Verde (Green) Valley. And north of Sedona's red rocks is Oak Creek Canyon, a tree-shaded cleft in the rocks with one of the state's most scenic stretches of highway running through it.

If you should fall in love with this country, don't be too surprised. People have been drawn to the region for hundreds of years. The Hohokam people farmed the fertile Verde Valley as long ago as A.D. 600, followed later by the Sinagua. Although these early tribes had disappeared by the time the first white settlers arrived in the 1860s, Apache and Yavapai tribes did inhabit the area. It was to protect settlers from these hostile tribes that the U.S. Army established Fort Verde here in 1871.

When Arizona became a U.S. territory in 1863, Prescott, due to its central location, was chosen as its capital. Although the town would eventually lose that title to Tucson and then to Phoenix, it was the most important city in Arizona for part of the late 19th century. Wealthy merchants and legislators rapidly transformed this pioneer outpost into a beautiful town filled with stately Victorian homes surrounding an imposing county courthouse.

Settlers were lured to this region not only by fertile land, but also by the mineral wealth that lay hidden in the ground. Miners founded a number of communities in central Arizona, among them Jerome. When the mines shut down, Jerome was almost completely abandoned, but now artists and craftspeople have moved in to reclaim and revitalize the old mining town.

In the middle of the 20th century, it was sunshine and a chance to ride the range that lured people to central Arizona, and many of those visitors headed to Wickenburg. Once called the dude-ranch capital of the world, Wickenburg still clings to its Western roots and has restored part of its downtown to its 1880s appearance. It is here you'll find most of the region's few remaining dude ranches, which now call themselves "guest ranches."

1 Wickenburg

53 miles NW of Phoenix; 61 miles S of Prescott; 128 miles SE of Kingman

Once known as the dude-ranch capital of the world, the town of Wickenburg, located in the desert northwest of Phoenix, attracted celebrities and families from all over the country. Those were the days when the West had only just stopped being wild, and spending the winter in Arizona was an adventure, not just a chance to escape winter weather. Today, although the area has only a handful of dude (or guest) ranches still in business, Wickenburg clings to its Wild West image. The dude ranches that remain range from rustic to luxurious, but a chance to ride the range is still the area's main attraction.

Wickenburg lies at the northern edge of the Sonoran Desert on the banks of the Hassayampa River, one of the last free-flowing rivers in the Arizona desert. The town was founded in 1863 by Prussian gold prospector Henry Wickenburg, who discovered what would eventually become the most profitable gold and silver mine in Arizona: The Vulture Mine. The mine closed in 1942 and is now operated as a tourist attraction.

When the dude ranches flourished back in the 1920s and 1930s, Wickenburg realized that visitors wanted a taste of the Wild West, so the town gave the tenderfoots what they wanted—trail rides, hayrides, cookouts, the works. Wickenburg has even preserved one of its downtown streets much as it may have looked in 1900. If you've come to Arizona searching for the West the way it used to be, Wickenburg is a good place to look. Just don't expect shootouts staged in the streets every day—this ain't Tombstone.

ESSENTIALS

GETTING THERE From Phoenix, take I-17 N to Arizona 74 W and then continue west on U.S. 60. From Prescott, take Arizona 89. If you're coming from the west, take U.S. 60 from I-10. U.S. 93 comes down from I-40 in northwestern Arizona.

VISITOR INFORMATION Contact the **Wickenburg Chamber of Commerce,** 216 N. Frontier St. (✆ **928/684-5479;** www.outwickenburgway.com). The visitor center is open Monday through Friday from 9am to 5pm, Saturday and Sunday from 10am to 2pm.

SPECIAL EVENTS **Gold Rush Days,** held on the second full weekend in February, is the biggest festival of the year in Wickenburg and has been for 60 years. Events include gold panning, a rodeo, and shootouts in the streets. On the second full weekend in November, the **Bluegrass Festival** features contests for fiddle and banjo. On the first weekend in December, Wickenburg holds its annual **Cowboy Poetry Gathering,** with lots of poetry and music.

EXPLORING THE AREA

A WALK AROUND TOWN

While Wickenburg's main attractions remain the guest ranches outside of town, a walk around downtown also provides a glimpse of the Old West. Most of the buildings here were built between 1890 and the 1920s (although a few are older), and although not all of them look their age, there is just enough Western character to make a stroll worthwhile (if it's not too hot).

The old **Santa Fe train station** is now the Wickenburg Chamber of Commerce, where you can pick up a map that tells a bit about the history of the town's buildings. The brick **post office,** almost across the street from the train station, once had a ride-up

Tips Wickenburg After Dark

These days, stargazing and telling stories around the campfire aren't the only things to do after dark. The **Del E. Webb Center for the Performing Arts,** 1090 S. Vulture Mine Rd. (© **928/684-6624;** www.delewebbcenter.org), brings a wide range of cultural performances to a town that once knew only horse operas.

window providing service to people on horseback. **Frontier Street** is preserved as it looked in the early 1900s. The covered sidewalks and false fronts are characteristic of frontier architecture; the false fronts often disguised older adobe buildings that were considered "uncivilized" by settlers from back east. The oldest building in town is the **Etter General Store,** adjacent to the Homestead Restaurant. The adobe-walled store was built in 1864 and has long since been disguised with a false wooden front. You can even go back to school at the **Garcia Little Red Schoolhouse,** 245 N. Tegner St. (© **928/684-7473**), which has a gift shop and is open Monday through Saturday from 10am to 4pm. You'll find the old schoolhouse next door to the Basha's supermarket.

Two of the town's most unusual attractions aren't buildings at all. The **Jail Tree,** behind the convenience store at the corner of Wickenburg Way and Tegner Street, is an old mesquite tree that served as the local hoosegow. Outlaws were simply chained to the tree. Their families would often come to visit and have a picnic in the shade of the tree. The second, equally curious, town attraction is the **Wishing Well,** which stands beside the bridge over the Hassayampa. Legend has it that anyone who drinks from the Hassayampa River will never tell the truth again. How the well adjacent to the river became a wishing well is unclear.

You'll also find a few art galleries around town, including the **Gold Nugget Art Gallery,** 274 E. Wickenburg Way (© **928/684-5849;** www.goldnuggetartgallery.com), which is housed in the oldest building in town (built in 1863) and features the works of more than 30 regional artists. If you're in the market for a new saddle or some Western wear, try **Ben's Saddlery,** 174 N. Tegner St. (© **928/684-2683**); or **Riata,** 70 E. Apache St. (© **928/684-4999**).

MUSEUMS & MINES

Desert Caballeros Western Museum ★★ Wickenburg thrives on its Western heritage, and inside this museum you'll find an outstanding collection of Western art depicting life on the range, including works by Albert Bierstadt, Charles Russell, Thomas Moran, Frederick Remington, Maynard Dixon, and other members of the Cowboy Artists of America. The Hays "Spirit of the Cowboy" collection is an impressive display of historical cowboy gear that alone makes this museum worth a stop.

21 N. Frontier St. © **928/684-2272.** www.westernmuseum.org. Admission $7.50 adults, $6 seniors, $1 children 6–16, free for children under 6. Mon–Sat 10am–5pm; Sun noon–4pm. Closed Mon July–Aug, New Year's Day, Easter, July 4th, Thanksgiving, and Christmas.

Robson's Arizona Mining World Boasting the world's largest collection of antique mining equipment, this private museum is a must for anyone fascinated by Arizona's rich mining history. Located on the site of an old mining camp and with the feel of a ghost town, this museum consists of more than 30 buildings filled with antiques and displays. You can pan for gold or hike through the desert to see ancient

Central Arizona

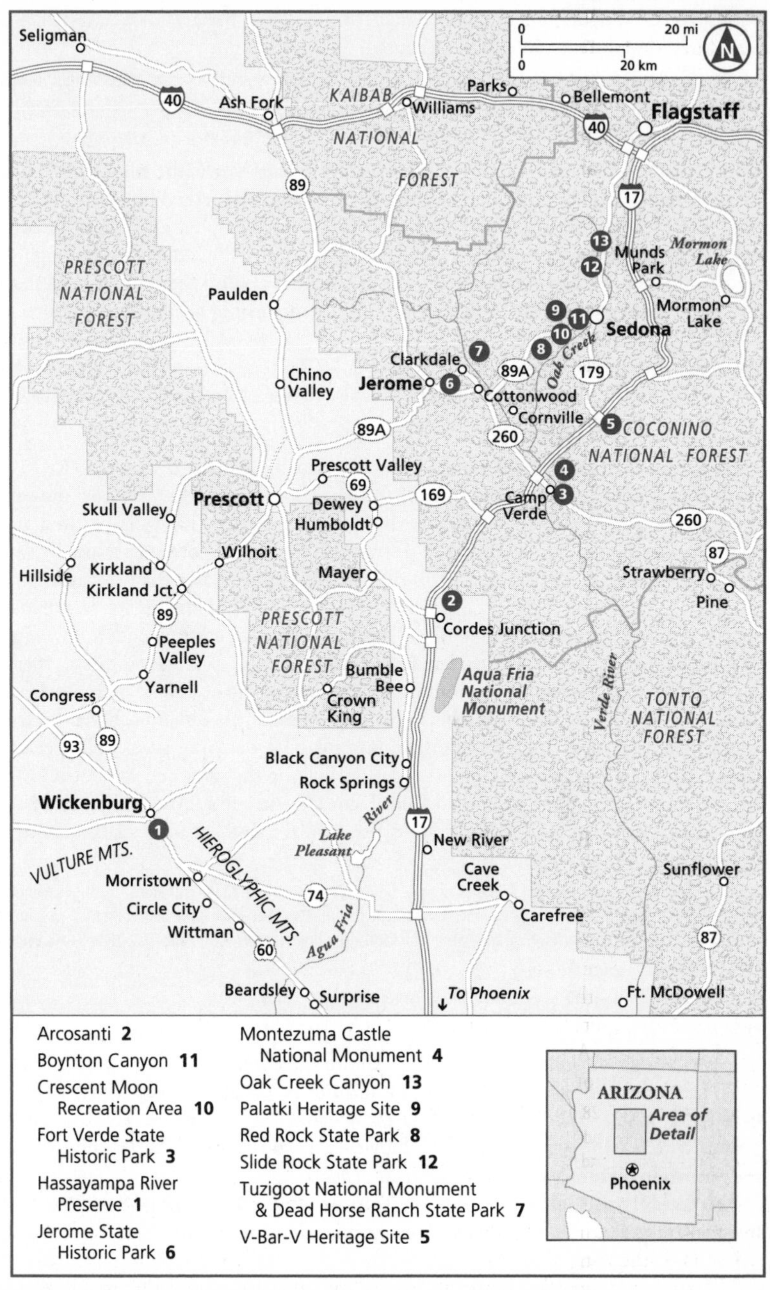

petroglyphs. Also on the property, you'll find Litsch's Bed & Breakfast (charging $90–$110 double; no credit cards accepted) and a restaurant.

Ariz. 71, 28 miles west of Wickenburg. ✆ **928/685-2609.** www.robsonsminingworld.com. Admission $5.50 adults, $5 seniors, free for children under 10. Oct–Apr Mon–Fri 9:30am–4pm, Sat–Sun 9:30am–5pm. Closed May–Sept. Head west out of Wickenburg on U.S. 60 and, after 20 miles, turn north on Ariz. 71.

The Vulture Mine *Kids* Lying at the base of Vulture Peak (the most visible landmark in the Wickenburg area), The Vulture Mine was first staked by Henry Wickenburg in 1863, fueling the small gold rush that helped populate this section of the Arizona desert. Today, The Vulture Mine has the feel of a ghost town, and though you can't go down into the old mine itself, you can wander around the aboveground shacks and mine structures on a self-guided tour. Mildly interesting for those who appreciate old mines, and fun for kids.

Vulture Mine Rd. ✆ **602/859-2743.** Admission $7 adults, $6 seniors, $5 children 6–12. Late Dec to Apr daily 9am–4pm; call for summer hours. Take U.S. 60 W out of town, turn left on Vulture Mine Rd., and drive 12 miles south.

A BIRDER'S PARADISE

Hassayampa River Preserve ★ At one time, the Arizona desert was laced with rivers that flowed for most, if not all, of the year. In the past 100-plus years, however, these rivers, and the riparian habitats they once supported, have disappeared at an alarming rate due to the damming of rivers and the lowering of water tables by wells. Riparian areas support trees and plants that require more water than is usually available in the desert, and this lush growth provides food and shelter for hundreds of species of birds, mammals, and reptiles. Today, the riparian cottonwood-willow forests of the desert Southwest are considered the country's most endangered forest type.

The Nature Conservancy, a nonprofit organization dedicated to purchasing and preserving threatened habitats, owns and manages the Hassayampa River Preserve, which is now one of the state's most important bird-watching sites (280 species of birds have been spotted here). Nature trails lead along the river beneath cottonwoods and willows, and past the spring-fed Palm Lake. On-site are a visitor center and bookshop. Free naturalist-guided walks are offered on the last Saturday of the month at 8:30am (reservations required).

49614 U.S. 60 (3 miles southeast of Wickenburg on U.S. 60). ✆ **928/684-2772.** www.nature.org. Suggested donation $5 ($3 for Nature Conservancy members). Mid-Sept to mid-May Wed–Sun 8am–5pm; mid-May to mid-Sept Fri–Sun 7–11am. Closed Thanksgiving, day after Thanksgiving, Christmas Eve, Christmas Day, New Year's Eve, and New Year's Day.

OUTDOOR PURSUITS

If you're in the area for more than a day or just can't spend another minute in the saddle, you can go out on a jeep tour and explore the desert backcountry, visit Vulture Peak, see some petroglyphs, or check out old mines. Call **B.C. Jeep Tours** (✆ **928/684-7901** or 928/231-1010; www.bcjeeptours.com), which charges $60 to $100 per person with a two-person minimum. However, if you've got time for only one jeep tour on your Arizona vacation, make it in Sedona.

Los Caballeros Golf Club, 1551 S. Vulture Mine Rd. (✆ **928/684-2704;** www.loscaballerosgolf.com), has been rated one of the best courses in the state. Greens fees are $135 in the cooler months.

Hikers should head southwest of town to the end of Vulture Mine Road (off U.S. 60) to climb Vulture Peak, which is a steep but rewarding climb best done in the cooler months. The views from up top (or even just the saddle near the top) are well worth the effort. There are sometimes spectacular wildflower displays here in the spring.

WHERE TO STAY

GUEST RANCHES

Flying E Ranch ★ Kids This is a working cattle ranch with 20,000 high, wide, and handsome acres for you and the cattle to roam. Family-owned since 1952, the Flying E attracts plenty of repeat business, with families finding it a particularly appealing and down-home kind of place. The main lodge features a spacious lounge where guests like to gather by the fireplace. Accommodations vary in size, but all have Western-style furnishings and either twin or king-size beds. Three family-style meals are served in the wood-paneled dining room, but there's no bar, so you'll need to bring your own liquor. There are also breakfast cookouts, lunch rides, and evening chuck-wagon dinners.

2801 W. Wickenburg Way, Wickenburg, AZ 85390. ✆ **888/684-2650** or 928/684-2690. Fax 928/684-5304. www.flyingeranch.com. 17 units. $285–$363 double. Rates include all meals. 2- to 4-night minimum stay. MC, V. Closed May–Oct. Drive 4 miles west of town on U.S. 60. **Amenities:** Dining room; outdoor pool; tennis court; exercise room; Jacuzzi; sauna; horseback riding ($35–$50 per person per day); horseshoes; lawn games; hayrides; guest rodeos. *In room:* A/C, TV, fridge.

Kay El Bar Guest Ranch ★ This is the smallest and oldest of the Wickenburg guest ranches, and its adobe buildings, built between 1914 and 1925, are listed on the National Register of Historic Places. The well-maintained ranch is quintessentially Wild West in style, and the setting, on the bank of the (usually dry) Hassayampa River, lends the ranch a surprisingly lush feel compared with the arid surrounding landscape. While the cottage and the Casa Grande room are the most spacious, the smaller rooms in the adobe main lodge have original Monterey-style furnishings and other classic 1950s dude-ranch decor. I like this place because it's so small you feel like you're on a friend's ranch.

Rincon Rd., off U.S. 93 (P.O. Box 2480), Wickenburg, AZ 85358. ✆ **800/684-7583** or 928/684-7593. Fax 928/684-4497. www.kayelbar.com. 11 units. $340–$425 double; $725–$815 cottage for 4. Rates do not include 15% service charge. Rates include all meals and horseback riding. 2- to 4-night minimum stay. Children 3 and under stay free in parent's room. MC, V. Closed May to mid-Oct. **Amenities:** Dining room; lounge; small outdoor pool; access to nearby health club; Jacuzzi; massage; laundry service; horseback riding. *In room:* Hair dryer, no phone.

Rancho de los Caballeros ★★ Located on 20,000 acres 2 miles west of Wickenburg, Rancho de los Caballeros is part of an exclusive country club–resort community and, as such, feels more like a resort than a guest ranch. However, the main lodge itself, with its flagstone floor, copper fireplace, and colorfully painted furniture, has a very Southwestern feel. Peace and quiet are the keynotes of a visit here, and most guests focus on golf (the golf course is one of the best in the state) and horseback riding. In addition, the ranch has a new spa called the Ranch House and offers skeet and trap shooting and guided nature walks. Bedrooms are filled with handcrafted furnishings, exposed-beam ceilings, Indian rugs, and, in some, tile floors and fireplaces. While breakfast and lunch are quite casual, dinner is more formal, with proper attire required.

1551 S. Vulture Mine Rd. (off U.S. 60 west of town), Wickenburg, AZ 85390. ✆ **800/684-5030** or 928/684-5484. Fax 928/684-9565. www.sunc.com. 79 units. Mid-Oct to mid-Dec and late Apr to early May $386–$412 double, $452–$490 suite; mid-Dec to late Apr $446–$486 double, $526–$596 suite. Rates do not include 15% gratuity charge. Rates include all meals. Riding, golf, and spa packages available. Children under 5 stay free in parent's room. MC, V. Closed early May to mid-Oct. **Amenities:** Dining room; 2 lounges; small outdoor pool; 18-hole golf course; 4 tennis courts; exercise room; access to nearby health club; full-service spa; bike rentals; children's programs; concierge; business center;

massage; babysitting; coin-op laundry; laundry service; dry cleaning; horseback riding ($35–$60 per ride). *In room:* A/C, TV, dataport, fridge, coffeemaker, hair dryer, iron, microwave.

WHERE TO DINE

Get a quick salad, sandwich, or coffee right in the center of downtown at the friendly **Pony Espresso Café,** 233 E. Wickenburg Way (✆ **928/684-0208;** www.ponyespressocafe.com).

House of Berlin GERMAN/CONTINENTAL Wickenburg may seem like an unusual place for an authentic German restaurant, but that's exactly what you'll find right downtown. The place is small and casual, and serves a mix of German and other Continental dishes. Local favorites include the Wiener schnitzel and *sauerbraten.*

169 E. Wickenburg Way. ✆ **928/684-5044.** Reservations recommended. Main courses $6.50–$15 lunch, $12–$18 dinner. MC, V. Tues 5–9pm; Wed–Sun 11:30am–2pm and 5–9pm.

EN ROUTE TO PRESCOTT

Between Wickenburg and Prescott, Arizona 89 climbs out of the desert at the town of **Yarnell,** which lies at the top of a steep stretch of road. The landscape around Yarnell is a jumble of weather-worn granite boulders that give the town a unique appearance. Several little crafts and antiques shops here are worth a stop, including the curiously named **Brand New Dead Things,** 22877 Arizona 89 (✆ **928/427-6393**), which is filled with all manner of natural curiosities and desert-inspired crafts. However, the town's main claim to fame is the **Shrine of St. Joseph of the Mountains** (✆ **928/778-5229;** www.stjoseph-shrine.org), which is known for its carved stone Stations of the Cross. Watch for the sign to the shrine as you drive through town.

2 Prescott

100 miles N of Phoenix; 66 miles SW of Sedona; 87 miles SW of Flagstaff

Prescott, the former territorial capital, is an Arizona anomaly; it doesn't seem like the Southwest at all. With its stately courthouse on a tree-shaded square, its well-preserved historic downtown business district, and its old Victorian homes, Prescott wears the air of the quintessential American small town, the sort of place where the Broadway show *The Music Man* might have been staged. Prescott has just about everything a small town should have: an 1890s saloon (The Palace), an old cattlemen's hotel (the Hassayampa Inn), a burger shop (Kendall's), and a brewpub (the Prescott Brewing Company). Add to this several small museums, a couple of other historic hotels, the strange and beautiful landscape of the Granite Dells, and the nearby Prescott National Forest, and you have a town that appeals to visitors with a diverse range of interests.

The town's pioneer history dates from 1863, when the Walker party discovered gold in the mountains of central Arizona. Soon miners were flocking to the area to seek their own fortunes. A year later, Arizona became a U.S. territory, and the new town of Prescott, located right in the center of Arizona, was made the territorial capital. Prescott lost its statewide influence when the capital moved to Phoenix, but because of the importance of ranching and mining in central Arizona, Prescott continued to be a major regional town. Today Prescott has become an upscale retirement community, as much for its historical heritage as for its mild year-round climate. In summer, Prescott is also a popular weekend getaway for Phoenicians; it is usually 20 degrees cooler here than it is in Phoenix.

ESSENTIALS

GETTING THERE Prescott is at the junction of Arizona 89, Arizona 89A, and Arizona 69. If you're coming from Phoenix, take the Cordes Junction exit (Exit 262) from I-17. From Flagstaff, the most direct route is I-17 to Arizona 169 to Arizona 69. From Sedona, just take Arizona 89A all the way.

Great Lakes Airlines (© **800/554-5111;** www.greatlakesav.com) flies between Prescott's Ernest A. Love Airport, on U.S. 89, and both Phoenix and Kingman. **Shuttle "U"** (© **800/304-6114** or 928/442-1000; www.shuttleu.com) provides service to Prescott from Sky Harbor Airport for $31 one-way, $52 round-trip.

VISITOR INFORMATION The **Prescott Chamber of Commerce** is at 117 W. Goodwin St. (© **800/266-7534** or 928/445-2000; www.prescott.org). The visitor center is open Monday through Friday from 9am to 5pm, and Saturday and Sunday from 10am to 2pm.

ORIENTATION Arizona 89 comes into Prescott on the northeast side of town, where it joins with Arizona 69 coming in from the east. Five miles north of town, Arizona 89A from Sedona also merges with Arizona 89. The main street into town is **Gurley Street,** which forms the north side of Courthouse Plaza. **Montezuma Street,** also known as Whiskey Row, forms the west side of the plaza. If you continue south on Montezuma Street, you'll be on Arizona 89 heading toward Wickenburg.

GETTING AROUND For car rentals, call **Enterprise** (© 800/261-7331) or **Hertz** (© 800/654-3131).

SPECIAL EVENTS The **World's Oldest Rodeo** (© **800/358-1888** or 928/445-3103; www.worldsoldestrodeo.com) is Prescott's biggest annual event and is held in early July. In mid-July, the Sharlot Hall Museum hosts the **Prescott Indian Art Market,** and on the third weekend in August, the **Arizona Cowboy Poets Gathering** takes place. In early June, there's **Territorial Days,** which includes special art exhibits, performances, tournaments, races, and lots of food and free entertainment. In December, the city is decked out with lights, and there are numerous holiday events.

EXPLORING THE TOWN

A walk around **Courthouse Plaza** should be your first introduction to Prescott. The stately old courthouse in the middle of the tree-shaded plaza sets the tone for the whole town. The building, far too large for a small regional town such as this, dates from the days when Prescott was the capital of the Arizona territory. Under the big shade trees, you'll find several bronze statues of cowboys and soldiers.

Surrounding the courthouse and extending north for a block is Prescott's **historic business district.** Stroll around admiring the brick buildings, and you'll realize that Prescott was once a very important place. Duck into an old saloon or the lobby of one of the historic hotels, and you'll understand that the town was also part of the Wild West.

To learn more about the history of Prescott, contact **Melissa Ruffner** at **Prescott Historical Tours** (© **928/445-4567**). Ms. Ruffner does her tours in Victorian costume and passes out copies of her book on the territorial history of Arizona. Tours cost $40 per couple.

Fort Whipple Museum Located north of town off U.S. 89 on the grounds of what is now a Veterans Administration hospital, this museum focuses on the history of this fort, which was active from 1863 to 1922 and has many stately officers' homes. Don't miss the display about Fiorello LaGuardia's time at the fort.

Veterans Administration campus, Building 11, 500 N. Hwy. 89. ✆ **928/445-3122.** Free admission. Thurs–Sat 10am–4pm.

Phippen Museum ★ If you're a fan of classic Western art, you won't want to miss this small museum. Located on a hill a few miles north of town, the Phippen is named after the first president of the prestigious Cowboy Artists of America organization and exhibits works by both established Western artists and newcomers. Also on display are artifacts and photos that help place the artwork in the context of the region's history. More than 100 Arizona artists are represented in the museum store. The **Phippen Western Art Show & Sale** is held each year on Memorial Day weekend.

4701 U.S. 89 N. ✆ **928/778-1385.** www.phippenartmuseum.org. Admission $5 adults, $4 seniors and students, free for children under 12. Tues–Sat 10am–4pm; Sun 1–4pm.

Sharlot Hall Museum ★ Opened in 1928 in a log home that once served as the governor's mansion of the Arizona territory, this museum was founded by Sharlot Hall, who served as the territorial historian from 1909 to 1911. In addition to the governor's "mansion," which is furnished much as it might have been when it was built, several other interesting buildings can be toured. With its traditional wood-frame construction, the Frémont House, which was built in 1875 for the fifth territorial governor, shows how quickly Prescott grew from a remote logging and mining camp into a civilized little town. The 1877 Bashford House reflects the Victorian architecture that was popular throughout the country around the end of the 19th century. The Sharlot Hall Building houses exhibits on Native American cultures and territorial Arizona. Every year in early summer, artisans, craftspeople, and costumed exhibitors participate in the **Folk Arts Fair.**

415 W. Gurley St. ✆ **928/445-3122.** www.sharlot.org. Admission $5 adults. May–Sept Mon–Sat 10am–5pm, Sun noon–4pm; Oct–Apr Mon–Sat 10am–4pm, Sun noon–4pm.

The Smoki Museum This interesting little museum, which houses a collection of Native American artifacts in a historic stone building, is named for the fictitious Smoki tribe. The tribe was dreamed up in 1921 by a group of non-Indians who wanted to inject some new life into Prescott's July 4th celebrations. Despite its phony origins, the museum contains genuine artifacts and basketry from many different tribes, mainly Southwestern. The museum also sponsors interesting lectures on Native American topics.

147 N. Arizona St. ✆ **928/445-1230.** www.smokimuseum.org. Admission $5 adults, $4 seniors, $3 students. Mon–Sat 10am–4pm; Sun 1–4pm. Closed Easter, Thanksgiving, Christmas, and Jan 1–15.

OUTDOOR PURSUITS

Prescott is situated on the edge of a wide expanse of high plains with the pine forests of **Prescott National Forest** at its back. Within the national forest are lakes, campgrounds, and many miles of hiking and mountain-biking trails. My favorite hiking and biking areas are Thumb Butte (west of town) and the Granite Mountain Wilderness (northwest of town).

Thumb Butte, a rocky outcropping that towers over the forest just west of town, is Prescott's most readily recognizable natural landmark. A 1.2-mile trail leads nearly to the top of this butte, and from the saddle near the summit, there's a panoramic vista of the entire region. The trail itself is very steep but paved much of the way. The summit of the butte is a popular rock-climbing spot. An alternative return trail makes a loop hike possible. To reach the trail head, drive west out of town on Gurley Street, which becomes Thumb Butte Road. Follow the road until you see the National Forest signs, after which there's a parking lot, picnic area, and trail head. The parking fee is $2.

The Granite Basin Recreation Area provides access to the **Granite Mountain Wilderness.** Trails lead beneath the cliffs of Granite Mountain, where you might spot peregrine falcons. For the best views, hike 1.5 miles to Blair Pass and then on up the Granite Mountain trail as far as you feel like going. To reach this area, take Gurley Street west from downtown, turn right on Grove Avenue, and follow it around to Iron Springs Road, which will take you northwest out of town to the signed road for the Granite Basin Recreation Area (less than 8 miles from downtown). There is a $2 parking fee here.

Both of the above areas also offer mountain-biking trails. Although the scenery isn't as spectacular as in the Sedona area, the trails are great. You can rent a bike and get maps and specific trail recommendations at **Ironclad Bicycles,** 710 White Spar Rd. (✆ **928/776-1755;** www.ironcladbicycles.com), which charges $24 to $48 per day for mountain bikes. This shop also rents bikes at **Encore Performance & Fabrication,** 2929 N. Arizona 89 (✆ **928/778-7910**), near the Peavine Trail (see below).

For maps and information on these and other hikes and bike rides in the area, stop by the **Bradshaw Ranger Station,** 344 S. Cortez St. (✆ **928/443-8000;** www.fs.fed.us/r3/prescott).

North of town 5 miles on Arizona 89 is an unusual and scenic area known as the **Granite Dells.** Jumbled hills of rounded granite suddenly jut from the landscape, creating a maze of huge boulders and smooth rock. In the middle of this dramatic landscape lies **Watson Lake,** the waters of which push their way in among the boulders to create one of the prettiest lakes in the state. On the highway side of the lake, you'll find **Watson Lake Park,** which has picnic tables and great views. Spring through fall (weather permitting) on Saturday and Sunday between 10am and 4pm, you can rent **canoes and kayaks** ($10–$15 per hr.) at the lake. Reservations aren't accepted, but you can call **Prescott Outdoors** (✆ **928/925-1410;** www.prescottoutdoors.com) to make sure they'll be at the lake with their boats.

For hiking in the Watson Lake area, I recommend heading to the scenic **Peavine Trail,** which is one of the most gratifying easy hikes in the state, To find the trail head, turn east onto Prescott Lake Parkway, which is between Prescott and the Granite Dells, and then turn left onto Sun Dog Ranch Road. This rails-to-trails path extends for several miles through the middle of the Granite Dells and is the best way to fully appreciate the Dells (you'll be away from both people and the highway). Although this is a fascinating, easy hike, it also makes a great, equally easy, mountain-bike ride that can be extended 7.5 miles on the Iron King Trail. Also accessible from this same trail head is the **Watson Woods Riparian Preserve,** which has some short trails through the wetlands and riparian zone along Granite Creek.

A couple of miles west of Watson Lake on Willow Creek Road, you can hike in **Willow Creek Park,** where several miles of trails lead through grasslands and groves of huge cottonwood trees adjacent to Willow Lake. The trails eventually lead to the edge of the Granite Dells. There's great bird-watching in the trees in this park, and there are even great blue heron and cormorant rookeries.

If you want to explore the area on horseback, try **Granite Mountain Stables,** 2400 Shane Dr. (✆ **928/771-9551;** www.granitemountainstables.com), which offers guided trail rides in the Prescott National Forest. A 1-hour ride is $35.

Reasonably priced golf is available at the 36-hole **Antelope Hills Golf Course,** 1 Perkins Dr. (✆ **800/972-6818** or 928/776-7888; www.antelopehillsgolf.com). Greens fees range from $38 to $55.

SHOPPING

Downtown Prescott is filled with antiques stores, especially along North Cortez Street, and is the best place in Arizona do some antiques shopping. For Native American crafts and Old West memorabilia, be sure to stop in at **Ogg's Hogan,** 111 N. Cortez St. (✆ **928/443-9856**). In the Hotel St. Michael's shopping arcade, check out **The Hotel Trading Post,** 110 S. Montezuma St. (✆ **928/778-7276**), which carries some genuine Native American artifacts at reasonable prices. Owner Ernie Lister also makes silver jewelry in the 19th-century Navajo style. In this same arcade, you'll find the **Prairie Rose Boutique,** 110 S. Montezuma St. (✆ **928/443-0909**), which has lots of beautiful women's Southwestern fashions. On the same block are both the **Arts Prescott Gallery,** 134 S. Montezuma St. (✆ **928/776-7717;** www.artsprescott.com), a cooperative of local artists; and **Van Gogh's Ear,** 156B S. Montezuma St. (✆ **928/776-1080;** www.vgegallery.com), which was founded by a splinter group from the co-op and actually has higher-quality art and crafts. Also on this block you'll find the **Newman Gallery,** 106-A S. Montezuma St. (✆ **928/442-9167;** www.newmangallery.net), which features the colorful Western-inspired pop-culture imagery of artist Dave Newman.

Want to sample some local wine while you're in the area? Head north of Prescott to **Granite Creek Vineyards,** 2515 N. Rd. 1 E., Chino Valley (✆ **928/636-2003;** www.granitecreekvineyards.com), which produces sulfite-free wines that are surprisingly good. The winery is open Friday through Sunday from 1 to 5pm. Call for directions.

WHERE TO STAY

EXPENSIVE

Hassayampa Inn ★ Built as a luxury hotel in 1927, the Hassayampa Inn, which is listed on the National Register of Historic Places, evokes the time when Prescott was the bustling territorial capital. In the lobby, exposed ceiling beams, wrought-iron chandeliers, and arched doorways all reflect the place's Southwestern heritage. Although guest rooms tend to be very small, each is unique and features either original furnishings or antiques. Some suites are very oddly configured; you might find the shower in one closet and the commode in another. One room is said to be haunted; any hotel employee will be happy to tell you the story of the ill-fated honeymooners whose ghosts supposedly reside here.

122 E. Gurley St., Prescott, AZ 86301. ✆ **800/322-1927** or 928/778-9434. www.hassayampainn.com. 68 units. $109–$159 double; $160–$249 suite. Children under 12 stay free in parent's room. AE, DC, DISC, MC, V. **Amenities:** Restaurant; lounge; exercise room; room service; laundry service; dry cleaning. *In room:* A/C, TV, dataport, hair dryer, iron, Wi-Fi.

Fun Fact **Haunted Hotels**

Jerome may be the region's top ghost town, but Prescott describes no fewer than three of its hotels as haunted. The Hassayampa Inn, St. Michael's Hotel, and Hotel Vendome all claim to have resident ghosts.

MODERATE

Hotel Vendome ★ Not quite as luxurious as the Hassayampa, yet not as basic as the St. Michael, the Vendome is a good middle-price choice for those who want to stay in a historic hotel. Built in 1917 as a lodging house, the restored brick building is only 2 blocks from the action of Whiskey Row, but far enough away that you can get a good night's sleep. Guest rooms are outfitted with new furnishings, but some of the bathrooms still contain original claw-foot tubs. Naturally, this hotel, like several others in town, has its own resident ghost.

230 S. Cortez St., Prescott, AZ 86303. ✆ **888/468-3583** or 928/776-0900. www.vendomehotel.com. 20 units. $99–$139 double; $139–$179 2-bedroom unit. Rates include continental breakfast. AE, DISC, MC, V. **Amenities:** Lounge; concierge. *In room:* A/C, TV, dataport, hair dryer, iron, free local calls.

Log Cabin Bed & Breakfast ★ This modern log house is located among the massive boulders of the Granite Dells, and although the inn is on the highway, it is set back a bit from the road. While the exterior of the Log Cabin reflects its name, the interior is more classic country style. One guest room has white wicker furniture, while another has a brass bed. Two of the rooms have claw-foot tubs, while my favorite room, the Cozy Fireside room, has a claw-foot tub, a gas fireplace, and a skylight.

3155 N. Hwy. 89, Prescott, AZ 86301. ✆ **888/778-0442** or 928/778-0442. Fax 928/445-0000. www.prescottlogcabin.com. 4 units. $129–$169 double. AE, DISC, MC, V. **Amenities:** Jacuzzi; massage. *In room:* A/C, Wi-Fi, no phone.

Rocamadour Bed & Breakfast for (Rock) Lovers ★★ The Granite Dells, just north of Prescott, is the area's most unforgettable feature. Should you wish to stay amid these jumbled boulders, there's no better choice than Rocamadour. Mike and Twila Coffey honed their innkeeping skills as owners of a 40-room château in France, and antique furnishings from that château can now be found throughout this inn. The most elegant pieces are in the Chambre Trucy, which also boasts an amazing underlit whirlpool tub. One cottage is built into the boulders and has a large whirlpool tub on its deck. The unique setting, engaging innkeepers, and thoughtful details everywhere you turn make this one of the state's must-stay inns.

3386 N. Hwy. 89, Prescott, AZ 86301. ✆ **888/771-1933** or 928/771-1933. 3 units. $149–$169 double; $219 suite. AE, DC, DISC, MC, V. Rates include full breakfast. *In room:* A/C, TV/VCR.

INEXPENSIVE

Hotel St. Michael *Value* Located right on Whiskey Row, this restored hotel, complete with resident ghost and the oldest elevator in Prescott, offers a historic setting at budget prices (don't expect the most stylish furnishings). All rooms are different; some have bathtubs but no showers. The casual Caffe St. Michael, where breakfast is served, overlooks Courthouse Plaza.

205 W. Gurley St., Prescott, AZ 86301. ✆ **800/678-3757** or 928/776-1999. Fax 928/776-7318. www.hotelstmichael.net. 72 units. $59–$99 double; $89–$119 suite. Rates include full breakfast. AE, DISC, MC, V. **Amenities:** Restaurant; access to nearby health club; shopping arcade. *In room:* A/C, TV, free local calls.

WHERE TO DINE

Grab picnic fare at **New Frontiers Natural Foods,** 1112 W. Iron Springs Rd. (✆ **928/445-7370**). For delicious baked goods, including savory turnovers, stop in at the **Pangaea Bakery,** 220 W. Goodwin St., Suite 1 (✆ **928/778-2953**), which is located half a block off Whiskey Row. The bakery is open Monday through Friday from 7am to 3pm, and Saturday from 8am to 3pm. For a quick, juicy burger or some ice cream, stop in at **Kendall's Famous Burgers & Ice Cream,** 113 S. Cortez St. (✆ **928/778-3658**), which is open Monday through Saturday from 11am to 8pm, and Sunday from 11am to 6pm. For coffee, try **Cuppers Coffee House,** 226 S. Cortez St. (✆ **928/445-1636**), which is in a house that was built in 1872; or **Prescott Coffee Roasters,** 318 W. Gurley St. (✆ **928/717-0191**), an Internet cafe 2 blocks west of Whiskey Row.

MODERATE

Murphy's ★ AMERICAN Murphy's, housed in an 1890 mercantile building that's on the National Register of Historic Places, has long been one of Prescott's favorite special-occasion restaurants. Sparkling leaded-glass doors usher diners into a high-ceilinged room with fans revolving slowly overhead. Many of the shop's original shelves can still be seen in the lounge area, and the restaurant does a good job of creating a historical ambience. The best bets on the menu are the mesquite-grilled meats, but the fish specials can also be good. You can save a bit of money by dining early and ordering one of the sunset dinners.

201 N. Cortez St. ✆ **928/445-4044.** www.murphysrestaurants.com. Reservations recommended. Main courses $7.50–$16 lunch, $12–$29 dinner. AE, DISC, MC, V. Sun–Thurs 11am–10pm; Fri–Sat 11am–11pm.

129½ ★ NEW AMERICAN Prescott, a classic small-town-America sort of place, may seem an odd location for a classic New York–style jazz club, but this restaurant has it down. It may not be in a basement and it isn't smoky, but everything else has just the right feel. Best of all, the restaurant has great food. Steaks are the specialty and can be had with an assortment of delicious sauces, such as rosemary cream, mushroom ragout, and pinot and green peppercorn (my personal favorite). Money-saving early dinners are served Tuesday through Thursday between 4 and 6pm.

129½ N. Cortez St. ✆ **928/443-9292.** www.fourcornersrestaurants.com. Reservations recommended. Main courses $6–$11 lunch, $16–$28 dinner. AE, DISC, MC, V. Tues–Thurs 11am–2pm and 4–9:30pm; Fri 11am–2pm and 5–10pm; Sat 5–10pm.

The Palace *Finds* SOUTHWESTERN/STEAKHOUSE/SEAFOOD The Palace is the oldest saloon in Arizona (in business for more than 120 years) and looks just the way it might have at the start of the 20th century. While the front of The Palace is centered on the old bar, most of the cavernous space is dedicated to a bustling dining room. The generous steaks are your best bet here. If you bump into someone carrying a shotgun, don't panic! It's probably the owner, who likes to dress the part of a Wild West saloonkeeper. There's live music Friday and Saturday nights, and on Sunday afternoons there's a honky-tonk piano player. Dinner shows are held a couple of times each month.

120 S. Montezuma St. ✆ **928/541-1996.** www.historicpalace.com. Reservations suggested on weekends. Main courses $7–$11 lunch, $11–$27 dinner. AE, DISC, MC, V. Sun–Thurs 11am–3:30pm and 4:30–9pm; Fri–Sat 11am–3:30pm and 4:30–10pm.

The Rose Restaurant ★★ CONTINENTAL This is Prescott's best restaurant and is a must for anyone staying in town. Year after year, The Rose, which is housed in a building that was constructed around 1900, continues to satisfy locals and visitors alike. Veal dishes can also be outstanding, and the pasta with scallops and Italian sausage is a curious combination of flavors that works well. The wine list includes plenty of reasonably priced options.

234 S. Cortez St. ✆ **928/777-8308.** www.theroserestaurant.com. Reservations recommended. Main courses $20–$38. AE, DC, DISC, MC, V. Wed–Sat 5–9pm; Sun 10am–2pm (Apr to mid-Dec) and 5–9pm.

INEXPENSIVE

Dinner Bell Café ★ *Finds* AMERICAN This casual little breakfast-and-lunch place is a big hit with local students and other people in the know who come to order either the waffles (served with a variety of toppings) or the thick, juicy burgers. The waffles are available at lunch, but I don't think you can get the burger at breakfast. The Dinner Bell has a split personality. Up front there's a classic old diner that's been in business since 1939, while in back there's a colorful modern space with walls that roll up. The creekside setting a block off Whiskey Row makes this a great little hideaway for a quick, casual meal.

321 W. Gurley St. ✆ **928/445-9888.** Main courses $5–$8. No credit cards. Mon–Fri 6:30am–2pm; Sat–Sun 7am–2pm.

Prescott Brewing Company AMERICAN/PUB FARE Popular primarily with a younger crowd, this brewpub keeps a good selection of its own beers on tap, but its cheap and filling meals are just as sought after. Fajitas are a specialty, along with such pub standards as fish and chips, bangers and mash, and not-so-standard spent-grain beer-dough pizzas and vegetarian dishes. The Caesar salad with chipotle dressing packs a wallop.

130 W. Gurley St. ✆ **928/771-2795.** www.prescottbrewingcompany.com. Main courses $7.50–$19. AE, DISC, MC, V. Sun–Thurs 11am–10pm; Fri–Sat 11am–11pm (pub stays open 2 hr. after kitchen closes).

Sweet Tart ★ *Finds* CAFE This little hole-in-the-wall makes the best pastries in Arizona. Not only that, I once had a chicken panini here that was the best I've ever had; the bread had a biscuitlike texture and was slathered with pesto. Before you walk through the door, make sure you're hungry enough for dessert because the pastry case here is absolutely irresistible. At breakfast, they have, among other treats, a variety of brioches, including blueberry and mixed-fruit. Currently, Sweet Tart is doing four-course dinners every Saturday night; call for reservations.

123 N. Cortez St. ✆ **928/443-8587.** Reservations required for dinner. Main courses $7–$10; prix-fixe dinners $45. AE, DISC, MC, V. Tues–Sat 7am–4pm; Sun 8am–3pm.

PRESCOTT AFTER DARK

Back in the days when Prescott was the territorial capital and a booming mining town, it supported dozens of rowdy saloons, most of which were concentrated along Montezuma Street on the west side of Courthouse Plaza. This section of town was known as **Whiskey Row,** and legend has it there was a tunnel from the courthouse to one of the saloons so lawmakers wouldn't have to be seen ducking into the saloons during regular business hours. On July 14, 1900, a fire consumed most of Whiskey Row. However, concerned cowboys and miners managed to drag the tremendously heavy bar of The Palace saloon across the street before it was damaged.

Today, Whiskey Row is no longer the sort of place where respectable women shouldn't be seen, although it does still have a few noisy saloons with genuine Wild West flavor. Most of them feature live country music on weekends and are the dark, dank sorts of places that provide solace to a cowboy after a long day's work. However, within a few blocks of Whiskey Row, you can hear country, folk, jazz, and rock at a surprisingly diverse assortment of bars, restaurants, and clubs. In fact, Prescott has one of the densest concentrations of live-music clubs in the state.

To see what this street's saloons looked like back in the old days, drop by **The Palace,** 120 S. Montezuma St. (✆ **928/541-1996;** www.historicpalace.com), which still has a classic bar up front. Just push through the swinging doors and say howdy to the fellow with the six-guns; he'll likely be the owner. These days, The Palace is more of a restaurant than a saloon, but there's live music on the weekends. A couple of times a month, there are also dinner theater performances. Call to find out if anything is happening while you're in town.

If you want to drink where the ranchers drink and not where the hired hands carouse, head upstairs to the **Jersey Lilly Saloon,** 116 S. Montezuma St. (© **928/541-7854**), which attracts a more well-heeled clientele than the street-level saloons. On weekends, there is live music in a wide range of styles. Just around the corner from The Palace and the Jersey Lilly is the **Prescott Brewing Company,** 130 W. Gurley St. (© **928/771-2795;** www.prescottbrewingcompany.com), which is today's answer to the saloons of yore, brewing and serving its own tasty microbrews. Good pub fare is also served. A block away you'll find the **Raven Café,** 142 N. Cortez St. (© **928/717-0009**), which is the most artsy and eclectic nightlife venue in town. Not only does the Raven have the best beer list in Prescott (with an emphasis on Belgian beers and American microbrews), but the entertainment lineup ranges from vintage movies on Tuesday nights to live jazz and salsa dancing.

The **Prescott Fine Arts Association,** 208 N. Marina St. (© **928/445-3286;** www.pfaa.net), sponsors plays, music performances, children's theater, and art exhibits. The association's main building, a former church built in 1899, is on the National Register of Historic Places. A block away, you'll find the **Elks Opera House,** 117 E. Gurley St. (© **888/858-ELKS** or 928/443-8541; www.cityofprescott.net/visitors/elks), which was built in 1905 and has been under renovation for several years now. **Yavapai College Performance Hall** (© **877/928-4253** or 928/776-2000) also stages a wide range of shows. And check the schedule at the Sharlot Hall Museum's **Blue Rose History Theater** (© **928/445-3122**).

3 Jerome

35 miles NE of Prescott; 28 miles W of Sedona; 130 miles N of Phoenix

Few towns anywhere in Arizona make more of an impression on visitors than Jerome, a historic mining town that clings to the slopes of Cleopatra Hill high on Mingus Mountain. The town is divided into two sections that are separated by an elevation change of 1,500 vertical feet, with the upper part of town 2,000 feet above the Verde Valley. On a clear day, the view from Jerome is stupendous—it's possible to see for more than 50 miles, with the red rocks of Sedona, the Mogollon Rim, and the San Francisco Peaks all visible in the distance. Add to the unforgettable views the abundance of interesting shops and galleries and the winding narrow streets, and you have a town that should not be missed.

Jerome had its start as a copper-mining town, but it was never easy to mine the ore here. For many years, the mountain's ore was mined using an 88-mile-long network of underground railroads. However, in 1918 a fire broke out in the mine tunnels, and mining companies were forced to abandon the tunnels in favor of open-pit mining.

Between 1883 and 1953, Jerome experienced an economic roller-coaster ride as the price of copper rose and fell. In the early 1950s, when it was no longer profitable to mine the copper ore of Cleopatra Hill, the last mining company shut down its operations, and almost everyone left town. By the early 1960s, Jerome looked as though it were on its way to becoming just another ghost town—but then artists who had discovered the phenomenal views and dirt-cheap rents began moving in, and slowly the would-be ghost town developed a reputation as an artists' community. Soon tourists

Fun Fact Jail Brakes?

One unforeseen hazard of open-pit mining next to a town built on a 30-degree slope was the effect dynamiting would have on Jerome. Mine explosions would regularly rock Jerome's world, and eventually buildings in town began sliding downhill. Even the town jail broke loose. Without jail brakes to stop it, the jail slid 225 feet downhill. (Now that's a jailbreak.)

began visiting to see and buy the artwork that was being created in Jerome, and old storefronts turned into galleries.

Jerome is now far from a ghost town, and on summer weekends the streets are packed with visitors browsing the galleries and crafts shops. The same remote and rugged setting that once made it difficult and expensive to mine copper has now become one of the town's main attractions. Because Jerome is built on a steep slope, streets through town switch back from one level of houses to the next, with narrow alleys and stairways connecting the different levels of town. All these winding streets, alleys, and stairways are lined with old brick and wood-frame buildings that cling precariously to the side of the mountain. The entire town has been designated a National Historic Landmark, and today, residences, studios, shops, and galleries stand side by side looking (externally, anyway) much as they did when Jerome was an active mining town.

ESSENTIALS

GETTING THERE Jerome is on Arizona 89A roughly halfway between Sedona and Prescott. Coming from Phoenix, take Arizona 260 from Camp Verde.

VISITOR INFORMATION Contact the **Jerome Chamber of Commerce** (✆ **928/634-2900;** www.jeromechamber.com) for information.

EXPLORING THE TOWN

Wandering the streets, soaking up the atmosphere, and shopping are the main pastimes in Jerome. But before you launch yourself on a shopping tour, you can learn about the town's past at the **Jerome State Historic Park,** off Arizona 89A on Douglas Road in the lower section of town (✆ **928/634-5381**). Located in a mansion built in 1916 as a home for mine owner "Rawhide Jimmy" Douglas and as a hotel for visiting mining executives, the Jerome State Historic Park contains exhibits on mining as well as a few of the mansion's original furnishings. From its perch on a hill above Douglas's Little Daisy Mine, the mansion overlooks Jerome and, dizzyingly far below, the Verde Valley. The mansion was constructed of adobe bricks made on the site and once contained a wine cellar, billiards room, marble shower, steam heat, and central vacuum system. Admission is $3, and the park is open daily (except Christmas) from 8am to 5pm.

To learn more about Jerome's history, stop in at the **Jerome Historical Society's Mine Museum,** 200 Main St. (✆ **928/634-5477;** www.jeromehistoricalsociety.org), which has some small and old-fashioned displays on mining. It's open daily from 9am to 5pm; admission is $2 for adults, $1 for seniors, and free for children 12 and under. For that classic mining-town tourist-trap experience, follow the signs up the hill from downtown Jerome to the **Gold King Mine** (✆ **928/634-0053**), where you can see lots of old, rusting mining equipment and maybe even catch a demonstration. The mine is open 9am to 5pm daily, and admission is $4 for adults, $3 for seniors, and $2 for children ages 6 to 12.

Most visitors come to Jerome for the shops, which offer an eclectic blend of contemporary art, chic jewelry, one-of-a-kind handmade fashions, and unusual imports. Of course, there are now also the inevitable ice cream parlors and shops full of tacky souvenirs. The **Raku Gallery,** 250 Hull Ave. (✆ **928/639-0239;** www.rakugallery.com), has gallery space on two floors and walls of glass across the back, with views of the red rocks of Sedona in the distance. The **Jerome Gallery,** 240 Hull Ave. (✆ **928/634-7033;** www.jeromegallery.com), has good-quality ceramics, jewelry, and home furnishings. On this same block, you'll also find **Nellie Bly,** 136 Main St. (✆ **928/634-0255;** www.nbscopes.com), with a room full of handmade kaleidoscopes (ask to see the ones in the back room). **Sky Fire,** 140 Main St. (✆ **928/634-8081**), features an interesting collection of Southwestern and ethnic gifts and furnishings. To see what local artists are creating, stop in at the **Jerome Artists Cooperative Gallery,** 502 Main St. (✆ **928/639-4276;** www.jeromeartistscoop.com), on the west side of the street where Hull Avenue and Main Street fork as you come up the hill into town. At this end of town, you'll also find **Pura Vida Gallery,** 501 School St. (✆ **928/634-0937;** www.puravidagallery.com), which has a fascinating and eclectic selection of fine art, jewelry, and unusual Southwest-inspired pieces of furniture. Don't miss the eclectic offerings of the **House of Joy,** 416 Hull Ave. (✆ **928/634-5339;** www.jeromesfinest.com).

If you're in the market for local art, be sure to drop by the **Old Jerome High School,** which is located on Arizona 89A downhill from the main part of town and is full of artists' studios. On the first Saturday of each month all of the studios here are open from 5 to 9pm for the Jerome Art Walk.

WHERE TO STAY

Connor Hotel of Jerome Housed in a renovated historic hotel, this lodging has spacious rooms with large windows; views of the valley, however, are limited. Although a few of the rooms are located directly above the hotel's popular bar, which can be quite noisy on weekends, most rooms are quiet enough to provide a good night's rest. Better yet, come on a weekday when the Harley-Davidson poseur crowd from the Scottsdale area isn't thundering through the streets on their hogs.

164 Main St. (P.O. Box 1177), Jerome, AZ 86331. ✆ **800/523-3554** or 928/634-5006. Fax 928/649-0981. www.connorhotel.com. 12 units. $90–$165 double. Children under 12 stay free in parent's room. AE, DISC, MC, V. Pets accepted. **Amenities:** Bar. *In room:* A/C, TV, dataport, fridge, coffeemaker, hair dryer, iron, free local calls.

Ghost City Inn With its long verandas on both floors, this restored old house is hard to miss as you drive into town from Clarkdale. It manages to capture the spirit of Jerome, with a mix of Victorian and Southwestern decor. Most bedrooms have great views across the Verde Valley (and these are definitely worth requesting). Two units feature antique brass beds. The rooms are on the small side, so if space is a priority, opt for the suite.

541 Main St. (P.O. Box T), Jerome, AZ 86331. ✆ **888/634-4678.** www.ghostcityinn.com. 6 units. $95–$120 double; $145 suite. Rates include full breakfast. AE, DISC, MC, V. Pets accepted ($20 nonrefundable deposit). No children under 14. **Amenities:** Jacuzzi. *In room:* TV/VCR, no phone.

WHERE TO DINE

The Asylum ★ *Finds* ECLECTIC As the name would imply, this restaurant (inside a former hospital building high above downtown Jerome) is a bit out of the ordinary. The bedpan full of candy at the front desk and the odd little notes in the menu will also make it absolutely clear that this place doesn't take much, other than good food, seriously. I like the distinctly Southwestern dishes, including the prickly-pear barbecued pork tenderloin with tomatillo salsa, and an unusual butternut-squash soup made with a cinnamon-lime cream sauce. Cocktails all get wacky loony-bin names, and there's also a superb, award-winning wine list.

200 Hill St. ✆ **928/639-3197.** www.theasylum.biz. Reservations recommended. Main courses $9–$13 lunch, $17–$28 dinner. AE, DISC, MC, V. Daily 11am–3:30pm and 5–9pm.

Flatiron Café BREAKFAST/LIGHT MEALS The tiny Flatiron Café is a simple breakfast-and-lunch spot in, you guessed it, Jerome's version of a flatiron building. The limited menu includes the likes of lox and bagels, a breakfast quesadilla, black-bean hummus, smoked-salmon quesadillas, fresh juices, and espresso drinks. It looks as though you could hardly squeeze in here, but there's more seating across the street. Definitely not your usual ghost-town lunch counter.

416 Main St. (at Hull Ave.). ✆ **928/634-2733.** Reservations not accepted. Most items $7–$10. MC, V. Thurs–Mon 8:30am–3:30pm.

4 The Verde Valley

Camp Verde: 20 miles E of Jerome; 30 miles S of Sedona; 95 miles N of Phoenix

Named by early Spanish explorers who were impressed by the sight of such a verdant valley in an otherwise brown desert landscape, the Verde Valley has long been a magnet for both wildlife and people. Today, the valley is one of Arizona's richest agricultural and ranching regions and is quickly gaining popularity with retirees. Cottonwood and Clarkdale, the valley's two largest towns, are old copper-smelting towns, while Camp Verde was an army post back in the days of the Indian Wars. All three towns have some interesting historic buildings, but it is the valley's two national monuments—Tuzigoot and Montezuma Castle—that are the main attractions.

These two national monuments preserve the ruins of Sinagua pueblos. Long before the first European explorers entered the Verde Valley, the Sinagua people were living by the river and irrigating their fields with its waters. By the time the first pioneers began settling in this region, the Sinaguas had long since moved on, and Apaches had claimed the valley as part of their territory. When settlers came into conflict with the Apaches, Fort Verde, now a state park, was established. Between this state park and the two national monuments, hundreds of years of Verde Valley history and prehistory can be explored. This valley is also the site of the most scenic railroad excursion in the state.

ESSENTIALS

GETTING THERE Camp Verde is just off I-17 at the junction with Arizona 260. The latter highway leads northwest through the Verde Valley for 12 miles to Cottonwood.

VISITOR INFORMATION Contact the **Cottonwood Chamber of Commerce,** 1010 S. Main St., Cottonwood (✆ **928/634-7593;** www.cottonwood.verdevalley.com).

FESTIVALS Avid birders may want to plan their visit to coincide with the annual **Verde Valley Birding & Nature Festival** (✆ **928/282-2202;** www.birdyverde.org), which is held the last weekend in April.

A RAILWAY EXCURSION

Verde Canyon Railroad ★★ When the town of Jerome was busily mining copper, a railway was built to link the booming town with the territorial capital at nearby Prescott. Because of the rugged mountains between Jerome and Prescott, the railroad was forced to take a longer but less difficult route north along the Verde River before turning south toward Prescott. Today, you can ride these same tracks aboard the Verde Canyon Railroad. The route through the canyon traverses both the remains of a copper smelter and unspoiled desert that is inaccessible by car and is part of Prescott National Forest. The views of the rocky canyon walls and green waters of the Verde River are quite dramatic, and if you look closely along the way, you'll see ancient Sinagua cliff dwellings. In late winter and early spring, nesting bald eagles can also be spotted. Of the two excursion train rides in Arizona, this is by far the more scenic (although the Grand Canyon Railway certainly has a more impressive destination). Live music and a very informative narration make the ride entertaining as well.

300 N. Broadway, Clarkdale. ✆ **800/320-0718.** www.verdecanyonrr.com. Tickets $55 adults, $50 seniors, $35 children 2–12; 1st-class tickets $80. Call or visit the website for schedule and reservations.

NATIONAL MONUMENTS & STATE PARKS

Dead Horse Ranch State Park You'll find this state park on the outskirts of Cottonwood, not far from Tuzigoot National Monument. Set on the banks of the Verde River, the park offers picnicking, fishing, swimming, hiking, mountain biking, and camping. Trails wind through the riparian forests along the banks of the river and visit marshes that offer good bird-watching; they also lead into the adjacent national forest, so you can get in many miles of scenic hiking and mountain biking. The ranch was named in the 1940s, when the children of a family looking to buy a ranch told their parents they wanted to buy the place with the dead horse by the side of the road.

675 Dead Horse Ranch Rd., Cottonwood. ✆ **928/634-5283.** www.pr.state.az.us. Admission $6 per car. Daily 8am–8pm. Closed Christmas. From Main St. on the east side of Cottonwood, drive north on N. 10th St.

Fort Verde State Historic Park Just south of Montezuma Castle and Montezuma Well, in the town of Camp Verde, you'll find Fort Verde State Historic Park. Established in 1871, Fort Verde was the third military post in the Verde Valley and was occupied until 1891, by which time tensions with the Indian population had subsided and made the fort unnecessary. The military had first come to the Verde Valley in 1865 at the request of settlers who wanted protection from the local Tonto Apache and Yavapai. The tribes, traditionally hunters and gatherers, had been forced to raid farms for food after their normal economy was disrupted by the sudden influx of settlers into the area. Between 1873 and 1875, most of the Indians in the area were rounded up and forced to live on various reservations. An uprising in 1882 led to the last clash between local tribes and Fort Verde's soldiers.

The state park, which covers 10 acres, preserves three officers' quarters, an administration building, and some ruins. The buildings that have been fully restored house exhibits on the history of the fort and what life was like here in the 19th century. With their gables, white picket fences, and shake-shingle roofs, the buildings of Fort Verde suggest that life at this remote post was not so bad, at least for officers. Costumed military reenactments are held here throughout much of the year; call for details.

125 E. Holloman St., Camp Verde. ✆ **928/567-3275.** www.pr.state.az.us. Admission $2 adults, free for children under 14. Daily 8am–5pm. Closed Christmas.

Montezuma Castle National Monument ★★ Despite the name, the ruins within this monument are neither castle nor Aztec dwelling—as the reference to Aztec ruler Montezuma implies. This Sinagua ruin is, however, one of the best-preserved cliff dwellings in Arizona. The site consists of two impressive stone pueblos that were, for some unknown reason, abandoned by the Sinagua people in the early 14th century.

The more intriguing of the two ruins is set in a shallow cave 100 feet up a cliff overlooking Beaver Creek. Construction on this five-story, 20-room village began sometime in the early 12th century. Because Montezuma Castle has been protected from the elements by the overhanging roof of the cave in which it was built, the original adobe mud that was used to plaster over the stone walls of the dwelling is still intact. Another structure, containing 45 rooms on a total of six levels, stands at the base of the cliff. This latter dwelling, which has been subjected to rains and floods over the years, is not nearly as well preserved as the cliff dwelling. In the visitor center, you'll see artifacts that have been unearthed from the two ruins.

Montezuma Well, located 11 miles north of Montezuma Castle (although still part of the national monument), is a spring-fed sinkhole that was a true oasis in the desert for native peoples. This sunken pond was formed when a cavern in the area's porous limestone bedrock collapsed. Underground springs quickly filled the sinkhole, which today contains a pond measuring more than 360 feet across and 65 feet deep. Over the centuries, the presence of year-round water attracted first the Hohokam and later the Sinagua peoples, who built irrigation canals to use the water for growing crops. Some of these channels can still be seen. An excavated Hohokam pit house, built around 1100, and Sinagua structures are clustered in and near the sinkhole. To reach Montezuma Well, take Exit 293 off I-17.

Exit 289 off I-17. ✆ **928/567-3322.** www.nps.gov/moca. Admission $5 adults ($8 w/Tuzigoot National Monument admission), free for children 16 and under; no charge to visit Montezuma Well. Memorial Day weekend to Labor Day weekend daily 8am–6pm; rest of year daily 8am–5pm.

Out of Africa Wildlife Park ★ *Kids* Lions and tigers and bears, oh my. And zebras and giraffes and wildebeests, oh yes. That's what you'll encounter at this sprawling wildlife park between Camp Verde and Cottonwood. The park includes both a "wildlife preserve" of large fenced predator enclosures and a "Serengeti Safari" area. In this latter area, you ride on a rugged safari vehicle through a vast enclosure populated by giraffes, zebras, ostriches, wildebeests, and other animals of the Serengeti. You may even get to feed a giraffe or zebra. The other half of the park is home to numerous lions, tigers, wolves, panthers, hyenas, and other large predators. All these carnivores are fed on Sunday, Wednesday, and Friday at 3pm, and following the feeders is a highlight of a visit to the park.

Verde Valley Justice Rd., Camp Verde. ✆ **928/567-2840.** www.outofafricapark.com. Admission $28 adults, $26 seniors, $20 children ages 3–12, free for children under 3. Wed–Sun 9:30am–5pm. Also open on many holiday Mon. Closed Thanksgiving, Christmas, and July 4th.

Tuzigoot National Monument Perched atop a hill overlooking the Verde River, this small, stone-walled pueblo was built by the Sinagua people and was inhabited between 1125 and 1400. The Sinagua, whose name is Spanish for "without water," were traditionally dry-land farmers relying entirely on rainfall to water their crops. When the Hohokam, who had been living in the Verde Valley since A.D. 600, moved on to more fertile land around 1100, the Sinagua moved into this valley. Their buildings progressed from individual homes called pit houses to the type of communal pueblo seen here at Tuzigoot.

An interpretive trail leads through the Tuzigoot ruins, explaining different aspects of Sinaguan life, and inside the visitor center is a small museum displaying many of the artifacts unearthed here. Desert plants, many of which were used by the Sinagua, are identified along the trail.

Just outside Clarkdale off Ariz. 89A. ✆ **928/634-5564.** www.nps.gov/tuzi. Admission $5 adults ($8 w/Montezuma Castle National Monument admission), free for children 16 and under. Memorial Day weekend to Labor Day weekend daily 8am–6pm; rest of year daily 8am–5pm. Closed Christmas.

OTHER VERDE VALLEY ATTRACTIONS & ACTIVITIES

IN & AROUND CAMP VERDE

Out on the edge of town, you'll find Camp Verde's top attraction—**Cliff Castle Casino,** 555 Middle Verde Rd. (✆ **800/381-SLOT** or 928/567-7900; www.cliffcastlecasino.net), at Exit 289 off I-17.

IN & AROUND COTTONWOOD & CLARKDALE

Cottonwood, 6 miles from Jerome, isn't nearly as atmospheric as the old copper-mining town up on the hill, but there are a few blocks of historic buildings filled with interesting shops. Old-town Cottonwood's **Main Street,** with its shops, galleries, cafes, and covered sidewalk, is a pleasant place for a stroll. Be sure to check out Ramona Stites's colorful landscape paintings at **Javadog Gallery,** 1023 N. Main St. (✆ **928/634-5217;** www.javadoggallery.com). From here, you can also walk the **Jail Trail,** which begins beside the old town jail (now a visitor center) and heads 1 mile through the cottonwood-willow forests along the banks of the Verde River. At its far end, the trail connects to Dead Horse Ranch State Park, which has many more miles of trails. There's good bird-watching along the Jail Trail, so bring your binoculars. This trail is part of the 6-mile Verde River Greenway, which protects the riparian forests along the riverbanks.

If it's a hot day, you may want to head up to **Sycamore Creek** to cool off in one of the creek's swimming holes. It's a 2-mile hike on Parson's Trail to the first swimming hole, but there are more farther up the creek. To reach the trail head for this hike, follow signs to Tuzigoot National Monument, and after crossing the bridge over the Verde River, turn left onto gravel Forest Road 131 (signed for the Sycamore Canyon Wilderness). The trail head is 11 miles up this road.

WHERE TO STAY

Hacienda de la Mariposa ★★ *Finds* This modern Santa Fe–style inn is set on the banks of Beaver Creek and is just up the road from Montezuma Castle National Monument. Guest rooms contain rustic Mexican furnishings, gas beehive-style fireplaces, small private patios, and lots of character. Bathrooms feature skylights and whirlpool tubs. With a patio overlooking the creek, the Mariposa Creekside room is my favorite. The little Casita de Milagros, a sort of cottage/massage room that serves as a gathering spot for guests, has a huge amethyst geode set into the ceiling. In a walled garden out back, you'll find a swimming pool only steps from the creek.

3875 Stagecoach Rd. (P.O. Box 310), Camp Verde, AZ 86322. ✆ **888/520-9095** or 928/567-1490. www.lamariposa-az.com. 5 units. $195–$225 double. AE, DISC, MC, V. No children. **Amenities:** Outdoor pool; Jacuzzi; massage. *In room:* A/C, TV/VCR, coffeemaker, hair dryer, free local calls.

WHERE TO DINE

Blazin' M Ranch Chuckwagon Suppers *Kids* AMERICAN Located adjacent to Dead Horse Ranch State Park, the Blazin' M Ranch is classic Arizona-style family entertainment—steaks and beans accompanied by cowboy music and comedy. This place is geared primarily toward the young 'uns, with pony rides, farm animals, and a little cow town for the kids to explore. If you're young at heart, you might enjoy the Blazin' M, but it's definitely more fun if you bring the whole family. One of the highlights is the gallery of animated woodcarvings, which features humorous Western scenes.

Off 10th St., Cottonwood. ✆ **800/937-8643** or 928/634-0334. www.blazinm.com. Reservations recommended. Dinner $35 adults, $33 seniors, $25 children ages 3–12. AE, DISC, MC, V. Mon–Sat gates open at 5pm, dinner at 6:30pm, show at 7:30pm. Closed Jan.

Old Town Café *Finds* CAFE The almond croissants at this European-style cafe in downtown Cottonwood are among the best I've ever had. If that isn't recommendation enough for you, there are also good salads and sandwiches, such as a grilled panini of smoked turkey, spinach, and tomatoes.

1025 "A" N. Main St., Cottonwood. ✆ **928/634-5980.** Reservations not accepted. Salads and sandwiches $6–$9. MC, V. Tues–Sat 8am–3pm.

5 Sedona & Oak Creek Canyon ★★★

66 miles NE of Prescott; 116 miles N of Phoenix; 106 miles S of the Grand Canyon

There is not a town anywhere in the Southwest, perhaps anywhere in the country, with a more beautiful setting than Sedona. On the outskirts of town, red-rock buttes, eroded canyon walls, and mesas rise into cerulean skies. Off in the distance, the Mogollon Rim looms, its forests of juniper and ponderosa pine dark against the rocks. With a wide band of rosy sandstone predominating in this area, Sedona has come to be known as red-rock country, and each evening at sunset, the rocks put on an unforgettable light show that is reason enough for a visit.

All this may sound perfectly idyllic, but if you lower your eyes from the red rocks, you'll see the flip side of Sedona—a sprawl of housing developments, highways lined with unattractive strip malls, and bumper-to-bumper traffic. Consequently, I have a love-hate relationship with Sedona. I love the setting and the views; I hate the crass commercialism and tourist-trap character that has taken over. (Wanna buy a timeshare?) However, not even the proliferation of timeshare sales offices disguised as "visitor information centers" can mar the beauty of the backdrop.

With national forest surrounding the city (and even fingers of forest extending into what would otherwise be the city limits), Sedona also has some of the best outdoor access of any city in the Southwest. All around town, alongside highways and down side streets in suburban neighborhoods, there are trail heads. Trek down any one of these trails and you leave the city behind and enter the world of the red rocks. Just don't be surprised if you come around a bend in the trail and find yourself in the middle of a wedding ceremony or a group of 30 people doing tai chi.

Located at the mouth of Oak Creek Canyon, Sedona was first settled by pioneers in 1877 and was named for the first postmaster's wife. Word of Sedona's beauty did not begin to spread until Hollywood filmmakers began using the region's red rock as backdrop to their Western films. Next came artists, lured by the landscapes and desert light (it was here in Sedona that the Cowboy Artists of America organization was formed). Although still much touted as an artists' community, Sedona's art scene these days is geared more toward tourists than toward collectors of fine art.

More recently, the spectacular views and mild climate were discovered by retirees. Sedona's hills are now alive with the sound of construction as ostentatious retirement mansions and celebrity trophy homes sprout from the dust like desert toads after an August rainstorm. Sedona is also a magnet for New Age believers, who come to experience unseen cosmic energy fields known as vortexes. The vortexes are such a powerful attraction that many New Age types have stayed in the area and have turned Sedona into a hotbed of alternative therapies. You can hardly throw a smudge stick around these parts without hitting a psychic (shouldn't they have seen it coming?). Most recently, mountain bikers have begun to ride the red rock, and word is spreading that the biking here is almost as good as up north in Moab, Utah.

The waters of Oak Creek were what first attracted settlers and native peoples to this area, and today this stream still lures visitors to Sedona—especially in summer, when the cool shade and even cooler creek waters are a glorious respite from the heat of the desert. Two of Arizona's finest swimming holes are located on Oak Creek only a few miles from Sedona, and one of these, Slide Rock, has been made into a state park.

With its drop-dead gorgeous scenery, dozens of motels and resorts, and plethora of good restaurants, Sedona makes an excellent base for exploring central Arizona. Several ancient Indian ruins (including an impressive cliff dwelling), the "ghost town" of Jerome, and the scenic Verde Canyon Railroad are all within easy driving distance, and even the Grand Canyon is but a long day trip away.

ESSENTIALS

GETTING THERE Sedona is on Arizona 179 at the mouth of Oak Creek Canyon. From Phoenix, take I-17 to Arizona 179 N. From Flagstaff, head south on I-17 until you see the turnoff for Arizona 89A and Sedona. Arizona 89A also connects Sedona with Prescott.

Sedona Phoenix Shuttle (© **800/448-7988** in Arizona, or 928/282-2066; www.sedona-phoenix-shuttle.com) operates several trips daily between Phoenix's Sky Harbor Airport and Sedona. The fare is $45 one-way, $85 round-trip.

VISITOR INFORMATION The **Sedona–Oak Creek Canyon Chamber of Commerce Visitor Center/Uptown Gateway Visitor Center,** 331 Forest Rd. (© **800/288-7336** or 928/282-7722; www.visitsedona.com), operates a visitor center at the corner of Arizona 89A and Forest Road near uptown Sedona. The visitor center is open Monday through Saturday from 8:30am to 5pm, and Sunday and holidays from 9am to 3pm.

You can also get information, as well as a Red Rock Pass for parking at area trail heads, at the **South Gateway Visitor Center,** Tequa Shopping Plaza, 7000 Ariz. 179, Village of Oak Creek (© **928/284-5324**), which is open daily from 8:30am to 5pm; or the **North Gateway Visitor Center,** Oak Creek Vista Overlook, Arizona 89A (© **928/282-4119**), which is open March 1 through November 1, weather permitting, daily from 9am to 4:30pm.

GETTING AROUND Whether traveling by car or on foot, you'll need to cultivate patience when trying to cross major roads in Sedona. Traffic here, especially on weekends, is some of the worst in the state. Also be prepared for slow traffic on roads that have good views; drivers are often distracted by the red rocks. You may hear or see references to the **"Y,"** which refers to the intersection of Arizona 179 and Arizona 89A between the Tlaquepaque shopping plaza and uptown Sedona.

Rental cars are available through **Enterprise** (© **800/261-7331**). You can also rent a jeep from **Farabee Jeep Rentals of Sedona** (© **928/282-8700;** www.farabeejeeprentals.com), which charges $125 for 4 hours and $185 for 8 hours. Or you can get around Sedona on the **Sedona Roadrunner,** a free shuttle bus that operates every 8 to 15 minutes between uptown, Tlaquepaque, and the Hillside Shops.

SPECIAL EVENTS The **Sedona International Film Festival** (© **928/282-1177;** www.sedonafilmfestival.com), held in late February or early March, always books

Sedona & Vicinity

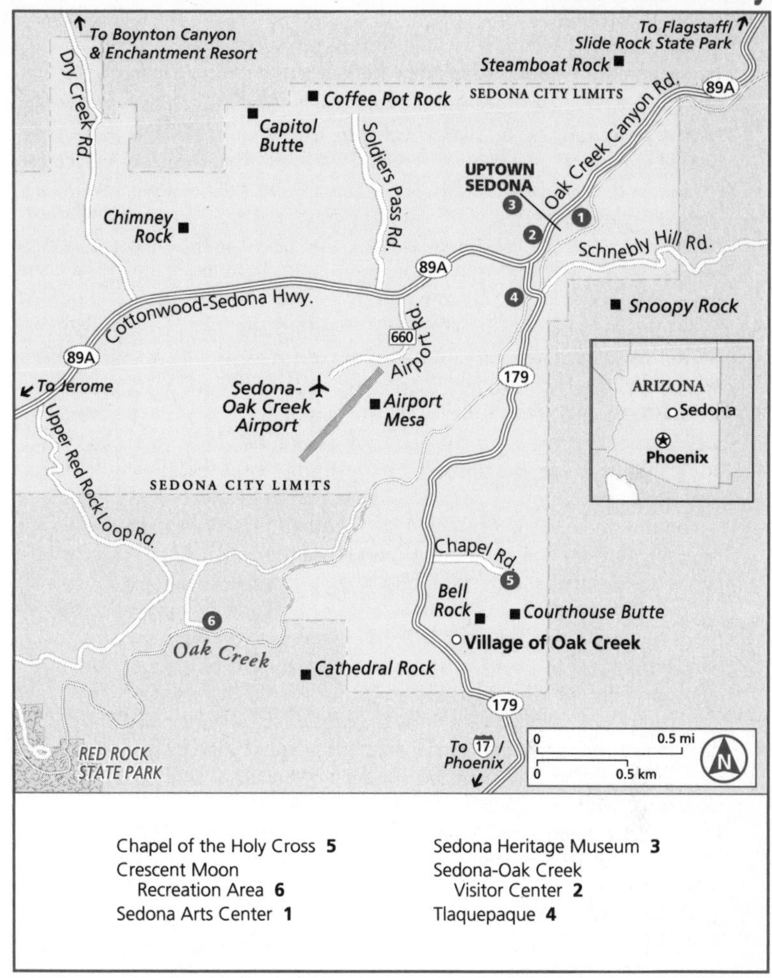

plenty of interesting films. In late September, **Sedona Jazz on the Rocks** (✆ **928/282-1985;** www.sedonajazz.com) brings world-class jazz to the area. In early December, Sedona celebrates the **Festival of Lights** (✆ **928/282-4838;** www.tlaq.com) at Tlaquepaque by lighting thousands of *luminarias* (paper bags partially filled with sand and containing a single candle). From mid-November until early January, more than a million lights illuminate Los Abrigados Resort (✆ **800/521-3131** or 928/282-1777; www.redrockfantasy.com) in a **Red-Rock Fantasy.**

EXPLORING RED-ROCK COUNTRY

The Grand Canyon may be Arizona's biggest attraction, but there's actually far more to do in Sedona. If you aren't an active type, there's the obvious option of just sitting down and gazing in awe at the rugged cliffs, needlelike pinnacles, and isolated buttes

Vortex Power

For many years now, Sedona has been one of the world's centers for the New Age movement, and large numbers of people make the pilgrimage here to experience the "power vortexes" of the surrounding red-rock country. Around town you'll see bulletin boards and publications advertising such diverse services as past-life regressions, crystal healing, angelic healing, tarot readings, reiki, axiatonal therapy, electromagnetic field balancing, soul recovery, channeling, aromatherapy, myofascial release, and aura photos and videos.

According to believers, a vortex is a site where the earth's unseen lines of power intersect to form a particularly powerful energy field. Psychic Page Bryant determined through channeling that there were four vortexes around Sedona. Scientists may scoff, but Sedona's vortexes have become so well known that the visitor centers have several handouts to explain them and a map to guide you to them. (Many of the most spectacular geological features of the Sedona landscape also happen to be vortexes.)

The four main vortexes are Bell Rock, Cathedral Rock, Airport Mesa, and Boynton Canyon. **Bell Rock** and **Airport Mesa** are both said to contain masculine or electric energy that boosts emotional, spiritual, and physical energy. **Cathedral Rock** is said to contain feminine or magnetic energy, good for facilitating relaxation. The **Boynton Canyon** vortex is considered an electromagnetic energy site, which means it has a balance of both masculine and feminine energy.

If you're not familiar with vortexes and want to learn more about the ones in Sedona, consider a vortex tour. These are offered by several companies, including **Earth Wisdom Jeep Tours** (✆ 800/482-4714 or 928/282-4714; www.earthwisdomtours.com), **Spirit Steps** (✆ 800/728-4562 or 928/282-4562; www.spiritsteps.org), and **Sedona Vortex Tours** (✆ 800/943-3266 or 928/282-2733; www.sedonaretreats.com). All three offer tours that combine aspects of Native American and New Age beliefs. Tours last 2½ to 3 hours and cost around $70 to $75 per person.

You can also stock up on books, crystals, and other spiritual supplies at stores such as **Crystal Magic,** 2978 W. Hwy. 89A (✆ **928/282-1622;** www.crystalmagicsedona.com), or **Center for the New Age,** 341 Hwy. 179 (✆ **888/881-6651** or 928/282-2085; www.sedonanewagecenter.com).

that rise from the green forest floor at the mouth of Oak Creek Canyon. Want to see more but don't want to break a sweat? Head out into the red rocks on a jeep tour or drift over the red rocks in a hot-air balloon. Want to go *mano a mano* with this wild landscape? Go for a hike, rent a mountain bike, or go horseback riding. (See "Organized Tours" and "Outdoor Pursuits" later in this chapter for details.)

Although **Schnebly Hill Road,** which climbs into the red rocks east of Sedona, is a rough dirt road, it's a must for superb views. This road is best driven in a high-clearance vehicle or SUV, but depending on how recently it has been maintained, it can be passable in a regular car. To reach this scenic road, head south out of Sedona on Arizona 179, turn left after you cross the bridge over Oak Creek, and head up the road, which starts out paved but soon turns to dirt. As this road climbs to the top of the Mogollon Rim, each switchback and cliff-edged bend in the road yields a new and more astonishing view. At the rim is the Schnebly Hill overlook, offering a view that just begs to be savored over a long picnic. If you don't feel comfortable doing this drive in your own vehicle, consider booking a jeep tour that heads up this way.

Just south of Sedona, on the east side of Arizona 179, you'll see the aptly named **Bell Rock.** There's a parking area at the foot of this formation, and trails lead up to the top. Adjacent to Bell Rock is **Courthouse Butte,** and to the west stands **Cathedral Rock.** From the Chapel of the Holy Cross (see "Attractions & Activities Around Town," below) on Chapel Road, you can see **Eagle Head Rock** (from the front door of the chapel, look three-quarters of the way up the mountain to see the eagle's head), the **Twin Nuns** (two pinnacles standing side by side), and **Mother and Child Rock** (to the left of the Twin Nuns).

If you head west out of Sedona on Arizona 89A and turn left onto Airport Road, you'll drive up onto **Airport Mesa,** which commands an unobstructed panorama of Sedona and the red rocks. About halfway up the mesa is a small parking area from which trails radiate. The views from here are among the best in the region, and the trails are very easy.

Boynton Canyon, located 8 miles west of the "Y," is a narrow red-rock canyon and is one of the most beautiful spots in the Sedona area. This canyon is also the site of the deluxe Enchantment resort, but hundreds of years before there were luxury casita suites here, there were Sinagua cliff dwellings. Several of these cliff dwellings can still be spotted high on the canyon walls. **Boynton Canyon Trail** leads 3 miles up into this canyon from a trail head parking area just outside the gates of Enchantment. To get to the trail head, drive west out of Sedona on Arizona 89A, turn right on Dry Creek Road, take a left at the first T intersection, and a right at the second T.

On the way to Boynton Canyon, look north from Arizona 89A, and you'll see **Coffee Pot Rock,** also known as Rooster Rock, rising 1,800 feet above Sedona. Three pinnacles, known as the **Three Golden Chiefs** by the Yavapai tribe, stand beside Coffee Pot Rock. As you drive up Dry Creek Road, on your right you'll see **Capitol Butte,** which resembles the U.S. Capitol.

To the west of Boynton Canyon, you can visit the well-preserved Sinagua cliff dwellings at **Palatki Heritage Site** (© **928/282-3854**). These small ruins, tucked under the red cliffs, are the best place in the area to get a feel for the ancient Native American cultures that once lived in this region. Among the ruins, you'll see numerous pictographs (paintings) created by the past residents of Palatki. Before heading out to these ruins, be sure you make a reservation by calling the number above. To reach the ruins, follow the directions to Boynton Canyon, but instead of turning right at the second T intersection, turn left onto unpaved Boynton Pass Road (Forest Rd., or FR, 152), which is one of the

---

***Fun Fact* The Name Game**

If you're having a hard time remembering which rock is which here in Sedona, you aren't alone. Cathedral Rock was originally named Courthouse Rock, but many years ago it was incorrectly marked on a map and the change stuck.

---

most scenic roads in the area. Follow this road to another T intersection and go right onto Forest Road 525, then veer right onto Forest Road 795, which dead-ends at the ruins. You can also get here by taking Arizona 89A W from Sedona to Forest Road 525, a gravel road leading north to Forest Road 795. To visit Palatki, you'll need a Red Rock Pass (see "The High Cost of Red-Rock Views," below); ruins are usually open daily from 9:30am to 3pm. The dirt roads around here become impassable to regular cars when they're wet, so don't try coming out here if the roads are at all muddy.

South of Arizona 89A and a bit west of the turnoff for Boynton Canyon is Upper Red Rock Loop Road, which leads to **Crescent Moon Recreation Area,** a National Forest Service recreation area that has become a must-see for visitors to Sedona. Its

The High Cost of Red-Rock Views

A quick perusal of any Sedona real-estate magazine will convince you that property values around these parts are as high as the Mogollon Rim. However, red-rock real estate is also expensive for those who want only a glimpse of the rocks. With the land around Sedona split up into several types of National Forest Service day-use sites, state parks, and national monuments, visitors find themselves pulling out their wallets just about every time they turn around to look at another rock. Here's the lowdown on what it's going to cost you to do the red rocks right.

A **Red Rock Pass** will allow you to visit Palatki Ruins and the V Bar V Ranch petroglyph site and park at any national forest trail head parking areas. The cost is $5 for a 1-day pass, $15 for a 7-day pass, and $20 for a 12-month pass. Passes are good for everyone in your vehicle. If you plan to be in the area for more than a week and also want to visit Grasshopper Point (a swimming hole), Banjo Bill (a picnic area), Call of the Canyon (the West Fork Oak Creek trail head), and Crescent Moon (Sedona's top photo-op site), you'll want to buy a **Red Rock Grand Annual Pass,** for $40. These sites each charge $7 admission per vehicle, so unless you plan on visiting at least three of them or expect to be around for more than a week, the Red Rock Grand Annual Pass is not a good deal.

There are also two state parks in the area—Slide Rock ($8–$10 per car) and Red Rock ($6 per car). Admission to the Montezuma Castle or Tuzigoot national monuments will cost you $5 per adult.

If there are two or more of you traveling together and you plan on visiting the Grand Canyon and three or four other national parks or monuments, you might want to consider getting an **America the Beautiful Pass** ($80). This pass is good for a year and will get you into any national park or national monument in the country. If you're 62 or older, definitely get an **America the Beautiful Senior Pass** ($10), which is good for the rest of your life. Persons with disabilities can get a free lifetime **America the Beautiful Access Pass.** Any of these three passes can be used in lieu of a Red Rock Pass.

For more information on the Red Rock passes, visit www.redrockcountry.org.

popularity stems from a beautiful photograph of Oak Creek with **Cathedral Rock** in the background—an image that has been reproduced countless times in Sedona promotional literature and on postcards. Hiking trails lead up to Cathedral Rock. Admission is $7 per vehicle (unless you have previously purchased a Red Rock Grand Annual Pass; see "The High Cost of Red-Rock Views," below). For more information, contact the Red Rock Ranger Station (© **928/282-4119;** www.fs.fed.us/r3/coconino).

If you continue on Red Rock Loop Road, you will come to **Red Rock State Park,** 4050 Red Rock Loop Rd. (© **928/282-6907**), which flanks Oak Creek. The views here take in many of the rocks listed above, and you have the bonus of being right on the creek (though swimming and wading are prohibited). Park admission is $6 per car. The park offers lots of guided walks and interpretive programs.

South of Sedona, near the junction of I-17 and Arizona 179, you can visit one of the premier petroglyph sites in Arizona. The rock art at the **V Bar V Heritage Site** covers a small cliff face and includes images of herons and turtles. To get here, take the dirt road that leads east for 2⅔ miles from the junction of I-17 and Arizona 179 to the Beaver Creek Campground. The entrance to the petroglyph site is just past the campground. From the parking area, it's about a half-mile walk to the petroglyphs, which are open Friday through Monday from 9:30am to 3:30pm. To visit this site, you'll need a Red Rock Pass or other valid pass. For information, contact the **Red Rock Ranger District** (© **928/282-4119;** www.fs.fed.us/r3/coconino).

OAK CREEK CANYON

The **Mogollon Rim** (pronounced "*mug*-ee-un" by the locals) is a 2,000-foot escarpment cutting diagonally across central Arizona and on into New Mexico. At the top of the Mogollon Rim are the ponderosa pine forests of the high mountains, while at the bottom the lowland deserts begin. Of the many canyons cutting down from the rim, Oak Creek Canyon is the most beautiful (and one of the few that has a paved road down through it). Arizona 89A runs through the canyon from Flagstaff to Sedona, winding its way down from the rim and paralleling Oak Creek. Along the way are overlooks, parks, picnic areas, campgrounds, cabin resorts, and small inns.

If you have a choice of how first to view Oak Creek Canyon, approach it from the north. Your first stop after traveling south from Flagstaff will be the **Oak Creek Canyon Vista,** which provides a view far down the valley to Sedona and beyond. The overlook is at the edge of the Mogollon Rim, and the road suddenly drops in tight switchbacks just south of here. You may notice that one rim of the canyon is lower than the other. This is because Oak Creek Canyon is on a geologic fault line; one side of the canyon is moving in a different direction from the other.

Although the top of the Mogollon Rim is a ponderosa pine forest and the bottom a desert, Oak Creek Canyon supports a forest of sycamores and other deciduous trees. There is no better time to drive scenic Arizona 89A than between late September and mid-October, when the canyon is ablaze with red and yellow leaves.

In the desert, swimming holes are powerful magnets during the hot summer months, and consequently, **Slide Rock State Park,** 6871 N. U.S. 89A (© **928/282-3034;** www.pr.state.az.us), located 7 miles north of Sedona on the site of an old homestead, is the most popular spot in all of Oak Creek Canyon. What pulls in the crowds of families and teenagers is the park's natural water slide and great little swimming hole. On hot days, the park is jammed with people splashing in the water and sliding over the algae-covered sandstone bottom of Oak Creek. Sunbathing and fishing are other popular pastimes. The park is open daily; admission is $8 per vehicle ($10 during the summer). There's another popular swimming area at **Grasshopper Point,** several miles closer to Sedona. Admission is $7 per vehicle, unless you have previously purchased a Red Rock Grand Annual Pass (see "The High Cost of Red-Rock Views," above, for details).

Within Oak Creek Canyon, several hikes of different lengths are possible. By far the most spectacular and popular is the 6-mile round-trip up the **West Fork of Oak Creek.** This is a classic canyon-country hike with steep canyon walls rising from the creek. At some points, the canyon is no more than 20 feet wide, with walls rising up more than 200 feet. You can also extend the hike many more miles up the canyon for an overnight backpacking trip. The trail head for the West Fork of Oak Creek hike is 9.5 miles up Oak Creek Canyon from Sedona at the Call of the Canyon Recreation Area, which charges a $7 day-use fee per vehicle unless you have already purchased a Red Rock Grand Annual Pass.

Stop by the Sedona–Oak Creek Chamber of Commerce for a free map of area hikes. The **Coconino National Forest's Red Rock Ranger Station,** which, at press time, was in a temporary space 2 miles east of I-17 at Exit 298 (Beaver Creek Rd.), is an even better source of hiking information. It's open Monday through Friday from 8am to 4:30pm. Sometime in 2008, the ranger station will relocate to a new facility on Arizona 179 south of the Village of Oak Creek.

If you get thirsty while driving through the canyon, hold out for **Garlands Indian Gardens Market,** 3951 N. Hwy. 89A (© **928/282-7702**), about 4 miles north of Sedona. Here, in the fall, you can get delicious organic apple juice made from apples grown in the canyon. For one last view down the canyon, stop at **Midgely Bridge** (watch for the parked cars and small parking area at the north end of the bridge).

ATTRACTIONS & ACTIVITIES AROUND TOWN

Sedona's most notable architectural landmark is the **Chapel of the Holy Cross,** 780 Chapel Rd. (© **928/282-4069**), a small church built right into the red rock on the south side of town. If you're driving up from Phoenix, you can't miss it—the chapel sits high above the road just off Arizona 179. With its contemporary styling, it is one of the most architecturally important modern churches in the country. Marguerite Brunswig Staude, a devout Catholic painter, sculptor, and designer, had the inspiration for the chapel in 1932, but it wasn't until 1957 that her dream was finally realized. The chapel's design is dominated by a simple cross forming the wall that faces the street. The cross and the starkly beautiful chapel seem to grow directly from the rock, allowing the natural beauty of the red rock to speak for itself. It's open Monday through Saturday from 9am to 6pm and Sunday from 10am to 6pm.

The **Sedona Arts Center,** 15 Art Barn Rd. at Arizona 89A (© **888/954-4442** or 928/282-3809; www.sedonaartscenter.com), near the north end of uptown Sedona, has a gallery that specializes in works by local and regional artists.

To learn a bit about the local history, stop by the **Sedona Heritage Museum,** 735 Jordan Rd. (© **928/282-7038;** www.sedonamuseum.org), in Jordan Historical Park. The museum, which is housed in a historic home, is furnished with antiques and contains exhibits on the many movies that have been filmed in the area. The farm was once an apple orchard, and there's still apple-processing equipment in the barn. Hours are daily from 11am to 3pm; admission is $3.

While Sedona isn't yet a resort spa destination on par with Phoenix or Tucson, it does have a few spas that might add just the right bit of pampering to your vacation. **Therapy on the Rocks,** 676 N. Hwy. 89A (© **928/282-3002;** www.myofascialrelease.com),

Moments Sunset at the Amitabha Stupa

There's just something about Sedona that brings out people's spirituality, and one of the latest spiritual attractions to find a home among the red rocks is the **Amitabha Stupa (✆ 928/300-4435;** www.stupas.org), a Tibetan Buddhist shrine erected in a residential neighborhood in west Sedona. The 36-foot-tall stupa is up a short path that winds through juniper trees festooned with prayer flags. The stupa is often visited by devout Buddhists, who leave offerings at the base of the stupa, but the public is welcome any time from dawn to dusk. To find the stupa, drive north from Arizona 89A on Andante Drive and turn left on Pueblo Drive. Park outside the gate on the right.

with its creekside setting, is a longtime local favorite that offers massage, myofascial release, and great views of the red rocks. For personal attention, try the little **Red Rock Healing Arts Center,** Creekside Plaza, 251 Hwy. 179 (✆ **888/31-9033** or 928/203-9933; www.redrockhealing.com), which is just up the hill from the Tlaquepaque shopping plaza and offers a variety of massages, wraps, scrubs, and facials. In the Village of Oak Creek, there's the **Hilton Spa,** at the Hilton Sedona Resort & Spa, 10 Ridge View Dr. (✆ **928/284-6900;** www.hiltonsedonaspa.com), offering a variety of treatments (try the Painted Desert clay wrap or Sedona stone massage). There are also exercise and yoga classes, a pool, and tennis courts. Prices for a 60-minute treatment range from $129 to $139.

It may be a bit premature to start calling Sedona the next Napa Valley, but there are a few wineries in the area. Two of them, both located in the community of Page Springs about 20 minutes west of Sedona, are open to the public for tastings. To reach these wineries, drive west from Sedona on Arizona 89A, and turn south on Page Springs Road. You'll first come to **Oak Creek Vineyards and Winery,** Page Springs Road (✆ **928/649-0290;** www.oakcreekvineyards.net), which is across the street from the Page Springs Fish Hatchery. The tasting room here is open Wednesday through Sunday from 11am to 5pm. At press time, this winery had plans to add a restaurant. **Page Springs Vineyards & Cellars,** 1500 N. Page Springs Rd. (✆ **928/639-3004;** www.pagespringscellars.com), is the more impressive and reliable of the two wineries, although as of 2006, they were still making most of their wines with grapes from California, not from their own vineyards. Rhone varietals are the specialty here. The tasting room is open Thursday through Sunday from 11am to 6pm. **Echo Canyon Vineyard & Winery** is my favorite local winery, but it is not generally open to the public. However, this winery can be visited on Jeep tours operated by Sun Country Adventures (✆ **877/783-6000;** www.scadventures.net). The 2½-hour tours cost $95 per person.

ORGANIZED TOURS

For an overview of Sedona, take a tour on the **Sedona Trolley** (✆ **928/282-4211;** www.sedonatrolley.com), which leaves several times daily on two separate tours. One tour visits the Tlaquepaque shopping plaza, the Chapel of the Holy Cross, and several art galleries, while the other goes out through west Sedona to Boynton Canyon and Enchantment Resort. Tours are $10 for adults ($19 for both tours) and $5 for children 12 and under ($9 for both tours).

The red-rock country surrounding Sedona is the city's greatest natural attraction, and there's no better way to explore it than by four-wheel-drive vehicle. Although you may end up feeling like every other tourist in town, you quite simply should not leave Sedona without going on a jeep tour. These tours will get you out onto rugged roads and 4×4 trails with spectacular views. The unchallenged leader in Sedona jeep tours is **Pink Jeep Tours,** 204 N. Hwy. 89A (✆ **800/873-3662** or 928/282-5000; www.pinkjeep.com), which has been heading deep into the Coconino National Forest since 1958. It offers tours ranging in length from 1½ to 4 hours, however, the 2-hour "Broken Arrow" tour ($72 adults, $54 children 12 and under) is the most adventurous and is the tour I recommend. Pink Jeep Tours also offers tours to Grand Canyon National Park.

If a jeep just isn't manly enough for you, how about a Hummer? Better yet, how about a Hummer that runs on enviro-friendly bio-diesel? **Hummer Affair,** 273 N. Hwy. 89A, Suite C (✆ **928/282-6656;** www.hummeraffair.com), will take you out in the red rocks in the ultimate off-road vehicle. One-hour tours run $40 to $69 ($29–$59 for children), but the 2-hour "Jeep Eater Tour" for $89 ($79 for children) is the most fun.

How about a chance to play cowboy? **A Day in the West,** 252 N. Hwy. 89A (✆ **800/973-3663** or 928/282-4320; www.adayinthewest.com), has its own private ranch for some of its jeep tours and horseback rides. There are cowboy cookouts, too. Prices range from $45 to $165.

If you'd like to have a very knowledgeable local tour guide show you around places you're interested in seeing at your own pace, I recommend getting in touch with Steve "Benny" Benedict at **Touch the Earth Adventures** (✆ **928/203-9132;** www.earthtours.com). Benny likes to take clients to spots that even many locals don't know about. Half-day excursions run $125 per person, and full-day outings are $225 per person.

For a tour of the Sedona area from a Native American perspective, contact **Way of the Ancients** (✆ **866/204-9243;** www.wayoftheancients.com), which offers 5-hour tours that cost $69 for adults and $59 for children. There are also excursions to the Hopi mesas ($139 for adults and $129 for children).

Just because it's too dark to see the red rocks doesn't mean there's nothing to see and do in Sedona at night. How about a tour of the heavens? **Evening Sky Tours** (✆ **866/701-0398** or 928/203-0006; www.eveningskytours.com) takes advantage of the dark night skies over Sedona to lead people on astronomy tours of the stars and planets. Tours cost $60 for adults and $20 for children.

As spectacular as Sedona is from the ground, it is even more so from the air. **Arizona Helicopter Adventures** (✆ **800/282-5141** or 928/282-0904; www.azheli.com) offers short flights to different parts of this colorful region. Prices start at $58 per person for a 12-minute flight. **Sky Safari Air Tours** (✆ **888/TOO-RIDE** or 928/204-5939; www.sedonaairtours.com) offers a variety of flights in small planes. A 15-minute air tour will run you $49 per person, while a 45-minute tour will cost $99. Flights as far afield as the Grand Canyon and Canyon de Chelly can also be arranged.

My favorite Sedona air tours are those offered by **Red Rock Biplane Tours** (✆ **888/TOO-RIDE** or 928/204-5939; www.sedonaairtours.com), which operates modern Waco open-cockpit biplanes. With the wind in your hair, you'll feel as though you've entered the world of Snoopy and the Red Baron. Tours lasting 20 to 60 minutes are offered; a 20-minute tour costs $89 per person with a two-person minimum.

If something a bit slower is more your speed, how about drifting over the sculpted red buttes of Sedona in a hot-air balloon? **Northern Light Balloon Expeditions** (✆ **800/230-6222** or 928/282-2274; www.northernlightballoon.com) charges $190 per person; **Red Rock Balloon Adventures** (✆ **800/258-3754;** www.redrockballoons.com) charges $195 per person; while **Sky High Balloon Adventures** (✆ **800/551-7597;** www.skyhighballoons.com), which floats over the Verde Valley and includes a "splash-and-dash" descent to the river, charges $180 per person.

OUTDOOR PURSUITS

Hiking is the most popular outdoor activity in the Sedona area, with dozens of trails leading off into the red rocks. The only problem is that nearly everyone who comes to Sedona wants to go hiking, so finding a little solitude along the trail can be difficult. Not surprisingly, the most convenient trail heads also have the most crowded trails. If you want to ditch the crowds, pick a trail head that is *not* on Arizona 179 or Arizona 89A. That means that if you stop at any of the trail heads in Oak Creek Canyon or between the Village of Oak Creek and Sedona, you'll likely encounter lots of other people along the trail. You'll enjoy your Sedona hikes more if you start from a trail heading down a side road. Among my personal favorites are the trails that originate at the end of Jordan Road in uptown Sedona, the Cathedral Rock Trail, which starts in a housing development between Sedona and the Village of Oak Creek, and the trails off Boynton Pass Road. ***Note:*** Don't forget to get your Red Rock Pass before heading out for a hike.

This said, the most convenient place to get some red dust on your boots is along the **Bell Rock Pathway,** which begins alongside Arizona 179 just north of the Village of Oak Creek. This trail winds around the base of Bell Rock and accesses many other trails that lead up onto the sloping sides of Bell Rock. It's about 5 miles to go all the way around Bell Rock. Unfortunately, this is one of the most popular hiking trails in the area and is always crowded.

You'll see fewer tourists if you head to the .75-mile **Cathedral Rock Trail,** which is also located between the Village of Oak Creek and uptown Sedona. The trail follows cairns (piles of rocks) up the slickrock slopes on the north side of Cathedral Rock. To reach this trail, turn off Arizona 179 at the sign for the Back o' Beyond housing development and watch for the trail head at the end of the paved road. For convenience and solitude, you can't beat the **Mystic Trail,** which begins at an unmarked roadside pull-off on Chapel Road halfway between Arizona 179 and the Chapel of the Holy Cross. This is an easy out-and-back trail that runs between a couple of housing developments, but once you're on the trail, you'll feel all alone.

Among the most popular trails in the Sedona area are those that lead into **Boynton Canyon** (site of Enchantment Resort). Here you'll glimpse ancient Native American ruins built into the red-rock cliffs. Although the scenery is indeed stupendous, the great numbers of other hikers on the trail detract considerably from the experience, and the parking lot usually fills up early in the day. The 1.5-mile **Vultee Arch Trail,** which leads to an impressive sandstone arch, is another great hike. The turnoff for the trail head is 2 miles up Dry Creek Road and then another 3½ miles on a very rough dirt road. The **Devil's Bridge Trail,** which starts on the same dirt road, is a little easier to get to and leads to the largest natural sandstone arch in the area. This one is a 1.8-mile round-trip hike.

For the hands-down best views in Sedona, hike all or part of the **Airport Mesa Trail,** a 3.5-mile loop that circles Airport Mesa. With virtually no elevation gain, this is an easy hike. You'll find the trail head about halfway to the top of Airport Mesa on

Airport Road. Try this one as early in the day as possible; by midday, the parking lot is usually full and it stays that way right through sunset.

For more information on hiking in Oak Creek Canyon (site of the famous West Fork Oak Creek Trail), see "Oak Creek Canyon," earlier. For more information on all these hikes, contact the **Coconino National Forest's Red Rock Ranger Station** (✆ **928/282-4119;** www.fs.fed.us/r3/coconino), which, at press time, was in a temporary space 2 miles east of I-17 at Exit 298 (Beaver Creek Rd.). The ranger district has plans to relocate to a site on Arizona 179 south of the Village of Oak Creek.

Sedona is rapidly becoming one of the Southwest's meccas for mountain biking. The red rock here is every bit as challenging and scenic as the famed slickrock country of Moab, Utah, and much less crowded. Using Sedona as a base, mountain bikers can ride year-round by heading up to Flagstaff in summer and down to the desert lowlands in winter. One of my favorite places to ride is around the base of Bell Rock. Starting at the trail head parking area just north of the Village of Oak Creek, you'll find not only the easy Bell Rock Path, but numerous more challenging trails.

Another great ride starts above uptown Sedona, where you can take the Jim Thompson Trail to Midgely Bridge or the network of trails that head toward Soldier Pass. The riding here is moderate and the views are superb. To reach these trails, take Jordan Road to a left onto Park Ridge Road, and follow this road to where it ends at a dirt trail head parking area. You can rent bikes from **Sedona Sports,** Creekside Plaza (below the "Y"), 251 N. Hwy. 179 (✆ **866/204-2377** or 928/282-1317; www.sedonasports.com), or **Mountain Bike Heaven,** 1695 W. Hwy. 89A (✆ **928/282-1312;** www.mountainbikeheaven.com). Rates are around $35 to $50 per day. **Sedona Bike & Bean,** 6020 Hwy. 179, Village of Oak Creek (✆ **928/284-0210;** www.bike-bean.com), across the street from the popular Bell Rock Pathway and its adjacent mountain-bike trails, rents bikes (and serves coffee). Bikes go for $40 to $50 for a full day. Any of these stores can sell you a good local trail map or Cosmic Ray's *Fat Tire Tales and Trails* guidebook to the best rides in Arizona. If you'd prefer to have a guide take you out on either a mountain-bike or a road-bike tour, contact **Sedona MTB Adventures** (✆ **888/984-1246** or 928/284-1246; www.sedonamtbadventures.com).

Trail Horse Adventures (✆ **800/723-3538;** www.trailhorseadventures.com) offers guided horseback trail rides. A 2-hour ride (that includes creek crossings) will cost you $75. There are also lunch and dinner rides. **Sedona Red Rock Jeep Tours,** 270 N. Hwy. 89A (✆ **800/848-7728** or 928/282-6826; www.redrockjeep.com), offers horseback rides ($85 for 2 hr.) that include transportation by jeep to the ranch where the rides are held.

Surprisingly, Sedona has not yet been ringed with golf courses. However, what few courses there are offer superb views to distract you from your game. The **Oakcreek Country Club,** 690 Bell Rock Blvd. (✆ **888/703-9489** or 928/284-1660; www.oakcreekcountryclub.com), south of town off Arizona 179, has stunning views from

---

Fun Fact **The Red Rocks Return**

Every year the Sedona Chamber of Commerce receives boxes of rocks sent by visitors who took home a few "souvenirs" from their Sedona vacation and then later felt pangs of guilt over having absconded with pieces of this beautiful landscape.

---

the course. Greens fees are $69 to $125. The **Sedona Golf Resort** ★★, 35 Ridge Trail Dr. (✆ **877/733-9885** or 928/284-9355; www.sedonagolfresort.com), south of town on Arizona 179, offers equally breathtaking views of the red rocks. Greens fees are $59 to $105.

SHOPPING

Ever since the Cowboy Artists of America organization was founded in Sedona back in 1965 (at what is now the Cowboy Club restaurant), this town has had a reputation as an artists' community. Today, with dozens of galleries around town, it's obvious that art is one of the driving forces behind the local economy. Most of Sedona's galleries specialize in traditional Western, contemporary Southwestern, and Native American art, and in some galleries, you'll see works by members of the Cowboy Artists of America. You'll find the greatest concentration of galleries and shops in the uptown area of Sedona (along Ariz. 89A just north of the "Y") and at Tlaquepaque.

With more than 40 stores and restaurants, **Tlaquepaque,** 336 Hwy. 179 (✆ **928/282-4838;** www.tlaq.com), at the bridge over Oak Creek on the south side of Sedona, bills itself as Sedona's arts-and-crafts village and is designed to resemble a Mexican village. (It was named after a famous arts-and-crafts neighborhood in the suburbs of Guadalajara.) The maze of narrow alleys and courtyards, with its fountains, chapel, and bell tower, is worth a visit even if you aren't in a buying mood. Most of the shops here sell high-end art. I wish all shopping centers were such fascinating places.

Unfortunately, many of Sedona's shops now specialize in cheap Southwestern gifts that have little to do with art, and weeding through the tackiness to find the real galleries can be difficult. One place to start is at **Hozho,** with a couple of Sedona's better galleries, on Arizona 179 just before you cross the Oak Creek bridge in Sedona.

Cowboy Corral ★ If you want to dress like Wyatt Earp or Annie Oakley, this shop can outfit you. Definitely not your standard urban cowboy shop, Cowboy Corral goes for the vintage look. 219 N. Hwy. 89A. ✆ **800/457-2279** or 928/282-2040. www.cowboycorral.com.

El Prado Located in the Tlaquepaque shopping center, this gallery features the unusual stone furniture of artist R. C. Albin and the fascinating copper wind sculptures of Lyman Whittaker. These aren't the sorts of things you can pack in your suitcase for the flight home, but if you've got a new retirement home here in Arizona, these pieces sure would look good in the garden. At Tlaquepaque, 336 Hwy. 179. ✆ **800/498-3300** or 928/282-7390. www.elpradogalleries.com.

Exposures International Gallery of Fine Art If you've got a big house and need some big art, this is the place to shop for it. Exposures is the largest gallery in the state and usually has lots of monument-size sculptures out front. My favorite artist here is Texas sculptor Bill Worrell. 561 Hwy. 179. ✆ **877/ART-SITE** or 928/282-1125. www.exposuresfineart.com.

Garland's Indian Jewelry ★★★ A great location in the shade of scenic Oak Creek Canyon and a phenomenal collection of concho belts, squash-blossom necklaces, and bracelets make this the best place in Arizona to shop for Indian jewelry. There are also lots of kachinas for sale. At Indian Gardens, 3953 W. Hwy. 89A (4 miles north of Sedona). ✆ **928/282-6632.** www.garlandsjewelry.com.

Garland's Navajo Rugs ★★★ Garland's isn't just the premier Navajo rug shop in Sedona; it has the largest selection of contemporary and antique Navajo rugs in the world. It also carries Native American baskets and pottery, Hopi kachina dolls, and Navajo sand paintings. 411 Hwy. 179. ✆ **928/282-4070.** www.garlandsrugs.com.

Geoffrey Roth Ltd. If you're in the market for some unique jewelry or a gorgeous handmade wrist watch, check out this shop in the Tlaquepaque shopping center. At Tlaquepaque, 336 Hwy. 179, Suite A102. ✆ **800/447-7684** or 928/282-7756. www.geoffreyrothltd.com.

George Kelly Fine Jewelers This is another great place to shop for beautiful jewelry. The designs are highly creative and incorporate a wide range of stones, even the occasional meteorite. At Hyatt Shops at Piñon Pointe, 101 N. Hwy. 89A. ✆ **928/282-8884.**

Hillside Sedona This shopping center just south of Tlaquepaque is dedicated to art galleries and upscale retail shops, along with a couple of good restaurants. The hillside location means there are some good views to be had while you shop. 671 Hwy. 179. ✆ **928/282-4500.** www.hillsidesedona.net.

Hoel's Indian Shop ★★ Located 10 miles north of Sedona in a private residence in Oak Creek Canyon, this Native American arts-and-crafts gallery is one of the finest in the region and sells pieces of the highest quality. It's a good idea to call before coming out to make sure the store will be open. 9589 N. Hwy. 89A. ✆ **928/282-3925.** www.hoelsindianshop.com.

Hummingbird House Looking for an unusual gift to take home to someone? Tired of the crowds of tourists at Tlaquepaque and in Uptown? Check out this hidden gift shop in an attractively restored historic general store set behind a picket fence. You'll find the shop on a back street behind the Burger King that's at the junction of Arizona 89A and Arizona 179. 100 Brewer Rd. ✆ **928/282-0705.**

Lanning Gallery In business for more than 2 decades, this gallery in the Hozho Center across Oak Creek from Tlaquepaque carries both classic and contemporary art, with an emphasis on colorful two-dimensional works. At Hozho Center, 431 Hwy. 179. ✆ **928/282-6865.** www.lanninggallery.com.

Ondie Towne USA Ladies, want to dress like a rock star or well-heeled cowgirl? This leather boutique is the place. Ondie Towne, who is of Cherokee descent, is a fashion designer who has designed leather outfits for a number of celebrities. There are clothes for men, too. 1195-B W. Hwy. 89A. ✆ **928/203-0980.** www.ondietowneusa.com.

Sedona Arts Center Members Gallery Located at the north end of uptown Sedona, this shop is the best place in town to see the work of area artists—everything from jewelry and fiber arts to photography and ceramics. Because it's a nonprofit shop, you won't pay any tax here. 15 Art Barn Rd. ✆ **928/282-3865.** www.sedonaartscenter.com.

Son Silver West For those who love everything Southwestern, this shop is a treasure-trove of all kinds of interesting stuff, including Native American and Hispanic art and crafts, antique *santo* (saint) carvings, antique rifles, imported pots, dried-chile garlands *(ristras),* and garden art. 1476 Hwy. 179 (on the south side of town). ✆ **928/282-3580.** www.sonsilverwest.com.

WHERE TO STAY

Sedona is one of the most popular destinations in the Southwest, with dozens of hotels and motels around town. However, across-the-board, accommodations here tend to be overpriced for what you get. (Blame it on the incomparable views.) My advice is to save money elsewhere on your trip and make Sedona the place where you splurge on a room with a view.

VERY EXPENSIVE

El Portal Sedona ★★ You just can't help but fall in love with this amazing inn. Owners Steve and Connie Segner and Lynda Bourgeois have done everything right, and the overall experience here makes this one of the very best lodgings in the state. Located adjacent to the Tlaquepaque shopping center and built of hand-formed adobe blocks, El Portal, with its pleasant central courtyard, is designed to resemble a 200-year-old hacienda and is a monument to fine craftsmanship. The inn is filled with Arts-and-Crafts–period antiques, including not only the furniture, but also the door knobs, hinges, and even air-conditioning vents. In the living room, the huge ceiling beams were salvaged from a railroad bridge over the Great Salt Lake. Each of the large guest rooms has its own distinctive character, from Arts and Crafts to cowboy chic (rustic log furniture). All but two rooms have whirlpool tubs, and many rooms have private balconies with red-rock views. Exquisite breakfasts and weekend dinners are served.

95 Portal Lane, Sedona, AZ 86336. ✆ **800/313-0017** or 928/203-9405. Fax 928/203-9401. www.elportalsedona.com. 12 units. $259–$550 double. Rates include afternoon hors d'oeuvres. 2-night minimum on weekends and holidays. AE, DC, DISC, MC, V. Pets accepted. Children under 6 discouraged. **Amenities:** Restaurant (New American); access to nearby health club and adjacent resort pools; concierge; massage; laundry service; guided hikes and Jeep tours. *In room:* A/C, TV/DVD, dataport, minibar, fridge, hair dryer, iron, high-speed Internet access, Wi-Fi, free local calls.

Enchantment Resort ★★★ Located at the mouth of Boynton Canyon, this resort more than lives up to its name. The setting is breathtaking, the pueblo-style architecture blends in with the landscape, and the affiliated Mii amo spa is one of the finest in the state. The individual casitas can be booked as two-bedroom suites, one-bedroom suites, or single rooms, but it's worth reserving a suite just so you can enjoy the casita living rooms, which feature high beamed ceilings and beehive fireplaces. All the rooms, however, have patios with dramatic views. Both the Yavapai Restaurant (p. 209) and a less formal bar and grill offer tables outdoors; lunch on the terrace should not be missed.

The Mii amo spa is actually a separate entity within the resort and has its own restaurant, guest rooms, and rates (see separate review, below). Enchantment Resort guests do, however, have access to the spa facilities and can avail themselves of treatments.

525 Boynton Canyon Rd., Sedona, AZ 86336. ✆ **800/826-4180** or 928/282-2900. Fax 928/282-9249. www.enchantmentresort.com. 220 units. $350–$450 double; $450–$550 junior suite; $750–$950 1-bedroom suite; $1,125–$1,525 2-bedroom suite. Rates do not include $22 resort fee. Children 12 and under stay free in parent's room. AE, DC, DISC, MC, V. **Amenities:** 3 restaurants (New American, Southwestern, spa cuisine); lounge; 7 pools; par-3 golf course; putting green; 7 tennis courts; croquet lawn; health club; full-service spa; Jacuzzi; bikes; children's programs; concierge; business center; room service; massage; babysitting; guest laundry; laundry service; dry cleaning. *In room:* A/C, TV/VCR, dataport, minibar, coffeemaker, hair dryer, iron, safe, high-speed Internet access, Wi-Fi.

Mii amo, a destination spa at Enchantment ★★★ This full-service health spa inside the gates of the exclusive Enchantment Resort may not be the largest spa in the state, but it easily claims the best location. Designed to resemble a modern Santa Fe–style pueblo from the outside, the spa backs up to red-rock cliffs and is shaded by cottonwood trees. Though small, Mii amo is well designed, with indoor and outdoor pools, a crystal grotto, and outdoor massage cabanas at the foot of the cliffs. Guest rooms, which open onto a courtyard, have a bold, contemporary styling (mixed with Indonesian art and artifacts) that makes them some of the finest accommodations in the state. All units have private patios and gas fireplaces. Mii amo is a world unto itself in this hidden canyon, and no other spa in Arizona has a more Southwestern feel.

525 Boynton Canyon Rd., Sedona, AZ 86336. ✆ **888/749-2137** or 928/203-8500. Fax 928/203-8599. www.miiamo.com. 16 units. 3-night packages: Apr–May and Sept–Oct $2,640–$4,440 double; Dec–Jan $2,040–$3,840 double; Feb–Mar,

June–Aug, and Nov $2,340–$4,140 double. Rates include 3 meals per day and 6 spa treatments. AE, DC, DISC, MC, V. **Amenities:** Restaurant (New American/spa cuisine); 2 pools (indoor and outdoor); exercise room; full-service spa with 24 treatment rooms and wide variety of body treatments; 3 Jacuzzis; bikes; concierge; room service; laundry service; dry cleaning. *In room:* A/C, TV, dataport, minibar, coffeemaker, hair dryer, iron, safe, high-speed Internet access, Wi-Fi.

EXPENSIVE

Adobe Village Graham Inn ★★ A garden full of bronze statues of children greets you when you pull up to this luxurious inn in the Village of Oak Creek, 6 miles south of uptown Sedona. The inn lies almost at the foot of Bell Rock and features a variety of themed accommodations. The villas, the Sundance room, and the Sedona suite are the most impressive rooms here. My favorite is the Purple Lizard villa, which opts for a colorful Taos-style interior and an amazing rustic canopy bed. The Wilderness villa resembles a luxurious log cabin. The Lonesome Dove villa is a sort of upscale cowboy cabin with a fireplace, potbellied stove, and round hot tub in a "barrel." Can you say *romantic?* This inn also operates the Adobe Grand Villas in West Sedona.

150 Canyon Circle Dr., Sedona, AZ 86351. ✆ **866/846-1425** or 928/284-1425. Fax 928/284-0767. www.sedonasfinest.com. 11 units. $199–$329 double; $389–$409 suite; $349–$479 villa. Rates include full breakfast. AE, DISC, MC, V. 2-night minimum weekends; 3-night minimum holidays. **Amenities:** Outdoor pool; Jacuzzi; concierge; room service; massage and spa services. *In room:* A/C, TV/VCR, dataport, coffeemaker, hair dryer, iron, free local calls.

Amara Resort and Spa ★★ Conveniently located yet secluded and with views of the red rocks and frontage on an Oak Creek swimming hole, this stylish boutique hotel offers the best of both worlds here in Sedona. This hip resort may seem like an odd fit for a town that has long boasted of its cowboy heritage, but the minimalist decor and Zen-inspired style are a welcome addition to the Sedona hotel scene. From the outside, the hotel fits right in with the red-rock surroundings, while inside, bold splashes of color contrast with black-and-white photos. Guest rooms all have balconies or patios, wonderful pillow-top beds, and furnishings in black and red. The resort's dining room draws on interesting flavor influences from around the globe. Try to arrange for a sunset dinner while you're here. The resort recently added a spa.

310 N. Hwy. 89A, Sedona, AZ 86336. ✆ **866/455-6610** or 928/282-4828. Fax 928/282-4825. www.amararesort.com. 100 units. $139–$248 double; $249–$500 suite. Children under 12 stay free in parent's room. AE, DC, DISC, MC, V. Pets accepted ($75). **Amenities:** 3 restaurants (New American, Mexican, American); 3 lounges; outdoor saltwater pool; exercise room; health club; full-service spa; Jacuzzi; sauna; concierge; courtesy shopping shuttle; business center; room service; massage; babysitting; laundry service; dry cleaning. *In room:* A/C, TV/DVD, dataport, minibar, fridge, coffeemaker, hair dryer, iron, high-speed Internet access, Wi-Fi, free local calls.

Briar Patch Inn ★★ *Value* If you're searching for tranquility or a romantic retreat amid the cool shade of Oak Creek Canyon, this is the place. Located 3 miles north of Sedona on the banks of Oak Creek, this inn's cottages are surrounded by beautiful grounds where bird songs and the babbling creek set the mood. The cottages date from the 1940s but have been attractively updated (some with flagstone floors), and a Western/rustic-Mexican style now predominates. Most units have fireplaces and kitchenettes. In summer, breakfast is often served on a creekside terrace while musicians play classical guitar and violin. There are also swimming holes and a stone gazebo for massages. All in all, the Briar Patch offers a delightful combination of solitude and sophistication. The only drawback is the lack of red-rock views from the tree-shaded location.

3190 N. Hwy. 89A, Sedona, AZ 86336. ✆ **888/809-3030** or 928/282-2342. Fax 928/282-2399. www.briarpatchinn.com. 18 units. $195–$385 double. Rates include full breakfast. Children under 4 stay free in parent's room. AE, MC, V. **Amenities:** Access to nearby health club; concierge; massage and spa services. *In room:* A/C, kitchen, fridge, coffeemaker, hair dryer, iron, no phone.

Canyon Villa ★★ Located in the Village of Oak Creek, 6 miles south of Sedona, this bed-and-breakfast offers luxurious accommodations and spectacular views of the red rocks. All rooms but one have views, as do the pool area, living room, and dining room. Guest rooms are varied in style—Victorian, Santa Fe, country, rustic—but no matter what the decor, the furnishings are impeccable. All rooms have balconies or patios, and several have fireplaces. Breakfast is a lavish affair meant to be lingered over, and in the afternoon there's an elaborate spread of appetizers.

40 Canyon Circle Dr., Sedona, AZ 86351. ✆ **800/453-1166** or 928/284-1226. Fax 928/284-2114. www.canyonvilla.com. 11 units. $189–$304 double. Rates include full breakfast. AE, DC, DISC, MC, V. No children under 11. **Amenities:** Outdoor saltwater pool; concierge. *In room:* A/C, TV, hair dryer, iron, Wi-Fi, free local calls.

Garland's Oak Creek Lodge ★ *Finds* Located 8 miles north of Sedona in the heart of Oak Creek Canyon, this may be the hardest place in the area to book a room. People have been coming here for so many years and like it so much that they reserve a year in advance (last-minute cancellations do occur, so don't despair). What makes the lodge so special? Maybe it's that you have to drive *through* Oak Creek to get to your log cabin. Maybe it's the beautiful gardens or the slow, relaxing atmosphere of an old-time summer getaway. The well-maintained cabins, most of which have air-conditioning, are rustic but comfortable; the larger ones have their own fireplaces. Meals include organic fruits and vegetables grown on the property, and there's a yoga pavilion overlooking the creek.

P.O. Box 152, Sedona, AZ 86339. ✆ **928/282-3343.** www.garlandslodge.com. 16 units. $225–$275 double (plus 15% service charge). Rates include breakfast and dinner. 2-night minimum. Children under 2 stay free in parent's room. MC, V. Closed mid-Nov to Mar and Sun year-round. **Amenities:** Dining room; lounge; tennis court; concierge; massage; babysitting. *In room:* No phone.

Hilton Sedona Resort & Spa ★★ This resort boasts not only one of the most breathtaking golf courses in the state, but also the best pool area north of Phoenix. While golf is the driving force behind most stays here, anyone looking for an active vacation will find plenty to keep themselves busy. Guest rooms are suites of varying sizes, with fireplaces and balconies or patios. The resort's restaurant plays up its views of the golf course and red rocks. About the only drawback to this place is that, because it's south of the Village of Oak Creek, it's a bit of a drive to the shops and restaurants of Sedona proper.

90 Ridge Trail Dr., Sedona, AZ 86351. ✆ **877/273-3762** or 928/284-4040. Fax 928/284-6940. www.hiltonsedona.com. 219 units. Mid-Feb to mid-Nov $169–$459 double; mid-Nov to mid-Feb $149–$339 double. Rates do not include $10 resort fee. Children under 18 stay free in parent's room. AE, DC, DISC, MC, V. Pets accepted ($50 nonrefundable deposit). **Amenities:** Restaurant (Southwestern/American); seasonal poolside snack bar; lounge; 3 pools; 18-hole golf course; 3 tennis courts; exercise room; full-service spa; 3 Jacuzzis; sauna; children's programs; concierge; business center; room service; massage; babysitting; guest laundry; laundry service; dry cleaning. *In room:* A/C, TV, dataport, minibar, coffeemaker, hair dryer, iron, safe, high-speed Internet access.

Las Posadas of Sedona ★ Located across the highway from the Hilton resort in the Village of Oak Creek, Las Posadas is a cross between an all-suites boutique hotel and a bed-and-breakfast inn. The big suites are in four separate buildings, and all have separate entrances and kitchenettes, which makes staying here a bit like having your own Sedona apartment. The difference is that here you get to go have a gourmet breakfast each morning in the main building. All the suites have gas fireplaces and a balcony or patio, and some suites have outdoor whirlpool spas. When you check in, you'll find not only a plate of freshly baked cookies, but also a plate of hors d'oeuvres in your room. Be sure to ask for a room with a view.

26 Avenida de Piedras, Sedona, AZ 86351. ✆ **888/284-5288** or 928/284-5288. Fax 928/284-4178. www.lasposadas ofsedona.com. 20 units. $189–$429 double. Rates include full breakfast. AE, DC, DISC, MC, V. No children under 12. **Amenities:** Outdoor pool; access to nearby health club; concierge; massage. *In room:* A/C, TV/DVD, dataport, kitchen, fridge, coffeemaker, hair dryer, iron, microwave, Wi-Fi, free local calls.

L'Auberge de Sedona ★★ If you had to forgo your vacation in France this year, consider a stay at this luxurious boutique resort on the banks of Oak Creek. Shaded by towering sycamore trees and with colorful flower gardens surrounding its many cottages, the resort is a sort of French country retreat in the middle of the desert. L'Auberge's cottages, which look like rustic log cabins from the outside, have a classic styling worthy of a luxury French country inn (leather couches, gorgeous beds, plush towels, wood-burning fireplaces). Although there are rooms in the main lodge, the much larger cottages are definitely worth the extra cost. The restaurant, which carries on the French theme in its decor and menu, has a creekside terrace during the summer.

301 L'Auberge Lane, Sedona, AZ 86336. ✆ **800/272-6777** or 928/282-1661. Fax 928/282-2885. www.lauberge.com. 56 units. $175–$375 double; $275–$525 cottage; $500–$800 2-bedroom cottage. Children under 18 stay free in parent's room. AE, DC, DISC, MC, V. Pets accepted ($35 fee). **Amenities:** Restaurant (French); lounge; access to nearby health club; small full-service spa; Jacuzzi; concierge; courtesy shopping shuttle; business center; babysitting; laundry service; dry cleaning. *In room:* A/C, TV, fridge, coffeemaker, hair dryer, iron, safe, high-speed Internet access, Wi-Fi.

The Lodge at Sedona ★★ Set amid pine trees a block off Arizona 89A in west Sedona, this large inn is decorated in the Arts and Crafts style, which makes it one of the more distinctive inns in Sedona. The best rooms are those on the ground floor. These tend to be large, and several are suites. Second-floor rooms are more economical and tend to be fairly small. Suites are only slightly more expensive than deluxe rooms, which makes the suites the best choices here. If you want views, book one of the small upstairs rooms or the Desert Trail, Copper Canyon, or Whispering Winds suite. Breakfasts are five-course affairs that will often tide you over until dinner.

125 Kallof Place, Sedona, AZ 86336. ✆ **800/619-4467** or 928/204-1942. Fax 928/204-2128. www.lodgeatsedona. com. 14 units. $170–$339 double. Rates include full breakfast. 2-night minimum on weekends. AE, DISC, MC, V. Dogs accepted ($35 per night). No children under 11. **Amenities:** Access to nearby health club; concierge; massage. *In room:* A/C, hair dryer, iron, Wi-Fi, no phone.

Saddle Rock Ranch ★ The stunning views alone make this one of Sedona's top lodging choices, but in addition, you get classic Western ranch styling in a 1926-vintage home that once belonged to Barry Goldwater. Walls of stone and adobe, huge exposed beams, and plenty of windows to take in the scenery are enough to enchant guests even before they reach their rooms. In one room you'll find Victorian elegance, in another an English canopy bed and stone fireplace. Dressing areas and private gardens add to the charm. The third room is a separate little cottage with a pine bed, flagstone floors, and a beamed ceiling. The pool and whirlpool have one of the best views in town. A trail leads up to Airport Mesa.

255 Rock Ridge Dr., Sedona, AZ 86336. ✆ **866/282-7640** or 928/282-7640. Fax 928/282-7640. www.saddlerock ranch.com. 3 units. $159–$229 double. Rates include full breakfast. MC, V. No children under 14. **Amenities:** Small outdoor pool; access to nearby health club; Jacuzzi; concierge; massage; laundry service; dry cleaning. *In room:* A/C, TV/VCR, fridge, coffeemaker, hair dryer, iron, Wi-Fi, free local calls.

Sedona Rouge Hotel & Spa ★★ This stylish boutique hotel is the newest luxury hotel in Sedona, and though it is located right on busy U.S. 89A in west Sedona, it has a very distinctive character that I like. Merging contemporary styling with North African details, the hotel manages to create an ambience that is very international in feel. Antique wrought-iron window grates from Tunisia decorate hallways, and guest rooms hold Moroccan-inspired tables. Bathrooms, with dual-head rain-type showers, are a real highlight. If you can, try to get a room on the third floor; these have vaulted ceilings that make the rooms seem larger. The tiny lobby is just off an enclosed courtyard with a splashing fountain. A rooftop patio has the best view at the hotel. This is a good pick for couples in a romantic mood.

2250 W. Hwy. 89A, Sedona, AZ 86336. ✆ **866/312-4111** or 928/203-4111. Fax 928/203-9094. www.sedonarouge.com. 77 units. Jan–Feb $169–$259 double; Mar–May and Sept–Oct $189–$289 double; June–Aug and Nov–Dec $179–$269 double. AE, DC, DISC, MC, V. Pets accepted ($100 refundable deposit, $50 fee). **Amenities:** Restaurant (New American); lounge; outdoor pool; exercise room; full-service spa; Jacuzzi; concierge; room service; massage; babysitting; laundry service; dry cleaning. *In room:* A/C, TV, dataport, fridge, coffeemaker, hair dryer, iron, high-speed Internet access, Wi-Fi, free local calls.

MODERATE

Best Western Inn of Sedona ★ Located about midway between uptown and west Sedona, this hotel has great views of the red rocks from its wide terraces and outdoor pool. Unfortunately, although the guest rooms are comfortable enough, not all of them have views. However, the modern Southwestern decor and the setting, surrounded by native landscaping and located beyond the tourist mainstream, make this an appealing choice.

1200 W. Hwy. 89A, Sedona, AZ 86336. ✆ **800/292-6344** or 928/282-3072. Fax 928/282-7218. www.innofsedona.com. 110 units. Mar–Oct $131–$209 double; Nov–Feb $115–$189 double. Rates include continental breakfast. Children 12 and under stay free in parent's room. AE, DC, DISC, MC, V. Pets accepted ($20 fee). **Amenities:** Small outdoor pool; Jacuzzi; concierge. *In room:* A/C, TV, dataport, fridge, coffeemaker, hair dryer, iron, high-speed Internet access.

Cedars Resort on Oak Creek Located right at the "Y" and set atop a 100-foot cliff, this motel has fabulous views across Oak Creek to the towering red rocks. Guest rooms are large and have been fairly recently refurbished. Creekside rooms have private balconies, but for the best views, ask for a king-size room. A long stairway leads down to the creek, and the shops of uptown Sedona are just a short walk away.

20 W. Hwy. 89A (P.O. Box 292), Sedona, AZ 86339. ✆ **800/874-2072** or 928/282-7010. Fax 928/282-5372. www.sedonacedarsresort.com. 38 units. $99–$149 double. Rates include continental breakfast. Children 12 and under stay free in parent's room. AE, DC, DISC, MC, V. **Amenities:** Small outdoor pool; exercise room; Jacuzzi; concierge; business center; massage. *In room:* A/C, TV, dataport, fridge, coffeemaker, hair dryer, iron, Wi-Fi, free local calls.

Forest Houses ★ *Finds* Set at the upper end of Oak Creek Canyon and built right on the banks of the creek, these rustic houses and apartments date back to the 1940s. Built by a stone sculptor, they feature artistic touches that set them apart from your average cabins. About half of the houses are built right on the creek, and some seem to grow straight from the rocks in the streambed. Terraces let you fully enjoy the setting. One of my favorite units is the two-bedroom Cloud House, with stone floors, peeled-log woodwork, and a loft. This property is certainly not for everyone (no phones, no TVs, and you have to drive through the creek to get here), but those who discover the Forest Houses often come back year after year.

9275 N. Hwy. 89A, Sedona, AZ 86336. ✆ **928/282-2999.** www.foresthousesresort.com. 15 units. $90–$145 double. 2- to 4-night minimum stay. AE, MC, V. Closed Jan to mid-Mar. Pets accepted ($20 deposit). *In room:* Kitchen, fridge, coffeemaker, no phone.

The Orchards Inn of Sedona ★★ Located in the heart of uptown Sedona and affiliated with L'Auberge de Sedona, the adjacent French country inn/resort (see review, above), this hotel claims an enviable location on a hillside above Oak Creek.

The views from the hillside setting are spectacular and are some of the best in Sedona. Despite the name, this is much more of a hotel than an inn, though the rooms have a very tasteful and comfortable classic style. Don't be discouraged when you drive up to the front door; though the hotel is located amid the uptown tourist crowds, it seems miles away once you check into your room and gaze out at the red rocks.

254 Hwy. 89A, Sedona, AZ 86336. ✆ **877/700-2944** or 928/282-2405. Fax 928/282-7818. www.orchardsinn.com. 41 units. $110–$220 double. Children under 12 stay free in parent's room. AE, DC, DISC, MC, V. **Amenities:** Restaurant (Regional American); small outdoor pool; access to nearby health club; Jacuzzi; concierge; room service; massage; babysitting; laundry service; dry cleaning. *In room:* A/C, TV, dataport, fridge, coffeemaker, hair dryer, iron, safe, high-speed Internet access.

INEXPENSIVE

Matterhorn Inn Located in the heart of the uptown shopping district, this choice is convenient to restaurants and shops, and all of the attractively furnished guest rooms have excellent views of the red-rock canyon walls. Although the Matterhorn is set above a row of shops fronting busy Arizona 89A, if you lie in bed and keep your eyes on the rocks, you'd never know there was so much going on below you. This place is a great value for Sedona.

230 Apple Ave., Sedona, AZ 86336. ✆ **800/372-8207** or 928/282-7176. www.matterhorninn.com. 23 units. Mar–Nov $99–$169 double; Dec–Feb $79–$149 double. Children under 5 stay free in parent's room. AE, MC, V. Pets accepted ($10 per day). **Amenities:** Small outdoor pool; access to nearby health club; Jacuzzi. *In room:* A/C, TV, dataport, fridge, coffeemaker, hair dryer, iron, Wi-Fi, free local calls.

Rose Tree Inn *Finds* This little inn, only a block from Sedona's uptown shopping district, is tucked amid pretty gardens (yes, there are lots of roses) on a quiet street. The property consists of an eclectic cluster of older buildings that have all been renovated. Each unit is furnished differently—one Victorian, one Southwestern, two with gas fireplaces. Four guest rooms have kitchenettes, making them good choices for families or for longer stays. The Rose Tree Inn also handles bookings for a pair of modern little apartments a block away. Called the Rooms Upstairs, these apartments are upstairs from and owned by a local architectural firm, and are an economical way to make yourself at home here in Sedona.

376 Cedar St., Sedona, AZ 86336. ✆ **888/282-2065** or 928/282-2065. www.rosetreeinn.com. 5 units. $98–$139 double. Children under 16 stay free in parent's room. AE, MC, V. **Amenities:** Access to nearby health club; concierge; laundry service. *In room:* A/C, TV/VCR, kitchen, fridge, coffeemaker, hair dryer, iron, microwave, Wi-Fi.

Sky Ranch Lodge This motel is located atop Airport Mesa and has the most stupendous vista in town. From here you can see the entire red-rock country, with Sedona filling the valley below. Although the rooms are fairly standard motel issue, some have such features as gas fireplaces, barn-wood walls, and balconies. Only the nonview units fall into the inexpensive category, but those great views are just steps away.

Airport Rd. (P.O. Box 2579), Sedona, AZ 86339. ✆ **888/708-6400** or 928/282-6400. Fax 928/282-7682. www.skyranchlodge.com. 94 units. $75–$189 double. AE, MC, V. Pets accepted ($10 per night). **Amenities:** Small outdoor pool; Jacuzzi; coin-op laundry. *In room:* A/C, TV, dataport, coffeemaker.

CAMPGROUNDS

Within Oak Creek Canyon along Arizona 89A, there are five National Forest Service campgrounds. **Manzanita,** 6 miles north of town, is both the largest and the most pleasant (and the only one open in winter). Other Oak Creek Canyon campgrounds include **Bootlegger,** 9 miles north of town; **Cave Springs,** 13 miles north of town; and **Pine Flat,** 12 miles north of town. All of these campgrounds charge $18 per night. The **Beaver Creek Campground,** 3 miles east of I-17 on Forest Road 618, which is an extension of Arizona 179 (take Exit 298 off I-17), is a pleasant spot near the V Bar V Heritage petroglyph site. Campsites here are $14 per night. For more information on area campgrounds, contact the **Coconino National Forest's Red Rock Ranger Station** (© **928/282-4119;** www.fs.fed.us/r3/coconino), which, at press time, was in a temporary space 2 miles east of I-17 at Exit 298 (Beaver Creek Rd.). The ranger district has plans to relocate to a site on Arizona 179 south of the Village of Oak Creek. Reservations can be made for Manzanita, Pine Flat, and Cave Springs campgrounds by contacting the **National Recreation Reservation Center** (© **877/444-6777** or 518/885-3639; www.reserveusa.com).

WHERE TO DINE

EXPENSIVE

Cowboy Club Grille & Spirits ★ SOUTHWESTERN With its big booths, huge steer horns over the bar, and cowboy gear adorning the walls, this restaurant looks like a glorified cowboy steakhouse—but this is big flavor country, and the menu isn't the sort any real cowboy would likely have anything to do with. Start out with fried cactus strips with black-bean gravy or perhaps a rattlesnake brochette. For an entree, be sure to try the buffalo sirloin, which is served with some flavorful sauce of the moment. At lunch, try the buffalo burger. Service is relaxed and friendly. The adjacent Silver Saddle Room is a more upscale spin on the same concept, with similar menu prices. It was in this building in 1965 that the Cowboy Artists of America organization was formed.

241 N. Hwy. 89A. © **928/282-4200.** www.cowboyclub.com. Reservations recommended. Main courses $7–$24 lunch, $10–$43 dinner. AE, DC, DISC, MC, V. Daily 11am–4pm and 5–10pm.

El Portal Sedona ★★ NEW AMERICAN/SOUTHWESTERN Although El Portal is primarily a deluxe inn, it also serves superb dinners on Wednesday through Saturday nights. While many of the diners are guests at the inn, the meals are open to the public by reservation. These dinners provide anyone who is not staying at this inn a chance to lounge around in the courtyard and living room/dining room, and get a sense for what it's like to stay here. The menu is short and usually includes less than a half-dozen entrees and an equal number of appetizers and salads. If the baked brie with roasted garlic and raspberry chipotle sauce is on the menu, don't even think of resisting. This dish is heavenly! Crab- and lobster-filled ravioli in a Manchego cheese sauce and spice-encrusted duck breast with shallot/cherry/pinot noir sauce are just two examples of the sorts of entrees you can expect.

95 Portal Lane. © **928/203-4942.** www.innsedona.com. Reservations required. Main courses $20–$45. AE, DC, DISC, MC, V. Wed–Sat 5:30–8pm.

The Heartline Café ★★ SOUTHWESTERN/INTERNATIONAL The heart line, from Zuni mythology, is a symbol of health and longevity; it is also a symbol for the healthful, creative food served here. To start with, don't miss the tea-smoked chicken dumplings with spicy peanut sauce or the Gorgonzola torte with caramelized pear. Memorable entrees include pecan-crusted local trout with Dijon cream sauce. Those searching out variety in vegetarian choices will find it here. The beautiful courtyard and traditionally elegant interior are good places to savor a meal accompanied by a selection from the reasonably priced wine list. The Heartline Café also has a takeout restaurant next door. It's a great place to stop to pick up a picnic lunch before heading out into the red rocks. This latter establishment is open Monday through Saturday from 11am to 7pm.

Tips Cocktails & More with a View

Since the main reason you're in Sedona is to enjoy the views of those amazing red rocks, it would be a shame not to take every possible opportunity to sit back and ogle the scenery. So why not sip a drink while you stare? In the morning, I like to get coffee and a pastry at **Wildflower Bread Company,** in the Shops at Piñon Point, 101 N. Hwy. 89A (© **928/204-2223;** www.wildflowerbread.com), which is in the shopping complex between uptown Sedona and the "Y." Although there's a bit of traffic noise here, the view of Snoopy Rock is hard to beat.

Later in the day, when my energy level flags from too much hiking and mountain biking, I get coffee at **Ravenheart Uptown,** 206 N. Hwy. 89A (© **928/282-1070**), and then grab a table outside on the terrace. This espresso place is on the very edge of uptown Sedona with absolutely nothing between you and the red rocks. If there weren't so much to do in the area, I could sit here all day.

When it's time to watch the sunset light show, I like head to the bar at uptown's **Vista Cantina & Restaurant,** 320 N. Hwy. 89A (© **928/282-0002**), which is located in Sinagua Plaza. This place does decent margaritas. Because there are just a handful of tables with views, try to arrive early. The view tables are tucked around behind the bar.

1610 W. Hwy. 89A. © **928/282-0785.** www.heartlinecafe.com. Reservations recommended. Main courses $8.25–$15 lunch, $16–$28 dinner. AE, DC, DISC, MC, V. Wed–Mon 11am–3pm and 5–9:30pm (no lunch on Tues in summer).

Reds ★★ NEW AMERICAN This lively bistro and bar is housed in the very stylish Sedona Rouge Hotel & Spa and serves contemporary comfort food in an equally contemporary setting. The brick oven turns out lots of great dishes, including a delicious mac-and-cheese skillet that is way better than anything your mom ever made you. The meatloaf is another classic that is tastier than any meatloaf has a right to be. If you're looking for something a bit more contemporary, try the seared ahi.

2250 W. Hwy. 89A. © **928/203-4599.** www.sedonarouge.com. Reservations recommended. Main courses $8–$12 lunch, $15–$28 dinner. AE, DISC, MC, V. Sun–Thurs 7:30–10:30am, 11:30am–2pm, and 5–9pm; Fri–Sat 7:30–10:30am, 11:30am–2pm, and 5–10pm.

René at Tlaquepaque ★★ CONTINENTAL/AMERICAN Although a formal dining experience and traditional French fare may seem out of place in a town that celebrates its cowboy heritage, René's makes fine dining seem as natural as mesquite-grilled steak and cowboy beans. Located in Tlaquepaque, the city's upscale south-of-the-border-themed shopping center, this restaurant is the best place in Sedona for a special meal. The house specialty here is rack of lamb, and if you like lamb, this dish should not be missed. More adventurous diners may want to try the excellent tenderloin of venison with whiskey–juniper berry sauce. Finish with a flambéed dessert and selections from the after-dinner drink cart.

At Tlaquepaque, 336 Ariz. 179, Suite 118. © **928/282-9225.** www.rene-sedona.com. Reservations recommended. Main courses $9–$16 lunch, $20–$42 dinner. AE, MC, V. Sun–Thurs 11:30am–2pm and 5:30–8:30pm; Fri–Sat 11:30am–2pm and 5:30–9pm.

Shugrue's Hillside Grill ★★ NEW AMERICAN/CONTINENTAL Located at the back of the Hillside Sedona shopping plaza, this is the most upscale outpost in a small chain of popular Arizona restaurants. Although the prices are high at dinner, if you come before the sun sets, you'll be treated to unforgettable views through the walls of glass. The extensive menu includes influences from around the world. For a starter, try the blackened shrimp saganaki. There are plenty of good steak and fish entrees, too.

671 Hwy. 179. © **928/282-5300.** www.shugrues.com. Reservations highly recommended. Main courses $8–$18 lunch, $21–$30 dinner. AE, DC, MC, V. Sun–Thurs 11:30am–3pm and 5–9pm; Fri–Sat 11:30am–3pm and 5–10pm.

Yavapai Restaurant ★★ SOUTHWESTERN The Yavapai Restaurant, at the exclusive Enchantment Resort, has the best views and most memorable setting of any restaurant in Sedona. It is also one of the town's most formal restaurants (no blue jeans allowed), which doesn't quite fit with the rugged setting but is in keeping with Enchantment's exclusive character. The menu changes regularly to take advantage of seasonal ingredients, but keep an eye out for venison dishes and veal chops with the sauce of the moment. Because the scenery is every bit as important as the food here, make sure you make dinner reservations to take in the sunset on the red rocks. You can also soak up the views at breakfast and lunch and save quite a bit of money.

At Enchantment Resort, 525 Boynton Canyon Rd. © **928/204-6000.** www.enchantmentresort.com. Reservations required. Main courses $15–$19 lunch, $27–$42 dinner; Sun brunch $40 for adults, $20 for children ages 5–11. AE, DISC, MC, V. Mon–Sat 6:30am–2:15pm, and 5:30–9:15pm; Sun 10:30am–2:15pm.

MODERATE

Cucina Rústica ★★ MEDITERRANEAN/SOUTHWESTERN With its various distinct dining rooms and numerous antique doors, this sister restaurant to west Sedona's wonderful Dahl & DiLuca (see below) feels like a luxurious villa. My personal favorite dining room has a central dome that is lit by what appear to be thousands of stars, but for a genuine starlit dinner, ask for a seat on the patio. Start with the *bruschetta pomodoro,* a tomato-and-basil appetizer that tastes like a bite of summer; then, when it comes time to order an entree, just ask for the *gamberi del capitano.* These grilled prawns, wrapped in radicchio and prosciutto, are among the best prawns I've ever had—positively ambrosial.

7000 Hwy. 179, Village of Oak Creek. © **928/284-3010.** www.cucinarustica.com. Reservations recommended. Main courses $12–$28. AE, DC, MC, V. Sun–Thurs 5–9; Fri–Sat 5–10pm.

Dahl & DiLuca ★★ ROMAN ITALIAN A faux-Tuscan villa interior, complete with a bar in a grotto, makes this the most romantic restaurant in Sedona, and the excellent Italian food makes it that much more unforgettable. Be sure to start with some of the *pane romano,* which, as far as I'm concerned, is the best garlic bread west of New York's Little Italy. Pasta predominates here, and portions are big. I like the linguine Siciliana with calamari and mushrooms. The kitchen also serves up a panoply of deftly prepared seafood, chicken, and vegetarian dishes. The eggplant Parmesan and portobello *alla griglia* are real standouts. Genial and efficient service, reasonably priced wines, and nightly live music make this place even more enjoyable.

2321 W. Hwy. 89A (in west Sedona diagonally across from the Safeway Plaza). © **928/282-5219.** www.dahl-diluca.com. Reservations recommended. Main courses $11–$28. AE, DISC, MC, V. Daily 5–10pm.

Fournos Restaurant ★ *Finds* MEDITERRANEAN In contrast to the glitz and modern Southwest decor of so many of Sedona's restaurants, Fournos is a refreshingly casual place run by the husband-and-wife team of Shirley and Demetrios Fournos. Step through the front door, and you almost have to walk through the kitchen to get to the handful of tables in the dining room. In the kitchen, chef Demetrios cooks up a storm, preparing such dishes as shrimp flambéed in ouzo and baked with feta; Cephalonian-style lamb shanks with herbs and potatoes; and Mykonos-style poached fish with a sauce of yogurt, onions, mayonnaise, and butter. Other specialties are rack of lamb and lamb Wellington.

3000 W. Hwy. 89A. ✆ **928/282-3331.** www.fournosrestaurant.com. Reservations highly recommended. Main courses $16–$21. AE, DISC, MC, V. Thurs–Sat seatings at 6 and 8pm.

INEXPENSIVE

Dining in Sedona tends to be expensive, so your best bets for economical meals are sandwich shops or ethnic restaurants. For breakfast, locals swear by the **Coffee Pot Restaurant,** 2050 W. Hwy. 89A (✆ **928/282-6626**). For filling sandwiches, try **Sedona Memories,** 321 Jordan Rd. (✆ **928/282-0032**), 1 block off Arizona 89A in the uptown shopping area. For vegetarian food, try **D'lish,** 3190 W. Hwy. 89A (✆ **928/203-9393;** www.dlishsedona.com). Having a picnic? You can stock up on exotic imported meats, cheeses, and other fun foods or get a gourmet sandwich to go at **Euro-Deli Sedona,** 3190 W. Hwy. 89A (✆ **928/282-4798;** eurodelisedona.com). If you're in the Village of Oak Creek and want a quick meal or some gourmet picnic ingredients, stop in at **A'Roma,** Tequa Plaza, 7000 Hwy. 179, Suite 114A (✆ **928/284-1556;** www.a-romasedona.com). Alternatively, head to **New Frontiers Natural Foods,** 1420 W. Hwy. 89A (✆ **928/282-6311**), for your picnic ingredients. When you need good espresso, perhaps for that long drive to the Grand Canyon, stop by **Ravenheart of Sedona,** at the Old Marketplace shopping center, 1370 W. Hwy. 89A, Suite 12 (✆ **928/282-5777;** www.ravenheartcoffee.net), or their uptown location at 206 N. Hwy. 89A (✆ **928/282-1070**).

Casa Bonita MEXICAN Located in the same shopping center as the Basha's super market, this casual and colorful Mexican restaurant is a local favorite. Both the food and the service are usually very reliable. I like the fried fish tacos, which are made with tartar sauce. I know this may not sound like an authentic Mexican recipe, but those tacos sure are tasty. Be sure to have a designated driver; the margaritas here are the best in town.

164 Coffee Pot Dr., Suite H. ✆ **928/282-2728.** Main courses $4–$15. AE, DISC, MC, V. Mon–Thurs 11am–9:30pm; Fri–Sun 11am–10pm.

The Hideaway Restaurant ITALIAN/DELI Hidden away at the back of a shopping plaza near the "Y," this casual family restaurant is as popular with locals as it is with visitors. Basic pizzas, subs, sandwiches, salads, and pastas are the choices here, and both the salad dressings and sausages are made on the premises. However, most people come for the knockout views. From the shady porch, you can see the creek below and the red rocks rising across the canyon. Lunch or an early sunset dinner is your best bet. The *paisano* (Sicilian sausage soup and a sandwich) lunch and antipasto salad are both good choices. Keep an eye out for hummingbirds and great blue herons.

Country Sq., 251 Ariz. 179. ✆ **928/282-4204.** Reservations accepted only for parties of 10 or more. Main courses $6–$16. AE, DISC, MC, V. Daily 11am–9pm.

Javelina Cantina ★ MEXICAN Although Javelina Cantina is part of a chain of Arizona restaurants, the formula works, and few diners leave disappointed. Sure, the restaurant is touristy, but what it has going for it is good Mexican food, a lively atmosphere, decent views, and a convenient location in the Hillside shops. The grilled fish tacos are tasty, as is the pork adobo sandwich. Other dishes worth trying include the salmon tostadas. There are also plenty of different margaritas and tequilas to accompany your meal. Expect a wait.

At Hillside Sedona shopping plaza, 671 Hwy. 179. © **928/203-9514.** www.javelinacantina.com. Reservations recommended. Main courses $8–$19. AE, DISC, MC, V. Daily 11:30am–9:30pm.

Oak Creek Brewery & Grill AMERICAN If you find yourself lost in the maze of shops at the Tlaquepaque shopping plaza, don't despair of finding sustenance before you find your way back to your car; just consult one of the shopping center maps and head to this casual second-floor brewpub. The menu features pizzas, smoked pork tenderloin with prickly pear–chipotle glaze, rotisserie chicken, and plenty of sandwiches—and it all goes well with the pub's beers. If you feel like having some fun, order the "Seven Dwarfs," a sampler of all the beers they brew here.

In Tlaquepaque Arts Village, Ariz. 179 downhill from the "Y." © **928/282-3300.** www.oakcreekpub.com. Reservations recommended. Main courses $10–$16 lunch, $12–$26 dinner. AE, DISC, MC, V. Daily 11am–9pm.

Picazzo's ★ PIZZA For down-home pizza in an upscale setting, nothing in Sedona can compare with this artistic pizza place. Throw in an attractive walled patio dining area and a view of Coffee Pot Rock, and you have one of the best values in town. There are good by-the-slice lunch specials, and during happy hour, there are half-price appetizers. Try the Southwestern pizza, which is made with salsa, spicy chicken or beef, pepper jack cheese, and black beans. Or how about a bacon cheeseburger pizza? Great setting, great view, great pizza, and best of all, by eating here you can avoid the crowds in uptown Sedona.

1855 W. Hwy. 89A. © **928/282-4140.** www.picazzos.com. Reservations not accepted. Pizzas $11–$23. AE, DC, MC, V. Sun–Thurs 11am–10pm; Fri–Sat 11am–11pm.

Red Planet Diner ★ Kids INTERNATIONAL With its flying saucer fountain out front and its totally cosmic decor, this casual diner is a UFO-spotter's dream come true. You can sip a mother-ship "vorttini" while you wait for your food, but most people come here for the milk shakes. Those shakes are best accompanied by a Roswell burger or maybe some Flash Gordon chili. The walls are plastered with photos of UFOs and images from old sci-fi movies. Unfortunately, you may sometimes feel as if aliens have kidnapped your waitress.

1655 W. Hwy. 89A. © **928/282-6070.** Reservations not accepted. Main courses $8–$16. AE, DISC, MC, V. Daily 10am–11pm.

SEDONA AFTER DARK

If you'd like to catch some live classical music while you're in town, check the schedule of **Chamber Music Sedona** (© **928/204-2415;** www.chambermusicsedona.org).

If you're searching for good microbrewed beer, head to the **Oak Creek Brewing Co.,** 2050 Yavapai Dr. (© **928/204-1300;** www.oakcreekbrew.com), north of Arizona 89A off Coffee Pot Drive. There's also the affiliated **Oak Creek Brewery and Grill** (© **928/282-3300;** www.oakcreekpub.com) in the Tlaquepaque shopping complex. If you're looking for some live music, check out **Olde Sedona Bar & Grille,** 1405 W. Hwy. 89A (© **928/282-5670;** www.oldesedona.com). Down in the Village of Oak Creek, you can do a little dancing at the **Full Moon Saloon,** 7000 Hwy. 179 (© **928/284-1872;** www.thefullmoonsaloon.com), which is located in the Tequa Plaza shopping center and has live music several nights a week.

6

The Grand Canyon & Northern Arizona

The Grand Canyon—the name is at once both entirely apt and entirely inadequate. How can words sum up the grandeur of 2 billion years of the earth's history sliced open by the power of a single river? Once an impassable and forbidding barrier to explorers and settlers, the Grand Canyon today is a magnet that attracts millions of visitors from all over the world each year. The pastel layers of rock weaving through the canyon's rugged ramparts, the interplay of shadows and light, the wind in the pines, and the croaking of ravens on the rim—these are the sights and sounds that never fail to transfix the hordes of visitors who gaze awestruck into the canyon's seemingly infinite depths.

While the Grand Canyon is undeniably the most amazing natural attraction anywhere in the state, northern Arizona contains other natural attractions that are also worthwhile, and certainly less crowded. Only 60 miles south of the great yawning chasm stand the San Francisco Peaks, the tallest of which, Humphreys Peak, rises to 12,643 feet. These peaks, sacred to the Hopi and Navajo, are ancient volcanoes that today are popular with skiers, hikers, and mountain bikers.

Volcanic eruptions 900 to 1,000 years ago helped turn the land east of the San Francisco Peaks into fertile farmland that allowed the Sinagua people to thrive in this otherwise inhospitable environment. Within a few hundred years, however, the Sinagua disappeared. Today the ruins of their ancient villages, scattered across lonely, windswept plains, are all that remain of their culture.

Just as the region once attracted Native Americans, it also attracted pioneers, who settled on the south side of the San Francisco Peaks. Amid expansive ponderosa pine forests now stands the city of Flagstaff, which at 7,000 feet in elevation is one of the highest cities in the U.S. Flagstaff is home to Northern Arizona University, whose students ensure that this is a lively, liberal town. Born of the railroads and named for a flagpole, Flagstaff is now the main jumping-off point for trips to the Grand Canyon. Because the city has preserved much of its Western heritage in its restored downtown historic district, it's well worth a visit on its own.

While it's the Grand Canyon that brings many people to northern Arizona, most visitors spend only a day or so in Grand Canyon National Park. So you may want to take a look at what else there is to do in this part of the state. If, on the other hand, you want only to visit the canyon, there are many different ways to accomplish this goal. You can do so in a group or alone; on foot or by raft; or from a mule, a train, or a helicopter. Regardless of what you decide, you'll find that the Grand Canyon more than lives up to its name.

1 The Grand Canyon South Rim ★★★

60 miles N of Williams; 80 miles NE of Flagstaff; 230 miles N of Phoenix; 340 miles N of Tucson

Whether you merely stand on the rim gazing in awe, spend several days hiking deep in the canyon, or ride the roller-coaster rapids of the Colorado River, a trip to the Grand Canyon is an unforgettable experience. A mile deep, 277 miles long, and up to 18 miles wide, the canyon is so large that it is positively overwhelming in its grandeur, truly one of the great natural wonders of the world. The cartographers who mapped this land were obviously deeply affected by the spiritual beauty of the canyon and named the landscape features accordingly. Their reverence is reflected in formations named for Solomon, Apollo, Venus, Thor, Zoroaster, Horus, Buddha, Vishnu, Krishna, Shiva, and Confucius.

Something of this reverence infects nearly every first-time visitor. Nothing in the slowly changing topography of the approach to the Grand Canyon prepares you for what awaits. You hardly notice the elevation gain or the gradual change from windswept sagebrush scrubland to ponderosa pine forest. Suddenly, it's there. No preliminaries, no warnings. Stark, quiet, a maze of cathedrals and castles sculpted by nature.

Layers of sandstone, limestone, shale, and schist give the canyon its colors, and the interplay of shadows and light from dawn to dusk creates an ever-changing palette of hues and textures. Formed by the erosive action of the Colorado River as it flows through the Kaibab Plateau, the Grand Canyon is an open book exposing the secrets of this region's geologic history. Geologists believe it has taken between 3 million and 6 million years for the Colorado River to carve the Grand Canyon, but the canyon's history extends much further back in time. Written in the canyon's bands of stone are more than 2 billion years of history.

Millions of years ago, vast seas covered this region. Sediments carried by sea water were deposited and, over millions of more years, those sediments were turned into limestone and sandstone. According to one theory, when the ancient seabed was thrust upward to form the Kaibab Plateau, the Colorado River began its work of cutting through the plateau. Today, 21 sedimentary layers, the oldest of which is more than a billion years old, can be seen in the canyon. Beneath all these layers, at the very bottom, is a stratum of rock so old that it has metamorphosed, under great pressure and heat, from soft shale to a much harder stone. Called Vishnu Schist, this layer is the oldest rock in the Grand Canyon and dates from 2 billion years ago.

In the more recent past, the Grand Canyon has been home to several Native American cultures, including the Ancestral Puebloans (Anasazi), who are best known for their cliff dwellings in the Four Corners region. About 150 years after the Ancestral Puebloans and Coconino peoples abandoned the canyon in the 13th century, another tribe, the Cerbat, moved into the area. Today, the Hualapai and Havasupai tribes, descendants of the Cerbat people, still live in and near the Grand Canyon on the south side of the Colorado River. On the North Rim lived the Southern Paiute, and in the east, the Navajo.

In 1540, Spanish explorer Garcia Lopez de Cárdenas became the first European to set eyes on the Grand Canyon, but it would be another 329 years before the first expedition traveled through the entire canyon. John Wesley Powell, a one-armed Civil War veteran, was deemed crazy when he set off to navigate the Colorado River in wooden boats. His small band of men spent 98 days traveling 1,000 miles down the Green and Colorado rivers. So difficult was the endeavor that when some of the expedition's boats were wrecked by powerful rapids, part of the group abandoned the journey and set out on foot, never to be seen again.

How wrong the early explorers were about this supposedly Godforsaken landscape. Instead of being abandoned as a worthless wasteland, the Grand Canyon has become one of the most important natural wonders on the planet, a magnet for people from all over the world. By raft, by mule, on foot, and in helicopters and small planes—approximately four million people each year come to gaze into this great chasm.

However, there have been those in the recent past who regarded the canyon as mere wasted space, suitable only for filling with water. Upstream of the Grand Canyon stands Glen Canyon Dam, which forms Lake Powell, while downstream lies Lake Mead, created by Hoover Dam. The same thing could have happened to the Grand Canyon, but luckily the forces for preservation prevailed. Today, the Grand Canyon is the last major undammed stretch of the Colorado River.

Named by early Spanish explorers for the pinkish color of its muddy waters, the Colorado River once carried immense loads of silt. Because much of the Colorado's silt load now gets deposited on the bottom of Lake Powell (behind Glen Canyon Dam), the water in the Grand Canyon is much clearer (and colder) than it once was. No longer does the river flow murky and pink from heavy loads of eroding sandstone.

While the waters of the Colorado are now clearer than before, the same cannot be said for the air in the canyon. Yes, you'll find smog here, smog that has been blamed on both Las Vegas and Los Angeles to the west and a coal-fired power plant to the east, near Page. Scrubbers installed on the power plant's smokestacks should help the park's air quality, but there isn't much to be done about smog drifting from the west.

But the most visible and frustrating negative impact on the park in recent years has been the traffic congestion at the South Rim during the busy months from spring to fall. With roughly four million people visiting the park each year, traffic during the summer months has become almost as bad at the South Rim as it is during rush hour in any major city, and finding a parking space can be the biggest challenge of a visit to Grand Canyon National Park. But don't let these inconveniences dissuade you from visiting. Despite the crowds, the Grand Canyon more than lives up to its name and is one of the most memorable sights on Earth.

ESSENTIALS

GETTING THERE

During the summer, if at all possible, travel to the park by some means other than car. Alternatives include taking the Grand Canyon Railway from Williams, flying into Grand Canyon Airport and then taking a taxi, taking the Open Road Tours bus service from Flagstaff, or coming to the park on a guided tour. There are plenty of scenic overlooks, hiking trails, restaurants, and lodges in the Grand Canyon Village area, and free shuttle buses operate along both Hermit Road and Desert View Drive.

BY CAR The South Rim of the Grand Canyon is 60 miles north of Williams and I-40 on Arizona 64 and U.S. 180. Flagstaff, the nearest city of any size, is 80 miles away. From Flagstaff, it's possible to take U.S. 180 directly to the South Rim or U.S. 89 to Arizona 64 and the east entrance to the park. This latter route is my preferred way of getting to the canyon since it sees slightly less traffic. Be sure you have plenty of gasoline in your car before setting out for the canyon; there are few service stations in this remote part of the state and what gas stations there are charge exorbitant prices.

Long waits at the entrance gates, parking problems, and traffic congestion have become the norm at the canyon during the popular summer months, and even during

The Grand Canyon & Northern Arizona

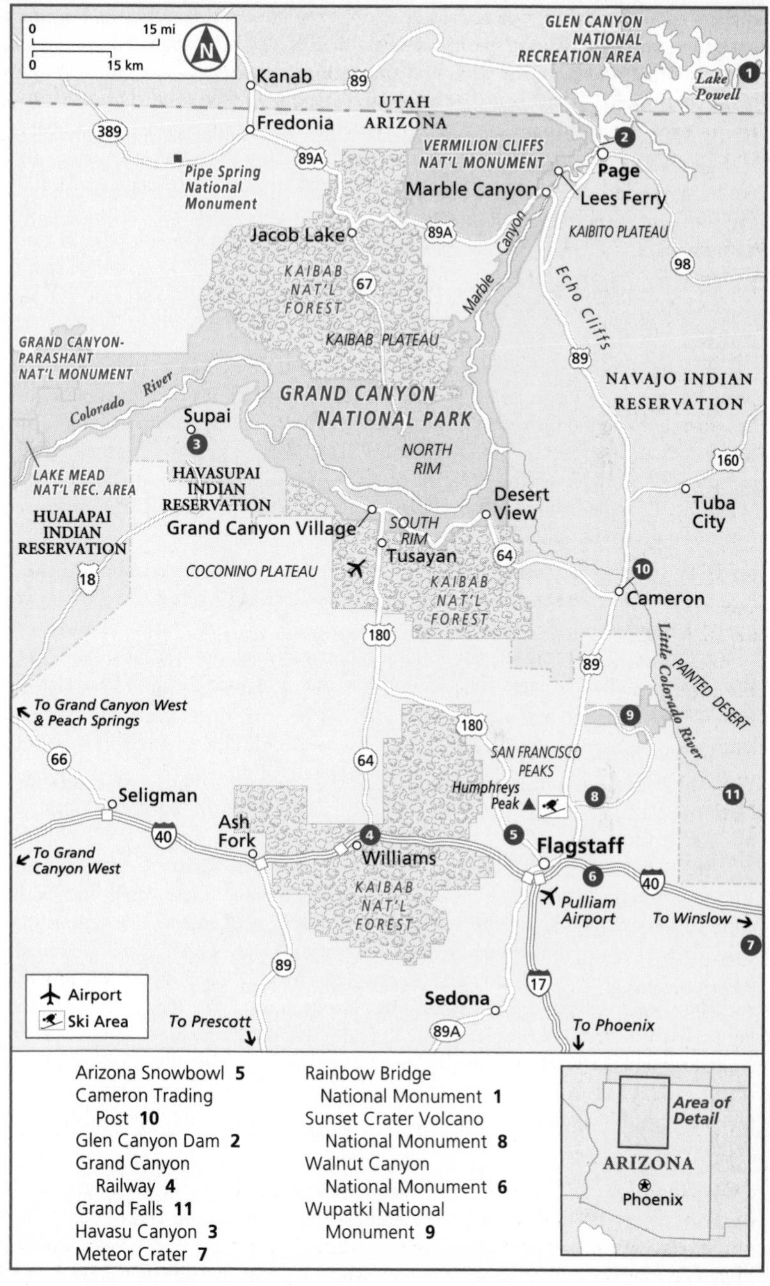

the spring and fall there can be backups at the entrance gates and visitors can have a hard time finding a parking space. However, in 2007, extra ticketing lanes were added at the south entrance to the park, and the park service was even experimenting with hand-held ticketing machines that help speed visitors on their way.

BY PLANE The Grand Canyon Airport is in Tusayan, 6 miles south of Grand Canyon Village. **Scenic Airlines** (© **800/634-6801;** www.scenic.com) flies from the North Las Vegas Airport and charges $218 to $318 round-trip. Alternatively, you can fly into Flagstaff and then arrange another mode of transportation the rest of the way to the national park (see "Flagstaff," later in this chapter, for details).

BY TRAIN The **Grand Canyon Railway** operates excursion trains between Williams and the South Rim of the Grand Canyon. See "Williams," later in this chapter, for details.

For long-distance connections, **Amtrak** (© **800/872-7245;** www.amtrak.com) provides service to Flagstaff and Williams. From Flagstaff, it's then possible to take a bus directly to Grand Canyon Village. From Williams, you can take the Grand Canyon Railway excursion train to Grand Canyon Village. ***Note:*** The Amtrak stop in Williams is undeveloped and is on the outskirts of town. If you plan to take an Amtrak train to Williams, a shuttle from the Grand Canyon Railway Hotel will pick you up where the Amtrak train drops you off.

BY BUS Bus service between Phoenix, Flagstaff, Williams, and Grand Canyon Village is provided by **Open Road Tours** (© **800/766-7117** or 602/997-6474; www.openroadtours.com). Between Phoenix and Flagstaff, adult fares are $42 one-way and $76 round-trip ($30 and $52 for children); between Flagstaff and the Grand Canyon (by way of Williams), fares are $27 one-way and $54 round-trip ($19 and $38 for children).

VISITOR INFORMATION

You can get advance information on the Grand Canyon by contacting **Grand Canyon National Park,** P.O. Box 129, Grand Canyon, AZ 86023 (© **928/638-7888;** www.nps.gov/grca).

When you arrive at the park, stop by the **Canyon View Visitor Center,** at Canyon View Information Plaza, 6 miles from the south entrance. Here you'll find exhibits, an information desk, and a shop selling maps, books, and videos. The center is open daily 8am to 5pm. Unfortunately, the information plaza, which is well designed for handling large crowds, has no adjacent parking, so you'll have to park where you can and then walk or take a free shuttle bus. The nearest places to park are at Mather Point, Market Plaza, park headquarters, and Yavapai Observation Station. If you're parked anywhere in Grand Canyon Village, you'll want to catch the Village Route bus. If you park at Yaki Point, you can take the Kaibab Trail Route bus. *The Guide,* a small newspaper full of useful information about the park, is available at both South Rim park entrances.

ORIENTATION

Grand Canyon Village is built on the South Rim of the canyon and divided roughly into two sections. At the east end of the village are the Canyon View Information Plaza, Yavapai Lodge, Trailer Village, and Mather Campground. At the west end are El Tovar Hotel and Bright Angel, Kachina, Thunderbird, and Maswik lodges, as well as several restaurants, the train depot, and the trail head for the Bright Angel Trail.

GETTING AROUND

As I mentioned earlier, the Grand Canyon Village area can be extremely congested, especially in summer. If possible, you may want to use one of the transportation options below to avoid the park's traffic jams and parking problems. To give you an idea, in summer you can expect at least a 20- to 30-minute wait at the South Rim entrance gate just to get into the park. You can cut the waiting time here by acquiring an America the Beautiful–National Parks & Federal Recreational Lands Pass, before arriving. These passes are available as an Annual Pass ($80), a lifetime Senior Pass (available to U.S. citizens and permanent residents 62 or older for $10), and a lifetime Access Pass (available free to U.S. citizens and permanent residents with permanent disabilities). With pass in hand, you can use the express lane.

BY BUS Free shuttle buses operate on four routes within the park. The **Village Route** bus circles through Grand Canyon Village throughout the day with frequent stops at the Canyon View Information Plaza, Market Plaza (site of a general store, bank, laundry, and showers), hotels, campgrounds, restaurants, and other facilities. The **Hermit's Rest Route** bus takes visitors to eight canyon overlooks west of Bright Angel Lodge (this bus does not operate Dec–Feb.). The **Kaibab Trail Route** bus stops at the Canyon View Information Plaza, Pipe Creek Vista, the South Kaibab trail head, and Yaki Point. This latter stop is the trail head for the South Kaibab Trail to the bottom of the canyon. The **Canyon View/Mather Point Route** is specifically for visitors who need mobility assistance and shuttles between the Mather Point parking lot and the Canyon View Information Center. There's also a Hikers' Express bus to Yaki Point. This bus stops at Bright Angel Lodge and the Back Country Information Office. Hikers needing transportation to or from Yaki Point when the bus is not running can use a taxi (© **928/638-2822** or 928/638-2631, ext. 6563).

Between mid-May and mid-October, **Trans Canyon** (© **928/638-2820**) offers shuttle-bus service between the South Rim and the North Rim. The vans leave the South Rim at 1:30pm and arrive at the North Rim at 6pm. The return trip leaves the North Rim at 7am, arriving back at the South Rim at 11:30am. The fare is $70 one-way and $130 round-trip; reservations are required.

BY CAR Service stations are outside the south entrance to the park in Tusayan, at Desert View near the east entrance (this station is seasonal), and east of the park at Cameron. Because of the long distances within the park and to towns outside the park, fill up before setting out on a drive. Gas at the canyon is very expensive.

BY TAXI Taxi service is available to and from the airport, trail heads, and other destinations (© **928/638-2822** or 928/638-2631, ext. 6563). The fare from the airport to Grand Canyon Village is $10 for up to two adults ($5 for each additional person).

FAST FACTS: The Grand Canyon

Accessibility Check *The Guide* for park programs, services, and facilities that are partially or fully accessible. You can also get *The Grand Canyon National Park Accessibility Guide* at park entrances, Canyon View Center, Yavapai Observation Station, Kolb Studio, Tusayan Museum, and Desert View Information Center. Temporary accessibility permits are available at the park entrances, Canyon View Information Plaza, Yavapai Observation Station, Kolb Studio,

El Tovar concierge desk, and Bright Angel Lodge transportation desk. The national park has wheelchairs available at no charge for temporary use inside the park. You can usually find one of these wheelchairs at the Canyon View Information Plaza. Wheelchair-accessible shuttle buses can be arranged a day in advance by calling the national park (✆ **928/638-0591**). Accessible tours can also be arranged by contacting any lodge transportation desk or by calling **Grand Canyon National Park Lodges** (✆ **928/638-2631**).

Banks & ATMs There's an ATM at the **Chase** bank (✆ **928/638-2437**) at Market Plaza, which is near Yavapai Lodge. The bank is open Monday through Thursday from 9am to 5pm and Friday from 9am to 6pm.

Climate The climate at the Grand Canyon is dramatically different from that of Phoenix, and between the rim and the canyon floor there's also a pronounced difference. The South Rim is at 7,000 feet and consequently gets very cold in winter. You can expect snow anytime between November and May, and winter temperatures can be below 0°F (–18°C) at night, with daytime highs in the 20s or 30s (minus single digits to single digits Celsius). Summer temperatures at the rim range from highs in the 80s (20s Celsius) to lows in the 50s (teens Celsius). The North Rim of the canyon, which is slightly higher than the South Rim and stays a bit cooler throughout the year, is open to visitors only from May to October because the access road is not kept cleared of snow in winter.

On the canyon floor, temperatures are considerably higher. In summer, the mercury can reach 120°F (49°C) with lows in the 70s (20s Celsius), while in winter, temperatures are quite pleasant with highs in the 50s (teens Celsius) and lows in the 30s (single digits Celsius). July, August, and September are the wettest months because of frequent afternoon thunderstorms. April, May, and June are the driest months, but it still might rain or even snow. Down on the canyon floor, there is much less rain year-round.

Fees The entry fee for Grand Canyon National Park is $25 per car (or $12 per person if coming in on foot or by bicycle). Your admission ticket is good for 7 days. Don't lose it, or you'll have to pay again to reenter the park.

Festivals The **Grand Canyon Music Festival** (✆ **800/997-8285** or 928/638-9215; www.grandcanyonmusicfest.org) is held each year in early to mid-September.

Hospitals & Clinics The **North County Community Health Center** (✆ **928/638-2551**) is on Clinic Drive, off Center Road (the road that runs past the National Park Service ranger office). The clinic is open daily from 8am to 6pm (shorter hours in winter). It provides 24-hour emergency service as well.

Laundry A coin-operated laundry is located near Mather Campground in the Camper Services building.

Lost & Found Report lost items or turn in found items at the Canyon View Information Plaza; call ✆ **928/638-7798.** For items lost or found at a hotel, restaurant, or lounge, call ✆ **928/638-2631.**

Parking If you want to avoid parking headaches, try using the lot at the Market Plaza (the general store), which is up a side road near Yavapai Lodge and the Canyon View Information Plaza. From this large parking area, a paved hiking trail leads to the historic section of the village in less than 1.5 miles, and most of the route is along the rim. Another option is to park at the Maswik Transportation Center parking lot, which is served by the Village Route shuttle bus.

Police In an emergency, dial ✆ **911.** Ticketing speeders is one of the main occupations of the park's police force, so obey the posted speed limits.

Post Office The post office is at Market Plaza near Yavapai Lodge. It's open Monday through Friday from 9am to 4:30pm and Saturday from 11am to 1pm.

Radio KSGC, 92.1 FM, provides news, music, the latest weather forecasts, and travel-related information for the Grand Canyon area.

Road Conditions Information on road conditions in the Grand Canyon area is available by calling ✆ **888/411-7623** or 928/638-7888.

Safety The most important safety tip to remember is to be careful near the edge of the canyon. Footing can be unstable and may give way. Also, be sure to keep your distance from wild animals, no matter how friendly they may appear. Avoid hiking alone if at all possible and keep in mind that the canyon rim is more than a mile above sea level (it's harder to breathe up here). Do not leave valuables in your car or tent.

DESERT VIEW DRIVE

While the vast majority of visitors to the Grand Canyon enter through the south entrance, head straight for Grand Canyon Village, and proceed to get caught up in traffic jams and parking problems, you can avoid much of this congestion and have a much more enjoyable experience if you enter the park through the east entrance. To reach the east entrance from Flagstaff, take U.S. 89 to Arizona 64. Following this route, you'll get great views of the canyon sooner after you enter the park and have fewer parking problems. Even before you reach the park, you can stop and take in views of the canyon of the Little Colorado River. These viewpoints are on the Navajo Reservation, and at every stop you'll have opportunities to shop for Native American crafts and souvenirs at the numerous vendors' stalls that can be found at virtually every scenic viewpoint on the Navajo Reservation.

Desert View Drive, the park's only scenic road open to cars year-round, extends for 25 miles from Desert View, which is just inside the park's east entrance, to Grand Canyon Village, the site of all the park's hotels and most of its other commercial establishments. Along Desert View Drive, you'll find not only good viewpoints, but several picnic areas. Much of this drive is through forests, and canyon views are limited, but where there are viewpoints, they are among the best in the park.

Desert View, with its trading post, general store, snack bar, service station, information center, bookstore, and historic watchtower, is the first stop on this scenic drive. With its large parking lot, Desert View seems much better designed for handling large numbers of tourists than does Grand Canyon Village and is a much better introduction to the national park than what visitors encounter when they enter from the south entrance (at Tusayan).

From anywhere at Desert View, the scenery is breathtaking, but the very best perspective here is from atop the **Desert View Watchtower.** Although the watchtower looks as though it was built centuries ago, it actually dates from 1932. Architect Mary Elizabeth Jane Colter, who is responsible for much of the park's historic architecture,

Tips **Pack a Lunch**

Lunch options are very limited inside Grand Canyon National Park so, if you are driving up from Flagstaff, I suggest packing a picnic lunch. Try stopping in at a grocery store in Flagstaff for supplies. Otherwise, you're going to be stuck eating burgers in a cafeteria when you could be sitting on the edge of the canyon gazing out at one of the most awe-inspiring vistas on Earth.

designed it to resemble the prehistoric towers that dot the Southwestern landscape. Built as an observation tower and rest stop for tourists, the watchtower incorporates Native American designs and art. The curio shop on the ground floor is a replica of a kiva (sacred ceremonial chamber) and has lots of interesting souvenirs, regional crafts, and books. The tower's second floor features work by Hopi artist Fred Kabotie. Covering the walls are pictographs incorporating traditional designs. On the walls and ceiling of the upper two floors are more traditional images by artist Fred Geary, this time reproductions of petroglyphs from throughout the Southwest. From the roof, which, at 7,522 feet above sea level, is the highest point on the South Rim, it's possible to see the Colorado River, the Painted Desert to the northeast, the San Francisco Peaks to the south, and Marble Canyon to the north. Coin-operated binoculars provide close-up views of some of the noteworthy landmarks of this end of the canyon. Several black-mirror "reflectoscopes" provide interesting darkened views of some of the most spectacular sections of the canyon. In the gift shop, you can get a pamphlet describing the watchtower in detail.

At **Navajo Point,** the next stop along the rim, the Colorado River and Escalante Butte are both visible, and there's a good view of the Desert View Watchtower. However, I suggest heading straight to **Lipan Point** ★★, where you get what I think are the South Rim's best views of the Colorado River. You can actually see several stretches of the river, including a couple of major rapids. From here you can also view the Grand Canyon supergroup: several strata of rock tilted at an angle to the other layers of rock in the canyon. Their angle indicates there was a period of geological mountain building before the depositing of layers of sandstone, limestone, and shale. The red, white, and black rocks of the supergroup are composed of sedimentary rock and layers of lava. One of the park's best-kept secrets, a little-known though very rugged trail, begins here at Lipan Point (see "Hiking the Canyon," below, for details).

The **Tusayan Museum** (daily 9am–5pm) is the next stop along Desert View Drive. This small museum is dedicated to the Hopi tribe and the Ancestral Puebloan people who inhabited the region 800 years ago; inside are artfully displayed exhibits on various aspects of Ancestral Puebloan life. Outside is a short self-guided trail through the ruins of an Ancestral Puebloan village. Free guided tours are available.

Next along the drive is **Moran Point,** from which you can see a bright-red layer of shale in the canyon walls. This point is named for 19th-century landscape painter Thomas Moran, who is known for his paintings of the Grand Canyon.

The next stop, **Grandview Point,** affords a view of Horseshoe Mesa, another interesting feature of the canyon landscape. The mesa was the site of the Last Chance Copper Mine in the early 1890s. Later that same decade, the Grandview Hotel was built and served canyon visitors until its close in 1908. The steep, unmaintained Grandview

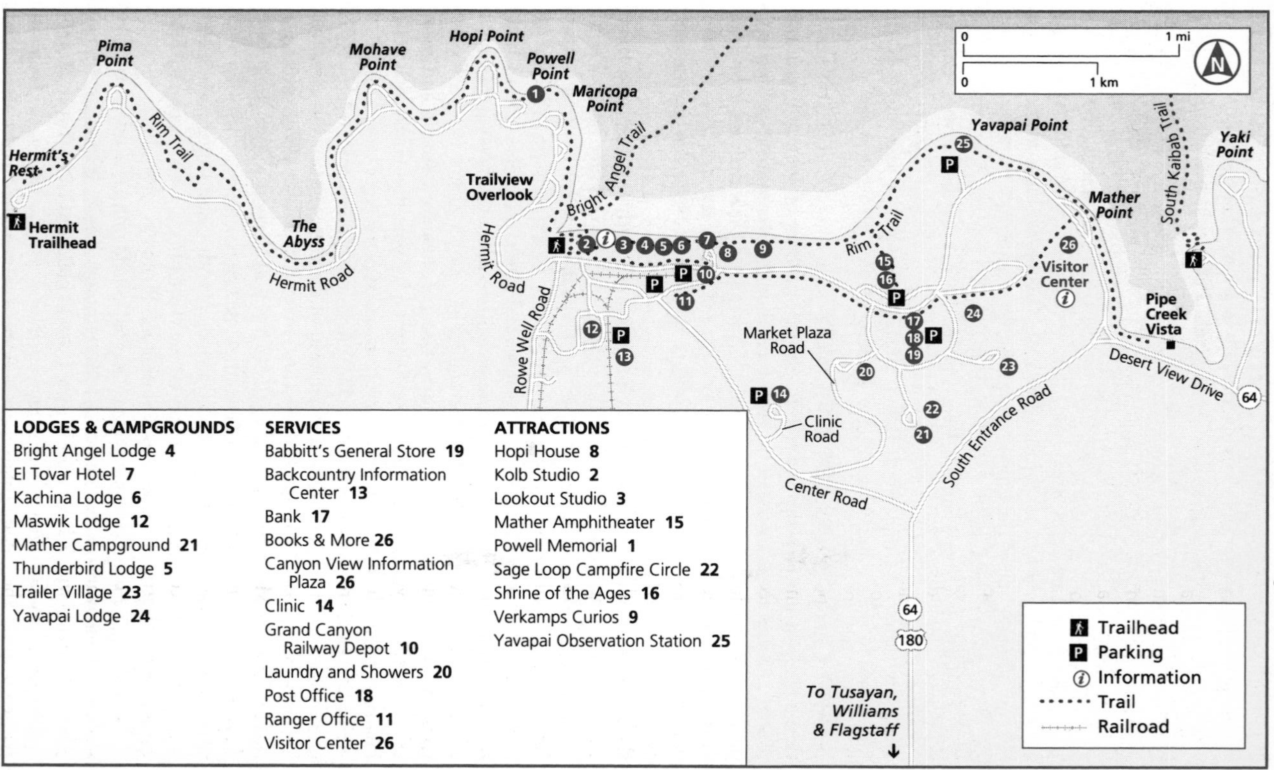

Pima Point
Mohave Point
Hopi Point
Powell Point
Maricopa Point
Hermit's Rest
Rim Trail
Hermit Trailhead
The Abyss
Hermit Road
Trailview Overlook
Bright Angel Trail
Hermit Road
Rowe Well Road
Yavapai Point
Rim Trail
Mather Point
South Kaibab Trail
Yaki Point
Visitor Center
Pipe Creek Vista
Market Plaza Road
Desert View Drive
64
Clinic Road
Center Road
South Entrance Road
0 1 mi
0 1 km
64
180
To Tusayan, Williams & Flagstaff
Trailhead
Parking
Information
Trail
Railroad
LODGES & CAMPGROUNDS
Bright Angel Lodge 4
El Tovar Hotel 7
Kachina Lodge 6
Maswik Lodge 12
Mather Campground 21
Thunderbird Lodge 5
Trailer Village 23
Yavapai Lodge 24
SERVICES
Babbitt's General Store 19
Backcountry Information Center 13
Bank 17
Books & More 26
Canyon View Information Plaza 26
Clinic 14
Grand Canyon Railway Depot 10
Laundry and Showers 20
Post Office 18
Ranger Office 11
Visitor Center 26
ATTRACTIONS
Hopi House 8
Kolb Studio 2
Lookout Studio 3
Mather Amphitheater 15
Powell Memorial 1
Sage Loop Campfire Circle 22
Shrine of the Ages 16
Verkamps Curios 9
Yavapai Observation Station 25

Trail leads down to Horseshoe Mesa from here. This trail makes a good less-traveled alternative to the South Kaibab Trail, although it is somewhat steeper.

The last stop along Desert View Drive is **Yaki Point,** which is no longer open to private vehicles. The park service would prefer it if you parked your car in Grand Canyon Village and took the Kaibab Trail Route shuttle bus from the Canyon View Information Plaza to Yaki Point. The reality is that people passing by in cars want to see what this viewpoint is all about and now park their cars alongside the main road and walk up the Yaki Point access road. The spectacular view from here encompasses a wide section of the central canyon. The large, flat-topped butte to the northeast is Wotan's Throne, one of the canyon's most readily recognizable features. Yaki Point is the site of the trail head for the South Kaibab Trail and consequently is frequented by hikers headed down to Phantom Ranch at the bottom of the canyon. The South Kaibab Trail is the preferred downhill hiking route to Phantom Ranch and is a more scenic route than the Bright Angel Trail. If you're planning a day hike into the canyon, this should be your number-one choice. Be sure to bring plenty of water.

GRAND CANYON VILLAGE & VICINITY

Grand Canyon Village is the first stop for the vast majority of the nearly four million people who visit the Grand Canyon every year (though I recommend coming in from the east entrance and avoiding the crowds). Consequently, it is the most crowded area in the park, but it also has the most overlooks and visitor services. Its many historic buildings add to the popularity of the village, which, if it weren't so crowded all the time, would have a pleasant atmosphere.

For visitors who have entered the park through the south entrance, that unforgettable initial gasp-inducing glimpse of the canyon comes at **Mather Point.** From this overlook, there's a short paved path to the Canyon View Information Plaza, but because you're allowed to park at Mather Point only for a maximum of 1 hour, you'll have to hurry if you want to take in the views and gather some park information.

Continuing west toward the village proper, you next come to **Yavapai Point,** which has the best view from anywhere in the vicinity of Grand Canyon Village. From here you can see the Bright Angel Trail, Indian Gardens, Phantom Ranch, and even the suspension bridge that hikers and mule riders use to cross the Colorado River near Phantom Ranch. Oh, yes, and of course you can also see the Colorado River. This viewpoint is a particularly great spot to take sunrise and sunset photos. Here you'll also find the historic **Yavapai Observation Station,** which houses a small museum and has big walls of glass to take in those extraordinary vistas. A paved pathway extends west from Yavapai Point for 3 miles, passing through Grand Canyon Village along the way. This trail also continues 2.5 miles east to the Pipe Creek Vista.

Continuing west from Yavapai Point, you'll come to a parking lot at park headquarters and a side road that leads to parking at the Market Plaza, which is one of the closest parking lots to the Canyon View Information Plaza.

West of these parking areas is Grand Canyon Village proper, where a paved pathway leads along the rim providing lots of good (though crowded) spots for taking pictures. The village is also the site of such historic buildings as **El Tovar Hotel** and **Bright Angel Lodge,** both of which are worth brief visits to take in the lodge ambience of their lobbies. Inside Bright Angel Lodge you'll find the **Bright Angel History Room,** which has displays on Mary Elizabeth Jane Colter and the Harvey Girls. Be sure to check out this room's fireplace, which is designed with all the same geologic layers that appear in the canyon. Adjacent to El Tovar are two historic souvenir and curio shops. **Hopi House Gift Store and Art Gallery,** the first shop in the park, was built in 1905 to resemble a Hopi pueblo and to serve as a place for Hopi artisans to work and sell their crafts. Today, it's full of Hopi and Navajo arts and crafts, including expensive kachina dolls, rugs, jewelry, and pottery. The nearby **Verkamps Curios** originally opened in a tent in 1898, but John Verkamp soon went out of business. The store reopened in 1905 and ever since has been the main place to look for souvenirs and crafts. Just inside the door is a 535-pound meteorite. Both shops are open daily; hours vary seasonally.

To the west of Bright Angel Lodge, two buildings cling precariously to the rim of the canyon. These are the Kolb and Lookout studios, both of which are listed on the National Register of Historic Places. **Kolb Studio** is named for Ellsworth and Emory Kolb, two brothers who set up a photographic studio on the rim of the Grand Canyon in 1904. The construction of this studio generated one of the Grand Canyon's first controversies—over whether buildings should be allowed on the canyon rim. Because the Kolbs had friends in high places, their sprawling studio and movie theater remained. Emory Kolb lived here until his death in 1976, by which time the studio had been listed as a historic building. It now serves as a bookstore, while the auditorium houses special exhibits. **Lookout Studio,** built in 1914 from a design by Mary Elizabeth Jane Colter, was the Fred Harvey Company's answer to the Kolb brothers' studio and incorporates architectural styles of the Hopi and the Ancestral Puebloans. The use of native limestone and an uneven roofline allow the studio to blend in with the canyon walls and give it the look of an old ruin. It now houses a souvenir store and two lookout points. Both the Kolb and Lookout studios are open daily; hours vary seasonally.

HERMIT ROAD

Hermit Road leads 8 miles west from Grand Canyon Village to Hermit's Rest, and mile for mile, it has the greatest concentration of breathtaking viewpoints in the park. Because it is closed to private vehicles March through November, it is also one of the most pleasant places to do a little canyon viewing or easy hiking during the busiest times of year: no traffic jams, no parking problems, and plenty of free shuttle buses operating along the route. Westbound buses stop at eight overlooks (Trailview, Maricopa Point, Powell Point, Hopi Point, Mohave Point, The Abyss, Pima Point, and Hermit's Rest); eastbound buses stop only at Mohave and Hopi points. From December to February, you can drive your own vehicle along this road, but keep in mind that winters usually mean a lot of snow, and the road can sometimes be closed due to hazardous driving conditions.

Because you probably won't want to stop at every viewpoint along this route, here are some tips to help you get the most out of an excursion along Hermit Road. First of all, keep in mind that the earlier you catch a shuttle bus, the more likely you are to avoid the crowds (buses start 1 hr. before sunrise, so photographers can get good shots of the canyon in dawn light). Second, remember that the closer you are to Grand Canyon Village, the larger the crowds will be. So, head out early and get a couple of miles between you and the village before getting off the shuttle bus.

The first two stops are **Trailview Overlook** and **Maricopa Point,** both on the paved section of the Rim Trail and within 1½ miles of the village, thus usually pretty crowded. If you just want to do a short, easy walk on pavement, get out at Maricopa Point and walk back to the village. From either overlook, you have a view of the Bright Angel Trail winding down into the canyon from Grand Canyon Village. The trail, which leads to the bottom of the canyon, crosses the Tonto Plateau about 3,000 feet below the rim. This plateau is the site of Indian Garden, where there's a campground in a grove of cottonwood trees. Because the views from these two overlooks are not significantly different from those in the village, I suggest skipping these stops if you've already spent time gazing into the canyon from the village.

Powell Point, the third stop, is the site of a memorial to John Wesley Powell, who, in 1869 with a party of nine men, became the first person to navigate the Colorado River through the Grand Canyon. Visible at Powell Point are the remains of the Orphan Mine, a copper mine that began operation in 1893. The mine went out of business because transporting the copper to a city where it could be sold was too expensive. Uranium was discovered here in 1954, but in 1966 the mine was shut down, and the land became part of Grand Canyon National Park. Again, I recommend continuing on to the more spectacular vistas that lie ahead.

The next stop is **Hopi Point,** which is one of the three best stops along this route. From here you can see a long section of the Colorado River far below you. Because of the great distance, the river seems to be a tiny, quiet stream, but in reality the section you see is more than 100 yards wide and races through Granite Rapids. Because Hopi Point juts into the canyon, it is one of the best spots in the park for taking sunrise and sunset photos; shuttle buses operate from 1 hour before sunrise to 1 hour after sunset.

The view is even more spectacular at the next stop, **Mohave Point.** Here you can see the river in two directions. Three rapids are visible from this overlook, and on a quiet day, you can sometimes even hear Hermit Rapids. As with almost all rapids in the canyon, Hermit Rapids are at the mouth of a side canyon where boulders loosened by storms and carried by flooded streams are deposited in the Colorado River. Don't miss this stop; it's got the best view on Hermit Road.

Next you come to **The Abyss,** the appropriately named 3,000-foot drop created by the Great Mojave Wall. This vertiginous view is one of the most awe-inspiring in the park. The walls of The Abyss are red sandstone that's more resistant to erosion than the softer shale in the layer below. Other layers of erosion-resistant sandstone have formed the free-standing pillars that are visible from here. The largest of these pillars is called the Monument. If you're looking for a good hike along this road, get out here and walk westward to either Pima Point (3 miles distant) or Hermit's Rest (4 miles away).

Tips Leave the Driving to Them

Now, I'm not a big fan of guided tours, but sometimes they just make a lot of sense. The Grand Canyon is one of those places, especially if you are usually the designated driver. Why should you have to keep your eyes on the road when there's all that gorgeous scenery right outside the window? Why not let someone else do the driving?

If you plan on making your visit to the Grand Canyon a day trip from Flagstaff rather than an overnight stay at the park, consider taking a tour with **American Dream Tours** (**✆ 888/203-1212** or 928/527-3369; www.americandreamtours.com). Not only will you get to enjoy the scenery more, but knowledgeable guides will fill you with fascinating information about the canyon. Tours are $88 for adults and $62 for children 10 and under (lower rates may be available on their website).

The **Pima Point** overlook, because it is set back from the road, is another good place to get off the bus. From here, the Rim Trail leads through the forest near the canyon rim, providing good views undisturbed by traffic on Hermit Road. From this overlook, it's also possible to see the remains of Hermit Camp on the Tonto Plateau. Built by the Santa Fe Railroad, Hermit Camp was a popular tourist destination between 1911 and 1930 and provided cabins and tents. Only foundations remain.

The final stop on Hermit Road is at **Hermit's Rest,** which was named for Louis Boucher, a prospector who came to the canyon in the 1890s and was known as the Hermit. The log-and-stone Hermit's Rest building, designed by Mary Elizabeth Jane Colter and built in 1914, is on the National Register of Historic Places and is one of the most fascinating structures in the park. With its snack bar, it makes a great place to linger while you soak up a bit of park history. The steep Hermit Trail, which leads down into the canyon, begins just past Hermit's Rest.

HIKING THE CANYON

No visit to the canyon is complete without journeying below the rim on one of the park's hiking trails. While the views don't necessarily get any better than they are from the top, they do change considerably. Gazing up at all those thousands of feet of vertical rock walls provides a very different perspective than that from atop the rim. Should you venture far below the rim, you also stand a chance of seeing fossils, old mines, petroglyphs, wildflowers, and wildlife. However, with around four million people visiting the Grand Canyon annually, you can forget about finding any solitude on the park's main hiking trails.

That said, there is no better way to see the canyon than on foot (my apologies to the mules), and a hike down into the canyon will likely be the highlight of your visit. You can get away from *most* of the crowds simply by heading down the Bright Angel or South Kaibab trail for 2 to 3 miles. Keep in mind, though, that these are the two busiest trails below the canyon rim and can see hundreds of hikers per day. If you want to see fewer other hikers and are in good shape, consider heading down the Grandview Trail or the Hermit Trail instead. If you're just looking for an easy walk that doesn't involve hiking back up out of the canyon, the Rim Trail is for you.

The Grand Canyon offers some of the most rugged and strenuous hiking anywhere in the United States, and for this reason anyone attempting even a short walk should be well prepared. Each year, injuries and fatalities are suffered by day hikers who set out without sturdy footgear or without food and adequate amounts of water. Even a 30-minute hike in summer can dehydrate you, and a long hike in the heat can necessitate drinking more than a gallon of water. So, carry and drink at least 2 quarts (2 liters) of water if you go for a day hike during the summer. Don't attempt to hike from the rim to the Colorado River and back in a day. Although there are very fit individuals who have managed the grueling hike to the bottom and back in a day, there are also plenty who have tried and died. Also remember that mules have the right of way.

DAY HIKES

Hikers tend to gravitate to loop trails, but here on the South Rim, you'll find no such trails. Thus, day hikers must reconcile themselves to out-and-back hikes. Still, the vastly different scenery in every direction makes out-and-back hikes here as interesting as any loop trail could be. The only problem is that the majority of the out-and-back trails are the reverse of what you'll find most other places. Instead of starting out by slogging up a steep mountain, you let gravity assist you in hiking down into the canyon. With little negative reinforcement and few natural turnaround destinations, it is easy to hike so far that the return trip back up the trail becomes an arduous death march. Know your limits and turn around before you become tired. On the canyon rim, the only hiking trail is the Rim Trail, while the Bright Angel, South Kaibab, Grandview, and Hermit trails all head down into the canyon.

For an easy, flat hike, your only option is the **Rim Trail,** which stretches from Pipe Creek Vista east of Grand Canyon Village to Hermit's Rest, 8 miles west of the village. Around 5 miles of this trail are paved, and the portion that passes through Grand Canyon Village is always the most crowded stretch of trail in the park. To the west of the village, after the pavement ends, the Rim Trail leads another 6.75 miles out to Hermit's Rest. For most of this distance, the trail follows Hermit Road, which means you'll have to deal with traffic noise (mostly from shuttle buses). To get the most enjoyment out of a hike along this stretch, I like to head out as early in the morning as possible (to avoid the crowds) and get off at The Abyss shuttle stop. From here it's a 4-mile hike to Hermit's Rest; for more than half of this distance, the trail isn't as close to the road as it is at the Grand Canyon Village end of the route. Plus, Hermit's Rest makes a great place to rest, and from here you can catch a shuttle bus back to the village. Alternatively, you could start hiking from Grand Canyon Village (it's just more than 8 miles from the west end of the village to Hermit's Rest) or any of the seven shuttle-bus stops en route, or take the shuttle all the way to Hermit's Rest and then hike back.

The **Bright Angel Trail,** which starts just west of Bright Angel Lodge in Grand Canyon Village, is the most popular trail into the canyon because it starts right where the greatest number of park visitors tend to congregate (near the ice-cream parlor and the hotels). It is also the route used by mule riders headed down into the canyon. Bear in mind that this trail follows a narrow side canyon for several miles down into the Grand Canyon and thus has somewhat limited views. For these reasons, this trail is worth avoiding if you're on foot. On the other hand, it's the only maintained trail into the canyon that has potable water, and there are four destinations along the trail that make good turnaround points. Both 1½ Mile Resthouse (1,131 ft. below the rim) and 3 Mile Resthouse (2,112 ft. below the rim) have water (except in winter, when the water is turned off). Keep in mind that these rest houses take their names from their distance from the rim; if you hike to 3 Mile Resthouse, you still have a 3-mile hike back up. Destinations for longer day hikes include Indian Garden (9 miles round-trip) and Plateau Point (12 miles round-trip), which are both just more than 3,000 feet below the rim. There is year-round water at Indian Garden.

The **South Kaibab Trail** ★★★ begins near Yaki Point east of Grand Canyon Village and is the preferred route down to Phantom Ranch. This trail also offers the best views of any of the day hikes into the canyon, so should you have time for only one day hike, make it this trail. From the trail head, it's 3 miles round-trip to Cedar Ridge and 6 miles round-trip to Skeleton Point. The hike is very strenuous, and no water is available along the trail.

If you're looking to escape the crowds and are an experienced mountain or desert hiker with good, sturdy boots, consider the unmaintained **Hermit Trail,** which begins at Hermit's Rest, 8 miles west of Grand Canyon Village at the end of Hermit Road. It's a 5-mile round-trip hike to Santa Maria Spring on a trail that loses almost all of its elevation (1,600–1,700 ft.) in the first 1.5 miles. Beyond Santa Maria Spring, the Hermit Trail descends to the Colorado River, but it is a 17-mile hike, one-way, from the trail head. Alternatively, you can do a 7-mile round-trip hike to Dripping Springs.

Water from either of these two springs must be treated with a water filter, iodine, or purification tablets, or by boiling for at least 10 minutes, so you're better off just carrying sufficient water for your hike. Hermit Road is closed to private vehicles from March to November, so chances are, you'll need to take the free shuttle bus out to the trail head. If you take the first bus of the day, you'll probably have the trail almost all to yourself.

The **Grandview Trail,** which begins at Grandview Point 12 miles east of Grand Canyon Village, is another steep and unmaintained trail that's a good choice for physically fit hikers. A strenuous 6-mile round-trip hike leads down to Horseshoe Mesa, 2,600 feet below the rim-top trail head. No water is available, so carry at least 2 quarts. Allow at least 7 hours for this rugged hike. Just to give you an idea of how steep this trail is, you'll lose more than 2,000 feet of elevation in the first .75 mile down to Coconino Saddle.

There's one other trail I have to tell you about, but you have to promise not to tell anyone else. This trail is so secret that the National Park Service doesn't mark it on any of its maps. It's called the **Tanner Trail,** and it starts just downhill from the beginning of the parking lot at Lipan Point near the east end of Desert View Drive. The Tanner Trail started out as a trail used by horse thieves to move stolen horses between Utah and Arizona. This is one of the shortest, steepest, and most challenging trails down into the canyon, and it is probably for good reason that the park service doesn't want you to know about it. They don't want to have to rescue you when you collapse from dehydration hiking back up.

There, now that you are suitably warned, let me tell you about the single best day-hiking experience I've ever had in the Grand Canyon. The Tanner Trail is so unknown that I hiked it twice in 2 days and saw only one other hiker. He was sitting at the top of the trail dripping with sweat after having hiked all the way to the Colorado River and back (this is an activity that the park service works hard to discourage people from attempting). Therein lies the beauty of this trail—you can have it all to yourself even when the park is packed with tourists! Of course, there is a cost. This trail is not for everyone. You must be in excellent shape, with good knees and strong quadriceps. Don't even think of setting foot on this trail unless you are wearing very sturdy boots with excellent ankle support. Take lots of water and drink it. Finally, remember that it will take you considerably longer to hike back up than it took you to hike down. So how far can you hike on this trail? Well, that's up to you. It's 3 miles and a 1,700-foot elevation drop to Escalante Butte, from which you get a good view of Marble Canyon, Hance Rapids, and the bottom of the canyon.

BACKPACKING

Backpacking the Grand Canyon is an unforgettable experience. Although most people are content to simply hike down to Phantom Ranch and back, there are many miles of trails deep in the canyon. Keep in mind, however, that to backpack the canyon, you'll need to do a lot of planning. A **Backcountry Use Permit** is required of all hikers planning to overnight in the canyon, unless you'll be staying at Phantom Ranch in one of the cabins or a dormitory.

Because a limited number of hikers are allowed into the canyon on any given day, it's important to make reservations as soon as it is possible to do so. Reservations are taken in person, by mail, by fax (but not by phone), and online. Contact the **Backcountry Information Center,** Grand Canyon National Park, P.O. Box 129, Grand Canyon, AZ 86023 (✆ **928/638-7875** Mon–Fri 1–5pm for information; fax 928/638-2125;

www.nps.gov/grca). The office begins accepting reservations on the first of every month for the following 5 months. Holiday periods are the most popular—if you want to hike over the Labor Day weekend, be sure you make your reservation on May 1. If you show up without a reservation, go to the Backcountry Information Center (daily 8am–noon and 1–5pm), adjacent to the Maswik Lodge, and put your name on the waiting list. When applying for a permit, you must specify your exact itinerary, and once in the canyon, you must stick to this itinerary. Backpacking fees include a nonrefundable $10 backcountry permit fee and a $5 per-person per-night backcountry camping fee. American Express, Diners Club, Discover, MasterCard, and Visa are accepted for permit fees. Keep in mind that you'll still have to pay the park entry fee when you arrive at the Grand Canyon.

There are **campgrounds** at Indian Garden, Bright Angel Campground (near Phantom Ranch), and Cottonwood, but hikers are limited to 2 nights per trip at each of these campgrounds (except Nov 15–Feb 28, when 4 nights are allowed at each campground). Other nights can be spent camping at undesignated sites in certain regions of the park.

The *Backcountry Trip Planner* contains information to help you plan your itinerary. It's available through the Backcountry Information Center (see contact information, above). Maps are available through the **Grand Canyon Association,** P.O. Box 399, Grand Canyon, AZ 86023 (© **800/858-2808** or 928/638-2481; www.grandcanyon.org), and at bookstores and gift shops within the national park, including Canyon View Information Plaza, Kolb Studio, Desert View Information Center, Yavapai Observation Station, Tusayan Museum, and, on the North Rim, Grand Canyon Lodge.

The best times of year to backpack are spring and fall. In summer, temperatures at the bottom of the canyon are frequently above 100°F (38°C), while in winter, ice and snow at higher elevations make footing on trails precarious (crampons are recommended). Plan to carry at least 2 quarts, and preferably 1 gallon, of water whenever backpacking in the canyon.

The Grand Canyon is an unforgiving landscape and, as such, many people might want a professional guide while backpacking through this rugged corner of the Southwest. To arrange a guided backpacking trip into the canyon, contact **Discovery Treks,** 28248 N. Tatum Blvd. Suite B1-414, Cave Creek, AZ 85331 (© **888/256-8731** or 480/247-9266; www.discoverytreks.com), which offers 3- to 5-day all-inclusive hikes into the canyon with rates ranging from $975 to $1,395 per person.

OTHER WAYS OF SEEING THE CANYON

BUS TOURS

If you'd rather leave the driving to someone else and enjoy more of the scenery, opt for a bus or van tour of one or more sections of the park. **Grand Canyon National Park Lodges** (© **928/638-2631;** www.grandcanyonlodges.com) offers several tours within the park. These can be booked by calling or stopping at one of the transportation desks, which are at Bright Angel, Maswik, and Yavapai lodges (see "Where to Stay," later in this chapter). Prices range from around $15 for a 1½-hour sunrise or sunset tour to around $40 for a combination tour to both Hermit's Rest and Desert View.

MULE RIDES ★

Mule rides into the canyon have been popular since the beginning of the 20th century, when the Bright Angel Trail was a toll road. After having a look at the steep drop-offs and narrow path of the Bright Angel Trail, you might decide this isn't exactly the place to trust your life to a mule. Never fear: Wranglers will be quick to reassure you they haven't lost a rider yet. Trips of various lengths and to different destinations are offered. The 1-day trip descends to Plateau Point, where there's a view of the Colorado River 1,300 feet below. This grueling trip requires riders to spend 6 hours in the saddle. Those who want to spend a night down in the canyon can choose an overnight trip to Phantom Ranch, where cabins and dormitories are available at the only lodge actually in the canyon. From November to March, a 3-day trip to Phantom Ranch is offered; other times of year, you'll ride down one day and back up the next. Mule trips range in price from $148 for a 1-day ride to $401 for an overnight ride to $566 for the 2-night ride. Couples get discounts on overnight rides.

Riders must weigh less than 200 pounds fully dressed; stand at least 4 feet, 7 inches tall; and speak fluent English. Pregnant women are not allowed on mule trips.

Because these trail rides are very popular (especially in summer), they often book up 6 months or more in advance (reservations are taken up to 13 months in advance). For more information or to make a reservation, contact **Xanterra Parks & Resorts** (✆ **888/297-2757** or 303/297-2757; www.grandcanyonlodges.com). If at the last minute (5 days or fewer from the day you want to ride) you decide you want to go on a mule trip, contact **Grand Canyon National Park Lodges** at its Arizona phone number (✆ **928/638-2631**) for the remote possibility that there may be space available. If you arrive at the canyon without a reservation and decide that you'd like to go on a mule ride, stop by the Bright Angel Transportation Desk to get your name put on the next day's waiting list.

THE GRAND CANYON RAILWAY ★★

In the early 20th century, most visitors to the Grand Canyon arrived by train, and it's still possible to travel to the canyon along the steel rails. The **Grand Canyon Railway** (✆ **800/843-8724** or 928/773-1976; www.thetrain.com), which runs from Williams to Grand Canyon Village, uses both 1950s-vintage diesel engines and, between Memorial Day and Labor Day, early-20th-century steam engines to pull 1920s and 1950s passenger cars. Trains depart from the Williams Depot, which is housed in the historic 1908 Fray Marcos Hotel and also contains a railroad museum, gift shop, and cafe. (Grand Canyon Railway also operates the adjacent Grand Canyon Railway Hotel.) At Grand Canyon Village, the trains use the 1910 log railway terminal in front of El Tovar Hotel.

Passengers have the choice of five classes of service: coach (which includes both Pullman and Budd cars), club class, first class, observation dome (upstairs in the dome car), and luxury parlor class. Actors posing as cowboys provide entertainment, including musical performances, aboard the train. The round-trip takes 8 hours, including a 3¼- to 3¾-hour layover at the canyon. Fares range from $65 to $170 for adults, $40 to $145 for children 11 to 16, and $30 to $95 for children 2 to 10 (not including tax or the park entry fee).

Not only is this a fun trip that provides great scenery and a trip back in time, but taking the train also allows you to avoid the traffic congestion and parking problems in Grand Canyon Village. When booking your train trip, you can also book a bus tour in the park, which will help you see more than you would on foot. The railway offers room/train packages as well.

In November, December, and January, there's the Polar Express with service to the North Pole and a visit from Santa.

A BIRD'S-EYE VIEW

Despite controversies over noise and safety (there have been a few crashes over the years), airplane and helicopter flights over the Grand Canyon remain one of the most popular ways to see this natural wonder. Personally, I would rather enjoy the canyon on foot or from a saddle. However, the volume of flights over the canyon each day would indicate that quite a few people don't share my opinion. If you want to join the crowds buzzing the canyon, you'll find several companies operating out of Grand Canyon Airport in Tusayan. Air tours last anywhere from 30 minutes to about 2 hours.

Companies offering tours by small plane include **Air Grand Canyon** (© **800/247-4726** or 928/638-2686; www.airgrandcanyon.com) and **Grand Canyon Airlines** (© **866/235-9422** or 928/638-2359; www.grandcanyonairlines.com). This latter company has been offering air tours since 1927 and is the oldest scenic airline at the canyon. Fifty-minute flights cost $99 to $119 for adults and $79 to $89 for children (including current $10 per person fuel surcharge).

Helicopter tours are available from **Maverick Airstar Helicopters** (© **888/261-4414** or 702/261-0007; www.airstar.com), **Grand Canyon Helicopters** (© **800/541-4537** or 928/638-2764; www.grandcanyonhelicoptersaz.com), and **Papillon Grand Canyon Helicopters** (© **800/528-2418** or 928/638-2419; www.papillon.com). Rates range from $145 to $175 for a 30-minute flight and from $205 to $235 for a 45- to 55-minute flight. Children sometimes receive a discount (usually around $20), and discounts can also be found on the various tour company websites.

INTERPRETIVE PROGRAMS

Numerous interpretive programs are scheduled throughout the year at various South Rim locations. Walks led by rangers explore different aspects of the canyon; rangers give geology talks, offer lectures on the cultural and natural resources of the canyon, lead nature hikes, organize trips to fossil beds, and hold stargazing gatherings. At Tusayan Ruin, guided tours are offered. Evening programs are held at Mather Amphitheater or the Shrine of the Ages. Consult your copy of *The Guide* for information on times and meeting points.

THE GRAND CANYON FIELD INSTITUTE

If you're the active type or would like to turn your visit to the Grand Canyon into more of an educational experience, you may want to consider doing a trip with the **Grand Canyon Field Institute** (© **866/471-4435** or 928/638-2485; www.grandcanyon.org/fieldinstitute). Cosponsored by Grand Canyon National Park and the Grand Canyon Association, the Field Institute schedules an amazing variety of guided, educational trips, such as challenging backpacking trips through the canyon (some for women only) and programs lasting anywhere from 1 to 18 days. Subjects covered include wilderness studies, geology, natural history, human history, photography, and art.

JEEP TOURS

If you'd like to explore parts of Grand Canyon National Park that most visitors never see, contact **Grand Canyon Jeep Tours & Safaris** (© **800/320-5337** or 928/638-5337; www.grandcanyonjeeptours.com), which offers three different tours that visit the park as well as the adjacent Kaibab National Forest. One tour stops at a lookout tower that affords an elevated view of the canyon, while another visits an Indian ruin and site of petroglyphs and cave paintings. Prices range from $45 to $104 for adults and $35 to $84 for children 12 and under.

RAFTING THE COLORADO RIVER ★★★

Rafting down the Colorado River as it roars and tumbles through the mile-deep gorge of the Grand Canyon is the adventure of a lifetime. Ever since John Wesley Powell ignored everyone who knew better and proved that it was possible to travel by boat down the tumultuous Colorado, running the big river has become a passion and an obsession with adventurers. Today, anyone from grade-schoolers to grandmothers can join the elite group of people who have made the run. However, be prepared for some of the most furious white water in the world.

Numerous companies offer trips through various sections of the canyon. You can spend as little as half a day on the Colorado (downstream from Glen Canyon Dam; see "Lake Powell & Page," in chapter 7) to as many as 19 days. You can go down the river in a huge motorized rubber raft (the quickest and noisiest way to see the entire canyon), a paddle- or oar-powered raft (more thrills and more energy expended on your part if you have to help paddle), or a wooden dory (the biggest thrill of all). In a motorized raft, you can travel the entire canyon from Lees Ferry to Lake Mead in only 8 days; however, you'll have to listen to the outboard motor whenever you aren't in the middle of a rapid. Should you opt for an oar- or paddle-powered raft or dory, expect to spend 5 to 6 days getting from Lees Ferry to Phantom Ranch, or 7 to 9 days getting from Phantom Ranch to Diamond Creek, just above Lake Mead. Aside from the half-day trips near Glen Canyon Dam, any Grand Canyon rafting trip will involve lots of monster rapids. Variables to consider include hiking in or out of Phantom Ranch for a combination rafting-and-hiking adventure.

Most trips start from Lees Ferry near Page and Lake Powell. It's also possible to start (or finish) a trip at Phantom Ranch, hiking in or out from either the North or South Rim. The main rafting season is April through October, but some companies operate year-round. Rafting trips tend to book up more than a year in advance, and most companies begin taking reservations between March and May for the following year's trips. Expect to pay between $220 and $280 per day for your white-water adventure, depending on the length of the trip and the type of boat used.

The following are some of the companies I recommend checking out when you start planning your Grand Canyon rafting adventure:

- **Arizona Raft Adventures,** 4050 E. Huntington Rd., Flagstaff, AZ 86004 (© **800/786-7238;** www.azraft.com); 6- to 16-day motor, oar, and paddle trips. Although this is not one of the larger companies operating on the river, it offers lots of different trips, including those that focus on natural history and photography. They also do trips in paddle rafts that allow you to help navigate and provide the power while shooting the canyon's many rapids.
- **Canyoneers,** P.O. Box 2997, Flagstaff, AZ 86003 (© **800/525-0924** or 928/526-0924; www.canyoneers.com); 3- to 7-day motorized-raft trips and 5- to 14-day oar-powered trips. Way back in 1938, this was the first company to take paying customers down the Colorado, and Canyoneers is still one of the top companies on the river. In 2007, Canyoneers' oar-powered trips were accompanied by a restored 1947 Grand Canyon cataract boat.
- **Diamond River Adventures,** P.O. Box 1300, Page, AZ 86040 (© **800/343-3121** or 928/645-8866; www.diamondriver.com); 4- to 8-day motorized-raft trips and 5- to 13-day oar trips. This is the only women-owned and -managed rafting company operating in the Grand Canyon.

- **Grand Canyon Expeditions Company,** P.O. Box O, Kanab, UT 84741 (✆ **800/544-2691** or 435/644-2691; www.gcex.com); 8-day motorized trips and 14- and 16-day dory trips. If you've got the time, I highly recommend these dory trips as among the most thrilling adventures in the world.
- **Hatch River Expeditions,** HC 67 Box 35, Marble Canyon, AZ 86036 (✆ **800/856-8966;** www.hatchriverexpeditions.com); 4- and 7-day motorized trips. The 4-day trips involve hiking either into the canyon or out of the canyon. On the 7-day trip, a helicopter lifts you out of the canyon at the end of the trip. This company has been in business since 1929 and claims to be the oldest commercial rafting company in the U.S. With so much experience, you can count on Hatch to provide you with a great trip.
- **Outdoors Unlimited,** 6900 Townsend Winona Rd., Flagstaff, AZ 86004 (✆ **800/637-7238** or 928/526-4511; www.outdoorsunlimited.com); 5- to 13-day oar and paddle trips. This company has been taking people through the canyon for nearly 40 years and usually sends them home very happy.
- **Wilderness River Adventures,** P.O. Box 717, Page, AZ 86040 (✆ **800/992-8022** or 928/645-3296; www.riveradventures.com); 4- to 8-day motorized-raft trips and 6-, 7-, 12-, and 14-day oar trips. The 4-day trips (actually 3½ days) involve hiking out from Phantom Ranch. This is one of the bigger companies operating on the canyon, and it offers a wide variety of trips, which makes it a good one to check with if you're not sure which type of trip you want to do.

For information on 1-day rafting trips at the west end of the Grand Canyon, see "Havasu Canyon & Grand Canyon West," later in this chapter. For information on half-day trips near Page, see "Lake Powell & Page," in chapter 7.

ACTIVITIES OUTSIDE THE CANYON

If you aren't completely beat at the end of the day, you might want to take in an evening of **Navajo dancing** at the Grand Hotel (✆ **928/638-3333**) in Tusayan; call for the schedule.

For a virtual Grand Canyon experience, you can see an IMAX movie at the **National Geographic Visitor Center,** Arizona 64/U.S. 180 (✆ **928/638-2468;** www.grandcanyonimaxtheater.com), in Tusayan outside the south entrance to the park. A short IMAX film covering the history and geology of the canyon is shown throughout the day on the theater's seven-story screen. Admission is $13 for adults and $9.60 for children 3 to 11. March to October, there are shows daily between 8:30am and 8:30pm; November to February, shows are daily between 10:30am and 6:30pm.

Outside the east entrance to the park, the **Cameron Trading Post** (✆ **800/338-7385** or 928/679-2231; www.camerontradingpost.com), at the crossroads of Cameron where Arizona 64 branches off U.S. 89, is the best trading post in the state. The original stone trading post, a historic building, now houses a gallery of Indian artifacts, clothing, and jewelry. This gallery sells museum-quality pieces, but even if you don't have $10,000 to drop on a rug or basket, you can still look around. The main trading post is a more modern building and is the largest trading post in northern Arizona. Don't miss the beautiful terraced gardens in back of the original trading post.

WHERE TO STAY

Keep in mind that the Grand Canyon is one of the most popular national parks in the country, and hotel rooms both within and just outside the park are in high demand. Make reservations as far in advance as possible. Don't expect to find a room if you head up here in summer without a reservation. You'll likely wind up driving back to Williams or Flagstaff to find a vacancy. There, is, however, one long-shot option. See "Inside the Park," below, for details. Who knows? You might get lucky.

INSIDE THE PARK

All hotels inside the park are operated by **Xanterra Parks & Resorts.** Reservations are taken up to 13 months in advance, beginning on the first of the month. If you want to stay in one of the historic rim cabins at Bright Angel Lodge, reserve at least a year in advance. However, rooms with shared bathrooms at Bright Angel Lodge are often the last in the park to book up, and although they're small and very basic, they're your best bet if you're trying to get a last-minute reservation.

To make reservations at any of the in-park hotels listed below, contact **Grand Canyon National Park Lodges/Xanterra Parks & Resorts,** 6312 S. Fiddlers Green Circle, Suite 600N, Greenwood Village, CO 80111 (© **888/297-2757** or 303/297-2757; www.xanterra.com or www.grandcanyonlodges.com). It is sometimes possible, due to cancellations and no-shows, to get a same-day reservation; it's a long shot, but it happens. Same-day reservations can be made by calling © **928/638-2631.** Xanterra accepts American Express, Diners Club, Discover, MasterCard, and Visa. Children 16 and under stay for free in their parent's room.

Expensive

El Tovar Hotel ★★ El Tovar Hotel, which first opened its doors in 1905 and was completely renovated in 2005, is the park's premier lodge. Built of local rock and Oregon pine by Hopi craftsmen, it's a rustic yet luxurious mountain lodge that perches on the edge of the canyon (although with views from only a few rooms). The lobby, entered from a veranda set with rustic furniture, has a small fireplace, cathedral ceiling, and log walls on which moose, deer, and antelope heads are displayed. Although guest rooms are comfortable and attractively decorated, the standard units are rather small, as are the bathrooms. For more leg room, book a deluxe unit. Suites, with private terraces and stunning views, are extremely spacious. El Tovar Dining Room (see "Where to Dine," below) is the best restaurant in the village. Just off the lobby is a cocktail lounge with a view.

78 units. $142–$205 double; $258–$322 suite. **Amenities:** Restaurant (Continental/Southwestern); lounge; concierge; tour desk; room service. *In room:* A/C, TV, dataport, fridge, hair dryer, iron, safe.

Moderate

Maswik Lodge Set back ¼ mile or so from the rim, the Maswik Lodge offers spacious rooms and cabins that have been comfortably modernized without losing their appealing rustic character. If you don't mind roughing it a bit, the 28 old cabins, which are available only in summer, have lots of character. These cabins have high ceilings and ceiling fans, and are my top choice away from the rim. If you crave modern appointments, lots of space, and predictably comfortable air-conditioned accommodations, opt for one of the large Maswik North rooms, all of which were renovated in 2006. Second-floor rooms have high ceilings and balconies, which makes them your other best bet away from the rim.

278 units. $77–$138 double (winter discounts available); $77 cabin. **Amenities:** Cafeteria; lounge; tour desk. *In room:* A/C, TV, fridge, coffeemaker, safe.

Thunderbird & Kachina Lodges If you want great views, these hotels are your best bets—but only if you get a room with a view. These two side-by-side hotels date from the 1960s and, with their dated styling, are a far cry from what you might imagine a national park hotel would look like. They do, however, have a couple of things going for them. They have the biggest windows of any of the four hotels right on the canyon rim, and major renovations a few years ago extensively modernized them. Try to get a second-story room on the canyon side of either hotel (these rooms at the Kachina Lodge get the nod for having *the* best views). Book early—these two lodges are some of the park's most popular accommodations. Just remember, if it's not a view room, you'll be staring at the parking lot. Unfortunately, when making reservations, you cannot request a view room. Good luck.

104 units. $139–$152 double. *In room:* TV, dataport, fridge, coffeemaker, hair dryer, iron, safe.

Yavapai Lodge Located in several buildings at the east end of Grand Canyon Village (a 1-mile hike from the main section of the village, but convenient to the Canyon View Information Plaza), the Yavapai is the largest lodge in the park and thus is where you'll likely wind up if you wait too long to make a reservation. Unfortunately, it's also the least-appealing hotel in the park. There are no canyon views, which is why Yavapai is less expensive than the Thunderbird and Kachina lodges. If you must stay here, try for a room in the nicer Yavapai East wing, which is set under shady pines. Rooms in this wing have air-conditioning. However, I recommend that you plan ahead and try to stay at one of the lodges right on the rim.

358 units. $97–$126 double; $76–$89 double in winter. **Amenities:** Cafeteria; tour desk. *In room:* TV.

Inexpensive

Bright Angel Lodge & Cabins ★ Bright Angel Lodge, which began operation in 1896 as a collection of tents and cabins on the edge of the canyon, is the most affordable lodge in the park, and, with its flagstone-floor lobby and huge fireplace, it has a genuine, if crowded, mountain-lodge atmosphere. It offers the greatest variety of accommodations in the park. The best and most popular units are the rim cabins, which should be booked a year in advance for summer. Outside the winter months, other rooms should be booked at least 6 months in advance. Most of the rooms and cabins feature rustic furnishings. The Buckey Suite, the oldest structure on the canyon rim, is arguably the best room in the park, with a canyon view, gas fireplace, and king-size bed. The tour desk, fireplace, museum, and restrooms account for the constant crowds in the lobby. This lodge was completely renovated in 2007.

86 units, 20 w/shared bathrooms. $52 double w/sink only; $58 double w/sink and toilet; $70–$143 double w/private bathroom; $92–$239 cabin. **Amenities:** 2 restaurants (American, steakhouse/Southwestern); lounge; ice-cream parlor; tour desk. *In room:* No phone.

Phantom Ranch ★ Built in 1922, Phantom Ranch is the only lodge at the bottom of the Grand Canyon and has a classic ranch atmosphere. Accommodations are in rustic stone-walled cabins or 10-bed gender-segregated dormitories. Evaporative coolers keep both the cabins and the dorms cool in summer. Make reservations as early as possible, and don't forget to reconfirm. It's also sometimes possible to get a room on the day of departure if there are any last-minute cancellations. To attempt this, you must put your name on the waiting list at the Bright Angel Lodge transportation desk the day before you want to stay at Phantom Ranch.

Family-style meals must be reserved in advance. The menu consists of beef-and-vegetable stew ($23), a vegetarian dinner ($23), and steak ($36). Breakfasts ($18) are hearty, and sack lunches ($10) are available as well. Between meals, the dining hall becomes a canteen selling snacks, drinks, gifts, and necessities. After dinner, it serves as a beer hall. There's a public phone here, and mule-back duffel transfer ($61) between Grand Canyon Village and Phantom Ranch can be arranged.

✆ **928/638-3283** for reconfirmations. 11 cabins, 40 dorm beds. $93 double in cabin; $34 dormitory bed. Mule-trip overnights (w/all meals and mule ride included) $369 for 1 person, $661 for 2 people. 2-night trips available Nov–Mar. **Amenities:** Restaurant (American); lounge. *In room:* No phone.

IN TUSAYAN (OUTSIDE THE SOUTH ENTRANCE)

If you can't get a reservation for a room in the park, this is the next closest place to stay. Unfortunately, this area can be very noisy because of the many helicopters and airplanes taking off from the airport. Also, hotels outside the park are very popular with tour groups, which during the busy summer months keep many hotels full. All of the hotels listed here are lined up along U.S. 180/Arizona 64.

Best Western Grand Canyon Squire Inn ★★ Kids If you prefer playing tennis to riding a mule, this may be the place for you. Of all the hotels in Tusayan, this one has the most resortlike feel due to its restaurants, lounges, and extensive recreational amenities. With so much to offer, it almost seems as if the hotel were trying to distract guests from the canyon itself. But even if you don't bowl or play tennis, you'll likely appreciate the large guest rooms with comfortable easy chairs and big windows. In the lobby, which is more Las Vegas glitz than mountain rustic, cases are filled with old cowboy paraphernalia. Down in the basement are an impressive Western sculpture, a waterfall wall, and even a bowling alley.

Ariz. 64 (P.O. Box 130), Grand Canyon, AZ 86023. ✆ **800/622-6966** or 928/638-2681. Fax 928/638-2782. www.grandcanyonsquire.com. 250 units. Mid-Mar to mid-Oct and late Nov to Dec $105–$195 double; mid-Oct to late Nov and Jan to mid-Mar $75–$155 double. Children 12 and under stay free in parent's room. AE, DC, DISC, MC, V. **Amenities:** 2 restaurants (Continental, American); 2 lounges; seasonal outdoor pool; 2 tennis courts; exercise room; Jacuzzi; sauna; game room; concierge; coin-op laundry. *In room:* A/C, TV, dataport, coffeemaker, hair dryer, iron, Wi-Fi, free local calls.

Grand Hotel ★★ With its mountain lodge–style lobby, this modern hotel lives up to its name and is your best bet outside the park. There's a flagstone fireplace, log-beam ceiling, and fake ponderosa-pine tree trunks holding up the roof. Just off the lobby are a dining room (with evening entertainment ranging from Native American dancers to country-music bands), a small bar that even has a few saddles for bar stools, and an espresso stand. Guest rooms are spacious, with a few Western touches, and some have small balconies.

Ariz. 64 (P.O. Box 3319), Grand Canyon, AZ 86023. ✆ **888/634-7263** or 928/638-3333. Fax 928/638-3131. www.grandcanyongrandhotel.com. 121 units. $99–$223 double. Children 17 and under stay free in parent's room. AE, DISC, MC, V. **Amenities:** Restaurant (American/Southwestern); lounge; indoor pool; exercise room; Jacuzzi; concierge; coin-op laundry. *In room:* A/C, TV, dataport, coffeemaker, hair dryer.

Holiday Inn Express–Grand Canyon Hotel This hotel has modern, well-designed—if a bit sterile and characterless—guest rooms. The Holiday Inn Express also manages an adjacent 32-suite property whose rooms have a Western theme. Although these suites are fairly pricey, they're among the nicest accommodations inside or outside the park.

Ariz. 64 (P.O. Box 3245), Grand Canyon, AZ 86023. ✆ **888/473-2269** or 928/638-3000. Fax 928/638-0123. www.grandcanyon.hiexpress.com. 194 units. $69–$162 double; $89–$250 suite. Rates include continental breakfast. Children under 18 stay free in parent's room. AE, DC, DISC, MC, V. **Amenities:** Indoor pool; Jacuzzi. *In room:* A/C, TV, dataport, hair dryer, iron, high-speed Internet access.

Quality Inn & Suites Canyon Plaza ★ The setting behind the IMAX theater and surrounded by parking lots is none too pretty, but guest rooms are relatively luxurious and the hotel is built around two enclosed skylit courtyards, one of which houses a restaurant and the other a bar and whirlpool. Guest rooms are large and comfortable, with balconies or patios; most also have minibars. The suites contain separate small living rooms, microwaves, and fridges. The hotel is very popular with tour groups.

P.O. Box 520, Grand Canyon, AZ 86023. ✆ **800/221-2222** or 928/638-2673. Fax 928/638-9537. www.grandcanyonqualityinn.com. 232 units. Mid-Mar to Oct $180 double, $240 suite; Nov to mid-Mar $100–$170 double, $160–$240 suite. Rates include continental breakfast. Children 18 and under stay free in parent's room. AE, DC, DISC, MC, V. **Amenities:** Restaurant (American); lounge; outdoor pool; 2 Jacuzzis. *In room:* A/C, TV, dataport, coffeemaker, hair dryer, high-speed Internet access.

Red Feather Lodge *Kids* With more than 200 units, this motel is often slow to fill up, so it's a good choice for last-minute bookings. Try to get one of the newer rooms, which are a bit more comfortable than the older ones. The pool here makes this place a good bet for families.

Ariz. 64 (P.O. Box 1460), Grand Canyon, AZ 86023. ✆ **800/538-2345** or 928/638-2414. Fax 928/638-2707. www.redfeatherlodge.com. 215 units. $80–$135 double. Rates include continental breakfast. Children under 18 stay free in parent's room. AE, DC, DISC, MC, V. Pets accepted ($50 deposit plus $10 per night). **Amenities:** Restaurant (American); seasonal outdoor pool; Jacuzzi. *In room:* A/C, TV, dataport, coffeemaker, hair dryer.

OTHER AREA ACCOMMODATIONS

Cameron Trading Post Motel ★★ *Finds* Located 54 miles north of Flagstaff on U.S. 89 at the junction with the road to the east entrance of the national park, this motel offers some of the most attractive rooms in the vicinity of the Grand Canyon and is part of one of the best trading posts in the state. The motel, adjacent to the historic Cameron Trading Post, is built around the shady oasis of the old trading post's terraced gardens. The garden terraces are built of sandstone, and there's even a picnic table made from a huge slab of stone. Guest rooms feature Southwestern-style furniture and attractive decor. Most have balconies, and some have views of the Little Colorado River (which, however, rarely has much water in it at this point). Don't miss the Navajo tacos in the dining room; the small ones are plenty big enough for a meal.

P.O. Box 339, Cameron, AZ 86020. ✆ **800/338-7385** or 928/679-2231. Fax 928/679-2501. www.camerontradingpost.com. 62 units. Jan–Feb $59–$69 double, $99–$129 suite; Mar–May $79–$89 double, $129–$159 suite; June to mid-Oct $99–$109 double, $149–$179 suite; mid-Oct to Dec $69–$79 double, $129–$159 suite. AE, DISC, MC, V. Pets accepted ($15 fee). **Amenities:** Restaurant. *In room:* A/C, TV, coffeemaker.

CAMPGROUNDS

Inside the Park

On the South Rim, there are two campgrounds and an RV park. **Mather Campground,** in Grand Canyon Village, has more than 300 campsites. Reservations can be made up to 6 months in advance and are highly recommended for stays between March and mid-November (reservations not accepted for other months). Contact the National Park Service Reservation Center (✆ **877/444-6777** or 518/885-3639; www.recreation.gov). Between late spring and early fall, don't even think of coming up here without a reservation; you'll just set yourself up for disappointment. If you don't have a reservation, your next best bet is to arrive in the morning, when sites are being vacated. Campsites are $18 per night ($15 per night mid-Nov to Feb; reservations not accepted).

Desert View Campground, with 50 sites, is 25 miles east of Grand Canyon Village and open from mid-May to mid-October only. No reservations are accepted. Campsites are $12 per night.

The **Trailer Village RV park,** with 84 RV sites, is in Grand Canyon Village and charges $27 per night (for two adults) for full hookup. Reservations can be made up to 13 months in advance by contacting **Grand Canyon National Park Lodges/ Xanterra Parks & Resorts,** 6312 S. Fiddlers Green Circle, Suite 600N, Greenwood Village, CO 80111 (✆ **888/297-2757** or 303/297-2757; www.xanterra.com or www.grandcanyonlodges.com). For same-day reservations, call ✆ **928/638-2631.**

Outside the Park

Two miles south of Tusayan is the U.S. Forest Service's **Ten-X Campground.** This campground has 70 campsites, is open May through September, and charges $10. It's usually your best bet for finding a site late in the day. This campground is open May through October, depending on the weather.

You can also camp just about anywhere within the **Kaibab National Forest,** which borders Grand Canyon National Park, as long as you are more than a quarter-mile away from Arizona 64/U.S. 180. Several dirt roads lead into the forest from the highway, and although you won't find designated campsites or toilets along these roads, you will find spots where others have obviously camped before. This so-called dispersed camping is usually used by campers who have been unable to find sites in campgrounds. One of the most popular roads for this sort of camping is on the west side of the highway between Tusayan and the park's south entrance. For more information, contact the **Tusayan Ranger District,** Kaibab National Forest, P.O. Box 3088, Grand Canyon, AZ 86023 (✆ **928/638-2443;** www.fs.fed.us/r3/kai).

WHERE TO DINE

INSIDE THE PARK

If you're looking for a quick, inexpensive meal, there are plenty of options. In Grand Canyon Village, choices include **cafeterias** at the Yavapai and Maswik lodges and a **delicatessen** at Canyon Village Marketplace on Market Plaza. The **Bright Angel Fountain,** at the back of the Bright Angel Lodge, serves hot dogs, sandwiches, and ice cream and is always crowded on hot days. My favorite place in the park to grab a quick bite is the **Hermit's Rest Snack Bar** at the west end of Hermit Road. The stone building that houses this snack bar was designed by Mary Elizabeth Jane Colter, who also designed several other buildings on the South Rim. At Desert View (near the east entrance to the park), there's the **Desert View Trading Post Cafeteria.** All of these places are open daily for all three meals, and all serve meals for $10 and under.

The Arizona Room SOUTHWESTERN Because this restaurant has the best view of the three dining establishments right on the South Rim, it is immensely popular. Add to this the fact that The Arizona Room has a menu (pan-seared salmon with melon salsa, baby back ribs with prickly pear or chipotle glaze) almost as creative as that of El Tovar Dining Room, and you'll understand why there is often a long wait for a table here. To avoid the wait, arrive early, which should assure you of getting a table with a good view out the picture windows. Once the sun goes down, the view is absolutely black, which means you could be dining anywhere—which would defeat the entire purpose. Because this restaurant is open for lunch part of the year, you've got another great option for dining with a billion-dollar view.

At the Bright Angel Lodge. ✆ **928/638-2631.** Reservations not accepted. Main courses $7.75–$12 lunch, $11–$26 dinner. AE, DC, DISC, MC, V. Daily 4:30–10pm (Mar–Oct also open for lunch daily 11:30am–3pm). Closed Jan–Feb.

Bright Angel Coffee Shop AMERICAN As the least expensive of the three restaurants right on the rim of the canyon, this casual Southwestern-themed coffeehouse in the historic Bright Angel Lodge stays packed throughout the day. Meals are simple and none too memorable, but if you can get one of the few tables near the windows, at least you get something of a view. The menu includes everything from burgers to Southwestern favorites such as tamales and fajitas to spaghetti (foods calculated to comfort tired and hungry hikers), but my favorite offerings are the bread bowls full of chili and stew. Wines are available, and service is generally friendly and efficient.

At the Bright Angel Lodge. ✆ **928/638-2631.** Reservations not accepted. Main courses $7–$16. AE, DC, DISC, MC, V. Daily 6:30–10pm.

El Tovar Dining Room ★★ CONTINENTAL/SOUTHWESTERN If you're staying at El Tovar, you'll want to have dinner in the hotel's rustic yet elegant dining room. But before making reservations at the most expensive restaurant in the park, be aware that few tables have views of the canyon. However, despite the limited views, the meals served here are the best in the park. The menu leans heavily to the spicy flavors of the Southwest, though plenty of milder, more familiar dishes are offered as well. The New York steak with crispy onion rings is a good bet, as is the wild salmon. Start your meal with the interesting little roulades (flavorful bite-size tortilla roll-ups). Service is generally quite good. Have a drink in the bar before dinner (you might even be able to snag a table with a view).

At El Tovar Hotel. ✆ **928/638-2631,** ext. 6432. Reservations highly recommended for dinner. Main courses $10–$15 lunch, $19–$30 dinner. AE, DC, DISC, MC, V. Daily 6:30–11am, 11:30am–2pm, and 5–10pm.

IN TUSAYAN (OUTSIDE THE SOUTH ENTRANCE)

In addition to the restaurants listed below, you'll find a steakhouse and a pizza place, as well as familiar chains such as McDonald's, Pizza Hut, and Wendy's.

Canyon Star Restaurant and Saloon ★ AMERICAN/MEXICAN This place aims to compete with El Tovar Dining Room and The Arizona Room, and serves the most creative Southwestern fare this side of the park boundary, plus you'll have live entertainment while you eat. Try the barbecued buffalo brisket (at lunch, go for the buffalo burger). Evening shows include performances of Native American songs and dances. This place is big, so there usually isn't too long a wait for a table, and even if there is, you can head for the saloon and saddle up a bar stool (some of the stools have saddles instead of seats) while you wait.

At the Grand Hotel, Ariz. 64. ✆ **928/638-3333.** Reservations not accepted. Main courses $7–$13 lunch, $15–$28 dinner. AE, DISC, MC, V. Daily 7–10am and 11am–10pm.

Coronado Room ★ CONTINENTAL/SOUTHWESTERN If you should suddenly be struck by an overpowering desire to have escargot for dinner, don't despair—head for the Best Western Grand Canyon Squire Inn. Now, I'm well aware that Best Western and escargot go together about as well as the Eiffel Tower and rattlesnake fritters, but this place really does serve classic Continental fare way out here in the Arizona high country. You'll probably want to stick to the steaks, though (or the wild game such as elk tournedos). You might also want to try a few of the Southwestern appetizers on the menu.

At the Best Western Grand Canyon Squire Inn, Ariz. 64. ✆ **928/638-2681.** Reservations recommended. Main courses $18–$29. AE, DC, DISC, MC, V. Daily 5–10pm.

2 The Grand Canyon North Rim ★★★

42 miles S of Jacob Lake; 216 miles N of Grand Canyon Village (South Rim); 354 miles N of Phoenix; 125 miles W of Page/Lake Powell

Although the North Rim of the Grand Canyon is only 10 miles from the South Rim as the crow flies, it's more than 200 miles by road, and because it is such a long drive from population centers such as Phoenix and Las Vegas, the North Rim is much less crowded than the South Rim. Additionally, due to heavy snowfall, the North Rim is open only from mid-May to late October or early November. There are also far fewer activities or establishments on the North Rim than there are on the South Rim (no helicopter or plane rides, no IMAX theater, no McDonald's). For these reasons, most of the millions who annually visit the Grand Canyon never make it to this side—and that is exactly why, in my opinion, the North Rim is a far superior place to visit. If Grand Canyon Village turns out to be more human zoo than the wilderness experience you expected, the North Rim will probably be much more to your liking, although crowds, traffic congestion, and parking problems are not unheard of here, either.

The North Rim is on the Kaibab Plateau, which is more than 8,000 feet high on average and takes its name from the Paiute word for "mountain lying down." The higher elevation of the North Rim means that instead of the mix of junipers interspersed with ponderosa pines of the South Rim, you'll see dense forests of ponderosa pines, Douglas firs, and aspens interspersed with large meadows. Consequently, the North Rim has a much more alpine feel than the South Rim. The elevation—1,000 feet higher than the South Rim—also means that the North Rim gets considerably more snow in winter than the South Rim. The highway south from Jacob Lake is not plowed in winter, when the Grand Canyon Lodge closes down.

ESSENTIALS

GETTING THERE The North Rim is at the end of Arizona 67 (the North Rim Pkwy.), reached from U.S. 89A. **Trans Canyon** (© **928/638-2820**) operates a shuttle between the North Rim and the South Rim of the Grand Canyon during the months the North Rim is open. The trip takes 5 hours; the fare is $70 one-way and $130 round-trip (reservations required).

FEES The park entry fee is $25 per car and is good for 1 week. Remember not to lose the little paper receipt that serves as your admission pass.

VISITOR INFORMATION For information before leaving home, contact **Grand Canyon National Park,** P.O. Box 129, Grand Canyon, AZ 86023 (© **928/638-7888;** www.nps.gov/grca). At the entrance gate, you'll be given a copy of *The Guide,* a small newspaper with information on park activities. There's also an **information desk** in the lobby of the Grand Canyon Lodge.

Tips An Important Note

Visitor facilities at the North Rim are open only from mid-May to mid-October. From mid-October to November (or until snow closes the road to the North Rim), the park is open for day use only. The campground may be open after mid-October, weather permitting.

EXPLORING THE PARK

While it's hard to beat the view from a rustic rocking chair on the terrace of the Grand Canyon Lodge, the best spots for seeing the canyon are Bright Angel Point, Point Imperial, and Cape Royal. **Bright Angel Point** is at the end of a half-mile trail near the Grand Canyon Lodge, and from here you can see and hear Roaring Springs, which are 3,600 feet below the rim and are the North Rim's only water source. You can also see Grand Canyon Village on the South Rim.

At 8,803 feet, **Point Imperial** is the highest point on the North Rim. A short section of the Colorado River can be seen far below, and off to the east the Painted Desert is visible. The Point Imperial/Nankoweap Trail leads north from here along the rim of the canyon. However, this area was burned in a forest fire in 2000.

Cape Royal is the most spectacular setting on the North Rim, and along the 23-mile road to this viewpoint you'll find several other scenic overlooks. Across the road from the **Walhalla Overlook** are the ruins of an Ancestral Puebloan structure, and just before reaching Cape Royal, you'll come to the **Angel's Window Overlook,** which gives you a breathtaking view of the natural bridge that forms Angel's Window. Once at Cape Royal, you can follow a trail across this natural bridge to a towering promontory overlooking the canyon.

Once you've had your fill of simply taking in the views, you may want to get out and stretch your legs on a trail or two. Quite a few day hikes of varying lengths and difficulty are possible. The shortest is the .5-mile paved trail to Bright Angel Point, along which you'll have plenty of company but also plenty of breathtaking views. If you have time for only one hike while you're here, make it down the **North Kaibab Trail.** This trail is 14 miles long and leads down to Phantom Ranch and the Colorado River. To hike the entire trail, you'll need to have a camping permit and be in very good physical condition (it's almost 6,000 ft. to the canyon floor). For a day hike, most people make Roaring Springs their goal. This hike is 9½ miles round-trip, involves a descent and ascent of 3,000 feet, and takes 7 to 8 hours. You can shorten this hike considerably by turning around at the Supai Tunnel, which is fewer than 1,500 feet below the rim at the 2-mile point. For a relatively easy hike away from the crowds, try the Widforss Point Trail.

If you want to see the canyon from a saddle, contact **Grand Canyon Trail Rides** (**© 435/679-8665;** www.canyonrides.com), which offers mule rides varying in length from 1 hour ($30) to a full day ($125).

EN ROUTE TO OR FROM THE NORTH RIM

Between Page and the North Rim of the Grand Canyon, U.S. 89A crosses the Colorado River at **Lees Ferry** in Marble Canyon. The original **Navajo Bridge** over the river here was replaced in 1995, and the old bridge is now open to pedestrians. From the bridge, which is 470 feet above the Colorado River, there's a beautiful view of Marble Canyon. At the west end of the bridge, you'll find the Navajo Bridge Interpretive Center, which is operated by the National Park Service and is partly housed in a stone building built during the Depression by the Civilian Conservation Corps (CCC). At the east end of the bridge, which is on the Navajo Reservation, interpretive signs tell the story of Lees Ferry from the Native American perspective.

Lees Ferry is the starting point for raft trips through the Grand Canyon, and for many years it was the only place to cross the Colorado River for hundreds of miles in either direction. This stretch of the river is now legendary among anglers for its trophy trout fishing. Lees Ferry has a 54-site campground (✆ **928/355-2320**); campsites are $10 per night and reservations are not accepted.

Lees Ferry Anglers (✆ **800/962-9755** or 928/355-2261; www.leesferry.com), 11 miles west of the bridge at Lees Ferry, is fishing headquarters for the region. Not only does it sell all manner of fly-fishing tackle and offer advice about good spots to try your luck, but it operates a guide service and rents waders and boats. A guide and boat costs $300 per day for one person, and $375 per day for two people. At Lees Ferry Lodge, there is also a fly shop, and you can hire a guide through **Ambassador Guides** (✆ **800/256-7596;** www.ambassadorguides.com), which charges $425 per day for one angler or two anglers if you go out in a boat. Lake Powell guide service is also available.

Continuing west, the highway passes under the **Vermilion Cliffs,** so named for their deep-red coloring. At the base of these cliffs are huge boulders balanced on narrow columns of eroded soil. The balanced rocks give the area an otherworldly appearance. Along this unpopulated stretch of road are a couple of very basic lodges.

Seventeen miles west of Marble Canyon you'll see a sign for **House Rock Ranch.** This wildlife area, managed by the Arizona Game and Fish Department, is best known for its herd of bison (American buffalo). From the turnoff, it's a 22-mile drive south on a gravel road to reach the ranch.

Along this same stretch of road, you'll find the gravel road that leads north to the **Coyote Buttes** ★★★, which are among the most unusual rock formations in Arizona. Basically, these striated conical sandstone hills are petrified sand dunes, which should give you a good idea of why one area of the Coyote Buttes is called The Wave. The buttes are a favorite of photographers. You must have a permit ($5 per person) to visit this area, and only 20 people are allowed to visit each day (with a maximum group size of six people). Reservations must be made 4 months in advance on the first of the month at exactly noon. With the exception of reservations for July and August, all available permits are usually reserved within a few minutes after noon. There's no actual trail to the buttes, so you have to navigate by way of the simple map that you'll be sent when you receive your permit. For more information, contact the **Arizona Strip Interpretive Association/Interagency Visitor Center,** 345 E. Riverside Dr., St. George, UT 84770 (✆ **435/688-3246;** www.az.blm.gov/asfo/asia.htm).

One last detour to consider before or after visiting the national park is an area known as the **East Rim.** This area lies just outside the park in Kaibab National Forest and can be reached by turning east on gravel Forest Road (FR) 611 about ¾ mile south of DeMotte Campground, which is a few miles north of the park entrance. Follow Forest Road 611 for 1½ miles to Forest Road 610 and turn south. Continue for 3 miles to the East Rim Viewpoint. Another good view can be had from the Marble viewpoint at the end of Forest Road 219, a 4-mile-long dead-end spur road off Forest Road 610 about 6 miles from the junction with FR 611. For more information, contact the **North Kaibab Ranger Station,** 430 S. Main St. (P.O. Box 248), Fredonia, AZ 86022 (✆ **928/643-7395;** www.fs.fed.us/r3/kai), or the **Kaibab Plateau Visitors Center,** HC 64, Arizona 67/U.S. 89A, Jacob Lake, AZ 86022 (✆ **928/643-7298**), which is open only during the summer.

NORTH OF THE PARK

To learn more about the pioneer history of this remote and sparsely populated region of the state (known as the Arizona Strip), continue west from Jacob Lake 45 miles on Arizona 389 to **Pipe Spring National Monument,** 406 N. Pipe Spring Rd., Fredonia (✆ **928/643-7105;** www.nps.gov/pisp), which preserves an early Mormon ranch house that was built in the style of a fort for protection from Indians. This "fort" was also known as Winsor Castle and occasionally housed the wives of polygamists hiding out from the law. Tours of Winsor Castle are offered throughout the day; a small museum contains exhibits on both Mormon settlers and the Paiute Indians who have long inhabited this region. In summer, there are living-history demonstrations. The monument is open daily (except New Year's Day, Thanksgiving, and Christmas) from 7am to 5pm June through August, and from 8am to 5pm the rest of the year. Admission is $5 per adult.

Southwest of Pipe Spring, in an area accessible only via long gravel roads, lies the **Grand Canyon-Parashant National Monument.** This monument preserves a vast and rugged landscape north of the east end of Grand Canyon National Park. The monument has no facilities and no paved roads. For more information, contact the Bureau of Land Management's **Interagency Information Center,** 345 E. Riverside Dr., St. George, UT 84790 (✆ **435/688-3200;** www.nps.gov/para).

If you're a fan of Native American rock art and are searching for a memorable and uncrowded adventure, make time to visit the remote **Snake Gulch,** west of Jacob Lake. The red-and-yellow pictographs in this remote canyon date from the Basketmaker period (300 B.C.–A.D. 800) and are among the most impressive and extensive in the state. The first shallow cave is about 2 miles from the trail head. Continue down the canyon for 2 or 3 miles to find many more shallow caves with pictographs. To reach the Snake Gulch trail head, drive ¼ mile south of Jacob Lake Visitor Center on Arizona 67, turn west on Forest Road 461, and follow this road and Forest Road 462 for about 9 miles. Turn south on Forest Road 422 and continue 2 miles, and then go west on Forest Road 423 for 1¼ miles to Forest Road 642. Drive north 2 miles on Forest Road 642 to the trail head at the end of the road. This route involves about 15 miles of driving on gravel roads that are passable to regular passenger vehicles unless there has been recent rain or snow. Alternatively, you can drive south from Fredonia on a good paved road (FR 422), which turns to gravel a short distance before the Forest Road 642 junction. Carry plenty of water, especially in summer, when it can be extremely hot here. Spring and fall are the best times to visit. For more information, contact the North Kaibab Ranger District, 430 S. Main St. (P.O. Box 248), Fredonia, AZ 86022 (✆ **928/643-7398**).

WHERE TO STAY

INSIDE THE PARK

Grand Canyon Lodge ★★ Perched right on the canyon rim, this classic mountain lodge is listed on the National Register of Historic Places and is as impressive a lodge as any you'll find in a national park. The stone-and-log main building has a soaring ceiling and a viewing room set up with chairs facing a wall of glass, and on either side of this room are flagstone terraces furnished with rustic chairs. Accommodations vary from standard motel units to rustic mountain cabins to comfortable modern cabins. My favorites are still the frontier cabins, which, although cramped and paneled with dark wood, capture the feeling of a mountain retreat better than any of the other options. A few units have views of the canyon, but most are tucked back away from the rim. The dining hall has two walls of glass to take in the awesome canyon views.

Xanterra Parks & Resorts, 6312 S. Fiddlers Green Circle, Suite 600N, Greenwood Village, CO 80111. ✆ **888/297-2757** or 303/297-2757, or 928/638-2611 for same-day reservations. Fax 303/297-3175. www.grandcanyonnorthrim.com. 205 units. $102–$147 double. Children 16 and under stay free in parent's room. AE, DC, DISC, MC, V. Closed mid-Oct to mid-May. **Amenities:** 2 restaurants (American); lounge; tour desk; coin-op laundry.

OUTSIDE THE PARK

North of the national park, the next closest lodgings are the Kaibab Lodge and the Jacob Lake Inn. You'll also find lots of budget accommodations in Kanab, Utah, 37 miles west of Jacob Lake.

Jacob Lake Inn This is one of only two lodges outside the entrance to the North Rim of Grand Canyon National Park, and, because it is at the crossroads of Jacob Lake, it is always a busy spot in summer. While most of the units here are old cabins that tend to be cramped and old fashioned, there are also two dozen modern motel-style rooms in a contemporary mountain rustic lodge. It is these latter rooms, which are the inn's only rooms with TVs, telephones, and high-speed Internet access, that I recommend. Sure, they're more expensive than the cabins, but they are the nicest rooms in the area. Be sure to stock up on cookies at the inn's bakery.

Ariz. 67/U.S. 89A, Jacob Lake, AZ 86022. ✆ **928/643-7232** or 928/643-7898. www.jacoblake.com. 69 units. $75–$122 cabin double; $94–$123 motel/lodge double. AE, DISC, MC, V. Pets accepted ($10 per night). **Amenities:** Restaurant (American); bakery; playground.

EN ROUTE TO THE PARK

If you don't have a reservation at the North Rim's Grand Canyon Lodge, you should call the places recommended below to see if you can get a reservation. If so, you can continue on to the North Rim the next morning. Lodges anywhere near the canyon fill up early in the day if they aren't already fully booked with reservations made months in advance.

Cliff Dwellers Lodge There isn't much else out this way except this remote lodge, which is affiliated with Lees Ferry Anglers and tends to stay filled up with trout anglers and rafters. The newer, more expensive rooms are standard motel units with combination tub/showers, while the older rooms, in an interesting stone-walled building, have knotty-pine walls and showers only. Despite the rusticity of these latter rooms, they are among my favorites in the area. The lodge is close to some spectacular balanced rocks, and it's about 11 miles east to Lees Ferry. The views are unforgettable.

U.S. 89A milepost 547 (H.C. 67, Box 30), Marble Canyon, AZ 86036. ✆ **800/962-9755** or 928/355-2261. Fax 928/355-2271. www.cliffdwellerslodge.com. 21 units. Mar–Nov $70–$80 double, $200 3-bedroom house; Dec–Feb $50 double, $150 3-bedroom house. AE, DISC, MC, V. **Amenities:** Restaurant (American). *In room:* A/C, TV, coffeemaker, no phone.

Lees Ferry Lodge at Vermilion Cliffs Located at the foot of the Vermilion Cliffs, 3½ miles west of the Colorado River, Lees Ferry Lodge, built in 1929 of native stone and rough-hewn timber beams, is a small place with simple, rustic accommodations. However, the lodge's restaurant serves as a sort of de facto community center for area residents, and owner Maggie Sacher is usually on hand to answer questions and share stories. Also, the patio seating area in front of the lodge has fabulous views. Boat rentals and fly-fishing guides can be arranged through the lodge. The restaurant here has a great, old-fashioned atmosphere. With its rustic character and friendly feel, this is my favorite place to stay in the area. Don't miss it.

U.S. 89A (H.C. 67, Box 1), Marble Canyon, AZ 86036. ✆ **800/451-2231** or 928/355-2231. www.leesferrylodge.com. 12 units. $53–$70 double. Children under 5 stay free in parent's room. AE, DISC, MC, V. Pets accepted. **Amenities:** Restaurant (American); game room. *In room:* A/C, coffeemaker, no phone.

Marble Canyon Lodge The Marble Canyon Lodge, built in the 1920s just 4 miles from Lees Ferry, is popular with both rafters and anglers. Accommodations vary considerably in size and age, with some rustic units in old stone buildings and newer motel-style rooms available as well. These latter rooms are the best in the area. You're right at the base of the Vermilion Cliffs here, and the views are great. In addition to the restaurant, there's a general store and fly shop where you can rent a boat or hire a guide. P.O. Box 6032, Marble Canyon, AZ 86036. ✆ **800/726-1789** or 928/355-2225. Fax 928/355-2227. www.mcg-leesferry.com. 56 units. $56–$72 double; $74–$88 cottage; $123–$136 apt. Children under 12 stay free in parent's room. AE, DISC, MC, V. Pets accepted. **Amenities:** Restaurant (American). *In room:* A/C, TV, no phone.

CAMPGROUNDS

Located just north of Grand Canyon Lodge, the **North Rim Campground,** with 75 sites and no hookups for RVs, is the only campground at the North Rim. It's open mid-May to mid-October. Reservations can be made up to 6 months in advance by calling the National Recreation Reservation Service (✆ **877/444-6777** or 518/885-3639; www.recreation.gov). Campsites cost $15 to $20 per night.

There are two nearby campgrounds outside the park in the Kaibab National Forest. They are **DeMotte Campground,** which is the closest to the park entrance and has 23 sites, and **Jacob Lake Campground,** which is 30 miles north of the park entrance and has 53 sites. Both charge between $14 and $16 per night and do not take reservations. They're open May 15 to November 1. You can also camp anywhere in the Kaibab National Forest as long as you're more than a quarter-mile from a paved road or water source. So if you can't find a site in a campground, simply pull off the highway in the national forest and park your RV or pitch your tent.

The **Kaibab Camper Village** (✆ **800/525-0924,** 928/643-7804 May 15–Oct 15, or 928/526-0924 other months; www.kaibabcampervillage.com) is a privately owned campground in the crossroads of Jacob Lake, 30 miles north of the park entrance. It's open from mid-May to mid-October and has around 100 sites. Rates are $13 for tent sites, $27 for RV sites with full hookups. Make reservations well in advance.

WHERE TO DINE

INSIDE THE PARK

Grand Canyon Lodge has a dining room with a splendid view. Because this restaurant is so popular, reservations are required for dinner. More casual choices at the lodge include a cafeteria and a saloon that serves light meals.

OUTSIDE THE PARK

Your only choices for a meal outside the park are the **Kaibab Lodge,** just north of the entrance, and the **Jacob Lake Inn** (✆ **928/643-7232;** www.jacoblake.com), 45 miles north at the junction with U.S. 89A.

3 Flagstaff ★★

150 miles N of Phoenix; 32 miles E of Williams; 80 miles S of Grand Canyon Village

With its wide variety of accommodations and restaurants, the great outdoors at the edge of town, three national monuments nearby, one of the state's finest museums, and a university that supports a lively cultural community, Flagstaff makes an ideal base for exploring much of northern Arizona.

The San Francisco Peaks, just north of the city, are the site of the Arizona Snowbowl ski area, one of the state's main winter playgrounds. In summer, miles of trails through these same mountains attract hikers and mountain bikers, and it's even possible to ride the chairlift for a panoramic vista that stretches 70 miles north to the

Grand Canyon. Of the area's national monuments, two preserve ancient Indian ruins and one an otherworldly landscape of volcanic cinder cones.

It was as a railroad town that Flagstaff made its fortunes, and after several years of renovations, the historic downtown offers a glimpse of the days when the city's fortunes rode the rails. The railroad still runs right through the middle of Flagstaff, much to the dismay of many visitors, who find that most of the city's inexpensive motels (and even some of the more expensive places) are too close to the busy tracks to allow them to get a good night's sleep.

ESSENTIALS

GETTING THERE Flagstaff is on I-40, one of the main east-west interstates in the United States. I-17 starts here and heads south to Phoenix. Arizona 89A connects Flagstaff to Sedona by way of Oak Creek Canyon. U.S. 180 connects Flagstaff with the South Rim of the Grand Canyon, and U.S. 89 connects the city with Page.

Pulliam Airport, 3 miles south of Flagstaff off I-17, is served by **US Airways** (© **800/428-4322**) from Phoenix. **Amtrak** (© **800/872-7245**) offers service to Flagstaff from Chicago and Los Angeles. The train station is at 1 E. Rte. 66.

VISITOR INFORMATION Contact the **Flagstaff Visitor Center,** 1 E. Rte. 66 (© **800/842-7293** or 928/774-9541; www.flagstaffarizona.org). The visitor center is open Monday through Saturday from 8am to 5pm and Sunday from 9am to 4pm.

ORIENTATION Downtown Flagstaff is just north of I-40. Milton Road, which at its southern end becomes I-17 to Phoenix, leads past Northern Arizona University on its way into downtown and becomes Route 66, which runs parallel to the railroad tracks. San Francisco Street is downtown's main street. Humphreys Street leads north out of town toward the San Francisco Peaks and the South Rim of the Grand Canyon.

GETTING AROUND Car rentals are available from **Avis** (© 800/331-1212), **Budget** (© 800/527-0700), **Enterprise** (© 800/261-7331), **Hertz** (© 800/654-3131), and **National** (© 800/227-7368).

Call **A Friendly Cab** (© 928/774-4444) if you need a taxi. **Mountain Line Transit** (© 928/779-6624) provides public bus transit around the city; the fare is $1.

OUTDOOR PURSUITS

Flagstaff is northern Arizona's center for outdoor activities. Chief among them is skiing at **Arizona Snowbowl** (© **928/779-1951;** www.arizonasnowbowl.com), on the slopes of Mount Agassiz, from which you can see all the way to the North Rim of the Grand Canyon. There are four chairlifts, 32 runs, 2,300 vertical feet of slopes, ski rentals, and a children's ski program. With an excellent mix of beginner, intermediate, and advanced slopes, and as the ski area that's most easily accessed from Phoenix, Snowbowl sees a lot of weekend traffic from the snow-starved denizens of the desert. Conditions are, however, very unreliable, and the ski area can be shut down for weeks on end due to lack of snow. All-day lift tickets are $46 for adults, $25 for children 8 to 12, $25 for seniors, and free for children under 8 and seniors over 70. In summer, you can ride a chairlift almost to the summit of Mount Agassiz and enjoy the expansive views across seemingly all of northern Arizona. The round-trip lift-ticket price is $10 for adults, $8 for seniors, and $6 for children 8 to 12. To get here, take U.S. 180 N from Flagstaff for 7 miles and turn right onto Snow Bowl Road.

When there's no snow on the ground, there are plenty of trails for hiking throughout the San Francisco Peaks, and many national forest trails are open to mountain

Moments White Buffalo, Watchable Wildlife & a Tiny Chapel

As you drive north to the Grand Canyon on U.S. 180, about 20 miles north of Flagstaff, be sure to watch for **Spirit Mountain Ranch,** mile marker 236.5 (© **928/606-2779;** www.sacredwhitebuffalo.com), which is home to a small herd of white buffalo. These animals are considered sacred by Native Americans. The buffalo can be visited daily between 9am and 4pm, and admission is $5.

Across the road from Spirit Mountain Ranch, you can walk the 1.5-mile **Kendrick Park Watchable Wildlife Trail.** Along this trail, you might spot elk, pronghorn antelope, or mule deer grazing in the meadow. Also in this valley is the rustic little **Chapel of the Holy Dove,** a roadside chapel with a wall of glass facing the forest.

bikes. Late September, when the aspens have turned a brilliant golden yellow, is one of the best times of year for a hike in Flagstaff's mountains. If you've got the stamina, do the **Humphreys Peak Trail,** which climbs 3,000 feet in 4.5 miles. Needless to say, the views from the 12,633-foot summit are stupendous. After all, this is the highest point in Arizona. To reach the trail head, take U.S. 180 N out of Flagstaff for 7 miles, turn right on Snow Bowl Road, and continue to the parking area by the ski lodge. This is my favorite Flagstaff area hike and is nearly as awe inspiring in its own way as hiking down into the Grand Canyon.

If you'd like a short hike with a big payoff, hike to **Red Mountain.** This hike is only about 2.5 miles round-trip, but leads to a fascinating red-walled cinder cone that long ago collapsed to reveal its strange interior walls. To find the trail head, drive north from Flagstaff toward the Grand Canyon on U.S. 180. At milepost 247, watch for a forest road leading west for about a quarter-mile to the trail-head parking area.

For information on other hikes in the Coconino National Forest, contact the **Peaks Ranger District,** 5075 N. Hwy. 89, Flagstaff (© **928/526-0866;** www.fs.fed.us/r3/coconino).

SEEING THE SIGHTS

Downtown Flagstaff—along Route 66, San Francisco Street, Aspen Avenue, and Birch Avenue—is the city's **historic district.** These old brick buildings are now filled with shops selling Native American crafts, works by local artists and artisans, Route 66 souvenirs, and various other Arizona mementos such as rocks, minerals, and crystals. Don't miss **Jonathan Day's Indian Arts,** 21 N. San Francisco St. (© **928/779-6099;** www.traditionalhopikachinas.com), a small shop with what just might be the best selection of traditional Hopi kachinas in the state. Also worth a visit is **The Artists Gallery,** 17 N. San Francisco St. (© **928/773-0958;** www.theartistsgallery.net). The historic district is worth a walk-through even if you aren't shopping.

MUSEUMS, PARKS & CULTURAL ACTIVITIES

The Arboretum at Flagstaff Covering 200 acres, this arboretum, the highest-elevation research garden in the U.S., focuses on plants of the high desert, coniferous forests, and alpine tundra, all of which are environments found in the vicinity of Flagstaff. On the grounds are a butterfly garden, an herb garden, a shade garden, and a passive solar greenhouse. There are guided tours daily at 11am and 1pm. The arboretum also has regularly scheduled birds-of-prey presentations.

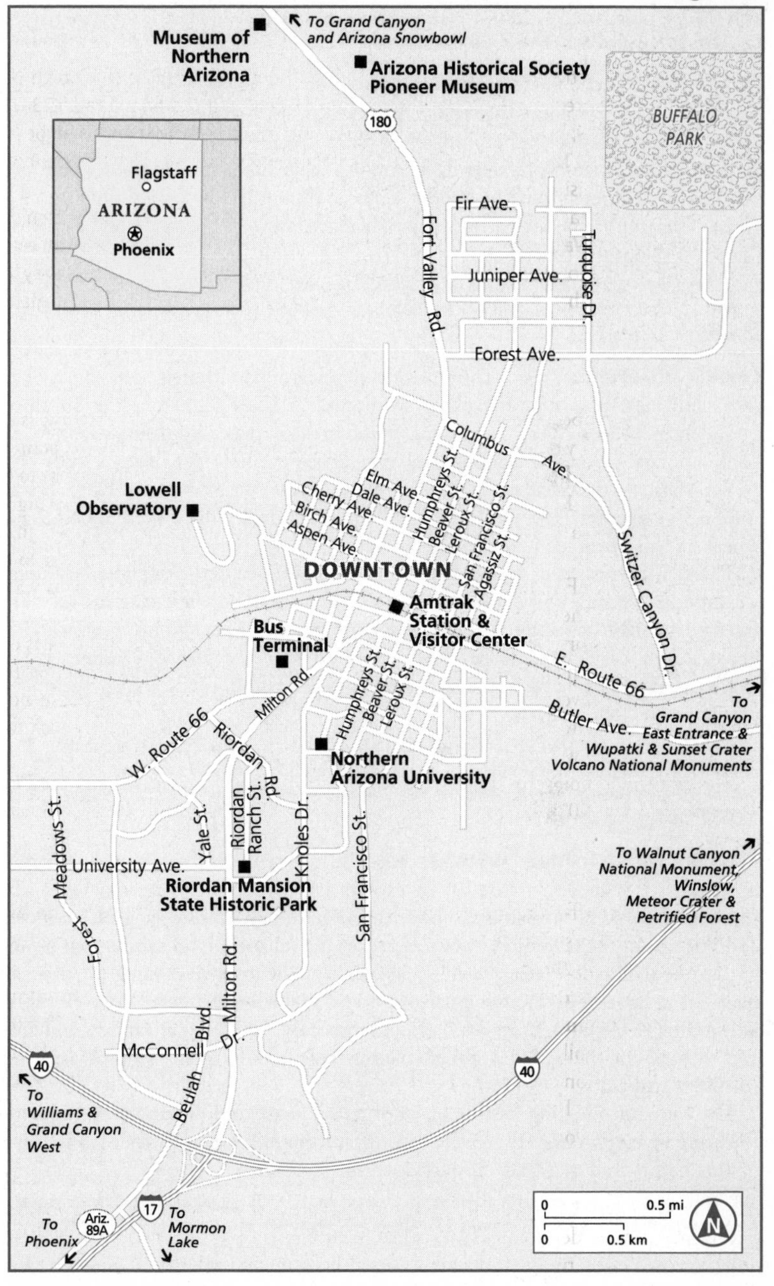

To Grand Canyon and Arizona Snowbowl
Museum of Northern Arizona
Arizona Historical Society Pioneer Museum
180
BUFFALO PARK
Flagstaff
ARIZONA
Phoenix
Fir Ave.
Fort Valley Rd.
Turquoise Dr.
Juniper Ave.
Forest Ave.
Columbus Ave.
Elm Ave.
Dale Ave.
Cherry Ave.
Birch Ave.
Aspen Ave.
Humphreys St.
Beaver St.
Leroux St.
San Francisco St.
Agassiz St.
Lowell Observatory
DOWNTOWN
Switzer Canyon Dr.
Amtrak Station & Visitor Center
Bus Terminal
E. Route 66
Milton Rd.
Butler Ave.
To Grand Canyon East Entrance & Wupatki & Sunset Crater Volcano National Monuments
W. Route 66
Riordan Rd.
Northern Arizona University
Meadows St.
Yale St.
Riordan Ranch St.
Knoles Dr.
San Francisco St.
University Ave.
Riordan Mansion State Historic Park
To Walnut Canyon National Monument, Winslow, Meteor Crater & Petrified Forest
Forest
Milton Rd.
Beulah Blvd.
McConnell Dr.
40
To Williams & Grand Canyon West
To Phoenix
Ariz. 89A
17
To Mormon Lake
0 0.5 mi
0 0.5 km
N

4001 S. Woody Mountain Rd. ✆ **928/774-1442.** www.thearb.org. Admission $5 adults, $2 children 6–17. Apr–Oct daily 9am–5pm. Guided tours at 11am and 1pm. Closed Nov–Mar.

Arizona Historical Society Pioneer Museum This small historical museum is housed in a stone building that was constructed in 1908 as a hospital for the indigent (in other words, a poor farm). Today, the old hospital contains a historical collection from northern Arizona's pioneer days. Among the exhibits are old photos and pieces of camera equipment used by Emery Kolb at his studio on the South Rim of the Grand Canyon. Barbed wire, livestock brands, saddles, and trapping and timber displays round out the collection.

2340 N. Fort Valley Rd. ✆ **928/774-6272.** www.arizonahistoricalsociety.org. Admission $3 adults, $2 seniors and students 12–18; free for all on 1st Sat of each month. Mon–Sat 9am–5pm. Closed New Year's Day, Thanksgiving, and Christmas.

Lowell Observatory ★ This historic observatory is located atop aptly named Mars Hill and is one of the oldest astronomical observatories in the Southwest. Founded in 1894 by Percival Lowell, the observatory has played important roles in contemporary astronomy. Among the work carried out here was Lowell's study of the planet Mars and the calculations that led him to predict the existence of Pluto. It wasn't until 13 years after Lowell's death that Pluto was finally discovered almost exactly where he had predicted it would be.

The facility consists of several observatories, a visitor center with numerous fun and educational exhibits, and outdoor displays. While it can be interesting to visit during the day, the main attraction is the chance to observe the stars and planets through the observatory's 24-inch telescope. Keep in mind that the telescope domes are not heated, so if you come up to stargaze, be sure to dress appropriately. Also, there are no programs on cloudy nights.

1400 W. Mars Hill Rd. ✆ **928/233-3211.** www.lowell.edu. Admission $6 adults, $5 seniors and students, $3 children 5–17. Mar–Oct daily 9am–5pm (tours on the hour 10am–4pm); Nov–Feb daily noon–5pm (tours on the hour 1–4pm). Telescope viewings: June–Aug Mon–Sat 5:30–9:30pm; Sept–May Wed and Fri–Sat 5:30–9:30pm. Closed Jan 1, Easter, Thanksgiving, and Dec 24–25.

Museum of Northern Arizona ★★ This small but surprisingly thorough museum is the ideal first stop on an exploration of northern Arizona. You'll learn, through state-of-the-art exhibits, about the archaeology, ethnology, geology, biology, and fine arts of the region. The cornerstone of the museum is an exhibit that explores life on the Colorado Plateau from 15,000 B.C. to the present. Among the other displays are a life-size kiva ceremonial room and a small but interesting collection of kachinas. The large gift shop is full of contemporary Native American arts and crafts, and throughout the summer special exhibits and sales focus on Hopi, Navajo, and Zuni arts and crafts.

The museum building itself is made of native stone and incorporates a courtyard featuring vegetation from the six life zones of northern Arizona. Outside is a short self-guided nature trail that leads through a narrow canyon.

3101 N. Fort Valley Rd. (3 miles north of downtown Flagstaff on U.S. 180). ✆ **928/774-5213.** www.musnaz.org. Admission $5 adults, $4 seniors, $3 students, $2 children 7–17. Daily 9am–5pm. Closed New Year's Day, Thanksgiving, and Christmas.

Riordan Mansion State Historic Park ★ Built in 1904 for local timber barons Michael and Timothy Riordan, this 13,000-square-foot mansion—Arizona's finest

Finds Grand Falls: The Chocolate Niagara

Calm down all you chocoholics. Grand Falls, 33 miles east of Flagstaff, only looks like liquid chocolate; it isn't a *real* chocolate waterfall. This said, it's still worth the drive out to see it. At 185 feet tall, these falls on the Little Colorado River are higher than Niagara Falls, although the falls do not carry nearly the volume of water that Niagara does. In fact, for most of the year, there's no water at all in Grand Falls. These falls only run during the spring snow-melt season (in years when there has been any snow) and after summer monsoons. Consequently, to see these falls, you need to have good timing. You also need a high clearance vehicle, since the last 10 miles of the route is on a washboard gravel road that can be impassable if it has rained recently.

To find Grand Falls, drive north from Flagstaff on U.S. 89A, and turn east on Townsend-Winona Road. Drive 8 miles to Leupp Road, and turn left. Follow this road 14 miles to Indian Route 70, which is immediately after the sign marking the boundary of the Navajo reservation (watch for a sign for GRAND FALLS BIBLE CHURCH). Turn north (left) onto this gravel road and drive 10 miles north to the Little Colorado River. Now turn around and go back ¼ mile to the unmarked rough dirt track on your right. The falls are a few hundred yards down this dirt road.

example of an Arts and Crafts–era building—is actually two houses connected by a large central hall. Each brother and his family occupied half of the house (they had the rooflines constructed differently so that visitors could tell the two sides apart). Although the mansion looks like a log cabin, it's actually faced with log slabs. Inside, mission-style furnishings and touches of Art Nouveau styling make it clear that this family was keeping up with the times. The west wing of the mansion holds displays on, among other things, Stickley furniture. Guided tours provide a glimpse into the lives of two of Flagstaff's most influential pioneers.

409 W. Riordan Rd. (off Milton Rd./Ariz. 89A, just north of the junction of I-40 and I-17). ✆ **928/779-4395.** www.azstateparks.com. Admission $6 adults, $2.50 children 7–13. May–Oct daily 8:30am–5pm; Nov–Apr daily 10:30am–5pm. Guided tours on the hour. Closed Christmas.

Sunset Crater Volcano National Monument ★ Dotting the landscape northeast of Flagstaff are more than 400 volcanic craters, of which Sunset Crater Volcano is the youngest. Taking its name from the colors of the cinders near its summit, Sunset Crater Volcano stands 1,000 feet tall and began forming in 1064. Over a period of 100 years, the volcano erupted repeatedly (creating the red-and-yellow cinder cone seen today) and eventually covered an area of 800 square miles with ash, lava, and cinders. A 1-mile interpretive trail passes through a desolate landscape of lava flows, cinders, and ash as it skirts the base of this volcano. If you want to climb to the top of a cinder cone, take the 1-mile Lenox Crater Trail. In the visitor center (at the west entrance to the national monument), you can learn more about the formation of Sunset Crater and about volcanoes in general. Near the visitor center is the small Bonito Campground, which is open from late May to mid-October.

14 miles north of Flagstaff off U.S. 89. ✆ **928/526-0502.** www.nps.gov/sucr. Admission $5 adults, free for children 16 and under (admission also valid for Wupatki National Monument). Daily sunrise–sunset; visitor center daily May–Oct 8am–5pm, Nov–Apr 9am–5pm. Visitor center closed Christmas.

Walnut Canyon National Monument ★ The remains of 300 small 13th-century Sinagua cliff dwellings can be seen in the undercut layers of limestone in this 400-foot-deep wooded canyon east of Flagstaff. These cliff dwellings, though not nearly as impressive as the ruins at Montezuma Castle National Monument (50 miles to the south) or Wupatki National Monument (20 miles to the north), are worth a visit for the chance to poke around inside the well-preserved rooms, which were well protected from the elements (and from enemies). The Sinagua were the same people who built and then abandoned the stone pueblos in Wupatki National Monument, and it is theorized that when the land to the north lost its fertility, the Sinagua began migrating southward, settling for 150 years in Walnut Canyon.

A self-guided trail leads from the visitor center on the canyon rim down 185 feet to a section of the canyon wall where 25 cliff dwellings can be viewed up close (some can even be entered). Bring binoculars so that you can scan the canyon walls for other cliff dwellings. From Memorial Day to Labor Day three times each month, there are guided hikes into the monument's backcountry (reservations required). There's also a picnic area near the visitor center.

7½ miles east of Flagstaff on Walnut Canyon Rd. (take Exit 204 off I-40). ✆ **928/526-3367**. www.nps.gov/waca. Admission $5 adults, free for children 16 and under. May–Oct daily 8am–5pm; Nov–Apr daily 9am–5pm; trail closes 1 hr. earlier. Visitor center closed Christmas.

Wupatki National Monument ★★ The landscape northeast of Flagstaff is desolate and windswept, a sparsely populated region carpeted with volcanic ash deposited in the 11th century. It comes as quite a surprise, then, to learn that this area contains hundreds of Native American habitation sites. The most impressive ruins are those left by the Sinagua (the name means "without water" in Spanish), who inhabited this area from around 1100 until shortly after 1200. The Sinagua people built small villages of stone similar to the pueblos on the nearby Hopi Reservation, and today the ruins of these ancient villages can be seen in this national monument.

The largest of the pueblos is Wupatki Ruin, in the southeastern part of the monument. Here the Sinagua built a sprawling three-story pueblo containing nearly 100 rooms. They also constructed what is believed to be a ball court which, although quite different in design from the courts of the Aztec and Maya, suggests that a similar game may have been played in this region. Another circular stone structure just below the main ruins may have been an amphitheater or dance plaza.

The most unusual feature of Wupatki, however, is a natural phenomenon: a blowhole, which may have been the reason this pueblo was constructed here. A network of small underground tunnels and chambers acts as a giant barometer, blowing air through the blowhole when the underground air is under greater pressure than the outside air. On hot days, cool air rushes out of the blowhole with amazing force.

Several other ruins within the national monument are easily accessible by car. They include Nalakihu, Citadel, and Lomaki, which are the closest to U.S. 89; and Wukoki, near Wupatki. Wukoki Ruin, built atop a huge sandstone boulder, is particularly picturesque. The visitor center is adjacent to the Wupatki ruins and contains interesting exhibits on the Sinagua and Ancestral Puebloan people who once inhabited the region.

33 miles north of Flagstaff off U.S. 89. ✆ **928/679-2365**. www.nps.gov/wupa. Admission $5 adults, free for children 16 and under (admission also valid for Sunset Crater Volcano National Monument). Daily sunrise–sunset. Visitor center daily 9am–5pm. Visitor center closed Christmas.

Moments **Join an Archaeological Dig**

Elden Pueblo, on the north side of Flagstaff on U.S. 89, is a small archaeological site that is open to the public free of charge. Although these Sinagua ruins are not much to look at, you can help out with the excavation of the site if you're interested. Each summer, the **Elden Pueblo Archaeological Project** (© **928/527-3452**) hosts a field school for members of the Arizona Archaeological Society (AAS). Field schools cost $100 per week (plus $30 to become an AAS member).

WHERE TO STAY

EXPENSIVE

The Inn at 410 ★★ Situated only 2 blocks from historic downtown Flagstaff, this restored 1894 Craftsman home is one of the best B&Bs in Arizona, providing convenience, pleasant surroundings, comfortable rooms, and delicious breakfasts. Guests can lounge and enjoy afternoon tea on the front porch, in the comfortable dining room, or out on the pleasant garden patio. Each guest room features a distinctive theme; my favorites are Canyon Memories and the Southwest Suite, which conjure up the inn's Western heritage. All rooms have fireplaces, and three have two-person whirlpool tubs. Some of the guest rooms are in an adjacent building, and these rooms are just as nice as those in the main house.

410 N. Leroux St., Flagstaff, AZ 86001. © **800/774-2008** or 928/774-0088. Fax 928/774-6354. www.inn410.com. 9 units. $165–$230 double. 2-night minimum on weekends Apr–Oct. Rates include full breakfast and afternoon refreshments. AE, MC, V. No children under 5. **Amenities:** Access to nearby health club; concierge; business center; massage; babysitting; guest laundry. *In room:* A/C, TV/DVD/VCR, fridge, coffeemaker, hair dryer, iron, Wi-Fi, no phone.

Shooting Star Inn ★ *Finds* Although this rustic inn has only two simply furnished rooms and is a bit out-of-the-way (about midway between Flagstaff and the Grand Canyon), it is so unusual I think you should know about it. It's definitely not for everyone, but a stay here just might be the most memorable part of a visit to northern Arizona. The modern log inn is an off-the-grid home, which means that electricity here is produced by an array of photovoltaic panels. Also, water is trucked in regularly because there is no source of water in the remote valley where the inn is located. The Shooting Star is operated by professional photographer Tom Taylor, whose real passion is astronomy; as part of your stay, you'll get to study the stars and planets through some of Taylor's many telescopes. Because the inn is so far from town, you may want to arrange to have Taylor cook dinners for you.

27948 N. Shooting Star Lane, Flagstaff, AZ 86001. © **928/606-8070.** www.shootingstarinn.com. 2 units. $175 double. Rates include full breakfast and astronomy program. AE, DISC, MC, V. *In room:* Wi-Fi, no phone.

MODERATE

England House Bed & Breakfast ★★ This B&B, just 3 blocks from Flagstaff's historic downtown, is a beautiful two-story Victorian red-sandstone house built in 1902. This old house, which opened as an inn in 2004, was lovingly restored by owners Richard and Laurel Dunn, who are devoted to details. Consequently, this inn has a delightful period authenticity. The three large guest rooms are on the second floor and are furnished with 1870s French antiques. There's also a small guest room, called The Pantry (though it isn't really *that* small), on the ground floor. One room even has a Tempur-Pedic mattress, while another has a feather bed. Breakfasts are served in a bright sunroom just off the kitchen.

614 W. Santa Fe Ave., Flagstaff, AZ 86001. ✆ **877/214-7350** or 928/214-7350. www.englandhousebandb.com. 4 units. $125–$195 double. Rates include full breakfast. DISC, MC, V. No children under 12. **Amenities:** Jacuzzi; concierge. *In room:* A/C, hair dryer, iron, Wi-Fi, no phone.

Little America Hotel ★ *Value* Set on 500 acres of pine forest and with a trail that winds for 2 miles through the property, this hotel on the east side of Flagstaff might seem at first to be little more than a giant truck stop. However, on closer inspection, you'll find that behind the truck stop stands a surprisingly luxurious and economical hotel set beneath shady pines. The decor is dated but fun, with a sort of French Provincial style predominating. Rooms vary in size, but all have small private balconies and were recently renovated.

2515 E. Butler Ave., Flagstaff, AZ 86004. ✆ **800/865-1410** or 928/779-7900. Fax 928/779-7983. www.littleamerica.com. 248 units. $89–$169 double; $99–$179 suite. Children 12 and under stay free in parent's room. AE, DC, DISC, MC, V. Take Exit 198 off I-40. **Amenities:** 3 restaurants (American, Continental, deli); lounge; outdoor pool; exercise room; Jacuzzi; children's playground; concierge; courtesy airport shuttle; business center; room service; coin-op laundry; laundry service; dry cleaning. *In room:* A/C, TV, dataport, fridge, coffeemaker, hair dryer, iron, safe, high-speed Internet access.

Radisson Woodlands Hotel Flagstaff ★★ With its elegant marble-floored lobby, the Woodlands Hotel is easily the most upscale lodging in Flagstaff. A white baby grand, a crystal chandelier, traditional European furnishings, and contemporary sculpture all add to the unexpected luxury in the public spaces, as do intricately carved pieces of furniture and architectural details from different Asian countries. Guest rooms are quite comfortable and have Sleep Number® beds.

1175 W. Rte. 66, Flagstaff, AZ 86001. ✆ **800/333-3333** or 928/773-8888. Fax 928/773-0597. www.radisson.com/flagstaffaz. 183 units. $99–$149 double; $129–$189 suite. AE, DC, DISC, MC, V. **Amenities:** 2 restaurants (Japanese, Continental); lounge; outdoor pool; exercise room; indoor and outdoor Jacuzzis; sauna; business center; room service; coin-op laundry; laundry service; dry cleaning. *In room:* A/C, TV, dataport, coffeemaker, hair dryer, iron, high-speed Internet access, Wi-Fi.

INEXPENSIVE

Historic Hotel Monte Vista This hotel is definitely not for everyone. Although it is historic, it is also a bit run-down and appeals primarily to young travelers who appreciate the low rates and the nightclub just off the lobby. So why stay here? In its day, the Monte Vista hosted the likes of Clark Gable, John Wayne, Carole Lombard, and Gary Cooper, and today, the hotel is haunted (ask at the front desk for the list of resident ghosts). Opened in 1927, the Monte Vista now has creatively decorated rooms that vary in size and decor. Although the hotel has plenty of old-fashioned flair, don't expect perfection. Check out a room first to see if this is your kind of place.

100 N. San Francisco St., Flagstaff, AZ 86001. ✆ **800/545-3068** or 928/779-6971. Fax 928/779-2904. www.hotelmontevista.com. 50 units, 5 w/shared bathrooms. May–Oct $70 double w/shared bathroom, $80–$130 double w/private bathroom, $120–$180 suite; Nov–Apr $65 double w/shared bathroom, $75–$125 double w/private bathroom, $115–$170 suite. AE, DISC, MC, V. Pets accepted ($25 deposit). **Amenities:** Restaurant (American); lounge; coin-op laundry. *In room:* TV, hair dryer.

Hotel Weatherford *Value* This place isn't fancy, but it has loads of character. As part of an ongoing restoration that has taken more than 20 years, this historic hotel in downtown Flagstaff has been steadily upgrading its rooms. Although only a few of the rooms have been renovated, budget-conscious fans of historic hotels will want to check them out. The distinctive stone-walled 1897 building has a wraparound veranda on its third floor, where you'll also find the beautifully restored Zane Grey Ballroom (now an elegant bar). Downstairs are a casual restaurant and the ever-popular Charly's Pub & Grill, which has been booking live rock, blues, and jazz acts for more than 2 decades.

23 N. Leroux St., Flagstaff, AZ 86001. ✆ **928/779-1919.** Fax 928/773-8951. www.weatherfordhotel.com. 10 units, 3 w/shared bathrooms. $70–$80 double; $105–$125 suite. Children under 12 stay free in parent's room. AE, DC, DISC, MC, V. **Amenities:** Restaurant (American/Southwestern); 2 lounges. *In room:* No phone.

WHERE TO DINE

If you're headed north to the Grand Canyon and need a good espresso to get you there, stop at **Late for the Train Espresso,** 1800 N. Fort Valley Rd. (✆ **928/773-0308;** www.lateforthetrain.com), on U.S. 180 as you drive north out of town. Just watch for the old gas station. There are other locations at 107 N. San Francisco St. (✆ **928/779-5975**) and 2880 S. Milton Rd., Suite 300 (✆ **928/213-8500**). If you need some good bread for a picnic or just want something sweet, try **House of Bread,** University Plaza Shopping Center, 1237 S. Plaza Way (✆ **928/774-5254;** www.houseofbreadflagstaff.com).

EXPENSIVE

Brix ★★ NEW AMERICAN Although it's a bit hard to find (tucked into a corner of an old brick carriage house), Brix, Flagstaff's most contemporary restaurant, is well worth searching out. The menu relies on fresh, seasonal ingredients, so it changes regularly. However, any time of year, you'll find a great selection of artisanal cheeses, which make a good starter to a meal here. The chef's creativity shines through in such seasonal entrees as pork chops with rhubarb-ginger compote, pan-roasted duck breast with quinoa fritters, and house-made pappardelle pasta with fava beans, roasted mushrooms, and cippolini onions. There's an excellent wine list to accompany the food.

413 N. San Francisco St. ✆ **928/213-1021.** www.brixflagstaff.com. Reservations recommended. Main courses $8.50–$12 lunch, $22–$30 dinner. AE, DISC, MC, V. Mon–Thurs 11am–2pm and 5–9pm; Fri 11am–2pm and 5–10pm; Sat 5–10pm.

Cottage Place Restaurant ★★ CONTINENTAL/NEW AMERICAN On the south side of the railroad tracks in a neighborhood mostly frequented by college students, Cottage Place is just what its name implies—an unpretentious little cottage. But despite the casual appearance, dining here is a formal affair. The menu, which tends toward the rich side, is primarily Continental, with Southwestern and Middle Eastern influences as well. The house specialties are chateaubriand and rack of lamb (both served for two); there are always a couple of choices for vegetarians as well. The appetizer sampler, with herb-stuffed mushrooms, charbroiled shrimp, and *tiropitas* (cheese-stuffed phyllo pastries), is a winner. There's a long, award-winning wine list.

126 W. Cottage Ave. ✆ **928/774-8431.** www.cottageplace.com. Reservations recommended. 3-course meals $22–$34. AE, MC, V. Wed–Sun 5–9:30pm.

Josephine's ★★ REGIONAL AMERICAN Housed in a restored Craftsman bungalow with a beautiful stone fireplace and a wide front porch for summer dining, this restaurant combines a historical setting with excellent food that draws on a wide range of influences. For these reasons, this is my favorite downtown Flagstaff restaurant. The thinly sliced ancho-marinated steak is a real winner. At lunch, try the crab-cake po' boy sandwich. There's a good selection of reasonably priced wines also. Be sure to save room for the molten chocolate cake or the unusual half-baked peanut butter–chocolate chip cookie.

503 N. Humphrey's St. ✆ **928/779-3400.** www.josephinesrestaurant.com. Reservations recommended. Main courses $8.75–$13 lunch, $19–$28 dinner. AE, DISC, MC, V. Mon–Fri 11am–2:30pm and 5–9pm; Sat 5–9pm.

MODERATE

Jackson's Grill at the Springs ★★ NEW AMERICAN Set on the outskirts of Flagstaff, this modern American bistro boasts the most attractive setting of any restaurant in town. The food here is also delicious, which makes this place well worth the 10-minute drive from downtown Flagstaff. Start with the spinach salad, which is made with prosciutto-wrapped shrimp, or the ahi tuna salad. The spit-roasted entrees are among the best bets here. If you are on your way between Flagstaff and Sedona late in the day, this makes a great place for dinner.

7055 N. U.S. 89A. ✆ **928/213-9332.** www.jacksonsgrillrestaurant.com. Reservations recommended on weekends. Main courses $12–$34. AE, DC, DISC, MC, V. Mon–Thurs 5–9:30pm; Fri–Sun 11am–3pm and 5–9:30pm.

Pasto ★ ITALIAN Located in downtown Flagstaff, Pasto has a lively urban feel and can get boisterous on the weekends. The food is some of the best in town and is always reliable. Casual yet sophisticated, Pasto is less formal than Cottage Place or Josephine's, so if you don't feel like getting dressed up after a day at the canyon, come here. As the restaurant's name implies, the menu includes a good assortment of pastas; however, I always go for the *osso buco.*

19 E. Aspen St. ✆ **928/779-1937.** www.pastorestaurant.com. Reservations recommended. Main courses $16–$28. AE, DC, DISC, MC, V. Tues–Sun 5–9pm.

INEXPENSIVE

Beaver Street Brewery *Value* BURGERS/PIZZA This big microbrewery, cafe, and billiards parlor on the south side of the railroad tracks serves up several good brews, and it also does great pizzas and salads. The Beaver Street pizza, made with roasted-garlic pesto, sun-dried tomatoes, fresh basil, and goat cheese, is particularly tasty. Robust salads include a Mongolian beef version with sesame-ginger dressing. This place stays packed with college students, but a good pint of ale helps any wait pass quickly, especially if you can grab a seat by the woodstove. The brewery also operates the adjacent **Beaver Street Brews and Cues,** 3 S. Beaver St., which has pool tables and a vintage bar.

11 S. Beaver St. ✆ **928/779-0079.** www.beaverstreetbrewery.com. Reservations not accepted. Main courses $9.50–$15. AE, DISC, MC, V. Sun–Thurs 11:30am–11pm; Fri–Sat 11:30am–midnight.

Karma Sushi Bar Tapas ★ JAPANESE Located on historic Route 66 directly across from the Flagstaff Visitor Center, this stylish sushi place has a fun Asian rustic feel. Clientele tends to be college students, not tourists, which is why I like to eat here. Of course, since this place specializes in sushi and small plates, it's a great place for a light meal, especially after one too many cowboy-size steaks. I'm a sucker for fancy sushi rolls, and here I like to get the caterpillar (freshwater eel, cucumber, crab, and avocado slices) and the black cat roll (tempura asparagus, spicy lobster, mango, and avocado, with black sesame seeds).

6 E. Rte. 66. ✆ **928/774-6100.** Reservations not accepted. Sushi $3.50–$12; main courses $8–$16. MC, V. Mon–Fri 11am–2pm and 5–10pm; Sat–Sun 5–10pm.

Macy's European Coffee House & Bakery COFFEEHOUSE/BAKERY Good espresso and baked goodies draw people in here the first time, but there are also decent vegetarian pasta dishes, soups, salads, and other college-town standbys. This is Flagstaff's counterculture hangout, attracting both students and professors. For the true Macy's experience, order one of the huge lattes and a scone or other pastry.

14 S. Beaver St. ✆ **928/774-2243.** Meals $4–$7.75. MC, V. Daily 6am–10pm.

FLAGSTAFF AFTER DARK

For events taking place during your visit, check *Flagstaff Live* (www.flaglive.com), a free weekly newspaper available at shops and restaurants downtown. The university has many musical and theatrical groups that perform throughout most of the year, and several clubs around town book a variety of live acts.

The Orpheum Theater, 15 W. Aspen St. (✆ **928/556-1580;** www.orpheumpresents.com), in downtown Flagstaff, gets the best of touring rock, folk, and country acts, so be sure to check the schedule while you're in town. In summer, be sure to find out what's showing at **Movies on the Square** (✆ **928/774-6929;** www.heritagesquaretrust.org), a free outdoor movie series shown at downtown Flagstaff's Heritage Square on Friday nights. There's also live entertainment before the movies, as well as on Thursday nights and Saturday and Sunday afternoons. Also, during the warmer months, there are regular outdoor concerts at the **Pine Mountain Amphitheater,** Fort Tuthill County Park (✆ **928/556-1580;** www.pinemountainamphitheater.com), which is located at Exit 337 off I-17 south of Flagstaff.

Flagstaff has three good brewpubs. My favorite is the **Beaver Street Brewery,** 11 S. Beaver St. (✆ **928/779-0079**), described under "Where to Dine," above. Also try **Flagstaff Brewing Co.,** 16 E. Rte. 66 (✆ **928/773-1442;** www.flagbrew.com), or **Mogollon Brewing Co.,** 15 N. Agassiz St. (✆ **928/773-8950;** www.mogbrew.com). This latter brewpub also has its own on-site still (the first such operation in Arizona) and makes prickly pear vodka. Climb the stairs to the **Wine Loft,** 17 N. San Francisco St. (✆ **928/773-9463**), a wine bar located above the Artists Gallery in downtown Flagstaff, and, if you're like me, you'll wish you had a place like this in your town. There's live music by local musicians several nights per week. I wouldn't think of leaving Flagstaff without hanging out here at least one evening. Also check out **Cuveé 928,** 6 E. Aspen Ave., Suite 110 (✆ **928/214-9463**), a wine bar right on Heritage Square in downtown Flagstaff.

For a livelier scene, check out the **Museum Club,** 3404 E. Rte. 66 (✆ **928/526-9434;** www.museumclub.com), a Flagstaff institution and one of America's classic roadhouses. Built in the early 1900s and often called the Zoo Club, this cavernous log saloon is filled with deer antlers, stuffed animals, and trophy heads. There's live music (mostly country) on weekends.

Other places around town with live music include **Charly's Pub & Grill,** 23 N. Leroux St. (✆ **928/779-1919;** www.weatherfordhotel.com), inside the historic Weatherford Hotel. This place has long been a popular student hangout featuring live blues and rock 7 nights a week. For a mellower scene, see what's on the schedule at the **Campus Coffee Bean,** 1800 S. Milton Rd. (✆ **928/556-0660**).

4 Williams

32 miles W of Flagstaff; 58 miles S of the Grand Canyon; 220 miles E of Las Vegas, NV

Although it's almost 60 miles south of the Grand Canyon, Williams is still the closest real town to the national park. Consequently, it has dozens of motels catering to those unable to get a room in or just outside the park. Founded in 1880 as a railroading and logging town, Williams also has a bit of Western history to boast about, which makes it an interesting place to explore for a morning or afternoon. Old brick commercial buildings dating from the late 19th century line the main street, while modest Victorian homes sit on the tree-shaded streets that spread south from the railroad tracks. In recent years, mid-20th–century history has taken center stage: Williams was the last town on historic Route 66 to be bypassed by I-40, and the town plays up its Route 66 heritage.

Most important for many visitors, however, is that Williams is where you'll find the Grand Canyon Railway depot. The excursion train that departs from here not only provides a fun ride on the rails, but serves as an alternative to dealing with traffic congestion in Grand Canyon National Park. Of course, there are also the obligatory on-your-way-to-the-Grand-Canyon tourist traps nearby.

Named for famed mountain man Bill Williams, the town sits at the edge of a ponderosa pine forest atop the Mogollon Rim. Surrounding Williams is the Kaibab National Forest. Within the forest and not far out of town are good fishing lakes, hiking and mountain-biking trails, and a small downhill ski area.

ESSENTIALS

GETTING THERE Williams is on I-40 just west of the junction with Arizona 64, which leads north to the South Rim of the Grand Canyon.

Amtrak (✆ **800/872-7245**) has service to Williams on its *Southwest Chief* line. There's no station, though—the train stops on the outskirts of town. However, a shuttle van from the Grand Canyon Railway Hotel will pick you up and drive you into town, and since most people coming to Williams by train are continuing on to the Grand Canyon on the Grand Canyon Railway, this arrangement works well.

For information on the **Grand Canyon Railway** excursion trains to Grand Canyon Village, see "Exploring the Area: Route 66 & Beyond," below.

VISITOR INFORMATION For information on the Williams area, including details on hiking, mountain biking, and fishing, contact the **City of Williams/Forest Service Visitor Center,** 200 W. Railroad Ave. (✆ **800/863-0546** or 928/635-4707; www.williamschamber.com). The visitor center, which includes some interesting historical displays, is open daily from 8am to 5pm (until 6:30pm in the summer). The shop carries books on the Grand Canyon and trail maps for the adjacent national forest.

EXPLORING THE AREA: ROUTE 66 & BEYOND

These days, most people coming to Williams are here to board the **Grand Canyon Railway** ★★, Grand Canyon Railway Depot, 233 N. Grand Canyon Blvd. (✆ **800/843-8724** or 928/773-1976; www.thetrain.com), which operates vintage steam and diesel locomotives and 1920s and 1950s coaches between Williams and Grand Canyon Village. Round-trip fares (not including tax or the national park entrance fee) range from $60 to $170 for adults, $40 to $145 for children 11 to 16, and $30 to $95 for children 2 to 10. Although this is primarily a day-excursion train, it's possible to ride up one day and return on a different day—just let the reservations clerk know. If you stay overnight, be sure you have a reservation at one of the hotels right in Grand Canyon Village; otherwise, you'll end up having to take a shuttle bus or taxi out of the park to your hotel, which can be inconvenient and add a bit to your daily costs.

Route 66 fans will want to drive Williams's main street, which, not surprisingly, is named Route 66. Along this stretch of the old highway, you can check out the town's vintage buildings, many of which house shops selling Route 66 souvenirs. There are also a few antiques stores selling collectibles from the heyday of the famous highway.

Both east and west of town are other parts of the "Mother Road" that you can drive. However, with the exception of the section that begins at Exit 139, these stretches are not very remarkable and are recommended only for die-hard fans of Route 66. East of town, take Exit 167 off I-40 and follow the graveled **Old Trails Highway** (the predecessor to Rte. 66). A paved section of Route 66 begins at Exit 171 on the north side of the interstate and extends for 7 miles to the site of the Parks General Store. From Parks, you can continue to Brannigan Park on a graveled section of Route 66.

West of Williams, take Exit 157 and go south. If you turn east at the T intersection, you'll be on a gravel section of the old highway; if you turn west, you'll be on a paved section. Another stretch can be accessed at Exit 106. If you continue another 12 miles west and take Exit 139, you'll be on the longest uninterrupted stretch of Route 66 left in the country. It extends from here through the town of **Seligman,** which has several interesting buildings, and all the way to Kingman.

WHERE TO STAY

MODERATE

Grand Canyon Railway Hotel ★★ This hotel is operated by the Grand Canyon Railway and combines modern comforts with the style of a classic Western railroad hotel. The high-ceilinged lobby features a large flagstone fireplace and original paintings of the Grand Canyon. The very comfortable guest rooms feature Southwestern styling; ask for a unit in the wing with the fitness room, pool, and hot tub. The hotel's elegant lounge, which features a 100-year-old English bar, serves simple meals, and there's a cafeteria-style restaurant adjacent. Although this hotel does not accept pets, they do have a pet "resort."

233 N. Grand Canyon Blvd., Williams, AZ 86046. ✆ **800/843-8724** or 928/635-4010. Fax 928/773-1610. www.thetrain.com. 298 units. Mid-Mar to mid-Oct and holidays $179 double; mid-Oct to Dec $119 double; Jan to mid-Mar $99 double. Railroad/hotel packages available (mid-Mar to mid-Oct and holidays $159 per person; mid-Oct to mid-Mar $119 per person). Children under 16 stay free in parent's room. AE, DISC, MC, V. **Amenities:** Restaurant (American); lounge; indoor pool; exercise room; Jacuzzi; children's playground; tour desk; room service; coin-op laundry. *In room:* A/C, TV, dataport, coffeemaker, hair dryer, iron, free local calls.

INEXPENSIVE

In addition to the following choices, there are numerous budget chain motels in Williams.

The Canyon Motel & RV Park ★ *Kids* *Finds* You'll find this updated 1940s Route 66 motor lodge on the eastern outskirts of Williams, tucked against the trees. While the setting and rooms in 1940s flagstone cottages are nice enough, the real attractions are the railroad cars parked in the front yard. You can stay in one of two 1929 cabooses or a 1950s Pullman car, which makes this a fun place to overnight if you plan to take the excursion train to the Grand Canyon. I prefer the caboose rooms, which have a more authentic feel. An indoor pool, a horseshoe pit, a swing set, and a nature trail provide plenty of entertainment for the whole family. There's also a deluxe RV park here.

1900 E. Rodeo Rd., Williams, AZ 86046. ✆ **800/482-3955** or 928/635-9371. Fax 928/635-4138. www.thecanyonmotel.com. 23 units. $40–$79 double; $115–$139 caboose; $69–$116 Pullman double. Children under 11 stay free in parent's room. DISC, MC, V. Pets accepted ($7 per night). **Amenities:** Restaurant (American); small indoor pool. *In room:* TV, fridge, coffeemaker, microwave, Wi-Fi, no phone.

The Red Garter Bed & Bakery ★ *Finds* The Wild West lives again at this restored 1897 bordello, but these days the only tarts that come with the rooms are in the bakery downstairs. Located across the street from the Grand Canyon Railway terminal at the top of a steep flight of stairs, this B&B sports high ceilings, attractive wood trim, and reproduction period furnishings. Walls in a couple of rooms have graffiti written by bordello visitors in the early 20th century. The great historical atmosphere makes this my favorite place to stay in Williams.

137 W. Railroad Ave., Williams, AZ 86046. ✆ **800/328-1484** or 928/635-1484. www.redgarter.com. 4 units. $120–$145 double. Lower rates off season (and online). Rates include continental breakfast. DISC, MC, V. No children under 8. **Amenities:** Bakery. *In room:* TV, Wi-Fi, no phone.

CAMPGROUNDS

There are several campgrounds near Williams in the Kaibab National Forest. They include **Cataract Lake,** 1 mile northwest of Williams on Cataract Lake Road, with 18 sites; **Dogtown Lake,** 6½ miles southeast of Williams off Fourth Street/County Road 73, with 52 sites; **Kaibab Lake,** 4 miles northeast of Williams off Arizona 64, with 63 sites; and **Whitehorse Lake,** 19 miles southeast of Williams off Fourth Street/County Road 73, with 94 sites. All campgrounds are first-come, first-served, and charge $10 to $15 per night.

WHERE TO DINE

Rod's Steak House STEAKHOUSE/SEAFOOD For a good dinner in Williams, just look for the red neon steer at the east end of town. The menu here may be short, but the food is reliable. Prime rib au jus, the house specialty, comes in three different weights to fit your hunger. If you're not in the mood for steak, opt for barbecued ribs, trout, or fried chicken.

301 E. Rte. 66. ✆ **928/635-2671.** www.rods-steakhouse.com. Reservations recommended. Main courses $6–$15 lunch, $12–$40 dinner. AE, DISC, MC, V. Mon–Sat 11am–9:30pm.

5 Havasu Canyon ★★ & Grand Canyon West

Havasu Canyon: 200 miles W of Grand Canyon Village; 70 miles N of Ariz. 66; 155 miles NW of Flagstaff; 115 miles NE of Kingman

Grand Canyon West: 240 miles W of Grand Canyon Village; 70 miles N of Kingman; 115 miles E of Las Vegas, NV

With roughly four million people each year visiting the South Rim of the Grand Canyon, and traffic congestion and parking problems becoming the most memorable aspects of many people's trips, you may want to consider an alternative to the South Rim. For most travelers, this means driving around to the North Rim; however, the North Rim is open only from mid-May to late October and is, unfortunately, not immune to parking problems and traffic congestion.

There are a couple of lesser-known alternatives. A visit to Havasu Canyon, on the Havasupai Indian Reservation, entails a 20-mile round-trip hike or horseback ride similar to that from Grand Canyon Village to Phantom Ranch, although with a decidedly different setting at the bottom of the canyon. Grand Canyon West, home to the much hyped SkyWalk, is on the Hualapai Indian Reservation and is primarily a tour bus destination for vacationers from Las Vegas. With bus tours, cafeteria-style restaurants, contrived attractions, and as much buzzing helicopter and small-plane traffic as any busy airport, Grand Canyon West is definitely someplace that is best appreciated by those who have very little time to spare but who desperately want to see something that looks like the Grand Canyon. This is also the only place where you can fly down into the canyon, which accounts for all the air traffic.

ESSENTIALS

GETTING THERE **Havasu Canyon** It isn't possible to drive all the way to Havasu Canyon's Supai village. The nearest road ends 8 miles from Supai at Hualapai Hilltop. This is the head for the trail into the canyon and is at the end of Indian Route 18, which runs north from Arizona 66. The turnoff is 7 miles east of Peach Springs and 31 miles west of Seligman.

The easiest and fastest (and by far most expensive) way to reach Havasu Canyon is by helicopter from Grand Canyon Airport. Flights are operated by **Papillon Grand Canyon Helicopters** (© **800/528-2418** or 928/638-2419; www.papillon.com). The round-trip air-and-ground day excursion is $555; it's also possible to arrange to stay overnight. Lower rates are usually available on this company's website.

Grand Canyon West If you're headed to Grand Canyon West, you've got a couple of options. The best route is to head northwest out of Kingman on U.S. 93. After 27 miles, turn right onto the Pearce Ferry Road (signed for Dolan Springs and Meadview). After 28 miles on this road, turn right onto Diamond Bar Road, which is signed for Grand Canyon West. Another 14 miles down this road brings you to the Hualapai Indian Reservation. A little farther along, you'll come to the Grand Canyon West Terminal (there's actually an airstrip here), where visitor permits and bus-tour tickets are sold. You can also drive to Grand Canyon West from Peach Springs via Buck and Doe Road, which adds almost 50 miles of gravel road to your trip and is not passable if it has rained any time recently.

VISITOR INFORMATION For information on Havasu Canyon, contact the **Havasupai Tourist Enterprises,** P.O. Box 160, Supai, AZ 86435 (© **928/448-2121** or 928/448-2141; www.havasupaitribe.com), which handles all campground reservations. For information on Grand Canyon West, contact **Destination Grand Canyon,** 6206 W. Desert Inn, Suite B, Las Vegas, NV 89146 (© **877/716-9378** or 702/878-9378; www.destinationgrandcanyon.com).

HAVASU CANYON ★★★

Imagine hiking for hours through a dusty brown landscape of rocks and cacti. The sun overhead is blistering and bright. The air is hot and dry. Rock walls rise higher and higher as you continue your descent through a mazelike canyon. Eventually, the narrow canyon opens into a wide plain shaded by cottonwood trees, a sure sign of water, and within a few minutes you hear the sound of a babbling stream. The water, when you finally reach it, is cool and crystal clear, a pleasant surprise. Following the stream, you pass through a dusty (usually cluttered and unkempt, some say dirty and depressing) Indian village of small homes. Not surprisingly, in a village 8 miles beyond the last road, every yard seems to be a corral for horses. Passing through the village, you continue along the stream. As the trail descends again, you spot the first waterfall.

The previously crystal-clear water is now a brilliant turquoise blue at the foot of the waterfall. The sandstone walls look redder than before. No, you aren't having a heat-induced hallucination—the water really is turquoise, and it fills terraces of travertine that form deep pools of cool water at the base of three large waterfalls. Together these three waterfalls form what many claim is the most beautiful spot in the entire state. I'm not going to argue with them.

This is Havasu Canyon, the canyon of the Havasupai tribe, whose name means "people of the blue-green waters." For centuries, the Havasupai have called this idyllic desert oasis home.

The waterfalls are the main attraction here, and most people are content to go for a dip in the cool waters, sun themselves on the sand, and gaze for hours at the turquoise waters. A trail leads all the way down to the Colorado River, but this is an overnight hike.

The Havasupai entry fee is $35 per person to visit Havasu Canyon, and everyone entering the canyon is required to register at the tourist office in the village of Supai. Because it's a long walk to the campground, be sure you have a confirmed reservation before setting out from Hualapai Hilltop. It's good to make reservations as far in advance as possible, especially for holiday weekends.

If you plan to hike down into the canyon, start early to avoid the heat of the day. The hike is beautiful, but it's 10 miles to the campground. The steepest part of the trail is the first mile or so from Hualapai Hilltop. After this section, it's relatively flat.

Through **Havasupai Tourist Enterprises** (© **928/448-2121** or 928/448-2141; www.havasupaitribe.com), you can hire a horse to carry you or your gear down into the canyon from Hualapai Hilltop. Horse rental costs $75 each way. Many people who hike in decide that it's worth the money to ride out, or at least have their backpacks carried out. Be sure to confirm your horse reservation a day before driving to Hualapai Hilltop. Sometimes no horses are available, and it's a long drive back to the nearest town. There are also pack mules that will carry your gear into and out of the canyon.

If you'd like to hike into Havasu Canyon with a guide, **Arizona Outback Adventures,** 16447 N. 91st St., Suite 101, Scottsdale, AZ 85260 (© **866/455-1601** or 480/945-2881; www.azoutbackadventures.com), leads 3- to 5-day hikes into Havasu Canyon and charges $1,375 to $1,625 per person. **Discovery Treks,** 28248 N. Tatum Blvd., Suite B1, no. 414, Cave Creek, AZ 85331 (© **888/256-8731;** www.discoverytreks.com), offers similar 3-day trips for $975 to $1,145 per person.

GRAND CANYON WEST

Located on the Hualapai Indian Reservation on the south side of the Colorado River, **Grand Canyon West** (© **877/716-9378** or 702/878-9378; www.destinationgrandcanyon.com) overlooks the little-visited west end of Grand Canyon National Park. Although the view is not as spectacular as at either the South Rim or the North Rim, Grand Canyon West is noteworthy for one thing: It is one of the only places where you can legally take a helicopter ride down into the canyon. This is possible because the helicopters operate on land that is part of the Hualapai Indian Reservation. At this point, the south side of the Colorado lies within the reservation, while the north side of the river is within Grand Canyon National Park. The tours are operated by **Papillon Helicopters** (© **888/635-7272** or 702/736-7243; www.papillon.com), which charges $149 to $204 per person for a quick trip to the bottom of the canyon and a boat ride on the Colorado River. ***Note:*** Lower rates may be available on their website.

Grand Canyon West is a self-styled major destination, with plans for a full-fledged resort and major airport in the future. In 2007, the first phase of this development, the much-publicized **Skywalk,** opened to the public. Contrary to what you may have read about this Vegas-style attraction, the SkyWalk is not over the Colorado River and is not in Grand Canyon National Park. The horseshoe-shaped glass observation platform juts over a side canyon of the Grand Canyon, and from the deck you can glimpse the Colorado River a short distance away and 4,000 feet below. However, you'll have to cough up $75 for the privilege of walking out on the SkyWalk for a view that is only marginally better than the view from solid ground. For your $75, you'll also get a guided **bus tour** along the rim of the canyon. The tours stop at Eagle Point, which is the site of the SkyWalk and a collection of traditional Native American dwellings, and at Guano Point, where bat guano was once mined commercially. As part of your package tour, you'll also get to visit Hualapai Ranch, a faux cow town where there are wagon and horseback rides, cowboy cookouts, and gunfight shows. Tours operate daily throughout the year and cost $50 per person (with lunch); $75 with lunch and the SkyWalk; $109 with a Hummer tour or horseback ride added on; and $199 with a helicopter ride down into the canyon and a brief boat trip on the Colorado River. Reservations are recommended. If you're coming from Kingman, allow at least 2 hours to get here.

Because this is about the closest spot to Las Vegas that actually provides a glimpse of the Colorado River and Grand Canyon National Park, the bus tours and helicopter rides are very popular with tour groups from Las Vegas. Busloads of visitors come and go throughout the day, and the air is always filled with the noise of helicopters ferrying people down into the canyon.

While I can recommend a trip out to Grand Canyon West only as a side trip from Las Vegas or for travelers who absolutely must fly down into the canyon, the drive out here is almost as scenic as the destination itself. Along Diamond Bar Road, you'll be driving below the Grand Wash Cliffs, and for much of the way, the route traverses a dense forest of Joshua trees.

OTHER AREA ACTIVITIES

If you long to raft the Grand Canyon but have only a couple of free days in your schedule to realize your dream, then you have just one option. Here at the west end of the canyon, it's possible to do a 1-day rafting trip that begins on the Hualapai Indian Reservation. These trips are operated by **Hualapai River Runners,** P.O. Box 246, Peach Springs, AZ 89434 (✆ **928/769-2219;** www.grandcanyonresort.com), a tribal rafting company, and run between March and October. Expect a mix of white water and flat water. Although it's not as exciting as longer trips in the main section of the canyon, you'll still plow through some pretty big waves. Be ready to get wet. These trips stop at a couple of side canyons where you can get out and do some exploring. One-day trips cost $299 per person.

If you aren't interested in (or can't afford) one of these rafting trips, you still might want to consider driving down to the bottom of the Grand Canyon. That's right, the Diamond Creek Road leads to the bottom of the canyon. This gravel road is on the Hualapai Indian Reservation and is the only place in the Grand Canyon where it is possible to drive to the Colorado River. Bear in mind that this is a rough road and you'll need a high-clearance vehicle and a permit ($12 per person). Get your permit at the Hualapai Lodge.

Also in this area, you can visit **Grand Canyon Caverns** (✆ **928/422-3223;** www.grandcanyoncaverns.com), just outside Peach Springs. The caverns, which are accessed via a 210-foot elevator ride, are open from Memorial Day to October 15 daily from 9am to 5pm (sometimes until 6pm), and other months daily from 10am to 4pm. Admission is $13 for adults, $9.95 for children 4 to 12. "Explorers' Tours" ($45) head off into parts of the caverns that aren't seen on the regular tour.

WHERE TO STAY & DINE

Grand Canyon Caverns Inn If you plan to hike or ride into Havasu Canyon, you'll need to be at Hualapai Hilltop as early in the morning as possible, and because it's a 3- to 4-hour drive to the trail head from Flagstaff, you might want to consider staying here at one of only two lodgings for miles around. As the name implies, this motel is built on the site of the Grand Canyon Caverns, which are open to the public. On the premises is a general store with camping supplies and food. For much of the year, this motel is used by Elderhostel and stays full.

Mile Marker 115, Rte. 66, Peach Springs, AZ 86434. © **877/422-4459,** 928/422-3223, or 928/422-4459. Fax 928/422-4471. www.grandcanyoncaverns.com. 48 units. $62–$72 double. AE, DISC, MC, V. Pets accepted ($25 deposit plus $5 per night). **Amenities:** Restaurant (American); lounge; seasonal outdoor pool; coin-op laundry. *In room:* A/C, TV.

Hualapai Lodge ★ *Finds* Located in the Hualapai community of Peach Springs, this lodge offers by far the most luxurious accommodations anywhere in the region. Guest rooms are spacious and modern, with a few bits of regional decor for character. Most people staying here are in the area to visit Grand Canyon West, to go rafting with Hualapai River Runners, or to hike in to Havasu Canyon. The dining room is just about the only place in town to get a meal.

900 Rte. 66, Peach Springs, AZ 86434. © **888/255-9550** or 928/769-2230. Fax 928/769-2372. www.grandcanyonresort.com. 60 units. Mid-Mar to Oct $100–$110 double; Nov to mid-Mar $80–$84 double. Children under 15 stay free in parent's room. AE, DC, DISC, MC, V. **Amenities:** Restaurant (Mexican/Native American/American); outdoor saltwater pool; exercise room; tour desk; coin-op laundry. *In room:* A/C, TV, dataport, coffeemaker, hair dryer.

IN HAVASU CANYON

Havasu Campground The campground is 2 miles below Supai village, between Havasu Falls and Mooney Falls, and the campsites are mostly in the shade of cottonwood trees on either side of Havasu Creek. Picnic tables are provided, but no firewood is available. Cutting any trees or shrubs is prohibited, so be sure to bring a camp stove. Spring water is available, but it needs to be purified before you drink it.

Havasupai Tourist Enterprises, P.O. Box 160, Supai, AZ 86435. © **928/448-2141** or 928/448-2121. 100 sites. $17 per person. MC, V.

Havasupai Lodge Located in Supai village, this lodge offers, aside from the campground, the only accommodations in the canyon. The two-story building features standard motel-style rooms that lack only TVs and telephones, neither of which is much in demand at this isolated retreat. The only drawback of this comfortable though basic lodge is that it's 2 miles from Havasu Falls and 3 miles from Mooney Falls. The Havasupai Café, across from the general store, serves breakfast, lunch, and dinner. It's a very casual place, and prices are high for what you get because all ingredients must be packed in by horse.

P.O. Box 159, Supai, AZ 86435. © **928/448-2111** or 928/448-2201. www.havasupaitribe.com. 24 units. $145 double. MC, V. **Amenities:** Restaurant nearby. *In room:* A/C, no phone.

6 Kingman

180 miles SW of Grand Canyon Village; 150 miles W of Flagstaff; 30 miles E of Laughlin, NV; 90 miles SE of Las Vegas, NV

Although Kingman is the only town of any size between the Grand Canyon and Las Vegas, it is primarily a place to gas up before heading out across the desert. However, if you have a couple of hours to spare, the city does have interesting little museums and downtown historic buildings. The town's other claim to fame is that it is on the longest extant stretch of historic Route 66.

That Kingman today is more way station than destination is not surprising, considering its history. In 1857, Lieut. Edward Fitzgerald Beale passed through this region leading a special corps of camel-mounted soldiers on a road-surveying expedition.

Some 60 years later, the road Beale surveyed would become the National Old Trails Highway, the precursor to Route 66. Gold and silver were discovered in the nearby hills in the 1870s, and in the early 1880s, the railroad laid its tracks through what would become the town of Kingman. Kingman flourished briefly around the start of the 20th century as a railroad town, and today, buildings constructed during this railroading heyday (including the historic Brunswick Hotel) give downtown a bit of historic character.

In the nearby hills, such mining towns as Oatman and Chloride sprang up and boomed until the 1920s, when the mines became unprofitable and were abandoned. However, the lure of gold and silver has never quite died in this area, and in nearby Oatman, the Gold Road Mine is still an operational mine, though giving tours now seems to generate more income than the actual mining of gold.

During the 1930s, as tens of thousands of the impoverished and unemployed followed Route 66 from the Midwest to Los Angeles, Kingman became a stop on the road to the promised land of California. Route 66 has long since been replaced by I-40, but the longest remaining stretch of the old highway runs east from Kingman to Ash Fork. Over the years, Route 66 has taken on legendary qualities, and today people come from all over the world searching for pieces of this highway's historic past.

Remember Andy Devine? No? Well, Kingman is more than happy to tell you all about its squeaky-voiced native-son actor. Devine starred in hundreds of short films and features in the silent-screen era, but he's perhaps best known as cowboy sidekick Jingles on the 1950s TV western *Wild Bill Hickok.* In the 1950s and 1960s, he hosted *Andy's Gang,* a popular children's TV show; and in the 1960s, he played Captain Hap on *Flipper.* Devine died in 1977, but here in Kingman his memory lives on—in a room in the local museum and every September when the town celebrates Andy Devine Days.

ESSENTIALS

GETTING THERE Kingman is on I-40 at the junction with U.S. 93 from Las Vegas. One of the last sections of old Route 66 (Ariz. 66) connects Kingman with Ash Fork.

Amtrak (✆ **800/872-7245**) offers rail service to Kingman from Chicago and Los Angeles. The station is at 106 Fourth St.

VISITOR INFORMATION The **Kingman AZ Visitors Bureau,** 120 W. Andy Devine Ave. (✆ **866/427-RT66** or 928/753-6106; www.kingmantourism.org), operates the Powerhouse Tourist Information & Visitor Center in this restored 1907 powerhouse, which also houses the Historic Route 66 Museum, a Route 66 gift shop, and a model railroad. The bureau is daily from 9am to 6pm (until 5pm Dec–Feb).

EXPLORING THE AREA

There isn't much to do right in Kingman, but while you're in town, you can learn more about local history at the **Mohave Museum of History and Arts,** 400 W. Beale St. (✆ **928/753-3195;** www.mohavemuseum.org). There's also plenty of Andy Devine memorabilia on display. The museum is open Monday through Friday from 9am to 5pm, Saturday and Sunday from 1 to 5pm. Admission is $4 for adults, $3 for seniors, free for children 12 and under. Afterwards, take a drive or a stroll around downtown Kingman to view the town's many historic buildings. (You can pick up a map at the museum.)

Get Your Kicks on Route 66

It was the Mother Road, the Main Street of America, and for thousands of Midwesterners devastated by the Dust Bowl days of the 1930s, the road to a better life. On the last leg of its journey from Chicago to California, Route 66 meandered across the vast empty landscape of northern Arizona.

Officially dedicated in 1926, Route 66 was the first highway in America to be uniformly signed from one state to the next. Less than half of the highway's 2,200-mile route was paved, and in those days, the stretch between Winslow and Ash Fork was so muddy in winter that drivers had their cars shipped by railroad between the two points. By the 1930s, however, the entire length of Route 66 had been paved, and the westward migration was underway.

The years following World War II saw Americans take to Route 66 in unprecedented numbers for a different reason. A new prosperity and reliable cars made travel a pleasure, and Americans set out to discover the West. Motor courts, cafes, and tourist traps sprang up along the highway's length, and these businesses increasingly turned to eye-catching signs and billboards to lure passing motorists. Neon lit up the once lonely stretches of highway.

By the 1950s, Route 66 just couldn't handle the traffic. After President Eisenhower initiated the National Interstate Highway System, Route 66 was slowly replaced by a four-lane divided highway. Many of the towns along the old highway were bypassed, and motorists stopped frequenting such roadside establishments as Pope's General Store and the Oatman Hotel. Many closed, while others were replaced by their more modern equivalents. Some, however, managed to survive, and they appear along the road like strange time capsules from another era, vestiges of Route 66's legendary past.

The **Wigwam Motel** (p. 283) in Holbrook is one of the most distinctive Route 66 landmarks. The wigwams (actually tepees) were built out of concrete around 1940 and still contain many of their original furnishings. Also in Holbrook are several rock shops with giant signs—and life-size concrete dinosaurs—that date from Route 66 days. Nighttime here comes alive with vintage neon.

Flagstaff, the largest town along the Arizona stretch of Route 66, became a major layover spot. Motor courts flourished on the road leading into town from the east. Today, this road has been officially renamed Route 66 by the city of Flagstaff, and a few of the old motor courts remain. Although you probably wouldn't want to stay in most of these old motels, their neon signs were once beacons in the night for tired drivers. Downtown Flagstaff has quite a few shops where you can pick up Route 66 memorabilia.

About 65 miles west of Flagstaff begins the longest remaining stretch of old Route 66. Extending for 160 miles from Ash Fork to Topock, this lonely blacktop passes through some of the most remote country in Arizona (and goes right through the town of Kingman). In Seligman, at the east end of this stretch of the highway, you'll find the **Snow Cap Drive-In** (✆ **928/422-3291**), which serves up fast food amid outrageous decor. Next door at **Angel & Vilma Delgadillo's Route 66 Gift Shop & Visitor's Center,** 217 E. Rte. 66 (✆ **928/422-3352;** www.route66giftshop.com), owned by John's uncle Angel, you'll be entertained by one of Route 66's most famous residents and an avid fan of the old highway. The walls of Angel's old one-chair barbershop are covered with photos and business cards of happy customers. Today, Angel's place is a Route 66 information center and souvenir shop, and Angel is president emeritus of the Route 66 Association of Arizona.

After leaving Seligman, the highway passes through such waysides as Peach Springs, Truxton, Valentine, and Hackberry. Before reaching Peach Springs, you'll come to **Grand Canyon Caverns,** once a near-mandatory stop for families traveling Route 66. In Hackberry, be sure to stop at the **Hackberry Store & Old Route 66 Visitor Center** (✆ **928/769-2605**), which is filled with Route 66 memorabilia as well as old stuff from the 1950s and 1960s. At Valle Vista, near Kingman, the highway goes into a 7-mile-long curve. Some claim it's the longest continuous curve on a U.S. highway.

After the drive through the wilderness west of Seligman, Kingman feels like a veritable metropolis; its bold neon signs once brought a sigh of relief to the tired and the hungry. Today, it boasts dozens of modern motels and is still primarily a resting spot for the road weary. **Mr. D'z Route 66 Diner,** a modern rendition of a 1950s diner (housed in an old gas station/cafe), serves burgers and blue-plate specials. Across the street at 120 W. Andy Devine Ave. is a restored powerhouse that dates from 1907 and is home to the **Historic Route 66 Association of Arizona** (✆ **928/753-5001;** www.azrt66.com), the **Historic Route 66 Museum** (✆ **928/753-9889;** www.kingmantourism.org/route66museum), and the **Kingman Area Chamber of Commerce Visitor Center.** Each year over the first weekend in May, Kingman is the site of the **Route 66 Fun Run,** which consists of a drive along 150 miles of old Route 66 between Topock and Seligman.

The last stretch of Route 66 in Arizona heads southwest out of Kingman through the rugged Sacramento Mountains. It passes through **Oatman,** which almost became a ghost town after the local gold-mining industry collapsed and the new interstate highway pulled money out of town. Today, mock gunfights and nosy wild burros entice motorists to stop, and shops playing up Route 66's heritage line the wooden sidewalks.

After dropping down out of the mountains, the road once crossed the Colorado River on a narrow metal bridge. Although the bridge is still there, it now carries a pipeline instead of traffic; cars must now return to the bland I-40 to continue their journey into the promised land of California.

If you're interested in historic homes, you can tour the **Bonelli House,** 430 E. Spring St. (✆ **928/753-3175**), a two-story stone home built in 1915 and furnished much as it may have been at that time. It's open Monday through Friday from 11am to 3pm, but before heading over, check at the Mohave Museum of History and Arts to see if a guide can show you around. Admission is by donation.

The **Historic Route 66 Museum,** 120 W. Andy Devine Ave. (✆ **928/753-9889;** www.kingmantourism.org/route66museum), has exhibits on the history of not just Route 66, but also the roads, railroads, and trails that preceded it. There's a great collection of old photos taken during the Depression, and even an "Okie" truck on display. You'll also see a Studebaker Champion and mock-ups of a gas station, diner, hotel lobby, and barbershop. Hours are daily from 9am to 6pm (until 5pm Dec–Feb); admission is $4 for adults, $3 for seniors, and free for children 12 and under.

When you're tired of the heat and want to cool off, head southeast of Kingman to **Hualapai Mountain Park,** 6250 Hualapai Mountain Rd. (✆ **928/681-5700;** www.mcparks.com), which is at an elevation of 7,000 feet and offers picnicking, hiking, mountain biking, camping, and rustic rental cabins built in the 1930s by the Civilian Conservation Corps. Daily admission to the park is $5.

GHOST TOWNS

Located 30 miles southwest of Kingman on what was once Route 66 is the busy little mining camp of **Oatman,** a classic Wild West ghost town full of tourist shops selling tacky souvenirs. Founded in 1906 when gold was discovered here, Oatman quickly grew into a lively town of 12,000 people and was an important stop on Route 66—even Clark Gable and Carole Lombard stayed here (on their honeymoon, no less). In 1942, when the U.S. government closed down many of Arizona's gold-mining operations, Oatman's population plummeted. Today, there are fewer than 250 inhabitants, and the once-abandoned old buildings have been preserved as a ghost town. The historic look of Oatman has attracted numerous filmmakers over the years; *How the West Was Won* is just one of the movies that was shot here.

One of Oatman's biggest attractions is its population of feral burros. These animals, which roam the streets of town begging for handouts, are descendants of burros used by gold miners. Be careful—they bite!

Daily staged shootouts in the streets and dancing to country music on weekend evenings are the other big draws, but you can also tour a gold mine. Tours operated by **Gold Road Mine Tours** (✆ **928/768-1600;** www.goldroadmine.com) take you underground and also show you all the topside workings of a modern gold mine. Tours last 1 hour; the cost is $12 for adults and $6 for children 12 and under. The mine is on historic Route 66 about 2½ miles east of Oatman.

And, of course, the Wild West isn't the Wild West if you don't spend some time in the saddle. **Oatman Stables** (✆ **928/768-3257;** www.oatmanstables.com) offers 1-hour horseback rides for $25 per person and 2-hour rides for $45.

Annual events staged here are among the strangest in the state. There are the bed races in January, a Fourth of July high-noon sidewalk egg fry, and a Labor Day burro biscuit toss. Saloons, restaurants, and a very basic hotel (where you can view the room Clark and Carole rented on their wedding night) provide food and lodging if you decide you'd like to soak up the Oatman atmosphere for a while. For more information, contact the **Oatman-Gold Road Chamber of Commerce,** P.O. Box 423, Oatman, AZ 86433 (✆ **928/768-6222;** www.oatmangoldroad.com).

Chloride, yet another quasi ghost town, is about 20 miles northwest of Kingman. The town was founded in 1862 when silver was discovered in the nearby Cerbat Mountains, and is named for a type of silver ore that was mined here. By the 1920s, there were 75 mines and 2,000 people in Chloride. When the mines shut down in 1944, the town lost most of its population. Today, there are around 150 year-round residents. For more information, contact the **Chloride Chamber of Commerce,** P.O. Box 268, Chloride, AZ 86431 (© **928/565-2204;** www.chloridearizona.com).

Much of the center of the town has been preserved as a historic district that includes, among other less-than-remarkable buildings, the oldest continuously operating post office in Arizona.

Every first and third Saturday of the month at high noon, Chloride comes alive when **The Immortal Gunfighters** (© **928/565-4109;** www.immortalgunfighters.com) stage gunfights at Cyanide Springs mock cow town. On the second and fourth Saturday of each month at high noon at Cyanide Springs, gunfight shows are staged by the **Wild Roses of Chloride** (www.chloridewildroses.com), an all-women gunfighters' group. Note that there are no shows in July or August. I guess the wild roses wilt in the heat.

Chloride's biggest attractions are the **Chloride murals,** painted by artist Roy Purcell in 1966. The murals, sort of colorful hippie images, are painted on the rocks on a hillside about a mile outside town. To find them, drive through town on Tennessee Avenue and continue after the road turns to dirt. You can also see old petroglyphs created by the Hualapai tribe on the hillside opposite the murals.

WHERE TO STAY

Most of the budget motel chains have branches in Kingman, and rates are among the lowest in the state. None of these motels are particularly recommendable, but if it's late in the day and you need a place to stay, you're more likely to find a cheap place here than in Las Vegas to the west or Williams to the east.

WHERE TO DINE

DamBar & Steak House STEAKHOUSE This steakhouse has long been Kingman's favorite place for dinner out. It's hard to miss—just look for the steer on the roof of a rustic wooden building. Inside, the atmosphere is very casual, with wooden booths and sawdust on the floor. Mesquite-broiled steaks are the name of the game here, but there are plenty of other hearty dishes as well.

1960 E. Andy Devine Ave. © **928/753-3523.** Reservations recommended on weekends and in summer. Main courses $7.50–$28. AE, DISC, MC, V. Daily 11am–10pm.

Mr. D'z Route 66 Diner AMERICAN This modern version of a vintage roadside diner is painted an eye-catching turquoise and pink. The retro color scheme continues inside, where you can snuggle into a booth or grab a stool at the counter. This place is a big hit with car buffs and people doing Route 66. Punch in a few 1950s tunes on the jukebox, and order up a Route 66 bacon cheeseburger and a root-beer float.

105 E. Andy Devine Ave. © **928/718-0066.** Main courses $4.75–$16. AE, MC, V. Daily 7am–9pm.

7

The Four Corners Region: Land of the Hopi & Navajo

Ready for a little trivia quiz? Where in the U.S. can you stand in four states at the same time? Give up? The answer is way up in the northeastern corner of Arizona, where this state meets New Mexico, Colorado, and Utah. This novelty of the United State's westward expansion has long captured the imagination of vacationing families looking for some way of entertaining the kids in the middle of the desert. "Hey, kids, wanna play Twister in four states at the same time?"

Known as Four Corners, this spot is the site of a Navajo Tribal Park. Pay your admission, and you, too, can experience the Four Corners state of mind. However, Four Corners is much more than a surveyor's gimmick. The term also refers to this entire region, most of which is Navajo and Hopi reservation land. The Four Corners region happens to have some of the most spectacular landscapes in the state, with majestic mesas, rainbow-hued deserts, towering buttes, multicolored cliffs, deep canyons, a huge cliff-rimmed reservoir, and even a meteorite crater. Among the most dramatic landscape features are the 1,000-foot buttes of Monument Valley, which for years have symbolized the Wild West of John Wayne movies and car commercials.

The Four Corners region is also home to Arizona's most scenic reservoir, Lake Powell, a flooded version of the Grand Canyon. With its miles of blue water mirroring red-rock canyon walls hundreds of feet high, Lake Powell is one of northern Arizona's curious contrasts—a vast artificial reservoir in the middle of barren desert canyons. Although 50 years ago there was a bitter fight over damming Glen Canyon to form Lake Powell, today the lake is among the most popular attractions in the Southwest.

Be forewarned, however: The Four Corners also claims some of the most desolate, wind-swept, and monotonous landscapes in the state, so be sure to fill up on both gas and coffee before heading out on the highway for another 100-mile drive to the next destination.

While this region certainly offers plenty of scenery, it also provides one of the nation's most fascinating cultural experiences. This is Indian country, the homeland of both the Navajo and the Hopi, tribes that have lived on these lands for hundreds of years and have adapted different means of surviving in this arid region. The Navajo, with their traditional log homes (called hogans) scattered across the countryside, were herders of sheep, goats, and cattle. The Hopi, on the other hand, congregated in villages atop mesas and built houses of stone. Today, the Hopi still grow corn and other crops at the foot of their mesas in much the same way the indigenous peoples of the Southwest have done for centuries.

These two tribes are only the most recent Native Americans to inhabit what many consider to be a desolate, barren wilderness. The Ancestral Puebloans (formerly called Anasazis) left their mark

The Four Corners Region

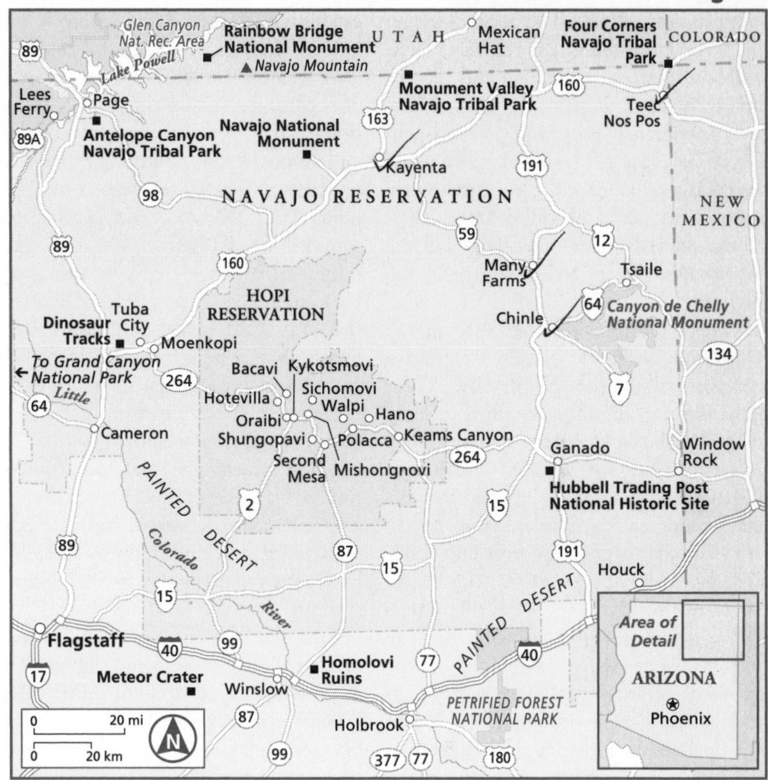

throughout the canyons of the Four Corners region. Their cliff dwellings date back 700 years or more, and here in Arizona, the most spectacular ruins are in Canyon de Chelly and Navajo national monuments. No one is sure why the Ancestral Puebloans moved up into the cliff walls, but there is speculation that unfavorable growing conditions brought on by drought may have forced them to use every possible inch of arable land. Likewise, no one is certain why the Ancestral Puebloans abandoned their cliff dwellings in the 13th century. With no written record, their disappearance may forever remain a mystery.

The Hopi, who claim the Ancestral Puebloans as their ancestors, have for centuries lived atop mesas in northeastern Arizona, and Oraibi, on Third Mesa, may be the oldest continuously inhabited community in the U.S. Most of the villages are built on three mesas, known simply as First, Second, and Third, which are numbered from east to west and are completely surrounded by the Navajo reservation. These villages have always maintained a great deal of autonomy, which over the years has sometimes led to fighting between villages. The appearance of missionaries and the policies of the Bureau of Indian Affairs have also created conflicts among and within villages.

The Navajo Reservation covers an area of 25,000 square miles (roughly the size of West Virginia) in northeastern Arizona and parts of New Mexico and Utah. It's the largest reservation in the U.S. and is home to nearly 200,000 Navajos. Although the reservation today has modern towns with supermarkets, malls, and hotels, many Navajo still follow a pastoral lifestyle as herders of goats and sheep. As you travel the roads of the reservation, you'll frequently encounter flocks of goats and sheep, and herds of cattle and horses. These animals have free range of the reservation and often graze beside the highway.

Unlike the pueblo tribes such as the Hopi and Zuni, the Navajo are relative newcomers to the Southwest. Their Athabascan language is most closely related to the languages spoken by Native Americans in the Pacific Northwest, Canada, and Alaska. It's believed that the Navajo migrated southward from northern Canada beginning around 1000, arriving in the Southwest sometime after 1400. At this time, they were still hunters and gatherers, but contact with the pueblo tribes, which had long before adopted an agricultural lifestyle, began to change the Navajo into farmers. When the Spanish arrived in the Southwest in the early 17th century, the Navajo began raiding Spanish settlements for horses, sheep, and goats and adopted a pastoral way of life, grazing their herds on the high plains and the canyon bottoms.

The continued raids, made even more successful with the acquisition of horses, put the Navajo in conflict with the Spanish settlers who were beginning to encroach on Navajo land. In 1805, the Spanish sent a military expedition into the Navajo's chief stronghold, Canyon de Chelly, and killed 115 people, who, by some accounts, may have been all women, children, and old men. This massacre, however, did not stop the conflicts between the Navajo and Spanish settlers.

In 1846, when this region became part of the United States, American settlers encountered the same problems that the Spanish had. Military outposts were established to protect the new settlers, and numerous unsuccessful attempts were made to establish peace. In 1863, after continued attacks, a military expedition led by Col. Kit Carson burned crops and homes late in the summer, effectively obliterating the Navajo's winter food supplies. Thus defeated, the Navajo were rounded up and herded 400 miles to an inhospitable region of New Mexico near Fort Sumner. This trek became known as the Long Walk. Living conditions at Fort Sumner were deplorable, and the land was unsuitable for farming. In 1868, however, the Navajo were allowed to return to their homeland.

Upon returning home, and after continued clashes with white settlers, the Navajo eventually settled into a lifestyle of herding. But today the Navajo have had to turn to many different livelihoods. Although weaving and silver work have become lucrative businesses, the amount of money these trades garner for the tribe as a whole is not significant. Many Navajo now take jobs as migrant workers. Gas and oil leases and coal mining on the reservation provide additional income.

Although the reservation covers an immense area, much of it is of little value other than as scenery. Fortunately, the Navajo have recognized the income potential of their spectacular land. Monument Valley is operated as a tribal park, as is the Four Corners park. Numerous Navajo-owned tour companies also operate on the reservation.

As you travel the reservation, you may notice small hexagonal buildings with rounded roofs. These are hogans, the traditional homes of the Navajo, and are usually made of wood and earth with the doorway facing east to greet the new day. At the Canyon de Chelly and Navajo national monument visitor centers, you can look inside hogans that are part of the parks' exhibits. If you take a tour at Canyon de Chelly or Monument Valley, you may have an opportunity to visit a privately owned hogan. Although most Navajo now live in modest houses or mobile homes, a family will usually also have a hogan for religious ceremonies.

The Navajo and Hopi reservations cover a vast area and are laced with a network of well-paved roads, as well as many unpaved roads that are not always passable to cars without four-wheel-drive. Keep your gas tank filled because distances are great, and keep an eye out for livestock on the road, especially at night.

1 Winslow

55 miles E of Flagstaff; 70 miles S of Second Mesa; 33 miles W of Holbrook

It's hard to imagine a town that could build its tourist fortunes on a mention in a pop song, but that is exactly what Winslow has done ever since the band the Eagles sang about "standin' on a corner in Winslow, Arizona," in their hit song "Take It Easy." On the corner of Second Street and Kinsley Avenue, the town even has an official Standin' on the Corner Park (complete with a mural of a girl in a flatbed Ford).

Popular songs aside, Winslow can claim a couple of more significant attractions. Right in town is La Posada, one of the Southwest's historic railroad hotels. Twenty miles west of town is mile-wide Meteor Crater. And east of town is Homolovi Ruins State Park, which has ancient ruins as well as extensive petroglyphs. If you happen to be a rock climber, you'll find great climbing routes in Chevelon Canyon south of town.

ESSENTIALS

GETTING THERE Winslow is on I-40 at the junction with Arizona 87, which leads north to the Hopi mesas and south to Payson. **Amtrak** (© **800/872-7245**) trains stop in Winslow at La Posada hotel, 501 E. Second Street.

VISITOR INFORMATION Contact the **Winslow Chamber of Commerce,** 101 E. Second St. (© **928/289-2434;** www.winslowarizona.org).

ONE BIG HOLE IN THE GROUND

Meteor Crater ★★ Northern Arizona has more than its fair share of natural attractions, and while most of the region's big holes in the ground were created by the slow process of erosion, there is one hole that has far more dramatic origins. At 550 feet deep and 2½ miles in circumference, the Barringer Meteorite Crater is the best-preserved meteorite impact crater on earth. The meteorite, which estimates put at roughly 150 feet in diameter, was traveling at 40,000 mph when it slammed into the earth 50,000 years ago. Within seconds, more than 175 million tons of rock had been displaced, leaving a gaping crater and a devastated landscape. Today, you can stand on the rim of the crater (there are observation decks and a short trail) and marvel at the power, equivalent to 20 million tons of TNT, which created this otherworldly setting. In fact, so closely does this crater resemble craters on the surface of the moon that in the 1960s, NASA came here to train Apollo astronauts.

On the rim of the crater, there's a small museum that features exhibits on astrogeology and space exploration, as well as a film on meteorites. On display are a 1,400-pound meteorite and an Apollo space capsule. Throughout the day, there are 1-hour hiking tours along the rim of the crater.

20 miles west of Winslow at Exit 233 off I-40. © **800/289-5898** or 928/289-5898. www.meteorcrater.com. Admission $15 adults, $13 seniors, $6 children 6–17. Memorial Day to mid-Sept daily 7am–7pm; mid-Sept to Memorial Day daily 8am–5pm. Closed Christmas.

OTHER AREA ATTRACTIONS

In downtown Winslow, near that famous corner, you'll find the little **Old Trails Museum,** 212 N. Kinsley Ave., at Second Street (© **928/289-5861**), which is something of a community attic and has exhibits on Route 66 and the Harvey Girls (who once worked in the nearby La Posada hotel; see the box, "Fred Harvey & His Girls," later in this chapter). The museum is open Monday through Saturday from 9am to 5pm. Admission is free.

Even if you aren't planning on staying the night at the restored **La Posada,** 303 E. Second St. (© **928/289-4366**), be sure to stop by just to see this historic railway hotel. Self-guided tours are available for a $2 donation.

On the windswept plains north of Winslow, 1¼ miles north of I-40 at Exit 257, is **Homolovi Ruins State Park** (© **928/289-4106;** www.azstateparks.com), which preserves more than 300 Ancestral Puebloan archaeological sites, several of which have been partially excavated. Although these ruins are not nearly as impressive as those at Wupatki or Walnut Canyon, a visit here will give you a better understanding of the interrelationship of the many ancient pueblos of this region. Also in the park are numerous petroglyphs; ask for directions at the visitor center. Admission is $5 per vehicle. The ruins are open daily during daylight hours, but the visitor center is open only from 8am to 5pm. There's also a campground, charging $10 to $20 per site.

Continuing north from the state park, you'll find the little-known and little-visited **Little Painted Desert** ★ (© **928/524-4757**), a 660-acre county park. To reach the park and its viewpoint overlooking the painted hills of this stark yet colorful landscape, continue north on Arizona 87 from Homolovi Ruins State Park for another 12 miles.

If you're in the market for some Route 66 memorabilia, drop by **Roadworks Gifts & Souvenirs,** 101 W. Second St. (© **928/289-5423;** www.roadworksroute66.com). Also, be sure to check out the **SNOWDRIFT Art Space,** 120 W. Second St. (© **928/289-8201;** www.snowdriftart.com), an art gallery opened by artist Daniel Lutzick, who was one of the people who helped get the historic La Posada hotel up and running again.

WHERE TO STAY

In addition to the following historic hotel, you'll find lots of budget chain motels in Winslow.

La Posada ★★ *Finds* What an unexpected beauty this place is! Designed by Mary Elizabeth Jane Colter, architect of many of the buildings on the South Rim of the Grand Canyon, this railroad hotel first opened in 1930. Colter gave La Posada the feel of an old Spanish hacienda and even created a fictitious history for the building. In the lobby are numerous pieces of original furniture as well as reproductions of pieces once found in the hotel. The nicest rooms are the large units named for famous guests—Albert Einstein, Howard Hughes, Harry Truman, Charles Lindbergh. The management's artistic flair comes across in these rooms, one of which (the Howard Hughes Room) has wide plank floors, murals, a fireplace, a rustic bed and armoire, Art Deco chairs, and a kilim rug. The bathroom is a classic of black-and-white tile and original fixtures. There are also rooms with whirlpool tubs. The hotel's Turquoise Room (see "Where to Dine," below) is by far the best restaurant in the entire Four Corners region. La Posada is in the process of being slowly but completely restored and is reason enough to overnight in Winslow.

303 E. Second St. (Rte. 66), Winslow, AZ 86047. © **928/289-4366.** Fax 928/289-3873. www.laposada.org. 37 units. $99–$149 double; $175 suite. AE, DC, DISC, MC, V. Pets accepted ($10 fee). **Amenities:** Restaurant (New

American/Southwestern); lounge; access to nearby health club; concierge; room service. *In room:* A/C, TV, hair dryer, iron, no phone.

WHERE TO DINE

Need some good coffee? Stop in at the **Seattle Grind Coffeehouse,** 106 E. Second St. (✆ **928/289-2859**), which has a very contemporary, art-gallery feel that could hold its own in any major metropolitan area. Right here in Winslow—no foolin'!

The Turquoise Room ★★ *Value* NEW AMERICAN/SOUTHWESTERN When Fred Harvey began his railroad hospitality career, his objective was to provide decent meals to the traveling public. (See "Fred Harvey & His Girls," on p. 290.) Here, in La Posada's reincarnated dining room, you'll get not just decent meals, but superb meals the likes of which you won't find anywhere else in northern Arizona. In summer, herbs and vegetables often come from the hotel's own gardens, and wild game is a specialty. Be sure to start your meal with the sweet-corn and black-bean soups, which are served side by side in the same bowl to create a sort of yin-yang symbol. On top of all this, you can watch the trains rolling by just outside the window.

At La Posada, 303 E. Second St. ✆ **928/289-2888.** www.theturquoiseroom.net. Reservations recommended. Main courses $8–$13 lunch, $16–$29 dinner. AE, DISC, MC, V. Daily 7am–2pm and 5–9pm.

2 The Hopi Reservation

67 miles N of Winslow; 250 miles NE of Phoenix; 100 miles SW of Canyon de Chelly; 140 miles SE of Page/Lake Powell

The Hopi Reservation, often referred to as Hopiland or just Hopi, is completely encircled by the Navajo Reservation and has at its center a grouping of mesas upon which the Hopi have lived for nearly 1,000 years. This remote region, with its flat-topped mesas and barren landscape, is the center of the universe for the Hopi people. Here the Hopi follow their ancient customs, and many aspects of pueblo culture remain intact. However, much of the culture is hidden from the view of visitors, and although the Hopi perform elaborate religious and social dances throughout the year, many of these dances are not open to outsiders.

The mesas are home to two of the oldest continuously inhabited villages in North America—Walpi and Old Oraibi. Although these two communities show their age and serve as a direct tie to the pueblos of the Ancestral Puebloan culture, most of the villages on the reservation are scattered collections of modern homes. These villages are not destinations unto themselves, but along Arizona 264 numerous crafts shops and studios sell kachinas, baskets, pottery, and silver jewelry. The chance to buy crafts directly from the Hopi is the main reason for a visit to this area, although you can also take a guided tour of Walpi village.

Important note: When visiting the Hopi pueblos, remember that you are a guest and your privileges can be revoked at any time. Respect all posted signs at village entrances, and remember that *photographing, sketching, and recording are prohibited in the villages and at ceremonies.* Also, kivas (ceremonial rooms) and ruins are off-limits.

ESSENTIALS

GETTING THERE This is one of the state's most remote regions. Distances are great, but highways are generally in good condition. Arizona 87 leads from Winslow to Second Mesa, and Arizona 264 runs from Tuba City in the west to the New Mexico state line in the east.

VISITOR INFORMATION For advance information, contact the **Office of Public Relations,** Hopi Tribe, P.O. Box 123, Kykotsmovi, AZ 86039 (✆ **928/734-3283;** www.hopi.nsn.us); or the **Hopi Cultural Preservation Office** (✆ **928/734-3612;** www.nau.edu/~hcpo-p).

THE VILLAGES

With the exception of Upper and Lower Moenkopi, which are near the Navajo town of Tuba City, and the recently settled Yuh Weh Loo Pah Ki community east of Keams Canyon, the Hopi villages are scattered along roughly 20 miles of Arizona 264. Although Old Oraibi is the oldest, there are no tours of this village, and visitors are not likely to feel very welcome here. Consequently, Walpi, the only village with organized tours, is the best place for visitors to learn more about life in the Hopi villages. I mention all of the Hopi villages below to provide a bit of history and perspective on this area, but for the most part, these villages (with the exception of Walpi and Old Oraibi) are not at all picturesque. However, most do have quite a few crafts galleries and stores selling silver jewelry.

FIRST MESA At the top of First Mesa is the village of **Walpi,** which was located lower on the slopes of the mesa until the Pueblo Revolt of 1680 brought on fear of reprisal from the Spanish. The villagers moved Walpi to the very top of the mesa so that they could better defend themselves in the event of a Spanish attack. Parts of Walpi today still look much like the Ancestral Puebloan villages of the Arizona canyons. Small stone houses seem to grow directly from the rock of the mesa top, and ladders jut from the roofs of kivas. The view from here stretches for hundreds of miles around.

Immediately adjacent to Walpi are the two villages of **Sichomovi,** which was founded in 1750 as a colony of Walpi, and **Hano,** which was founded by Tewa peoples who were most likely seeking refuge from the Spanish after the Pueblo Revolt. Neither of these villages has the ancient character of Walpi. At the foot of First Mesa is **Polacca,** a settlement founded in the late 1800s by Walpi villagers who wanted to be closer to the trading post and school.

SECOND MESA Second Mesa is today the center of tourism in Hopiland, and this is where you'll find the Hopi Cultural Center. Villages on Second Mesa include **Shungopavi,** which was moved to its present site after Old Shungopavi was abandoned in 1680 following the Pueblo Revolt. Old Shungopavi is said to be the first Hopi village and was founded by the Bear Clan. Shungopavi is notable for its silver jewelry and its coiled plaques (flat baskets).

Mishongnovi, which means "place of the black man," is named for the leader of a clan that came here from the San Francisco Peaks around 1200. The original Mishongnovi village, located at the base of the mesa, was abandoned in the 1690s, and the village was reestablished at the current site atop the mesa. The Snake Dance is held here during odd-numbered years. It is doubtful that these dances will be open to non-Hopis, although you could try calling Mishongnovi's Community Development Office (see "Visitor Information," above) to check.

Sipaulovi, which is located on the eastern edge of the mesa, was founded after the Pueblo Revolt of 1680.

THIRD MESA **Oraibi,** which the Hopi claim is the oldest continuously occupied town in the United States, is located on Third Mesa. The village dates from 1150 and, according to legend, was founded by people from Old Shungopavi. A Spanish mission was established in Oraibi in 1629, and the ruins are still visible north of the village.

Today, Oraibi is a mix of old stone houses and modern ones, usually of cinder block. Wander around Oraibi, and you'll likely be approached by village women and children offering to sell you various local crafts and the traditional blue-corn *piki* bread. You may also be invited into someone's home to see the crafts they have to offer. For this reason, Old Oraibi is the most interesting village in which to shop for local crafts.

For centuries, Oraibi was the largest of the Hopi villages, but in 1906, a schism arose due to Bureau of Indian Affairs policies, and many of the villagers left to form **Hotevilla.** This is considered the most conservative of the Hopi villages and has had frequent confrontations with the federal government. **Kykotsmovi,** also known as Lower Oraibi or New Oraibi, was founded in 1890 by villagers from Oraibi who wanted to be closer to the school and trading post. This village is the seat of the Hopi Tribal Government. **Bacavi** was founded in 1907 by villagers who had helped found Hotevilla but who later decided that they wanted to return to Oraibi. The people of Oraibi would not let them return, and rather than go back to Hotevilla, they founded a new village.

MOENKOPI This village is 40 miles to the west of the Hopi mesas. Founded in 1870 by people from Oraibi, Moenkopi sits in the center of a wide green valley where plentiful water makes farming more reliable. Moenkopi is only a few miles from Tuba City off U.S. 160 and is divided into the villages of Upper Moenkopi and Lower Moenkopi.

EXPLORING THE WORLD OF THE HOPI

Start your visit to the Hopi pueblos at the **Hopi Cultural Center,** on Arizona 264 in Second Mesa (✆ **928/734-6650**). This combination museum, motel, and restaurant is the tourism headquarters for the area. The museum is open Monday through Friday from 8am to 5pm; in summer, it's also open Saturday and Sunday from 9am to 3pm. You might also find the museum open on Saturdays in spring and fall. Admission is $3 for adults and $1 for children 13 and under.

The most rewarding Hopi village to visit is **Walpi** ★, on First Mesa. Guided tours of this tiny village are offered daily between 9:30am and 4pm (9am–5pm in summer). Admission is $8 for adults and $5 for youths 5 to 17. To sign up for a tour, drive to the top of First Mesa (in Polacca, take the road that says FIRST MESA VILLAGE) and continue through the village to **Ponsi Hall Visitor Center** (✆ **928/737-2262**), where you'll see signs for the tours. The tours, which last 1 hour, are led by Hopis who will tell you the history of the village and explain a bit about the local culture. Similar tours are also offered by **Village of Walpi Tour Services** (✆ **928/737-9556** or 928/737-9377). These tours are offered Monday through Friday from 8:30am to 4pm. The cost is $5.

CULTURAL TOURS

To get the most out of a visit to the Hopi mesas, it is best to book a guided tour. With a guide, you will probably learn much more about this rather insular culture than you ever could on your own. Tour companies frequently use local guides and stop at the homes of working artisans. This all adds up to a more in-depth and educational visit to one of the oldest cultures on the continent.

Bertram Tsavadawa at **Tsavadawa's Ancient Pathways** (✆ **928/797-8145;** www.ancientpathwaystours.com) specializes in tours to Hopi petroglyph sites. These are sites that are not open to the public unless you are with a Hopi guide. Tours also visit Old Oraibi. The cost is $75 per person for a 3-hour tour and $165 for a 6-hour tour.

DANCES & CEREMONIES

The Hopi have developed the most complex religious ceremonies of any of the Southwest tribes. The masked kachina dances for which they are most famous are held from January to July. However, most kachina dances are closed to the non-Hopi public. Social dances (usually open to the public) are held August through February. If you're on the reservation during these months, ask if any dances are taking place. Who knows? You might get lucky. Snake Dances (usually closed to the non-Hopi public) are held August through December.

Kachinas, whether in the form of dolls or masked dancers, are representative of the spirits of everything from plants and animals to ancestors and sacred places. More than 300 kachinas appear on a regular basis in Hopi ceremonies, and another 200 appear occasionally. The kachina spirits are said to live in the San Francisco Peaks to the southwest and at Spring of the Shadows in the east. According to legend, the kachinas lived with the Hopi long ago, but the Hopi people made the kachinas angry, causing them to leave. Before departing, though, the kachinas taught the Hopi how to perform their ceremonies.

Today, the kachina ceremonies, performed by men wearing elaborate costumes and masks, serve several purposes. Most important, they bring clouds and rain to water the all-important corn crop, but they also ensure health, happiness, long life, and harmony in the universe. As part of the kachina ceremonies, dancers often bring carved wooden kachina dolls to village children to introduce them to the various spirits.

The kachina season lasts from the winter solstice until shortly after the summer solstice. The actual dates for dances are determined by the position of the sun and are usually announced only shortly before the ceremonies are to be held. Preparations for the dances take place inside kivas (circular ceremonial rooms) that are entered from the roof by means of a ladder; the dances themselves are usually held in a village square or street.

With ludicrous and sometimes lewd mimicry, clowns known as *koyemsi, koshares,* and *tsukus* entertain spectators between the dances, bringing a lighthearted counterpoint to the very serious nature of the kachina dances. Non-Hopis attending dances have often become the focus of attention for these clowns.

Despite the importance of the kachina dances, it is the **Snake Dance** that has captured the attention of many non-Hopis. The Snake Dance involves the handling of both poisonous and nonpoisonous snakes. The ceremony takes place over 16 days, with the first 4 days dedicated to collecting snakes from the four cardinal directions. Later, footraces are held from the bottom of the mesa to the top. On the last day of the ceremony, the actual Snake Dance is performed. Men of the Snake Society form pairs of dancers—one to carry the snake in his mouth and the other to distract the snake with an eagle feather. When all the snakes have been danced around the plaza, they are rushed down to their homes at the bottom of the mesa to carry the Hopi prayers for rain to the spirits of the underworld.

Due to the disrespectful attitude of some past visitors, many ceremonies and dances are now closed to non-Hopis. However, a couple of Hopi villages do allow visitors to attend some of their dances. The best way to find out about attending dances is to contact the **community development office** of the individual villages (see phone numbers under "Visitor Information," above).

SHOPPING

Most visitors come to the reservation to shop for Hopi crafts. Across the reservation, dozens of small shops sell crafts and jewelry of different quality, and some homes, especially at the foot of First Mesa, have signs indicating that they sell crafts. Shops often sell the work of only a few individuals, so you should stop at several to get an idea of the variety of work available. Also, if you tour Walpi or wander around in Oraibi, you will likely be approached by villagers selling various crafts, including kachina dolls. The quality is not usually as high as that in shops, but then, neither are the prices.

At Keams Canyon, almost 30 miles east of the cultural center, you'll find **McGee's Indian Art Gallery** (✆ **928/738-2295;** www.hopiart.com), which is the best place to shop for high-quality contemporary kachina dolls. This shop is adjacent to a grocery store and has been a trading post for more than 100 years.

If you're in the market for Hopi silver jewelry, stop in at **Hopi Fine Arts** (✆ **928/737-2222;** www.hopifinearts.net), which is at the foot of Second Mesa at the junction of Arizona 264 and Arizona 87. This shop also has a good selection of kachina dolls and some beautiful coil and wicker plaque baskets.

One of the best places to get a quick education in Hopi art and crafts is **Tsakurshovi** (✆ **928/734-2478**), a tiny shop 1½ miles east of the Hopi Cultural Center on Second Mesa. This shop has a huge selection of traditional kachina dolls and also has lots of jewelry. Janice and Joe Day, the owners, are very friendly and are always happy to share their expertise with visitors. This is also where you can buy a "Don't Worry Be Hopi" T-shirt.

If you're interested in kachina dolls, be sure to visit Oraibi's **Monongya Gallery** (✆ **928/734-2344**), a big building right on Arizona 264 outside of Oraibi. It usually has one of the largest selections of kachina dolls in the area. Also in Oraibi is **Hamana So-o's Arts & Crafts** (✆ **928/607-0176**), which is in an old stone house from which owner Sandra Hamana sells primarily artwork and crafts based on kachina images.

WHERE TO STAY & DINE

If you've brought your food along, you'll find picnic tables just east of Oraibi on top of the mesa. These tables have an amazing view!

Hopi Cultural Center Restaurant & Inn Although it isn't much, this simple motel makes the best base for anyone planning to spend a couple of days shopping for crafts in the area. Because it is the only lodging for miles around, be sure you have a reservation before heading up for an overnight visit. Guest rooms are comfortable enough, though the grounds are quite desolate. The restaurant has a salad bar and serves American and traditional Hopi meals, including *piki* bread (a paper-thin bread made from blue corn) and Hopi stew with hominy, lamb, and green chile. There's also a museum.

P.O. Box 67, Second Mesa, AZ 86043. ✆ **928/734-2401.** Fax 928/734-6651. www.hopiculturalcenter.com. 33 units. Mar 15–Oct 15 $95–$100 double; Oct 16–Mar 14 $70–$75 double. Children 12 and under stay free in parent's room. AE, DISC, MC, V. **Amenities:** Restaurant (American/Hopi); shopping arcade. *In room:* A/C, TV, coffeemaker, free local calls.

EN ROUTE TO OR FROM THE HOPI MESAS

On the west side of the reservation, in Tuba City, is the **Tuba City Trading Post,** Main Street and Moenave Avenue (✆ **928/283-5441**). This octagonal trading post was built in 1906 of local stone and is designed to resemble a Navajo hogan (there's also a real hogan on the grounds). The trading post sells Native American crafts, with an emphasis on books, music, and jewelry. Across the parking lot from the trading post you'll find **Hogan Espresso,** Main Street and Moenave Avenue (✆ **800/644-8383** or 928/283-4545), one of the few places on the reservation where you can get espresso. Behind

A Native American Crafts Primer

The Four Corners region is taken up almost entirely by the Navajo and Hopi reservations, so Native American crafts are ubiquitous. You'll see jewelry for sale by the side of desolate roads, Navajo rugs in tiny trading posts, and Hopi kachinas being sold out of village homes. The information below will help you make an informed purchase.

Hopi Kachina Dolls These elaborately decorated wooden dolls are representations of spirits of plants, animals, ancestors, and sacred places. Traditionally, they were given to children to initiate them into the pantheon of kachina spirits. These spirits play important roles in ensuring rain and harmony in the universe. Kachinas have long been popular with collectors, and Hopi carvers have changed their style over the years to cater to the collectors' market. Older kachinas were carved from a single piece of cottonwood, sometimes with arms simply painted on. This older style is much simpler and stiffer than the contemporary style that emphasizes action poses and realistic proportions. A great deal of carving and painting goes into each kachina, and prices today are in the hundreds of dollars for even the simplest. Currently very popular with tourists and collectors are the *tsuku,* or clown kachinas, which are usually painted with bold horizontal black-and-white stripes and are often depicted in humorous situations or carrying slices of watermelon. In the past few years, young carvers have been returning to the traditional style of kachina, so you now are finding more of these simpler images for sale.

Navajo Silver Work While the Hopi create overlay silver work from sheets of silver and the Zuni use silver work simply as a base for their skilled lapidary or stone-cutting work, the Navajo silversmiths highlight the silver itself. Silversmithing did not catch on with the Navajo until the 1880s, when Lorenzo Hubbell, who had established a trading post in the area, decided to hire Mexican silversmiths as teachers. The earliest pieces of Navajo jewelry were replicas of Spanish ornaments, but as the Navajo silversmiths became more proficient, they began to develop their own designs. The squash-blossom necklace, with its horseshoe-shape pendant, is perhaps the most distinctive Navajo design.

Hopi Overlay Silver Work Most Hopi silver work is done in the overlay style, which was introduced to Hopi artisans after World War II, when the

the trading post, you'll find the new **Explore Navajo Interactive Museum,** Main Street and Moenave Avenue (✆ **928/283-4545**), a small museum in a giant tentlike structure that was used at the 2002 Salt Lake City Olympics. Although small, the museum provides a good introduction to Navajo culture. There is also a good Navajo code talkers exhibit here. The museum is open Monday through Saturday 10am to 8pm, and Sunday noon to 8pm. Admission is $9 for adults, $7 for seniors, and $6 for children ages 6 to 12.

G.I. Bill provided funds for Hopi soldiers to study silversmithing at a school founded by Hopi artist Fred Kabotie. The overlay process basically uses two sheets of silver, one with a design cut from it. Heat fuses the two sheets, forming a raised image. Designs often borrow from other Hopi crafts such as basketry and pottery, and from ancient Ancestral Puebloan pottery. Belt buckles, earrings, bolo ties, and bracelets are all popular.

Hopi Baskets On Third Mesa, wicker plaques and baskets are made from rabbit brush and sumac, and colored with bright aniline dyes. On Second Mesa, coiled plaques and baskets are created from dyed yucca fibers. Throughout the reservation, yucca-fiber sifters are made by plaiting over a willow ring.

Hopi Pottery Most Hopi pottery is produced on First Mesa. Contemporary Hopi pottery comes in a variety of styles, including a yellow-orange ware decorated with black-and-white designs. White pottery with red-and-black designs is also popular. Hopi pottery designs tend toward geometric patterns. Nampeyo, who died in 1942, is the most famous Hopi potter. She is credited with bringing Hopi pottery to the attention of non-Hopi collectors. Today, members of the Nampeyo family are still active as potters.

Navajo Rugs After they acquired sheep and goats from the Spanish, the Navajo learned weaving from the pueblo tribes, and by the early 1800s, their weavings were widely recognized as being the finest in the Southwest. The Navajo women primarily wove blankets, but by the end of the 19th century, the craft began to die out when it became more economical to purchase a ready-made blanket. When Lorenzo Hubbell set up his trading post, he immediately recognized a potential market in the East for the woven blankets—if they could be made heavy enough to be used as rugs. Although today the cost of Navajo rugs, which take hundreds of hours to make, has become almost prohibitively expensive, there are still enough women practicing the craft to keep it alive.

The best rugs are those made with homespun yarn and natural vegetal dyes. (Commercially manufactured yarns and dyes are increasingly used to keep costs down.) There are more than 15 regional styles of rugs and quite a bit of overlapping and borrowing. Bigger and bolder patterns are likely to cost quite a bit less than very complex and highly detailed patterns.

If you happen to be in Tuba City on a Friday morning, be sure to check out the **Tuba City Flea Market** (**© 928/283-3284**), where you'll find not only deals on the necessities of life on the reservation, but also Navajo jewelry and traditional fare such as mutton stew, grilled mutton, and fry bread. You'll find the flea market east of the Quality Inn; go east on Edgewater Drive, and turn right at the sign for the refuse transfer station.

On the western outskirts of Tuba City, on U.S. 160, you'll find **Van's Trading Co.** (**© 928/283-5343**), in the corner of a large grocery store. Van's has a dead-pawn auction on the 15th of each month at 3pm (any pawned item not reclaimed by the owner by a specified date is considered "dead pawn"). The auction provides opportunities to buy older pieces of Navajo silver-and-turquoise jewelry.

In mid-October, Tuba City is the site of the **Western Navajo Fair** (www.westernnavajofair.com), which sells Native American crafts.

West of Tuba City and just off U.S. 160, you can see **dinosaur footprints** ★ preserved in the stone surface of the desert. There are usually a few people waiting at the site to guide visitors to the best footprints (these guides will expect a tip of $1–$2). The scenery out your car window is some of the strangest in the region—red-rock sandstone formations that resemble petrified sand dunes.

The **Cameron Trading Post** ★ (✆ **800/338-7385** or 928/679-2231; www.camerontradingpost.com), 16 miles south of the junction of U.S. 160 and U.S. 89, is well worth a visit. The main trading post is filled with souvenirs but has large selections of rugs and jewelry as well. In the adjacent stone-walled gallery are museum-quality Native American artifacts (with prices to match). The trading post includes a motel, convenience store, and gas station.

WHERE TO STAY

Quality Inn Navajo Nation Located in the bustling Navajo community of Tuba City (where you'll find gas stations, fast-food restaurants, and grocery stores), this modern hotel is adjacent to the historic Tuba City Trading Post and is actually a more attractive place to stay in this region than the Hopi Cultural Center. The hotel offers comfortable rooms of average size, but the green lawns, shade trees, and old trading post (complete with hogan) are what really set this place apart. This hotel is also the site of the new Explore Navajo Interactive Museum and has an Internet cafe.

Main St. and Moenave Ave. (P.O. Box 247), Tuba City, AZ 86045. ✆ **800/644-8383** or 928/283-4545. Fax 928/283-4144. www.qualityinntubacity.com. 80 units. Apr–Oct $105–$140 double; Nov–Mar $85–$115 double. Children 18 and under stay free in parent's room. AE, DC, DISC, MC, V. Pets accepted ($10 deposit). **Amenities:** Restaurant (American/Mexican/Navajo); business center; coin-op laundry. *In room:* A/C, TV, coffeemaker, hair dryer, iron, safe, microwave, high-speed Internet access, free local calls.

3 The Petrified Forest & Painted Desert ★

25 miles E of Holbrook; 90 miles E of Flagstaff; 118 miles S of Canyon de Chelly; 180 miles N of Phoenix

Petrified wood has long fascinated people, and although it can be found in almost every state, the "forest" of downed logs in northeastern Arizona is by far the most extensive. But don't head out this way expecting to see standing trees of stone with leaves and branches intact. Though there is enough petrified timber scattered across this landscape to fill a forest, it is, in fact, in the form of logs and not standing trees. Many a visitor has shown up expecting to find some sort of national forest of stone trees. The reality is much less impressive than the petrified forest of the imagination.

However, this area is still unique. When, in the 1850s, this vast treasure-trove of petrified wood was discovered scattered like kindling across the landscape, enterprising people began exporting it wholesale to the East. Within 50 years, so much had been removed that in 1906 several areas were set aside as the Petrified Forest National Monument, which, in 1962, became a national park. A 27-mile scenic drive winds through the petrified forest (and a small corner of the Painted Desert), providing a fascinating high-desert experience.

It may be hard to believe when you drive across this arid landscape, but at one time this area was a vast steamy swamp. That was 225 million years ago, when dinosaurs and huge amphibians ruled the earth and giant now-extinct trees grew on the high ground around the swamp. Fallen trees were washed downstream, gathered in piles in still backwaters, and eventually covered over with silt, mud, and volcanic ash. As water seeped through this soil, it dissolved the silica in the volcanic ash and redeposited this silica inside the cells of the logs. Eventually, the silica recrystallized into stone to form petrified wood, with minerals such as iron, manganese, and carbon contributing the distinctive colors.

This region was later inundated with water, and thick deposits of sediment buried the logs ever deeper. Eventually, the land was transformed yet again as a geologic upheaval thrust the lake bottom up above sea level. This upthrust of the land cracked the logs into the segments we see today. Wind and water gradually eroded the landscape to create the Painted Desert, and the petrified logs were once again exposed on the surface of the land.

ESSENTIALS

GETTING THERE The north entrance to Petrified Forest National Park is 25 miles east of Holbrook on I-40. The south entrance is 20 miles east of Holbrook on U.S. 180.

FEES The entry fee is $10 per car. The park is open daily from 8am to 5pm (7am–7pm in summer).

VISITOR INFORMATION For further information on the Petrified Forest or the Painted Desert, contact **Petrified Forest National Park,** P.O. Box 2217, Petrified Forest, AZ 86028 (✆ **928/524-6228;** www.nps.gov/pefo). For information on Holbrook and the surrounding region, contact the **Holbrook Chamber of Commerce,** 100 E. Arizona St. (✆ **800/524-2459** or 928/524-6558; www.ci.holbrook.az.us).

EXPLORING A UNIQUE LANDSCAPE

Petrified Forest National Park has both a north and a south entrance. If you are coming from the west, it's better to start at the southern entrance and work your way north along the park's 27-mile scenic road, which has more than 20 overlooks. This way, you'll see the most impressive displays of petrified logs early in your visit and save the Painted Desert vistas for last. If you're coming from the east, start at the northern entrance and work your way south.

The **Rainbow Forest Museum** (✆ **928/524-6228**), just inside the south entrance to the park, is the best place to begin your tour. Here you can learn all about petrified wood, watch an introductory film, and otherwise get oriented. Exhibits chronicle the area's geologic and human history. There are also displays on the reptiles and dinosaurs that once inhabited this region. The museum sells maps and books and also issues free backpacking permits. It's open daily from 8am to 5pm. Adjacent to the museum is a snack bar.

The **Giant Logs self-guided trail** starts behind the museum. The trail winds across a hillside strewn with logs that are 4 to 5 feet in diameter. Almost directly across the parking lot from the museum is the entrance to the **Long Logs** and **Agate House** areas. On the 1.6-mile Long Logs trail, you can see more big trees, while at Agate House, a 2-mile round-trip hike will lead you to the ruins of a pueblo built from colorful petrified wood. These two trails can be combined into a 2.6-mile hike.

Heading north, you'll pass by the unusual formations known as **The Flattops.** These structures were caused by the erosion of softer mineral deposits from beneath a harder and more erosion-resistant layer of sandstone. The Flattops is one of the park's wilderness areas. The **Crystal Forest** is the next stop to the north, named for the beautiful amethyst and quartz crystals once found in the cracks of petrified logs. Concern over the removal of these crystals was what led to the protection of the petrified forest. A .75-mile loop trail winds past the logs that once held the crystals.

At the **Jasper Forest Overlook,** you can see logs that include petrified roots, and a little bit farther north, at the **Agate Bridge** stop, you can see a petrified log that forms a natural agate bridge. Continuing north, you'll reach **Blue Mesa,** where pieces of petrified wood form capstones over easily eroded clay soils. As wind and water wear away at the clay beneath a piece of stone, the balance of the stone becomes more and more precarious until it eventually comes toppling down. A 1-mile loop trail here leads into the park's badlands.

Erosion has played a major role in the formation of the Painted Desert, and to the north of Blue Mesa you'll see some of the most interesting erosional features of the area. It's quite evident why these hills of sandstone and clay are known as **The Teepees.** The layers of different color are due to manganese, iron, and other minerals in the soil.

By this point, you've probably seen as much petrified wood as you'd ever care to see, so be sure to stop at **Newspaper Rock,** where instead of staring at more ancient logs, you can see a dense concentration of petroglyphs left by generations of Native Americans. At nearby **Puerco Pueblo,** the park's largest archaeological site, you can view the remains of homes built by the people who created the park's petroglyphs. This pueblo was probably occupied around A.D.1400. Don't miss the petroglyphs on its back side.

North of Puerco Pueblo, the road crosses I-40. From here to the Painted Desert Visitor Center, there are eight overlooks onto the southernmost edge of the **Painted Desert.** Named for the vivid colors of the soil and stone that cover the land here, the Painted Desert is a dreamscape of pastels washed across a barren expanse of eroded hills. The colors are created by minerals dissolved in sandstone and clay soils that were deposited during different geologic periods. There's a picnic area at Chinde Point overlook. At Kachina Point, you'll find the **Painted Desert Inn,** a renovated historic building that, unfortunately, does not offer overnight accommodations. From here, there's access to the park's other wilderness area. The inn, which was built in 1924 and expanded by the Civilian Conservation Corps, is noteworthy for both its architecture and the Fred Kabotie murals on the interior walls. Hours are 9am to 5pm daily. Between Kachina Point and Tawa Point, you can do an easy 1-mile round-trip hike along the rim of the Painted Desert. An even more interesting route leads down into the Painted Desert from behind the Painted Desert Inn.

Fun Fact **Rock Talk**

Gift shops throughout this region sell petrified wood in all sizes and colors, natural and polished. This petrified wood does not come from the national park, but is collected on private land in the area. No piece of petrified wood, no matter how small, may be removed from Petrified Forest National Park.

Just inside the northern entrance to the park is the **Painted Desert Visitor Center** (✆ **928/524-6228**), open daily 8am to 5pm, where you can watch a short film that explains the process by which wood becomes fossilized. Adjacent to the visitor center are a cafeteria, a bookshop, and a gas station.

OTHER REASONS TO LINGER IN HOLBROOK

Although the Petrified Forest National Park is the main reason for visiting this area, you might want to stop by downtown Holbrook's **Old West Museum,** 100 E. Arizona St. (✆ **928/524-6558**), which also houses the Holbrook Chamber of Commerce visitor center. This old and dusty museum has exhibits on local history but is most interesting for its old jail cells. It's open Monday through Friday from 8am to 5pm (and Sat–Sun 8am–4pm in summer); admission is free. On weekday evenings between June and mid-August, the Holbrook Chamber sponsors Native American dances on the lawn in front.

Although it is against the law to collect petrified wood inside Petrified Forest National Park, there are several rock shops in Holbrook where you can buy pieces of petrified wood in all shapes and sizes. You'll find them lined up along the main street through town and out on U.S. 180, the highway leading to the south entrance of Petrified Forest National Park. The biggest and best of these rock shops is **Jim Gray's Petrified Wood Co.,** 147 Hwy. 180 (✆ **928/524-1842;** www.petrifiedwoodco.com), which has everything from raw rocks to $24,000 petrified-wood coffee tables. This store also has a fascinating display of minerals and fossils. It's open daily from 8am to 6pm (longer hours in summer) and is well worth a stop.

In town on the north side of I-40 is **McGee's Gallery,** 2114 N. Navajo Blvd. (✆ **800/524-9183** or 928/524-1876; mcgeeshopitraders.com), a Native American crafts gallery with a wide selection of typical crafts at reasonable prices. There's a particularly good collection of kachina dolls here.

If you're interested in petroglyphs, you may want to schedule a visit to the **Rock Art Ranch** ★ (✆ **928/288-3260**), southwest of Holbrook on part of the old Hashknife Ranch, which was the largest ranch in the country during the late 19th century. Within the bounds of this ranch, pecked into the rock walls of Chevelon Canyon, are hundreds of Ancestral Puebloan petroglyphs. The setting, a narrow canyon that is almost invisible until you are right beside it, is enchanting, making this the finest place in the state to view petroglyphs. Tours (reservations required) are available Monday through Saturday year-round (call to get rate information and directions to the ranch).

WHERE TO STAY

Holbrook, the town nearest to Petrified Forest National Park, offers lots of budget chain motels charging very reasonable rates.

Wigwam Motel *Finds* If you're willing to sleep on a saggy mattress for the sake of reliving a bit of Route 66 history, don't miss this collection of concrete wigwams (tepees, actually). This unique motel was built in the 1940s, when unusual architecture was springing up all along famous Route 66. The motel has been owned by the same family since it was built and still has the original rustic furniture. Old cars are kept in the parking lot for an added dose of Route 66 character.

811 W. Hopi Dr., Holbrook, AZ 86025. ✆ **928/524-3048.** Fax 928/524-9335. www.galerie-kokopelli.com/wigwam. 15 units. $48–$54 double. MC, V. Pets accepted. *In room:* A/C, TV.

Tips **No Smoke Signals Necessary**

If you're driving in to Arizona from New Mexico, you can get information on the state at the **Painted Cliffs Welcome Center,** Grants Road, Lupton (✆ **928/688-2448**), which is at Exit 359 off I-40. The visitor center is open daily from 8am to 5pm.

WHERE TO DINE

While there are plenty of inexpensive restaurants in Holbrook, none is particularly memorable or recommendable. Your best bet is to drive over to Winslow to The Turquoise Room at La Posada hotel.

4 The Window Rock & Ganado Areas

74 miles NE of Petrified Forest National Park; 91 miles E of Second Mesa; 190 miles E of Flagstaff; 68 miles SE of Canyon de Chelly National Monument

Window Rock, the capital of the Navajo nation, is less than a mile from the New Mexico state line and is named for a huge natural opening in a sandstone cliff just outside town. Today, that landmark is preserved as the **Window Rock Tribal Park,** located 2 miles north of Arizona 264. As the Navajo nation's capital, Window Rock is the site of government offices, a museum and cultural center, and a zoo. A few miles to the west is the St. Michaels Historical Museum, in the community of St. Michaels. About a half-hour's drive west of St. Michaels is the Hubbell Trading Post, in the community of Ganado.

ESSENTIALS

GETTING THERE To reach Window Rock from Flagstaff, take I-40 east to Lupton and go north on Indian Route 12.

VISITOR INFORMATION For advance information, contact **Navajo Tourism,** P.O. Box 663, Window Rock, AZ 86515 (✆ **928/810-8501;** www.discovernavajo.com).

SPECIAL EVENTS Unlike the village ceremonies of the pueblo-dwelling Hopi, Navajo religious ceremonies tend to be held in the privacy of family hogans. However, the public is welcome to attend the numerous fairs, powwows, and rodeos held throughout the year. The biggest of these is the **Navajo Nation Fair** (✆ **928/871-7055;** www.navajonationfair.com), held in Window Rock in early September. It features traditional dances, a rodeo, a powwow, a parade, a Miss Navajo Pageant, and arts-and-crafts exhibits and sales.

EXPLORING THE AREA

Hubbell Trading Post National Historic Site ★ Located just outside the town of Ganado, 26 miles west of Window Rock, the Hubbell Trading Post was established in 1876 by Lorenzo Hubbell and is the oldest continuously operating trading post on the Navajo Reservation. Hubbell did more to popularize the arts and crafts of the Navajo people than any other person and was in large part responsible for the revival of Navajo weaving in the late 19th century.

Much more than just a place to trade crafts for imported goods, trading posts were for many years the main gathering spot for meeting people from other parts of the reservation and served as a sort of gossip fence and newsroom. Hubbell Trading Post is still in use today, and in the trading post's general store, you'll see basic foodstuffs (not much variety here) and bolts of the cloth Navajo women use for sewing their traditional skirts and blouses. However, today the trading post is more a living museum. Visitors can explore the grounds on their own or take a guided tour ($2), and can often watch Navajo weavers in the slow process of creating a rug.

The rug room is filled with a variety of traditional and contemporary Navajo pieces. And although it's possible to buy a small 12×18-inch rug for around $100, most cost thousands of dollars. In another room are baskets, kachinas, and jewelry by Navajo, Hopi, and Zuni artisans. Twice a year, in May and August, there are auctions of Native American crafts here at the trading post.

Ariz. 264, Ganado. ✆ **928/755-3475.** www.nps.gov/hutr. Free admission. May to mid-Sept daily 8am–6pm; mid-Sept to Apr daily 8am–5pm. Closed New Year's Day, Thanksgiving, and Christmas.

Navajo Museum, Library & Visitor's Center This museum and cultural center is housed in a large modern building patterned after a traditional hogan. Inside you'll see temporary exhibits of contemporary crafts and art, as well as exhibits on contemporary Navajo culture. There's also a gift shop here.

Ariz. 264 at Post Office Loop Rd. (across from the Navajo Nation Inn), Window Rock. ✆ **928/871-7941.** Free admission. Mon and Sat 8am–5pm; Tues–Fri 8am–8pm.

Navajo Nation Zoo & Botanical Park *Kids* Located in back of the Navajo Nation Inn, this zoo and botanical garden features animals and plants that are significant in Navajo history and culture. Bears, cougars, and wolves are among the creatures you'll see. Although small, this zoo participates in the wolf recovery program that is reintroducing Mexican wolves into the wild. The setting, which includes several sandstone "haystack" rocks, is very dramatic, and some of the animal enclosures are quite large and incorporate natural rock outcroppings.

Ariz. 264, Window Rock. ✆ **928/871-6574** or 928/871-6573. Free admission. Mon–Sat 10am–5pm. Closed New Year's Day, Thanksgiving, and Christmas.

St. Michaels Historical Museum In the community of St. Michaels, 4 miles west of Window Rock, this museum chronicles the lives and influence of Franciscan friars who started a mission in this area in the 1670s. The museum is in a small building adjacent to the impressive stone mission church. Back in the early years of the 20th century, a friar here photographed the Navajo of the area, and the chance to see some of these historical photos is one of the best reasons to visit this museum.

St. Michaels, just south of Ariz. 264. ✆ **928/871-4171.** Free admission. Memorial Day to Labor Day daily 9am–4pm. Closed other months.

SHOPPING

The **Hubbell Trading Post,** although a National Historic Site, is still an active trading post and has an outstanding selection of rugs, as well as lots of jewelry (see

---

Tips What Time Is It?

The Navajo nation observes daylight saving time, contrary to the rest of the state, so if you're coming from elsewhere in Arizona, the time here will be 1 hour later in months when daylight saving is in effect. The Hopi Reservation, however, does not observe daylight saving time, even though it is completely surrounded by the Navajo Reservation.

Tips **Buying Crafts**

All over the Navajo Reservation, you'll see roadside stalls selling jewelry and crafts. While you can sometimes get quality merchandise and bargain prices at these stalls, you'll usually find better items at trading posts, museum shops, park gift shops, and established shops where you receive some guarantee of quality.

"Exploring the Area," above). In Window Rock, be sure to visit the **Navajo Arts and Crafts Enterprise** (✆ **866/871-4095** or 928/871-4095), which is next to the Quality Inn Navajo Nation Capital and has been operating since 1941. Here you'll find silver-and-turquoise jewelry, Navajo rugs, baskets, pottery, and Native American clothing. The store is open Monday through Friday from 9am to 9pm, Saturday from 10am to 9pm, and Sunday from 10am to 6pm.

WHERE TO STAY

Navajoland Days Inn This modern hotel is 2 miles west of Window Rock near the historic St. Michaels Mission and is centrally located for exploring west to the Hopi mesas, north to Canyon de Chelly, and south to Petrified Forest National Park. With its indoor pool and exercise room, this is your best bet in the area. There's a Denny's out front, which is about as good as it gets in this corner of the state.

392 W. Hwy. 264, St. Michaels, AZ 86511. ✆ **800/329-7466** or 928/871-5690. Fax 928/871-5699. www.daysinn.com. 73 units. $70–$90 double; $90–$150 suite. Children 12 and under stay free in parent's room. AE, DC, DISC, MC, V. Pets accepted ($20). **Amenities:** Restaurant (American); indoor pool; exercise room; Jacuzzi; sauna; coin-op laundry. *In room:* A/C, TV, dataport, coffeemaker, hair dryer, iron, high-speed Internet access, free local calls.

Quality Inn Navajo Nation Capital ★ This hotel is in Window Rock, the administrative center of the Navajo Reservation. The rooms feature rustic Southwestern-style furnishings and are the best you'll find on the reservation. The restaurant serves American and traditional Navajo dishes, including mutton stew and fry bread.

48 W. Hwy. 264 (P.O. Box 2340), Window Rock, AZ 86515. ✆ **800/662-6189** or 928/871-4108. Fax 928/871-5466. www.qualityinnwindowrock.com. 56 units. Apr–Oct $69–$105 double; Nov–Mar $65–$100 double. Rates include full breakfast. Children 18 and under stay free in parent's room. AE, DC, DISC, MC, V. Pets accepted ($50 deposit). **Amenities:** Restaurant (American/Navajo); coin-op laundry. *In room:* A/C, TV, fridge, coffeemaker, hair dryer, iron, microwave, high-speed Internet access, free local calls.

WHERE TO DINE

In Window Rock, your best bet is the **Quality Inn Navajo Nation Capital** (see "Where to Stay," above), which serves moderately priced American, Mexican, and Navajo food. Try the Navajo tacos or mutton stew. The restaurant is open Monday through Friday from 6am to 9pm and on Saturday and Sunday from 7am to 6pm.

At the **Chihootso Indian Market** (✆ **928/871-4698**), at the junction of Arizona 264 and Navajo Route 12, you'll find several tiny restaurants that specialize in traditional Navajo dishes such as mutton stew and fry bread. On weekends there's also a crafts/flea market in the parking lot here. Hours vary.

5 Canyon de Chelly National Monument ★★★

68 miles NW of Window Rock; 222 miles NE of Flagstaff; 110 miles SE of Navajo National Monument; 110 miles SE of Monument Valley Navajo Tribal Park

It's hard to imagine narrow canyons less than 1,000 feet deep being more spectacular than the Grand Canyon, but in some ways Canyon de Chelly National Monument is just that. Gaze down from the rim at an ancient cliff dwelling as the whinnying of horses and clanging of goat bells drift up from far below, and you'll be struck by the continuity of human existence. For nearly 5,000 years, people have called these canyons home, and today the canyon is the site of not only prehistoric dwelling sites, but also the summer homes of Navajo farmers and sheepherders.

Canyon de Chelly National Monument consists of two major canyons—Canyon de Chelly (which is pronounced "canyon duh shay" and is derived from the Navajo word *tsegi,* meaning "rock canyon") and Canyon del Muerto (Spanish for "Canyon of the Dead")—and several smaller canyons. The canyons extend for more than 100 miles through the rugged slickrock landscape of northeastern Arizona, draining the seasonal snowmelt runoff from the Chuska Mountains.

In summer, Canyon de Chelly's smooth sandstone walls of rich reds and yellows contrast sharply with the deep greens of corn, pastures, and cottonwoods on the canyon floor. Vast stone amphitheaters form the caves in which the Ancestral Puebloans built their homes, and as you watch shadows and light paint an ever-changing canyon panorama, it's easy to see why the Navajo consider this sacred ground. With mysteriously abandoned cliff dwellings and breathtaking natural beauty, Canyon de Chelly is as worthy of a visit as the Grand Canyon.

ESSENTIALS

GETTING THERE From Flagstaff, the easiest route to Canyon de Chelly is I-40 to U.S. 191 to Ganado. At Ganado, drive west on Arizona 264 and pick up U.S. 191 N to Chinle. If you're coming down from Monument Valley or Navajo National Monument, Indian Route 59, which connects U.S. 160 and U.S. 191, is an excellent road with plenty of beautiful scenery.

FEES Monument admission is free.

VISITOR INFORMATION Before leaving home, you can contact **Canyon de Chelly National Monument,** P.O. Box 588, Chinle, AZ 86503 (© **928/674-5500;** www.nps.gov/cach), for information. The visitor center is open daily 8am to 5pm (MST, not Navajo Reservation time). The monument itself is open daily from sunrise to sunset.

SPECIAL EVENTS The annual **Central Navajo Fair** is held in Chinle in August.

EXPLORING THE CANYON

Your first stop should be the **visitor center,** in front of which is an example of a traditional crib-style hogan, a hexagonal structure of logs and earth that Navajos use as both a home and a ceremonial center. Inside the visitor center, a small museum explores the history of Canyon de Chelly, and there's often a silversmith demonstrating Navajo jewelry-making techniques. Interpretive programs are offered at the monument Memorial Day to Labor Day. Check at the visitor center for daily activities, such as campfire programs and natural-history programs.

From the visitor center, most people tour the canyon by car. Very different views of the monument's system of canyons are provided by the 15-mile North Rim and 16-mile South Rim drives. The North Rim Drive overlooks Canyon del Muerto, while the South Rim Drive overlooks Canyon de Chelly. With stops, the drive along either rim road can easily take 2 to 3 hours. If you have time for only one, make it the South Rim Drive, which provides both a dramatic view of Spider Rock and the chance to hike down into the canyon on the only trail you can explore without hiring a guide. If, on the other hand, you're more interested in the history and prehistory of this area, opt for the North Rim Drive, which overlooks several historically significant sites within the canyon.

THE NORTH RIM DRIVE

The first stop on the North Rim is the **Ledge Ruin Overlook.** On the opposite wall, about 100 feet up from the canyon floor, you can see the Ledge Ruin. This site was occupied by the Ancestral Puebloans between 1050 and 1275. Nearby, at the unmarked Dekaa Kiva Viewpoint, you can see a lone kiva (circular ceremonial building). This structure was reached by means of toeholds cut into the soft sandstone cliff wall.

The second stop is the **Antelope House Overlook,** which is the all-around most interesting overlook in the monument. Not only do you get to hike .25 mile over the rugged rim-rock landscape, but you get to view ruins, rock art, and impressive cliff walls. The Antelope House ruin takes its name from the antelope paintings, believed to date back to the 1830s, on a nearby cliff wall. Beneath the ruins of Antelope House, archaeologists have found the remains of an earlier pit house dating from A.D. 693. Although most of the Ancestral Puebloan cliff dwellings were abandoned sometime after a drought began in 1276, Antelope House had already been abandoned by 1260, possibly because of damage caused by flooding. Across the wash from Antelope House, an ancient tomb, known as the Tomb of the Weaver, was discovered by archaeologists in the 1920s. The tomb contained the well-preserved body of an old man wrapped in a blanket of golden eagle feathers and accompanied by cornmeal, shelled and husked corn, pine nuts, beans, salt, and thick skeins of cotton. Also visible from this overlook is Navajo Fortress, a red-sandstone butte that the Navajo once used as a refuge from attackers. A steep trail once led to the top of Navajo Fortress, and by using log ladders that could be pulled up into the refuge, the Navajo were able to escape their attackers.

The third stop is **Mummy Cave Overlook,** named for two mummies found in burial urns below the ruins. Archaeological evidence indicates that this giant amphitheater consisting of two caves was occupied for 1,000 years, from A.D. 300 to 1300. In the two caves and on the shelf between are 80 rooms, including three kivas. The central structure between the two caves includes an interesting three-story building characteristic of the architecture in Mesa Verde in New Mexico. Archaeologists speculate that a group of Ancestral Puebloans migrated here from New Mexico. Much of the original plasterwork is still intact and indicates that the buildings were colorfully decorated.

Tips **Taking Photos on the Reservations**

Before taking a photograph of a Navajo, always ask permission. If it's granted, a tip of $1 or more is expected. Photography is not allowed at all in Hopi villages.

The fourth and last stop on the North Rim is the **Massacre Cave Overlook,** which got its name after an 1805 Spanish military expedition killed more than 115 Navajo at this site. The Navajo at the time had been raiding Spanish settlements that were encroaching on their territory. Accounts of the battle at Massacre Cave differ. One version claims there were only women, children, and old men taking shelter in the cave, but the official Spanish records claim 90 warriors and 25 women and children were killed. Also visible from this overlook is Yucca Cave, which was occupied about 1,000 years ago.

THE SOUTH RIM DRIVE

The South Rim Drive climbs slowly but steadily, and at each stop you're a little bit higher above the canyon floor. Near the mouth of the canyon is the **Tunnel Overlook,** where a short narrow canyon feeds into Chinle Wash, a wash formed by the streams that cut through the canyons of the national monument. *Tsegi* is a Navajo word meaning "rock canyon," and at the nearby **Tsegi Overlook,** that's just what you'll see when you gaze down from the viewpoint.

The next stop is the **Junction Overlook,** so named because it overlooks the junction of Canyon del Muerto and Canyon de Chelly. Here you can see the Junction Ruin, which has 10 rooms and a kiva. Ancestral Puebloans occupied this ruin during the Great Pueblo Period, which lasted from around 1100 until shortly before 1300. First Ruin, which is perched precariously on a long narrow ledge, is also visible. In this ruin are 22 rooms and two kivas. Good luck picking out the two canyons in this maze of curving cliff walls.

The third stop is **White House Overlook,** from which you can see the 80-room White House Ruins, which are among the largest ruins in the canyon. These buildings were inhabited between 1040 and 1275. From this overlook, you have your only opportunity to descend into Canyon de Chelly without a guide or ranger. The **White House Ruins Trail** ★★ descends 600 feet to the canyon floor and crosses Chinle Wash before reaching the White House Ruins. The buildings of this ruin were constructed both on the canyon floor and 50 feet up the cliff wall in a small cave. Although you cannot enter the ruins, you can get close enough to get a good look. Do not wander off this trail, and please respect the privacy of the Navajo living here. The 2.5-mile round-trip hike takes about 2 hours. Be sure to carry water.

Notice the black streaks on the sandstone walls above the White House Ruins. These streaks, known as desert varnish, are formed by seeping water, which reacts with iron in the sandstone (iron is what gives the walls their reddish hue). To create the canyon's many petroglyphs, Ancestral Puebloan artists would chip away at the desert varnish. Later, the Navajo used paints to create pictographs of animals and historical events, such as the Spanish military expedition that killed 115 Navajo at Massacre Cave. Many of these petroglyphs and pictographs can be seen if you take a guided tour into the canyon.

The fifth stop is **Sliding House Overlook.** These ruins were built on a narrow shelf and appear to be sliding down into the canyon. Inhabited from about 900 until 1200, Sliding House contained between 30 and 50 rooms. This overlook is already more than 700 feet above the canyon floor, with sheer walls giving the narrow canyon a very foreboding appearance.

On the last access road to the canyon rim, you'll come to the **Face Rock Overlook,** which provides yet another dizzying glimpse of the ever-deepening canyon. Here you gaze 1,000 feet down to the bottom. However, it is the next stop—**Spider Rock**

Fred Harvey & His Girls

Unless you grew up in the Southwest and can remember back to pre–World War II days, you may have never heard of Fred Harvey and the Harvey Girls. But if you spend much time in northern Arizona, you're likely to run into quite a few references to the Harvey Girls and their boss.

Fred Harvey was the Southwest's most famous mogul of railroad hospitality and an early promoter of tourism in the Grand Canyon State. Harvey, who was working for a railroad in the years shortly after the Civil War, developed a distaste for the food served at railroad stations. He decided he could do a better job and in 1876 opened his first Harvey House railway-station restaurant for the Santa Fe Railroad. By the time of his death in 1901, Harvey operated 47 restaurants, 30 diners, and 15 hotels across the West.

The women who worked as waitresses in the Harvey House restaurants came to be called Harvey Girls. Known for their distinctive black dresses, white aprons, and black bow ties, Harvey Girls had to adhere to very strict behavior codes and were the prim and proper women of the late-19th- and early-20th-century American West. In fact, in the late 19th century, they were considered the only real "ladies" in the West, aside from schoolteachers. So celebrated were they in their day that in the 1940s, Judy Garland starred in a Technicolor MGM musical called *The Harvey Girls.* Garland played a Harvey Girl who battles the evil town dance-hall queen (played by Angela Lansbury) for the soul of the local saloonkeeper.

Overlook—that offers the monument's most spectacular view. This viewpoint overlooks the junction of Canyon de Chelly and Monument Canyon. The monolithic pinnacle known as Spider Rock rises 800 feet from the canyon floor, its two freestanding towers forming a natural monument. Across the canyon from Spider Rock stands the similarly striking **Speaking Rock,** which is connected to the far canyon wall.

OTHER WAYS TO SEE THE CANYON

Access to the floor of Canyon de Chelly is restricted; unless you're on the White House Ruins Trail (see "The South Rim Drive," above), you must be accompanied by an authorized guide in order to enter the canyon. **Navajo guides** usually charge $15 to $25 per hour with a 3-hour minimum and will lead you into the canyon on foot or in your own four-wheel-drive vehicle. **De Chelly Tours** (**✆ 928/674-3772;** www.dechellytours.com) charges $20 per hour, with a 3-hour minimum, to go out in your four-wheel-drive vehicle; if it supplies the vehicle, the cost goes up to $125 for three people for 3 hours. Similar tours are offered by **Canyon de Chelly Tours** (**✆ 928/674-5433** or 928/349-1600; www.canyondechellytours.com), which will take you into the canyon in a jeep or a Unimog truck (a powerful four-wheel-drive off-road vehicle). Unimog tours are $50 to $52 for adults and $35 to $37 for children 12 and under. Tours depart from the Holiday Inn parking lot. Reservations are recommended. The monument visitor center also maintains a list of guides.

Another way to see Canyon de Chelly and Canyon del Muerto is on what locals call **shake-and-bake tours** ★, via a six-wheel-drive truck. In summer, these excursions really live up to the name. (In winter, the truck is enclosed to keep out the elements.) The trucks operate out of **Thunderbird Lodge** (✆ **800/679-2473;** www.tbirdlodge.com) and are equipped with seats in the bed. Tours make frequent stops for photographs and to visit ruins, Navajo farms, and rock art. Half-day trips cost around $41 per person ($32 for children 12 and under), while full-day tours cost around $67 for all ages. Full-day tours, offered spring through fall, leave at 9am and return at 5pm.

If you'd rather use a more traditional means of transportation, you can go on a guided horseback ride. To leave the crowds behind, drive east along South Rim Drive to **Totsonii Ranch** ★ (✆ **928/755-6209;** www.totsoniiranch.com), which is 1¼ miles past where the pavement ends. Rides from here visit a remote part of the canyon (including the Spider Rock area) and cost $15 per group per hour for the guide and $15 per person per hour. Totsonii Ranch also offers overnight rides for $335 per person and 2-night rides for $515 per person.

If you're physically fit and like hiking, consider hiring a guide to lead you down into the canyon. Hikes can start at the White House Ruin trail, near the Spider Rock overlook, or from near the Antelope House overlook. These latter two starting points are trails that are not open to the public without a guide and should be your top choices. The hike from Antelope House gets my vote for best option for a hike. Guides can be hired at the monument visitor center. Guides charge $15 per hour for up to 15 people.

SHOPPING

The **Thunderbird Lodge Gift Shop,** in Chinle (✆ **800/679-2473** or 928/674-5841), is well worth a stop while you're in the area. It has a huge collection of rugs, as well as good selections of pottery and plenty of souvenirs. In the canyon wherever visitors gather (at ruins and petroglyph sites), you're likely to encounter craftspeople selling jewelry and other types of handwork. These craftspeople, most of whom live in the canyon, accept cash, personal checks, traveler's checks, and sometimes credit cards.

WHERE TO STAY & DINE

Holiday Inn–Canyon de Chelly ★★ Located between the town of Chinle and the national monument entrance, this modern hotel is on the site of the old Garcia Trading Post, which has been incorporated into the restaurant and gift-shop building (although the building no longer has any historical character). All guest rooms have patios or balconies, and most face the cottonwood-shaded pool courtyard. Because Canyon de Chelly truck tours leave from the parking lot here and because the restaurant serves the best food in town, this should be your top choice for a room in Chinle.

Indian Rte. 7 (P.O. Box 1889), Chinle, AZ 86503. ✆ **800/465-4329** or 928/674-5000. Fax 928/674-8264. www.holiday-inn.com/chinle-garcia. 108 units. $69–$159 double. Children under 18 stay free in parent's room; children 12 and under eat for free. AE, DC, DISC, MC, V. **Amenities:** Restaurant (American/Navajo); outdoor pool; exercise room; concierge; room service; coin-op laundry. *In room:* A/C, TV, dataport, coffeemaker, hair dryer, iron, high-speed Internet access, Wi-Fi.

Tips Forget About Wine with Dinner

Alcohol is prohibited on both Navajo and Hopi reservations. Unfortunately, however, despite this prohibition, drunk drivers are a problem on the reservation, so stay alert.

Thunderbird Lodge Built on the site of an early trading post right at the mouth of Canyon de Chelly, the Thunderbird Lodge is the closest hotel to the national monument. The red-adobe construction of the lodge itself is reminiscent of ancient pueblos, and the presence on the property of an old stone-walled trading post gives this place lots of character. Guest rooms have both ceiling fans and air-conditioning. The old trading post now serves as a cafeteria, but there is a gift shop with a rug room on-site. P.O. Box 548, Chinle, AZ 86503. ✆ **800/679-2473** or 928/674-5841. Fax 928/674-5844. www.tbirdlodge.com. 74 units. Apr to mid-Nov $101–$106 double, $145 suite; mid-Nov to Mar $65 double, $91 suite. Children 2 and under stay free in parent's room. AE, DC, DISC, MC, V. Pets accepted. **Amenities:** Restaurant (American/Navajo); tour desk. *In room:* A/C, TV, Wi-Fi, free local calls.

CAMPGROUNDS

Adjacent to the Thunderbird Lodge is the free **Cottonwood Campground,** which has around 100 sites but does not take reservations. On South Rim Drive 10 miles east of the Canyon de Chelly visitor center is another option, the private **Spider Rock Campground** (✆ **928/674-8261;** www.spiderrockcampground.com), which has more than 30 spaces and charges $10 to $12 per night. This campground also has a couple of hogans for rent for $29 to $39 per night. The next nearest campgrounds are at **Tsaile Lake** and **Wheatfields Lake,** both south of the town of Tsaile on Indian Route 12. Tsaile is at the east end of the North Rim Drive.

6 Navajo National Monument ★

110 miles NW of Canyon de Chelly; 140 miles NE of Flagstaff; 60 miles SW of Monument Valley; 90 miles E of Page

Navajo National Monument, located 30 miles west of Kayenta and 60 miles northeast of Tuba City, encompasses three of the largest and best-preserved Ancestral Puebloan cliff dwellings in the region—Betatakin (Talastima), Keet Seel (Kawestima), and Inscription House. It's possible to visit both Betatakin and Keet Seel, but, due to its fragility, Inscription House is closed to the public. The name Navajo National Monument is a bit misleading. Although the Navajo do inhabit the area now, the cliff dwellings were built by Kayenta Ancestral Puebloans, who were the ancestral Hopi and Pueblo peoples. The Navajo did not arrive in this area until centuries after the cliff dwellings had been abandoned.

For reasons unknown, the well-constructed cliff dwellings here were abandoned around the middle of the 13th century. Tree rings suggest that a drought in the latter part of the 13th century prevented the Ancestral Puebloans from growing sufficient crops. In Tsegi Canyon, however, there's another theory for the abandonment. The canyon was usually flooded each year by spring and summer snowmelt, which made farming quite productive, but in the mid-1200s, weather patterns changed and streams began cutting deep into the soil, forming narrow little canyons called arroyos, which lowered the water table and made farming much more difficult.

ESSENTIALS

GETTING THERE Navajo National Monument can be reached by taking U.S. 89 N to U.S. 160 to Arizona 564 N.

FEES Monument admission is free.

VISITOR INFORMATION For information, contact **Navajo National Monument,** HC 71 Box 3, Tonalea, AZ 86044 (✆ **928/672-2700;** www.nps.gov/nava). Spring through fall, the visitor center is Monday through Friday from 8am to 5pm and Saturday and Sunday from 8am to 7pm; in winter the visitor center is open daily from 9am to 5pm. The monument is open daily from sunrise to sunset.

EXPLORING THE MONUMENT

A visit to Navajo National Monument is definitely not a point-and-shoot experience. You're going to have to expend some energy if you want to see what this monument is all about. The shortest distance you'll have to walk is 1 mile, which is the round-trip from the visitor center to the Betatakin overlook. However, if you want to actually get close to these ruins, you're looking at strenuous day or overnight hikes.

Your first stop should be the **visitor center,** which has informative displays on the Ancestral Puebloan and Navajo cultures, including numerous artifacts from Tsegi Canyon. You can also watch a couple of short films or a slide show.

The only one of the monument's three ruins that can be seen easily is **Betatakin** ★, which means "ledge house" in Navajo. Built in a huge amphitheater-like alcove in the canyon wall, Betatakin was occupied only from 1250 to 1300 and may have housed 125 people. A 1-mile round-trip paved trail from the visitor center leads to overlooks of Betatakin. The strenuous 5-mile round-trip hike to Betatakin itself is led by a ranger, takes 3 to 5 hours, and involves descending more than 600 feet to the floor of Tsegi Canyon and later returning to the rim. Between late May and early September, these guided hikes are offered twice a day and leave the visitor center at 8:15 and 11am (MST, not Navajo Reservation time). Other months, tours leave weekends at 10am, but call to make sure the tour will be going out. These hikes are offered on a first-come, first-served basis. All participants should carry 1 to 2 quarts of water. This is a fascinating hike, and because the number of hikers is limited, you won't feel like you're shoulder to shoulder with a herd of tourists.

Keet Seel ★, which means "broken pieces of pottery" in Navajo, has a much longer history than Betatakin, with occupation beginning as early as A.D. 950 and continuing until 1300. At one point, Keet Seel may have housed 150 people. The 17-mile round-trip hike is quite strenuous. During the summer, hikers usually stay overnight at a primitive campground near the ruins, but in the winter, the hike is done as a day hike. You must carry enough water for your trip—up to 2 gallons in summer—because none is available along the trail. These hikes are offered daily between Memorial Day and Labor Day. You can apply for a permit 6 months in advance.

WHERE TO STAY

There is no lodge at the national monument, but there are two free campgrounds that have a total of 48 campsites. One is open year-round, and one is open April through September. The nearest reliable motels are 30 miles away in Kayenta. See the section on Monument Valley, below, for details.

7 Monument Valley Navajo Tribal Park ★★★

60 miles NE of Navajo National Monument; 110 miles NW of Canyon de Chelly; 200 miles NE of Flagstaff; 150 miles E of Page

In its role as sculptor, nature has, in the north central part of the Navajo Reservation, created a garden of monoliths and spires unequaled anywhere on earth. Whether you've ever been here or not, you've almost certainly seen Monument Valley before. This otherworldly landscape has been an object of fascination for years, and since Hollywood director John Ford first came here in the 1930s, it has served as backdrop for countless movies, TV shows, and commercials.

Located 30 miles north of Kayenta and straddling the Arizona-Utah state line (you actually go into Utah to get to the park entrance), Monument Valley is a vast flat plain punctuated by natural sandstone cathedrals. These huge monoliths rise up from the sagebrush with sheer walls that capture the light of the rising and setting sun and transform it into fiery hues. Evocative names including the Mittens, Three Sisters, Camel Butte, Elephant Butte, the Thumb, and Totem Pole reflect the shapes the sandstone has taken under the erosive forces of nature.

While it may at first seem as if this strange landscape is a barren wasteland, it is actually still home to a few hardy Navajo families. The Navajo have been living in the valley for generations, herding their sheep through the sagebrush scrublands, and some families continue to reside here today. In fact, human habitation in Monument Valley dates back hundreds of years. Within the park are more than 100 Ancestral Puebloan archaeological sites, ruins, and petroglyphs dating from before 1300.

ESSENTIALS

GETTING THERE Monument Valley Navajo Tribal Park is 200 miles northeast of Flagstaff. Take U.S. 89 north to U.S. 160 to Kayenta, which is 23 miles south of Monument Valley and 29 miles east of Navajo National Monument. Then drive north on U.S. 163.

FEES Admission to the park is $5 per person (free for children 9 and under). ***Note:*** Because this is a tribal park and not a federal park, America the Beautiful passes are not valid here.

VISITOR INFORMATION For information, contact **Monument Valley Navajo Tribal Park** (✆ **435/727-5874** or 435/727-5870; www.navajonationparks.org). May through September, the park is open daily from 6am to 8pm; between October and April, it's open daily from 8am to 5pm. The park is closed on Christmas and is open only from 8am to noon on Thanksgiving.

EXPLORING THE PARK

This is big country and, like the Grand Canyon, is primarily a point-and-shoot experience for most visitors. Because this is reservation land and people still live in Monument Valley, most backcountry and off-road travel are prohibited unless you're with a licensed guide. So basically, with one exception, your options for seeing the park are limited. You can take a few pictures from the overlook at the visitor center, drive the park's Valley Drive (a scenic but very rough 17-mile dirt road), take a jeep or van tour, or go on a guided hike or horseback ride. At the visitor center, you'll find a small museum, a great gift shop, and a restaurant with a knockout view. Adjacent to the visitor center is a campground, and a picnic area is a quarter-mile away.

Although Valley Drive is best driven in a high-clearance vehicle, plenty of people drive the loop in rental cars and other standard passenger vehicles. Take it slow, and you should do fine. However, if the first stretch of rocky, rutted road convinces you to change your mind about the drive, just return to the visitor center and book a jeep or van tour and let someone else pay the repair bills. Along the loop drive, you'll pass 11 very scenic viewpoints that provide ample opportunities for photographing the valley's many natural monuments. At many of these viewpoints, you'll also encounter Navajos selling jewelry and other crafts. At John Ford's Point, so named because it was a favorite shooting location for film director John Ford, you may even get the chance to photograph a Navajo on horseback posed in front of all that spectacular scenery. He'll expect a dollar.

Moments **Monumental Sunsets**

Be sure to save some film on your camera (or storage space in your digital camera) for sunset at Monument Valley. Sure, these rocks are impressive at noon, but as the sun sets and the shadows lengthen, they are positively enchanting—making up one of the most spectacular sites in America.

Tip: If you're trying to decide whether to take a tour, here's some little-publicized information that might help you with your decision. Most tours don't just drive the 17-mile loop; they go off into a part of the valley that is closed to anyone who is not on a tour. This part of the valley is, in my opinion, the most beautiful. You'll get close-up looks at several natural arches and stop at some beautiful petroglyphs. Before booking a tour, make sure that the tour will go to this "closed" section of the valley. There are always plenty of jeep tour companies waiting for business in the park's main parking lot. If you've managed to get a room at Goulding's Lodge, which is my favorite hotel in the area and should be your first choice, then your best bet is to go out with **Goulding's Tours** (© **435/727-3231;** www.gouldings.com), which has its office right at the lodge (see "Where to Stay & Dine," below), just a few miles from the park entrance. Goulding's offers 3½-hour tours ($42 for adults, $27 for children under 8) and full-day tours ($75 for adults, $57 for children). **Monument Valley Simpson's Trailhandler Tours** (© **435/727-3362;** www.trailhandlertours.com), which charges $40 for a 2½-hour tour, is another reliable company to try, as is **Sacred Monument Tours** (© **435/727-3218** or 928/380-4527; www.monumentvalley.net), which charges $46 for a 2-hour jeep tour and $82 for a 4-hour sunrise or sunset tour.

The traditional way to explore this quintessentially Wild West landscape, however, is from the back of a horse, a la John Wayne. I recommend going out with **Diné Trail Ride Tours** (© **435/419-0135** or 928/697-3776), which starts its rides from John Ford's Point, about halfway around Valley Drive. Trail rides range in price from $35 for a half-hour ride to $95 for a half-day ride. Alternatively, try **Sacred Monument Tours** (© **435/727-3218** or 928/380-4527; www.monumentvalley.net), which charges from $50 for a 1-hour horseback ride up to $290 for an all-day ride.

Because the jeep and van tours are such a big business here, there's a steady stream of the vehicles on Valley Drive throughout the day. One way to get away from the rumble of engines is to go out on a guided hike. These are offered by **Sacred Monument Tours** (© **435/727-3218** or 928/380-4527; www.monumentvalley.net), which charges between $57 and $165 per person for hikes of different lengths. **Kéyah Hózhóní Tours** (© **928/309-7440;** www.monumentvalley.com) also offers hiking tours and overnight camping trips; call for rates. Keep in mind that summers can be very hot here.

The exception to the no-traveling-off-road rule is the 3.25-mile **Wildcat Trail** ★★, a loop trail that circles West Mitten Butte and provides the only opportunity to get close to this picturesque butte. As you circle the butte, you'll get all kinds of different perspectives, even one that completely eliminates the "thumb." Because this is the park's only option for unguided hiking, it is a not-to-be-missed excursion and one of the most memorable hikes in the state. In summer, be sure to carry plenty of water.

ACTIVITIES OUTSIDE THE PARK

Before leaving the area, you might want to visit **Goulding's Museum & Trading Post,** at Goulding's Lodge (see "Where to Stay & Dine," below). This old trading post was the home of the Gouldings for many years and is set up as they had it back in the 1920s and 1930s. There are also displays about the many movies that have been shot here. The trading post hours vary with the seasons; admission is by $2 suggested donation.

Inside Kayenta's Burger King, which is next door to the Hampton Inn, there's an interesting exhibit on the Navajo code talkers of World War II. The code talkers were Navajo soldiers who used their own language to transmit military messages, primarily in the South Pacific.

WHERE TO STAY & DINE

In addition to the lodgings listed here, you'll find several budget motels north of Monument Valley in the Utah towns of Mexican Hat and Bluff. When it's time for a meal, try the View Restaurant, which is in the park's visitor center and more than lives up to its name. Alternatively, try the Stagecoach Dining Room at Goulding's. The Navajo steak, served atop fry bread, is great! If you need a latte to get you on down the road, stop by **Shepherd's Eyes** (**© 928/697-3368**), an espresso bar and Internet cafe ¼ mile west of the junction of U.S. 160 and U. S. 163. This cafe also serves Navajo tea, which is made from a wild plant that grows in the area.

Best Western Wetherill Inn Located in Kayenta a mile north of the junction of U.S. 160 and U.S. 163, and 20 miles south of Monument Valley, the Wetherill Inn offers neither the convenience of Goulding's Lodge nor the amenities of the nearby Holiday Inn or Hampton Inn. The rooms, however, are comfortable enough. A cafe next door serves Navajo and American food.

1000 Main St. (P.O. Box 175), Kayenta, AZ 86033. **© 800/780-7234** or 928/697-3231. Fax 928/697-3233. www.bestwestern.com/wetherillinn. 54 units. May 1–Oct 15 $125–$135 double; Oct 16–Nov 15 and Apr $80–$85 double; Nov 16–Mar 31 $65–$70 double. Children 12 and under stay free in parent's room. Rates include continental breakfast. AE, DC, DISC, MC, V. **Amenities:** Indoor pool; tour desk. *In room:* A/C, TV, dataport, coffeemaker, hair dryer, iron, free local calls.

Goulding's Lodge ★ This is the only lodge actually located in Monument Valley and should be your first hotel choice in the area. Because this is the most popular hotel in the area, be sure to make your reservation well in advance. Goulding's offers superb views from the private balconies of its large guest rooms. The restaurant serves Navajo and American dishes, and its views are enough to make any meal an event. Unfortunately, although the setting is memorable, the service can be somewhat lacking. The lodge also has a museum and a video library that includes a few films that have been shot in Monument Valley.

P.O. Box 360001, Monument Valley, UT 84536. **© 435/727-3231.** Fax 435/727-3344. www.gouldings.com. 62 units. Mar 15–Nov 15 $123–$175 double; Nov 16–Mar 14 $73–$83 double. Children 8 and under stay free in parent's room. AE, DC, DISC, MC, V. Pets accepted ($10 fee). **Amenities:** Restaurant (American/Navajo); indoor pool; exercise room; tour desk; coin-op laundry; grocery store; gas station. *In room:* A/C, TV/DVD, dataport, fridge, coffeemaker, hair dryer, iron, high-speed Internet access, Wi-Fi, free local calls.

Hampton Inn–Navajo Nation In the center of Kayenta, this is the newest lodging in the area and, as such, should be your second choice after Goulding's. The hotel is built in a modern Santa Fe style and has spacious, comfortable guest rooms. It's adjacent to the Navajo Cultural Center and a Burger King that has an interesting display on the Navajo code talkers of World War II.

Fun Fact More Big Rocks

Monument Valley isn't the only place in this region with impressive rocks. Just north of Kayenta, on the road to Monument Valley, you'll pass by El Capitan, a huge plug of volcanic rock that rises from the desert floor. Of course, when you pull over to take a picture, you can also shop for cheap jewelry at Navajo vendors' stalls. East of Kayenta on U.S. 160, watch for the red sandstone cliffs known as Baby Rocks. East of Tuba City, also on U.S. 160, watch for the two sandstone towers known as Elephant Feet.

U.S. 160 (P.O. Box 1219), Kayenta, AZ 86033. © **800/426-7866** or 928/697-3170. Fax 928/697-3189. www.hampton-inn.com. 73 units. $64–$137 double. Rates include continental breakfast. Children under 18 stay free in parent's room. AE, DC, DISC, MC, V. Pets accepted ($20 nonrefundable deposit). **Amenities:** Restaurant (American/Navajo); small outdoor pool; room service; coin-op laundry. *In room:* A/C, TV, dataport, coffeemaker, hair dryer, iron, high-speed Internet access.

Holiday Inn–Kayenta This Holiday Inn, right in the center of Kayenta, is very popular with tour groups and is almost always crowded. Although the grounds are dusty and a bit run-down, the rooms are spacious and clean. I like the poolside units best. Part of the hotel's dining room is designed to look like an Ancestral Puebloan ruin, and the menu offers both American and Navajo cuisine.

U.S. 160 and U.S. 163 (P.O. Box 307), Kayenta, AZ 86033. © **888/465-4329** or 928/697-3221. Fax 928/697-3349. www.holiday-inn.com. 163 units. Nov–Apr $69–$999 double, $89–$119 suite; May–June $119–$149 double, $149–$179 suite; July–Oct $139–$169 double, $179–$209 suite. Children 18 and under stay free in parent's room; children 12 and under eat free. AE, DC, DISC, MC, V. **Amenities:** Restaurant (American/Navajo); small outdoor pool; exercise room; room service; coin-op laundry. *In room:* A/C, TV, dataport, coffeemaker, hair dryer, iron, high-speed Internet access.

CAMPGROUNDS

If you're headed to Monument Valley Navajo Tribal Park, you can camp in the park at the **Mitten View Campground** (© **435/727-5874** or 435/727-5870), which has 99 sites and charges $10 per night from April to September ($5 per night the rest of the year, when there are no facilities or running water). Another option, just outside the park, is **Goulding's Campground** (© **435/727-3231;** www.gouldings.com), which charges $22 to $36 per night. There are also small cabins that go for $69 per night. This campground is open year-round (limited services Nov to mid-Mar) and has an indoor pool, hot showers, a playground, and a coin-op laundry.

DRIVING ON TO COLORADO OR NEW MEXICO: THE FOUR CORNERS MEET

It seems like a supremely silly reason to drive miles out of your way, but lots of people feel they just have to visit the **Four Corners Monument Navajo Tribal Park** (© **928/871-6647**). Why? So they can stand in four states—Arizona, Colorado, Utah, and New Mexico—at once and get their photo taken. Located north of Teec Nos Pos in the very northeast corner of the state, this park is the only place in the United States where the corners of four states come together. The scenery is not exactly the most dramatic in the region, and the exact point is just a cement pad surrounded by flags and vendors stalls. The park also has a few picnic tables and a snack bar serving, among other things, Navajo fry bread. The park is open daily from 7am to 8pm between mid-May and mid-September, and from 8am to 5pm between mid-September and mid-May. The park is closed on New Year's Day, Thanksgiving, and Christmas. Admission is $3 for adults, free for children 6 and under.

8 Lake Powell ★★ & Page

272 miles N of Phoenix; 130 miles E of Grand Canyon North Rim; 130 miles NE of Grand Canyon South Rim

Had the early Spanish explorers of Arizona suddenly come upon Lake Powell after traipsing for months across desolate desert, they would have either taken it for a mirage or fallen to their knees and rejoiced. Imagine the Grand Canyon filled with water, and you have a pretty good picture of Lake Powell. Surrounded by hundreds of miles of parched desert, this reservoir, created by the damming of the Colorado River at Glen Canyon, seems unreal when first glimpsed. Yet real it is, and it draws everyone in the region toward its promise of relief from the heat.

Construction of the Glen Canyon Dam came about despite the angry outcry of many who felt that this canyon was even more beautiful than the Grand Canyon and should be preserved in its natural state. Preservationists lost the battle, and construction of the dam began in 1960, with completion in 1963. It took another 17 years for Lake Powell to fill to capacity. Today, the lake is a watery powerboat playground, and houseboats and water-skiers cruise where birds and waterfalls once filled the canyon with their songs and sounds. These days most people seem to agree, though, that Lake Powell is as amazing a sight as the Grand Canyon, and it draws almost as many visitors each year as its downriver neighbor. In the past few years, however, Lake Powell has lost some of its luster as a prolonged drought in the Southwest has left the lake's water level down by roughly 100 feet. Although this has left a bathtub-ring effect on the shores of the lake, it has also exposed wide expanses of beach in the Wahweap area.

While Lake Powell is something of a man-made wonder of the world, one of the natural wonders of the world—Rainbow Bridge—can also be found on the shores of the lake. Called *nonnozhoshi,* or "the rainbow turned to stone," by the Navajo, this is the largest natural bridge on Earth and stretches 275 feet across a side canyon off Lake Powell.

The town of Page, originally a camp constructed to house the workers who built the dam, has many motels and restaurants, and is the main base for many visitors who come to explore Lake Powell.

ESSENTIALS

GETTING THERE Page is connected to Flagstaff by U.S. 89. Arizona 98 leads southeast onto the Navajo Indian Reservation and connects with U.S. 160 to Kayenta and Four Corners. The Page Airport is served by **Great Lakes Airlines (© 800/554-5111** or 307/433-2899; www.greatlakesav.com), which flies from Phoenix. Round-trip airfares start around $200.

FEES Admission to Glen Canyon National Recreation Area is $15 per car (good for 1 week). There is also a $16-per-week boat fee if you bring your own boat.

VISITOR INFORMATION For further information on the Lake Powell area, contact the **Glen Canyon National Recreation Area** (**© 928/608-6404;** www.nps.gov/glca); the **Page-Lake Powell Chamber of Commerce,** 608 Elm St., Page (**© 888/261-7243** or 928/645-2741; www.pagelakepowellchamber.org); or the **John Wesley Powell Memorial Museum,** 6 N. Lake Powell Blvd., Page (**© 888/597-6873** or 928/645-9496; www.powellmuseum.org). You can also go to www.powellguide.com.

GETTING AROUND Rental cars are available at the Page Airport from **Avis** (✆ **800/331-1212** or 928/645-2024).

GLEN CANYON NATIONAL RECREATION AREA

Until the flooding of Glen Canyon formed Lake Powell, this area was one of the most remote regions in the contiguous 48 states. However, since the construction of Glen Canyon Dam at a spot where the canyon of the Colorado River was less than a third of a mile wide, this remote and rugged landscape has become one of the country's most popular national recreation areas. Today, the lake and much of the surrounding land is designated the Glen Canyon National Recreation Area and attracts around two million visitors each year. The otherworldly setting amid the slickrock canyons of northern Arizona and southern Utah is a tapestry of colors, the blues and greens of the lake contrasting with the reds and oranges of the surrounding sandstone cliffs. This interplay of colors and vast desert landscapes easily makes Lake Powell the most beautiful of Arizona's many reservoirs.

Built to provide water for the desert communities of the Southwest and West, **Glen Canyon Dam** stands 710 feet above the bedrock and contains almost 5 million cubic yards of concrete. The dam also provides hydroelectric power, and deep within its massive wall of concrete are huge power turbines. Although most Lake Powell visitors are more interested in water-skiing and powerboating than they are in drinking water and power production, there would be no lake without the dam, so any visit to this area ought to start at the **Carl Hayden Visitor Center** (✆ **928/608-6404**), which is located beside the dam on U.S. 89 just north of Page. Here you can tour the dam and learn about its construction. Between mid-May and mid-September, the visitor center is open daily from 8am to 6pm; December to February, it's open daily 8am to 4pm; other months, it's open daily 8am to 5pm.

More than 500 feet deep in some places, and bounded by nearly 2,000 miles of shoreline, **Lake Powell** is a maze of convoluted canyons where rock walls often rise hundreds of feet straight out of the water. In places, the long, winding canyons are so narrow there isn't even room to turn a motorboat around. The only way to truly appreciate this lake is from a boat, whether a houseboat, a runabout, or a sea kayak. Water-skiing, riding personal watercrafts, and fishing have long been the most popular on-water activities, and consequently, you'll be hard-pressed to find a quiet corner of the lake if you happen to be a solitude-seeking sea kayaker. However, with so many miles of shoreline, you're bound to find someplace to get away from it all. Your best bet for solitude is to head up-lake from Wahweap Marina. This will get you away from the crowds and into some of the narrower reaches of the lake.

In addition to the Carl Hayden Visitor Center mentioned above, there's the **Bullfrog Visitor Center,** in Bullfrog, Utah (✆ **435/684-7423**). In April, it's open intermittently from 8am to 5pm; May through Labor Day, it's open daily from 8am to 5pm (closed Labor Day–Mar).

BOAT & AIR TOURS

There are few roads penetrating the Glen Canyon National Recreation Area, so the best way to appreciate this rugged region is by boat. If you don't have your own boat, you can at least see a small part of the lake on a boat tour. A variety of tours depart from **Wahweap Marina** (✆ **800/528-6154** or 928/645-2433; www.lakepowell.com). The ***Canyon Princess*** does a 1-hour tour ($14 for adults, $11 for children) that, unfortunately, doesn't really show you much more of the lake than you can see from shore. The *Canyon Princess* also offers sunset dinner cruises ($65). A better choice for those with limited time or finances would be the **Antelope Canyon Cruise** ($35 for adults, $28 for children). To see more of the lake, opt for the full-day tour to Rainbow Bridge (see below for details).

The Glen Canyon National Recreation Area covers an immense area, much of it only partially accessible by boat. If you'd like to see more of the area than is visible from car or boat, consider taking an air tour with **Westwind Scenic Air Tours** (© **800/245-8668** or 928/645-2494; www.westwindairservice.com), which offers several tours of northern Arizona and southern Utah, including flights over Rainbow Bridge and Monument Valley. Sample rates are $138 for a 35- to 45-minute flight over Rainbow Bridge ($124 for children 16 and under) and $245 for a 75-minute flight over Monument Valley ($221 for children). There are also tours that include a 2-hour jeep tour at Monument Valley. These tours are $280 for adults and $252 for children.

RAINBOW BRIDGE NATIONAL MONUMENT

Roughly 40 miles up Lake Powell from Wahweap Marina and Glen Canyon Dam, in a narrow side canyon of the lake, rises **Rainbow Bridge** ★★★, the world's largest natural bridge and one of the most spectacular sights in the Southwest. Preserved in Rainbow Bridge National Monument, this natural arch of sandstone stands 290 feet high and spans 275 feet. Carved by wind and water over the ages, Rainbow Bridge is an awesome reminder of the powers of erosion that have sculpted this entire region into the spectacle it is today.

Rainbow Bridge is accessible only by boat or on foot (a hike of 14 miles minimum), and, of course, going by boat is by far the more popular method. **Lake Powell Resorts and Marinas** (© **800/528-6154** or 928/645-2433; www.lakepowell.com) offers full-day tours ($116 for adults, $81 for children) that not only get you to Rainbow Bridge in comfort, but also cruise through some of the most spectacular scenery on earth. Tours include a box lunch and a bit more exploring after visiting Rainbow Bridge. Currently, because the lake's water level is so low from years of drought, the boat must stop between 1 and 1¼ miles from Rainbow Bridge, so if you aren't able to walk this distance, you won't even be able to see the sandstone arch.

Rainbow Bridge National Monument (© **928/608-6200;** www.nps.gov/rabr) is administered by Glen Canyon National Recreation Area. For information on hiking to Rainbow Bridge, contact the **Navajo Parks and Recreation Department,** P.O. Box 2520, Window Rock, AZ 86515 (© **928/871-6647;** www.navajonationparks.org). The hike to Rainbow Bridge is about a 25-mile round-trip hike, should be done as an overnight backpacking trip, and requires a Navajo Nation permit. Permits are available through the Navajo Parks and Recreation Department, at the **Cameron Visitor Center** (© **928/679-2303**), in the community of Cameron near the turnoff for the Grand Canyon, and at the **Antelope Canyon Park Office** (© **928/698-2808**), 7 miles south of Page on Navajo Route 20 (beside the LeChee Chapter House).

ANTELOPE CANYON

If you've spent any time in Arizona, chances are you've noticed photos of a narrow sandstone canyon only a few feet wide. The walls of the canyon seem to glow with an inner light, and beams of sunlight slice the darkness of the deep slot canyon. Sound familiar? If you've seen such a photo, you were probably looking at Antelope Canyon (sometimes called Corkscrew Canyon). Located 2½ miles southeast of Page off Arizona 98 (at milepost 299), this photogenic canyon comprises the **Antelope Canyon Navajo Tribal Park** ★★★ (© **928/698-2808**), which is on the Navajo Indian Reservation and

Fun Fact **So, What's with the Bathtub Ring?**

You'll notice that the red-rock cliff walls above the waters of Lake Powell are no longer red but are instead coated with what looks like a layer of white soap scum. Those are calcium carbonate deposits left on the rock over the past few years after a drought caused the lake level to drop more than 130 feet. Currently, the lake level is around 100 feet below what is known as full pool (when the reservoir is full).

is divided into upper and lower canyons. The entry fee is $6 for adults, free for children 7 and under. April through October, Antelope Canyon is open daily from 8am to 5pm; November through March, hours vary and closures are common.

There are currently two options for visiting Antelope Canyon. The most convenient and reliable way is to take a 1½-hour tour with **Antelope Canyon Adventures** (✆ **866/645-5501** or 928/645-5501; www.jeeptour.com) or **Antelope Canyon Tours** (✆ **866/645-9102** or 928/645-9102; www.antelopecanyon.com), both of which charge $20 (plus Navajo permit fee) per adult for a basic tour. Photographic tours cost between $35 and $62. If you don't want to deal with crowds of tourists ogling the rocks and snapping pictures with their point-and-shoots, I recommend heading out with **Overland Canyon Tours** (✆ **928/608-4072;** www.overlandcanyontours.com) to nearby Canyon X, which is much less visited than Antelope Canyon and is a good choice for serious photographers who want to avoid the crowds.

Alternatively, at both the upper and lower canyons, you'll find Navajo guides collecting park entry fees and fees for guide services. These guides charge $15 ($10 for children ages 6–12 at the lower section of the canyon). Upper Antelope Canyon is a short drive up a sandy stream bed from the highway, while Lower Antelope Canyon is a short walk from the parking area just off the highway. You'll get more out of your experience if you go on one of the guided tours mentioned above, but you'll save a little money by visiting the canyon on your own. For more information, contact **Antelope Canyon Navajo Tours** (✆ **928/698-3384;** www.navajotours.com).

Just remember that if there is even the slightest chance of rain anywhere in the region, you should not venture into this canyon, which is subject to flash floods. In the past, people who have ignored bad weather predictions have been killed by such floods.

WATERSPORTS

While simply exploring the lake's maze of canyons on a narrated tour is satisfying enough for many visitors, the most popular activities are still houseboating, water-skiing, riding personal watercrafts, and fishing. Five marinas (only Wahweap is in Arizona) help boaters explore the lake. At the **Wahweap Marina** (✆ **800/528-6154** or 928/645-2433; www.lakepowell.com), you can rent various types of boats, along with personal watercrafts and water skis. Rates in summer range from about $330 to $473 per day, depending on the type of boat. Personal watercrafts go for $283 per day, and sea kayaks rent for $28 to $34 per day. Weekly rates are also available. For information on renting houseboats, see "Where to Stay," below.

If roaring engines aren't your speed, you might want to consider exploring Lake Powell by sea kayak. While afternoon winds can sometimes make paddling difficult, mornings are often quiet. With a narrow sea kayak, you can even explore canyons too small for powerboats. Rentals are available at **Twin Finn Diving,** 811 Vista Ave. (✆ **928/**

645-3114; www.twinfinn.com). Sea kayaks rent for $45 to $55 per day, and sit-on-top kayaks for $35 to $45. Multiday kayak tours are operated by **Hidden Canyon Kayak** (✆ **800/343-3121** or 928/645-8866; www.diamondriver.com/kayak), which charges $760 to $1,000 for 4- to 6-day trips. Guided kayak trips are also offered by **Kayak Powell** (✆ **888/854-7862;** www.kayaklakepowell.com), which charges $85 for a half-day tour and $725 for a 4-day tour. Kayak rentals are also available for $45 to $60 per day.

While most of Glen Canyon National Recreation Area consists of the impounded waters of Lake Powell, the recreation area also contains a short stretch of the Colorado River that still flows swift and free. If you'd like to see this stretch of river, try a float trip from Glen Canyon Dam to Lees Ferry, operated by **Colorado River Discovery** (✆ **888/522-6644;** www.raftthecanyon.com) between March and November. Half-day trips cost $64 for adults and $54 for children ages 4 to 11. Try to reserve at least 2 weeks in advance.

If you have a boat (your own or a rental), avail yourself of some excellent year-round fishing. Smallmouth, largemouth, and striped bass, as well as walleye, catfish, crappie, and carp, are all plentiful. Because the lake lies within both Arizona and Utah, you'll need to know which state's waters you're fishing in whenever you cast your line out, and you'll need the appropriate license. (Be sure to pick up a copy of the Arizona and Utah state fishing regulations, or ask about applicable regulations at any of the marinas.) You can arrange licenses to fish the entire lake at **Lake Powell Resorts and Marinas** (✆ **928/645-2433**), which also sells bait and tackle and can provide you with advice on fishing this massive reservoir. Other marinas on the lake also sell licenses, bait, and tackle. The best season is March through November, but walleye are most often caught during the cooler months. If you'd rather try your hand at catching enormous rainbow trout, try downstream of the Glen Canyon Dam, where cold waters provide ideal conditions for trophy trout. Unfortunately, there isn't much access to this stretch of river. You'll need a trout stamp to fish for the rainbows. If you want a guide to take you where the fish are biting, contact Bill McBurney at **Ambassador Guide Service** (✆ **800/256-7596;** www.ambassadorguides.com).

If you're just looking for a good place for a swim near Lake Powell Resort, take the Coves Loop just west of the marina. Of the three coves, the third one, which has a

---

Finds Acrophobes, Beware!

If you have a fear of heights, there are a couple of places in the Page area that you should never visit. On the other hand, if you want some great views, then don't miss the following two scenic vistas.

As you drive down the hill from Page on Lake Powell Boulevard (the road toward Glen Canyon Dam from Page), go straight through the intersection instead of turning right toward the dam. Here you'll find a parking area and a short path to a viewing platform perched on the edge of sheer cliff walls. Below lie the clear green waters of the Colorado River, while upstream looms Glen Canyon Dam.

If you're up for a short hike, grab the camera and head to the **Horseshoe Bend** ★ viewpoint. Horseshoe Bend is a huge loop of the Colorado River, and the viewpoint is hundreds of feet above the water on the edge of a cliff. It's about a half-mile to the viewpoint from the trail head, which is 5 miles south of the Carl Hayden Visitor Center on U.S. 89 just south of milepost 545.

---

sandy beach, is the best. The Chains area, another good place to jump off the rocks and otherwise lounge by the lake, is outside Page down a rough dirt road just before you reach Glen Canyon Dam. The view underwater at Lake Powell is as scenic as the view above it; to explore the underwater regions of the canyon, contact **Twin Finn Diving Center,** 811 Vista Ave. (✆ **928/645-3114;** www.twinfinn.com), which charges $45 a day for scuba gear and also rents snorkeling equipment.

OTHER OUTDOOR PURSUITS

If you're looking for a quick, easy hike with great views, head north on North Navajo Drive from downtown Page. At the end of this street is the main trail head for Page's **Rimview Trail.** This trail runs along the edge of Manson Mesa, upon which Page is built, and has views of Lake Powell and miles of red-rock country. The entire loop trail is 8 miles long, but if you want to do a shorter hike, I recommend the stretch of trail heading east (clockwise) from the trail head. If you happen to have your mountain bike with you, the trail is a great ride.

At Lees Ferry, a 39-mile drive from Page at the southern tip of the national recreation area, you'll find three short trails (Cathedral Wash, River, and Spencer). The 2-mile **Cathedral Wash Trail** is the most interesting of the three day hikes and follows a dry wash through a narrow canyon with unusual rock formations. The trail head is at the second turnout after turning off U.S. 89A. Be aware that this wash is subject to flash floods. The **River Trail** is a 2-mile round-trip hike along the river and starts at the boat ramp. The **Spencer Trail,** which begins along the River Trail, leads up to the top of a 1,700-foot cliff for spectacular views of Marble Canyon. Lees Ferry is also the southern trail head for famed **Paria Canyon** ★, a favorite of canyoneering backpackers. This trail is 38 to 47 miles long (depending on where you start) and follows the meandering route of a narrow slot canyon for much of its length. Most hikers start from the northern trail head, which is in Utah on U.S. 89. For more information on hiking in Paria Canyon, contact the **Arizona Strip Interpretive Association/Interagency Visitor Center,** 345 E. Riverside Dr., St. George, UT 84770 (✆ **435/688-3246;** www.az.blm.gov/asfo/asia.htm).

The 27-hole **Lake Powell National Golf Course** ★, 400 Clubhouse Dr. (✆ **928/645-2023;** www.golflakepowell.com), is one of the most spectacular in the state. The fairways wrap around the base of the red-sandstone bluff atop which sits the town of Page. The views stretch on forever, and in places, eroded sandstone walls come right down to the greens. Greens fees are $60.

OTHER AREA ATTRACTIONS

Between April and October, you can learn about Navajo culture at **Navajo Village Heritage Center** (✆ **928/660-0304;** www.navajo-village.com), a museum and living-history center on the northeast corner of Ariz. 98 and Coppermine Road (on the south side of Page). Programs here include demonstrations by weavers, silversmiths, and other artisans. Prices range from $40 for a 2-hour tour ($30 for children) to $55 for a 4-hour tour ($40 for children). Both tours include dinner and traditional dances. Reservations are required. During the day, there are also 30-minute walk-through tours ($5). Although this is definitely a tourist attraction, you will come away with a better sense of Navajo culture.

John Wesley Powell Memorial Museum In 1869, one-armed Civil War veteran John Wesley Powell and a small band of men spent more than 3 months fighting the rapids of the Green and Colorado rivers to become the first people to travel the length of the Grand Canyon. It is for this intrepid—some said crazy—adventurer that Lake Powell is named and to whom this small museum is dedicated. Besides documenting the Powell expedition with photographs, etchings, artifacts, and dioramas, the museum displays Native American artifacts ranging from Ancestral Puebloan pottery to contemporary Navajo and Hopi crafts. The museum also acts as an information center for Page, Lake Powell, and the surrounding region.

6 N. Lake Powell Blvd. ✆ **888/597-6873** or 928/645-9496. www.powellmuseum.org. Admission $5 adults, $3 seniors, $1 children 5–12, free for children 4 and under. Mid-Feb to Nov Mon–Fri 9am–5pm (sometimes open on weekends in summer, but call to be sure). Closed Dec to mid-Feb.

WHERE TO STAY

HOUSEBOATS

Although there are plenty of hotels and motels in and near Page, the most popular accommodations here are not waterfront hotel rooms, but houseboats, which function as floating vacation homes. With a houseboat, which is as easy to operate as a car, you can explore Lake Powell's beautiful red-rock country, far from any roads. No special license or prior experience is necessary, and plenty of hands-on instruction is given before you leave the marina. Because Lake Powell houseboating is extremely popular with visitors from all over the world, it's important to make reservations as far in advance as possible, especially if you plan to visit in summer.

Antelope Point Resort & Marina ★★ Kids At this marina, you can rent some of the newest and most luxurious houseboats on the lake (the larger ones even have outdoor hot tubs). There are both 59-foot and 70-foot boats available, ranging in quality from deluxe to luxury. Speed boats ($295–$395 per day) and sea kayaks ($25 per day) can also be rented and are a great way to explore smaller waterways that your houseboat can't navigate. To reach the marina, head east out of Page on Arizona 98 and drive 5 miles to the signed Antelope Point Marina turnoff.

Antelope Point Marina, P.O. Box 4180, Page, AZ 86040. ✆ **800/255-5561**. Fax 480/998-7399. www.antelopepointlakepowell.com. Early June to early Sept $7,494–$9,595 per week; lower rates other months. 3-, 4-, and 5-night rates also available. AE, DC, DISC, MC, V. *In room:* A/C, TV/DVD, kitchen, fridge, coffeemaker, no phone.

Lake Powell Resorts & Marinas ★ Kids This is the original houseboat-rental operation on Lake Powell, and houseboats here range in size from 44 to 75 feet, sleep anywhere from 8 to 12 people, and come complete with showers and a fully equipped kitchen. The only things you really need to bring are bedding and towels. If you're coming in the summer, splurge on a boat with some sort of cooling system.

100 Lakeshore Dr., Page, AZ 86040. ✆ **800/528-6154** or 602/278-8888. Fax 602/331-5258. www.lakepowell.com. Early June to late Sept $1,404–$11,545 per week; lower rates other months. 3-, 4-, 5-, and 6-night rates also available on most houseboats. AE, DISC, MC, V. Pets accepted. *In room:* Kitchen, fridge, no phone.

HOTELS & MOTELS

Best Western Arizonainn Perched right at the edge of the mesa on which Page is built, this modern motel has a fine view across miles of desert, as do half of the guest rooms. The hotel's pool has a 100-mile view.

716 Rimview Dr., Page, AZ 86040. ✆ **800/826-2718** or 928/645-2466. Fax 928/645-2053. www.bestwestern.com. 103 units. Mid-Apr to mid-May $79–$109 double; mid-May to mid-Oct $89–$109 double; mid-Oct to mid-Apr $49–$69 double. Rates include continental breakfast. Children under 18 stay free in parent's room. AE, DC, DISC, MC, V. Pets accepted ($10 fee). **Amenities:** Small outdoor pool; exercise room; Jacuzzi; courtesy airport shuttle; coin-op laundry; dry cleaning. *In room:* A/C, TV, dataport, coffeemaker, hair dryer, iron, high-speed Internet access, free local calls.

Courtyard by Marriott ★ Located at the foot of the mesa on which Page is built and adjacent to the Lake Powell National Golf Course, this is the top in-town choice. It's also the closest you'll come to a golf resort in this corner of the state. Although you'll pay a premium for views of the golf course or lake, it's a worthwhile investment. Guest rooms are larger than those at most area lodgings. Moderately priced meals are served in a casual restaurant that has a terrace overlooking the distant lake. The 18-hole golf course has great views of the surrounding landscape.

600 Clubhouse Dr. (P.O. Box 4150), Page, AZ 86040. ✆ **800/321-2211** or 928/645-5000. Fax 928/645-5004. www.courtyard.com. 153 units. $89–$149 double. Children under 18 stay free in parent's room. AE, DC, DISC, MC, V. **Amenities:** Restaurant (Southwestern/American); lounge; outdoor pool; 18-hole golf course; exercise room; Jacuzzi; room service; coin-op laundry; dry cleaning. *In room:* A/C, TV, dataport, coffeemaker, hair dryer, iron, high-speed Internet access, Wi-Fi.

Lake Powell Resort ★ Simply because it is right on the lake, this hotel at the sprawling Wahweap Marina 5 miles north of Page should be your first lodging choice in the area. As the biggest and busiest hotel in the area, the Lake Powell Resort features many of the amenities and activities of a resort, but it is often overwhelmed by busloads of tour groups. Consequently, don't expect very good service. Guest rooms are arranged in several long two-story wings, and every unit has either a balcony or a patio. Half of the rooms have lake views; those in the west wing have the better vantage point, as the east wing overlooks a coal-fired power plant. The Rainbow Room (see "Where to Dine," below) offers fine dining. Because of all the tour groups that stay here, getting a reservation can be difficult.

100 Lakeshore Dr. (P.O. Box 1597), Page, AZ 86040. ✆ **800/528-6154** or 928/645-2433. Fax 928/645-1031. www.lakepowell.com. 348 units. May–Sept $119–$189 double, $217 suite; Oct–Apr $89–$139 double, $195 suite. Children under 18 stay free in parent's room. AE, DISC, MC, V. Pets accepted. **Amenities:** 2 restaurants (American/Southwestern, pizza); snack bar; lounge; 2 outdoor pools; exercise room; Jacuzzi; sauna; boat rentals; children's programs; tour desk; room service; coin-op laundry. *In room:* A/C, TV, fridge, coffeemaker, hair dryer, iron.

CAMPGROUNDS

There are campgrounds at **Wahweap** (✆ **928/645-2433**) and **Lees Ferry** (✆ **928/355-2320**) in Arizona, and at Bullfrog, Hite, and Halls Crossing in Utah. Some scrubby trees provide a bit of shade at the Wahweap site, but the wind and sun make this a rather bleak spot in summer. Nevertheless, because of the lake's popularity, these campgrounds stay packed for much of the year. Wahweap charges $19 to $34 per night and Lees Ferry charges $10; reservations are not accepted.

WHERE TO DINE

The Dam Bar & Grille AMERICAN This theme restaurant is a warehouse-size space designed to conjure up images of the interior of Glen Canyon Dam. Inside, cement walls, hard hats, and a big transformer that sends out bolts of neon "electricity" will put you in a "dam" good mood. Sandwiches, pastas, and steaks dominate the menu, but the rotisserie chicken is my favorite dish. The lounge area is a popular local hangout, and next door is the affiliated Gunsmoke Saloon nightclub.

644 N. Navajo Dr. ✆ **928/645-2161.** www.damplaza.com. Reservations recommended in summer. Main courses $7–$23. AE, DISC, MC, V. Mon–Sat 10am–10pm; Sun 4–10pm.

Rainbow Room AMERICAN/SOUTHWESTERN With sweeping vistas of Lake Powell through the walls of glass, the Rainbow Room is both Page's top restaurant and its most touristy. Be prepared for a wait; this place regularly feeds busloads of tourists. The menu is short but usually includes a few dishes with Southwestern flavor.

At Lake Powell Resort, 100 Lakeshore Dr. ✆ **928/645-1162.** Reservations recommended. Main courses $7–$15 lunch, $16–$26 dinner. AE, DISC, MC, V. Daily 6am–2pm and 5–9pm.

8

Eastern Arizona's High Country

Cactus and desert landscapes are what come to mind when most people think of Arizona. But that's only part of the picture. Arizona actually has more mountainous country than Switzerland and more forest than Minnesota, and most of these mountains and forests are here in the highlands of eastern Arizona.

In this sparsely populated region, towns with such apt names as Alpine, Lakeside, and Pinetop have become summer retreats for the residents of the state's low-lying, sun-baked deserts. Folks from Phoenix and its surrounding cities discovered long ago how close the cool mountain forests are. In only a few hours, you can drive up from the cacti and creosote bushes to the meadows and pine forests of the White Mountains.

Dividing the arid lowlands from the cool pine forests of the highlands is the Mogollon Rim (pronounced *Mug*-ee-un by the locals), a 2,000-foot escarpment that stretches for 200 miles from central Arizona into New Mexico. Along this impressive wall, the climatic and vegetative change is dramatic, with sunshine at the base and snow squalls at the top. This area was made famous by Western author Zane Grey, who lived in a cabin near Payson and set many of his novels in this scenic yet oft-overlooked part of Arizona. Fans of Grey's novels can follow in the author's footsteps and visit a small museum with an exhibit dedicated to Grey.

Trout fishing, hiking, horseback riding, and hunting are the main warm-weather pastimes of eastern Arizona, and when winter weather reports from up north have Phoenicians dreaming about snow (it's true, they really do), many head to the White Mountains for a bit of skiing. Sunrise Park Resort, operated by the White Mountain Apache Tribe, is the state's biggest and busiest downhill ski area. There are also plenty of cross-country ski trails in the area.

Much of eastern Arizona is Apache reservation land. Recreational activities abound here, but remember that the Apache tribe requires visitors to have reservation fishing permits and outdoor recreation permits. Fishing is particularly popular on the reservation, which isn't surprising, considering there are 400 miles of trout streams and 25 lakes stocked with rainbow and brown trout.

1 Payson & the Mogollon Rim Country

94 miles NE of Phoenix; 90 miles SE of Flagstaff; 90 miles SW of Winslow; 100 miles W of Pinetop-Lakeside

Payson, 94 miles from Phoenix and 5,000 feet above sea level, is one of the closest places for Phoenicians to find relief from the summer heat, and though it is not quite high enough to be considered the mountains, it certainly isn't the desert (summer temperatures are 20 degrees cooler than in the Valley of the Sun). The 2,000-foot-high, 200-mile-long Mogollon Rim, the region's main attraction, is only 22 miles north of town, and the surrounding Tonto National Forest provides opportunities for hiking,

Eastern Arizona's High Country

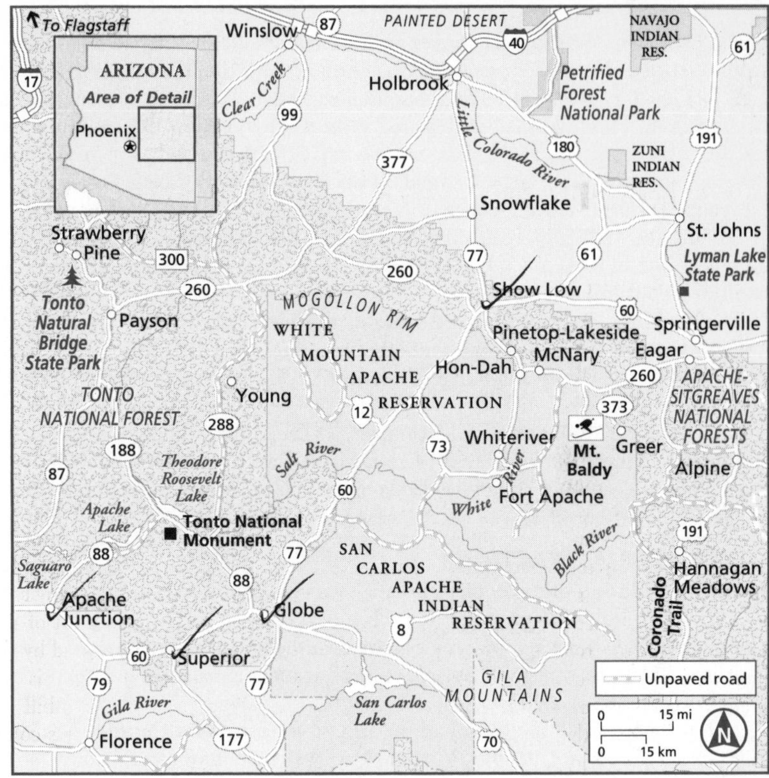

swimming, fishing, and hunting. The nearly perfect climate of Payson has also made the town a popular retirement spot. Summer highs are usually in the 80s or 90s (30s Celsius), while winter highs are usually in the 50s and 60s (teens Celsius).

ESSENTIALS

GETTING THERE Arizona 87, the Beeline Highway, connects Payson to Phoenix and Winslow. Arizona 260 runs east from Payson, climbing the Mogollon Rim and continuing into the White Mountains.

VISITOR INFORMATION Contact the **Rim Country Regional Chamber of Commerce,** 100 W. Main St., Payson (✆ **800/672-9766** or 928/474-4515; www.rimcountrychamber.com).

SPECIAL EVENTS The **World's Oldest Continuous Rodeo** takes place on the third weekend in August.

OUTDOOR PURSUITS

The area's most popular attraction is **Tonto Natural Bridge State Park,** 10 miles northwest of Payson on Arizona 87 (✆ **928/476-4202;** www.azstateparks.com), which preserves the largest natural travertine bridge in the world. In 1877, gold prospector David Gowan, while being chased by Apaches, became the first white man to see this natural bridge, which stands 183 feet high and 150 feet across at its widest point. Although it sounds very impressive, this natural bridge looks nothing like the sandstone arches in southern Utah and seems more like a tunnel than a free-standing arch. This state park also preserves a historic lodge built by Gowan's nephew and the nephew's sons. The lodge has been restored to the way it looked in 1927. Admission to the park is $3 per person. From Memorial Day to Labor Day, the park is open daily from 8am to 7pm; April, May, September, and October, it's open daily from 8am to 6pm; and November through March, it's open daily from 9am to 5pm. Closed on Christmas.

If you'd like to go horseback riding, try **Kohl's Ranch Stables,** on Highway 260, 17 miles north of Payson (✆ **928/478-0030**). Rates range from $30 for a 1-hour ride to $120 for a half-day ride.

The **Highline Trail** is a 50-mile hike along the lower slope of the Mogollon Rim. You can find out more about this and other area trails, as well as which are open to mountain bikes, at the **Payson Ranger Station,** 1009 E. Hwy. 260 (✆ **928/474-7900**), at the east end of town.

You can also hike this area in the company of llamas that will carry your gear for you. John and Joyce Bittner of **Fossil Creek Llama Ranch** (✆ **928/476-5178;** www.fossilcreekllamas.com) offer half-day llama hikes ($65 per person). Overnight stays in a tepee "bed-and-breakfast" can also be arranged for $85.

OTHER AREA ATTRACTIONS

About 5 miles north of town, off Arizona 87 on Houston Mesa Road, you can visit the ruins of **Shoofly Village,** in the Tonto National Forest. This village was first occupied nearly 1,000 years ago by peoples related to the Hohokam and Salado. It once contained 87 rooms, though today only rock foundations remain. An interpretive trail helps bring the site to life.

To learn more about the history of the area, stop by the **Rim Country Museum,** 700 Green Valley Pkwy. (✆ **928/474-3483;** www.rimcountrymuseums.com), which has displays on the region as well as a special Zane Grey exhibit and a reconstruction of the cabin Grey lived in during his time in the Payson area. The museum, located in Green Valley Park, is housed in the oldest forest ranger station and residence still standing in the Southwest. The museum is open Wednesday through Monday from 10am to 4pm. Admission is $3 for adults, $2.50 for seniors, and $2 for children 12 to 18. Nearby, you'll also find the affiliated **Museum of Rim Country Archaeology,** 510 W. Main St. (✆ **928/468-1128**), which has interesting displays on the Native American cultures that once inhabited this area. Admission is $2.50 for adults, $2 for seniors, and $1.50 for students ages 12 to 18. This museum is open Wednesday through Sunday from noon to 4pm.

If you're feeling lucky, spend some time and money at the **Mazatzal Casino** (✆ **800/777-PLAY** or 928/474-6044; www.777play.com), half a mile south on Arizona 87. The casino is run by the Tonto Apaches.

SCENIC DRIVES

Scenic drives through this region are popular with visitors. One of the most popular drives is along the top of the Mogollon Rim on 45-mile-long **Forest Road 300.** The road clings to the edge of the rim and has numerous views of the forest far below and plenty of places to stop, including lakes, picnic areas, trail heads, and campgrounds. This good gravel road can be negotiated in summer in a standard passenger car. In winter, however, the road is not maintained. From Payson, to access the rim road, head east on Arizona 260 or north on Arizona 87 for 30 miles and watch for signs.

About 15 miles north of Payson on Arizona 87 is the village of **Pine,** and another 3 miles beyond this, the village of **Strawberry.** Here, in a quiet setting in the forest, you'll find a few shops selling antiques and crafts and, in Pine, the small **Pine-Strawberry Museum,** Arizona 87, Pine (✆ **928/476-3547;** www.pinestrawhs.org), a small museum that chronicles the history of this area. May 15 to October 15, the museum is open Monday through Thursday from 10am to 2pm and Friday through Sunday from 10am to 4pm; other months the museum is open Monday through Saturday from 10am to 2pm. If you leave Arizona 87 in Strawberry and drive west 1¾ miles on Fossil Creek Road, you'll come to the old **Strawberry Schoolhouse,** a restored log building dating from 1885. The schoolhouse is open mid-May to mid-October Saturday from 10am to 4pm and Sunday from noon to 4pm (between mid-June and early Aug, the schoolhouse is also open Fri and Mon 10am–4pm).

Another interesting drive starts west of the Strawberry Schoolhouse. If you continue west on this road, you'll be on the gravel **Fossil Creek Road** ★★, which leads 10 miles down into a deep and spectacular canyon. It's a bit hair-raising, but if you like views, it's well worth the white knuckles and dust. At the bottom, **Fossil Creek** offers some of the most idyllic little swimming holes you could ever hope to find. If you make it down here on a weekday, you just might have a swimming hole all to yourself.

WHERE TO STAY

Majestic Mountain Inn Although located in town, this hotel was built in an attractive, modern mountain-lodge style that makes it the most appealing place to stay right in Payson. There's a large stone chimney and fireplace in the lobby, and all of the deluxe and luxury rooms have fireplaces. The luxury units also have tile floors and a double whirlpool tub facing the fireplace. The standard rooms aren't as spacious or luxurious, but are still quite comfortable.

602 E. Ariz. 260, Payson, AZ 85541. ✆ **800/408-2442** or 928/474-0185. www.majesticmountaininn.com. 50 units. $69–$159 double. Children under 18 stay free in parent's room. AE, DC, DISC, MC, V. Pets accepted ($20 1st night, $10 additional nights). **Amenities:** Outdoor pool; access to nearby health club. *In room:* A/C, TV/VCR, dataport, fridge, coffeemaker, hair dryer, iron, free local calls.

CAMPGROUNDS

East of Payson on Arizona 260 are several national forest campgrounds. These include **Upper Tonto Creek** and **Christopher Creek** campgrounds. The former campground does not take reservations, but the latter does. Information is available from the **Payson Ranger Station,** 1009 E. Ariz. 260 (✆ **928/474-7900;** www.fs.fed.us/r3/tonto), at the east end of town.

WHERE TO DINE

Cucina Paradiso ★ ITALIAN Although it's nothing fancy, this casual Italian restaurant on the north side of Payson is one of the best restaurants in town. Calamari is a specialty of the house, and the calamari Caesar salad is a tasty spin on a classic. There's also a good calamari *fra diavolo* made with a spicy white wine–tomato sauce. The Florentine ravioli in creamy red sauce is another good bet.

512 N. Beeline Hwy. ✆ **928/468-6500.** www.cucinaparadiso.com. Reservations recommended. Main courses $6.50–$10 lunch, $12–$16 dinner. AE, DC, DISC, MC, V. Mon–Thurs 11am–8:30pm; Fri 11am–9pm; Sat–Sun 3–9pm.

Fargo's Steakhouse ★ STEAKS This modern steakhouse next door to the Majestic Mountain Inn is the classiest restaurant in town and has a contemporary mountain-lodge atmosphere. The menu doesn't break any new ground, but you can get reliable steaks. Start with tenderloin skewers with Cajun dipping sauce or the bacon-wrapped scallops. Steak eaters on a diet will want to consider the black and bleu Caesar salad.

620 E. Ariz. 260. ✆ **928/474-7455.** www.fargossteakhouse.com. Reservations recommended. Main courses $7.50–$14 lunch, $17–$31 dinner. AE, DC, DISC, MC, V. Sun–Thurs 11am–9pm; Fri–Sat 11am–10pm.

2 Pinetop-Lakeside

90 miles NE of Payson; 185 miles NE of Phoenix; 50 miles S of Holbrook; 140 miles SE of Flagstaff

With dozens of motels and cabin resorts strung along Arizona 260 as it passes through town, Pinetop-Lakeside, actually two towns that grew together over the years, is the busiest community in the White Mountains. At first glance, it's easy to dismiss the town as one long commercial strip, what with all the shopping centers and budget motels, but Pinetop-Lakeside has spent many years entertaining families during the summer months, and it has plenty of diversions to keep visitors busy. You just have to look a little harder than you might in nearby Greer.

With Apache and Sitgreaves National Forests on one side and the unspoiled lands of the White Mountain Apache Indian Reservation on the other, Pinetop-Lakeside is well situated for anyone who enjoys the outdoors. Nearby are several lakes with good fishing; nearly 200 miles of hiking, mountain-biking, and cross-country ski trails; horseback riding; and downhill skiing. Although summer is the busy season, Pinetop-Lakeside becomes something of a ski resort in winter. Sunrise Park ski area is only 30 miles away, and on weekends the town is packed with skiers.

Pinetop-Lakeside is definitely the family destination of the White Mountains, so if you're looking for a romantic weekend or solitude, continue farther into the White Mountains to Greer or Alpine.

ESSENTIALS

GETTING THERE Pinetop-Lakeside is located on Arizona 260.

VISITOR INFORMATION For information on this area, contact the **Pinetop-Lakeside Chamber of Commerce,** 102C W. White Mountain Blvd., Lakeside (✆ **800/573-4031** or 928/367-4290; www.pinetoplakesidechamber.com).

OUTDOOR PURSUITS

Old forts and casinos aside, it's the outdoors (and the cool weather) that really draws people here. Fishing, hiking, mountain biking, and horseback riding are among the most popular activities. If you want to saddle up, call **Porter Mountain Stables,** 4048 Porter Mountain Rd. (✆ **928/368-5306** or 928/368-5800), which charges $27 for a 1-hour ride. At the end of your ride, you can even have a meal at the stable's affiliated steakhouse.

Meandering through the forests surrounding Pinetop-Lakeside are the 180 miles of trails of the **White Mountains Trail system.** Many of these trails are easily accessible (in fact, some are right in town) and are open to both hikers and mountain bikers. The trails at Pinetop's **Woodland Lake Park** are among my favorites. The park is just off Arizona 260 near the east end of Pinetop and has 6 miles of trails, including a paved path around the lake. For a panoramic vista of the Mogollon Rim, hike the short, flat **Mogollon Rim Interpretive Trail** off Arizona 260 on the west side of Lakeside.

For another short but pleasant stroll, check out the **Big Springs Environmental Study Area,** on Woodland Road in Lakeside. This quiet little preserve encompasses a small meadow through which flows a spring-fed stream. There is often good bird-watching here. You can spot more birds at Woodland Lake Park, mentioned above, and at **Jacques Marsh,** 2 miles north of Arizona 260 on Porter Mountain Road in Lakeside. For more information on area trails, contact the **Lakeside Ranger District,** 2022 W. White Mountain Blvd., Lakeside (✆ **928/368-5111**), on Arizona 260 in Lakeside, or the **Pinetop-Lakeside Chamber of Commerce** (see "Visitor Information," above).

If you're up here to catch the big one, area lakes hold native Apache trout, as well as stocked rainbows, browns, and brookies. This is also the southernmost spot in the United States where you can fish for arctic graylings. Right in the Pinetop-Lakeside area, try **Rainbow Lake,** which is a block south of Arizona 260 in Lakeside and has boat rentals available; **Woodland Lake,** in Woodland Lake Park, toward the east end of Pinetop and just south of Arizona 260; or **Show Low Lake,** east of Lakeside and north of Arizona 260. On the nearby White Mountain Apache Indian Reservation, there's good fishing in **Hawley Lake** and **Horseshoe Lake,** both of which are east of Pinetop-Lakeside and south of Arizona 260. If you plan to fish at either of these latter two lakes, be sure to get a reservation fishing license ($6 per day). Licenses are available at the **Hon-Dah Service Station,** at Arizona 260 and Arizona 73 (✆ **928/369-4311**); **Hon-Dah Ski & Outdoor Sport,** also at Arizona 260 and Arizona 73 (✆ **877/CAN-HUNT**); and, during the summer, **Hawley Lake Store,** south of Arizona 260 between Hon-Dah and Sunrise (✆ **928/335-7511**).

Several area golf courses are open to the public, including **Pinetop Lakes Golf & Country Club,** Buck Springs Road, Pinetop-Lakeside (✆ **928/369-4531;** www.pinetoplakesgolf.com), considered one of the best executive courses in the state (play this one if you have time for only one round while you're in the area); **Silver Creek Golf Club,** 2051 Silver Lake Blvd., Show Low (✆ **928/537-2744;** www.silvercreekgolfclub.com); and the **Show Low Golf Club,** 860 N. 36th Dr., Show Low (✆ **928/537-4564**).

About 50 miles south of Show Low, U.S. 60 crosses a bridge over the narrow, scenic canyon of the Salt River. This stretch of the river is a favorite of white-water rafters, and several companies offer rafting trips of varying lengths. Try **Wilderness Aware Rafting** (✆ **800/462-7238;** www.inaraft.com), **Canyon Rio Rafting** (✆ **800/272-3353;** www.canyonrio.com), or **Mild to Wild Rafting** (✆ **800/567-6745;** www.mild2wildrafting.com). Prices are between $114 and $124 for a day trip.

OTHER AREA ATTRACTIONS

If you're curious to learn more about the Apaches, drive south from Pinetop-Lakeside to the **Apache Cultural Center & Museum** (✆ **928/338-4625;** http://wmat.us/wmaculture.shtml), in the town of Fort Apache, which, along with the White Mountain Apache Reservation, was established in 1870 by the U.S. government. The cultural center, approximately 22 miles south of Pinetop on Arizona 73, includes a museum with small but informative exhibits on Apache culture. Outside the cultural center and down a short trail is a reconstructed Apache village. The cultural center is open Monday through Friday (plus Sat in summer) from 8am to 5pm. Admission is $5 for adults, $3 for seniors and students, and free for children under 10. You'll get much more out of your visit if you take one of the cultural center's 1½-hour guided tours, which are available by advance reservation only and include a visit to nearby Kinishba ruins. The tours cost $10. The cultural center is on the grounds of a former Indian school that is now called the Fort Apache Historic Park and includes more than 20

Tips A Pleasant Valley Detour

For a bit of back-roads adventure, head south from the Mogollon Rim to the remote community of Young, which sits in the middle of the aptly named Pleasant Valley. The town can be reached only via well-graded gravel roads—24 miles of gravel if you come from the north, 32 miles from the south—which is why a trip to Young is an adventure.

Why visit Young? Most people come just to see the land that spawned the worst range war and family feud in the West. Known as the Pleasant Valley War or Graham-Tewksbury Feud, it likely erupted over conflicts about sheep grazing in the valley, and eventually the feud took dozens of lives. Zane Grey memorialized the 1880s range war in his novel *To the Last Man.*

You'll find Young on Arizona 288, which heads south from Arizona 260 about midway between Payson and Heber, and connects to Arizona 88 north of Globe (near Theodore Roosevelt Lake).

historic buildings, but don't expect to see a Hollywood-style fort. These old buildings are, for the most part, dreary and in need of restoration.

Also in this area are the **Kinishba Ruins,** up a gravel road 2 miles west of Fort Apache on Arizona 73 and then 3 miles down a rough gravel road. This 200-room pueblo ruin is more than 1,000 years old and was visited by Coronado when he passed through in search of the Seven Cities of Cíbola. Get directions to the ruins at the Cultural Center.

For more information on visiting the White Mountain Apache Reservation, contact the **White Mountain Apache Tribe Office of Tourism** (© **877/338-9628;** www.wmat.nsn.us), also located in Fort Apache Historic Park.

If you're looking for something to do after dark, head out to the **Hon-Dah Casino,** 777 Hwy. 260 (© **800/929-8744** or 928/369-0299; www.hon-dah.com), owned and operated by the White Mountain Apache Tribe. It's open daily round-the-clock and is at the junction of Arizona 73 and Arizona 260, about 4 miles east of Pinetop-Lakeside.

WHERE TO STAY

Hon-Dah Resort Casino & Conference Center ★ This hotel, adjacent to the Hon-Dah Casino a few miles east of Pinetop-Lakeside, is the largest and most luxurious lodging in the White Mountains. As with most casino hotels, it was designed to impress. The portico is big enough to hold a basketball court, and inside the front door is an artificial rock wall upon which are mounted stuffed animals, including a cougar, a bobcat, a bear, ducks, and even a bugling elk. Guest rooms are, for the most part, very spacious.

777 Ariz. 260 (at junction w/Ariz. 73), Pinetop, AZ 85935. © **800/929-8744** or 928/369-0299. www.hon-dah.com. 128 units. $89–$109 double; $150–$180 suite. AE, DC, DISC, MC, V. **Amenities:** Restaurant (American); 2 lounges; year-round outdoor pool; Jacuzzi; sauna; video arcade; room service; coin-op laundry; casino. *In room:* A/C, TV, dataport, fridge, coffeemaker, hair dryer, iron, Wi-Fi.

Lake of the Woods Kids Set on its own private lake right on Arizona 260, Lake of the Woods is a rustic mountain resort that caters primarily to families. Cabins and houses range from tiny to huge, with rustic and modern side by side. The smallest sleep two or three, while the largest can take up to 20; all have kitchens and fireplaces.

Some are on the edge of the lake, while others are tucked away under the pines; be sure to request a location away from the busy highway and ask for a newer cabin, as the accommodations vary considerably in quality. Kids, in particular, love this place: They can fish in the lake, row a boat, or play in the snow.

2244 W. White Mountain Blvd. (P.O. Box 777), Lakeside, AZ 85929. ✆ **928/368-5353.** www.lakeofthewoodsaz.com. 33 units. $79–$212 cabin for 2 people. 3- to 5-night minimum stay in summer and on some holidays. Children under 2 stay free in parent's cabin. MC, V. Pets accepted. **Amenities:** Exercise room; 2 Jacuzzis; sauna; boat rentals; game room; coin-op laundry; playground. *In room:* TV, kitchen, fridge, coffeemaker, microwave, no phone.

CAMPGROUNDS

There are numerous campgrounds in the Pinetop-Lakeside area, including Fool Hollow, Lewis Canyon, and Lakeside. Of these, **Fool Hollow Lake Recreation Area** (✆ **928/537-3680;** www.azstateparks.com) is the nicest. There are also numerous campgrounds nearby on the White River Apache Indian Reservation. For information about these campgrounds, contact the **White Mountain Apache Tribe Wildlife and Outdoor Recreation Division** (✆ **928/338-4385,** ext. 234) or the **White Mountain Apache Tribe Office of Tourism** (✆ **877/338-9628;** www.wmat.nsn.us).

WHERE TO DINE

Charlie Clark's Steak House STEAKHOUSE/SEAFOOD Charlie Clark's, the oldest steakhouse in the White Mountains, has been serving up thick, juicy steaks since 1938 (before that, during Prohibition, the building was used as a sort of backwoods speak-easy). Mesquite-broiled steaks and chicken, as well as seafood and prime rib, fill the menu. To find the place, just look for the building with a horse statue on the roof.

1701 E. White Mountain Blvd., Pinetop. ✆ **888/333-0259** or 928/367-4900. www.charlieclarks.com. Reservations not accepted. Main courses $7–$18 lunch, $14–$40 dinner. AE, DC, DISC, MC, V. Sun–Thurs 11am–9pm; Fri–Sat 11am–10pm.

3 Greer & Sunrise Park ★

51 miles SE of Show Low; 98 miles SE of Holbrook; 222 miles NE of Phoenix

The tiny community of Greer, set in the lush meadows on either side of the Little Colorado River and surrounded by forests, is by far the most picturesque mountain community in Arizona. The elevation of 8,525 feet usually ensures plenty of snow in winter and pleasantly cool temperatures in summer, and together these two factors have turned Greer into something of an upscale mountain getaway that's popular among lowlanders with an eye for aesthetics. Modern log homes are springing up all over the valley, but Greer is still free of the sort of strip-mall developments that have forever changed the character of Payson and Pinetop-Lakeside.

The Little Colorado River, which flows through the middle of Greer on its way to the Grand Canyon, is little more than a babbling brook up here. Still, it's known for trout fishing, one of the main draws in these parts. In winter, cross-country skiing, ice-skating, ice fishing, and sleigh rides are popular. Greer is also the closest community to Sunrise Park ski area, which is what gives the village its ski-resort atmosphere.

ESSENTIALS

GETTING THERE From Phoenix, take U.S. 87 N to Payson and then go east on Arizona 260, or take U.S. 60 E from Phoenix through Globe and Show Low to Arizona 260 E. Greer is just a few miles south of Arizona 260 on Arizona 373.

VISITOR INFORMATION Online, contact the **Greer Business Association** (www.greerarizona.com).

OUTDOOR PURSUITS

Winter is one of the busiest seasons in Greer because the town is so close to the **Sunrise Park Resort** ski area (✆ **800/772-7669** or 928/735-7669; www.sunriseskipark.com). Located just off Arizona 260 on Arizona 273, this ski area, the largest and most popular in Arizona, is operated by the White Mountain Apache Tribe. It usually opens in November, but thaws and long stretches without snow can make winters a bit unreliable. Snow-making machines do, however, enhance the natural snowfall. Although there are some good advanced runs, beginner and intermediate skiers will be in heaven. I've rarely seen so many green runs starting from the uppermost lifts of a ski area, which makes it a very family-oriented place. At the top of 11,000-foot Apache Peak, a day lodge provides meals and a view that goes on forever. A ski school offers a variety of lessons. Lift tickets cost $45 for adults and $26 for children. Ski rentals are available here and at numerous shops in Pinetop-Lakeside.

More than 13 miles of groomed cross-country ski trails wind their way through forests of ponderosa pines and across high snow-covered meadows at Sunrise. These trails begin at the **Sunrise General Store** (✆ **800/772-7669,** ext. 2180), located at the turnoff for the downhill area. All-day trail passes are $7. When there is enough snow, there are also good opportunities for cross-country skiing in Greer, which has 35 miles of developed trails. At 8,500 feet, the alpine scenery is quiet and serene.

Come summer, the cross-country ski trails become **mountain-biking trails** and, when combined with the nearby **Pole Knoll trail system,** provide mountain bikers with 35 miles of trails of varying degrees of difficulty. Sunrise Park Resort also opens up its slopes to mountain bikers. Bikes can be rented for around $30 for 3 hours; a lift ticket for the day will run you another $18.

This area offers some of the finest mountain hiking in Arizona, and my favorite area trail is up 11,590-foot **Mount Baldy** ★, the second-highest peak in Arizona. This peak lies on the edge of the White Mountain Apache Indian Reservation and is sacred to the Apaches. Consequently, the summit is off-limits to non-Apaches. There are two trail heads for the hike. The most popular and scenic route begins 6 miles south of Sunrise Park ski area (off the gravel extension of Ariz. 273) and follows the West Fork of the Little Colorado River. This trail climbs roughly 2,000 feet and is moderately strenuous, and the high elevation often leaves lowland hikers gasping for breath.

For an easier hike, the **Butler Canyon Trail** is a 1-mile nature trail through Butler Canyon north of Greer. To reach the trail head, take East Fork Road, which is 4 miles south of Arizona 260. From the south end of Greer, the **East Fork Trail** eventually leads to Mount Baldy. This trail starts with a steep 600-foot climb but then becomes a much easier ascent. Another good choice for a day hike is the **West Fork Trail,** which begins north of Greer on Osborne Road and meanders through forests and meadows. The turnoff for the trail head is 4¼ miles south of Arizona 260.

Hikers can also catch a lift up Apache Peak at Sunrise Park Resort, which keeps its lifts running in summer for hikers and anyone else interested in the view from up high. A single-ride lift ticket is $10 for adults and $5 for children.

The three Greer Lakes on the outskirts of town—Bunch, River, and Tunnel reservoirs—are popular fishing spots. All three hold brown and rainbow trout. On **River Reservoir,** try the shallows at the south end. On **Tunnel Reservoir,** you can often do well from shore, especially if you're fly-fishing, though there is a boat launch. However,

Finds A Cocoon of Creativity

The **Butterfly Lodge Museum** (✆ **928/735-7514;** www.wmonline.com/butterfly lodge.htm) is a restored historic cabin built in 1914. Owned by James Willard Schultz (a writer) and his son Hart Merriam Schultz (a painter), the museum is a memorial to these two unusual and creative individuals who once called Greer home. It's just off Arizona 373 between Arizona 260 and Greer. It's open Memorial Day to Labor Day Thursday through Sunday (and holidays) from 10am to 5pm. Admission is $2 for adults and $1 for youths 12 to 17.

Big Lake, south of Greer, has the best fishing reputation here. Fishing is also good on **Sunrise Lake;** be sure to get a White Mountain Apache Indian Reservation fishing license ($6 per day for adults, available at the Sunrise General Store).

Sunrise Lake, near the Sunrise Park ski area, is a popular spot in the summer. Boat rentals are available at the **Sunrise Lake Marina** (✆ **928/735-7669,** ext. 2155). A fishing boat with an outboard motor rents for $60 per day.

WHERE TO STAY

IN GREER

Amberian Peaks Lodge & Restaurant ★ Set on a hillside at the upper end of the valley, this luxurious lodge is just a few steps away from the waters of the Little Colorado River, which at this point is little more than a creek. The lodge, with its two-story stone fireplace, log construction, and wide expanse of decks, is a great place to soak up Greer's mountain-getaway atmosphere. There's a wide range of room styles, suites, and a few cabins to choose from, with the emphasis on comfort and tranquility. On clear nights, a telescope is sometimes set up on the deck for stargazing.

One Main St. (P.O. Box 1), Greer, AZ 85927. ✆ **800/556-9997** or 928/735-9977. Fax 928/735-9920. www.thepeaks atgreer.com. 16 units. Mid-May to mid-Oct and mid-Dec to mid-Apr $135–$285 double, $205–$225 suite; mid-Apr to mid-May and mid-Oct to mid-Dec $115–$160 double, $180–$260 suite. Rates include continental breakfast. Children under 4 stay free in parent's room. AE, DISC, MC, V. 2-night minimum on weekends, 3-night minimum on holidays. **Amenities:** Restaurant (American); lounge; exercise room; 2 Jacuzzis; sauna; game room; massage. *In room:* TV/VCR/DVD, fridge, safe, microwave, Wi-Fi.

Hidden Meadow Ranch ★★ Although this luxurious guest ranch isn't located right in Greer, it is far and away the best place to stay in the region. Set on 150 acres of pine forests, the ranch offers accommodations in large modern log cabins that are rustic yet elegant and have wood-burning fireplaces, slate-tiled bathrooms, soaking tubs, and loft bedrooms. The dining room here, which might be featuring elk tenderloin when you visit, serves the best food in the White Mountains. In summer, horseback riding and fly fishing are the most popular activities, while in winter there are sleigh rides and cross-country skiing. Elk, deer, and wild turkeys are all regular visitors to the meadows here.

P.O. Box 300, Greer, AZ 85927. ✆ **866/333-4080** or 928/333-1000. Fax 928/333-1010. www.hiddenmeadow.com. 10 units. $550–$595 double. Rates include all meals and ranch activities. AE, DC, DISC, MC, V. Pets accepted. **Amenities:** Restaurant (New American); canoeing; horseback riding. *In room:* Fridge, coffeemaker, microwave, Wi-Fi.

Snowy Mountain Inn *Kids* Set back from the main road down a gravel driveway and shaded by tall pines, the Snowy Mountain Inn has a remote yet comfortable feel about it. The modern cabins, although a bit cramped inside, are great for family vacations; they come equipped with gas fireplaces, porches, and sleeping lofts, and some have private hot tubs as well. Surrounding the log cabins and main lodge are 10 acres of private forest, so guests have plenty of room to roam. There's a 1½-acre trout pond on the property, and a playground for the kids. The lodge has a sports bar for a restaurant.

38721 Rte. 373, Greer, AZ 85927. ✆ **888/766-9971** or 928/735-7576. Fax 928/735-7705. www.snowymountaininn.com. 8 units. $175–$225 cabin. AE, DISC, MC, V. Pets accepted ($15 per day). **Amenities:** Restaurant; lounge; children's playroom; guest laundry. *In room:* TV/VCR, kitchen, fridge, coffeemaker, microwave, no phone in cabins.

CAMPGROUNDS

In the immediate vicinity of Greer are a couple of nice campgrounds in Apache and Sitgreaves National Forests. Contact the **National Recreation Reservation Service** (✆ **877/444-6777** or 518/885-3639; www.recreation.gov) to make reservations for both the **Rolfe C. Hoyer Campground** ($16 per night), 1 mile north of Greer on Arizona 373; and the **Winn Campground** ($14 per night), 12 miles southwest of Greer on Arizona 273 (the road past Sunrise Park Resort). Because of its proximity to Greer and the Greer Lakes, Rolfe C. Hoyer is your best choice in the area. There are also several campgrounds nearby on the White Mountain Apache Indian Reservation (no reservations accepted).

WHERE TO DINE

Molly Butler Lodge ★ Although it may not look it, this restaurant has been in business since 1910 and is one of the oldest restaurants in the state. However, the Molly Butler has been much updated over the years and now sports a sort of 1970s mountain rustic look. While the menu sticks to simple fare, it's the most reliable menu in town. The steaks are your best choices, but the chili's good, too. The bar here is a favorite après-fishing hangout.

109 Main St. ✆ **866/288-3167** or 928/735-7226. Main courses $10–$24. AE, DISC, MC, V. Nov to mid-May daily 5–9pm; mid-May to Oct daily 11am–9pm.

4 Springerville & Eagar

56 miles E of Show Low; 82 miles SE of Holbrook; 227 miles NE of Phoenix

Together the adjacent towns of Springerville and Eagar constitute the northeastern gateway to the White Mountains. Although the towns themselves are at the foot of the mountains, the vistas from around Springerville and Eagar take in all the area's peaks. The two towns also like to play up their Wild West backgrounds—in fact, John Wayne liked the area so much that he had a ranch along the Little Colorado River just west of Eagar. Today, large ranches still run their cattle on the windswept plains north of Springerville and Eagar.

Volcanic activity between 300,000 and 700,000 years ago gave the land north of Springerville and Eagar its distinctive character. This area, known as the Springerville Volcanic Field, is the third-largest volcanic field of its kind in the continental United States (the San Francisco Field near Flagstaff and the Medicine Lake Field in California are both larger). The Springerville Volcanic Field covers an area bigger than the state of Rhode Island and contains 405 extinct volcanic vents. The many cinder cones dotting the landscape give this region a unique appearance. For a brochure outlining a tour of the volcanic field, contact the Springerville-Eagar Regional Chamber of Commerce (see "Visitor Information," below).

ESSENTIALS

GETTING THERE Springerville and Eagar are in the northeast corner of the White Mountains at the junction of U.S. 60, U.S. 180/191, and Arizona 260. From Phoenix, there are two routes: Arizona 87 N to Payson and then Arizona 260 E, or U.S. 60 E to Globe and then north to Show Low and on to Springerville (or you can take Ariz. 260 from Show Low to Springerville). From Holbrook, take U.S. 180 southeast to St. Johns and U.S. 180/191 S to Springerville. From southern Arizona, U.S. 191 is very slow but very scenic.

VISITOR INFORMATION For information on the Springerville and Eagar areas, contact the **Springerville-Eagar Regional Chamber of Commerce** (✆ **928/333-2123;** www.springerville-eagarchamber.com).

INDIAN RUINS

Casa Malpais Visitor Center and Museum ★ *Finds* The Casa Malpais ruins are unique in that the pueblo, which dates from 1250 and was occupied until about 1400, was built to take advantage of existing caves. Many of these caves form a system of catacomb-like rooms under the pueblo. The only way to visit the ruin is on guided tours that leave from the Casa Malpais museum, which is located in downtown Springerville. At the museum, you'll find exhibits on both the Mogollon people and dinosaurs that once roamed this region.

318 E. Main St., Springerville. ✆ **928/333-5375.** Guided tours $7 adults, $5 seniors and children. Museum daily 8am–4pm. Tours daily 9 and 11am and 2pm (weather permitting). Closed Thanksgiving and Christmas.

Lyman Lake State Park Within this state park are the early Ancestral Puebloan ruins of Rattlesnake Point Pueblo, as well as petroglyphs that date back thousands of years. Some of the petroglyphs are accessible only by boat, and during the summer months you can see them on guided tours Saturday and Sunday mornings at 10am. There are also summer tours to the ruins.

18 miles north of Springerville. ✆ **928/337-4441.** www.azstateparks.com. Admission $5 per car. Park daily daylight hours, visitor center daily 8am–5pm; tours May–Sept Sat–Sun.

MUSEUMS

A couple of small museums are worth a look if you have the time. The **Reneé Cushman Art Collection** is housed in the L.D.S. (Mormon) Church in Springerville. It consists of one woman's personal collection of European art and antiques. Among the works are an etching attributed to Rembrandt and three pen-and-ink drawings by Tiepolo. The antique furniture dates back to the Renaissance. The museum is open by appointment only. Contact the **Springerville-Eagar Regional Chamber of Commerce** (✆ **928/333-2123;** www.Springerville-eagarchamber.com) for information on arranging a visit.

Local history and old automated musical instruments are the focus of the X Diamond Ranch's **Little House Museum** (✆ **928/333-2286;** www.xdiamondranch.com), 7 miles west of Eagar on South Fork Road, off Arizona 260. Tales of colorful Wild West characters as told by the guide are as much a part of the museum as the displays themselves. Museum visits are by reservation only and cost $8 for adults and $4 for children under 12. Here on the X Diamond Ranch, a ruin site is open to the public.

OUTDOOR PURSUITS

Lyman Lake State Park (✆ **928/337-4441;** www.azstateparks.com), 18 miles north of Springerville, is popular for lake fishing. And if it's high summer and you feel like swimming, this is the place for a dip.

Alternatively, you can head out to the **X Diamond Ranch** (© **928/333-2286;** www.xdiamondranch.com), off Arizona 260 between Eagar and Greer (take C.R. 4124). The ranch maintains a section of the Little Colorado River as a fishing habitat. The half-day fishing rate is $30, while a full day costs $40. Horseback rides are also available, with options ranging from 1 hour ($25) to a full day ($150).

For a chance to see pronghorn antelope, elk, and mule deer, head south of Eagar to the **Sipe White Mountain Wildlife Area.** This grassy valley at the foot of the White Mountains was once a cattle ranch, and today the old ranch house serves as a visitor center that's open during the summer months. Several miles of hiking trails wind through forest and pasture and past lakes and ponds. There's good bird-watching here, too. Sipe is 5 miles down a gravel road that begins 2 miles south of Eagar off U.S. 180/191. For more information, contact the Arizona Game & Fish Department, Pinetop Regional Office, 2878 E. White Mountain Blvd., Pinetop (© **928/367-4281;** www.gf.state.az.us).

WHERE TO STAY

X Diamond Ranch Long known for its Little House Museum and trout fishing on the Little Colorado River, this ranch also rents a variety of cabins. Activities include fishing, horseback riding, and touring the ranch's archaeological site ($12 for a tour). There's no restaurant on the premises, but cabins have full kitchens.

P.O. Box 113, Greer, AZ 85927. © **928/333-2286.** www.xdiamondranch.com. 6 units. Apr–Oct $110–$175 double; Nov–Mar $95–$155 double. Children under 2 stay free in parent's room. AE, DISC, MC, V. Off Ariz. 260 between Eagar and Greer (take C.R. 4124). **Amenities:** Horseback riding. *In room:* TV, kitchen, fridge, coffeemaker, no phone in some units.

CAMPGROUNDS

Lyman Lake State Park (© **928/337-4441;** www.azstateparks.com), 18 miles north of Springerville on U.S. 180/191, has a campground with sites going for $12 to $22 per night. It's very popular with water-skiers, so don't expect much peace and quiet.

5 The Coronado Trail ★

Alpine: 28 miles S of Springerville; 75 miles E of Pinetop-Lakeside; 95 miles N of Clifton

Winding southward from the Springerville-Eagar area to Clifton and Morenci, the Coronado Trail (U.S. 191) is one of the most remote and little-traveled paved roads in the state. Because this road is so narrow and winding, it's slow going—meant for people who aren't in a hurry to get anywhere anytime soon. If you are *not* prone to carsickness, you may want to take a leisurely drive down this scenic stretch of asphalt.

The Coronado Trail is named for the Spanish explorer Francisco Vásquez de Coronado, who came to Arizona in search of gold in the early 1540s. Although he never found it, his party did make it as far north as the Hopi pueblos and would have traveled through this region on their march northward from Mexico. Centuries later, the discovery of huge copper reserves would make the fortunes of the towns of Clifton and Morenci, at the southern end of the Coronado Trail.

Alpine, at the northern end of the Coronado Trail, is the main base for today's explorers, who tend to be outdoor types in search of uncrowded trails and trout streams where the fish are biting. Located near the New Mexico state line, Alpine offers a few basic lodges and restaurants, plus easy access to the region's many trails.

This area is known as the Alps of Arizona, and Alpine's picturesque setting in the middle of a wide grassy valley at 8,030 feet certainly lives up to this image. Alpine is

It's Not the Grand Canyon, but . . .

The twin towns of Clifton and Morenci are home to one of Arizona's biggest holes in the ground. However, the hole here was not carved by a mighty river or created by the impact of a meteorite. No, this humongous hole is the Phelps Dodge Mining Company's open-pit copper mine, and it's the largest such mine in Arizona. Want to see just how big it is? Find out on a **Morenci Mine Tour** (© **877/646-8687;** www.phelpsdodge.com/community-environment). The 2 ½-hour tours are offered on Friday and Saturday at 8:30am and 1pm, and cost $8 for adults, $7 for seniors, and $4 for youths 9 to 17 (children younger than 9 are not permitted on the tour).

surrounded by the Apache and Sitgreaves National Forests, which together have miles of trails and several campgrounds. In spring, wildflowers abound and the trout fishing is excellent. In summer, there's hiking on forest trails. In autumn, the aspens in the Golden Bowl on the mountainside above Alpine turn a brilliant yellow, and in winter, visitors come for the cross-country skiing and ice fishing.

ESSENTIALS

GETTING THERE Alpine is 28 miles south of Springerville and Eagar at the junction of U.S. 191, which continues south to Clifton and Morenci, and U.S. 180, which leads east into New Mexico.

VISITOR INFORMATION For more information on the region, contact the **Alpine Area Chamber of Commerce,** P.O. Box 410, Alpine, AZ 85920 (© **928/339-4330;** www.alpinearizona.com). For outdoor information, contact the Apache and Sitgreaves National Forests' **Alpine Ranger District,** P.O. Box 469, Alpine, AZ 85920 (© **928/339-4384;** www.fs.fed.us/r3/asnf).

OUTDOOR PURSUITS

Fall, when the aspens turn the mountainside gold, is one of the most popular times of year in this area—there are only a few places in Arizona where fall color is worth a drive, and this is one of them.

Not far outside Alpine, there's cross-country skiing at the **Williams Valley Winter Recreation Area,** which doubles as a mountain-biking trail system in summer.

If you're looking to fish, try **Luna Lake,** east of Alpine off U.S. 180. Here at the lake, you'll also find some easy-to-moderate mountain-bike trails that usually offer good wildlife-viewing opportunities. The best hike in the area is the trail up **Escudilla Mountain,** just outside Alpine, where you'll see some of the best autumn displays of aspens. The Escudilla National Recreation Trail leads 3 miles to the summit of the mountain (6-mile round-trip) and involves more than 1,300 feet of elevation gain.

Summer or winter, **Hannagan Meadows,** 23 miles south of Alpine, is the place to be. Here you'll find excellent hiking, mountain biking, and cross-country ski trails. Hannagan Meadows also provides access to the **Blue Range Primitive Area,** which is popular with hikers. The Eagle Trail, which starts 5 miles south of Hannagan Meadows off Eagle Creek Road, is a good place to spot wildlife. It is in the remote wilderness areas near here that a Mexican gray wolf recovery project has been underway for several years. The reintroduction has so far met with mixed success, as wolves have been killed by cars, people, disease, and even mountain lions. Some wolves have had to be recaptured because they strayed out of the area set aside for them or because they had encounters with humans.

WHERE TO STAY & DINE

Between Springerville-Eagar and Clifton-Morenci, there are nearly a dozen National Forest Service campgrounds. If fishing and boating interest you, head to **Luna Lake Campground,** just east of Alpine on U.S. 180, where the daily campsite fee is $10. Reserve a Luna Lake campsite through the National Recreation Reservation Service (✆ **877/444-6777;** www.recreation.gov). For a more tranquil forest setting, try **Hannagan Campground** (reservations not accepted), which makes a good base for exploring the Coronado Trail. For information on these campgrounds, contact the **Alpine Ranger District** (✆ **928/339-4384**).

If you're looking for someplace to eat, Alpine has a couple of basic restaurants.

Hannagan Meadow Lodge Located 22 miles south of Alpine at an elevation of 9,100 feet, this rustic lodge dates back to 1926 and is set amid cool forests on the winding route of the Coronado Trail. With both rustic cabins and bed-and-breakfast lodge rooms, this place offers plenty of variety and is a good spot for a quiet getaway or a family vacation. In summer, the lodge is a base for exploring the hundreds of miles of hiking trails in the area, while in winter the lodge rents cross-country skis and snowshoes to its guests.

HC 61, P.O. Box 335, Alpine, AZ 85920. ✆ **928/339-4370.** www.hannaganmeadow.com. 17 units. $50–$100 suite; $80–$175 cabin. Children stay free in parent's room. Lodge room rates include full breakfast. MC, V. Pets accepted in cabins ($10 per day). **Amenities:** Restaurant (American); bike rentals; game room; horseback riding (May–Oct). *In room:* No phone.

Tal-Wi-Wi Lodge Located 3 miles north of Alpine on U.S. 191, Tal-Wi-Wi Lodge is nothing fancy—just a rustic lodge popular with anglers and hunters—but it's the best choice in the area. The deluxe rooms come with a hot tub or woodstove (one unit has both), heat sources that are well appreciated on cold winter nights (Alpine is often the coldest town in Arizona). The furnishings are rustic yet comfortable, and the wood-paneled walls and large front porches give the lodge a classic country flavor. The dining room serves country breakfasts and dinners.

U.S. 191 (P.O. Box 169), Alpine, AZ 85920. ✆ **800/476-2695** or 928/339-4319. Fax 928/339-1962. www.talwiwilodge.com. 20 units. $69–$99 double. 3-night minimum stay on holidays. MC, V. Pets accepted ($10 per day). **Amenities:** Restaurant (American); lounge. *In room:* Coffeemaker, Wi-Fi, no phone.

9

Tucson

Encircled by mountain ranges and bookended by the two units of Saguaro National Park, Tucson is Arizona's second-largest city, and for the vacationer it has everything that Phoenix has to offer, plus a bit more. There are world-class golf resorts, excellent restaurants, art museums and galleries, an active cultural life, and, of course, plenty of great weather. Tucson also has a long history that melds Native American, Hispanic, and Anglo roots. And with a national park, a national forest, and other natural areas just beyond the city limits, Tucson is a city that celebrates its Sonoran Desert setting.

At Saguaro National Park, you can marvel at the massive saguaro cacti that have come to symbolize the desert Southwest, while at the Arizona–Sonora Desert Museum (actually a zoo), you can acquaint yourself with the myriad flora and fauna of this region. Take a hike or a horseback ride up one of the trails that leads into the wilderness from the edge of the city, and you may even meet up with a few desert denizens on their own turf. Look beyond the saguaros and prickly pears, and you can find a desert oasis, complete with waterfalls and swimming holes, and, a short drive from the city, a pine forest that's home to the southernmost ski area in the country.

Founded by the Spanish in 1775, Tucson was built on the site of a much older Native American village, and the city's name comes from the Pima Indian word *chukeson,* which means "spring at the base of black mountain," a reference to the peak now known simply as "A Mountain." From 1867 to 1877, Tucson was the territorial capital of Arizona, but eventually the capital was moved to Phoenix. Consequently, Tucson did not develop as quickly as Phoenix and still holds on to some of its Hispanic and Western heritage.

Tucson has a history of valuing quality of life over development, which sets it apart from the Phoenix area. Back in the days of urban renewal, its citizens turned back the bulldozers and managed to preserve at least some of the city's old Mexican character. Likewise, today, in the face of the sort of sprawl that has given Phoenix the feel of a landlocked Los Angeles, advocates for controlled growth are fighting hard to preserve both Tucson's desert environment and the city's unique character. However, the seemingly inevitable sprawl has now ringed much of Tucson with vast suburbs, though as yet, the city is far from becoming another Phoenix.

The struggle to retain an identity distinct from other Southwestern cities is ongoing, and despite long, drawn-out attempts to breathe life into the city's core, downtown Tucson has little to offer visitors other than an art museum, a convention center, a few historic neighborhoods, and a couple of good restaurants. There are currently plans for a major downtown renaissance project known as Rio Nuevo that, it is hoped, will reinvigorate downtown Tucson.

Despite this minor shortcoming, Tucson remains Arizona's most beautiful and most livable city. With the Santa Catalina Mountains for a backdrop, Tucson boasts one of the most dramatic settings in the Southwest, and whether you're taking in the mountain vistas from the tee box of the 12th hole, the saddle of a palomino, or a table for two, I'm sure you'll agree that Tucson makes a superb vacation destination.

1 Orientation

Not nearly as large and spread out as Phoenix and the Valley of the Sun, Tucson is small enough to be convenient, yet large enough to be sophisticated. The mountains ringing Tucson are bigger and closer to town than those in the Phoenix and Scottsdale area, which gives Tucson a more dramatic skyline. The desert is also closer and more easily accessed here than in Phoenix.

ARRIVING

BY PLANE Located 6 miles south of downtown, **Tucson International Airport** (© 520/573-8000; www.tucsonairport.org) is served by the following major airlines: **Alaska/Horizon** (© 800/252-7522; www.alaskaair.com), **American** (© 800/433-7300; www.aa.com), **Continental** (© 800/523-3273; www.continental.com), **Delta** (© 800/221-1212; www.delta.com), **Frontier** (© 800/432-1359; www.flyfrontier.com), **JetBlue Airways** (© 800/538-2583; www.jetblue.com), **Northwest/KLM** (© 800/225-2525; www.nwa.com), **Southwest** (© 800/435-9792; www.southwest.com), **United** (© 800/864-8331; www.ual.com), and **US Airways** (© 800/428-4322; http://usairways.com).

Visitor centers in both baggage-claim areas can give you brochures and reserve a hotel room if you haven't done so already.

Many resorts and hotels in Tucson provide free or competitively priced airport shuttle service. **Arizona Stagecoach** (© **520/889-1000;** www.azstagecoach.com) operates 24-hour van service to downtown Tucson and the foothills resorts. Fares to downtown are around $20 one-way and $38 round-trip ($23 and $44 for a couple), and to the foothills resorts around $36 one-way and $62 round-trip ($42 and $74 for a couple). It takes between 45 minutes and 1 hour to reach the foothills resorts. To return to the airport, it's best to call at least a day before your scheduled departure.

You'll also find taxis waiting outside baggage claim, or you can call **Yellow Cab** (© **520/624-6611**) or **Allstate Cab** (© **520/881-2227**). The flag-drop rate at the airport is $4.50, and then $2 per mile. A taxi to downtown costs around $23, to the foothills resorts about $26 to $46.

Sun Tran (© **520/792-9222;** www.suntran.com), the local public transit system, operates bus service to and from the airport. The fare is $1. Route no. 6, to downtown, runs Monday through Friday from about 4:50am to 7:20pm, Saturday from about 7:15am to 6:15pm, and Sunday from about 6:20am to 5:20pm. Departures are every 30 minutes on weekdays and every hour on weekends. It takes 40 to 50 minutes to reach downtown. Route no. 11 operates on a similar schedule and travels along Alvernon Road to the midtown area.

BY CAR **I-10,** the main east-west interstate across the southern United States, passes through Tucson and connects to Phoenix. **I-19** connects Tucson with the Mexican border at Nogales. **Arizona 86** heads southwest into the Tohono O'odham Indian Reservation, and **Arizona 79** leads north toward Florence and eventually connects with **U.S. 60** into Phoenix.

If you're headed downtown, take the Congress Street exit off I-10. If you're coming from the north and going to one of the foothills resorts north of downtown, you'll probably want to take the Ina Road exit off I-10.

BY TRAIN Tucson is served by **Amtrak** (✆ **800/872-7245;** www.amtrak.com) passenger rail service. The *Sunset Limited,* which runs between Orlando and Los Angeles, stops in Tucson. The **train station** is at 400 E. Toole Ave. (✆ **520/623-4442**), in the heart of downtown and within walking distance of the Tucson Convention Center, El Presidio Historic District, and a few hotels. You'll see taxis waiting to meet the train.

BY BUS **Greyhound** (✆ **800/231-2222** or 520/792-3475; www.greyhound.com) connects Tucson to the rest of the United States through its extensive system. The bus station is currently at 471 W. Congress St., but this is a temporary location. Call at the time you are traveling to confirm the station location.

VISITOR INFORMATION

The **Metropolitan Tucson Convention & Visitors Bureau (MTCVB),** 100 S. Church Ave. (at Broadway), Suite 7199 (✆ **800/638-8350** or 520/624-1817; www.visittucson.org), is an excellent source of information on Tucson and environs. The visitor center is open Monday through Friday from 8am to 5pm, Saturday and Sunday from 9am to 4pm.

CITY LAYOUT

MAIN ARTERIES & STREETS Tucson is laid out on a grid that's fairly regular in the downtown areas but becomes less orderly the farther you go from the city center. In the flatlands, major thoroughfares are spaced at 1-mile intervals, with smaller streets filling in the squares created by the major roads. In the foothills, where Tucson's most recent growth has occurred, the grid system breaks down completely because of the hilly terrain.

The main **east-west roads** are (from south to north) 22nd Street, Broadway Boulevard, Speedway Boulevard, Grant Road (with Tanque Verde Rd. as an extension), and Ina Road/Skyline Drive/Sunrise Road. The main **north-south roads** are (from west to east) Miracle Mile/Oracle Road, Stone/Sixth Avenue, Campbell Avenue, Country Club Road, Alvernon Road, and Swan Road. **I-10** cuts diagonally across the Tucson metropolitan area from northwest to southeast.

In **downtown Tucson,** Congress Street and Broadway Boulevard are the main east-west streets; Stone Avenue, Sixth Avenue, and Fourth Avenue are the main north-south streets.

FINDING AN ADDRESS Because Tucson is laid out on a grid, finding an address is relatively easy. The zero (or starting) point for all Tucson addresses is the corner of Stone Avenue, which runs north and south, and Congress Street, which runs east and west. From this point, streets are designated either north, south, east, or west. Addresses usually, but not always, increase by 100 with each block, so that an address of 4321 E. Broadway Blvd. should be 43 blocks east of Stone Avenue. In the downtown area, many of the streets and avenues are numbered, with numbered streets running east and west, and numbered avenues running north and south.

STREET MAPS The best way to find your way around Tucson is to pick up a free map at the visitor center at the airport or at the MTCVB (see "Visitor Information,"

Tucson at a Glance

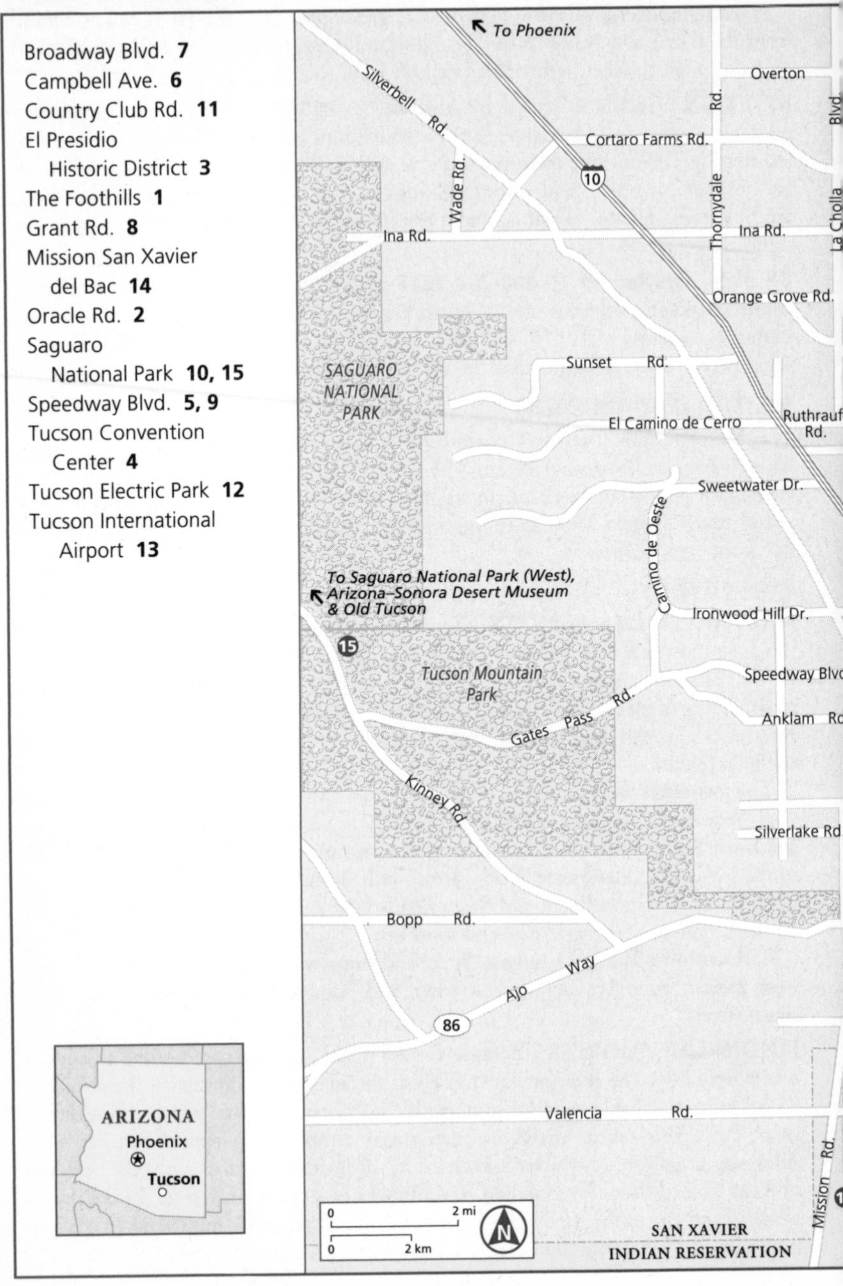

CORONADO NATIONAL FOREST
Hardy Rd.
Magee Rd.
Tohono Chul Park
Ina Rd.
La Canada Dr.
Orange Grove Rd.
Skyline Dr.
Kolb Rd.
Sabino Canyon Rd.
Sabino Canyon Park
Sunrise Dr.
Hacienda del Sol Rd.
Swan Rd.
Craycroft Rd.
River Rd.
Wetmore Rd.
Roger Rd.
Prince Rd.
Romero Rd.
Flowing Wells Rd.
Snyder Rd.
Bear Canyon Rd.
To Mount Lemmon
Catalina Hwy.
Miracle Mile
Ft. Lowell Rd.
Ft. Lowell Park
Tanque Verde Rd.
Grant Rd.
Oracle Rd.
Stone Ave.
Euclid Ave.
Campbell Ave.
Tucson Blvd.
Country Club Rd.
Alvernon Way
Speedway Blvd.
6th St.
5th St.
Grande Ave.
Congress
Broadway Blvd.
Historic Districts
Reid Park
Wilmot Rd.
Sentinel Peak Park
22nd St.
To Saguaro National Park (East)
Tucson Greyhound Park
36th St.
Golf Links Rd.
Ajo Way
Escalante Rd.
Pantano Rd.
Camino Seco
Kino Blvd.
DAVIS MONTHAN AFB
Irvington Rd.
Palo Verde Rd.
Drexel Rd.
12th Ave.
6th Ave.
Valencia Rd.
Los Reales Rd.
Tucson International Airport
To Nogales
10
19
210

above). The maps handed out by car-rental agencies are not very detailed but will do for some purposes. Local gas stations also sell detailed maps.

NEIGHBORHOODS IN BRIEF

Downtown This is Tucson's main business district, and though it incorporates parts of two historic districts, it has little to offer visitors who aren't in town for an event at the Tucson Convention Center, which dominates much of downtown. There are a few art galleries and a good restaurant or two in the area, but for the most part, downtown is a 9-to-5 business district. The main reason most visitors find themselves in downtown is to stop in at the Metropolitan Tucson Convention & Visitors Bureau visitor center.

El Presidio Historic District Named for the Spanish military garrison that once stood here, the neighborhood is bounded by Alameda Street on the south, Main Avenue on the west, Franklin Street on the north, and Church Avenue on the east. El Presidio was the city's most affluent neighborhood in the 1880s, and large homes from that period have been restored and now house restaurants, arts-and-crafts galleries, and a bed-and-breakfast inn. The Tucson Museum of Art anchors the neighborhood.

Barrio Histórico District Another 19th-century neighborhood, the Barrio Histórico is bounded on the north by Cushing Street, on the west by the railroad tracks, on the south by 18th Street, and on the east by Stone Avenue. The Barrio Histórico is characterized by Sonoran-style adobe row houses that directly abut the street with no yards, a style typical in Mexican towns. A few restaurants and galleries dot the neighborhood, but most restored buildings serve as offices and private residences. This remains a borderline neighborhood where restoration is a slow, ongoing process, so try to avoid it late at night.

Fourth Avenue Running from University Boulevard in the north to Ninth Street in the south, Fourth Avenue is the favored shopping district of cash-strapped college students. Shops specialize primarily in ethnic and used/vintage clothing as well as handcrafted items from around the world. Twice a year, in spring and late fall, the street is closed to traffic for a street fair. Plenty of restaurants, bars, and clubs also make this the city's favorite college nightlife district.

University District/Midtown Northeast of downtown Tucson, this part of the city is actually a collection of different neighborhoods surrounding the University of Arizona. Just to the west of the university campus, you'll find the sort of shops and restaurants you'd expect adjacent to a university. On the east side, you'll find neighborhoods that are home to the historic Arizona Inn and a few other hotels. Stretching north from the university is Campbell Avenue, which has one of the greatest concentrations of interesting budget restaurants in the city.

East Tucson This part of the city includes pretty much everything east of the University District all the way to the eastern unit of Saguaro National Park. Within east Tucson you'll find not only numerous business and all-suites hotels, but also lots of restaurants and both the national park and Sabino Canyon Recreation Area. Be prepared to spend quite a bit of time in your car as you drive this sprawling section of the city.

The Foothills This huge area in northern Tucson houses the city's most affluent neighborhoods. Elegant shopping plazas, modern malls, world-class resorts, golf courses, and expensive residential neighborhoods are surrounded by hilly desert at the foot of the Santa Catalina Mountains.

2 Getting Around

BY CAR

Unless you plan to stay by the pool or on the golf course, you'll want to rent a car. Luckily, rates are fairly economical. At press time, Dollar was charging $133 per week ($171 with taxes and surcharges included) for a compact car with unlimited mileage in Tucson. See "Getting Around Arizona" in chapter 2 for general tips on car rentals in Arizona.

The following agencies have offices at Tucson International Airport as well as other locations in the area. Because taxes and surcharges add up to 30% or more on car rentals at the airport, you may want to consider renting at some other location, where you can avoid paying some of these fees. Among the Tucson car-rental agencies are **Alamo** (© 800/462-5266 or 520/573-4740), **Avis** (© 800/331-1212 or 520/294-1494), **Budget** (© 800/527-0700 or 520/573-8476), **Dollar** (© 800/800-3665), **Enterprise** (© 800/261-7331 or 520/573-5250), **Hertz** (© 800/654-3131 or 520/573-5201), and **National** (© 800/227-7368 or 520/573-8050).

Downtown Tucson is still a relatively easy place to find a parking space, and parking fees are low. There are two huge parking lots at the south side of the Tucson Convention Center, a couple of small lots on either side of the Tucson Museum of Art (one at Main Ave. and Paseo Redondo, south of El Presidio Historic District, and one at the corner of Council St. and Court Ave.), and parking garages beneath the main library (101 N. Stone Ave.) and El Presidio Park (on Alameda St.). You'll find plenty of metered parking on the smaller downtown streets. Almost all Tucson hotels and resorts provide free parking.

Lanes on several major avenues in Tucson change direction at rush hour to facilitate traffic flow, so pay attention to signs that tell you the time and direction of traffic.

BY PUBLIC TRANSPORTATION

BY BUS Covering much of the Tucson metropolitan area, **Sun Tran** (© **520/792-9222;** www.suntran.com) public buses are $1 for adults and students, 40¢ for seniors, and free for children 5 and under. Day passes are available on buses for $2.

The **Ronstadt Transit Center,** at Congress Street and Sixth Avenue, is served by about 30 regular and express bus routes to all parts of Tucson. The bus system does *not* extend to such tourist attractions as the Arizona–Sonora Desert Museum, Old Tucson, Saguaro National Park, or the foothills resorts, and thus is of limited use to visitors. However, Sun Tran does provide a shuttle for sports games and special events. Call the above phone number for information.

BY TROLLEY Although they don't go very far, the restored electric streetcars of **Old Pueblo Trolley** (© **520/792-1802;** www.oldpueblotrolley.org) are a fun way to get from the Fourth Avenue shopping district to the University of Arizona. The trolleys operate on Friday from 6 to 10pm, Saturday from noon to midnight, and Sunday from noon to 6pm. The fare is $1 for adults and 50¢ for children 6 to 12. The fare on Sunday is only 25¢ for all riders. Friday and Saturday all-day passes are $2.50 for adults and $1.25 for children.

T.I.C.E.T., or Tucson Inner City Express Transit (© **520/747-3778**), operates five free downtown-area shuttles, only two of which are of much use to visitors. The Orange Route, which has stops near the visitor center, the Tucson Convention Center, the Tucson Children's Museum, Old Town Artisans, and the Tucson Museum of Art, operates Monday through Friday and runs every 20 minutes between 6am and 6pm. The Red Route, which links downtown with the numerous museums at the University of Arizona, operates Monday through Friday every 20 minutes between 6:30am and 5:30pm.

BY TAXI

If you need a taxi, you'll have to phone for one. **Yellow Cab** (© **520/624-6611**) and **Discount Cab** (© **520/388-9000**) provide service throughout the city. The flag-drop rate is between $2.25 and $2.50, and after that it's $1.75 to $1.80 per mile. Although distances in Tucson are not as great as those in Phoenix, it's still a good 10 or more miles from the foothills resorts to downtown Tucson, so expect to pay at least $10 for a taxi. Most resorts have shuttle vans or can arrange taxi service to major attractions.

ON FOOT

Downtown Tucson is compact and easily explored on foot, and many old streets in the downtown historic neighborhoods are narrow and much easier to appreciate if you leave your car in a parking lot. Also, although several major attractions—including the Arizona–Sonora Desert Museum, Old Tucson Studios, Saguaro National Park, and Sabino Canyon—can be reached only by car, they require quite a bit of walking once you arrive. These attractions often have uneven footing, so be sure to bring a good pair of walking shoes.

FAST FACTS: Tucson

Babysitters Most hotels can arrange a sitter for you, and many resorts feature special programs for children on weekends and throughout the summer. If your hotel can't help, call **A-1 Sitting Service** (© **520/881-1578**), which will send a sitter to your hotel.

Car Rentals See "Getting Around," above.

Dentist Call the Arizona Dental Association (© **800/866-2732**) for a referral.

Doctor For a doctor referral, ask at your hotel or call University Medical Center (© **520/694-8888**).

Emergencies For fire, police, or medical emergency, phone © **911.**

Eyeglass Repair **Alvernon Optical** (www.alvernonoptical.com) has several stores around town where you can have your glasses repaired or replaced. Locations include 440 N. Alvernon Way (© **520/327-6211**), 6987 N. Oracle Rd. (© **520/297-2501**), and 7123 E. Tanque Verde Rd. (© **520/296-4157**).

Hospitals The **Tucson Medical Center** is at 5301 E. Grant Rd. (© **520/327-5461**). The **University Medical Center** is at 1501 N. Campbell Ave. (© **520/694-0111**).

Information See "Visitor Information" in "Orientation," above.

Internet Access Internet access is free at downtown's **Joel D. Valdez Library,** at 101 N. Stone Ave. (© **520/791-4393**). Also, try FedEx Kinko's locations around the city.

Lost Property If you lose something at the airport, call ✆ **520/573-8156;** if you lose something on a Sun Tran bus, call ✆ **520/792-9222.**

Newspapers & Magazines The *Arizona Daily Star* is Tucson's morning daily, while the *Tucson Citizen* is the afternoon daily. The *Tucson Weekly* is the city's news-and-arts journal, published on Thursday.

Pharmacies Contact **Walgreens (✆ 800/WALGREENS;** www.walgreens.com) for the Walgreens pharmacy that's nearest you; some are open 24 hours a day.

Police In case of an emergency, phone ✆ **911.**

Post Office There's a post office in downtown Tucson at 141 S. Sixth Ave. (✆ **800/275-8777** or 520/903-1958; www.usps.com), open Monday through Friday from 8:30am to 5pm.

Radio **KXCI** (91.3 FM) has an alternative mix of programming and is a favorite with local Tucsonans, while **KUAT** (90.5 FM) has all-classical programming and is a good station for news. **KUAZ** (89.1 FM) is the National Public Radio station.

Safety Tucson is surprisingly safe for a city of its size. However, the Downtown Arts District isn't all that lively after dark and attracts a lot of street people and panhandlers. Be particularly alert if you're down here for a performance of some sort. Just to the south of downtown lies a poorer section of the city that's best avoided after dark unless you are certain of where you're going. Otherwise, take the same precautions you would in any other city.

When driving, be aware that many streets in the Tucson area are subject to flooding when it rains. Heed warnings about possible flooded areas and don't try to cross a low area that has become flooded. Find an alternate route instead.

Taxes In addition to the 5.6% sales tax levied by the state, Tucson levies a 2% city sales tax. Car-rental taxes, surcharges, and fees add up to around 30% on weekly rentals. The hotel tax in the Tucson area is generally between 11.5% to 12%.

Taxis See "Getting Around," above.

Weather For the local weather forecast, call the **National Weather Service (✆ 520/881-3333).**

3 Where to Stay

Although Phoenix still holds the title of Resort Capital of Arizona, Tucson is not far behind, and this city's resorts boast much more spectacular settings than most comparable properties in Phoenix and Scottsdale. As far as nonresort accommodations go, Tucson has a wider variety than Phoenix—partly because several historic neighborhoods have become home to bed-and-breakfast inns. The presence of several guest ranches within a 20-minute drive of Tucson also adds to the city's diversity of accommodations. Business and budget travelers are well served with all-suite and conference hotels, as well as plenty of budget chain motels.

At the more expensive hotels and resorts, summer rates, usually in effect from May to September or October, are often less than half what they are in winter. Surprisingly, temperatures usually aren't unbearable in May or September, which makes these good times to visit if you're looking to save money. When making late spring or early fall reservations, always be sure to ask when rates are scheduled to go up or down. If you

Tucson Accommodations

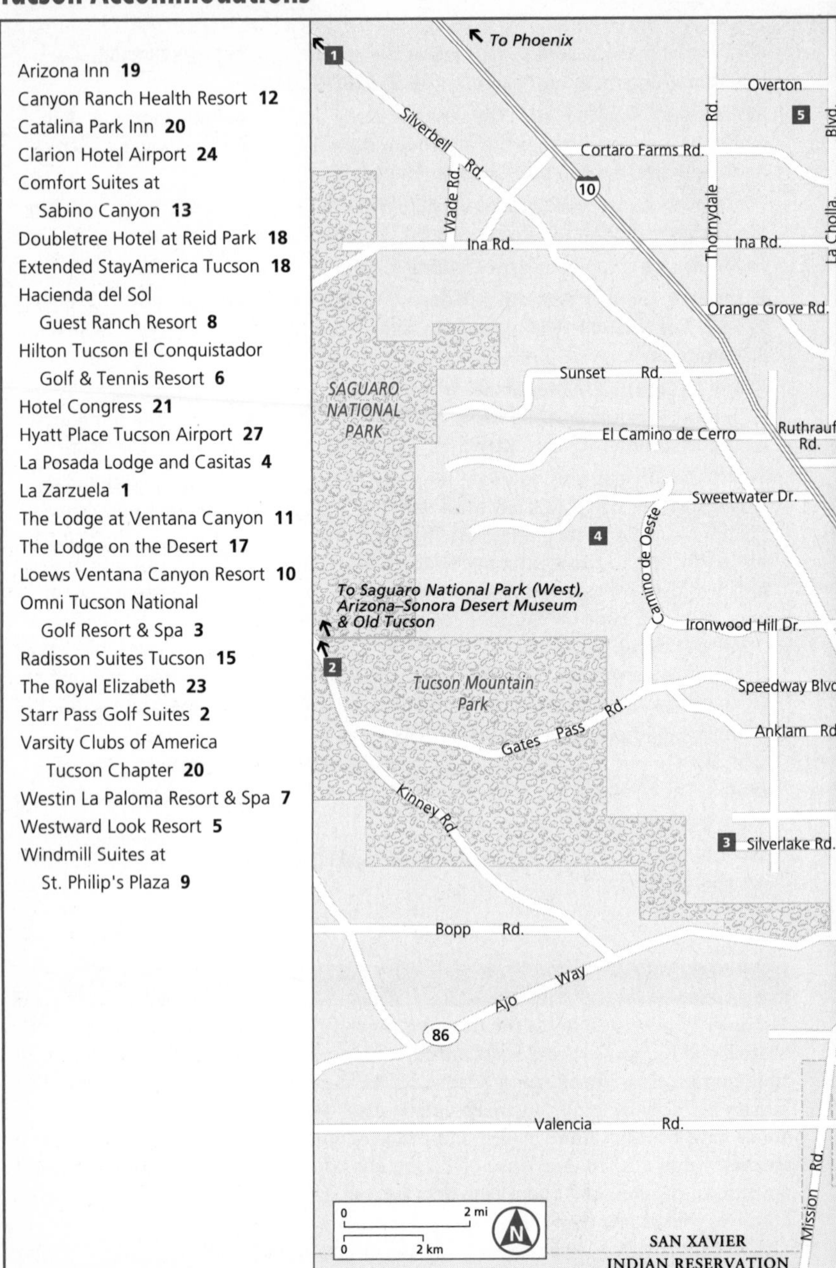

Arizona Inn 19
Canyon Ranch Health Resort 12
Catalina Park Inn 20
Clarion Hotel Airport 24
Comfort Suites at Sabino Canyon 13
Doubletree Hotel at Reid Park 18
Extended StayAmerica Tucson 18
Hacienda del Sol Guest Ranch Resort 8
Hilton Tucson El Conquistador Golf & Tennis Resort 6
Hotel Congress 21
Hyatt Place Tucson Airport 27
La Posada Lodge and Casitas 4
La Zarzuela 1
The Lodge at Ventana Canyon 11
The Lodge on the Desert 17
Loews Ventana Canyon Resort 10
Omni Tucson National Golf Resort & Spa 3
Radisson Suites Tucson 15
The Royal Elizabeth 23
Starr Pass Golf Suites 2
Varsity Clubs of America Tucson Chapter 20
Westin La Paloma Resort & Spa 7
Westward Look Resort 5
Windmill Suites at St. Philip's Plaza 9
To Phoenix
Overton
Cortaro Farms Rd.
Silverbell Rd.
Wade Rd.
10
Thornydale Rd.
La Cholla Blvd.
Ina Rd.
Ina Rd.
Orange Grove Rd.
Sunset Rd.
SAGUARO NATIONAL PARK
El Camino de Cerro
Ruthrauff Rd.
Sweetwater Dr.
Camino de Oeste
To Saguaro National Park (West), Arizona–Sonora Desert Museum & Old Tucson
Ironwood Hill Dr.
Tucson Mountain Park
Speedway Blvd.
Gates Pass Rd.
Anklam Rd.
Kinney Rd.
Silverlake Rd.
Bopp Rd.
Ajo Way
86
Valencia Rd.
Mission Rd.
0
2 mi
0
2 km
N
SAN XAVIER INDIAN RESERVATION

CORONADO NATIONAL FOREST
Hardy Rd.
Magee Rd.
Tohono Chul Park
Ina Rd.
La Canada Dr.
Orange Grove Rd.
Skyline Dr.
Kolb Rd.
Sabino Canyon Rd.
Sabino Canyon Park
Hacienda del Sol Rd.
Sunrise Dr.
River Rd.
Flowing Wells Rd.
Wetmore Rd.
Roger Rd.
Prince Rd.
Swan Rd.
Craycroft Rd.
Snyder Rd.
Bear Canyon Rd.
To Mount Lemmon
Catalina Hwy.
Miracle Mile
Ft. Lowell Rd.
Ft. Lowell Park
Tanque Verde Rd.
Grant Rd.
Oracle Rd.
Stone Ave.
Euclid Ave.
Campbell Ave.
Tucson Blvd.
Country Club Rd.
Alvernon Way
Speedway Blvd.
6th St.
5th St.
Grande Ave.
Congress
Broadway Blvd.
Historic Districts
Reid Park
Randolph Park
Wilmot Rd.
Sentinel Peak Park
22nd St.
Tucson Greyhound Park
36th St.
Golf Links Rd.
To Saguaro National Park (East)
Ajo Way
Escalante Rd.
Pantano Rd.
Camino Seco
DAVIS MONTHAN AFB
Irvington Rd.
Kino Blvd.
Drexel Rd.
Palo Verde Rd.
12th Ave.
6th Ave.
Valencia Rd.
Los Reales Rd.
Tucson International Airport
To Nogales
ARIZONA
Phoenix
Tucson

aren't coming to Tucson specifically for the winter gem and mineral shows, then you'll save quite a bit if you avoid the last week in January and the first 2 weeks in February, when hotels around town generally charge exorbitant rates.

Most hotels offer special packages, weekend rates, various discounts (such as for AARP or AAA members), and free accommodations for children, so it helps to ask when you reserve. Nearly all hotels have smoke-free and wheelchair-accessible rooms.

BED & BREAKFASTS If you're looking to stay in a B&B, several agencies can help. The **Arizona Association of Bed and Breakfast Inns** (www.arizona-bed-breakfast.com) has several members in Tucson. **Mi Casa Su Casa** (✆ **800/456-0682** or 480/990-0682; www.azres.com) will book you into one of its many home-stays (informal B&Bs) in the Tucson area or elsewhere in the state, as will **Arizona Trails Travel Services** (✆ **888/799-4284** or 480/837-4284; www.arizonatrails.com), which also books tour and hotel reservations.

DOWNTOWN & THE UNIVERSITY AREA

EXPENSIVE

Arizona Inn ★★★ With its pink-stucco buildings and immaculately tended flower gardens, the Arizona Inn is a 14-acre oasis of tranquility in central Tucson. Gracious, welcoming, and comfortable, it's an unforgettable place to spend a vacation. Originally opened in 1930 by Isabella Greenway, Arizona's first congresswoman, the inn is still family owned and operated, and is imbued with a gracious character and Old Arizona charm you won't find elsewhere in the state. Playing a game of croquet, taking high tea in the library (complimentary), or lounging by the pool, I always feel as if this were my second home. It's easy to imagine a time when guests would spend the entire winter here. Guest rooms vary in size and decor, but most have a mix of reproduction antiques and original pieces custom made for the inn years ago by disabled World War I veterans. Guest rooms also have such modern amenities as DVD players (and access to a library of films featuring actors and actresses who were once inn guests). Some units have gas fireplaces, and most suites have private patios or enclosed sun porches. The inn's main dining room (p. 343) is a casually elegant space. Fragrant flowering trees and vines surround the small pool.

2200 E. Elm St., Tucson, AZ 85719. ✆ **800/933-1093** or 520/325-1541. Fax 520/881-5830. www.arizonainn.com. 95 units. Mid-Jan to mid-Apr from $319 double, from $469 suite; mid-Apr to May from $229 double, from $369 suite; June to mid-Sept from $179 double, from $289 suite; mid-Sept to mid-Dec from $229 double, from $369 suite; mid-Dec to mid-Jan $259 double, from $359 suite. Summer rates include full breakfast and complimentary evening ice-cream fountain. Children 12 and under stay free in parent's room. AE, DC, MC, V. **Amenities:** 3 restaurants (Continental/American, International); 2 lounges; heated outdoor pool; 2 Har-Tru clay tennis courts; well-equipped exercise room; saunas; bikes; concierge; business center; room service; massage; babysitting; laundry service; dry cleaning; croquet; table tennis; badminton. *In room:* A/C, TV/DVD, dataport, fridge, coffeemaker, hair dryer, iron, safe, high-speed Internet access, free local calls.

The Lodge on the Desert ★★ Dating from 1936 and set amid neatly manicured lawns and gardens, The Lodge on the Desert is a classic old Arizona resort. The lush and relaxing retreat looks a lot like the Arizona Inn (though not nearly as deluxe, and without the superb service). Guest rooms are in hacienda-style adobe buildings tucked amid cacti and orange trees. Rooms feature a mix of contemporary and Southwestern furnishings; many units have beamed ceilings or fireplaces, and some have tile floors and also patios. The small pool has a good view of the Catalinas.

306 N. Alvernon Way, Tucson, AZ 85711. ✆ **800/456-5634** or 520/325-3366. Fax 520/327-5834. www.lodgeonthedesert.com. 35 units. Mid-Jan to mid-Apr $189–$299 double; mid-Apr to mid-May and mid-Sept to mid-Jan

$129–$204 double; mid-May to mid-Sept $89–$154 double. Rates include full breakfast. Children under 6 stay free in parent's room. AE, DC, DISC, MC, V. Pets accepted ($50 deposit plus $20 per night). **Amenities:** Restaurant (American/Continental); lounge; small outdoor pool; access to nearby health club; concierge; laundry service; dry cleaning. *In room:* A/C, TV, coffeemaker, hair dryer, iron, Wi-Fi.

MODERATE

Catalina Park Inn ★★ Close to downtown and overlooking a shady park, this 1927 home has been lovingly restored by owners Mark Hall and Paul Richard. From the outside, the inn has the look of a Mediterranean villa, while many interesting and playful touches enliven the classic interior. The huge Catalina Room in the basement is one of my favorites. Not only does it conjure up the inside of an adobe, but it has a whirlpool tub in a former cedar closet. Two upstairs rooms have balconies, while two units in a separate cottage across the garden offer more contemporary styling than the rooms in the main house.

309 E. First St., Tucson, AZ 85705. ✆ **800/792-4885** or 520/792-4541. www.catalinaparkinn.com. 6 units. $136–$166 double (lower rates late spring through fall). Rates include full breakfast. AE, DISC, MC, V. No children under 10. **Amenities:** Concierge. *In room:* A/C, TV/DVD, dataport, hair dryer, iron, high-speed Internet access, Wi-Fi, free local calls.

Doubletree Hotel Tucson at Reid Park ★★ This in-town high-rise hotel, with its pleasant orange-tree-shaded pool area, is midway between the airport and downtown Tucson, and is something of an in-town budget resort (the Randolph Park municipal golf course is right across the street). Guest rooms boast bright colors and bold contemporary designs, and there's a big exercise room by the pool. Although the hotel does a lot of convention business and sometimes feels crowded, the gardens, with their citrus trees (feel free to pick the fruit) and lawns, are always tranquil. Guest rooms are divided between a nine-story tower that offers views of the valley (even-numbered rooms face the pool, odd-numbered rooms face the mountains) and a two-story building with patio rooms overlooking the garden and pool area.

445 S. Alvernon Way, Tucson, AZ 85711. ✆ **800/222-TREE** or 520/881-4200. Fax 520/323-5225. www.dtreidpark.com. 295 units. Jan–May $199–$314 double, $349–$439 suite; June–Aug $99–$124 double, $199–$309 suite; Sept–Dec $155–$184 double, $255–$309 suite. Children under 18 stay free in parent's room. AE, DC, DISC, MC, V. Pets accepted ($25 fee). **Amenities:** 2 restaurants (Southwestern, American); 2 lounges; outdoor pool; 3 tennis courts; exercise room; Jacuzzi; concierge; car-rental desk; business center; room service; laundry service; dry cleaning. *In room:* A/C, TV, dataport, coffeemaker, hair dryer, iron, high-speed Internet access.

The Royal Elizabeth ★★ A block from the Temple of Music and Art, The Royal Elizabeth is an 1878 Victorian adobe home that features an unusual combination of architectural styles that makes for a uniquely Southwestern-style inn. In classic 19th-century Tucson fashion, the old home looks thoroughly unpretentious from the outside, but inside you'll find beautiful woodwork and gorgeous Victorian-era antique furnishings. Guest rooms open off a large, high-ceilinged central hall. The immediate neighborhood isn't as attractive as the nearby El Presidio neighborhood, but art galleries, the Tucson Museum of Art, and several good restaurants are within walking distance.

204 S. Scott Ave., Tucson, AZ 85701. ✆ **877/670-9022** or 520/670-9022. Fax 928/833-9974. www.royalelizabeth.com. 6 units. Aug–May $155–$245 double; June–Aug $115–$165 double. Rates include full breakfast. Children under 10 stay free in parent's room. AE, DISC, MC, V. **Amenities:** Outdoor heated pool; access to nearby health club; Jacuzzi; concierge; business center; massage. *In room:* A/C, TV/VCR/DVD, dataport, fridge, hair dryer, iron, safe, Wi-Fi, free local and long-distance calls.

Varsity Clubs of America Tucson Chapter ★ You've heard of sports bars, but have you ever heard of a sports hotel? That's what the Varsity Club is, and throughout the hotel there's loads of PAC-10 memorabilia and other sports-theme artwork on display.

Although this is a timeshare condo hotel, the rates are so good for what you get that I have to tell you about this place. All the suites here have full kitchens and separate master bedrooms.

3855 E. Speedway Blvd., Tucson, AZ 85716. ✆ **800/521-3131** or 520/318-3777. Fax 520/327-0110. www.ilxresorts.com. 60 units. Dec–Mar $150 1-bedroom suite, $225 2-bedroom suite; Apr–June and Oct–Nov $115 1-bedroom suite, $175 2-bedroom suite; July–Sept $75 1-bedroom suite, $125 2-bedroom suite. Children under 18 stay free in parent's room. AE, DC, DISC, MC, V. Pets accepted ($20 per night). **Amenities:** Restaurant (American); lounge; outdoor pool; exercise room; Jacuzzi; business center; massages. *In room:* A/C, TV/VCR, dataport, kitchen, fridge, coffeemaker, hair dryer, iron, safe, microwave.

INEXPENSIVE

Hotel Congress *Finds* Located in the heart of downtown Tucson, the Hotel Congress, built in 1919 to serve railroad passengers, once hosted John Dillinger. Today, it operates as a budget hotel and youth hostel. Although the place is utterly basic, the lobby has loads of Southwestern elegance. Guest rooms remain true to their historical character, with antique telephones and old radios, so don't expect anything fancy (like TVs). Most bathrooms have tubs or showers, but a few have both. There's the classic little Cup Cafe off the lobby (think Edward Hopper meets Gen X), as well as a tiny Western Tap Room bar. At night, the Club Congress (p. 386) is a popular (and loud) dance club (pick up earplugs at the front desk).

311 E. Congress St., Tucson, AZ 85701. ✆ **800/722-8848** or 520/622-8848. Fax 520/792-6366. www.hotelcongress.com. 40 units. $59–$109 double. AE, DC, DISC, MC, V. Pets accepted ($10 per night). **Amenities:** Restaurant; lounge; nightclub. *In room:* Wi-Fi.

EAST TUCSON

EXPENSIVE

Radisson Suites Tucson ★★ *Value* With large and very attractive rooms, this all-suite hotel is a good choice for both those who need plenty of space and those who want to be in the east-side business corridor. The five-story brick building is arranged around two long garden courtyards, one of which has a large pool and whirlpool. In fact, the pool and gardens are among the nicest at any nonresort hotel in Tucson and are the best reasons to stay here. Some rooms have Sleep Number® beds, and rooms on the fourth and fifth floors on the east side have nice mountain views.

6555 E. Speedway Blvd., Tucson, AZ 85710. ✆ **888/201-1718** or 520/721-7100. Fax 520/721-1991. www.radisson.com/suites_tucson. 299 suites. Oct–May $159–$219 double; June–Sept $124–$149 double. Children under 18 stay free in parent's room. AE, DC, DISC, MC, V. Pets accepted ($50 fee). **Amenities:** Restaurant (international); lounge; outdoor pool; exercise room; access to nearby health club; Jacuzzi; concierge; courtesy shopping shuttle; business center; room service; coin-op laundry; laundry service; dry cleaning. *In room:* A/C, TV, dataport, fridge, coffeemaker, hair dryer, iron, microwave, high-speed Internet access, Wi-Fi.

MODERATE

Comfort Suites at Sabino Canyon ★ Although it looks rather stark from the outside and shares a parking lot with a shopping center, this Comfort Suites is surprisingly pleasant inside. Built around four tranquil and lushly planted garden courtyards, the hotel has (for the most part) large rooms, some of which have kitchenettes. This is a good economical choice close to Sabino Canyon, the Mount Lemmon Highway, and Saguaro National Park's east unit.

7007 E. Tanque Verde Rd., Tucson, AZ 85715. ✆ **800/424-6423** or 520/298-2300. Fax 520/298-6756. www.choicehotels.com. 90 units. Jan to mid-Apr $99–$179 double; mid-Apr to mid-May and late Sept to Dec $89–$169 double; mid-May to late Sept $72–$95 double. Rates include continental breakfast and evening social hour Mon–Fri. Children 18 and under stay free in parent's room. AE, DC, DISC, MC, V. Pets accepted ($15 per night). **Amenities:** Small outdoor pool; access to nearby health club; Jacuzzi; coin-op laundry; dry cleaning. *In room:* A/C, TV, dataport, fridge, coffeemaker, hair dryer, iron, microwave, Wi-Fi, free local calls.

INEXPENSIVE

Extended StayAmerica Tucson ★ With no pool or exercise room and maid service only if you pay extra or stay for more than a week, this eastside hotel is pretty basic, but the rooms are clean and the rates are low. Guest rooms also have full kitchens, so you can save even more money on your Tucson stay by doing a little cooking in your room.

5050 E. Grant Rd., Tucson, AZ 85712. ✆ **800/804-3724** or 520/795-9510. Fax 520/795-9504. www.extendedstayamerica.com. 120 units. $75–$100 double (lower weekly rates). Children under 18 stay free in parent's room. AE, DISC, MC, V. Pets accepted ($25 per night, $75 maximum). **Amenities:** Coin-op laundry. *In room:* A/C, TV, dataport, kitchen, fridge, coffeemaker, iron, microwave, Wi-Fi, free local calls.

THE FOOTHILLS

VERY EXPENSIVE

Hilton Tucson El Conquistador Golf & Tennis Resort ★★★ Although this large resort is a bit out-of-the-way, the view of the Santa Catalina Mountains rising behind El Conquistador makes this northern foothills resort one of my favorites in Tucson. Sunsets are truly spectacular! Most guest rooms are built around a central courtyard with manicured lawns and a large oasis of swimming pools, one of which has a long water slide. Consequently, this place is a great choice for families. All rooms feature Southwestern-influenced contemporary furniture, spacious marble bathrooms, and balconies or patios. Be sure to ask for a mountain-view room. While golf on the resort's three courses is the favorite pastime, nongolfers have plenty of options, too.

10000 N. Oracle Rd., Tucson, AZ 85704. ✆ **800/325-7832** or 520/544-5000. Fax 520/544-1222. www.hiltonelconquistador.com. 428 units. Jan to late May $209–$319 double, from $359 suite; late May to early Sept $119–$209 double, from $179 suite; early Sept to Dec $149–$259 double, from $239 suite. Rates do not include $10 daily service fee. Children under 18 stay free in parent's room. AE, DC, DISC, MC, V. Valet parking $11. Pets accepted ($50 deposit). **Amenities:** 5 restaurants (Southwestern, steakhouse, Mexican, American); 2 lounges; 4 pools; 1 9-hole and 2 18-hole golf courses; 31 tennis courts; 7 racquetball courts; basketball court; volleyball court; 2 exercise rooms; spa; 5 Jacuzzis; saunas; bike rentals; children's programs; concierge; tour desk; business center; shopping arcade; room service; massage; babysitting; laundry service; dry cleaning; horseback riding. *In room:* A/C, TV, dataport, minibar, coffeemaker, hair dryer, iron, safe, high-speed Internet access, Wi-Fi.

The Lodge at Ventana Canyon ★★★ Golf is the name of the game at this boutique resort set within a gated country-club community at the base of the Santa Catalina Mountains. The third hole of the resort's Tom Fazio–designed Mountain Course plays across a deep ravine, which makes it one of the most photographed holes in Tucson. Though small, this exclusive lodge offers plenty of big-resort amenities and places an emphasis on personal service. The accommodations are in spacious suites, most of which have walls of windows facing the Catalinas, modern mission-style furnishings, small kitchens, and large bathrooms with oversize tubs (some are even old-fashioned footed tubs). All the rooms were renovated in 2006. A few units have balconies, cathedral ceilings, and spiral stairs that lead to sleeping lofts.

6200 N. Clubhouse Lane, Tucson, AZ 85750. ✆ **800/828-5701** or 520/577-1400. Fax 520/577-4065. www.thelodgeatventanacanyon.com. 50 units. Jan to early Apr $279–$549 1-bedroom suite, $449–$729 2-bedroom suite; early Apr to mid-May $189–$419 1-bedroom suite, $359–$619 2-bedroom suite; mid-May to early Sept $99–$175 1-bedroom suite, $189–$275 2-bedroom suite; early Sept to Dec $179–$399 1-bedroom suite, $349–$599 2-bedroom suite. Rates do not include $20 nightly service charge. Children under 18 stay free in parent's room. AE, DC, DISC, MC, V. Pets accepted ($50 fee). **Amenities:** Restaurant (New American); lounge; snack bar; outdoor pool; 2 acclaimed 18-hole golf courses; 12 tennis courts; exercise room; full-service spa; concierge; room service; massage; coin-op laundry; laundry service; dry cleaning. *In room:* A/C, TV, dataport, kitchen, coffeemaker, hair dryer, iron, microwave, high-speed Internet access.

Loews Ventana Canyon Resort ★★★ *Kids* For breathtaking scenery, fascinating architecture, and superb resort facilities (including two Tom Fazio golf courses, a full-service spa, and lots of options for kids), no other Tucson resort can compare. The Santa Catalina Mountains rise behind the property, and flagstone floors in the lobby lend a rugged but luxurious appeal. Guest rooms have balconies that overlook city lights or mountains. Bathrooms include tubs for two, and some rooms have fireplaces. Both the Ventana Room (p. 351) and the Flying V Bar & Grill are among the best restaurants in Tucson, and both have great views. The lobby lounge serves afternoon tea before becoming an evening piano bar. In addition to numerous other amenities, there are jogging and nature trails and a playground.

7000 N. Resort Dr., Tucson, AZ 85750. ✆ **800/234-5117** or 520/299-2020. Fax 520/299-6832. www.loewshotels.com/hotels/tucson. 398 units. Early Jan to late May from $365 double, from $750 suite; late May to early Sept from $150 double, from $295 suite; early Sept to early Jan from $325 double, from $700 suite. Children under 18 stay free in parent's room. AE, DC, DISC, MC, V. **Amenities:** 5 restaurants (New American, steakhouse, American); 2 lounges; 2 outdoor pools; 2 acclaimed 18-hole golf courses; 8 tennis courts; croquet court; exercise room; full-service spa; 2 Jacuzzis; saunas; bike rentals; children's programs; concierge; tour desk; courtesy shuttle; business center; 24-hr. room service; massage; babysitting; laundry service; dry cleaning. *In room:* A/C, TV, dataport, minibar, fridge, hair dryer, iron, safe, high-speed Internet access.

Omni Tucson National Golf Resort & Spa ★★★ As the name implies, golf is the driving force at this boutique resort, which for many years was the site of the annual Tucson Open PGA golf tournament. So, if you don't have your own clubs, you might feel out of place. Then again, you could just avail yourself of the superb full-service spa. Most of the spacious guest rooms cling to the edges of the golf course and have their own patios or balconies. At press time, this resort was undergoing a major renovation and only a limited number of rooms were available. The renovation is expected to continue until late 2008, and by then, the rooms here should be some of the best and most luxurious in town.

2727 W. Club Dr. (off Magee Rd.), Tucson, AZ 85742. ✆ **800/THE-OMNI** or 520/297-2271. Fax 520/297-7544. www.omnitucsonnational.com. 167 units. Jan–Apr $279–$459 double, $309–$499 suite; May and Sept–Dec $169–$299 double, $209–$359 suite; June–Aug $109–$209 double, $139–$299 suite. Rates do not include $12 nightly service charge. Children under 18 stay free in parent's room. AE, DC, DISC, MC, V. Pets accepted ($50 nonrefundable deposit). **Amenities:** 2 restaurants (American, Southwestern); lounge; 2 large pools; 2 18-hole golf courses; 4 tennis courts; basketball court; health club; full-service spa; 3 Jacuzzis; children's programs; concierge; business center; 24-hr. room service; massage; laundry service. *In room:* A/C, TV, dataport, minibar, coffeemaker, hair dryer, iron, safe, high-speed Internet access.

The Westin La Paloma Resort & Spa ★★★ *Kids* If grand scale is what you're looking for, this is the place. Everything about The Westin La Paloma is big—big portico, big lobby, big pool area—and from the resort's sunset-pink mission-revival buildings, there are big views. While adults will appreciate the resort's tennis courts, exercise facilities, and poolside lounge chairs, kids will love the 177-foot water slide. Guest rooms are in 27 low-rise buildings surrounded by desert landscaping. Couples should opt for the king rooms (ask for a mountain or golf-course view if you don't mind spending a bit more). French-inspired Southwestern cuisine is the specialty at Janos (p. 350), which is one of Tucson's finest restaurants.

3800 E. Sunrise Dr., Tucson, AZ 85718. ✆ **800/WESTIN-1** or 520/742-6000. Fax 520/577-5878. www.westinlapalomaresort.com. 487 units. Jan to late May $249–$479 double, from $445 suite; late May to mid-Sept $119–$169 double, from $245 suite; mid-Sept to Dec $209–$279 double, from $375 suite. Rates do not include $11 daily service fee.

Children under 18 stay free in parent's room. AE, DC, DISC, MC, V. Valet parking $12. Pets accepted. **Amenities:** 5 restaurants (Southwestern, American, swim-up bar and grill); 2 lounges; 5 pools (1 for adults only); 27-hole golf course; 10 tennis courts; racquetball court; volleyball court; health club; full-service Red Door Spa by Elizabeth Arden; 4 Jacuzzis; children's programs; concierge; car-rental desk; business center; shopping arcade; salon; 24-hr. room service; massage; babysitting; laundry service; dry cleaning. *In room:* A/C, TV, dataport, minibar, coffeemaker, hair dryer, iron, safe, high-speed Internet access, Wi-Fi.

EXPENSIVE

Hacienda del Sol Guest Ranch Resort ★★ *Finds* With its colorful Southwest styling, historical character, mature desert gardens, and ridgetop setting, Hacienda del Sol is one of Tucson's most distinctive hotels. The lodge's basic rooms, set around flower-filled courtyards, are evocative of old Mexican inns and have rustic and colorful character, with a decidedly artistic flair. If you prefer more modern, spacious accommodations, ask for a suite; if you want loads of space and the chance to stay where Katharine Hepburn and Spencer Tracy may have stayed, ask for a casita. With large terraces for alfresco dining, The Grill (p. 350) is one of Tucson's best restaurants.

5601 N. Hacienda del Sol Rd., Tucson, AZ 85718. ✆ **800/728-6514** or 520/299-1501. www.haciendadelsol.com. 30 units. Early Jan to May $175–$280 double, $345–$355 suite, $395–$495 casita; June–Sept $99–$154 double, $165–$185 suite, $185–$300 casita; Oct to early Jan $155–$250 double, $320–$330 suite, $360–$485 casita. 2-night minimum stay weekends and holidays. Children under 12 stay free in parent's room. AE, DC, DISC, MC, V. Pets accepted ($50). **Amenities:** Restaurant (regional American); lounge; small outdoor pool; access to nearby health club; Jacuzzi; room service; massage; dry cleaning; horseback riding. *In room:* A/C, TV, dataport, minibar, fridge, coffeemaker, hair dryer, iron, high-speed Internet access, Wi-Fi.

Westward Look Resort ★★ *Value* This reasonably priced resort, with the desert at its doorstep and a nature trail through the cacti, is a favorite of mine. Built in 1912 as a private estate, Westward Look is the oldest resort in Tucson, and although it doesn't have a golf course, it has riding stables, an excellent spa, and plenty of tennis courts. The large guest rooms have a Southwestern flavor and private patios or balconies with city views. For the ultimate in Southwest luxury, opt for one of the stargazer spa suites, which have outdoor hot tubs. The Gold Room (p. 349) serves excellent Continental and Southwestern cuisine and utilizes herbs and vegetables grown on-site. If you aren't a golfer but do enjoy resort amenities, this is one of your best bets in Tucson.

245 E. Ina Rd., Tucson, AZ 85704. ✆ **800/722-2500** or 520/297-1151. Fax 520/297-9023. www.westwardlook.com. 244 units. Jan–Apr $179–$395 double; May $149–$199 double; June–Sept $89–$189 double; Oct–Dec $169–$295 double. Rates do not include $12 daily resort fee. Children under 18 stay free in parent's room. AE, DC, DISC, MC, V. **Amenities:** 2 restaurants (Continental/Southwestern, American); lounge; 3 pools; 8 tennis courts; exercise room; full-service spa; 3 Jacuzzis; bike rentals; concierge; tour desk; car-rental desk; business center; room service; massage; laundry service; dry cleaning, executive-level rooms; horseback riding. *In room:* A/C, TV, dataport, minibar, coffeemaker, hair dryer, iron, high-speed Internet access, Wi-Fi.

MODERATE

La Posada Lodge and Casitas ★★ Although this hotel fronts busy Oracle Road, once you check in and park yourself on your patio overlooking the pool or the grassy courtyard, you'll forget all about the traffic out front. There are several different types of rooms here, but my favorites are the "Western" style rooms, which have a sort of retro south-of-the-border decor that includes headboards painted with classic Mexican scenes. Casitas, which are the largest and most expensive rooms here, have a similar decor. There are also some fun rooms with a 1950s retro feel. The attractive rooms, pleasant pool area, and on-site Mexican restaurant together make this an excellent and economical choice.

5900 N. Oracle Rd., Tucson, AZ 85704. ✆ **800/810-2808** or 520/887-4800. Fax 520/293-7543. www.laposadalodge.com. 72 units. $89–$149 double. Rates include continental breakfast. Children under 18 stay free in parent's room. AE, DC, DISC, MC, V. Pets accepted ($50 fee). **Amenities:** Restaurant (Mexican); lounge; outdoor pool; exercise room; Jacuzzi; laundry service; dry cleaning. *In room:* A/C, TV, dataport, fridge, coffeemaker, hair dryer, iron, microwave, high-speed Internet access, free local calls.

Windmill Suites at St. Philip's Plaza ★ *Value* Located on the edge of the foothills in the St. Philip's Plaza shopping center, this hotel offers both a good location and good value. There are good restaurants and upscale shops right across the parking lot. Bikes are available to guests, and out the hotel's back door is a paved pathway along the Rillito River (which is usually bone dry). Accommodations are spacious and have double vanities, wet bars, and two TVs—basically, everything you need for a long, comfortable stay.

4250 N. Campbell Ave., Tucson, AZ 85718. ✆ **800/547-4747** or 520/577-0007. Fax 520/577-0045. www.windmill inns.com. 122 units. Feb–Mar $165–$185 double; Apr–May and Oct–Jan $115–$159 double; June–Sept $89–$130 double. Rates include continental breakfast. Children under 18 stay free in parent's room. AE, DC, DISC, MC, V. Pets accepted. **Amenities:** Outdoor pool; exercise room; access to nearby health club; Jacuzzi; bikes; business center; coin-op laundry; laundry service; dry cleaning. *In room:* A/C, TV, fridge, hair dryer, iron, microwave, free local calls.

WEST OF DOWNTOWN

EXPENSIVE

La Zarzuela ★★ When I come to the desert, I want to be *in* the desert, not in the middle of the city. That's why I love this modern B&B. It sits high on a hill surrounded by saguaros and is just down a dirt road from Tucson Mountain Park, which is every bit as beautiful as Saguaro National Park. La Zarzuela has four colorfully decorated guest rooms spread around this sprawling modern Santa Fe–style building. The pool and hot tub are built on the edge of the desert, while courtyards and patios have splashes of colorful flowers in their landscaping. It's all very Southwestern, the perfect place to stay if you want to explore the desert. For all this seclusion, the inn is surprisingly close to downtown Tucson.

455 N. Camino de Oeste (P.O. Box 86030), Tucson, AZ 85754. ✆ **888/848-8225.** www.zarzuela-az.com. 5 units. $275–$325 double. Rates include full breakfast and evening wine and hors d'oeuvres. 2-night minimum. MC, V. Closed June 15–Sept 15. No children under 18. **Amenities:** Outdoor pool; access to nearby health club; Jacuzzi; concierge; massage; laundry service. *In room:* A/C, TV/DVD, fridge, coffeemaker, hair dryer, iron, high-speed Internet access, free local calls.

Starr Pass Golf Suites ★★ Located 3 miles west of I-10, Starr Pass is the most economically priced golf resort in the city. It's a condominium resort, however, which means you won't find the sort of service you get at other resorts. Accommodations are in privately owned Santa Fe–style casitas rented as two-bedroom units, master suites, or standard hotel-style rooms. The small hotel-style rooms are a bit cramped and not nearly as lavishly appointed as the master suites, which are more comfortable and have fireplaces, full kitchens, balconies, and a Southwestern style throughout. The desert-style 27-hole golf course is one of the best courses in the city. There are also hiking/biking trails on the property.

3645 W. Starr Pass Blvd., Tucson, AZ 85745. ✆ **800/503-2898** or 520/670-0500. Fax 520/670-0427. www.shell hospitality.com. 80 units. Jan to late May $179 double, $309 suite, $429 casita; late May to Sept $89 double, $139 suite, $199 casita; Oct–Dec $119 double, $179 suite, $249 casita. Children under 18 stay free in parent's room. AE, DC, DISC, MC, V. **Amenities:** 2 restaurants (steakhouse, American); lounge; outdoor pool; 27-hole golf course; 2 tennis courts; exercise room; Jacuzzi. *In room:* A/C, TV, fridge, coffeemaker, hair dryer, microwave, high-speed Internet access.

MODERATE

Casa Tierra Adobe Bed & Breakfast Inn ★ If you've come to Tucson to be in the desert, then this secluded B&B west of Saguaro National Park is well worth considering. Built to look as if it has been here since Spanish colonial days, the modern adobe home is surrounded by cactus and palo verde trees. There are great views across a landscape full of saguaros to the mountains, and sunsets are enough to take your breath away. Guest rooms, which have wrought-iron sleigh beds, open onto a central courtyard surrounded by a covered seating area. The two outdoor hot tubs make perfect stargazing spots, and there are a couple of telescopes on the property.

11155 W. Calle Pima, Tucson, AZ 85743. ✆ **866/254-0006** or 520/578-3058. www.casatierratucson.com. 4 units. $135–$195 double, $200–$325 suite. Rates include full breakfast. 2-night minimum stay. AE, DISC, MC, V. Closed June 16–Aug 14. **Amenities:** Exercise room; Jacuzzi; concierge; massage. *In room:* A/C, dataport, fridge, hair dryer, iron, microwave, Wi-Fi, free local calls.

NEAR THE AIRPORT

MODERATE

Clarion Hotel Airport Located just outside the airport exit, this hotel provides convenience and some great amenities, including a complimentary nightly cocktail reception and midnight snacks. Accommodations are generally quite large. King rooms are particularly comfortable, while poolside units are convenient for swimming and lounging.

6801 S. Tucson Blvd., Tucson, AZ 85706. ✆ **800/424-6423** or 520/746-3932. Fax 520/889-9934. www.clarionhotel.com. 188 units. Jan–Feb $109–$189 double; Mar–May $89–$119 double; June–Aug $69–$99 double; Sept–Dec $79–$119 double. Rates include full breakfast and cocktail hour. Children 18 and under stay free in parent's room. AE, DC, DISC, MC, V. **Amenities:** Restaurant (American); lounge; outdoor pool; exercise room; Jacuzzi; courtesy airport shuttle; room service; coin-op laundry; laundry service; dry cleaning. *In room:* A/C, TV, dataport, fridge, coffeemaker, hair dryer, iron, high-speed Internet access.

Hyatt Place Tucson Airport Okay, I know the airport location is none too appealing and that this is primarily a business-travelers' hotel, but it's just so pretty and well-designed that you should consider it. The suites all have separate sitting and sleeping areas with 42-inch wall-hung flat-panel TVs that can be angled to either area. Unusual features include electronic self-service check-in kiosks, continental (free) or hot (charge) breakfasts, and a tiny lounge area to one side of the lobby. You can even get a light meal here if you don't feel like going out to a restaurant for dinner.

6885 S. Tucson Blvd., Tucson, AZ 85709. ✆ **800/492-8847** or 520/295-0405. Fax 520/295-9140. www.hyattplace.com. 120 units. $99–$249 double. Rates include continental breakfast. Children under 18 stay free in parent's room. AE, DC, DISC, MC, V. **Amenities:** Restaurant (American); lounge; outdoor pool; exercise room; business center; coin-op laundry; laundry service; dry cleaning. *In room:* A/C, TV, dataport, fridge, coffeemaker, hair dryer, iron, high-speed Internet access, Wi-Fi.

OUTLYING AREAS

NORTH OF TUCSON

Across the Creek at Aravaipa Farms ★★ *Finds* Located 60 miles north of Tucson on Aravaipa Creek, this B&B is a romantic getaway near one of the state's most spectacular desert wilderness areas. Because the inn is 3 miles up a gravel road and then across a stream (high-clearance vehicles recommended), it's a long way to a restaurant. Consequently, innkeeper Carol Steele provides all meals. Guests entertain themselves hiking in the Aravaipa Canyon Wilderness, bird-watching, and cooling off in the creek. The casitas are eclectically decorated with a mix of folk art and rustic Mexican furnishings, and have tile floors, stone-walled showers, and shady verandas.

For a romantic weekend or a vigorous vacation, this inn makes an ideal base. Carol also rents out a house.

89395 Aravaipa Rd., Winkelman, AZ 85292. ✆ **520/357-6901.** www.aravaipafarms.com. 5 units. Mar–May $325 double; June–Feb $285 double. Rates include all meals. 2-night minimum stay weekends and holidays. No credit cards. Children by prior arrangement. **Amenities:** Dining room; outdoor swimming pool. *In room:* Fridge, coffeemaker, no phone.

C.O.D. Ranch and Retreat ★ Located 25 minutes north of the Tucson city limits, this place is primarily used by groups and family reunions. However, the remote location and the rustic ranch setting (that includes two restored 1880s adobe houses) make this lovingly restored ranch an ideal spot for a tranquil getaway between the desert and the mountains. The decor is a mix of rustic Mexican furnishings and contemporary works by regional artists. Several of the casitas have full kitchens, and two have fireplaces. The ranch borders Oracle State Park, and a section of the Arizona Trail is within a few miles. Horseback rides and guided nature walks can be arranged.

P.O. Box 241, Oracle, AZ 85623. ✆ **800/868-5617** or 520/615-3211. www.codranch.com. 20 units. $125–$275 double. Rates include full breakfast. Children 12 and under stay free in parent's room. AE, MC, V. Pets accepted. **Amenities:** Pool; Jacuzzi; bike rentals; massage; laundry service; horseback riding. *In room:* A/C, microwave, high-speed Internet access, free local calls.

SOUTH OF TUCSON

Chuparosa Inn ★ Tucked amid the shady trees of Madera Canyon, this rustic inn is built of stone and wood, and, with its tower at the front entrance, looks a bit like a miniature castle or a chalet. In other words, this place is beautiful and is a delightful place to stay if you have come up the canyon to do some bird-watching, which is the objective of many of the inn's guests. By the way, the inn's name is a Spanish term for "hummingbirds," and if you visit in the warmer months, you're likely to see plenty of the colorful little birds (14 species have been spotted here). There are also regularly scheduled hummingbird banding programs here.

1300 W. Madera Canyon Rd., Madera Canyon, AZ 85614. ✆ **520/393-7370.** www.chuparosainn.com. 3 units. $130 double; $150 suite. Rates include continental breakfast. 2-night minimum on weekends, holidays, and Mar–May. MC, V. Children over 12 are welcome. *In room:* A/C, kitchenette, fridge, coffeemaker, hair dryer, iron, microwave, no phone.

Santa Rita Lodge Nature Resort This lodge in the shady depths of Madera Canyon is used almost exclusively by bird-watchers and hikers, and getting a room in late spring, when the birds are out, can be difficult. March through August, the lodge even offers guided bird walks ($20 per person). The rooms and cabins are large and comfortable. The nearest restaurants are 13 miles away, so you should bring food for your stay.

1218 S. Madera Canyon Rd., Madera Canyon, AZ 85614. ✆ **520/625-8746.** Fax 520/625-1956. www.santaritalodge.com. 12 units. $85–$98 double. MC, V. Pets accepted June–Feb ($25 per day). *In room:* A/C, TV/DVD, kitchen, fridge, coffeemaker, microwave.

SPAS

Canyon Ranch Health Resort ★★★ Canyon Ranch, one of America's premier health spas, offers the sort of complete spa experience that's available at only a handful of places around the country. On staff are doctors, nurses, psychotherapists and counselors, fitness instructors, massage therapists, and tennis and golf pros. Services offered include health and fitness assessments; health, nutrition, exercise, and stress-management evaluations; fitness classes; massage therapy; therapeutic body treatments; facials, manicures, pedicures, and haircuts; makeup consultations; cooking demonstrations; and art classes. Guests stay in a variety of spacious and very comfortable accommodations. Three gourmet, low-calorie meals are served daily.

8600 E. Rockcliff Rd., Tucson, AZ 85750. ✆ **800/742-9000** or 520/749-9000. Fax 520/239-8535. www.canyonranch.com. 185 units. Sept to early June 4-night packages from $3,280 double; early June to Aug 4-night packages from $2,450 double. Rates include all meals and a variety of spa services and programs. AE, DC, DISC, MC, V. Pets accepted. No children under 14 (with exception of infants in the care of personal nannies). **Amenities:** 2 dining rooms; 11,000-sq.-ft. aquatic center and 3 outdoor pools; 7 tennis courts; racquetball and squash courts; 7 exercise rooms; 80,000-sq.-ft. spa complex; 8 Jacuzzis; saunas; steam rooms; bikes; concierge; courtesy airport shuttle; salon; room service; massage; guest laundry; laundry service; dry cleaning. *In room:* A/C, TV/DVD, dataport, hair dryer, iron, safe, high-speed Internet access, free local calls.

Miraval Life in Balance Resort and Spa ★★★ Focusing on what it calls "life balancing," Miraval emphasizes stress management, self-discovery, and relaxation rather than facials and mud baths. To this end, activities at the all-inclusive resort include meditation, tai chi, Pilates, and yoga; more active types can go hiking, mountain biking, rock climbing, and horseback riding. Miraval offers lifestyle-management workshops, fitness/nutrition consultations, exercise classes, an "equine experience" program, massage, and skin care and facials. The spa's main pool is a gorgeous three-tiered leisure pool surrounded by waterfalls and desert landscaping. Guest rooms, many of which have views of the Santa Catalina Mountains, are done in a Southwestern style. Most of the bathrooms have showers but no tubs.

5000 E. Via Estancia Miraval, Catalina, AZ 85739. ✆ **800/232-3969.** Fax 520/825-5163. www.miravalresorts.com. 102 units. Mid-Jan to late May and mid-Oct to Dec $1,260–$1,300 double; late May to mid-Oct $940 double. Rates do not include 17.5% service charge. Rates include all meals, classes, and a $110 per-person per-day credit for spa service, a round of golf, or private consultation. AE, DC, DISC, MC, V. No children. **Amenities:** 2 restaurants; lounge; 2 snack areas; 4 pools; 2 tennis courts; croquet lawn; superbly equipped exercise room; spa; 5 Jacuzzis; saunas; steam rooms; concierge; car-rental desk; courtesy airport shuttle; business center; massage; laundry service; dry cleaning; horseback riding. *In room:* A/C, TV/DVD, dataport, fridge, coffeemaker, hair dryer, iron, safe, high-speed Internet access, Wi-Fi, free local calls.

GUEST RANCHES

Lazy K Bar Guest Ranch ★ In operation as a guest ranch since 1936, the Lazy K Bar Ranch covers more than 200 acres and is adjacent to Saguaro National Park's west unit. Ranch activities include trail rides, guest rodeos, cookouts, and wagon rides, as well as nature talks, guided hikes, rappelling, and stargazing. Guest rooms vary in size and comfort level (some have fireplaces and private patios); try for one of the newest units, which are absolutely gorgeous. Family-style meals consist of hearty American ranch food, with cookouts offered twice a week.

8401 N. Scenic Dr., Tucson, AZ 85743. ✆ **800/321-7018** or 520/744-3050. Fax 520/744-7628. www.lazykbar.com. 24 units. Oct to mid-Dec $340–$445 double; mid-Dec to Apr $360–$505 double; May and Sept $250–$345 double. Rates include all meals and horseback riding. Children under 3 stay free in parent's room. AE, DISC, MC, V. Closed June–Aug. **Amenities:** Dining room; lounge; small outdoor pool; access to nearby health club; Jacuzzi; game room; courtesy airport shuttle (limited hours); massage; coin-op laundry; horseback riding. *In room:* A/C, no phone.

Tanque Verde Ranch ★★ Want to spend long days in the saddle but don't want to give up resort luxuries? Then Tanque Verde Ranch, which was founded in 1868 and still has some of its original buildings, is for you. This is far and away the most luxurious guest ranch in Tucson. The ranch borders Saguaro National Park and the Coronado National Forest, so there's plenty of room for horseback riding. There are also nature trails and a nature center, and at the end of the day, the spa provides ample opportunities to recover from too many hours in the saddle. Guest rooms are spacious and comfortable, with fireplaces and patios in many units. Some casitas are quite large and are among the most luxurious accommodations in the state. The dining room, which overlooks the Rincon Mountains, sets impressive buffets.

14301 E. Speedway Blvd., Tucson, AZ 85748. ✆ **800/234-DUDE** or 520/296-6275. Fax 520/721-9426. www.tanqueverderanch.com. 74 units. Mid-Dec to Apr $420–$640 double; May–Sept $330–$440 double; Oct to mid-Dec $370–$515 double. Rates include all meals and ranch activities. Children 3 and under $15 extra. AE, DC, DISC, MC, V. **Amenities:** Dining room; lounge; 3 pools (indoor and outdoor); 5 tennis courts; exercise room; small full-service spa; 2 Jacuzzis; saunas; bike rentals; children's programs; courtesy airport shuttle with 4-night stay; massage; babysitting; coin-op laundry; laundry service; dry cleaning; horseback riding; children's playground. *In room:* A/C, dataport, fridge, coffeemaker, hair dryer, iron.

White Stallion Ranch ★ *Kids* Set on 3,000 acres of desert, the White Stallion Ranch is perfect for those who crave wide-open spaces. Operated since 1965 by the True family, this spread has a more authentic feel than any other guest ranch in the area. A variety of horseback rides are offered Monday through Saturday, and a petting zoo keeps kids entertained. There are also nature trails, guided nature walks and hikes, hayrides, weekly rodeos, and team cattle penning. Guest rooms vary considerably in size and comfort, from tiny, spartan single units to deluxe two-bedroom suites. Renovated rooms are worth requesting.

9251 W. Twin Peaks Rd., Tucson, AZ 85743. ✆ **888/977-2624** or 520/297-0252. Fax 520/744-2786. www.wsranch.com. 42 units. Sept $234–$272 double, $292–$332 suite; Oct to mid-Dec, Jan, and late Apr to mid-June $286–$332 double, $352–$404 suite; mid-Dec to Jan 1 and Feb to late Apr $324–$392 double, $414–$476 suite. Rates do not include 15% service charge. Rates include all meals. 4- to 6-night minimum stay in winter. Children under 3 stay free in parent's room. No credit cards. Closed mid-June to Aug 31. **Amenities:** Dining room; lounge; small outdoor pool; tennis court; exercise room; small spa; Jacuzzi; sauna; bikes; children's programs; concierge; courtesy airport shuttle; business center; massage; coin-op laundry; horseback riding. *In room:* A/C, hair dryer, no phone.

4 Where to Dine

Variety, they say, is the spice of life, and Tucson certainly dishes up plenty of variety (and spice) when it comes to eating out. Tucson is a city that lives for spice, and in the realm of fiery foods, Mexican reigns supreme. There's historical Mexican at El Charro Café and El Minuto Cafe, *nuevo* Mexican at Café Poca Cosa and J Bar, and family-style Mexican at Casa Molina. So if you like Mexican food, you'll find plenty of places in Tucson to get all fired up.

On the other hand, if Mexican leaves you cold, don't despair—there are plenty of other restaurants serving everything from the finest French cuisine to innovative American, Italian, and Southwestern food. The latter is almost as prevalent in Tucson as Mexican food, and you should be sure to dine at a Southwestern restaurant early in your visit. This cuisine can be brilliantly creative, and after trying it, you may want *all* your meals to be Southwestern.

Foodies fond of the latest culinary trends will find plenty of spots to satisfy their cravings. Concentrations of creative restaurants can be found along East Tanque Verde Road and at foothills resorts and shopping plazas. On the other hand, if you're on a tight dining budget, look for early-bird dinners, which are quite popular with retirees.

DOWNTOWN

MODERATE

Café Poca Cosa ★★ *Value* NUEVO MEXICAN The cuisine served at this stylish downtown restaurant is the creation of owner/chef Suzana Davila and has been compared to the dishes dreamed up in *Like Water for Chocolate.* Although ostensibly Mexican, this food is not just *any* Mexican food; it's imaginative and different and is served in a bold and angular space that belies the location on the ground floor of a parking garage. Expect such creations as grilled beef with a jalapeño chile and tomatillo sauce, and chicken with a dark mole sauce made with Kahlúa, chocolate, almonds, and chiles. The menu is posted on portable blackboards, so you never know what you might find on any given day. However, I always opt for the *plato* Poca Cosa, a trio of dishes chosen by the chef. This lively restaurant is an excellent value.

110 E. Pennington St. ✆ **520/622-6400.** www.cafepococosainc.com. Reservations highly recommended. Main courses $12–$13 lunch, $18–$23 dinner. MC, V. Tues–Thurs 11am–9pm; Fri–Sat 11am–10pm.

El Charro Café ★ SONORAN MEXICAN El Charro, housed in an old stone building in El Presidio Historic District, is Tucson's oldest family-operated Mexican restaurant and is legendary around these parts for its unusual *carne seca,* a traditional air-dried beef that is a bit like shredded beef jerky. To see how they make *carne seca,* just glance up at the restaurant's roof as you approach. The large metal cage up there is filled with beef drying in the desert sun. You'll rarely find *carne seca* on a Mexican menu outside of Tucson, so indulge while you're here.

The adjacent **¡Toma!** (p. 387), a colorful bar/cantina, is under the same ownership. There are other El Charro locations at 6310 E. Broadway (✆ **520/745-1922**), 4699 E. Speedway Blvd. (✆ **520/325-1922**), and 100 W. Orange Grove (✆ **520/615-1922**).

311 N. Court Ave. ✆ **520/622-1922.** www.elcharrocafe.com. Reservations recommended for dinner. Main courses $6–$19. AE, DC, DISC, MC, V. Sun–Thurs 11am–9pm; Fri–Sat 11am–10pm.

INEXPENSIVE

Café à la C'Art SALADS/SANDWICHES Located in the courtyard on the grounds of the Tucson Museum of Art, this cafe serves up tasty sandwiches and makes a good lunch spot if you're downtown wandering the Presidio neighborhood or touring the museum. Try the gingered apricot-almond chicken-salad croissant or the Cuban sandwich, which is made with roasted pork and ham. Wash it all down with some fresh lemonade, and be sure to save room for dessert.

150 N. Main Ave. ✆ **520/628-8533.** Reservations not accepted. Sandwiches and salads $7.25–$9.25. DISC, MC, V. Mon–Fri 11am–3pm.

El Minuto Cafe MEXICAN El Minuto, located downtown at the edge of the Barrio Histórico next to El Tiradito shrine, is a meeting ground for both Anglos and Latinos who come for the lively atmosphere and Mexican home cooking. In business since 1936, this establishment is a neighborhood landmark and a prototype that other Mexican restaurants often try to emulate. Cheese crisps (Mexican pizza) are a specialty, and enchiladas, especially *carne seca,* are tasty. This is a fun place for people-watching—you'll find all types, from kids to businessmen in suits.

354 S. Main Ave. ✆ **520/882-4145.** Reservations not accepted. Main courses $6–$15. AE, DISC, MC, V. Sun–Thurs 11am–10pm; Fri–Sat 11am–11pm.

CENTRAL TUCSON & THE UNIVERSITY AREA

EXPENSIVE

Arizona Inn ★★ FRENCH/AMERICAN The dining room at the Arizona Inn, one of the state's first resorts, is consistently excellent. The pink-stucco pueblo-style buildings are surrounded by neatly manicured gardens that have matured gracefully, and it's romantic to dine in the courtyard or on the bar patio overlooking the colorful gardens. The menu changes regularly, but includes a good balance of classics such as vichyssoise and bouillabaisse and Southwestern-inspired dishes such as a grilled

Tucson Dining

Anthony's in the Catalinas **13**
Arizona Inn **26**
Beyond Bread **24**
Bistro Zin **18**
Bluefin Seafood Bistro **8**
Café à la C'Art **2**
Café Poca Cosa **3**
Candela Restaurant **6**
Casa Molina (3) **22, 33, 36**
Cuvée World Bistro **31**
The Dish Bistro & Wine Bar **30**
El Charro Café (2) **1, 40**
El Corral Restaurant **17**
El Cubanito Restaurant **27**
El Guero Canelo **23**
El Minuto Cafe **28**
Feast **32**
Firecracker Bistro **35**
Ghini's French Café **20**
The Gold Room **9**
The Grill **16**
HiFalutin Rapid Fire Western Grill **10**
Janos **15**
J Bar **15**
Kingfisher Bar & Grill **29**
Little Anthony's Diner **41**
Lovin' Spoonfuls **21**
McMahon's Prime Steakhouse **34**
Miguel's **11**
Pastiche Modern Eatery **21**
Pinnacle Peak Steakhouse **37**
Tavolino Ristorante Italiano **5**
Teresa's Mosaic Café **4**
Terra Cotta **14**
Tohono Chul Tea Room **7**
Ventana Room **42**
Vivace Restaurant **19**
Wildflower **8**
Yoshimatsu Healthy Japanese Food & Café **25**
Zona 78 **12**

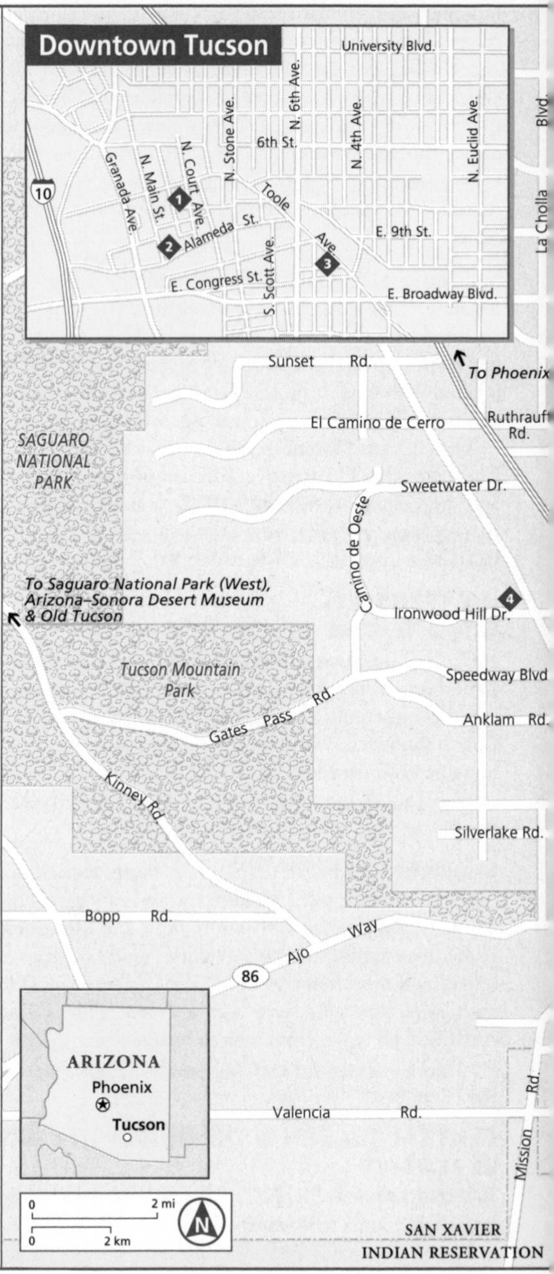

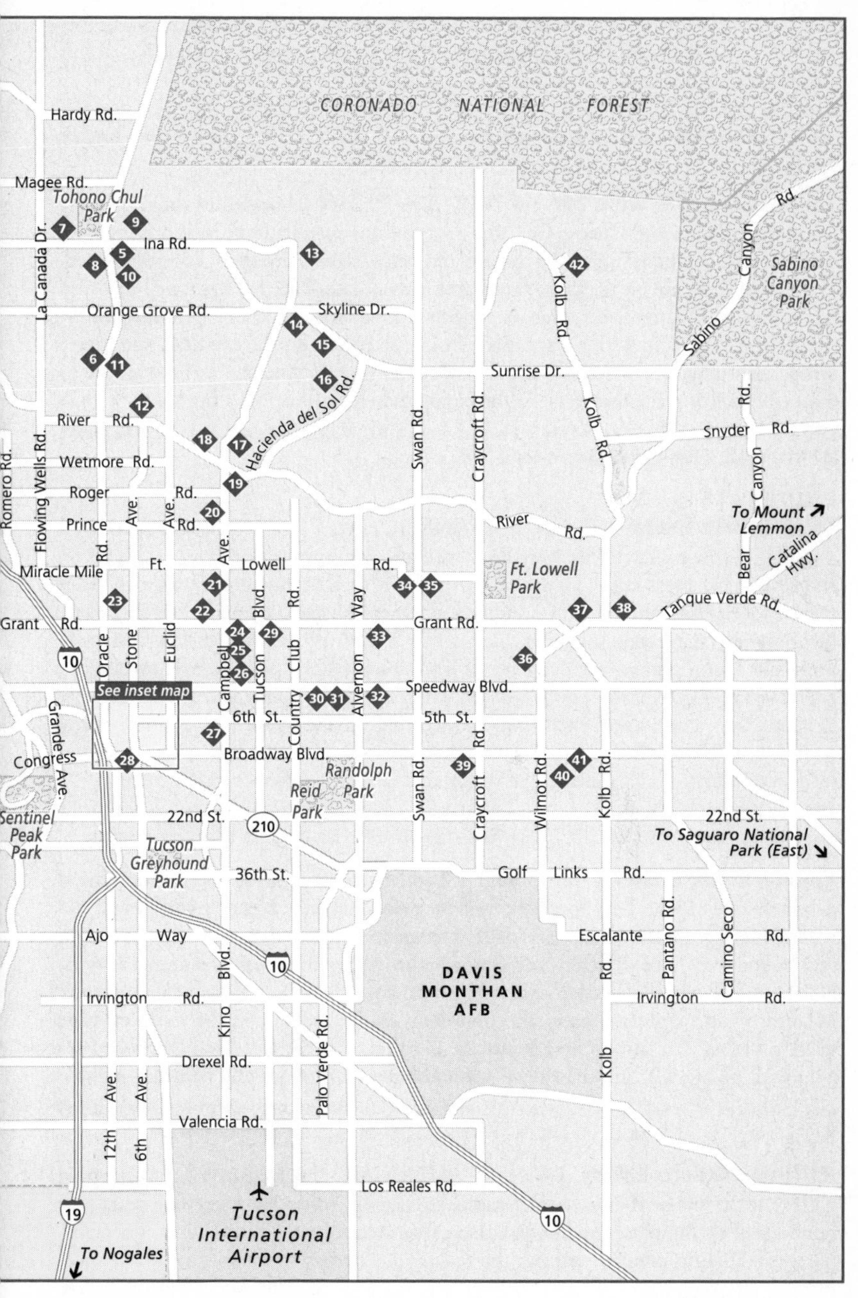
CORONADO NATIONAL FOREST
Hardy Rd.
Magee Rd.
Tohono Chul Park
Ina Rd.
La Canada Dr.
Orange Grove Rd.
Skyline Dr.
Sabino Canyon Rd.
Sabino Canyon Park
Kolb Rd.
Sunrise Dr.
Hacienda del Sol Rd.
River Rd.
Snyder Rd.
Wetmore Rd.
Romero Rd.
Flowing Wells Rd.
Roger Rd.
Prince Rd.
Swan Rd.
Craycroft Rd.
Bear Canyon Rd.
To Mount Lemmon
Catalina Hwy.
River Rd.
Ft. Lowell Park
Miracle Mile
Ft. Lowell Rd.
Tanque Verde Rd.
Grant Rd.
Oracle Rd.
Stone Ave.
Euclid Ave.
Campbell Ave.
Tucson Blvd.
Country Club Rd.
Alvernon Way
Speedway Blvd.
See inset map
6th St.
5th St.
Grande Ave.
Congress
Broadway Blvd.
Randolph Park
Reid Park
Wilmot Rd.
Sentinel Peak Park
22nd St.
Tucson Greyhound Park
36th St.
Golf Links Rd.
To Saguaro National Park (East)
Ajo Way
Escalante Rd.
Pantano Rd.
Camino Seco
DAVIS MONTHAN AFB
Kino Blvd.
Irvington Rd.
Drexel Rd.
Palo Verde Rd.
12th Ave.
6th Ave.
Valencia Rd.
Los Reales Rd.
Tucson International Airport
To Nogales
10
19
210
7
9
5
8
10
13
42
14
15
6
11
16
12
18
17
19
20
21
34
35
23
22
37
38
24
29
33
25
36
26
30
31
32
27
28
39
41
40

shrimp "martini" with watermelon salsa and salmon with a chile-scallion glaze. Presentation is artistic, and fresh ingredients are emphasized. The homemade ice creams are fabulous. On weekends, you might catch some live music.

2200 E. Elm St. ✆ **520/325-1541.** www.arizonainn.com. Reservations recommended. Main courses $10–$19 lunch, $27–$37 dinner; tasting menu $45–$60 ($60–$80 with wine). AE, DC, MC, V. Daily 6:15–10am, 11:30am–2pm, and 6–10pm.

The Dish Bistro & Wine Bar ★★ NEW AMERICAN Located in the rear of the Rumrunner Wine and Cheese Co., this tiny, minimalist restaurant is brimming with urban chic. On a busy night, the space could be construed as either cozy or crowded, so if you like it more on the quiet side, come early or late. The chef has a well-deserved reputation for daring dishes such as chorizo-stuffed veal chops with trumpet mushrooms; and lamb loin with a glaze made from star anise, allspice, sassafras, and maple syrup. Naturally, because this place is associated with a wine shop, the wine list is great; the well-informed servers will be happy to help you choose a bottle.

3200 E. Speedway Blvd. ✆ **520/326-1714.** www.dishbistro.com. Reservations highly recommended. Main courses $17–$34. AE, MC, V. Tues–Thurs 5–9pm; Fri–Sat 5–10pm.

MODERATE

Cuvée World Bistro ★★ *Value* INTERNATIONAL This stylish restaurant in a shopping center on busy Speedway Boulevard affects a sort of Moroccan-palace decor, and if you take a seat in the lounge, you can sprawl on a banquette covered with plush pillows for a thoroughly romantic and hedonistic experience. The menu travels all over the globe for inspiration and then blends flavors and textures in deliciously creative ways. The menu changes regularly, but if you see something (perhaps wild-mushroom cakes) served over avocado pesto, order it. This pesto is so creamy and rich it ought to be made into a spa treatment! Almost everything on the menu here sounds utterly tempting, and with prices so reasonable, you might want to come back a few times and work your way through the list. On Friday and Saturday nights, there's live music.

3352 E. Speedway Blvd. ✆ **520/881-7577.** www.cuveebistro.com. Reservations recommended. Main courses $9–$15 lunch, $16–$22 dinner. AE, DC, DISC, MC, V. Mon–Thurs 11am–10pm; Fri 11am–midnight; Sat 4:30pm–midnight.

Kingfisher Bar & Grill ★ SEAFOOD If you're serious about seafood, Kingfisher is definitely one of your best bets. The freshest seafood, artfully blended with bright flavors and imaginative ingredients, is deftly prepared as appetizers, sandwiches, and main dishes. You may have difficulty deciding whether to begin with Hama Hama oysters, house-smoked trout, or scallop *ceviche*—so why not tackle them all and call it a meal? Meat eaters and vegetarians will also find items on the menu, and the warm cabbage salad is a must. The atmosphere is upscale and lively, the bar and late-night menu are a hit with night owls, and there's live jazz and blues on Monday and Saturday nights.

2564 E. Grant Rd. ✆ **520/323-7739.** www.kingfisherbarandgrill.com. Reservations recommended. Main courses $8–$12 lunch, $16–$23 dinner. AE, DC, DISC, MC, V. Mon–Fri 11am–midnight; Sat–Sun 5pm–midnight.

Pastiche Modern Eatery ★★ NEW AMERICAN Located in a little shopping plaza that has lots of Tucson character, this high-energy bistro has for several years now been one of *the* hip places to dine in Tucson. The colorful artwork and vibrant contemporary food fairly shout *trendy,* but the restaurant manages to appeal to a broad spectrum of the population. From thyme-crusted sea bass to pumpkin ravioli with sage brown butter, there's enough here to keep everyone at the table happy. Light eaters can get half-orders of entrees and desserts. The crowded bar is a popular watering hole that turns out tasty margaritas. There's also an adjacent wine-and-gift shop that has interesting picnic fare and free wine tastings on Friday evenings from 5 to 6:30pm.

3025 N. Campbell Ave. ✆ **520/325-3333.** www.pasticheme.com. Reservations recommended. Main courses $7–$28. AE, DC, DISC, MC, V. Mon–Fri 11:30am–midnight; Sat–Sun 4:30pm–midnight.

INEXPENSIVE

Beyond Bread ★ AMERICAN/BAKERY Although ostensibly a bakery, this place is really a bustling sandwich shop that also sells great breads and pastries. You can even get hot breakfasts here, but I much prefer a latte and a selection from the pastry case. The sandwich list is long, with both hot and cold varieties, and they all come on the great bread that's baked here on the premises. Most of the sandwiches are so big that you could split them between two people if you weren't too hungry.

There's another Beyond Bread over on the east side of town at Monterey Village, 6260 E. Speedway Blvd. (✆ **520/747-7477**).

3026 N. Campbell Ave. ✆ **520/322-9965.** www.beyondbread.com. Reservations not accepted. Main dishes $4.25–$9.25. AE, MC, V. Mon–Fri 6:30am–8pm; Sat 7am–8pm; Sun 7am–6pm.

El Cubanito Restaurant ★ CUBAN Located across the street from the University of Arizona, this place is popular with students. During spring-training season (Mar), the restaurant is also popular with Cuban baseball players. What draws diners back to this nondescript place are the reasonably priced Cuban specialties, including various stews and Cuban sandwiches (meat- and cheese-filled baguettes pressed and warmed on the grill). The fried plantains are also worth trying, and the fruity shakes made with mango, banana, papaya, or other tropical fruits are delicious.

1150 E. Sixth St. ✆ **520/623-8020.** Reservations not accepted. Main courses $6.75–$10. MC, V. Mon–Sat 11am–7pm.

El Guero Canelo *Finds* MEXICAN The first time I stopped in at El Guero Canelo for one of their famous Sonoran hot dogs, a teenage mariachi band started playing *La Bamba* just as I ordered my meal. It was a Sunday afternoon, and the place was packed with local Hispanic families. The sun was shining in through 20-foot-tall walls of glass, and just about everything in the restaurant was painted in the colors of the Mexican flag (green, white, and red). The hot dog, wrapped in bacon and slathered with beans and salsa, was good, but it wasn't nearly as memorable as the restaurant scene itself. For a slice of authentic Tucson culture, this place is not to be missed. The original El Guero Canelo is at 5201 S. 12th Ave. (✆ **520/295-9005**).

2480 N. Oracle Rd. ✆ **520/882-8977.** www.elguerocanelo.com. Main courses $1.25–$6.50. No credit cards. Mon–Sat 6:30am–midnight; Sun 7am–midnight.

Feast ★ *Finds* INTERNATIONAL This place is not only a casual sit-down restaurant, but also a gourmet to-go place; it's the perfect place to pick up food for a sunset picnic dinner at Sabino Canyon Recreation Area or Saguaro National Park. The menu changes regularly, but you may find a sandwich made with roast pork and quince paste. Other possibilities are gnocchi with house-made sausage or white seafood lasagna.

4122 E. Speedway Blvd. ✆ **520/326-9363** or 520/326-6500. www.eatatfeast.com. Reservations not accepted. Main courses $8–$15. AE, DISC, MC, V. Tues–Sun 11am–9pm.

Ghini's French Café ★ *Finds* FRENCH A French cafe and breakfast spot in the middle of Tucson? *Mais oui!* This casual little spot is a real gem. The owner is from Marseille and reproduces plenty of favorites from the home country. At breakfast, there are flaky croissants, a Marseille-style omelet made with anchovies, and wonderful

Provençal-style fried eggs with tomatoes, garlic, and thyme. Lunchtime brings interesting salads, sandwiches made from baguettes, and a good range of simple pastas. Everything is available to go.

1803 E. Prince Rd. ✆ **520/326-9095.** www.ghiniscafe.com. Reservations not accepted. Sandwiches and pastas $6.25–$10. AE, DISC, MC, V. Tues–Sat 6:30am–3pm; Sun 8am–2pm.

Lovin' Spoonfuls ★ VEGAN Chili dogs, turkey sandwiches, tuna melts, bacon cheeseburgers. The menu at this casual little place may not sound too interesting until you realize that not one of those dishes actually has meat in it. This is a vegan restaurant, so there are no eggs or dairy products to be seen (or tasted), either. If you're already a vegetarian or vegan, you may not want to eat anywhere else while you're in Tucson.

2990 N. Campbell Ave., Suite 120. ✆ **520/325-7766.** www.lovinspoonfuls.com. Main courses $6.25–$11. DISC, MC, V. Mon–Sat 9:30am–9pm; Sun 10am–3pm.

Yoshimatsu Healthy Japanese Food & Café ★ JAPANESE I found out about this unusual place from a friend who had recently been to Japan and raved about this restaurant's authenticity. However, that's only part of the story. Not only is there a long menu of health-conscious Japanese dishes, but the decor in this ultracasual place is truly outrageous, with little glass cases displaying all manner of Japanese toys and action figures. The *okonomiyaki,* sort of a Japanese pizza, is one of my favorite dishes here, and for a truly bizarre treat, try the green-tea milkshake. There's also a stylish little sushi bar attached to the restaurant.

2660 N. Campbell Ave. ✆ **520/320-1574.** Reservations not accepted. Main dishes $6.50–$17. MC, V. Sat–Thurs 11:30am–2:30pm and 5–8:45pm; Fri 11:30am–2:30pm and 5–9:45pm.

EAST TUCSON

MODERATE

Le Delice ★★ FRENCH I know that desert hiking and French food go together about as well as the Eiffel Tower and enchiladas, but if you've been out hiking in Sabino Canyon all morning and you're starving, you don't have a whole lot of decent choices near the canyon. That's why Le Delice is such a delicious option. You can duck in for a pastry or a quick pick from the to-go case, or you can sit down and savor a classic quiche Lorraine, salad Lyonnaise, or steak frite. If its dinner time, you might want to pull on a clean shirt and change out of your hiking boots before dining on sweetbreads, coq au vin, or duck a l'orange.

7245 E. Tanque Verde Rd. ✆ **520/290-9714.** www.le-delice.com. Reservations recommended at dinner. Main courses $7–$15 lunch, $8.75–$35 dinner. AE, DC, MC, V. Tues–Sat 7am–8:30pm; Sun–Mon 7am–2:30pm.

Sky Blue Wasabi ★ *Finds* JAPANESE The same old friend who first took me to Yoshimatsu (see above) also brought me to this little out-of-the-way Japanese restaurant on Tucson's east side. With lots of blue lights and a contemporary feel, this place feels as though it ought to be in some upscale shopping center in the foothills; instead you'll find it tucked amid office buildings and shopping plazas just south of Broadway. While you can get a show at one of the teppanyaki tables, the real reason to eat here is the special sushi rolls. Do not miss, I repeat, do not miss, the Sky Blue Wasabi ultimate roll, which is made with lobster, shrimp, and 24-karat gold leaf! Likewise, try the Sky Blue Wasabi roll, which is made with eel and topped with fresh strawberries. Trust me, it works.

250 S. Craycroft Rd., no. 100. ✆ **520/747-0228.** Reservations recommended on weekends. Main courses $5–$14 lunch, $12–$30 dinner; sushi $4–$15. MC, V. Mon–Thurs 11am–2pm and 5–10pm; Fri 11am–2pm and 5–11pm; Sat 5–11pm; Sun 5–9pm.

INEXPENSIVE

Casa Molina MEXICAN Casa Molina, which sports a festive atmosphere, has been Tucson's favorite family-run Mexican restaurant for many years and is usually abuzz with families, groups, and couples. The margaritas are inexpensive yet tasty, and the *carne seca* shouldn't be missed. Light eaters will enjoy a layered *topopo* salad made with tortillas, refried beans, chicken, lettuce, celery, avocado, tomato, and jalapeños. The food is good, and the service efficient.

Other locations include 3001 N. Campbell Ave. (✆ **520/795-7593**) and 4240 E. Grant Rd. (✆ **520/326-6663**).

6225 E. Speedway Blvd. (near Wilmot Rd.). ✆ **520/886-5468.** www.casamolina.com. Reservations recommended. Dinners $6.50–$18. AE, DC, DISC, MC, V. Daily 11am–10pm.

Little Anthony's Diner *Kids* AMERICAN This place is primarily for kids, although lots of big kids enjoy the 1950s music and decor. The menu includes such offerings as a Jailhouse Rock burger and Chubby Checker triple-decker club sandwich. Daily specials and bottomless soft drinks make feeding the family fairly inexpensive. A video-game room will keep your kids entertained while you finish your milkshake. If you want to make a night of it (and you make a reservation far enough in advance), you can take in an old-fashioned melodrama next door at the Gaslight Theatre. Together, these two places make for a fun night out with the family.

7010 E. Broadway Blvd. (in back of the Gaslight Plaza). ✆ **520/296-0456.** Burgers and sandwiches $4.75–$9. MC, V. Mon 11am–9pm; Tues–Thurs 11am–10pm; Fri 11am–11pm; Sat 10:30am–11pm; Sun 10:30am–10pm.

THE FOOTHILLS

EXPENSIVE

Anthony's in the Catalinas ★★ NEW AMERICAN/CONTINENTAL From the moment you drive up and let the valet park your car, Anthony's, housed in a modern Italianate building overlooking the city, exudes Southwestern elegance. The waiters are smartly attired in tuxedos, and guests (the cigar-and-single-malt foothills set) are nearly as well dressed. In such a rarefied atmosphere, you'd expect only the finest meal and service, and that's exactly what you get. The house-smoked salmon and oysters Rockefeller are both fitting beginnings, followed by the likes of chateaubriand with béarnaise sauce. Wine is not just an accompaniment, but also a reason for dining out at Anthony's; at more than 100 pages, the wine list may be the most extensive in the city. Don't miss out on the next best part of a meal here (after the wine)—the day's soufflé (order early).

6440 N. Campbell Ave. ✆ **520/299-1771.** www.anthonyscatalinas.com. Reservations highly recommended. Main courses $24–$41 dinner. AE, DC, DISC, MC, V. Daily 5:30–10pm.

The Gold Room ★★ SOUTHWESTERN/CONTINENTAL With its contemporary Southwestern decor, menu of creative contemporary fare and updated comfort foods, superb views of the city far below, and expansive terrace for alfresco dining, The Gold Room is one of the best places in Tucson for a memorable Southwestern dining experience. Think jerked chicken with prickly pear–jalapeño glaze, sugar-and-spice scallops with truffle risotto, and beef tenderloin served with house-made green-chile tater tots. The length of the wine list is staggering, and there's a welcome range of

Moments **Market Timing**

Sunday mornings are a great time to stop by St. Philip's Plaza. No, this isn't a church, it's a shopping center, and on Sunday mornings, there is a wonderful little farmers' market. You can pick up organic bread, prickly-pear cactus juice and jelly, homemade tamales, Mexican cheeses, and plenty of produce. Stock up here and then head to Sabino Canyon Recreation Area for a picnic.

prices. Desserts are decadently rich, so be sure to save room. Although you can eat here on the cheap at lunch, the restaurant is most remarkable at night, when the cityscape of Tucson twinkles in the distance.

At the Westward Look Resort, 245 E. Ina Rd. ✆ **520/917-2930.** Reservations recommended. Main courses $10–$16 lunch, $19–$29 dinner; Sun brunch $25. AE, DISC, MC, V. Mon–Sat 7–11am, 11:30am–2pm, and 5:30–10pm; Sun 11am–1:30pm and 5:30–10pm.

The Grill ★★ REGIONAL AMERICAN Great food, historical Southwest character, views, live jazz—this place has it all. Located in a 1920s hacienda-style building at a former foothills dude ranch, The Grill is one of Tucson's best restaurants, so don't leave town without having at least one meal here. For openers, try the grilled andouille sausage with cornbread and prickly-pear chorizo sauce. Despite the price, the dry-aged New York strip steak is deservedly the most popular entree on the menu and is big enough for two people to share. Sunday brunch here is a real treat. The main patio overlooks the Catalinas and the fairways of The Westin La Paloma's golf course. Thursday through Sunday, the restaurant's Terraza del Sol bar has live music.

At the Hacienda del Sol Guest Ranch Resort, 5601 N. Hacienda del Sol Rd. ✆ **520/529-3500.** www.haciendadelsol.com. Reservations recommended. Main courses $23–$38; Sun brunch $32. AE, DC, DISC, MC, V. Mon–Sat 5:30–10pm; Sun 10am–1:30pm and 5:30–10pm.

Janos ★★★ SOUTHWESTERN/REGIONAL AMERICAN Janos Wilder, Tucson's most celebrated chef, is not only a world-class chef; he's a real sweetheart, too. Should you happen to bump into him while dining here, he'll make you feel as though you've been a regular at his restaurant for years. It is this conviviality—which spills over into all aspects of a meal here—that makes Janos one of my favorite restaurants in the entire state. Consequently, this luxuriously appointed restaurant, which is just outside the front door of The Westin La Paloma, is my top choice for a special-occasion dinner while in Tucson. The menu changes both daily and seasonally, with such complex offerings as beef tournedos with foie gras butter and truffle sauce and lamb chops with a complex spicy Southwestern rub.

At The Westin La Paloma, 3770 E. Sunrise Dr. ✆ **520/615-6100.** www.janos.com. Reservations highly recommended. Main courses $28–$45; 5-course tasting menu $80 ($115 with wine). AE, DC, MC, V. Mon–Thurs 5:30–9pm; Fri–Sat 5:30–9:30pm.

McMahon's Prime Steakhouse ★★ STEAKHOUSE/SEAFOOD If a perfectly done steak is what you're craving, then McMahon's is the place. This restaurant serves some of the best steaks in Tucson, and with a decidedly modern opulence, McMahon's boasts an atmosphere calculated to impress (a large glass-walled wine room dominates the main dining room). You can drop a bundle on dinner here, but no more than you'd spend at such high-end restaurants as Janos or the Ventana Room. The main difference is that your choices at McMahon's are simpler: steak, seafood, or steak and seafood. You'd be wasting a night out, though, if you didn't order a steak. There's a separate piano lounge and cigar bar.

2959 N. Swan Rd. ✆ **520/327-7463.** www.metrorestaurants.com. Reservations recommended. Main courses $9–$20 lunch, $18–$50 dinner. AE, DC, DISC, MC, V. Mon–Fri 11:30am–10pm; Sat–Sun 5–10pm.

Miguel's ★★ NUEVO LATINO If you're staying at one of the foothills resorts and just can't get enough south-of-the-border cuisine, this is another good bet. Be sure to start your meal with the guacamole and the lobster "cigars" with a reduction of guava and serrano chiles. The bacon-wrapped Guaymas shrimp and the seafood-stuffed chile relleno are favorites of mine, but there are also flavorful steaks and lots of seafood dishes. The tequila selection here is one of the best in Tucson, and the margaritas are delicious. If you can, eat before the sun goes down; there are views of the Santa Catalinas and the city.

At La Posada, 5900 N. Oracle Rd. ✆ **520/887-3777.** www.miguelstucson.com. Reservations recommended. Main courses $14–$29. AE, DISC, MC, V. Oct–May Sun–Thurs 11am–3pm and 5–10pm, Fri–Sat 11am–3pm and 5–11pm; June–Sept Sun–Thurs 5–10pm, Fri–Sat 5–11pm.

Ventana Room ★★★ NEW AMERICAN The Ventana Room is Tucson's poshest and most classically elegant restaurant, as you'll immediately guess from the wall of wine bottles just inside the door. *Ventana* means "window" in Spanish, and the views through the windows of this restaurant are every bit as memorable as the food. Be sure you make an early dinner reservation so that you can catch the sunset. Although you may have trouble concentrating on your food, do try; you wouldn't want to miss any of the subtle nuances. The tasting menus are designed to provide you with a delicious variety of flavors and textures. Ingredients are flown in from all over the world, so you never know what may show up on the menu. In the restaurant's rarefied atmosphere, you'll be pampered by a bevy of waiters providing professional and unobtrusive service. For superb French-inspired cuisine and gorgeous views, this restaurant just can't be beat.

At Loews Ventana Canyon Resort, 7000 N. Resort Dr. ✆ **520/615-5494.** www.ventanaroom.com. Reservations highly recommended. Jackets recommended for men. Prix-fixe menus $75–$105. AE, DC, DISC, MC, V. Tues–Thurs 6–9:30pm; Fri–Sat 6–10pm. Closed mid-Aug to mid-Sept.

MODERATE

Bistro Zin ★★ REGIONAL AMERICAN Sophisticated and urbane, Bistro Zin, Tucson's premier wine bar/restaurant, affects an urban feel with its wine-colored walls decorated with black-and-white photos of jazz greats. It's all very classy and cool, and with more than 20 different wine flights available on any given day, this is the perfect place to sample wines from around the world. There's also plenty of good food to accompany the many wines. The duck breast with seasonal fruit-flavored sauce is always a good bet.

At Joesler Village, 1865 E. River Rd., Suite 101. ✆ **520/299-7799.** www.foxrestaurantconcepts.com. Reservations recommended. Main courses $8–$13 lunch, $14–$29 dinner. AE, DISC, MC, V. Mon–Thurs 11am–10pm; Fri–Sat 4–11:30pm; Sun 5–9pm.

Bluefin Seafood Bistro ★ SEAFOOD Sure, this is the middle of the desert, but there's only so much beef you can eat on a week's vacation. If you've had enough steak to start your own ranch and are craving a nice bouillabaisse, this is a good choice. Adopting a sort of New Orleans styling, Bluefin is a sister restaurant to the ever-popular and always-reliable Kingfisher in central Tucson (p. 346). The menu is extensive; in addition to that bouillabaisse, you can get simply prepared grilled fish served with a choice of sauces. Personally, I go for the rock shrimp–chipotle salsa.

In Casas Adobes Shopping Center, 7053 N. Oracle Rd. ✆ **520/531-8500.** www.bluefinseafoodbistro.com. Reservations recommended. Main courses $8.50–$12 lunch, $16–$28 dinner. AE, DISC, MC. V. Sun–Wed 11am–9:30pm; Thurs–Sat 11am–midnight.

Firecracker Bistro ★ PAN-ASIAN With a menu that knows no boundaries and wild architectural touches that include flames issuing from torches atop the building and faux tree trunks in the bar, Firecracker is one of Tucson's liveliest restaurants. Hip decor aside, it's the large portions and reasonable prices that keep people coming back. The spicy vegetarian lettuce-cup appetizers (sort of roll-your-own burritos) are a fun finger-food starter. Seafood is definitely the strong suit here, and the wok-charred chunks of salmon covered with cilantro pesto are just about the best thing on the menu.

2990 N. Swan Rd. (at Fort Lowell). ✆ **520/318-1118.** www.metrorestaurants.com. Reservations recommended. Main courses $9–$23 lunch, $11–$23 dinner. AE, DC, DISC, MC, V. Mon–Thurs 11am–10pm; Fri 11am–10:30pm; Sat 4–10:30pm; Sun 4–10pm.

J Bar ★★★ SOUTHWESTERN The mouthwatering culinary creations of celebrity chef Janos Wilder at half-price? Sounds impossible, but that's pretty much what you'll find at this casual bar and grill adjacent to the famed foothills restaurant. Ask for a seat out on the heated patio, and with the lights of Tucson twinkling in the distance, dig into the best nachos you'll ever taste—here made with chorizo sausage and chili con queso. No matter what you order, you'll likely find that the ingredients and flavor combinations are most memorable. Who can forget spicy jerked pork with cranberry–habañero chutney or Yucatán-style plantain-crusted chicken with green coconut-milk curry? You won't want to miss sampling one of the *postres* (desserts). The dark chocolate–jalapeño sundae may sound unusual, but it's delicious.

At The Westin La Paloma, 3770 E. Sunrise Dr. ✆ **520/615-6100.** www.janos.com. Reservations highly recommended. Main courses $15–$28. AE, DC, MC, V. Mon–Sat 5–9:30pm.

Tavolino Ristorante Italiano ★ ITALIAN Located in a shopping center at the corner of Oracle and Ina roads, this is not the Italian restaurant of your youth. Forget the red-and-white checked tablecloths; Tavolino Ristorante Italiano has a hip urban trattoria personality. Because it's small, it stays packed and boisterous. Sure, there's a nice antipasto plate, but I'd opt for the eggplant stuffed with salmon mousse. For an entree, I like the lamb chops, which are pounded thin and tender.

In La Toscana Village Shopping Center, 7090 N. Oracle Rd. ✆ **520/531-1913.** Reservations recommended. Main courses $15–$22. AE, DC, MC, V. Mon–Sat 5:30–10pm.

Terra Cotta ★★ REGIONAL AMERICAN/SOUTHWESTERN Terra Cotta is Arizona's original Southwestern restaurant and is one of my favorite places to eat in Tucson. The combination of reasonably priced creative Southwestern cooking, a casual atmosphere with loads of contemporary Southwestern appeal, and lots of local artwork makes Terra Cotta truly distinctive and an Arizona classic. I always start my meals here with the rich-and-creamy garlic custard, which is served with warm salsa vinaigrette and herbed hazelnuts. The poblano chiles rellenos stuffed with either shrimp or adobo pork are another of my must-haves, as is the chutney-stuffed pork chop. A large brick oven turns out creative pizzas, while salads, sandwiches, and small plates flesh out the long menu.

3500 E. Sunrise Dr. ✆ **520/577-8100.** www.dineterracotta.com. Reservations recommended. Main courses $9–$14 lunch, $14–$27 dinner. AE, DC, DISC, MC, V. Daily 4–10pm (call for seasonal lunch hours).

Vivace Restaurant ★★ NORTHERN ITALIAN With a beautiful Tuscan-inspired setting, this restaurant serves reasonably priced, creative dishes. The atmosphere is lively and the food down-to-earth. For starters, consider indulging in the luscious antipasto platter for two, containing marinated artichokes, prosciutto, roasted red peppers, grilled asparagus, and herbed goat cheese. Pasta dishes, such as penne with sausage and roasted-pepper sauce, come nicely presented and in generous portions. But it's the crab-filled chicken breast that is most memorable. The wine list has plenty of selections, many fairly reasonably priced.

At St. Philip's Plaza, 4310 N. Campbell Ave. ✆ **520/795-7221.** Reservations recommended. Main courses $9–$17 lunch, $15–$29 dinner. AE, DC, DISC, MC, V. Mon–Thurs 11:30am–9pm; Fri–Sat 11:30am–10pm.

Wildflower ★★ NEW AMERICAN Stylish comfort food in large portions is the order of the day at this chic and casually elegant north Tucson bistro. A huge wall of glass creates minimalist drama, and large flower photographs on the walls enhance the bright and airy decor. The heaping plate of fried calamari with mizuna greens is a good bet for a starter, and entrees run the gamut from a comforting meatloaf to herb-crusted rack of lamb. Pasta and salmon also both show up in reliable guises. With so many tempting, reasonably priced dishes to sample, Wildflower is a foodie's delight.

At Casas Adobes Shopping Plaza, 7037 N. Oracle Rd. (at Ina Rd.). ✆ **520/219-4230.** www.foxrestaurantconcepts.com. Reservations recommended. Main courses $8–$15 lunch, $15–$29 dinner. AE, DC, DISC, MC, V. Mon–Thurs 11am–3pm and 5–9pm; Fri 11am–3pm and 5–10pm; Sat 5–10pm; Sun 5–9pm.

INEXPENSIVE

Candela Restaurant ★ *Finds* PERUVIAN/LATIN AMERICAN It's easy to miss this nondescript little restaurant, which is tucked into an older shopping plaza on Oracle Road south of Ina. However, keep looking. When you find it, you're in for a real treat if you enjoy trying new cuisines. As soon as you sit down, you'll be brought a basket of salty banana chips and a spicy dipping sauce. Make sure you order at least one dish with quinoa, a tiny South American grain. I love the quinoa salad, which is made with avocados, olive oil, and balsamic vinegar. Another must-have is the *pescado sudado* (steamed fish). If you see *chicha morada* on the menu, try it. It's an unusual purple corn drink that tastes much better than it sounds.

5845 N. Oracle Rd. ✆ **520/407-0111.** Reservations recommended on weekends. Main courses $6–$8 lunch, $14–$25 dinner. AE, DISC, MC, V. Mon–Fri 11am–2:30pm and 5–9pm; Sat–Sun noon–9pm.

HiFalutin Rapid Fire Western Grill ★ AMERICAN The first time I walked into this lively Western grill, I was absolutely hooked. The smell of burning juniper filled the restaurant, and I could almost taste the steaks. It wasn't until my second visit that I discovered the aroma was actually incense. Still, this place knows how to set the mood, and they come through with tasty comfort food with a Western twist. Get anything with the marinated flank steak, and you won't be disappointed. You can get it tossed with pasta, in a salad, or just plain straight up. Wash it all down with one of the great margaritas they serve, and you definitely have a highfalutin kind of meal.

6780 N. Oracle Rd. ✆ **520/297-0518.** www.hifalutintucson.com. Reservations recommended. Main courses $9–$25. AE, DC, DISC, MC, V. Daily 11am–9pm.

Tohono Chul Tea Room REGIONAL AMERICAN Located in a brick territorial-style building in 49-acre Tohono Chul Park (p. 367), this is one of the most tranquil restaurants in the city, and the garden setting provides a wonderful opportunity to experience the desert. Before or after lunching on grilled raspberry-chipotle chicken or tortilla soup, you can wander through the park's desert landscaping and admire the many species of cacti. The patios, surrounded by natural vegetation and plenty of potted flowers, are frequented by many species of birds. The adjacent gift shop offers Mexican folk art, nature-themed toys, household items, T-shirts, and books.

7366 N. Paseo del Norte (1 block west of the corner of Ina and Oracle roads in Tohono Chul Park). ✆ **520/797-1222.** www.tohonochulpark.org. Reservations accepted only for parties of 6 or more. Main courses $7–$11. AE, MC, V. Daily 8am–5pm.

Zona 78 ★ *Finds* PIZZA I'm a sucker for good pizza, and the pizza here is the best in Tucson. Maybe it's the big stone oven they use or maybe it's all the locally grown organic produce, but whatever it is, this place does it right. Try the Tuscany, an oval pizza covered with Italian sausage, mozzarella, kalamata olives, fennel, garlic, onions, and mushrooms. This pie is just bursting with flavors. To really get the most out of a visit to Zona 78, you need to bring enough people so that you can order the big antipasto plate or the cheese-and-fruit plate, which has lots of great imported cheeses. If you're not that hungry, try the Tuscan bean-and-spinach soup.

78 W. River Rd. ✆ **520/888-7878.** www.zona78.com. Reservations accepted only for parties of 8 or more. Main courses $7.50–$19. AE, DISC, MC, V. Mon–Thurs 11am–10pm; Fri–Sat 11am–11pm; Sun 4–9pm.

WEST TUCSON

MODERATE

Teresa's Mosaic Café ★ *Finds* MEXICAN A mile or so west of I-10, this casual Mexican restaurant, with colorful mosaic tile tables, mirror frames, and kitchen counter, is hidden behind a McDonald's on the corner of Grant and Silverbell roads but is well worth finding for breakfast or lunch. Try the *chilaquiles* or chorizo and eggs for breakfast, and don't pass up the fresh lemonade or *horchata* (spiced rice milk). This is an especially good spot for a meal if you're on your way to the Arizona–Sonora Desert Museum, Old Tucson, or Saguaro National Park's west unit.

2456 N. Silver Mosaic Rd. ✆ **520/624-4512.** Reservations recommended. Main courses $4.75–$16. DC, DISC, MC, V. Mon–Sat 7:30am–9pm; Sun 7:30am–2pm.

COWBOY STEAKHOUSES

El Corral Restaurant *Value* STEAKHOUSE El Corral is another of Tucson's fun, inexpensive, and atmospheric steakhouses. Good prime rib and cheap prices have made this place hugely popular with retirees and families. The restaurant doesn't accept reservations, so expect long lines or come before or after regular dinner hours. Inside, the hacienda building has a genuine old-timey feeling, with flagstone floors and wood paneling that make it dark and cozy. In keeping with the name, there's a traditional corral fence of mesquite branches around the restaurant parking lot. Prime rib is the house specialty, but there are steaks, chicken, pork ribs, and burgers.

2201 E. River Rd. ✆ **520/299-6092.** www.elcorraltucson.com. Reservations not accepted. Complete dinner $9–$19. AE, DC, DISC, MC, V. Mon–Thurs 5–10pm; Fri–Sun 4:30–10pm.

Pinnacle Peak Steakhouse ★ *Kids* STEAKHOUSE Located in Trail Dust Town (see the "Especially for Kids" section in "Seeing the Sights," below), a Wild West–themed shopping, dining, and family entertainment center, the Pinnacle Peak Steakhouse specializes in family dining in a fun cowboy atmosphere. Stroll the wooden sidewalks past the opera house and saloon to the grand old dining rooms of the restaurant. Once through the doors, you'll be surprised at the authenticity of the place, which really does resemble a dining room in Old Tombstone. Be prepared for crowds—this place is very popular with tour buses. Oh, and by the way, wear a necktie into this place, and it will be cut off! Actually, lots of people wear ties just so they can have them added to the collection tacked to the ceiling.

6541 E. Tanque Verde Rd. ✆ **520/296-0911.** www.pinnaclepeaktucson.com. Reservations not accepted. Main courses $8–$19. AE, DC, DISC, MC, V. Mon–Fri 5–10pm; Sat–Sun 4:30–10pm.

LATE-NIGHT NOSHING

If the movie didn't let out until 10pm and the popcorn wasn't enough to fill you up, where do you go to satisfy your hunger? Try **Kingfisher,** 2564 E. Grant Rd. (✆ **520/323-7739**), or **Pastiche Modern Eatery,** 3025 N. Campbell Ave. (✆ **520/325-3333**), both of which stay open on Friday and Saturday until midnight. (For more information, see the reviews of Kingfisher and Pastiche earlier in this chapter.)

BAKERIES, CAFES & QUICK BITES

For the best espresso in Tucson, head to **Raging Sage Coffee Roasters,** 2458 N. Campbell Ave. (✆ **520/320-5203**); prices are high, but the espresso here sure is tasty. The **Epic Café,** 743 N. Fourth Ave. (✆ **520/624-6844**), is a counter-cultural college hangout with colorful artwork, delicious scones, and other light fare. With comfy couches and a place to plug in your laptop, the **Coffee X Change,** 2443 N. Campbell Ave. (✆ **520/327-6783**), makes a good stop between downtown and the foothills. If you're a tea person, be sure to check out **Seven Cups,** 2516 E. Sixth St. (✆ **520/881-4072;** www.sevencups.com), a traditional Chinese tearoom in a hip residential neighborhood near the University of Arizona.

For eight-layer cakes and light food in an edgy atmosphere, I like to buzz over to **The Cup Cafe,** at Hotel Congress, 311 E. Congress St. (✆ **520/798-1618**). At **La Baguette Bakery,** 1797 E. Prince Rd. (✆ **520/322-6297**), which is affiliated with Ghini's French Café (p. 347), you can get all kinds of delicious French pastries. On the east side of the city, check out the sweet treats at **Something Sweet Dessert Lounge,** 5319 E. Speedway Blvd. (✆ **520/881-7735;** www.somethingsweet-dl.com), where "bigger is better" seems to be the order of the day. **AJ's Fine Foods,** 2805 E. Skyline Dr. (✆ **520/232-6340;** www.ajsfinefoods.com), a gourmet supermarket in the shopping center at the northwest corner of Skyline Drive and Campbell Avenue, is another good place to grab a pastry. If it's a hot day, head to **Frost, A Gelato Shoppe,** 7131 N. Oracle Rd., Suite 101 (✆ **520/797-0188;** www.frostgelato.com), a great little gelateria in the Casas Adobes shopping center.

When I need a quick lunch, I head for the nearest **Baggins Gourmet Sandwiches** for a delicious sandwich. Baggins has several locations, three of which are at East Speedway Boulevard and Kolb Road (✆ **520/290-9383**), Campbell Avenue and Fort Lowell Road (✆ **520/327-1611**), and downtown at Church Avenue and Pennington Street (✆ **520/792-1344**). Good pizza can be had at **Magpies Gourmet Pizza,** downtown at 605 N. Fourth Ave. (✆ **520/628-1661**), 4654 E. Speedway Blvd. (✆ **520/795-5977**), 105 S. Houghton Rd. (✆ **520/751-9949**), 7159 E. Tanque Verde Rd. (✆ **520/546-6526**), and 7315 Oracle Rd. (✆ **520/297-2712**). **Wild Oats Market** is a good place to get picnic supplies: organic fruit, delicious baked goods, cheese, meats, and wine. Locations are at 3360 E. Speedway Blvd. (✆ **520/795-9844**) and 7133 N. Oracle Rd. (✆ **520/297-5394**).

5 Seeing the Sights

Go west, young man (and woman). That's what you'll need to do if you're visiting Tucson and want to immerse yourself in the desert Southwest or the cinematic Wild West. Out past the western outskirts of Tucson, where the cactus grows and the tumbleweed blows, you'll find not only the west unit of Saguaro National Park (with the biggest and best stands of saguaro cactus), but also the Arizona–Sonora Desert Museum (one of the nation's top zoological parks) and Old Tucson Studios (film site over the years for hundreds of Westerns). Put these three attractions together for one long day of getting to know Tucson, and you have the city's best family outing (and you can bet the kids will be beat by the end of the day).

The Shrine That Stopped a Freeway

The southern Arizona landscape is dotted with roadside shrines, symbols of the region's Hispanic and Roman Catholic heritage. Most are simple crosses decorated with plastic flowers and dedicated to people who have been killed in auto accidents. One shrine, however, stands out from all the rest. It is Tucson's El Tiradito (The Castaway), which is dedicated to a sinner. Not only does this crumbling shrine attract the devout, but it once also stopped a freeway.

El Tiradito, on South Granada Avenue at West Cushing Street, is the only shrine in the United States dedicated to a sinner buried in unconsecrated soil. Several stories tell of how this shrine came to be, but the most popularly accepted one tells of a young shepherd who fell in love with his mother-in-law some time in the 1880s. When the father-in-law found his wife in the arms of this young man, he shot the son-in-law. The young shepherd stumbled from his in-laws' house and fell dead beside the dusty street. Because he had been caught in the act of adultery and died without confessing his sins, his body could not be interred in the church cemetery, so he was buried where he fell.

The people of the neighborhood soon began burning candles on the spot to try to save the soul of the young man, and eventually people began burning candles in hopes that their own wishes would come true. They believed that if the candle burned through the night, their prayers would be answered. The shrine eventually grew into a substantial little structure and in 1927 was dedicated by its owner to the city of Tucson. In 1940, the shrine became an official Tucson monument.

However, such status was not enough to protect the shrine from urban renewal, and when the federal government announced that it would level the shrine when it built a new freeway through the center of Tucson, the city's citizens were outraged. Their activities and protests led the shrine to be named to the National Register of Historic Places. Thus protected, the shrine could not be destroyed, and the freeway was moved a few hundred yards to the west.

To this day, devout Catholics from the surrounding neighborhood still burn candles at the shrine that stopped a freeway. A visit after dark, perhaps in conjunction with dinner next door at El Minuto (p. 343), a popular Mexican restaurant, is a somber experience that will easily convince you of how important this shrine is to the neighborhood.

Moments **Driving the Catalina Highway**

Within a span of only 25 miles, the Catalina Highway climbs roughly 1 mile in elevation from the lowland desert landscape of cacti and ocotillo bushes to forests of ponderosa pines. Passing through several different life zones, this route is the equivalent of driving from Mexico to Canada. When you look at it this way, the $5 use fee is small compared to what a flight to Canada would cost (and that fee will also get you into Sabino Canyon). Along the way, there are numerous overlooks, some of which are nauseatingly vertiginous. Other spots are particularly popular with rock climbers. There are numerous hiking trails, picnic areas, and campgrounds along the route. For more information, contact the **Coronado National Forest Santa Catalina Ranger District,** 5700 N. Sabino Canyon Rd. (✆ **520/749-8700;** www.fs.fed.us/r3/coronado).

THE TUCSON AREA'S (MOSTLY) NATURAL WONDERS

Arizona–Sonora Desert Museum ★★★ *Kids* Don't be fooled by the name. This is a zoo, and it's one of the best in the country. The Sonoran Desert of central and southern Arizona and parts of northern Mexico contains within its boundaries not only arid lands, but also forested mountains, springs, rivers, and streams. To reflect this diversity, exhibits here encompass the full spectrum of Sonoran Desert life—from plants to insects to fish to reptiles to mammals—and all are on display in very natural settings. Coyotes and javelinas (peccaries) seem very much at home in their compounds, which are surrounded by fences that are nearly invisible and that make it seem as though there is nothing between you and the animals. You'll also see black bears and mountain lions, tarantulas and scorpions, prairie dogs and desert bighorn sheep. However, my favorite exhibit is the walk-in hummingbird aviary.

The grounds here are quite extensive, so wear good walking shoes; a sun hat of some sort is also advisable. Don't be surprised if you end up staying here hours longer than you had intended. If you get hungry, there are two excellent dining options—the cafeteria-style Ironwood Terraces and the more upscale Ocotillo Café. You'll find this zoological park 14 miles west of downtown.

2021 N. Kinney Rd. ✆ **520/883-2702.** www.desertmuseum.org. Admission Sept–May $12 adults, $4 children 6–12; June–Aug $9 adults, $2 children 6–12. Oct–Feb daily 8:30am–5pm; Mar–Sept daily 7:30am–5pm. From downtown Tucson, go west on Speedway Blvd., which becomes Gates Pass Rd., and follow the signs.

Colossal Cave Mountain Park *Kids* It seems nearly every cave in the Southwest has its legends of bandits and buried loot, and Colossal Cave is no exception. A tour through this cavern, which isn't exactly colossal but is certainly impressive, combines a bit of Western lore with a bit of geology for an experience that both kids and adults will enjoy. Although there was much damage to the formations here before the cave was protected, the narrow passageways and dramatic lighting keep the 45-minute tours interesting. For more adventurous types, there are tours into little-visited parts of the cave. This private park also offers horseback riding ($27 for a 1-hr. ride) and has a small museum and picnic areas as well as snack bars.

16721 E. Old Spanish Trail Rd., Vail. ✆ **520/647-7275.** www.colossalcave.com. Cave admission $8.50 adults, $5 children 6–12, in addition to $5 per car for park entry. Mar 16–Sept 15 Mon–Sat 8am–6pm, Sun and holidays 8am–7pm; Sept 16–Mar 15 Mon–Sat 9am–5pm, Sun and holidays 9am–6pm. Take Old Spanish Trail southeast from east Tucson, or take I-10 and get off at the Vail exit.

Tucson Attractions

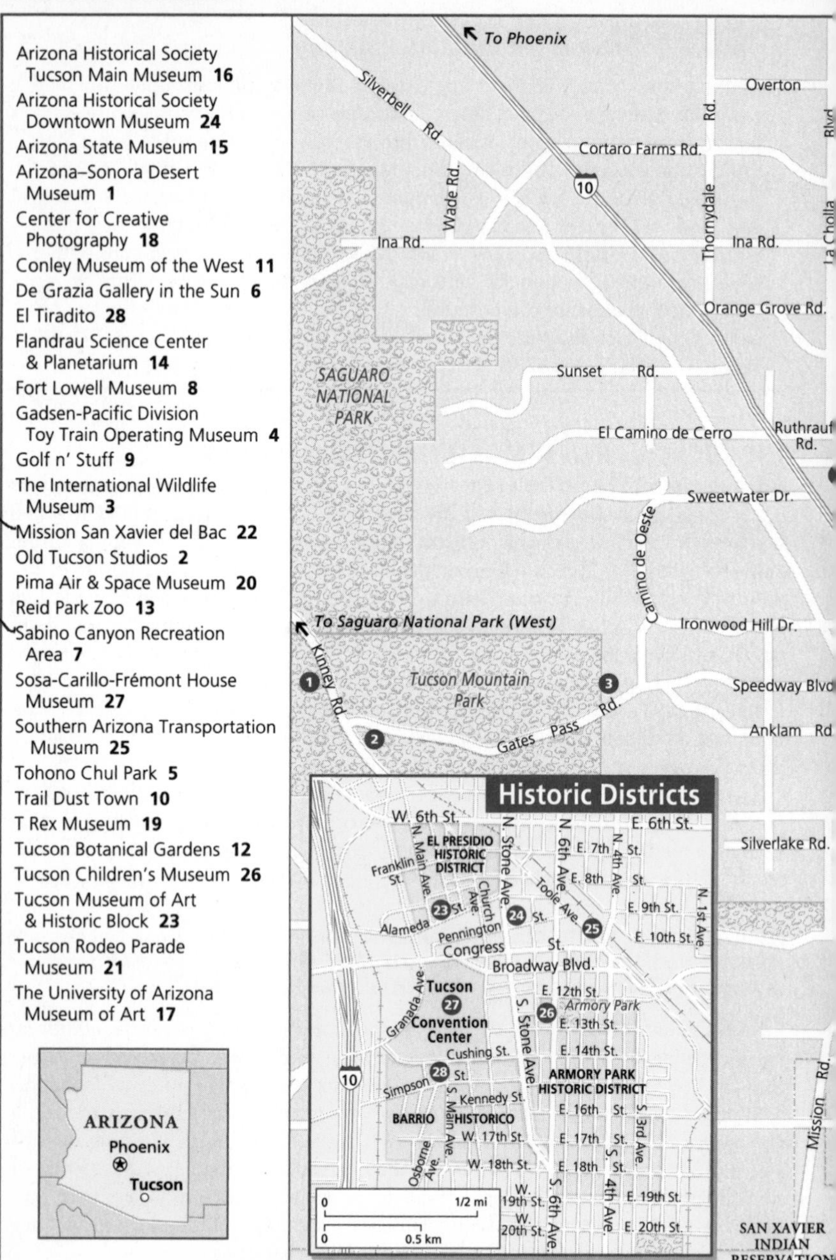
Arizona Historical Society Tucson Main Museum 16
Arizona Historical Society Downtown Museum 24
Arizona State Museum 15
Arizona–Sonora Desert Museum 1
Center for Creative Photography 18
Conley Museum of the West 11
De Grazia Gallery in the Sun 6
El Tiradito 28
Flandrau Science Center & Planetarium 14
Fort Lowell Museum 8
Gadsen-Pacific Division Toy Train Operating Museum 4
Golf n' Stuff 9
The International Wildlife Museum 3
Mission San Xavier del Bac 22
Old Tucson Studios 2
Pima Air & Space Museum 20
Reid Park Zoo 13
Sabino Canyon Recreation Area 7
Sosa-Carillo-Frémont House Museum 27
Southern Arizona Transportation Museum 25
Tohono Chul Park 5
Trail Dust Town 10
T Rex Museum 19
Tucson Botanical Gardens 12
Tucson Children's Museum 26
Tucson Museum of Art & Historic Block 23
Tucson Rodeo Parade Museum 21
The University of Arizona Museum of Art 17
ARIZONA
Phoenix
Tucson
To Phoenix
Silverbell Rd.
Overton
Cortaro Farms Rd.
Wade Rd.
Thornydale Rd.
La Cholla
Ina Rd.
Orange Grove Rd.
SAGUARO NATIONAL PARK
Sunset Rd.
El Camino de Cerro
Ruthrauff Rd.
Sweetwater Dr.
Camino de Oeste
To Saguaro National Park (West)
Ironwood Hill Dr.
Kinney Rd.
Tucson Mountain Park
Gates Pass Rd.
Speedway Blvd
Anklam Rd
Silverlake Rd.
Mission Rd.
SAN XAVIER INDIAN RESERVATION
Historic Districts
W. 6th St.
E. 6th St.
N. Main Ave.
EL PRESIDIO HISTORIC DISTRICT
N. Stone Ave.
N. 6th Ave.
E. 7th St.
N. 4th Ave.
Franklin St.
E. 8th St.
Church Ave.
Toole Ave.
E. 9th St.
N. 1st Ave.
Alameda St.
Pennington St.
E. 10th St.
Congress St.
Broadway Blvd.
Granada Ave.
Tucson Convention Center
E. 12th St.
Armory Park
S. Stone Ave.
E. 13th St.
Cushing St.
E. 14th St.
ARMORY PARK HISTORIC DISTRICT
Simpson St.
Kennedy St.
S. Main Ave.
BARRIO HISTORICO
E. 16th St.
S. 3rd Ave.
W. 17th St.
E. 17th St.
Osborne Ave.
W. 18th St.
E. 18th St.
S. 4th Ave.
S. 6th Ave.
W. 19th St.
E. 19th St.
W. 20th St.
E. 20th St.
0 1/2 mi
0 0.5 km

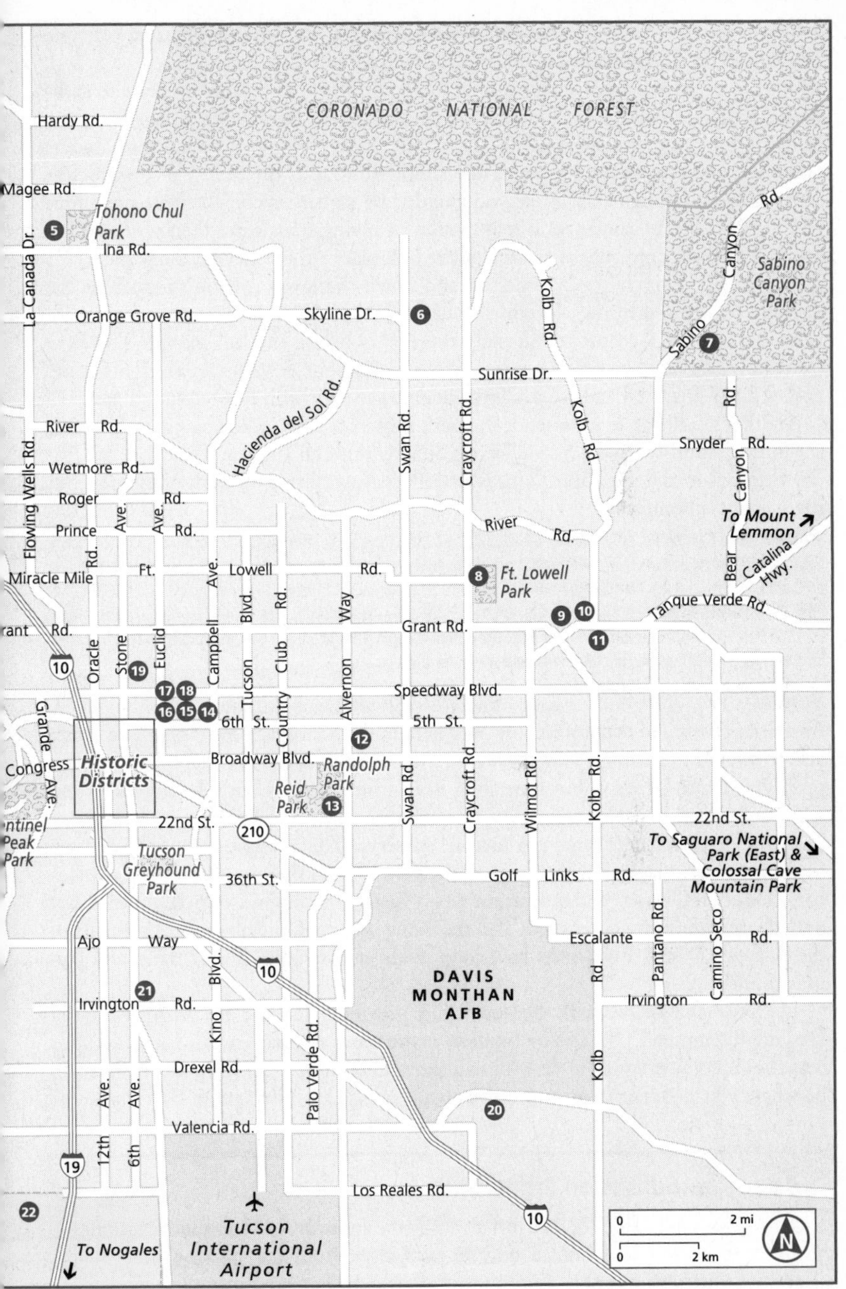

CORONADO NATIONAL FOREST
Hardy Rd.
Magee Rd.
Tohono Chul Park
Ina Rd.
La Canada Dr.
Orange Grove Rd.
Skyline Dr.
Kolb Rd.
Sabino Canyon Park
Sabino Canyon Rd.
Sunrise Dr.
Hacienda del Sol Rd.
Swan Rd.
Craycroft Rd.
River Rd.
Wetmore Rd.
Snyder Rd.
Bear Canyon Rd.
Roger Rd.
Prince Rd.
Flowing Wells Rd.
To Mount Lemmon
Catalina Hwy.
Miracle Mile
Ft. Lowell Rd.
Ft. Lowell Park
Tanque Verde Rd.
Grant Rd.
Oracle Rd.
Stone Ave.
Euclid Ave.
Campbell Ave.
Tucson Blvd.
Country Club Rd.
Alvernon Way
Speedway Blvd.
6th St.
5th St.
Grande Ave.
Congress
Historic Districts
Broadway Blvd.
Randolph Park
Reid Park
Wilmot Rd.
22nd St.
Sentinel Peak Park
210
To Saguaro National Park (East) & Colossal Cave Mountain Park
Tucson Greyhound Park
36th St.
Golf Links Rd.
Ajo Way
Escalante Rd.
Pantano Rd.
Camino Seco Rd.
Kino Blvd.
DAVIS MONTHAN AFB
Irvington Rd.
Palo Verde Rd.
Drexel Rd.
12th Ave.
6th Ave.
Valencia Rd.
Los Reales Rd.
Tucson International Airport
To Nogales
10
19
0 2 mi
0 2 km
N
5 6 7 8 9 10 11 12 13 14 15 16 17 18 19 20 21 22

Sabino Canyon Recreation Area ★★ Located at the base of the Santa Catalina Mountains on the northeastern edge of the city, Sabino Canyon is a desert oasis and, with its impressive desert scenery, hiking trails, and stream, is a fabulous place to commune with the desert for a morning or an afternoon. The chance to splash in the canyon's waterfalls and swim in natural pools (water conditions permitting) attracts many visitors, but it is just as enjoyable simply to gaze at the beauty of crystal-clear water flowing through a rocky canyon guarded by saguaro cacti. There are numerous picnic tables in the canyon, and many miles of hiking trails wind their way into the mountains from here, making it one of the best places in the city for a day hike.

A narrated tram shuttles visitors up and down the lower canyon throughout the day, and between April and November (but not July or Aug), there are moonlight tram rides three times each month (usually the nights before the full moon). The Bear Canyon tram is used by hikers heading to the picturesque Seven Falls, which are at the end of a 2.5-mile trail and are my favorite destination within this recreation area.

Another good way to experience the park is by bicycling up the paved road during the limited hours when bikes are allowed: Sunday through Tuesday, Thursday, and Friday before 9am and after 5pm. This is a strenuous uphill ride for most of the way, but the scenery is beautiful.

5900 N. Sabino Canyon Rd. ✆ **520/749-8700**, 520/749-2861 for shuttle information, or 520/749-2327 for moonlight shuttle reservations. www.fs.fed.us/r3/coronado or www.sabinocanyon.com. Parking $5 (also good for driving the Catalina Hwy.). Sabino Canyon tram ride $7.50 adults, $3 children 3–12; Bear Canyon tram ride $3 adults, $1 children 3–12. Park daily dawn–dusk. Sabino Canyon tram rides daily 9am–4:30pm (July to mid-Dec Mon–Fri 9am–4pm, Sat–Sun 9am–4:30pm); Bear Canyon tram rides daily 9am–4:30pm. Take Grant Rd. east to Tanque Verde Rd., continuing east; at Sabino Canyon Rd., turn north and watch for the sign.

Saguaro National Park ★★★ Saguaro cacti are the quintessential symbol of the American desert and occur naturally only here in the Sonoran Desert. Sensitive to fire and frost, and exceedingly slow to mature, these massive, treelike cacti grow in great profusion around Tucson but have long been threatened by both development and plant collectors. In 1933, to protect these desert giants, the federal government set aside two large tracts of land as a saguaro preserve. This preserve eventually became Saguaro National Park. The two units of the park, one on the east side of the city (Rincon Mountain District) and one on the west (Tucson Mountain District), preserve not only dense stands of saguaros, but also the many other wild inhabitants of this part of the Sonoran Desert. Both units have loop roads, nature trails, hiking trails, and picnic grounds.

The west unit of the park, because of its proximity to both the Arizona–Sonora Desert Museum and Old Tucson Studios, is the more popular area to visit (and your best choice if you're trying to do a lot in a short amount of time). This also happens to be where you'll see the most impressive stands of saguaros. Be sure to take the scenic

---

Moments **Sunset on Signal Hill**

A hike to Signal Hill, located off the Bajada Loop Drive in Saguaro National Park's west unit and only a quarter-mile walk from the parking area, will reward you with not only a grand sunset vista away from the crowds at Gates Pass, but also the sight of dozens of petroglyphs.

Bajada Loop Drive, where you'll find good views and several hiking trails (the Hugh Morris Trail involves a long, steep climb, but great views are the reward). To reach the west unit of the park, follow Speedway Boulevard west from downtown Tucson (it becomes Gates Pass Blvd.).

The east section of the park contains an older area of saguaro "forest" at the foot of the Rincon Mountains. This section is popular with hikers because most of it has no roads. It has a visitor center, a loop scenic drive, a picnic area, and a trail open to mountain bikes (the paved loop drive is a great road-bike ride). To reach the east unit of the park, take Speedway Boulevard east, then head south on Freeman Road to Old Spanish Trail.

Rincon Mountain District visitor center: 3693 S. Old Spanish Trail. ✆ **520/733-5153.** Tucson Mountain District visitor center: 2700 N. Kinney Rd. ✆ **520/733-5158.** www.nps.gov/sagu. Entry fee $10 per car, $5 per hiker or biker. Daily 7am–sunset; visitor centers daily 9am–5pm; open to hikers 24 hr. a day. Visitor centers closed Christmas.

HISTORIC ATTRACTIONS BOTH REAL & REEL

Mission San Xavier del Bac ★ Called the White Dove of the Desert, Mission San Xavier del Bac, an active Roman Catholic church serving the San Xavier Indian Reservation, is a blindingly white adobe building that rises from a sere, brown landscape. Considered the finest example of mission architecture in the Southwest, the beautiful church was built between 1783 and 1797, and incorporates Moorish, Byzantine, and Mexican Renaissance architectural styles. The church, however, was never actually completed, which only becomes apparent when the two bell towers are compared. One is topped with a dome, while the other has none.

Colorful murals cover the interior walls, and behind the altar are elaborate decorations. To the left of the main altar, in a glass sarcophagus, is a statue of St. Francis Xavier, the mission's patron saint, who is believed to answer the prayers of the faithful. A visit to San Xavier's little museum provides a bit of historical perspective and a chance to explore more of the mission. To the east of the church, atop a small hill, you'll find not only an interesting view of the church, but also a replica of the famous grotto in Lourdes, France. There are often food stalls selling fry bread in the parking lot in front of the church.

1950 W. San Xavier Rd. ✆ **520/294-2624.** www.sanxaviermission.org. Free admission; donations accepted. Daily 8am–5pm. Take I-19 S 9 miles to Exit 92 and turn right.

Old Tucson Studios ★★ Kids Despite the name, this is not the historical location of the old city of Tucson—it's a Western town originally built as the set for the 1939 movie *Arizona.* In the years since, Old Tucson has been used during the filming of John Wayne's *Rio Lobo, Rio Bravo,* and *El Dorado;* Clint Eastwood's *The Outlaw Josey Wales;* Kirk Douglas's *Gunfight at the O.K. Corral;* Paul Newman's *The Life and Times of Judge Roy Bean;* and, more recently, *Tombstone* and *Geronimo.*

Today, however, Old Tucson is far more than just a movie set. In addition to serving as a site for film, TV, and advertising productions (call ahead to find out if any filming is scheduled), it has become a Wild West theme park with diverse family-oriented activities and entertainment. Throughout the day, there are staged shootouts in the streets, stunt demonstrations, a cancan musical revue, and other performances. Train and kiddie rides, restaurants, and gift shops round out the experience.

201 S. Kinney Rd. ✆ **520/883-0100.** www.oldtucson.com. Admission $17 adults, $11 children 4–11. Daily 10am–4pm. Closed Thanksgiving, Dec 24–25, and occasional special events. Take Speedway Blvd. west, continuing in the same direction when it becomes Gates Pass Blvd., and turn left on S. Kinney Rd.

Moments **Seeing It All from "A Mountain"**

The best way to get a feel for the geography of the Tucson area is to drive to the top of a mountain—but not just any mountain. "A Mountain" (officially called Sentinel Peak) rises just to the west of downtown Tucson on the far side of I-10. The peak gets its common name from the giant whitewashed letter "A" (for University of Arizona) near the summit. To get here, drive west to the end of Congress Street and turn left on Sentinel Peak Road. The park is open Monday through Saturday from 8am to 8pm and Sunday from 8am to 6pm.

ART MUSEUMS

Center for Creative Photography Have you ever wished you could see an original Ansel Adams print up close, or perhaps an Edward Weston or a Richard Avedon? You can at the Center for Creative Photography. Originally conceived by Ansel Adams, the center now holds more than 60,000 master prints by more than 2,000 of the world's best photographers, making it one of the best and largest collections in the world. The center mounts fascinating exhibits year-round and is also a research facility that preserves the photographic archives of more than 60 photographers, including Adams. While the main gallery is open on a regular basis, you must make an appointment to view images from the archives.

University of Arizona campus, 1030 N. Olive Rd. (east of Park Ave. and Speedway Blvd.). ✆ **520/621-7968.** www.creativephotography.org. Admission by donation. Mon–Fri 9am–5pm; Sat–Sun noon–5pm. Closed major holidays. Bus: 1, 4, 5, or 6.

De Grazia Gallery in the Sun Southwestern artist Ettore "Ted" De Grazia was a Tucson favorite son, and his home, a sprawling, funky adobe building in the foothills, is a city landmark and now serves as a museum for this prolific artist. De Grazia is said to be the most reproduced artist in the world because many of his images of big-eyed children were used as greeting cards during the 1950s and 1960s. Today De Grazia's images seem trite and maudlin, but in his day he was a very successful artist. This gallery is packed with original paintings, so it may surprise you to learn that, near the end of his life, De Grazia burned several hundred thousand dollars' worth of his paintings in a protest of IRS inheritance taxes. The gift shop has lots of reproductions and other objects with De Grazia images.

6300 N. Swan Rd. ✆ **800/545-2185** or 520/299-9191. www.degrazia.org. Free admission. Daily 10am–4pm. Closed New Year's Day, Easter, Thanksgiving, and Christmas.

Tucson Museum of Art & Historic Block ★ This museum complex is one of the two best reasons to venture into downtown Tucson (the other is El Charro Café). The museum includes galleries housed in historic adobe homes, a courtyard frequently used to display sculptures, and a large modern building that frequently mounts the most interesting exhibits in town. The *Palice Pavilion—Art of the Americas* exhibit is a highlight of the museum. This exhibit consists of a large collection of pre-Columbian art that represents 3,000 years of life in Mexico and Central and South America. This collection is housed in the historic Stevens/Duffield House, which also contains Spanish colonial artifacts and Latin American folk art. The noteworthy Goodman Pavilion of Western Art comprises an extensive collection that depicts cowboys, horses, and the wide-open spaces of the American West. The museum has also preserved five historic homes on this same block, all open to the public. See "History Museums & Landmark Buildings," below, for details.

140 N. Main Ave. ✆ **520/624-2333.** www.tucsonarts.com. Admission $8 adults, $6 seniors, $3 students, free for children 12 and under; free on 1st Sun of each month. Tues–Sat 10am–4pm; Sun noon–4pm. Closed major holidays. All downtown-bound buses.

The University of Arizona Museum of Art ★★ With European and American works from the Renaissance to the 20th century, the art collections at this museum are even more extensive and diverse than those of the Tucson Museum of Art. Tintoretto, Rembrandt, Picasso, O'Keeffe, Warhol, and Rothko are all represented. Another attraction, the *Retablo of Ciudad Rodrigo,* consists of 26 paintings from 15th-century Spain that were originally placed above a cathedral altar. The museum also has an extensive collection of 20th-century sculpture that includes more than 60 clay and plaster models and sketches by Jacques Lipchitz.

University of Arizona campus, Park Ave. and Speedway Blvd. ✆ **520/621-7567.** www.artmuseum.arizona.edu. Free admission. Tues–Fri 9am–5pm; Sat–Sun noon–4pm. Closed major holidays. Bus: 1, 4, 5, or 6.

HISTORY MUSEUMS & LANDMARK BUILDINGS

In addition to the attractions listed below, downtown Tucson has a couple of historic neighborhoods that are described in "Walking Tour—Downtown Historic Districts," later in this chapter. Among the more interesting buildings are those maintained by the Tucson Museum of Art and located on the block surrounding the museum. These restored homes date from 1850 to 1907, and are all built on the former site of the Tucson presidio. A map and brochures are available at the museum's front desk, and free (with admission to the museum) guided tours of the historic block and Corbett House are available.

Arizona Historical Society Downtown Museum If you want to learn more about the history of Tucson, this is the museum to visit. Exhibits cover Spanish presidio days, American army days, merchants, and schools. Through the use of artifacts and old photos, these exhibits help bring the city's past to life. One of the most curious exhibits focuses on the gangster John Dillinger, who was arrested here in Tucson.

140 N. Stone Ave. ✆ **520/770-1473.** www.arizonahistoricalsociety.org. Admission $3 adults, $2 seniors and students ages 12–18, free for children under 12; free on 1st Fri of each month. Mon–Fri 10am–4pm. Closed major holidays. All downtown-bound buses.

Arizona Historical Society Tucson Main Museum As the state's oldest historical museum, this repository of all things Arizonan is a treasure-trove for the history

---

Finds The Conley Museum of the West

Although little more than a room at the back of the **Mark Sublette Medicine Man Gallery,** 7000 E. Tanque Verde Rd. (✆ **520/722-7798;** www.medicinemangallery.com), the **Conley Museum of the West** packs a lot into a tiny space. You can see not only 19th- and 20th-century pieces by some of the biggest names in Western art, but also Indian artifacts and art, Spanish colonial antiquities, and historical maps dating back to 1739. This place is a must for fans of Western art. The museum is open Monday through Saturday from 10am to 5pm and Sunday from 1 to 4pm. Admission is free.

---

buff. If you've never explored a real mine, you can do the next best thing by exploring the museum's full-scale reproduction of an underground mine tunnel. You'll see an assayer's office, miner's tent, stamp mill, and blacksmith's shop in the mining exhibit. A transportation exhibit displays stagecoaches and the horseless carriages that revolutionized life in the Southwest, while temporary other exhibits also give a pretty good idea of what it was like back then.

949 E. Second St. ✆ **520/628-5774.** www.arizonahistoricalsociety.org. Admission $5 adults, $4 seniors and students ages 12–18, free for children under 12; free for all on the 1st Sat of each month. Mon–Sat 10am–4pm. Closed major holidays. Bus: 1, 4, 5, or 6.

Arizona State Museum This museum, which is the oldest anthropological museum in the Southwest, houses *Paths of Life: American Indians of the Southwest,* one of the state's most interesting exhibits on prehistoric and contemporary Native American cultures of the Southwest. The exhibit focuses on 10 different tribes from around the Southwest and northern Mexico, not only displaying a wide range of artifacts, but also exploring the lifestyles and cultural traditions of Indians living in the region today. In addition, the museum showcases a collection of some 20,000 ceramic pieces. This pottery spans 2,000 years of life in the desert Southwest.

University of Arizona campus, 1013 E. University Blvd. at Park Ave. ✆ **520/621-6302.** www.statemuseum.arizona.edu. Admission $3 suggested donation. Mon–Sat 10am–5pm; Sun noon–5pm. Closed major holidays. Bus: 1, 4, 5, or 6.

Fort Lowell Museum Located in Fort Lowell Park, this museum is on the site of a cavalry outpost that was in operation between 1873 and 1891. The museum chronicles the history of life at the fort, and some of the ruins of the original fort can still be seen. Before it was a fort, this site was a Hohokam village, and artifacts uncovered from archaeological digs are also on display. Renowned medical researcher Walter Reed, who discovered how yellow fever is transmitted, served as base surgeon here in 1876. A display focusing on medical facilities at the fort explains that, despite Hollywood's version of history, injury from Indian attacks was not the biggest medical problem during the wars with the Apaches.

2900 N. Craycroft Rd. ✆ **520/885-3832.** www.arizonahistoricalsociety.org. Admission $3 adults, $2 seniors and students ages 12–18, free for children under 12; free for all on the 1st Sat of each month. Wed–Sat 10am–4pm. Closed major holidays. Bus: 34.

Sosa-Carillo-Frémont House Museum Located on the shady grounds of the modern Tucson Convention Center, the Sosa-Carillo-Frémont House is a classic example of Sonoran-style adobe architecture. Originally built in the 1870s, the house was rented in 1878 to territorial governor John Charles Frémont, who had led a distinguished military career as an explorer of the West. The building has been restored in the style of this period, and all rooms are decorated with period antiques. The flat roof is made of pine beams called *vigas,* which were traditionally covered with saguaro cactus ribs and topped by a layer of hard-packed mud. From November through mid-April, this museum offers six different tours of historic Tucson ($10 for adults, free for children under 12) on Thursday and Saturday mornings at 10am.

151 S. Granada Ave. (in the Tucson Convention Center complex). ✆ **520/622-0956.** Admission $3 adults, $2 seniors and students ages 12–18, free for children under 12; free on 1st Sat of each month. Wed–Sat 10am–4pm. Closed major holidays. All downtown-bound buses.

Southern Arizona Transportation Museum Housed in a building adjacent to the former Southern Pacific Railroad Depot, which was built in 1941 and restored in 2004, this little museum is worth a visit as much for the opportunity to wander

Value Passport to Tucson

The **Tucson Attractions Passport** is a great way to save money on admissions to many of the city's top attractions. The passport, available at the downtown Visitors Center, 100 S. Church St. (✆ **800/638-8350** or 520/624-1817; www.tucson passport.com), costs $15 and gets you two-for-one admissions to the Arizona–Sonora Desert Museum, Old Tucson Studios, Biosphere 2, the Pima Air & Space Museum, Tohono Chul Park, the Tucson Museum of Art, Kartchner Caverns State Park, and many other attractions in Tucson and across southern Arizona.

around the depot grounds as to see the museum's exhibits. The exhibits focus on the history of the railroad in southern Arizona. On the grounds are an old steam engine (open to the public Sat 10am–1pm) and a statue of Doc Holliday and Wyatt Earp.

414 N. Toole Ave. ✆ **520/623-2223.** www.tucsonhistoricdepot.org. Free admission. Tues–Thurs 11am–3pm; Fri–Sat 10am–4pm; Sun 11am–3pm. All downtown-bound buses.

Tucson Rodeo Parade Museum A parade must be pretty special to warrant its own museum, and Tucson's Fiesta de los Vaqueros Rodeo Parade is indeed special. It's the longest nonmotorized parade in the country and includes all manner of horse-drawn carriages, buggies, and wagons. If you don't plan on being in town for the rodeo, you can still see lots of those old horse-drawn vehicles at this museum. Included in the collection is the original surrey with the fringe on top that was used in the filming of *Oklahoma* (which was shot not in Oklahoma but in southern Arizona near the town of Patagonia). There's also a beautiful carriage that was used by Ava Gardner during the filming of *The Life and Times of Judge Roy Bean.* There are more than 150 vehicles on display here, as well as a wide variety of other displays focusing on the early history of Tucson. The only drawback of this fascinating museum is that it's open for only a couple of months each year (mid-Dec and early Jan to mid-Mar).

4823 S. Sixth Ave. ✆ **520/294-1280.** www.tucsonrodeoparade.com. Admission $5; free for children under 16. Mon–Sat 9:30am–3:30pm. Closed mid-Mar to mid-Dec, last week of Dec, and certain days during rodeo week (late Feb). Bus: 6, 8, 11, or 26.

SCIENCE & TECHNOLOGY MUSEUMS

Biosphere 2 *Overrated* For 2 years, beginning in September 1991, four men and four women were locked inside this airtight, 3-acre greenhouse in the desert 35 miles north of Tucson near the town of Oracle. During their tenure in Biosphere 2 (earth is considered Biosphere 1), they conducted experiments on how the earth, basically a giant greenhouse, manages to support all the planet's life forms. Today there are no longer any people living in Biosphere 2, and the former research facility is operated more as a tourist attraction than as a science center. Tours take visitors inside the giant greenhouse and into the mechanisms that helped keep this sealed environment going for 2 years. The strangest sight is the giant "lung" that allowed for the expansion and contraction of the air within Biosphere 2. Although the building, which sits in the middle of desert hill country, is an impressive sight, the tours are something of a letdown.

32540 S. Biosphere Rd. (off Ariz. 77 at mile marker 96.5). ✆ **520/838-6200.** www.bio2.com. Admission $20 ages 13 and older, $13 children 6–12. Daily 9am–4pm. Closed Thanksgiving and Christmas. Take Oracle Rd. north out of Tucson and continue north on Ariz. 77 until you see the sign.

Flandrau Science Center & Planetarium Located on the University of Arizona campus, Flandrau Planetarium is the most convenient place in Arizona to do a little stargazing through a professional telescope. As such, it should be on the itinerary of anyone coming to Tucson (unless it happens to be cloudy). The planetarium theater presents a variety of programs on the stars, and the exhibit halls contain a large mineral collection and hands-on science exhibits. However, the best reason to visit is to gaze through the planetarium's 16-inch telescope.

University of Arizona campus, 1601 E. University Blvd., at Cherry Ave. © **520/621-STAR.** www.flandrau.org. Telescope viewing free. $2.50 per person. Wed 6–9pm; Thurs–Fri 9am–3pm and 6–9pm; Sat noon–9pm; Sun noon–5pm. Telescope viewing (weather permitting) Wed–Sat 7–10pm. Closed major holidays. Bus: 1, 3, 4, 5, 9, or 15.

The International Wildlife Museum This castlelike building (modeled after a French Foreign Legion fort), located on the road that leads to the Arizona–Sonora Desert Museum, is a natural-history museum filled with stuffed animals in lifelike poses and surroundings. Animals from all over the world are displayed, and there are exhibits of extinct animals, including the Irish elk and the woolly mammoth. Among the more lifelike displays are the predator-and-prey exhibits. There are also fascinating exhibits of butterflies and other unusual insects.

4800 W. Gates Pass Rd. © **520/629-0100.** www.thewildlifemuseum.org. Admission $7 adults, $5.50 seniors and students, $2.50 children 4–12. Mon–Fri 9am–5pm; Sat–Sun 9am–6pm. Closed Thanksgiving and Christmas. Take Speedway Blvd. W., continuing in the same direction when it becomes Gates Pass Blvd. The museum is 5 miles west of I-10.

Pima Air & Space Museum ★ Located just south of Davis Monthan Air Force Base, the Pima Air & Space Museum houses one of the largest collections of historic aircraft in the world. On display are more than 250 aircraft, including an X-15 (the world's fastest aircraft), an SR-71 Blackbird, several Russian MiGs, a "Superguppy," and a B-17G "Flying Fortress." Tours are available.

The museum also offers guided tours of Davis Monthan's AMARC (Arizona Maintenance and Regeneration Center) facility, which goes by the name of the Boneyard. Here, thousands of mothballed military planes are lined up in neat rows under the Arizona sun. Tours last just under an hour and cost $6 for adults and $3 for children 12 and under. Tour reservations (© **520/574-0462**) should be made about a week in advance.

6000 E. Valencia Rd. © **520/574-0462.** www.pimaair.org. Admission Nov–May $14 adults, $11 seniors and military, $9 children 7–12; June–Oct $12 adults, $9.75 seniors and military, $8 children 7–12. Daily 9am–5pm. Closed Thanksgiving and Christmas. Take the Valencia Rd. exit from I-10 and drive east 2 miles to the museum.

Titan Missile Museum ★ If you've ever wondered what it would be like to have your finger on the button of a nuclear missile, here's your opportunity to find out. This deactivated intercontinental ballistic missile (ICBM) silo is now a museum—and is the only museum in the country that allows visitors to descend into a former missile silo. There's a huge Titan missile on display, and, even without its nuclear warhead, it is a terrifying sight. The guided tours do a great job of explaining not only the ICBM system, but also what life was like for the people who worked here. Operated by the Pima Air & Space Museum, this museum is located 25 miles south of Tucson near the community of Green Valley. On the first Saturday of each month, there is a special reservation-only "Beyond the Blast Doors" tour that takes visitors into areas not on the normal tour. There are also special tours on Tuesdays at 2pm. Other special tours are also available, and it is even possible to spend the night in the silo. Contact the museum for details.

1580 W. Duval Mine Rd., Sahuarita (Exit 69 off I-19). ✆ **520/625-7736.** Admission $8.50 adults, $7.50 seniors, $5 children 7–12; Beyond the Blast Door Tour $18 adults, $16 seniors, $9.95 children 8–12. Daily 9am–5pm. Closed Thanksgiving and Christmas. Take I-19 south to Green Valley; take Exit 69 W a half-mile to main entrance.

PARKS, GARDENS & ZOOS

See "The Tucson Area's (Mostly) Natural Wonders," earlier in this chapter, for details on the Arizona–Sonora Desert Museum, the region's premier zoo.

Reid Park Zoo *Kids* Although small and overshadowed by the Arizona–Sonora Desert Museum, the Reid Park Zoo makes a fun in-town destination if you have the kids along. The zoo has good Africa, Asia, and South America enclosures that include African and Asian elephants, white rhinoceroses, giraffes, anteaters, capybaras (the largest rodents in the world), and rheas (sort of like ostriches). Get here early, when the animals are more active and before the crowds hit. If you've got the kids along, there's a good playground in the adjacent park.

1030 S. Randolph Way (at 22nd St. between Country Club Rd. and Alvernon Way). ✆ **520/791-4022.** www.tucsonzoo.org. Admission $6 adults, $4 seniors, $2 children 2–14. Daily 9am–4pm. Closed Christmas. Bus: 7.

Tohono Chul Park ★★ Although this park covers fewer than 50 acres, it provides an excellent introduction to the plant and animal life of the desert. You'll see a forest of cholla cacti as well as a garden of small pincushion cacti. From mid-February to April, the wildflower displays here are gorgeous (if enough rain has fallen in the previous months). The park also includes an ethnobotanical garden; a garden for children that encourages them to touch, listen, and smell; a demonstration garden; natural areas; an exhibit house for art displays; a tearoom (p. 353) that's great for breakfast, lunch, or afternoon tea; and two very good gift shops. Park docents lead guided tours throughout the day. There are also bird walks and many other special events throughout the cooler months of the year.

7366 N. Paseo del Norte (off Ina Rd. west of the intersection with Oracle Rd.). ✆ **520/742-6455.** www.tohonochulpark.org. Admission $5 adults, $4 seniors, $3 students, $2 children ages 5–12; free for all on 1st Tues of every month. Grounds daily 8am–5pm (visitors may remain until sunset). Exhibit house daily 9am–5pm. Tearoom daily 8am–5pm. Buildings closed New Year's Day, July 4th, Thanksgiving, and Christmas (free admission to grounds on these days).

Tucson Botanical Gardens Set amid residential neighborhoods in midtown Tucson, these gardens are an oasis of greenery and, though small, are well worth a visit if you happen to be interested in desert plant life, landscaping, or gardening. On the 5½-acre grounds, there are a dozen different gardens that not only have visual appeal, but are also educational. You can learn about creating a garden for birds or for butterflies, and then see what sort of crops the Native Americans of this region have traditionally grown. A sensory garden stimulates all five senses. In past years, there has been a tropical butterfly house here from fall through spring.

2150 N. Alvernon Way. ✆ **520/326-9686.** www.tucsonbotanical.org. Admission $5 adults, $2.50 children 6–12. Daily 8:30am–4:30pm. Closed New Year's Day, July 4th, Thanksgiving, and Dec 24–25. Bus: 11.

ESPECIALLY FOR KIDS

In addition to the museums listed below, two of the greatest places to take kids in the Tucson area are the Arizona–Sonora Desert Museum and Old Tucson Studios. Kids will also get a kick out of the Sabino Canyon tram ride, the Reid Park Zoo, Flandrau Science Center & Planetarium, and the Pima Air & Space Museum. All are described in detail earlier in this chapter.

Kids All Aboard!

If you've got kids who idolize Thomas the Tank Engine, then you'd better schedule your Tucson visit for the second or fourth Sunday of the month. On those days (with a few exceptions), the **Gadsden-Pacific Division Toy Train Operating Museum,** 3975 N. Miller Ave. (✆ **520/888-2222;** http://hometown.aol.com/ienglish), sends out little engines that think they can. The trains chug around a variety of layouts built in different model railroad gauges. The museum is open from 12:30 to 4:30pm 2 days each month. Admission is free. In July and August, the museum is closed.

They'll also enjoy **Trail Dust Town,** 6541 E. Tanque Verde Rd. (✆ **520/296-5442;** www.traildusttown.com), a Wild West–themed shopping and dining center. It has a full-size carousel, a scaled-down train to ride, shootout shows, and miniature golf next door. Basically, it's a sort of scaled-down Old Tucson. If the kids are into miniature golf, take them to **Golf n' Stuff,** 6503 E. Tanque Verde Rd. (✆ **520/296-2366;** www.golfnstuff.com), which is right next door to Trail Dust Town. Not only is there a miniature golf course, there are bumper boats, go-karts, batting cages, laser tag, a climbing wall, and a video-game arcade. Between these two side-by-side attractions, you've got plenty to keep the family entertained for hours.

T Rex Museum ★ If you've got kids who are crazy for dinosaurs, be sure to bring them to this little homegrown private museum that likes to make learning about dinosaurs fun. There are exhibits of live insects and reptiles to give context to the fossils that are on display, and videos about dinosaurs are screened throughout the day.

100 E. Drachman St. ✆ **520/792-2884.** www.trexmuseum.org. Admission $5 per person. Mon–Sat 10am–5pm; Sun noon–5pm. Closed Easter, July 4th, Thanksgiving, and Christmas. Bus: 10 or 16.

Tucson Children's Museum This museum, in the historic Carnegie Library in downtown Tucson, is filled with fun and educational hands-on activities. Exhibits include a bakery and farmers' market and an electricity gallery. Expect to find such perennial kid favorites as a fire truck, a toy train, and dinosaur sculptures. Activities are featured daily.

200 S. Sixth Ave. ✆ **520/792-9985.** www.tucsonchildrensmuseum.org. Admission $7 adults, $5 seniors, $3.50 children 2–16; free 1 day each month (call for date). Tues–Sat 10am–5pm; Sun noon–5pm. Closed Thanksgiving and Christmas. All downtown-bound buses.

WALKING TOUR DOWNTOWN HISTORIC DISTRICTS

Start: Arizona Historical Society Downtown Museum.

Finish: Hotel Congress.

Time: 5 hours.

Best Times: Weekends, when restaurants aren't packed at lunch.

Worst Times: Summer, when it's just too hot to do any walking.

Tucson has a long and varied cultural history, which is most easily seen on a walking tour of the downtown historic neighborhoods. Start your explorations in El Presidio Historic District, which is named for the Presidio of San Augustín del Tucson (founded 1775), the Spanish garrison built here to protect the San Xavier del Bac Mission from the Apaches. For many years, the presidio was the heart of Tucson, and although no original buildings still stand, there is a recent reconstruction of part of the presidio, and numerous structures from the mid–19th century remain.

After finding a parking space at the large public lot at the corner of Court Avenue and Council Street, walk 1 block east on Council Street to Church Avenue and 1 block south to the corner of Washington Street, where you'll find a reconstruction of part of the:

❶ Tucson Presidio

Opened in 2007, this reconstruction of part of the Spanish fort that was the birthplace of Tucson is built of adobe blocks. Inside the walls and in an adjacent adobe building, you'll find displays on the early history of Tucson.

From the presidio building, walk 1 block south on Church Avenue and 1 block east on Alameda Street to Stone Avenue. Cross Stone, turn right, and walk half a block to the:

❷ Arizona Historical Society Downtown Museum

This museum, at 140 N. Stone Ave., is housed in the Wells Fargo bank building and is the perfect introduction to the history of Tucson. Spend an hour or so here getting acquainted with the city's past, and you'll get much more out of the rest of this walking tour.

From the museum, head west 2 blocks on Alameda Street, turn right on Court Avenue, and continue north for a block to Tucson's premier crafts market:

❸ Old Town Artisans

This adobe building, at 201 N. Court Ave., dates from 1862 and has numerous rooms full of interesting (and occasionally tacky) Southwestern crafts (see "Shopping," later in this chapter, for details). The central courtyard has shady gardens. You could spend hours browsing through the assortment of crafts here, but keep in mind you've still got a long walk ahead of you.

Across Meyer Avenue from this building's southwest corner is:

❹ La Casa Cordova

This building, at 175 N. Meyer Ave., dates from about 1848 and is one of the oldest in Tucson. Although the art museum owns five historic homes on this block, this is the only one that has been restored to look as it might have in the late 1800s. Each year from November to March, this building exhibits a very elaborate *nacimiento,* a Mexican folk-art nativity scene, with images from the Bible and Latin American history rolled into one miniature landscape full of angels, greenery, and Christmas lights.

Through a colorful gate just to the south of La Casa Cordova is the entrance to the:

❺ Tucson Museum of Art

This museum houses collections of pre-Columbian and Western art, as well as exhibits of contemporary works. A visit will not only allow you to see plenty of art, but will also provide a glimpse inside a couple of historic homes that now serve as museum galleries.

After touring the museum, walk back up Meyer Avenue; at the end of the block, you will find the:

❻ Romero House

This 1868 house may incorporate part of the original presidio wall, but it has been extensively altered over the years. At one time it even served as a gas station. The Romero House now contains the Tucson Museum of Art School.

From the Romero House, turn left onto Washington Street and then left again onto Main Avenue. The first building you'll come to on this side of the art museum's historic block is the:

❼ Corbett House

This restored mission-revival-style building, at 180 N. Main Ave., was built in 1907. The house, which is set back behind a green lawn, is strikingly different from the older, Sonoran-style adobe homes on this block. On Tuesday at 11am, the Tucson Museum of Art offers a guided tour of the Corbett House.

Next door to this home is the:

8 Stevens House

Located at 150 N. Main Ave., this is a Sonoran-style row house completed in 1866. It currently houses the museum's collection of pre-Columbian, Spanish colonial, and Latin American folk art, as well as a cafe, and is entered through the art museum's courtyard.

Next door is the:

9 Fish House

This house, at 120 N. Main Ave., was built in 1867 on the site of old Mexican barracks. Named for Edward Nye Fish, a local merchant, it now houses the museum's Western-art collection. Some of the walls of this house are 2 feet thick, and ceilings in some places are made from old packing crates.

From here, head back up Main Avenue; on your right at the far end of the next block, you'll reach the:

10 Julius Kruttschnidt House

This house, at 297 N. Main Ave., dates from 1886 and houses a bed-and-breakfast inn. Victorian trappings, including a long veranda, disguise the adobe origins of this unique and beautifully restored home.

Across Main Avenue from the B&B is the:

11 Steinfeld House

This house, at 300 N. Main Ave., was built in 1900 in California mission-revival style and was designed by Henry Trost, Tucson's most noted architect. It served as the original Owl's Club, a gentlemen's club for some of Tucson's most eligible bachelors of the time.

Another block north on Main Avenue stands the:

12 Owl's Club Mansion

This impressive mansion, at 378 N. Main Ave., was built in 1902 and designed by Henry Trost in the mission-revival style, albeit with a great deal of ornamentation. It replaced the Steinfeld House as home to the bachelors of the Owl's Club.

TAKE A BREAK

If you started your tour late in the morning, you're probably hungry by now. Continue north on Main Avenue to Franklin Street and walk east on Franklin to Court Avenue. Turn right onto Court, and you will find **El Charro Café** (p. 343), Tucson's oldest Mexican restaurant. Be sure to order *carne seca,* the house specialty.

From here, continue south on Court Avenue and cross Alameda Street to reach:

13 El Presidio Park/Plaza de las Armas

This was once the parade ground for the presidio and is now a shady gathering spot for everyone from downtown office workers to the homeless. Here on the plaza, you'll see a life-size bronze statue of a presidio soldier, as well as a statue commemorating the Mormon Battalion's visit to Tucson in 1846.

Just to the east of the park is the very impressive:

14 Pima County Courthouse

Built in 1928, this courthouse, at 115 N. Church Ave. incorporates Moorish, Spanish, and Southwestern architectural features, including a colorful tiled dome. A portion of the original presidio wall is in a glass case inside the building.

From the courthouse, continue south 2 blocks (across two pedestrian bridges) to the colorfully painted:

15 La Placita Village

This complex of offices and restaurants, at 110 S. Church Ave., was designed to resemble a Mexican village. It houses Tucson's visitor center and also incorporates the Samaniego House, a Sonoran-style row house that dates from the 1880s.

Adjacent to La Placita Village is the:

Walking Tour: Downtown Historic Districts

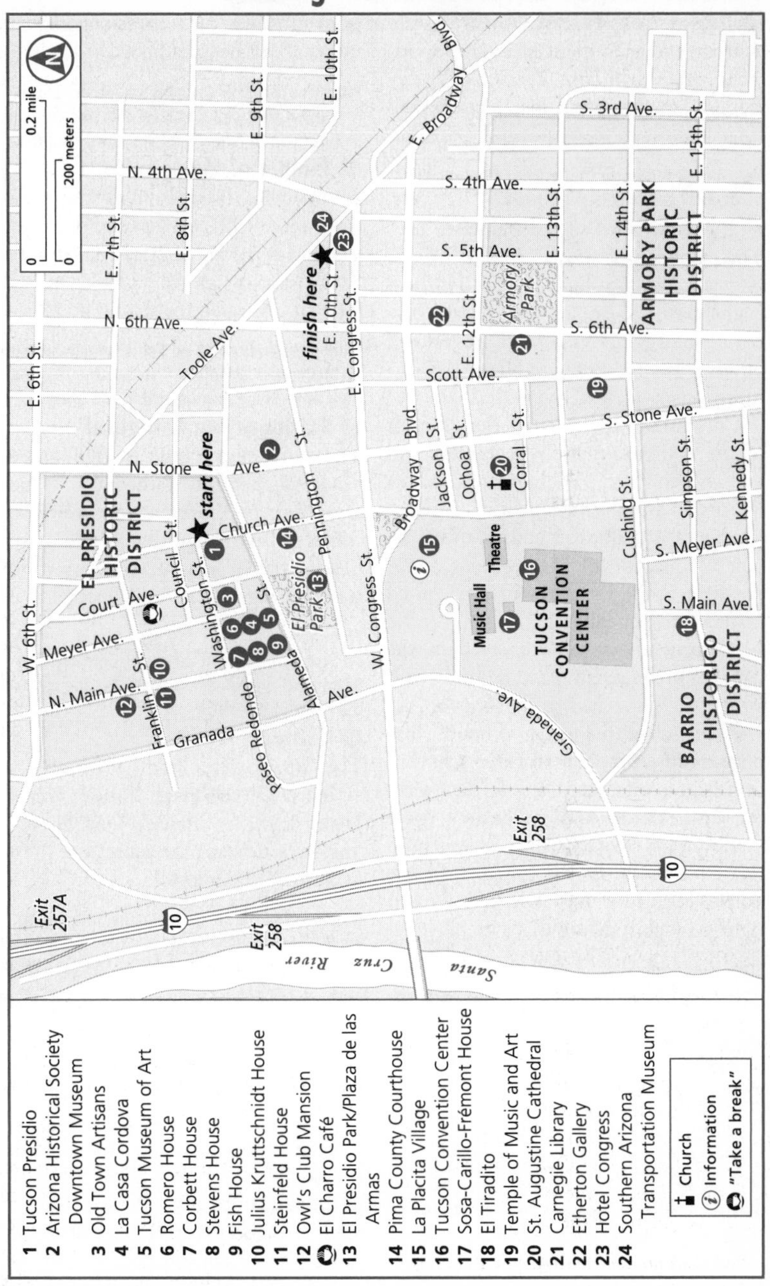

⓰ Tucson Convention Center

This sprawling complex includes a sports arena, grand ballroom, concert hall, theater, pavilions, meeting halls, gardens, and some interesting sculptures and fountains.

Near the fountains in the center of the convention center complex is the historic:

⓱ Sosa-Carillo-Frémont House

This adobe structure, located at 151 S. Granada Ave., was built in the 1850s and later served as the home of territorial governor John C. Frémont. The restored building is open to the public and is furnished in the style of the period.

Continue south through the grounds of the convention center complex, and you will come to Cushing Street, across which lies the Barrio Histórico District. With its 150 adobe row houses, this is the largest collection of 19th-century Sonoran-style adobe buildings in the United States. In the early 1970s, the entire neighborhood was almost razed in the name of urban renewal and highway construction. About half of downtown Tucson, including the neighborhoods that once stood on the site of today's convention center, was razed before the voices for preservation and restoration were finally heard. In fact, if it had not been for the activism of the residents of the Barrio Histórico, I-10 would now run right through much of this area.

Start your exploration of the northern (and more restored) blocks of the Barrio Histórico neighborhood by crossing Cushing Street and then turning down Main Avenue, where you will find, on the west side of the street in the first block:

⓲ El Tiradito

El Tiradito (The Castaway) is the only shrine in the United States dedicated to a sinner buried in unconsecrated soil, and people still light candles here in hopes of having their wishes come true.

Wander a while through the Barrio Histórico District, admiring the Sonoran-style homes that are built right out to the street. Many of these homes sport colorfully painted facades, signs of the ongoing renovation of this neighborhood.

From the corner of Cushing Street and South Meyer Avenue, walk 3 blocks east and turn left on South Scott Avenue, where you'll find the:

⓳ Temple of Music and Art

This building, located at 330 S. Scott Ave., was built in 1927 as a movie and stage theater and is the home of the Arizona Theatre Company (p. 389). Don't miss the little art gallery on the second floor.

From here, walk north on Scott Avenue, turn left on McCormick Street/13th Street, and then turn right onto Stone Avenue, which will bring you to:

⓴ St. Augustine Cathedral

The cathedral was built in 1896 and was modeled after the Cathedral of Querétaro, Mexico. Above the door, you'll see a statue of Saint Augustine as well as symbols of the Arizona desert—the horned toad, the saguaro, and the yucca.

From here, walk east on Corral Street, turn left on Scott Avenue, and then turn right on 12th Street and right again on Sixth Avenue to reach the front of the old:

㉑ Carnegie Library

The library dates from 1901 and was designed by celebrated Tucson architect Henry Trost. The building now houses the Tucson Children's Museum (see "Especially for Kids," above).

Now head north on Sixth Avenue. In 1 block, you'll pass the:

㉒ Etherton Gallery

This second-floor gallery (p. 380), upstairs from the popular Barrio restaurant, has long been one of Tucson's top contemporary art galleries.

Continue 1 more block north and turn right on Congress Street. In 1 block, you will see on the far side of the street the:

㉓ Hotel Congress

This hotel, located at 311 E. Congress St., was built as a railroad hotel in 1919 and once hosted John Dillinger, infamous public enemy number one. Today, the restored budget lodging (p. 334) is popular with

European travelers and students, and has a classic Western-style lobby. There's a cafe here, and the lobby is well worth a stroll-through.

Walk out the back door of the Hotel Congress and cross the street to the:

㉔ Southern Arizona Transportation Museum

This small museum, at 414 N. Toole Ave., is on the grounds of the historic 1941 Southern Pacific Railroad Depot. Outside is an old steam locomotive, and inside are exhibits on the early days of railroads in southern Arizona. On the depot grounds, keep an eye out for the statue of Wyatt Earp and Doc Holliday.

6 Organized Tours

Learning Expeditions, a program run by the **Arizona State Museum,** occasionally offers scholar-led archaeological tours. For information, contact the marketing department at the museum (✆ **520/626-8381;** www.statemuseum.arizona.edu).

For a look at a completely different sort of excavation, head 15 miles south of Tucson to the **ASARCO Mineral Discovery Center,** 1421 W. Pima Mine Rd., Sahuarita (✆ **520/625-7513;** www.mineraldiscovery.com), where you can tour a huge open-pit copper mine and learn about copper mining past and present. The center is open Tuesday through Saturday from 9am to 5pm; admission is free. November through April, 1-hour mine tours are offered five times a day. These tours cost $6 for adults, $5 for seniors, and $4 for children 5 to 12. To get here, drive south from Tucson on I-19 and take Exit 80. You might want to combine this tour with a visit to the nearby Titan Missile Museum.

Want to taste raw cactus, learn about cholla-extraction devices, and hold a live tarantula or snake? Call **Sunshine Jeep Tours** (✆ **520/742-1943;** www.sunshinejeeptours.com), which has a two-person minimum and charges $130 for the first two people and then, after the minimum is met, charges $50 for adults, $35 for children 11 to 15, and $25 for children 6 to 10. On these tours, you'll head out across a private ranch northwest of Tucson and pass through some of the densest stands of saguaro cacti in the state.

7 Outdoor Pursuits

BICYCLING Tucson is one of the best bicycling cities in the country, and the dirt roads and trails of the surrounding national forest and desert are perfect for mountain biking. Rentals at **Fair Wheel Bikes,** 1110 E. Sixth St. (✆ **520/884-9018**), go for $40 per day for road bikes and $30 per day for mountain bikes.

If you'd rather confine your pedaling to paved surfaces, there are some great options around town. The number-one choice in town for cyclists in halfway decent shape is the road up **Sabino Canyon** (p. 360). Keep in mind, however, that bicycles are allowed on this road only 5 days a week and then only before 9am and after 5pm (the road is closed to bikes all day Wed and Sat). For a much easier ride, try the **Rillito River Park path,** which currently has a 1-mile paved section between Swan and Craycroft roads and a 6-mile paved section between Campbell Avenue and I-10. The trail parallels River Road and the usually dry bed of the Rillito River, and if you've got knobby tires, you can link the two paved sections or continue west past La Cholla Road after the pavement ends. Another option close to downtown is the 7-mile **Santa**

Cruz River Park path, which runs along both sides of the usually dry Santa Cruz River and extends from West Grant Road to Irvington Road.

If mountain biking is more your speed, there are lots of great rides in the Tucson area. For an easy and very scenic dirt-road loop through forests of saguaros, head to the west unit of Saguaro National Park (p. 360) and ride the 6-mile **Bajada Loop Drive.** You can turn this into a 12-mile ride (half on paved road) by starting at the Red Hills Visitor Center.

BIRD-WATCHING Southern Arizona has some of the best bird-watching in the country, and although the best spots are south of Tucson, there are a few places around the city that birders will enjoy seeking out. Call the **Tucson Audubon Society's Rare Bird Alert** (✆ **520/798-1005**) to find out which birds have been spotted in the area lately.

The city's premier birding spot is the **Sweetwater Wetland,** a man-made wetland just west of I-10 and north of Prince Road. These wetlands were created as part of a wastewater treatment facility and now have an extensive network of trails that wind past numerous ponds and canals. There are several viewing platforms and enough different types of wildlife habitat that the area attracts a wide variety of bird species. To find the wetlands, take I-10 south to the Prince Road exit, and at the end of the exit ramp, turn right onto Sweetwater Drive. If you're driving west on Prince Road, go to the end of the road, turn right on Business Center Drive, turn left on River Park Road (which becomes Commerce Dr.), take the first left (probably unmarked), and then turn left again on Sweetwater Drive. Note that the wetlands are closed on Monday mornings from late March to mid-November.

Roy P. Drachman Agua Caliente Park, 12325 E. Roger Rd. (off N. Soldier Trail), in the northeast corner of the city, is just about the best place in Tucson to see birds. The year-round warm springs here are a magnet for dozens of species, including waterfowl, great blue herons, black phoebes, soras, and vermilion flycatchers. To find the park, follow Tanque Verde Road east 6 miles from the intersection with Sabino Canyon Road and turn left onto Soldier Trail. Watch for signs.

Other good places include **Sabino Canyon Recreation Area** (p. 360), the path to the waterfall at **Loews Ventana Canyon Resort** (p. 336), and the **Rillito River path** between Craycroft and Swan roads.

The best area for bird-watching is **Madera Canyon National Forest Recreation Area** ★ (✆ **520/281-2296;** www.fs.fed.us/r3/coronado), about 40 miles south of the city in the Coronado National Forest. Because of the year-round water here, Madera Canyon attracts a surprising variety of bird life. Avid birders flock to this canyon from around the country in hopes of spotting more than a dozen species of hummingbirds and an equal number of flycatchers, warblers, tanagers, buntings, grosbeaks, and many rare birds not found in any other state. However, before birding became a hot activity, this canyon was popular with families looking to escape the heat down in Tucson, and the shady picnic areas and trails still get a lot of use by those who don't carry binoculars. If you're heading out for the day, arrive early—parking is very limited. To reach Madera Canyon, take the Continental Road/Madera Canyon exit off I-19; from the exit, it's another 12 miles southeast. The canyon is open daily from dawn to dusk for day use; there is a $5 day-use fee. There's also a campground ($10 per night). For information on the canyon's Santa Rita Lodge and Chuparosa Inn, see p. 340.

GOLF Although there aren't quite as many golf courses in Tucson as in Phoenix, this is still a golfer's town. For last-minute tee-time reservations, contact **Standby Golf** (✆ **800/655-5345;** www.discountteetimes.com). No fee is charged for this service.

In addition to public and municipal links, numerous resort courses allow nonguests to play. Perhaps the most famous of these are the two 18-hole courses at **Ventana Canyon Golf and Racquet Club** ★, 6200 N. Clubhouse Lane (✆ **520/577-4015**). These Tom Fazio–designed courses offer challenging desert target-style play that is nearly legendary. The 3rd hole on the Mountain Course is one of the most photographed holes in the West. In winter, greens fees are $115 to $195 (slightly less if you are staying at Loews Ventana Canyon Resort or The Lodge at Ventana Canyon).

As famous as the Ventana Canyon courses is the 27-hole **Omni Tucson National Golf Resort and Spa** ★, 2727 W. Club Dr. (✆ **520/575-7540** or 520/297-2271; www.tucsonnational.com), a traditional course that is perhaps more familiar to golfers due to the fact that it was for many years the site of the annual Tucson Open. One of the 9-hole courses here was rebuilt as a desert-style target course in 2005, which makes this a good place for an introduction to desert golfing. If you are not staying at the resort, greens fees are $185 in winter, $70 in summer.

El Conquistador Country Club, 10555 N. La Cañada Dr., Oro Valley (✆ **520/544-1800;** www.elconquistadorcc.com), with two 18-hole courses and a 9-hole course, offers stunning (and very distracting) views of the Santa Catalina Mountains. Greens fees are $55 to $125 in winter.

At **Starr Pass Country Club & Spa,** 3645 W. Starr Pass Blvd. (✆ **800/503-2898** or 520/670-0400; www.starrpasstucson.com), the fairways play up to the narrow Starr Pass, which was once a stagecoach route. Greens fees are $199 in winter.

There are many public courses around town. The **Arizona National,** 9777 E. Sabino Greens Dr. (✆ **520/749-3636;** www.arizonanationalgolfclub.com), incorporates stands of cacti and rocky outcroppings into the course layout. Greens fees are $135 to $165 in winter. **The Golf Club at Vistoso,** 955 W. Vistoso Highlands Dr. (✆ **877/548-1110** or 520/797-9900; www.vistosogolf.com), has a championship desert course, with fees of $129 to $175 in winter. **Heritage Highlands Golf & Country Club,** 4949 W. Heritage Club Blvd., Marana (✆ **520/579-7000;** www.heritagehighlands.com), is a championship desert course at the foot of the Tortolita Mountains; greens fees are $115 in winter.

Tucson Parks and Recreation operates five municipal golf courses, of which the **Randolph** and **Dell Urich,** 600 S. Alvernon Way (✆ **520/791-4161**), are the premier courses. The former has been the site of Tucson's LPGA tournament. Greens fees for 18 holes at these two courses are $42 to $56 in winter. Other municipal courses include **El Rio,** 1400 W. Speedway Blvd. (✆ **520/791-4229**); **Silverbell,** 3600 N. Silverbell Rd. (✆ **520/791-5235**); and **Fred Enke,** 8251 E. Irvington Rd. (✆ **520/791-2539**). This latter course is the city's only desert-style golf course. Greens fees for 18 holes at these three courses are $36 to $50 in winter. For general information and tee-time reservations for any of the municipal courses, visit **www.tucsoncitygolf.com**.

HIKING Tucson is nearly surrounded by mountains, most of which are protected as city and state parks, national forest, or national park, and within these public areas are hundreds of miles of hiking trails.

Saguaro National Park (✆ **520/733-5153**) flanks Tucson on both the east and west, with units accessible off Old Spanish Trail east of Tucson and past the end of Speedway Boulevard west of the city. In these areas, you can observe Sonoran Desert vegetation and wildlife, and hike among the huge saguaro cacti for which the park is named. For saguaro-spotting, the west unit is the better choice. See p. 360 for details.

Tucson Mountain Park, at the west end of Speedway Boulevard, is adjacent to Saguaro National Park and preserves a similar landscape. The parking area at Gates Pass, on Speedway, is a favorite sunset spot.

Sabino Canyon (p. 360), off Sabino Canyon Road, is one of Tucson's best hiking areas, but is also the city's most popular recreation area. A cold mountain stream here cascades over waterfalls and forms pools that make great swimming holes. The 5-mile round-trip **Seven Falls Trail,** which follows Bear Canyon deep into the mountains, is the most popular hike in the recreation area. You can take a tram to the trail head or add extra miles by hiking from the main parking lot.

With the city limits pushing right to the boundary of the Coronado National Forest, there are some convenient hiking options in Tucson's northern foothills. The **Ventana Canyon Trail** begins at a parking area adjacent to the Loews Ventana Canyon Resort (off Sunrise Dr. west of Sabino Canyon Rd.) and leads into the Ventana Canyon Wilderness. A few miles west, there's the **Finger Rock Trail,** which starts at the top of the section of Alvernon Road accessed from Skyline Drive. There are actually a couple of trails starting here, so you can hike for miles into the desert. Over near the Westward Look Resort is the **Pima Canyon Trail,** which leads into the Ventana Canyon Wilderness and is reached off Ina Road just east of Oracle Road. Both of these trails provide classic desert canyon hikes of whatever length you feel like (a dam at 3 miles on the latter trail makes a good turnaround point). Just south of the Hilton Tucson El Conquistador Golf & Tennis Resort, you'll find the **Linda Vista Trail,** which begins just off Oracle Road on Linda Vista Boulevard. This trail lies at the foot of Pusch Ridge and winds up through dense stands of prickly-pear cactus. Higher up on the trail, there are some large saguaros. Because this trail is shaded by Pusch Ridge in the morning, it's a good choice for a morning hike on a day that's going to be hot.

Catalina State Park, 11570 N. Oracle Rd. (✆ **520/628-5798;** www.azparks.gov/Parks/parkhtml/catalina.html), is set on the rugged northwest face of the Santa Catalina Mountains, between 2,500 and 3,000 feet high. Hiking trails here lead into the Pusch Ridge Wilderness; however, the park's best day hike is the 5.5-mile round-trip to **Romero Pools,** where small natural pools of water set amid the rocks are a refreshing destination on a hot day (expect plenty of other people on a weekend). This hike involves about 1,000 feet of elevation gain. Admission to the park is $6 per vehicle ($3 between Memorial Day weekend and Labor Day weekend). Adjacent to the park are horseback-riding stables, and within the park is an ancient Hohokam ruin.

One of the reasons Tucson is such a livable city is the presence of the cool (and, in winter, snow-covered) pine forests of 8,250-foot Mount Lemmon. Within the **Mount Lemmon Recreation Area,** at the end of the Catalina Highway, are many miles of trails, and the hearty hiker can even set out from down in the lowland desert and hike up into the alpine forests (although it's easier to hike from the top down). For a more leisurely excursion, drive up onto the mountain to start your hike. However, be aware that in winter, there can be snow atop Mount Lemmon. There is a $5-per-vehicle charge to use any of the sites within this recreation area. Even if you plan to only pull off at a roadside parking spot and ogle the view of the desert far below, you'll need to stop at the roadside ticket kiosk at the base of the mountain and pay your fee. For more information, contact the **Coronado National Forest Santa Catalina Ranger District,** 5700 N. Sabino Canyon Rd. (✆ **520/749-8700;** www.fs.fed.us/r3/coronado).

HORSEBACK RIDING If you want to play cowboy or just go for a leisurely ride through the desert, there are plenty of stables around Tucson where you can saddle up.

In addition to renting horses and providing guided trail rides, some of the stables below offer sunset rides with cookouts. Although reservations are not always required, they're a good idea. You can also opt to stay at a guest ranch and do as much riding as your muscles can stand.

Pusch Ridge Stables, 13700 N. Oracle Rd. (✆ **520/825-1664;** www.puschridge stables.com), is adjacent to Catalina State Park and Coronado National Forest. Rates are $30 for 1 hour, $50 for 2 hours, and $40 for a sunset ride.

Over on the east side of Tucson, there's **Spanish Trail Outfitters** (✆ **520/749-0167;** www.spanishtrailoutfitters.com), which leads rides into the foothills of the Santa Catalina Mountains off Sabino Canyon Road. Rates are $35 for a 1-hour ride, $55 for a 2-hour or sunset ride.

HOT-AIR BALLOONING The ballooning season in Tucson runs October through April. **Balloon America** (✆ **520/299-7744;** www.balloonridesusa.com) offers flights over the desert ($225) or a more adventurous trip over the foothills of the Santa Catalina Mountains ($475). **Fleur de Tucson Balloon Tours** (✆ **520/529-1025;** www.fleurdetucson.net) offers rides over the Tucson Mountains, Saguaro National Park, and the Avra Valley. Rates are $225 to $250 per person, including brunch and a champagne toast.

SKIING Located 35 miles from Tucson (a 1-hr. drive), **Mount Lemmon Ski Valley** (✆ **520/576-1400**) is the southernmost ski area in the United States and offers 21 runs for experienced downhill skiers as well as beginners. The season here isn't very reliable, so be sure to call first to make sure it's open. Locals recommend not using your own skis or snowboard (too many exposed rocks). The ski area often opens only after a new dump of snow, so be sure to call the road-condition information line (✆ **520/547-7510**) before driving up. In a good year, the season runs from December to April.

TENNIS The **Randolph Tennis Center,** 50 S. Alvernon Way (✆ **520/791-4896;** www.randolphtenniscenter.com), convenient to downtown, is the Southwest's largest public tennis facility and offers 25 lighted courts. During the day, court time is $2.50 per person for 1½ hours; at night, it's $10 per court. Many of the city's hotels and resorts also provide courts for guest use.

WILDFLOWER-VIEWING Bloom time varies from year to year, but April and May are good times to view native wildflowers in the Tucson area. While the crowns of white blossoms worn by saguaro cacti are among the most visible blooms in the area, other cacti are far more colorful. **Saguaro National Park** (p. 360) and **Sabino Canyon** (p. 360) are among the best local spots to see saguaros, other cactus species, and various wildflowers in bloom. If you feel like heading farther afield, the wildflower displays at **Picacho Peak State Park** (p. 164), between Tucson and Casa Grande, are the most impressive in the state.

8 Spectator Sports

BASEBALL The **Colorado Rockies** (✆ **520/327-9467**) pitch spring-training camp in March at Hi Corbett Field, 3400 E. Camino Campestre, in Reid Park (at Randolph Way and E. Broadway). Tickets are $2 to $15. Both the **Chicago White Sox** and the **Arizona Diamondbacks** have their spring-training camps and exhibition games at Tucson Electric Park, 2500 E. Ajo Way (✆ **866/672-1343** or 520/434-1367; www.kinosportscomplex.com), on the south side of the city near the airport. Tickets range from $5 to $16.

Tucson Electric Park is also where you can watch the **Tucson Sidewinders** (© **520/434-1021;** www.tucsonsidewinders.com), the AAA affiliate team of the Arizona Diamondbacks. The season runs April through early September; tickets are $6 to $9.

FOOTBALL The **University of Arizona Wildcats** (© **800/452-2287** or 520/621-2287; www.arizonaathletics.com), a Pac-10 team, play at UA's Arizona Stadium.

GOLF TOURNAMENTS The **World Golf Championships–Accenture Match Play Championship** (© **866/942-2672;** www.pgatour.com), Tucson's main PGA tournament, is held in late February at The Gallery Golf Club at Dove Mountain. Daily tickets are $30 to $50.

HORSE/GREYHOUND RACING **Rillito Park Race Track,** 4502 N. First Ave. (© **520/293-5011**), the birthplace of both the photo finish and organized quarter-horse and Arabian racing, hosts quarter-horse and thoroughbred racing for one month each winter. The ponies run on weekends from mid-February to early March, and admission is $3 to $5.

Greyhounds race year-round at **Tucson Greyhound Park,** 2601 S. Third Ave. (© **520/884-7576;** www.tucdogtrak.com). Grandstand admission is $1.25. Races are held Monday through Saturday from 7:40pm. To reach the track, take Exit 261 off I-10.

9 Spas

If you'd prefer a massage to a round on the links, consider spending a few hours at a spa. While full-service health spas can cost $400 to $500 or more per day, for under $100 you can avail yourself of a spa treatment or two (massages, facials, seaweed wraps, loofah scrubs, and the like) and maybe even get to spend the day lounging by the pool at some exclusive resort. Spas are also great places (for both men and women) to while away an afternoon if you couldn't get a tee time at that golf course you wanted to play or if it happens to be raining.

The **Elizabeth Arden Red Door Spa,** at The Westin La Paloma Resort & Spa, 3666 E. Sunrise Dr. (© **520/742-7866,** ext. 7890; www.reddoorspas.com), focuses on skin-care services, but there are plenty of body wraps and massages available as well. With a 50-minute treatment (mostly $110–$130), you can use the spa's facilities for the day. However, unlike other spas in town, the Red Door is more about relaxation than staying fit, so you won't find aerobics classes or a pool here. Spa packages range in price from $199 to $552.

For a variety of services and a gorgeous location, you just can't beat **The Lakeside Spa & Tennis Center at Loews Ventana Canyon Resort,** 7000 N. Resort Dr. (© **520/529-7830;** www.loewshotels.com), which is wedged between the rugged Catalinas and manicured fairways of one of the most fabled golf courses in the state. Soothed by the scent of aromatherapy, you can treat yourself to herbal wraps, mud treatments, different styles of massage, specialized facials, complete salon services, and much more. Fifty-minute treatments run $100 to $125. With any 50-minute body treatment, you get use of the spa's facilities and pool and can attend any fitness classes being held that day.

With six locations around the Tucson area, **Gadabout Day Spa** (www.gadabout.com) offers the opportunity to slip a relaxing visit to a spa into a busy schedule. Mud baths, facials, and massages as well as hair and nail services are available, and body treatments and massages range from about $40 for a quick massage to $364 for a full day at the spa. You'll find Gadabout at the following locations: St. Philip's Plaza, 1990 E. River

Rd. (© **520/577-2000**); 6393 E. Grant Rd. (© **520/885-0000**); 3207 E. Speedway Blvd. (© **520/325-0000**); Sunrise-Kolb, 6960 E. Sunrise Dr. (© **520/615-9700**); and 8303 N. Oracle Rd. (© **520/742-0000**). The sixth location is Gadabout Man, 2951 N. Swan Rd. (© **520/325-3300**).

10 Shopping

Although the Tucson shopping scene is overshadowed by that of Scottsdale and Phoenix, Tucson does provide a respectable diversity of merchants. Tucsonans have a strong sense of their place in the Southwest, and this is reflected in the city's shopping opportunities. Southwestern clothing, food, crafts, furniture, and art abound (and often at reasonable prices), as do shopping centers built in a Southwestern architectural style.

The city's population center has moved steadily northward, so it is in the northern foothills that you'll find most of the city's large enclosed shopping malls as well as the more tasteful small shopping plazas specializing in boutiques and galleries.

In downtown Tucson, on Fourth Avenue, between Congress Street and Speedway Boulevard, more than 50 shops, galleries, and restaurants make up the **Fourth Avenue historic shopping and entertainment district.** The buildings here were constructed in the early 1900s, and the proximity to the University of Arizona helps keep this district bustling. Many of the shops cater primarily to student needs and interests. Through the underpass at the south end of Fourth Avenue is Congress Street, the heart of the **Downtown Arts District,** where there are still a few art galleries (most, however, have moved to the foothills). Both areas are primarily hangouts for college students.

El Presidio Historic District around the Tucson Museum of Art is the city's center for crafts shops. This area is home to Old Town Artisans and the Tucson Museum of Art museum shop. The city's **"Lost Barrio"** section, on the corner of Southwest Park Avenue and 12th Street (a block off Broadway), is a good place to look for Mexican imports and Southwestern-style home furnishings at good prices.

ANTIQUES & COLLECTIBLES

In addition to the places listed below, a great concentration of antiques shops can be found along Grant Road between Campbell Avenue and Alvernon Way.

American Antique Mall This antiques mall has 100 dealers and is one of the largest such places in southern Arizona. For sale are all manner of collectibles and a few antiques. 3130 E. Grant Rd. © **520/326-3070.** www.americanantiquemall.com.

Eric Firestone Gallery ★★ Collectors of Stickley and other Arts and Crafts furniture will not want to miss this impressive gallery, which is located in one of the historic buildings at Joesler Village shopping plaza. In addition to the furniture, there are period paintings and accessories. At Joesler Village, 4425 N. Campbell Ave. © **520/577-7711.** www.ericfirestonegallery.com.

Michael D. Higgins & Son Located next door to the Eric Firestone Gallery, this little shop specializes in pre-Columbian artifacts but also carries African, Asian, and even ancient Greek and Roman pieces. At Joesler Village, 4429 N. Campbell Ave. © **520/577-8330.** www.mhiggins.com.

Morning Star Antiques In a shop that adjoins Morning Star Traders (see "Native American Art, Crafts & Jewelry," below), Morning Star Antiques carries an excellent selection of antique Spanish and Mexican furniture, as well as other unusual and rustic pieces. 2000 E. Speedway Blvd. ✆ **520/881-3060.** www.morningstartraders.com.

Primitive Arts Gallery This is the best gallery in Tucson for pre-Columbian art, with an eclectic mix of ancient artifacts focusing on ceramics. You'll also find a smattering of other artifacts, from Greek urns to contemporary Argentine *mate* gourds. At Broadway Village, 3026 E. Broadway. ✆ **520/326-4852.**

ART

Tucson's gallery scene is not as concentrated as that in many other cities. Most Tucson galleries have in the past few years abandoned downtown in favor of the foothills and other more affluent suburbs. The current art hot spot is the corner of Campbell Avenue and Skyline Drive, where you'll find **El Cortijo,** a stylishly modern Southwestern shopping plaza that has several contemporary art galleries and an upscale restaurant. Behind this complex, at 6420 N. Campbell Avenue, is a small courtyard complex that is home to **Sanders Galleries** (✆ **520/299-1763;** www.sandersgalleries.com) and **Settlers West Galleries** (✆ **520/299-2607;** www.settlerswest.com), both of which specialize in Western art, as well as **Gallery West** (✆ **520/529-7002;** www.indianartwest.com), which specializes in American Indian art. On the southwest corner of the intersection, you'll find the **Medicine Man Gallery Foothills,** 2890 E. Skyline Dr. (✆ **520/299-7798;** www.medicinemangallery.com).

Davis Dominguez Gallery Located just a couple of blocks off Fourth Avenue in downtown Tucson, this huge gallery features some of the best and most creative contemporary art in the city. A couple of other contemporary art galleries on the same block make this the best place in Tucson to see cutting-edge art. 154 E. Sixth St. ✆ **866/629-9759** or 520/629-9759. www.davisdominguez.com.

Dinnerware Contemporary Art Gallery *Contemporary* is the key word at this gallery. Artists represented tend to have a very wide range of styles and media, so you never know what you'll find. Regardless, you can be sure it will be at the cutting edge of Tucson art. 101 W. Sixth St. ✆ **520/792-4503.** www.dinnerwarearts.com.

El Presidio Gallery Long one of Tucson's premier galleries, El Presidio deals primarily in traditional and contemporary paintings of the Southwest, and is located in a large, modern space in El Cortijo Arts Annex. Contemporary works tend toward the large and bright, and are favorites for decorating foothills homes. At El Cortijo Arts Annex, 3001 E. Skyline Dr. ✆ **800/487-7069** or 520/299-1414. www.elpresidiogallery.com.

Etherton Gallery For more than 25 years, this gallery has been presenting some of the most distinctive art to be found in Tucson, including contemporary and historical photographs. A favorite of museums and serious collectors, Etherton Gallery isn't afraid to present work with strong themes. 135 S. Sixth Ave. ✆ **520/624-7370.** www.ethertongallery.com. Also a smaller location at the Temple of Music and Art, 330 S. Scott Ave. (✆ **520/624-7370**).

Jane Hamilton Fine Art This gallery's boldly colored contemporary art really stands out, and much of the artwork reflects a desert aesthetic. At Joesler Village, 1825 E. River Rd., Suite 111. ✆ **800/555-3051** or 520/529-4886. www.janehamiltonfineart.com.

Mark Sublette Medicine Man Gallery ★★★ This gallery has the finest and most tasteful traditional Western art you'll find just about anywhere in Arizona. Artists represented include Ed Mell, Maynard Dixon, and Howard Post, and most of the gallery's artists have received national attention. There's an excellent selection of Native American crafts as well; see "Native American Art, Crafts & Jewelry," below, for more details. The gallery is also the site of the Conley Museum of the West, a small collection of Western art and old maps. There's another Mark Sublette Gallery in the foothills at 2890 E. Skyline Dr., Suite 190 (✆ **520/299-7798**). At Santa Fe Sq., 7000 E. Tanque Verde Rd. ✆ **800/422-9382** or 520/722-7798. www.medicinemangallery.com.

Philabaum Contemporary Art Glass For more than 25 years, this gallery has been exposing Tucson to the latest trends in contemporary glass art. The gallery is full of lovely and colorful pieces by Tucson's own Tom Philabaum and more than 100 other artists from around the country. In St. Philip's Plaza, 4280 N. Campbell Ave., Suite 105. ✆ **520/299-1939**. www.philabaumglass.com.

BOOKS

Chain bookstores in the Tucson area include **Barnes & Noble,** 5130 E. Broadway Blvd. (✆ **520/512-1166**) and 7325 N. La Cholla Blvd., Suite 100, in the Foothills Mall (✆ **520/742-6402**); and **Borders,** 4235 N. Oracle Rd. (✆ **520/292-1331**) and 5870 E. Broadway Blvd., at the Park Place Mall (✆ **520/584-0111**).

Bookman's This big bookstore, housed in a former supermarket, is crammed full of used books and recordings, and has long been a favorite of Tucsonans. There are other Bookman's stores at 6230 E. Speedway Blvd. (✆ **520/748-9555**) and 3733 W. Ina Rd. (✆ **520/579-0303**). 1930 E. Grant Rd. ✆ **520/325-5767**. www.bookmans.com.

Clues Unlimited If you forgot to pack your vacation reading, drop by this fun little store. Not only can you shop for the latest Carl Hiassen or other mystery, but you can say hi to Sophie, the resident pot-bellied pig. Broadway Village, 123 S. Eastbourne St. ✆ **520/326-8533**. www.cluesunlimited.com.

CRAFTS

Details Art & Design If you enjoy highly imaginative and colorful crafts with a sense of humor, you'll get a kick out of this place. Unexpected objets d'art turn up in the forms of clocks, ceramics, glass, and other media. At El Cortijo Gallery Row, 3001 E. Skyline Dr., no. 103. ✆ **520/577-1995**. www.detailsart.com.

Obsidian Gallery Contemporary crafts by nationally recognized artists fill this gallery. You'll find luminous glass art, unique and daring jewelry, imaginative ceramics, and much more. At St. Philip's Plaza, 4320 N. Campbell Ave. (at River Rd.). ✆ **520/577-3598**. www.obsidian-gallery.com.

Old Town Artisans ★ Housed in a restored 1850s adobe building covering an entire city block of El Presidio Historic District, this unique shopping plaza houses half a dozen different shops brimming with traditional and contemporary Southwestern designs. There's also free Wi-Fi in the courtyard here. 201 N. Court Ave. ✆ **800/782-8072** or 520/623-6024. www.oldtownartisans.com.

Tucson Museum of Art Shop The museum's gift shop offers a colorful and changing selection of Southwestern crafts, mostly by local and regional artists. 140 N. Main Ave. ✆ **520/624-2333**. www.tucsonarts.com.

FASHION

See also the listing for the Beth Friedman Collection under "Jewelry," below. For cowboy and cowgirl attire, see "Western Wear," below.

Dark Star Leather If you're in the market for a distinctive leather jacket, belt, or purse, be sure to stop by this little locally owned shop in Plaza Palomino. Exotic

Tips Seeing Stars

Amateur astronomers, take note. Because of all the great star-viewing opportunities in southern Arizona, Tucson has a large number of stargazers, and they all shop at **Stellar Vision Astronomy Shop,** 1835 S. Alvernon Way (✆ **520/571-0877**). This store is packed with telescopes of all shapes and sizes, as well as books and star charts.

leathers are used in the one-of-a-kind designs. You can sometimes find great deals on sale items. At Plaza Palomino, 2940 N. Swan Rd. ✆ **520/881-4700.** www.darkstarleather.com.

Maya Palace This shop features ethnic-inspired but sophisticated women's clothing in natural fabrics. The friendly staff helps customers of all ages put together a Southwestern chic look, from casual to dressy. Shops can also be found at El Mercado, 6332 E. Broadway Blvd. (✆ **520/748-0817**), and at Casas Adobes Plaza, 7057 N. Oracle Rd. (✆ **520/575-8028**). At Plaza Palomino, 2960 N. Swan Rd. ✆ **520/325-6411.** www.mayapalacetucson.com.

Rochelle K Fine Women's Apparel With everything from the latest in the little black dress to draping silks and casual linens, Rochelle K attracts a well-heeled clientele. You'll also find beautiful accessories and jewelry here. At Casas Adobes Plaza, 7039 N. Oracle Rd. ✆ **520/797-2279.** www.rochellek.com.

GIFTS & SOUVENIRS

B&B Cactus Farm This plant nursery is devoted exclusively to cacti and succulents, and is worth a visit just to see the amazing variety on display. It's a good place to stop on the way to or from Saguaro National Park East. The store can pack your purchase for traveling or ship it anywhere in the United States. 11550 E. Speedway Blvd. ✆ **520/721-4687.** www.bandbcactus.com.

DAH Rock Shop ★ If you can't make it to Tucson for the annual gem and mineral shows, don't despair. At this cluttered shop, you can pick through shelves crammed with all manner of rare minerals and strange stones. 3401 N. Dodge St. ✆ **520/323-0781.**

Native Seeds/SEARCH ★★ Gardeners, cooks, and just about anyone in search of an unusual gift will likely be fascinated by this tiny shop, which is operated by a nonprofit organization dedicated to preserving the biodiversity offered by native Southwest seeds. The shelves are full of heirloom beans, corn, chiles, and other seeds from a wide variety of native desert plants. There are also gourds and inexpensive Tarahumara Indian baskets, bottled sauces and salsas made from native plants, and books about native agriculture. 526 N. Fourth Ave. ✆ **866/622-5561** or 520/622-5561. www.nativeseeds.org.

Picánte Designs The plethora of Hispanic-themed icons and accessories here include *milagros,* Day of the Dead skeletons, Mexican crosses, jewelry, greeting cards, and folk art from around the world. This is a great place to shop for distinctive south-of-the-border kitschy gifts. 2932 E. Broadway. ✆ **520/320-5699.**

Tohono Chul Museum Shops ★ The two shops here are packed with Mexican folk art, nature-themed toys, household items, T-shirts, and books. These shops are an absolute must after a visit to surrounding Tohono Chul Park, which is landscaped with desert plants. Add a meal at the park's tearoom, and you've got a good afternoon's outing. For a description of the park, see p. 367. 7366 N. Paseo del Norte (1 block west of the corner of Ina and Oracle roads in Tohono Chul Park). ✆ **520/742-6455.** www.tohonochulpark.org.

UN Center/UNICEF If your tastes run to ethnic imports, be sure to check out this great little gift shop. Not only is there lots of cool stuff from all over the world, but when you buy something here, you'll be helping underprivileged children. Monterey Village, 6242 E. Speedway Blvd. ✆ **520/881-7060.** www.unitednationscenter.com.

JEWELRY

In addition to the stores mentioned below, see the listing for the Obsidian Gallery under "Crafts," above.

Beth Friedman Collection This shop sells a well-chosen collection of jewelry by Native American craftspeople and international designers. It also carries some extravagant cowgirl get-ups in velvet and lace, as well as contemporary women's fashions. At Joesler Village, 1865 E. River Rd., Suite 121. ✆ **520/577-6858.** www.bethfriedmanonline.com.

Turquoise Door The contemporary Southwestern jewelry here is among the most stunning in the city, made with opals, diamonds, lapis lazuli, amethysts, and the ubiquitous turquoise. At St. Philip's Plaza, 4330 N. Campbell Ave. (at River Rd.). ✆ **520/299-7787.** www.turquoisedoorjewelry.com.

MALLS & SHOPPING CENTERS

Foothills Mall This large factory-outlet mall and discount shopping center has, among many other stores, a Nike Factory Store, Off 5th Saks Fifth Avenue Outlet, and Barnes & Noble, as well as a brewpub and a couple of good restaurants. 7401 N. La Cholla Blvd. (at Ina Rd.). ✆ **520/219-0650.** www.shopfoothillsmall.com.

Plaza Palomino Built in the style of a Spanish hacienda with a courtyard and fountains, this little shopping center is home to some of Tucson's most interesting specialty shops, as well as galleries and restaurants. There's a farmers' market here on Saturday mornings. Southeast corner of North Swan and Fort Lowell roads. ✆ **520/320-6344.** www.plazapalomino.com.

St. Philip's Plaza This upscale Southwestern-style shopping center contains a couple of good restaurants, a luxury beauty salon/day spa, and numerous shops and galleries, including Bahti Indian Arts and Turquoise Door jewelry. On Sunday mornings, there is a farmers' market. Makes a great one-stop Tucson shopping outing. 4280 N. Campbell Ave. (at River Rd.). ✆ **520/529-2775.** www.stphilipsplaza.com.

Tucson Mall The foothills of northern Tucson have become shopping-center central, and this is the largest of the malls. You'll find more than 200 retailers in this busy, two-story skylit complex. 4500 N. Oracle Rd. ✆ **520/293-7330.** www.shoptucsonmall.com.

MEXICAN & LATIN AMERICAN IMPORTS

In addition to the shops mentioned below, the **"Lost Barrio,"** on the corner of Southwest Park Avenue and 12th Street (a block south of Broadway), is a good place to look for Mexican imports and Southwestern-style home furnishings at good prices.

Antigua de Mexico This warehouse-like shop is absolutely packed with crafts from Mexico—oversize ceramics and painted plates, wooden and wrought-iron furniture, and punched-metal frames and framed mirrors. Smaller items include crucifixes and candlesticks. 3235 W. Orange Grove Rd. ✆ **520/742-7114.**

Zócalo Although large pieces, including colonial-style furniture, constitute much of the inventory here, there are also decorator items such as Mexican ceramics, glassware, and Mexican-style paintings. A visit to Zócalo provides an opportunity to wander around Broadway Village, an interesting little historic shopping plaza. 3016 E. Broadway Blvd. ✆ **520/320-1236.** www.zocalomexicanfurniture.com.

NATIVE AMERICAN ART, CRAFTS & JEWELRY

Bahti Indian Arts Family-owned for more than 50 years, this store sells exquisitely made Native American crafts—jewelry, baskets, sculpture, paintings, books, weavings, kachina dolls, Zuni fetishes, and much more. At St. Philip's Plaza, 4280 N. Campbell Ave., Suite 100. ✆ **520/577-0290.** www.bahti.com.

Gallery West Located right below Anthony's in the Catalinas restaurant, this tiny shop specializes in very expensive Native American artifacts (mostly pre-1940s) such as New Mexico Pueblo pots, Apache and Pima baskets, 19th-century Plains Indian beadwork, Navajo weavings, and kachinas. There is also plenty of both contemporary and vintage jewelry. 6420 N. Campbell Ave. (at Skyline Dr.). ✆ **520/529-7002.** www.indianartwest.com.

Kaibab Courtyard Shops ★ In business since 1945, this store offers one of the best selections of Native American art and crafts in Tucson. You can find high-quality jewelry, Mexican pottery and folk arts, home furnishings, glassware, kachinas, and rugs. 2837–2841 N. Campbell Ave. ✆ **520/795-6905.**

Mark Sublette Medicine Man Gallery This shop has the best and biggest selection of old Navajo rugs in the city, and perhaps even in the entire state. There are also Mexican and other Hispanic textiles, Acoma pottery, basketry, and other Indian crafts, as well as artwork by cowboy artists. The gallery is the site of the Conley Museum of the West. There's another Mark Sublette Gallery in the foothills at 2890 E. Skyline Dr., Suite 190 (✆ **520/299-7798**). At Santa Fe Sq., 7000 E. Tanque Verde Rd. ✆ **800/422-9382** or 520/722-7798. www.medicinemangallery.com.

Morning Star Traders ★★★ With hardwood floors and a museumlike atmosphere, this store features museum-quality goods: antique Navajo rugs, kachinas, furniture, and a huge selection of old Native American jewelry. This just may be the best store of its type in the entire state. An adjoining shop, Morning Star Antiques, carries an impressive selection of antique furniture (see "Antiques & Collectibles," above). 2020 E. Speedway Blvd. ✆ **520/881-2112.** www.morningstartraders.com.

Silverbell Trading Not your run-of-the-mill crafts store, Silverbell specializes in regional Native American artwork, such as baskets and pottery, and carries unique pieces that the shop owner handpicks. Items such as stone Navajo corn maidens, Zuni fetishes, and figures carved from sandstone are among the highlights. At Casas Adobes Plaza, 7119 N. Oracle Rd. ✆ **520/797-6852.** www.silverbelltrader.com.

WESTERN WEAR

Arizona Hatters Arizona Hatters carries the best names in cowboy hats, from Stetson to Bailey to Resistol, and the shop specializes in custom-fitting hats to the customer's head and face. You'll also find bolo ties, belts, and other accessories here. 2790 N. Campbell Ave. ✆ **520/292-1320.** www.azhatters.com.

Stewart Boot Manufacturing Co. Boots that fit so well you don't even need socks. That's how a Tucson friend described the custom-made cowboy boots turned out by this South Tucson bootmaker. You'll have to wait for your boots, though, since, all the boots sold here are made to order. 30 W. 28th St. ✆ **520/622-2706.**

Western Warehouse If you want to put together your Western-wear ensemble under one roof, this is the place. It's the largest such store in Tucson and can deck you and your kids out in the latest cowboy fashions, including hats and boots. In Northwest Plaza, 3719 N. Oracle Rd. (at Prince Rd). ✆ **520/293-1808.** www.westernwarehouse.com.

11 Tucson After Dark

Tucson after dark is a much easier landscape to negotiate than the vast cultural sprawl of the Phoenix area. Rather than having numerous performing-arts centers all over the suburbs as in the Valley of the Sun, Tucson has a more concentrated nightlife scene. The **Downtown Arts District** is the center of the action, with the Temple of Music and Art, the Tucson Convention Center Music Hall, and several nightclubs. The **University of Arizona campus,** a mile away, is another hot spot for entertainment.

The free *Tucson Weekly* contains thorough listings of concerts, theater and dance performances, and club offerings. The entertainment section of the *Arizona Daily Star* ("Caliente") and the *Tucson Citizen*'s "Calendar" both come out each Thursday and are good sources of information for what's going on around town.

THE CLUB & MUSIC SCENE

COMEDY

Laffs Comedy Caffè This stand-up comedy club features local and professional comedians from around the country Thursday through Saturday nights. A full bar and a limited menu are available. At the Village, 2900 E. Broadway Blvd., Suite 154. ✆ **520/323-8669.** www.laffscomedyclub.com. Cover $7 Thurs, $10 Fri–Sat.

COUNTRY

Cactus Moon Café A 20- to 40-something crowd frequents this large and glitzy nightclub, which features primarily country music (with dance lessons several nights each week). Keep in mind, though, that some nights of the week may have rock instead of country. Check the schedule before putting on your boots. 5470 E. Broadway Blvd. (at Craycroft Rd.). ✆ **520/748-0049.** www.cactusmoon.net. Cover $2–$5.

The Maverick: King of Clubs The Maverick, in different incarnations and different locations around town, has been Tucson's favorite country music dance club since 1962. Currently it's located in a modern space out in east Tucson and is open Tuesday through Sunday nights, with live country music Thursday through Saturday nights. 6622 E. Tanque Verde Rd. ✆ **520/298-0430.** mavericktucson.com. No cover to $5.

DANCE CLUB

El Parador Restaurant Tropical decor and an abundance of potted plants set the mood for live Latin dance music and salsa lessons on Friday nights. The music starts at 9:30pm and dance lessons start at 10:15pm. On Saturday, DJs spin more salsa music, and every other Saturday night there's a live band. Customers of this "all ages" club range from 20- to 60-somethings. 2744 E. Broadway. ✆ **520/881-2808.** www.elparadortucson.com. Cover $6.

JAZZ

To find out what's happening on the local jazz scene, contact the **Tucson Jazz Society** (✆ **520/903-1265;** www.tucsonjazz.org). This organization's website lists various jazz nights at restaurants all over Tucson. Some of those restaurants include **Old Pueblo Grill,** 60 N. Alvernon Way (✆ **520/326-6000**), with live jazz on Sunday nights; and **Acacia at St. Philip's Plaza,** 4340 N. Campbell Ave. (✆ **520/232-0101**), with live jazz Thursday through Saturday nights, plus a jazz brunch on Sunday.

The Grill ★★ No other jazz venue in Tucson has more flavor of the Southwest than this restaurant lounge, perched high on a ridge-top overlooking the city. There's live music (mostly jazz) Thursday through Sunday nights. At Hacienda del Sol Guest Ranch Resort, 5601 N. Hacienda del Sol Rd. ✆ **520/529-3500.** www.haciendadelsol.com.

MARIACHI

Tucson is the mariachi capital of the United States, and no one should visit without spending at least one evening listening to some of these strolling minstrels.

La Fuente ★★ La Fuente is one of the largest Mexican restaurants in Tucson and serves up good food, but what really draws the crowds is the live mariachi music. If you just want to listen and not have dinner, you can hang out in the lounge. The mariachis perform Wednesday through Sunday nights. 1749 N. Oracle Rd. ✆ **520/623-8659.** www.lafuenterestaurant.com.

ROCK, BLUES & REGGAE

Chicago Bar Transplanted Chicagoans love to watch their home teams on the TVs at this neighborhood bar, but there's also live music nightly. Sure, blues gets played a lot, but so do reggae and rock and about everything in between. 5954 E. Speedway Blvd. ✆ **520/748-8169.** www.chicagobartucson.com. No cover to $5.

Club Congress Just off the lobby of the restored Hotel Congress (now a budget hotel catering to younger travelers), Club Congress is Tucson's main alternative-music venue. There are usually a couple of nights of live music each week, and over the years such bands as Nirvana, Dick Dale, and the Goo Goo Dolls have played here, although more recently, the club has tended to book primarily local and regional acts. 311 E. Congress St. ✆ **520/622-8848.** www.hotelcongress.com. Cover $4–$15.

The Rialto Theatre This renovated 1919 vaudeville theater, although not a nightclub, is now Tucson's main venue for performances by bands that are too big to play across the street at Club Congress (Shawn Colvin, Los Lobos, Beck). 318 E. Congress St. ✆ **520/740-1000.** www.rialtotheatre.com. Tickets $10–$35.

THE BAR, LOUNGE & PUB SCENE

Arizona Inn If you're looking for a quiet, comfortable scene, the piano music in the Audubon Lounge at the Arizona Inn is sure to soothe your soul. The lounge, which has been restored to its original appearance, has a classic feel, and the resort's gardens are beautiful. 2200 E. Elm St. ✆ **520/325-1541.**

Cascade Lounge ★ This is Tucson's ultimate piano bar. With a view of the Catalinas, the plush lounge is perfect for romance or relaxation at the start or end of a night on the town. Tuesday through Sunday nights, there's live piano music or a jazz band, and on Fridays and Saturdays, there's a DJ and dancing. At Loews Ventana Canyon Resort, 7000 N. Resort Dr. ✆ **520/299-2020.**

Cushing Street Bar & Restaurant Located on the edge of the Barrio Histórico district just south of the Tucson Convention Center, this restaurant/bar is in a historic adobe building and has loads of old Tucson character. There's also live music on weekends. 198 W. Cushing St. ✆ **520/622-7984.** www.cushingstreet.com.

58° & Holding This combination wine shop and wine bar in east Tucson is a good bet for a glass or two of wine in a relaxing setting. There are Wednesday-night wine tastings as well. There's a second wine bar in the foothills at St. Philip's Plaza, 4280 Campbell Rd., Suite 27 & 55 (© **520/299-5804**). 5340 E. Broadway Blvd. © **520/747-5858.** www.58degrees.com.

Gentle Ben's Brewing Co. Located just off the UA campus, Gentle Ben's, a big, modern place with plenty of outdoor seating, is Tucson's favorite microbrewery and, not surprisingly, attracts primarily a college crowd. 865 E. University Blvd. © **520/624-4177.** www.gentlebens.com.

The Kon Tiki With a Polynesian luau theme, this joint is not some modern-day designer's idea of what the 1950s were like; this is the real thing. Tiki lovers rejoice, but be careful, those sweet tropical cocktails can pack a Hawaiian punch! 4625 E. Broadway Blvd. © **520/323-7193.** www.kontiki-tucson.com.

Nimbus Brewing ★ Located in a warehouse district on the south side of Tucson, this brewpub is basically the front room of Nimbus's brewing and bottling facility. The beer is good, and there's live bluegrass, rock, or jazz on a regular basis. Hard to find, and definitely a local scene. 3850 E. 44th St. (2 blocks east of Palo Verde Rd.). © **520/745-9175.** www.nimbusbeer.com.

The Shelter Housed in an unusual round building that supposedly was once a fallout shelter (thus the name of the bar), this place is totally retro, with lots of JFK memorabilia on the walls. There are even vintage pinball machines. Fun and funky. 4155 E. Grant Rd. © **520/326-1345.**

Thunder Canyon Brewery This big brewpub is your best bet in Tucson for handcrafted ales and is the most convenient brewpub for anyone staying at a foothills resort. At Foothills Mall, 7401 N. La Cholla Blvd. (at Ina Rd.). © **520/797-2652.** www.thundercanyonbrewery.com.

¡Toma! ★ This bar, set in El Presidio Historic District and owned by the family that operates El Charro Café next door, has a fun and festive atmosphere complete with a Mexican hat fountain/sculpture in the courtyard. Drop by for cheap margaritas during happy hour (daily 3–6pm). 311 N. Court Ave. © **520/622-1922.**

COCKTAILS WITH A VIEW

Most of the best views in town are at foothills resorts; luckily, they don't mind sharing with nonguests. The lounge at **Anthony's in the Catalinas** also has a great view.

Desert Garden Lounge If you'd like a close-up view of the Santa Catalina Mountains, drop by the Desert Garden Lounge (at sunset, perhaps). The large lounge has live piano music several nights a week. At The Westin La Paloma, 3800 E. Sunrise Dr. © **520/742-6000.**

SPORTS BARS

Famous Sam's With nearly a dozen branches around the city, Famous Sam's (www.famoussams.com) keeps a lot of Tucson's sports fans happy with its cheap prices and large portions. Other convenient locations include 7930 E. Speedway Blvd. (© **520/290-9666**) and 2320 N. Silverbell Rd. (© **520/884-7267**). 1830 E. Broadway Blvd. © **520/884-0119.**

GAY & LESBIAN BARS & CLUBS

To find out about other gay bars around town, keep an eye out for the *Observer,* Tucson's newspaper for the gay, lesbian, and bisexual community. You'll find it at **Antigone Books,** 411 N. Fourth Ave. (✆ **520/792-3715;** www.antigonebooks.com), as well as at the bars listed here.

Ain't Nobody's Bizness Located in a small shopping plaza in midtown, this bar has long been *the* lesbian gathering spot in Tucson. There are pool tables, a dance floor, and a quiet, smoke-free room where you can duck out of the noise. Lately, this bar has also been doing nights for gay men as well, so check the schedule. 2900 E. Broadway Blvd., Suite 118. ✆ **520/318-4838.** www.aintnobodysbizness-az.com.

IBT's Located on funky Fourth Avenue, IBT's has long been the most popular gay men's dance bar in town. The music ranges from 1980s retro to hip-hop, and regular drag shows add to the fun. There's always an interesting crowd. 616 N. Fourth Ave. ✆ **520/882-3053.** www.ibts.net.

THE PERFORMING ARTS

To a certain extent, Tucson is a clone of Phoenix when it comes to the performing arts. Three of Tucson's major companies—the Arizona Opera Company, Ballet Arizona, and the Arizona Theatre Company—spend half their time in Phoenix. This means that whatever gets staged in Phoenix also gets staged in Tucson. This city does, however, have its own symphony and manages to sustain a diversified theater scene as well.

Usually, the best way to purchase tickets is directly from the company's box office. Tickets to Tucson Convention Center events (but not the symphony or the opera) and other venues around town may be available by calling **Ticketmaster** (✆ **520/321-1000;** www.ticketmaster.com) or by stopping by the **TCC box office,** 250 S. Church Ave. (✆ **520/791-4101;** www.cityoftucson.org/tcc).

PERFORMING-ARTS CENTERS & CONCERT HALLS

Tucson's largest performance venue is the **Tucson Convention Center (TCC) Music Hall,** 260 S. Church Ave. (✆ **520/791-4101;** www.cityoftucson.org/tcc). It's the home of the Tucson Symphony Orchestra and where the Arizona Opera Company usually performs when it's in town. This hall hosts many touring companies. The box office is open Monday through Friday from 10am to 6pm, Saturday from 10am to 4pm, and Sunday from noon to 4pm.

The centerpiece of the Tucson theater scene is the **Temple of Music and Art,** 330 S. Scott Ave. (✆ **520/622-2823**), a restored historic theater dating from 1927. The 605-seat Alice Holsclaw Theatre is the Temple's main stage, but there's also the 90-seat Cabaret Theatre. You'll also find an art gallery and gift shop here. The box office is normally open Monday through Friday from 10am to 6pm (or until curtain time if there is a show scheduled), Saturday and Sunday from noon to 6pm (or curtain).

University of Arizona Centennial Hall, 1020 E. University Blvd. at Park Avenue (✆ **520/621-3341;** www.uapresents.org), on the UA campus, is Tucson's other main performance hall. It stages performances by touring national musical acts, international companies, and Broadway shows. A big stage and excellent sound system permit large-scale productions. The box office is open Monday through Friday from 10am to 6pm and Saturday from noon to 5pm (closed Sat in summer).

Originally opened in 1930, downtown Tucson's **Fox Theatre,** 17 W. Congress St. (✆ **520/624-1515;** www.foxtucsontheatre.org), is a restored 1930s movie palace that is now the city's most beautiful place to catch live music, a play, or even a classic or independent film. The box office is open Monday through Friday from 10am to 6pm and Saturday from 10am to 2pm.

The **Center for the Arts Proscenium Theatre,** Pima Community College (West Campus), 2202 W. Anklam Rd. (✆ **520/206-6986**), is another good place to check for classical music performances. It offers a wide variety of shows.

OUTDOOR VENUES & SERIES

Weather permitting, Tucsonans head to Reid Park's **DeMeester Outdoor Performance Center,** at Country Club Road and East 22nd Street (✆ **520/791-4873**), for performances under the stars. This amphitheater stages live theater performances, as well as frequent concerts.

The **Tucson Jazz Society** (✆ **520/903-1265;** www.tucsonjazz.org), which manages to book a few well-known jazz musicians each year, sponsors different series at various locations around the city. Tickets are usually between $15 and $30.

CLASSICAL MUSIC, OPERA & DANCE

Both the **Tucson Symphony Orchestra** (✆ **520/882-8585** or 520/792-9155; www.tucsonsymphony.org), which is the oldest continuously performing symphony in the Southwest, and the **Arizona Opera Company** (✆ **520/293-4336** or 520/321-1000; www.azopera.com), the state's premier opera company, perform at the Tucson Convention Center Music Hall. Symphony tickets run $18 to $47; opera tickets are $35 to $140.

If you want to catch some economical classical music, check out the schedule at the **University of Arizona College of Fine Arts School of Music and Dance** (✆ **520/621-1162;** www.music.arizona.edu). Performances are held between September and April, and include classical music and opera performances held in the Music Building's Crowder and Holsclaw halls, both of which are near the intersection of Speedway Boulevard and Park Avenue on the UA campus. Equally worthwhile are the performances by the UA Dance Ensemble, which are staged in the **Stevie Eller Dance Theatre,** a little jewel box of a building. The bold contemporary architecture of this building makes seeing a performance here a double treat. Call the above number for information on performances.

THEATER

Tucson doesn't have a lot of theater companies, but what few it does have stage a surprisingly diverse sampling of both classic and contemporary plays.

Arizona Theatre Company (ATC; ✆ **520/622-2823;** www.aztheatreco.org), which performs at the Temple of Music and Art, splits its time between Tucson, Phoenix, and Mesa, and is the state's top professional theater company. Each season sees a mix of comedy, drama, and Broadway-style musical shows; tickets cost $27 to $48.

The **Invisible Theatre,** 1400 N. First Ave. (✆ **520/882-9721;** www.invisibletheatre.com), a tiny theater in a converted laundry building, has been home to Tucson's most experimental theater for more than 35 years (it does off-Broadway shows and musicals). Tickets go for about $22 to $25.

The West just wouldn't be the West without good old-fashioned melodramas, and the **Gaslight Theatre,** 7010 E. Broadway Blvd. (✆ **520/886-9428;** www.grandmatonyspizza.com), is where evil villains, stalwart heroes, and defenseless heroines pound the boards. You can boo and hiss, cheer and sigh as the predictable stories unfold on stage. It's all great fun for kids and adults, with plenty of pop-culture references thrown into the mix. Tickets are $16 for adults, $14 for students and seniors, and $7 for children 12 and under. Performances are held Tuesday through Sunday, with two shows nightly Tuesday through Saturday, plus a Sunday matinee. Tickets sell out a month in advance, so get them as soon as possible. On Monday nights, you can catch interesting live music performances.

CASINOS

Casino del Sol Located 15 miles southwest of Tucson off I-19 (take the Valencia Rd. exit and drive west) and operated by the Pascua Yaqui tribe, this is one of the two largest casinos in southern Arizona. There are plenty of slot machines, plus keno, bingo, and a card room. 7406 S. Camino de Oeste. ✆ **800/344-9435.** www.casinodelsol.com.

Desert Diamond Casino Operated by the Tohono O'odham tribe and just off I-19 south of Tucson, this casino offers the same variety of slot and video poker machines found at other casinos in the state. A card room, bingo, and keno round out the options. A free shuttle will bring you out to the casino from your hotel. Exit 80 (Pima Mine Rd.) off I-19. ✆ **866/332-9467** or 520/393-2700. www.desertdiamondcasino.com.

10

Southern Arizona

Although southern Arizona has its share of prickly pears and saguaros, much of this region has more in common with the Texas plains than it does with the Sonoran Desert. In the southeastern corner of the state, the mile-high grasslands, punctuated by forested mountain ranges, have long supported vast ranches where cattle range across wide-open plains. It was here that some of America's most legendary Western history took place—Wyatt Earp and the Clantons shot it out at Tombstone's O.K. Corral; Doc Holliday played his cards; and Cochise and Geronimo staged the last Indian rebellions.

Long before even the prospectors and outlaws arrived, this region had gained historical importance as the first part of the Southwest explored by the Spanish. As early as 1540, a Spanish expedition led by Francisco Vásquez de Coronado passed through this region, and today a national memorial near Hereford commemorates Coronado's journey.

Nearly 150 years later, Father Eusebio Francisco Kino founded a string of Jesuit missions across the region the Spanish called the Pimeria Alta, an area that would later become northern Mexico and eventually southern Arizona. Converting the Indians and building mission churches, Father Kino left a long-lasting mark on this region. Two of the missions he founded—San Xavier del Bac (p. 361), 9 miles south of present-day Tucson; and San José de Tumacácori south of Tubac (see the listing for Tumacácori National Historical Park, below)—still stand.

More than 450 years after Coronado marched through this region, the valley of the San Pedro River is undergoing something of a population explosion, especially in the town of Sierra Vista, where retirement communities sprawl across the landscape. Nearby, in the once nearly abandoned copper-mining town of Bisbee, urban refugees and artists have taken up residence and opened numerous galleries and B&Bs, making this one of the most interesting small towns in the state.

The combination of low deserts, high plains, and even higher mountains has given this region a fascinating diversity of landscapes. Giant saguaros cover the slopes of the Sonoran Desert throughout much of southern Arizona, and in the western parts of this region, organ pipe cacti reach the northern limit of their range. In the cool mountains, cacti give way to pines, and passing clouds bring snow and rain. Narrow canyons and broad valleys, fed by the rain and snowmelt, provide habitat for hundreds of species of birds and other wildlife. For many birds usually found only south of the border, this is the northernmost limit of their range. Consequently, southeastern Arizona has become one of the nation's most important bird-watching spots.

The region's mild climate has also given rise to the state's small wine industry. A handful of wineries and vineyards in southeastern Arizona make touring the wine country a favorite weekend excursion for residents of Tucson and Phoenix.

1 Organ Pipe Cactus National Monument ★★

135 miles S of Phoenix; 140 miles W of Tucson; 185 miles SE of Yuma

Located roughly midway between Yuma and Tucson, Organ Pipe Cactus National Monument is a preserve for the rare cactus for which the monument is named. The organ pipe cactus resembles the saguaro cactus in many ways, but instead of forming a single main trunk, organ pipes have many trunks, some 20 feet tall, that resemble—you guessed it—organ pipes.

This is a rugged region with few towns or services. To the west lie the inaccessible Cabeza Prieta National Wildlife Refuge and the Barry M. Goldwater Air Force Range (a bombing range), and to the east is the large Tohono O'odham Indian Reservation. The only motels in the area are in the small town of Ajo, a former company town that was built to house the workers at a now-abandoned copper mine. The downtown plaza, with its tall palm trees and arched and covered walkways, has the look and feel of a Mexican town square. Be sure to gas up your car before leaving Ajo.

ESSENTIALS

GETTING THERE From Tucson, take Arizona 86 W to Why and turn south on Arizona 85. From Yuma, take I-8 E to Gila Bend and drive south on Arizona 85.

FEES The park entry fee is $8 per car.

VISITOR INFORMATION For information, contact **Organ Pipe Cactus National Monument** (© **520/387-6849;** www.nps.gov/orpi). The visitor center is open daily from 8am to 5pm, although the park itself is open 24 hours a day. The visitor center is closed Thanksgiving, Christmas, and all federal holidays during the summer.

EXPLORING THE MONUMENT

Two well-graded gravel roads lead through different sections of this large national monument. Puerto Blanco Drive, formerly a long loop drive, is currently a 5-mile route leading only to the Red Tanks trail head, while Ajo Mountain Drive is a 21-mile one-way loop. Guides available at the park's visitor center explain natural features of the landscape along both drives. There are also a number of hiking trails along the roads, but many of these trails are now closed to the public due to safety concerns surrounding the use of this area by illegal immigrants crossing the border from Mexico. Be sure to check with the national monument before planning any hikes. In the winter, there are guided tours of Ajo Mountain Drive.

WHERE TO STAY

There are two campgrounds within the park. Campsites are $8 in primitive **Alamo Campground** and $12 in more developed **Twin Peaks Campground.** The nearest lodgings are in Ajo, with several old and very basic motels as well as a B&B. There are also plenty of budget chain motels in the town of Gila Bend, 70 miles north of the monument.

Guest House Inn Bed & Breakfast Built in 1925 as a guesthouse for mining executives, this B&B has attractive gardens in the front yard, a mesquite thicket off to one side, and a modern Southwestern feel to its interior decor. Guest rooms are simply furnished with reproduction antique and Southwestern furnishings. There are sunrooms on both the north and the south sides of the house.

700 Guest House Rd., Ajo, AZ 85321. © **520/387-6133.** www.guesthouseinn.biz. 4 units. $89 double. Rates include full breakfast. DC, MC, V. *In room:* A/C, fridge, hair dryer, iron, microwave, Wi-Fi, no phone.

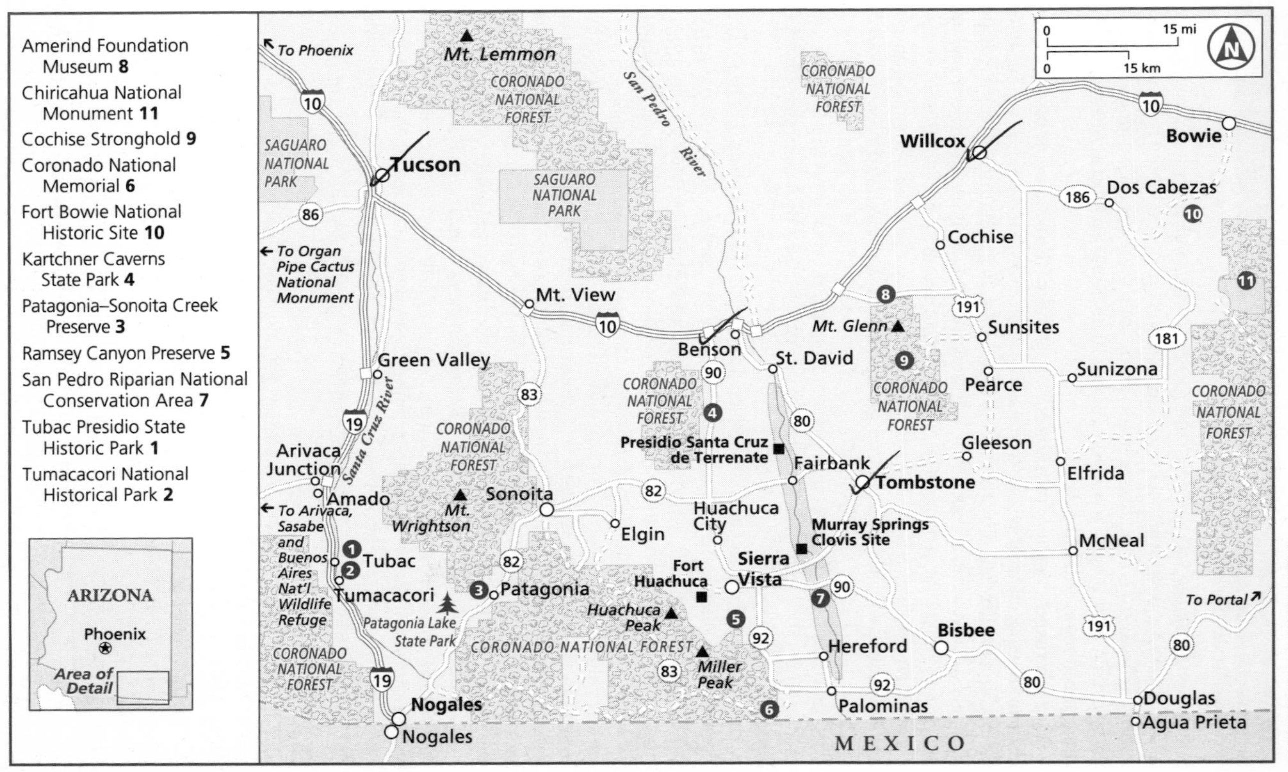
Amerind Foundation Museum 8
Chiricahua National Monument 11
Cochise Stronghold 9
Coronado National Memorial 6
Fort Bowie National Historic Site 10
Kartchner Caverns State Park 4
Patagonia–Sonoita Creek Preserve 3
Ramsey Canyon Preserve 5
San Pedro Riparian National Conservation Area 7
Tubac Presidio State Historic Park 1
Tumacacori National Historical Park 2
ARIZONA
Phoenix
Area of Detail
0 15 mi
0 15 km
N
To Phoenix
Mt. Lemmon
CORONADO NATIONAL FOREST
SAGUARO NATIONAL PARK
Tucson
San Pedro River
Willcox
Bowie
Dos Cabezas
Cochise
To Organ Pipe Cactus National Monument
Mt. View
Benson
St. David
Mt. Glenn
Sunsites
Pearce
Sunizona
Green Valley
Santa Cruz River
Arivaca Junction
Amado
Presidio Santa Cruz de Terrenate
Fairbank
Tombstone
Gleeson
Elfrida
Sonoita
Mt. Wrightson
To Arivaca, Sasabe and Buenos Aires Nat'l Wildlife Refuge
Elgin
Huachuca City
Murray Springs Clovis Site
McNeal
Tubac
Tumacacori
Patagonia
Fort Huachuca
Sierra Vista
Patagonia Lake State Park
Huachuca Peak
To Portal
Bisbee
Hereford
CORONADO NATIONAL FOREST
Miller Peak
Nogales
Nogales
Palominas
Douglas
Agua Prieta
MEXICO
10
86
83
19
90
80
82
92
191
186
181

2 Tubac ★★ & Buenos Aires National Wildlife Refuge ★

45 miles S of Tucson; 21 miles N of Nogales; 84 miles W of Sierra Vista

Located in the fertile valley of the Santa Cruz River 45 miles south of Tucson, Tubac is one of Arizona's largest arts communities and home to a developing retirement community. The town's old buildings house more than 80 shops selling fine arts, crafts, unusual gifts, and lots of Southwest souvenirs, making Tubac one of southern Arizona's most popular destinations.

In 1691, Father Eusebio Francisco Kino established Tumacácori as one of the first Spanish missions in what would eventually become Arizona. At that time, Tubac was a Pima Indian village, but by the 1730s, the Spanish began settling here in the region they called Pimeria Alta. After a Pima uprising in 1751, Spanish forces were sent into the area to protect the settlers, and in 1752 Tubac became a presidio (fort).

Although the European history of this area is more than 300 years old, the area's human habitation dates far back into prehistory. Archaeologists have found evidence that there have been people living along the Santa Cruz River for nearly 10,000 years. The Hohokam lived in the area from about A.D. 300 until their mysterious disappearance around 1500, and when the Spanish arrived some 200 years later, they found the Pima people inhabiting this region.

Tubac's other claim to fame is as the site from which Juan Bautista de Anza III, the second commander of the presidio, set out in 1775 to find an overland route to California. De Anza led 240 settlers and more than 1,000 head of cattle on this grueling expedition, and when the group finally reached the coast of California, they founded the settlement of San Francisco. A year after de Anza's journey to the Pacific, the garrison was moved from Tubac to Tucson, and, with no protection, Tubac's settlers moved away from the area. Soldiers were once again stationed here beginning in 1787, but lack of funds caused the closure of the presidio again when, in 1821, Mexican independence brought Tubac under a new flag. It was not until this region became U.S. territory that settlers returned, and by 1860, Tubac was the largest town in Arizona.

After visiting Tubac Presidio State Historic Park and Tumacácori National Historical Park to learn about the area's history, you'll probably want to spend some time browsing through the shops. Keep in mind, however, that many of the local artists leave town in summer, prompting local shops to close on weekdays. The shops are open daily during the busy season of October through May.

ESSENTIALS

GETTING THERE The Santa Cruz Valley towns of Amado, Tubac, and Tumacácori are all due south of Tucson on I-19.

VISITOR INFORMATION For information on Tubac and Tumacácori, contact the **Tubac Chamber of Commerce** (© **520/398-2704;** www.tubacaz.com), or the **Tubac-Santa Cruz Visitor Center,** 4 Plaza Rd. (© **520/398-0007;** www.toursantacruz.com).

SPECIAL EVENTS Each year in February, artists from all over the country participate in the **Tubac Festival of the Arts.** On the third weekend in October, **Juan Bautista de Anza Days** commemorates Capt. Juan Bautista de Anza's 1775 westward trek that led to the founding of San Francisco.

ART & HISTORY IN THE SANTA CRUZ VALLEY

Tubac Center of the Arts ★ Tubac is an arts community, and this Spanish colonial building serves as its center for cultural activities. Throughout the season, the center features workshops, traveling exhibitions, juried shows, an annual crafts show, and theater and music performances. The quality of the art at these shows is generally better than what's found in most of the surrounding stores. There is also a good little gift shop here.

9 Plaza Rd. ✆ **520/398-2371.** www.tubacarts.org. Admission by donation. Mon–Sat 10am–4:30pm; Sun 1–4:30pm. Closed mid-May to Labor Day and major holidays.

Tubac Presidio State Historic Park Although little remains of the old presidio (fort) but buried foundation walls, this small park does a good job of presenting the region's Spanish colonial history. The nearby Tumacácori mission (see below) was founded in 1691, but it was not until 1752 that Tubac Presidio was established in response to a Pima Indian uprising. In 1775, the presidio's military garrison was moved to Tucson, and, with no protection from raiding Apaches, most of Tubac's settlers left the area. A military presence was reestablished in 1787, but after Mexican independence in 1821, insufficient funds led to the presidio's closing. Villagers once again abandoned Tubac because of Apache attacks. After the Gadsden Purchase, Tubac became part of the United States and was again resettled.

Park exhibits focus on the Spanish soldiers, Native Americans, religion, and contemporary Hispanic culture in southern Arizona. Also on the grounds is the old Tubac School, built in 1885 and the oldest schoolhouse in the state. Living-history presentations are staged October through March on Sundays between 1 and 4pm. Among the characters you'll meet are Spanish soldiers, settlers, and friars.

Presidio Dr. ✆ **520/398-2252.** www.azstateparks.com. Admission $3 adults ($2 between Memorial Day and Labor Day), free for children under 14. Daily 8am–5pm. Closed Christmas.

Tumacácori National Historical Park ★ Founded in 1691 by Jesuit missionary and explorer Father Eusebio Francisco Kino, San José de Tumacácori mission was one of the first Anglo settlements in what is today Arizona. Father Kino's mission was to convert the Pima Indians, and for the first 60 years, the mission was successful. However, in 1751, during the Pima Revolt, the mission was destroyed. For the next 70 years, this mission struggled to survive, but during the 1820s, an adobe mission church was constructed. Today, the mission ruins are a silent and haunting reminder of the role that Spanish missionaries played in settling the Southwest. Much of the old adobe mission church still stands, and the Spanish architectural influences can readily be seen. A small museum contains exhibits on mission life and the history of the region. On weekends between October and April, Native American and Mexican craftspeople give demonstrations of indigenous arts. January through April, on the nights of the full moon, the monument stays open until 9pm, and guided tours are available. On the second Wednesday of the month from October to March, there are special living-history tours to the nearby ruins of San Cayetano de Calabazas mission. These tours are by reservation and cost $10 per person. **La Fiesta de Tumacácori,** a celebration of Indian, Hispanic, and Anglo cultures, is held the first weekend of December.

1891 E. Frontage Rd. ✆ **520/398-2341.** www.nps.gov/tuma. Admission $3 adults, free for children under 16. Daily 8am–5pm. Closed Thanksgiving and Christmas. Take I-19 to Exit 29; Tumacácori is 3 miles south of Tubac.

Finds Going Nuts in Sahuarita

As you drive south from Tucson to Tubac, you pass through the town of Sahuarita, which is home to one of the largest pecan farms in the country. More than 6,000 acres surrounding Sahuarita are planted in pecan trees. At **The Pecan Store,** 1625 E. Sahuarita Rd., Sahuarita (✆ **800/327-3226** or 520/791-2062; www.pecanstore.com), you can go "nuts" stocking up on everything from fresh pecans to chocolate toffee pecans to mesquite-spiced pecans (my personal favorite).

SHOPPING

While tourist brochures like to tout Tubac as an artists' community, the town is more of a Southwest souvenir mecca. There are a few genuine art galleries here, but you have to look hard amid the many tourist shops to find the real gems.

Some of the better fine art in the area is at the **Karin Newby Gallery,** Mercado de Baca, 19 Tubac Rd. (✆ **888/398-9662** or 520/398-9662; www.karinnewbygallery.com), which also has a large sculpture garden. For traditional Western art, some by members of the prestigious Cowboy Artists of America, visit **Big Horn Galleries,** 37 Tubac Rd. (✆ **520/398-9209;** www.bighorngalleries.com).

If you're in the market for jewelry, visit **Blackstar,** E. Frontage Road (✆ **520/398-0451;** www.blackstarmines.com), in nearby Amado. This store specializes in locally mined opal and other exotic gemstones. You'll find the gallery at Exit 48 off I-19.

If you want to take the flavor of the area home, stop in at **The Chile Pepper,** on Tubac Road in downtown Tubac (✆ **520/398-2921**), for gourmet foods with a Southwestern accent. Down near Tumacácori National Historical Park, you'll find all things hot (chiles, hot sauces, salsas) arranged on the shelves of one of the more genuine Tubac-area institutions, the **Santa Cruz Chile & Spice Company,** 1868 E. Frontage Rd. (✆ **520/398-2591;** www.santacruzchili.com), a combination store and packing plant. There's an amazing assortment of familiar and obscure spices for sale. In back, you can see various herbs being prepared and packaged. The shop is open Monday through Saturday from 8am to 5pm.

BUENOS AIRES NATIONAL WILDLIFE REFUGE ★

If you're a bird-watcher, you'll definitely want to make the trip to **Buenos Aires National Wildlife Refuge,** P.O. Box 109, Sasabe, AZ 85633 (✆ **520/823-4251;** www.fws.gov/southwest/refuges/arizona/buenosaires/index.html), about 28 miles from Tubac. To get here, head north from Tubac on I-19 to Arivaca Junction, then drive west on a winding two-lane road. The refuge begins just outside the small community of Arivaca.

Your first stop should be **Arivaca Cienega,** a quarter of a mile east of Arivaca. *Cienega* is Spanish for "marsh," and that is exactly what you'll find here. A boardwalk leads across this marsh, which is fed by seven springs that provide year-round water and consequently attract an amazing variety of bird life. This is one of the few places in the United States where you can see a gray hawk, and vermilion flycatchers are quite common. Other good birding spots within the refuge include **Arivaca Creek,** 2 miles west of Arivaca, and **Aguirre Lake,** a half-mile north of the refuge headquarters and visitor center, which is off Arizona 286 north of Sasabe.

The **visitor center** is a good place to spot one of the refuge's rarest birds, the masked bobwhite quail. These quail disappeared from Arizona in the late 19th century, but have been reintroduced in the refuge. Other birds you might spot outside the visitor center include Bendire's thrashers, Chihuahuan ravens, canyon towhees, and green-tailed towhees. The visitor center is open daily from 7:30am to 4pm (closed Thanksgiving, Christmas, New Year's Day, and summer weekends).

Other wildlife in the refuge includes pronghorn antelopes, javelinas, coatimundis, white-tailed deer, mule deer, and coyotes. Guided birding and other tours are offered weekends November through April. Call for details; some walks require reservations. There is primitive **camping** at nearly 100 designated spots along rough gravel roads. Look for the brown campsite signs along the road, and bring your own water.

These roads also offer good mountain biking. If you're looking for a strenuous hike, try the **Mustang Trail.** The trail climbs from Arivaca Creek, 2 miles west of Arivacain, to the surrounding dry hills and makes for a 5-mile round-trip hike.

OTHER OUTDOOR PURSUITS

Linking Tubac with Tumacácori is the 8-mile **de Anza Trail,** which follows the Santa Cruz River for much of its route and passes through forests and grasslands. This trail is part of the **Juan Bautista de Anza National Historic Trail,** which stretches from Nogales to San Francisco and commemorates the overland journey of the Spanish captain who, in 1775 and 1776, led a small band of colonists overland to California. These settlers founded what is now the city of San Francisco. Today, bird-watching is the most popular activity along the trail. History buffs will also get to see an excavation of part of the Spanish colonial settlement of Tubac. The most convenient trail head is beside Tubac Presidio State Historic Park. **Rex Ranch** (✆ **800/547-2696** or 520/398-2914; www.rexranch.com) offers horseback rides for $35 per hour.

If golf is more your speed, you can play a round at the **Tubac Golf Resort** (✆ **520/398-2211;** www.tubacgolfresort.com), just north of Tubac off East Frontage Road. Greens fees range from $39 to $109 in the winter.

WHERE TO STAY

IN AMADO

The Inn at Amado Territory Ranch ★ This modern inn just off I-19 at the crossroads of Amado is built in the territorial style and captures the feel of an old Arizona ranch house. Guest rooms are outfitted in a mix of Mexican rustic furnishings and reproduction East Coast antiques, just as homes would have been furnished in Arizona 100 years ago. Rooms on the second floor feature balconies with views across the farm fields of the Santa Cruz Valley, while those on the ground floor have patios. The inn holds high teas twice a week, and the Amado Café is right next door.

Moments **The Ruby Road**

If you enjoy scenic drives and don't mind gravel roads, you won't want to pass up the opportunity to drive the Ruby Road from Arivaca through Coronado National Forest to **Peña Blanca Lake** and **Nogales.** This road winds its way through the mountains just north of the Mexican border, passing Arivaca Lake before reaching picturesque Peña Blanca Lake, where the pavement resumes. Along the way, you'll pass the privately owned ghost town of **Ruby** (✆ **520/744-4471**), which is open to the public Thursday through Sunday (admission $12). Call first to make sure the caretaker is available. If you want to camp, you'll find a couple of campgrounds at Peña Blanca Lake.

3001 E. Frontage Rd. (P.O. Box 81), Amado, AZ 85645. ✆ **888/398-8684** or 520/398-8684. Fax 520/398-8186. www.amado-territory-inn.com. 9 units. Nov–June $130–$145 double; July–Oct $105–$115 double. Rates include full breakfast. AE, DISC, MC, V. Pets accepted. **Amenities:** Restaurant (American/Greek); massage. *In room:* A/C, hair dryer, Wi-Fi, no phone.

The Rex Ranch ★ *Finds* With its classic Southwestern styling and location adjacent to the de Anza Trail, this place is truly a hidden getaway. Just getting to this remote property is something of an adventure, since you have to drive *through* the Santa Cruz River to reach it. When you see the pink-walled mission-revival building in the middle of the desert, you'll know you've arrived someplace distinctly different. Although not all of the guest rooms are as attractively decorated as the public areas, the new rooms and the more recently renovated rooms are quite comfortable. Primarily a conference center and economical spa, the ranch offers a wide variety of spa treatments and massages. The attractive little dining room is one of this area's best restaurants (see Cantina Romantica under "Where to Dine," below).

131 Amado Montosa Rd. (P.O. Box 636), Amado, AZ 85645. ✆ **800/547-2696** or 520/398-2914. www.rexranch.com. 30 units. Oct to mid-Dec $115–$125 double, $160 suite; mid-Dec to May $135–$175 double, $205 suite; June–Sept $95–$105 double, $125 suite. Rates include continental breakfast. AE, DISC, MC, V. 2-night minimum stay. **Amenities:** Restaurant (Southwestern/New American); outdoor pool; spa; Jacuzzi; mountain-bike rentals; horseback riding; concierge; massage. *In room:* A/C, fridge, coffeemaker, Wi-Fi, no phone.

IN TUBAC

Tubac Golf Resort ★★ *Value* This economical golf resort is built on the Otero Ranch, which dates back to 1789 and is the oldest Spanish land-grant ranch in the Southwest. With its green fairways, the resort is a lush oasis amid the dry hills of the Santa Cruz Valley. The ranch has been undergoing extensive renovations in recent years and is now both a modern golf resort and a secluded hideaway capable of competing with resorts in Tucson. This resort has more a classic Southwestern ambience than most of the Tucson golf resorts, and because it is fairly small, it has a low-key feel that I like. The red-tile roofs and brick archways throughout the resort conjure up the Spanish heritage, while guest rooms are spacious and modern and set amid expansive lawns. Casitas have patios, beamed ceilings, and beehive fireplaces; newer rooms are worth requesting. Oh, yes, and watch out for cows grazing on the golf course.

1 Otero Rd. (P.O. Box 1297), Tubac, AZ 85646. ✆ **800/848-7893** or 520/398-2211. Fax 520/398-9261. www.tubacgolfresort.com. 98 units. $109–$229 double; $139–$359 suite. Children under 12 stay free in parent's room. AE, DISC, MC, V. Pets accepted ($25 fee). **Amenities:** 3 restaurants (Continental, Mexican); lounge; outdoor pool; 27-hole golf course; tennis court; exercise room; spa; Jacuzzi; bike rental; business center; shopping arcade; room service; massage; babysitting; coin-op laundry; laundry service. *In room:* A/C, TV, dataport, fridge, coffeemaker, hair dryer, iron, safe.

WHERE TO DINE

In addition to the restaurants mentioned below, the **Tubac Golf Resort** (see "Where to Stay," above) has a good restaurant.

IN AMADO

Amado Café MEDITERRANEAN/AMERICAN This restaurant, in a handsome territorial-style building just off I-19, is a good bet for lunch or dinner. The best part of the experience is sitting out back on the rustic flagstone patio, listening to the gurgling fountain, and contemplating the view of the mountains in the distance. The menu includes sandwiches, salads, stuffed grape leaves, and prime rib.

3001 E. Frontage Rd. (Exit 48 off I–19), Amado. ✆ **520/398-9211.** Reservations not necessary. Main courses $7.50–$11 lunch, $11–$22 dinner. AE, DISC, MC, V. Tues–Sat 11:30am–2pm and 5–8pm; Sun 11:30am–2pm.

Starry, Starry Nights

Southern Arizona's clear skies and the absence of lights in the surrounding desert make the night sky here as brilliant as anywhere on earth. This fact has not gone unnoticed by the world's astronomers—southern Arizona has come to be known as the Astronomy Capital of the World.

Many observatories are open to the public, but you'll need to make tour reservations well in advance. In addition to the ones listed below, the **Flandrau Science Center & Planetarium** (p. 366) in Tucson offers public viewings. In Flagstaff, there are public viewing programs at the **Lowell Observatory** (p. 248).

The **Smithsonian Institution Fred Lawrence Whipple Observatory** (✆ **520/670-5707;** www.cfa.harvard.edu/flwo/visitcenter.html), located atop 8,550-foot Mount Hopkins, is the largest observatory operated by the Smithsonian Astrophysical Observatory. Six-hour tours of the observatory are offered mid-March through November Monday, Wednesday, and Friday, and cost $7 for adults, $2.50 for children 6 to 12; no children under 6 allowed. Reservations are required and should be made 4 to 6 weeks in advance. No food is available here, so bring a picnic lunch. The observatory's visitor center (Mon–Fri 8:30am–4:30pm; closed federal holidays) is located on Mount Hopkins Road, near Amado (take Exit 56 off I-19, drive south 3 miles, and turn left on Elephant Head Road and then right on Mount Hopkins Road).

Located in the Quinlan Mountains atop 6,875-foot Kitt Peak, **Kitt Peak National Observatory** ★ (✆ **520/318-8726;** www.noao.edu/kpno) is the largest and most famous astronomical observatory in the region. This is the area's only major observatory to offer public nighttime viewing. Day visitors, however, must be content with a visitor center (daily 9am–3:45pm), museum, and guided tour. Tours are held at 10am, 11:30am, and 1:30pm. Admission is by $2 per person suggested donation, and tours are $3.50 for adults and $2 for children ages 6 to 12. The observatory is 56 miles southwest of Tucson off Arizona 86. Nighttime stargazing (reservations required; call 4–8 weeks in advance) costs $39 adults; $34 students, seniors, and children under 18. The visitor center is closed Thanksgiving, Christmas, and New Year's Day.

The **Mount Graham International Observatory** near the town of Safford offers 7-hour tours that include lunch but do not include viewing through the observatory's telescopes. Tours are arranged through **Eastern Arizona College's Discovery Park Campus,** 1651 W. Discovery Park Blvd., Safford (✆ **928/428-6260;** www.discoverypark.com). The tours are held on Saturdays between early May and mid-November, and cost $40 (reservations required).

Situated on the grounds of the privately owned Vega-Bray Observatory, an amateur observatory with six telescopes and a planetarium, the **Astronomer's Inn** ★, 1311 S. Astronomer's Rd., Benson, AZ 85602 (✆ **520/586-7906;** www.astronomersinn.com), is one of the most unusual lodgings in the state. The inn provides guests with not only a bed for the night, but a chance to observe the night sky and the sun through the observatory's telescopes. Viewing programs range from $59 to $130 per night. The inn is located 4 miles outside Benson; call for directions. Rates are $85 to $129 double.

Cantina Romantica ★★ SOUTHWESTERN/NEW AMERICAN Located in a historic adobe hacienda at The Rex Ranch resort (see "Where to Stay," above), 6 miles north of Tubac, Cantina Romantica is a culinary oasis in this neck of the woods. The menu has a metropolitan flair and includes the likes of pecan-crusted pork roulade and dry-aged filet mignon with mushroom-cabernet sauce. The setting is rustic and colorful, and the restaurant is reached by driving *through* the Santa Cruz River. Because the route to the restaurant is so unusual and because The Rex Ranch is so colorful, you should be sure to schedule an early dinner so you can enjoy the sights.

131 Amado Montosa Rd., Amado. ✆ **520/398-2914.** Reservations required. Main courses $13–$33. AE, DISC, MC, V. Wed–Sun 5:30–9pm. Call ahead during summer; restaurant may be closed.

IN TUBAC & TUMACACORI

If you need a latte while you're in town, stop by the **Tubac Deli & Coffee Co.,** 6 Plaza Rd. (✆ **520/398-3330;** tubacdeli.com).

Nob Hill Gourmet Market and Fine Dining ★ NEW AMERICAN Until this restaurant opened, there was nowhere right in Tubac for its new well-heeled residents to enjoy a white-tablecloth dinner. Actually, this is much more than someplace to sit down to trout stuffed with lemon and fennel or a filet mignon with truffle-port demi-glaze. There's also a small but well-stocked gourmet market, so you can pack some goodies and wander down to the Santa Cruz River for a picnic in the woods.

In Plaza de Anza, 10 Avenida Goya, Suite B. ✆ **520/398-1010.** www.nobhilltubac.com. Main courses $7.50–$13 lunch, $17–$32 dinner. AE, MC, V. Daily 11am–3pm and 5–8:30pm.

Shelby's Bistro Located behind a small shopping plaza and across a little foot bridge, this casual place has a very pleasant patio and is a great spot for lunch. The lunch menu is a mix of pastas, salads, sandwiches, and pizzas; in the evening, there's prime rib, lobster, and steaks. Try the Sonoran spice-rubbed chicken breast.

In Mercado de Baca, 19 Tubac Rd. ✆ **520/398-8075.** Reservations not necessary. Main courses $9.25–$33 dinner. MC, V. Sun–Tues 11am–4pm; Wed–Sat 11am–4pm and 5–9pm.

Wisdom's Cafe *Finds* MEXICAN Located between Tubac and Tumacácori (look for the giant chicken statues out front), this roadside diner is a Santa Cruz Valley institution, in business since 1944. With a cement floor and walls hung with old cowboy stuff, it feels a bit like a cross between a cave and an old barn. The menu is short but includes some twists on standard Mexican fare, including tostadas, tacos, and enchiladas made with turkey. Don't eat too much, though, or you won't have room for this restaurant's main draw—huge fruit burritos that are basically Mexican fruit pies.

1931 E. Frontage Rd., Tumacácori. ✆ **520/398-2397.** www.wisdomscafe.com. Reservations not necessary. Main dishes $4.50–$15. AE, DISC, MC, V. Mon–Sat 11am–3pm and 5–8pm.

3 Nogales

63 miles S of Tucson; 175 miles S of Phoenix; 65 miles W of Sierra Vista

Situated on the Mexican border, the twin towns of Nogales, Arizona, and Nogales, Sonora, Mexico (known jointly as Ambos Nogales), form a bustling border community. All day long, U.S. citizens cross into Mexico to shop for bargains on Mexican handicrafts, pharmaceuticals, tequila, and Kahlúa, while Mexican citizens cross into the United States to buy products not available in their country.

ESSENTIALS

GETTING THERE Nogales is the last town on I-19 before the Mexican border. Arizona 82 leads northeast from town toward Sonoita and Sierra Vista.

VISITOR INFORMATION Contact the Nogales Chamber of Commerce, 123 W. Kino Park Way (✆ **520/287-3685;** www.nogaleschamber.com).

EXPLORING NORTH & SOUTH OF THE BORDER

Most people who visit Nogales, Arizona, are here to cross the border to Nogales, Mexico. The favorable exchange rate makes shopping in Mexico very popular with Americans, although many of the items for sale in Mexico can be found at lower prices in Tucson. Many people now cross the border specifically to purchase prescription drugs, and pharmacies line the streets near the border crossing.

A couple of miles outside Nogales on the road to Patagonia, you'll see signs for the **Arizona Vineyards Winery,** 1830 Patagonia Rd. (✆ **520/287-7972**), open daily from 10am to 6pm. You may not think of Arizona as wine country, but the Spanish began growing grapes and making wine when they arrived centuries ago.

Nogales, Mexico, is a typical border town filled with tiny shops selling crafts and souvenirs. Some of the better deals are on wool rugs, which cost a fraction of what a Navajo rug costs but are not nearly as well made. Pottery is another popular buy. My personal favorites are the ceramic sinks and hand-blown glass tumblers and pitchers. Dozens of restaurants serve simple Mexican food and cheap margaritas.

Many good shops and restaurants in Nogales, Mexico, are within walking distance of the border, so unless you plan to continue farther into Mexico, it's not a good idea to take your car. There are numerous pay parking lots and garages on the U.S. side of the border. If you should take your car into Mexico, be sure to get Mexican auto insurance beforehand—your U.S. auto insurance will not be valid. There are plenty of insurance companies set up along the road leading to the border.

Most businesses in Nogales, Mexico, accept U.S. dollars. You may bring back $800 worth of merchandise duty-free, including 1 liter of liquor (if you are 21 or older). If planned regulations go into effect in January 2008, all U.S. citizens crossing the border into Mexico will need to have a passport. However, border states have been fighting these new regulations, and implementation may be delayed.

WHERE TO STAY

Esplendor Resort at Rio Rico ★★ *Value* Just a few miles north of Nogales, Esplendor is a secluded hilltop golf resort with great views across the Santa Cruz Valley and amenities that are similar to what you'll find at many Tucson resorts. Rooms are done in a very tasteful Spanish colonial decor, have attractive tile work in the bathrooms, and are some of the prettiest in southern Arizona. The only drawback is that

---

Finds These Boots Were Made for Ridin'

Cowboys and cowgirls in search of the ultimate pair of boots should be sure to schedule a visit to Nogales's **Paul Bond Boot Company,** 915 W. Paul Bond Dr. (✆ **520/281-0512;** www.paulbondboots.com), where, in 2007, 90-year-old Paul Bond was still designing boots that are absolute works of art and that sell for as much as $1,000 or more. You can also get custom-made boots for under $500. This bootmaker has been in business in Nogales since the 1950s.

---

the resort's Robert Trent Jones golf course is a short drive away on the far side of the freeway. The dining room serves good food and has very nice views. The resort is a good place to just get away from it all, but it also makes a good base for exploring east to Patagonia and west to Buenos Aires National Wildlife Refuge.

1069 Camino Caralampi, Rio Rico, AZ 85648. ✆ **800/288-4746** or 520/281-1901. Fax 520/281-7132. www.hhandr.com/esplendor. 180 units. $89–$139 double; $199–$450 suite. Children under 12 stay free in parent's room. AE, DC, DISC, MC, V. Pets accepted ($50 deposit). **Amenities:** 3 restaurants (Southwestern/Continental, American); 2 lounges; Olympic-size outdoor pool; 18-hole golf course; 4 tennis courts; access to nearby health club; exercise room; Jacuzzi; sauna; concierge; business center; massage; babysitting; laundry service; horseback riding. *In room:* A/C, TV, dataport, fridge, coffeemaker, hair dryer, iron, high-speed Internet access, Wi-Fi.

Hacienda Corona de Guevavi ★ *Finds* Few lodging places anywhere in Arizona capture the character of the state better than this historic hilltop ranch house outside of Nogales. Originally the headquarters of the Guevavi Ranch, the sprawling home was once a favorite getaway for John Wayne and had been abandoned when Phil and Wendy Stover bought the hacienda and embarked on a major restoration. Today the inn, which is built around courtyards and quiet gardens, has five very tastefully decorated guest rooms, all but one of which reflect the inn's Southwestern heritage (La Patrona is my favorite room). The one room that does not have a Southwestern flavor has the feel of a room at an African safari lodge. There is also a casita (guesthouse) available for families.

348 S. River Rd., Nogales, AZ 85628. ✆ **520/287-6503.** Fax 520/287-9312. www.haciendacorona.com. 6 units. $175–$225 double. Rates include full breakfast and evening hors d'oeuvres. DISC, MC, V. No children under 8 in main house. Pets accepted in casita. **Amenities:** Outdoor pool; concierge. *In room:* A/C, fridge, hair dryer, iron, no phone.

WHERE TO DINE

La Roca Restaurant ★ *Finds* MEXICAN Built into a cliff and cool as a cave, La Roca conjures up images of colonial Mexico. White-jacketed waiters provide a level of professional service found only in the most expensive establishments north of the border. Folk art and paintings in the spacious rooms seem to make the interior glow, and at night the place is lit with candles ensconced on the stone walls. The Guaymas shrimp and chicken *mole* are our longtime favorites. Don't miss the margaritas. Downstairs from the restaurant, you'll find a shop selling high-end Mexican pottery, furniture, antiques, and hand-woven rugs.

Calle Elias 91, Nogales, Mexico. ✆ **011/52/631/312-0760.** www.larocarestaurant.com. Main courses $8.50–$19. MC, V. Daily 11am–midnight. Walk through the border checkpoint, continue 300 ft., cross the railroad tracks on your left, and look for a narrow side street along the base of the cliff you saw as you crossed into Mexico. The restaurant is about 100 ft. down this street. After dark, solo travelers might want to avoid this restaurant if they are on foot.

4 Patagonia ★★ & Sonoita ★

Patagonia: 18 miles NW of Nogales; 60 miles SE of Tucson; 171 miles SE of Phoenix; 50 miles SW of Tombstone

A mild climate, numerous good restaurants, bed-and-breakfast inns, and a handful of wineries have turned the small communities of Patagonia and Sonoita into a favorite weekend getaway for Tucsonans. Sonoita Creek, one of the only perennial streams in southern Arizona, attracts an amazing variety of bird life and, consequently, also attracts flocks of bird-watchers from all over the country.

Patagonia and Sonoita are only about 12 miles apart, but they have decidedly different characters. Patagonia is a sleepy little hamlet with tree-shaded streets, old adobe buildings, and a park in the middle of town. The town's main draw, especially for bird-watchers, is the Nature Conservancy preserve on the edge of town. Sonoita, on the other hand, sits out on the windswept high plains and is really a highway crossroads, not a town. The landscape around Sonoita, however, is filled with expensive new homes on small ranches, and not far away are the vineyards of Arizona's wine country.

ESSENTIALS

GETTING THERE Sonoita is at the junction of Arizona 83 and Arizona 82. Patagonia is 12 miles southwest of Sonoita on Arizona 82.

VISITOR INFORMATION The **Patagonia Area Business Association Visitor's Center,** 307 McKeown Ave. (✆ **888/794-0060** or 520/394-9186; www.patagonia az.com), inside Mariposa Books in the center of Patagonia, is open Monday through Saturday from 10am to 5pm and Sunday from 11am to 4pm.

BIRD-WATCHING, WINE TASTING & OTHER AREA ACTIVITIES

Patagonia, 18 miles northwest of Nogales on Arizona 82, is a historic old mining and ranching town 4,000 feet up in the Patagonia Mountains. Surrounded by higher mountains, the little town has for years been popular with film and television crews. Among the films that have been shot here over the years are *Oklahoma!, Red River, A Star Is Born,* and *David and Bathsheba.* TV programs filmed here have included *Little House on the Prairie* and *The Young Riders.* Today, however, bird-watching and tranquility draw most people to this remote town.

The **Patagonia–Sonoita Creek Preserve** (✆ **520/394-2400;** www.nature.org) is owned by the Nature Conservancy and protects 2 miles of Sonoita Creek riparian (riverside) habitat, which is important to migratory birds. More than 300 species of birds have been spotted at the preserve, which makes it a popular destination with birders from all over the country. Among the rare birds that can be seen are 22 species of flycatchers, kingbirds, and phoebes, plus the Montezuma quail. A forest of cottonwood trees, some of which are 100 feet tall, lines the creek and is one of the best remaining examples of such a forest in southern Arizona. At one time, these forests grew along all the rivers in the region. To reach the sanctuary, which is just outside Patagonia on a dirt road that parallels Arizona 82, turn west on Fourth Avenue and then south on Pennsylvania Street, cross the creek, and continue about 1 mile. From April to September, hours are Wednesday through Sunday from 6:30am to 4pm; from October to March, hours are Wednesday through Sunday from 7:30am to 4pm. Admission is $5 ($3 for Nature Conservancy members). On Saturday at 9am, there are naturalist-guided walks through the preserve; reservations are not required.

On your way to or from the Nature Conservancy Preserve, be sure to drop by **Paton's Birder's Haven,** which is basically the backyard of Marion Paton. Numerous hummingbird feeders and a variety of other feeders attract an amazing range of birds to the yard, making this a favorite stop of avid birders who are touring the region. If you're heading out to the Nature Conservancy preserve, watch for the BIRDER'S HAVEN sign at 477 Pennsylvania Rd. after you cross the creek.

Another required birders' stop in the area is at the **Patagonia Roadside Rest Area** 4¼ miles south of Patagonia on Arizona 82. This pull-off is a good place to look for rose-throated becards, varied buntings, and zone-tailed hawks.

Avid birders will also want to visit **Las Cienegas National Conservation Area** (✆ **520/258-7200;** www.az.blm.gov/nca/lascienegas/lascieneg.htm), which has grasslands, wetlands, and oak forests. This is a good place to look for the rarely seen gray hawk. Access is off the east side of Arizona 83, about 7 miles north of Sonoita.

Patagonia Lake State Park (✆ **520/287-6965;** www.azstateparks.com), about 7 miles south of Patagonia off Arizona 82, is a popular boating and fishing lake that was formed by the damming of Sonoita Creek. The lake is 2½ miles long and stocked in winter with rainbow trout. Other times of year, people fish for bass, crappie, bluegill, and catfish. Park facilities include a picnic ground, campground, and swimming beach. There is also good bird-watching here—elegant trogons, which are among the most beautiful of southern Arizona's rare birds, have been spotted. The park day-use fee is $7 ($8 holidays and summer weekends). Campsites are $12 to $25. Adjacent to the park, you'll find the **Sonoita Creek State Natural Area** (✆ **520/287-2791**), a 5,000-acre preserve along the banks of Sonoita Creek. During much of the year, the natural area operates boat tours several mornings each week. These tours focus on the birds and history of the area. There are also guided hikes and guided bird-watching outings. Call the number above for information and reservations.

If you'd like to have a local birding guide take you out and help you identify the area's many species of flycatchers, contact Matt Brown at the **Patagonia Birding & Butterfly Co.** (✆ **520/604-6300;** www.lifebirds.com). If you want to do some horseback riding, **Coronado Outfitters** (✆ **520/394-0187;** www.coronadooutfitters.com) offers 1-hour rides for $25 and half-day rides for $75. **Arizona Horseback Experience** (✆ **520/455-5696;** www.horsebackexperience.com) also does trail rides in this area. A 3-hour ride is $85 and a wine-tasting ride to a local winery is $160.

Sonoita proper is little more than a crossroads with a few shops and restaurants, but surrounding the community are miles of rolling grasslands that are a mix of luxury-home "ranchettes" and actual cattle ranches, all of which have spectacular big-sky views. Out on those high plains, vineyards have made Sonoita Arizona's own little wine country. Most of the wineries are located in or near the village of Elgin, which is 10 miles east of Sonoita. Right in Sonoita, you'll find **Dos Cabezas Wine Works** (✆ **602/622-0399;** www.doscabezaswinery.com), which is located on Arizona 82 in the middle of town. The winery's tasting room is open Friday through Sunday from 10:30am to 4:30pm. Just west of Elgin, you'll find **Callaghan Vineyards,** 336 Elgin Rd. (✆ **520/455-5322;** www.callaghanvineyards.com), which is open for tastings Friday through Sunday from 11am to 3pm. This winery produces by far the best wines in the region and, perhaps, the best wines in the state. The two other area wineries don't do nearly as good a job, but you can be the judge yourself. In the ghost town of Elgin, there's the **Village of Elgin Winery** (✆ **520/455-9309;** www.elginwines.com), which is open daily from 10am to 5pm. Three miles south of Elgin, you'll find **Sonoita Vineyards,** on Elgin-Canelo Road (✆ **520/455-5893;** www.sonoitavineyards.com), which is open daily from 10am to 4pm. The above tasting-room hours are subject to change, so you might want to call ahead.

While in Patagonia, be sure to check out the interesting shops and galleries around town. You'll also find interesting books and gifts at **Mariposa Books,** 317 McKeown Ave. (✆ **520/394-9186**). **Mesquite Grove Gallery,** 371 McKeown Ave. (✆ **520/394-2358**), has a good selection of works by area artists. At **Global Arts Gallery,** 315 McKeown Ave. (✆ **520/394-0077**), you'll find a wide range of ethnic arts, fine art, jewelry, and women's clothing. Also be sure to visit **La Galeria Dia de los Muertos,** 266 Naugle Ave. (✆ **520/394-2035**). This little cottage, associated with a Patagonia gift shop, was the creation of Grayce Arnold. She assembled a collection of hundreds of Mexican skeleton figures, which are created for Mexico's Dia de los Muertos (Day of the Dead) celebration. The gallery is open daily from 10am to 5pm.

WHERE TO STAY

IN PATAGONIA

Circle Z Ranch ★ In business since 1926, this is the oldest continuously operating dude ranch in Arizona. Over the years, it has served as a backdrop for numerous movies and TV shows, including *Gunsmoke* and John Wayne's *Red River*. The 6,500-acre ranch on the banks of Sonoita Creek is bordered by the Nature Conservancy's Patagonia–Sonoita Creek Sanctuary, Patagonia State Park, and the Coronado National Forest. Miles of trails ensure everyone gets in plenty of riding in desert hills, grasslands, or riparian forest along the creek. The adobe cottages provide an authentic ranch feel that's appreciated by guests hoping to find a genuine bit of the Old West.

Ariz. 82 (between Nogales and Patagonia), P.O. Box 194, Patagonia, AZ 85624. ✆ **888/854-2525** or 520/394-2525. Fax 520/394-2058. www.circlez.com. 24 units. $2,360–$3,300 double per week. Rates do not include 15% service charge. Lower rates for children 15 and under. Nightly rates sometimes available, with 3-night minimum. Rates include all meals and horseback riding. MC, V. Closed early May to late Oct. **Amenities:** Dining room; BYOB lounge; outdoor pool; tennis court; game room; guest laundry; horseback riding. *In room:* No phone.

Duquesne House B&B ★ This old adobe building 1 block off Patagonia's main street was built in 1898 as miners' apartments. The unusual little building, with its shady front porch, is your best choice for overnight accommodations in Patagonia. Each unit has its own entrance, sitting room, and bedroom, and is decorated in quintessentially Southwestern style. My favorite room has an ornate woodstove and claw-foot tub. At the back of the house, an enclosed porch overlooks the garden.

357 Duquesne Ave. (P.O. Box 162), Patagonia, AZ 85624. ✆ **520/394-2732.** 4 units. $99 double. Rate includes full breakfast. No credit cards. *In room:* A/C, no phone.

IN SONOITA

La Hacienda de Sonoita ★ Located on the east side of Sonoita and not too far out of town, this hacienda-style B&B has unobstructed views that stretch to the distant mountain ranges surrounding these high plains. The inn is built around a central courtyard, which has a bubbling fountain and covered porches. There's also another covered porch that looks out to the eastern views. The decor in the guest rooms ranges from rancho deluxe to cowboy chic. My personal favorite is the Grand Canyon Room.

34 Swanson Rd. (P.O. Box 408), Sonoita, AZ 85637. ✆ **520/455-5308.** Fax 520/455-5309. www.haciendasonoita.com. 4 units. $115–$140 double. Children under 12 stay free in parent's room. AE, MC, V. *In room:* A/C, no phone.

Sonoita Inn Housed in a barnlike building, the Sonoita Inn plays up the area's ranching history. The building was originally constructed by the owner of the famed Triple Crown–winning thoroughbred Secretariat, and in 1999 it was converted into an inn. The lobby, with its wooden floors, huge fireplace, and ranch brands for decoration, is cool and dark (a welcome escape on hot summer days). Guest rooms feature Indian rugs and 1950s-inspired bedspreads for a retro cowboy touch. Although it's right on Sonoita's main road, the fascinating decor more than makes up for the less-than-quiet location. The Mountain View Room on the second floor has the best view. A popular steakhouse is adjacent to the inn.

At intersection of Ariz. 82 and Ariz. 83, P.O. Box 99, Sonoita, AZ 85637. ✆ **800/696-1006** or 520/455-5935. www.sonoitainn.com. 18 units. $99–$149 double. Rates include deluxe continental breakfast. Children under 18 stay free in parent's room. AE, DISC, MC, V. Pets accepted ($25 per night). *In room:* A/C, TV/VCR, free local calls.

WHERE TO DINE

IN PATAGONIA

For good coffee and pastries, check out **Gathering Grounds,** 319 McKeown Ave. (✆ **520/394-2097**), which also serves ice cream and has a deli. Looking for nightlife? Don't miss **La Mision de San Miguel,** 335 McKeown St. (✆ **520/394-0123;** www.lamisionpatagonia.com), which looks like an old mission but inside is a Mexican-inspired bar with live music and dancing on Friday and Saturday nights.

Santo's Mexican Cafe *Finds* MEXICAN This place is about as nondescript and basic as a roadside diner can be, but the Mexican food served here is always fresh and flavorful. If the weather is good, sit out front under the canopy that shades the patio. This place is a favorite of birders.

328 Naugle Ave. ✆ **520/394-2597.** Reservations not accepted. Main dishes $6–$8.25. MC, V. Tues–Wed 7am–3pm; Thurs–Sun 7am–8pm.

Velvet Elvis Pizza Company ITALIAN This casual hangout sums up the unusual character of Patagonia's residents. Faux-finished walls ooze artiness, while paeans to pop culture include shrines to both the Virgin Mary and Elvis. The menu features a variety of pizzas, but if you can remember to plan a day in advance, you should call in an order for the Inca pizza (made with a quinoa-flour crust). Add an organic salad and accompany it with some fresh juice, microbrew, espresso, or wine.

292 Naugle Ave. ✆ **520/394-2102.** www.velvetelvispizza.com. Reservations not accepted. Pizzas $12–$45; other dishes $6.50–$16. MC, V. Thurs–Sun 11:30am–8:30pm.

IN SONOITA

Grab good breads and pastries, hot breakfasts, and sandwiches at the **Grasslands Bakery/ Café,** 3119 Ariz. 83 (✆ **520/455-4770;** www.grasslandsbakery.com), which is an outpost of organic foods. There are even tastings of organic wines and loads of house-made salsas, jams, and other items for sale. The bakery is open Thursday through Sunday from 8am to 3pm.

Café Sonoita ★ AMERICAN A tiny place with just a handful of tables, this cafe serves some of the best food in the area and has long been a favorite with locals. The menu, which changes daily and is limited to a handful of dishes that are listed on a blackboard, is surprisingly creative. Ingredients are always fresh, which is why the menu changes all the time, and there are local wines to accompany the meals. Although you can get straightforward traditional fare such as steaks and prime rib, the best reason to eat here is the more creative dishes.

3280 Ariz. 82 (at the east end of town). ✆ **520/455-5278.** www.cafesonoita.com. Reservations accepted only for parties of 4 or more. Main courses $5.50–$8.75 lunch; $8.50–$18 dinner. DISC, MC, V. Wed–Thurs 5–8pm; Fri–Sat 11am–2:30pm and 5–8pm.

Canela ★ SOUTHWESTERN This is the most upscale restaurant at the crossroads of Sonoita and was an instant hit when it opened. The menu changes frequently to take advantage of what's fresh and seasonal, but may include Hubbard squash soup flavored with Indian spices and pumpkin seeds, mussels in a green-chile–white-wine broth, or fennel-crusted venison flank steak served with pecan cous-cous. If you're looking for the quintessential Arizona wine-country restaurant, this is it.

3252 Ariz. 82. ✆ **520/455-5873.** Reservations recommended. Main courses $15–$21. AE, DISC, MC, V. Thurs–Sun 5–10pm.

The Steak Out ★ STEAKHOUSE This is ranch country, and this big barn of a place is where the ranchers head when they want a good steak. A classic cowboy atmosphere prevails—there's even a mounted buffalo head just inside the front door. The restaurant's name and the scent of a mesquite fire should be all the hints you need about what to order—a grilled steak, preferably the exceedingly tender filet mignon. Wash it down with a margarita, and you've got the perfect cowboy dinner.

At intersection of Ariz. 82 and Ariz. 83. ✆ **520/455-5205.** Reservations recommended. Main courses $10–$35. AE, DISC, MC, V. Mon–Thurs 5–9pm; Fri 5–10pm; Sat 11am–10pm; Sun 11am–9pm.

5 Sierra Vista & the San Pedro Valley ★

70 miles SE of Tucson; 189 miles SE of Phoenix; 33 miles SW of Tombstone; 33 miles W of Bisbee

Located at an elevation of 4,620 feet above sea level, Sierra Vista is blessed with the perfect climate—never too hot, never too cold. This fact more than anything else has contributed to Sierra Vista becoming one of the fastest-growing cities in Arizona. Although the city itself is a modern, sprawling community outside the gates of the U.S. Army's Fort Huachuca, it is wedged between the Huachuca Mountains and the valley of the San Pedro River. Consequently, Sierra Vista makes a good base for exploring the region's natural attractions.

Within a few miles' drive of town are the San Pedro Riparian National Conservation Area, Coronado National Memorial, and the Nature Conservancy's Ramsey Canyon Preserve. No other area of the United States attracts more attention from birders, who come in hopes of spotting some of the 300 species that have been sighted in southeastern Arizona. About 25 miles north of town is Kartchner Caverns State Park, the region's biggest attraction.

ESSENTIALS

GETTING THERE Sierra Vista is at the junction of Arizona 90 and Arizona 92 about 35 miles south of I-10. Sierra Vista Municipal Airport is served by **Great Lakes Airlines** (✆ **800/554-5111;** www.greatlakesav.com) from Phoenix.

VISITOR INFORMATION The **Sierra Vista Convention & Visitors Bureau,** 3020 Tacoma St. (✆ **800/288-3861** or 520/417-6960; www.visitsierravista.com), can provide information on the area. To find the visitor center if you're coming from the north, take the Arizona 90 Bypass, turn right on Coronado Drive, turn left on Tacoma Street, and continue to the Oscar Yrun Community Center.

SPECIAL EVENTS In February, cowboy poets, singers, and musicians come together at the **Cochise Cowboy Poetry & Music Gathering** (✆ **800/288-3861** or 520/417-6960; www.cowboypoets.com).

ATTRACTIONS AROUND BENSON

While Kartchner Caverns is the main draw in the Benson area, you may also want to visit the remarkable **Singing Wind Bookshop** (✆ **520/586-2425**), on a ranch down a dirt road north of town. The store has been in business more than 30 years and started out with just a couple of shelves of books. Now the inventory is well into the thousands, with an emphasis on the Southwest, natural sciences, and children's literature. To get here, take Exit 304 from I-10 in Benson. Drive north 2¼ miles and take a right (east) at the sign that says SINGING WIND ROAD. Drive to the end, opening and closing the gate. The store is open daily from 9am to 5pm.

Finds Navajo Rugs

If you happen to be in the market for a Navajo rug, get in touch with Steve Getzwiller at **Nizhoni Ranch Gallery** (✆ **520/455-5020;** www.navajorug.com), which is located outside Sonoita. Here you'll find one of Arizona's best selections of contemporary and old Navajo rugs.

Tucson may have Old Tucson Studios, but Benson has **Mescal** (✆ **520/883-0100**). This Western-town movie set is operated by Old Tucson Studios and has been used for years in the making of Westerns, as well as TV shows and commercials. Hour-long walking tours of Mescal are offered and provide a feel for the many movies that have been shot here. While Old Tucson Studios feels like an amusement park, this place seems like an old ghost town. For fans of old Westerns, this is a must. Tours are available Tuesday, Thursday, and Saturday between 10am and 2pm, and cost $8 per person. Roughly 35 miles east of Tucson, take Exit 297 off I-10, then head north for 3 miles on Mescal Road. When the pavement ends, head west for ½ mile on the dirt road to the town, which is visible on the hill ahead.

Kartchner Caverns State Park ★★ These caverns are among the largest and most beautiful in the country, and because they are wet caverns, stalactites, stalagmites, soda straws, and other cave formations are still growing. Within the caverns are two huge rooms, each larger than a football field with ceilings more than 100 feet high. These two rooms can be visited on two separate tours. On the shorter Rotunda/Throne Room Tour, you will see, in the Rotunda Room, thousands of delicate soda straws. The highlight, though, is the Throne Room, at the center of which is a 58-foot-tall column. The second, and longer, tour visits the Big Room and leads past many strange and rare cave formations. Within the park are several miles of aboveground hiking trails. A campground charging $22 per night provides a convenient place to stay in the area.

Because the caverns are a popular attraction and tours are limited, try to make a reservation in advance, especially if you want to visit on a weekend. However, it is sometimes possible to get same-day tickets if you happen to be passing by.

Off Ariz. 90, 9 miles south of Benson. ✆ **520/586-CAVE.** www.azstateparks.com. Admission $5 per car; Rotunda/Throne Room Tour $19 adults, $9.95 children 7–13, free for children under 7; Big Room Tour $23 adults, $13 children 7–13, children under 7 not allowed. Park daily 7:30am–6pm; cave tours approximately every 20 min. 8am–5pm. Closed Christmas.

ATTRACTIONS AROUND SIERRA VISTA

Arizona Folklore Preserve Set beneath the shady cottonwoods and sycamores of Ramsey Canyon, the Arizona Folklore Preserve is the brainchild of Dolan Ellis, Arizona's official state balladeer, and his wife, Rose. Ellis was first appointed back in 1966 and has been writing songs about Arizona for more than 40 years. He performs most weekends and often welcomes musical guests to his performance hall.

56 Folklore Trail. ✆ **520/378-6165.** www.arizonafolklore.com. Admission $12 adults, $6 students 17 and under. Showtime Sat–Sun 2pm. Reservations required. Take Ariz. 92 south from Sierra Vista and turn right onto Ramsey Canyon Rd.

Fort Huachuca Historical Museum Fort Huachuca, an army base at the mouth of Huachuca Canyon just west of Sierra Vista, was established in 1877. The buildings of the old post have been declared a National Historic Landmark, and one is now a museum dedicated to the many forts that once dotted the Southwest. Interesting aspects of the exhibits include quotes by soldiers that give an idea of what it was like to serve back then. The associated **U.S. Army Military Intelligence Museum,** at Hungerford and Cristi streets, has displays on early code machines, surveillance drones, and other pieces of equipment formerly used for intelligence gathering.

At the Fort Huachuca U.S. Army base, Grierson Rd., Sierra Vista. ✆ **520/533-5736.** Suggested donation $2. Mon–Fri 9am–4pm; Sat–Sun 1–4pm. Closed New Year's Day, Thanksgiving, and Christmas.

BIRDING HOT SPOTS & OTHER NATURAL AREAS

Bird-watching is big business in these parts, with birders' B&Bs, bird refuges, and even birding festivals. The **Southwest Wings Birding Festival** (✆ **520/678-8237;** www.swwings.org), one of southern Arizona's biggest annual birding events, is held each year in early August in Sierra Vista.

If you'd like to join a guided bird walk along the San Pedro River or up Carr Canyon in the Huachuca Mountains, an owl-watching night hike, or a hummingbird banding session, contact the **Southeastern Arizona Bird Observatory** (✆ **520/432-1388;** www.sabo.org), which also has a public bird-viewing area at its headquarters 2 miles north of the Mule Mountain Tunnel on Arizona 80 north of Bisbee (watch for Hidden Meadow Lane). Most activities take place between April and September, and cost $15 to $65. Workshops and tours are also offered.

Serious birders who want to add lots of rare birds to their life lists might want to take a guided tour. Your best bet is **Mark Pretti Nature Tours** (✆ **520/803-6889;** www.markprettinaturetours.com), run by the former resident naturalist at Ramsey Canyon Preserve. A half-day birding tour costs $120 and a full-day tour costs $200 to $220. Three-day ($625) and 8-day ($1,250) trips are also offered. Other reliable area guides include Wezil Walraven of **Wezil Walraven Bird Tours** (✆ **520/234-0123;** www.wrensandravens.com) and Melody Kehl of **Melody's Outdoor Adventures** (✆ **888/296-9437** or 520/296-9437; www.ebiz.netopia.com/outdoor). **High Lonesome Birdtours** (✆ **800/743-2668** or 520/458-9446; www.hilonesome.com), another local tour company, charges about $975 per person for a 4-day birding trip. You can also attend birding-oriented seminars offered by **Sky Island Field Seminars** (✆ **866/900-1146** or 520/558-1146; www.skyislandfieldseminars.com).

In addition to the birding hot spots listed below, there are a few other places that serious birders should not miss. **Garden Canyon,** on Fort Huachuca, has 8 miles of trails, and 350 species of birds have been sighted. There are also Indian pictographs a 10-minute drive up the canyon's rough dirt road (high-clearance vehicle recommended). This is a good place to look for elegant trogons and Mexican spotted owls. Get directions at the fort's front gate, and be prepared to show your license, vehicle registration, and proof of vehicle insurance. The canyon is open to the public daily during daylight hours.

South of Ramsey Canyon off Arizona 92, you'll find **Carr Canyon,** which has a road that climbs up through the canyon to some of the higher elevations in the Huachuca Mountains. Keep your eyes open for buff-breasted flycatchers, red crossbills, and red-faced warblers. The one-lane road is narrow and winding (usually navigable by passenger car), and not for the acrophobic. It climbs 5 miles up into the mountains and goes to Reef Townsite, an old mining camp.

The **Environmental Operations Park,** 3 miles east of Arizona 92 on Arizona 90, is a grasslands and wetlands restoration site at Sierra Vista's sewage treatment facility,

Moments **Hummingbird Heaven**

If it's summer and you're looking to add as many hummingbirds to your life list as possible, take a drive up Miller Canyon (south of Ramsey Canyon) to **Beatty's Miller Canyon Guest Ranch and Orchard,** 2173 E. Miller Canyon Rd., Hereford (© **520/378-2728;** www.beattysguestranch.com), where a public hummingbird-viewing area is set up. A total of 15 species of hummers have been sighted here, and several times, 14 species have been seen in one day.

and is a good place to see yellow-headed blackbirds, ducks, peregrines, and harriers from fall to spring. The area is open daily.

Coronado National Memorial About 20 miles south of Sierra Vista is a 5,000-acre preserve dedicated to Francisco Vásquez de Coronado, the first European to explore this region. In 1540, Coronado, leading more than 700 people, left Compostela, Mexico, in search of the fabled Seven Cities of Cíbola, said to be rich in gold and jewels. Sometime between 1540 and 1542, Coronado led his band of weary men and women up the valley of the San Pedro River, which this monument overlooks. At the visitor center, you can learn about Coronado's fruitless quest for riches and check out the wildlife observation area. Outside the visitor center, a trail leads three-quarters of a mile to 600-foot-long Coronado Cave. (You'll need to bring your own flashlight and get a permit at the visitor center if you want to explore this cave.) After stopping at the visitor center, drive up to 6,575-foot Montezuma Pass, which is in the center of the memorial and provides far-reaching views of Sonora, Mexico, to the south, the San Pedro River to the east, and several mountain ranges and valleys to the west. Along the .75-mile round-trip Coronado Peak Trail, you'll also have good views of the valley and can read quotations from the journals of Coronado's followers. There are also some longer trails where you'll see few other hikers.

4101 E. Montezuma Canyon Rd., Hereford. © **520/366-5515.** www.nps.gov/coro. Free admission. Daily 9am–5pm. Closed Thanksgiving and Christmas. Take Ariz. 92 south from Sierra Vista to S. Coronado Memorial Drive and continue 5 miles to the visitor center.

Ramsey Canyon Preserve ★ Each year, beginning in late spring, a buzzing fills the air in Ramsey Canyon, but it's not the buzzing of the bees. This preserve is home to 14 species of hummingbirds, and it is the whirring of these diminutive birds' wings that fills the air. Wear red clothing when you visit, and you're certain to attract the little avian dive bombers, which will mistake you for the world's largest flower. Situated in a wooded gorge in the Huachuca Mountains, this Nature Conservancy preserve covers only 380 acres. However, because Ramsey Creek, which flows through the canyon, is a year-round stream, it attracts a wide variety of wildlife, including bears, bobcats, and nearly 200 species of birds. A short nature trail leads through the canyon, and a second trail leads higher up the canyon. April and May are the busiest times here, while May and August are the best times to see hummingbirds. Guided walks are offered March through October.

27 Ramsey Canyon Rd., off Ariz. 92, 5 miles south of Sierra Vista. © **520/378-2785.** www.nature.org. Admission $5 ($3 for Nature Conservancy members); free on 1st Sat of each month. Feb–Oct daily 8am–5pm; Nov–Jan Thurs–Mon 9am–4pm. Closed New Year's Day, Thanksgiving, and Christmas.

San Pedro Riparian National Conservation Area ★ Over the past century, roughly 90% of Arizona's free-flowing year-round rivers and streams have disappeared due to human use of desert waters. These rivers and streams once supported riparian areas that provided water, food, and protection to myriad plants, animals, and even humans. You can get an idea of what such riparian areas were like by visiting this sprawling preserve, which is located 8 miles east of Sierra Vista. Fossil findings from this area indicate that people were living along this river as long as 11,000 years ago. At that time, this area was a swamp, not a desert. Today, the San Pedro River is all that remains of this ancient wetland, and, due to an earthquake a century ago, much of the San Pedro's water now flows underground. Don't expect a wide, rushing river when you visit the San Pedro; what you'll see here would be called a creek anywhere but Arizona. Still, the water attracts wildlife, especially birds, and the conservation area is very popular with birders, who have a chance of spotting more than 300 species here.

Also within the riparian area is the **Murray Springs Clovis Site,** where 16 spear points and the remains of a 10,000-year-old mammoth kill were found in the 1960s. Although there isn't much to see other than some trenches, there are numerous interpretive signs along the short trail through the site. It's just north of Arizona 90 about 5 miles east of Sierra Vista.

For a glimpse of the region's Spanish history, visit the ruins of the **Presidio Santa Cruz de Terrenate,** about 20 miles northeast of Sierra Vista off Arizona 82 near the ghost town of Fairbank. This military outpost was established in 1775 or 1776 but was never completed due to the constant attacks by Apaches. Today only decaying adobe walls remain. To reach this site, take Arizona 82 E from U.S. 90 and drive north 1¾ miles on Ironhorse Ranch Road, which is at milepost 60. It's a 1¼-mile hike to the site. To visit **Fairbank** ghost town, drive Arizona 82 to the bridge over the San Pedro River. Here you'll find the remains of several buildings from the heyday of this former railroad town. Fairbank, which was founded in the 1880s to serve nearby silver-mining towns, once had a population of nearly 15,000 people. Today, only one of the old buildings has been restored and opened to the public. The old Fairbank School is now the **Schoolhouse Museum and Store** (✆ **520/459-2555**) and is open Friday through Sunday from 9:30am to 4:30pm. From Fairbank, several miles of hiking trails lead along the San Pedro River. You can walk to two other ghost towns, Millville and Charleston, but there is very little to see at either of these old town sites. It is also possible to walk from Fairbank to the ruins of the Presidio Santa Cruz de Terrenate.

For bird-watching, the best place is the system of trails at the Arizona 90 crossing of the San Pedro. Here you'll find the **San Pedro House** (✆ **520/508-4445**), a 1930s ranch that is operated as a visitor center and bookstore. It's open daily from 9:30am to 4:30pm and has information on guided walks and hikes, bird walks, bird-banding sessions, and other events that are scheduled throughout the year. Outside the old ranch house, there's a huge old cottonwood tree.

Ariz. 90. ✆ **520/458-3559.** www.az.blm.gov/nca/spnca/spnca-info.htm. Free admission. Parking areas open sunrise–sunset.

Finds A Holy Bird Sanctuary

In the community of St. David, 5 miles south of Benson on Arizona 80, you'll find the **Holy Trinity Monastery** (✆ **520/720-4642**), which is near the banks of the San Pedro River and has a 1.3-mile birding trail.

OTHER OUTDOOR PURSUITS

Horseback riding at Fort Huachuca's **Buffalo Corral** (✆ **520/533-5220**) is a good deal $12 to $14 per person per hour for trail rides. Special family rates are available.

Hikers will find numerous trails in the Huachuca Mountains west of Sierra Vista. There are trails at Garden Canyon on Fort Huachuca, at Ramsey Canyon Preserve, at Carr Canyon in Coronado National Forest, and within Coronado National Memorial. See "Birding Hot Spots & Other Natural Areas," above, for details. For information on hiking in the Coronado National Forest, contact the **Sierra Vista Ranger District,** 5990 S. Hwy. 92 (✆ **520/378-0311;** www.fs.fed.us/r3/coronado), 8 miles south of Sierra Vista.

WHERE TO STAY

IN BENSON

Holiday Inn Express ★ If you're looking for lodging close to Kartchner Caverns, try this off-ramp budget hotel in Benson. The hotel's lobby is done in Santa Fe style with flagstone floors and rustic Southwestern furniture. Guest rooms are strictly hotel modern, but they are roomy and reliable.

630 South Village Loop, Benson, AZ 85602. ✆ **888/465-4329** or 520/586-8800. Fax 520/586-1370. www.bensonaz.hiexpress.com. 62 units. $93–$229 double. Rates include continental breakfast. Children under 18 stay free in parent's room. AE, DC, DISC, MC, V. **Amenities:** Outdoor pool; exercise room; access to nearby health club; coin-op laundry. *In room:* A/C, TV, dataport, fridge, coffeemaker, hair dryer, iron, high-speed Internet access, Wi-Fi, free local calls.

IN HEREFORD

Ash Canyon Bed & Breakfast ★ With a single "casita" (little house), this secluded birders' B&B may be small, but if you're serious about birds, this is *the* place to stay in the area. People come from all over the country to sit on owner/innkeeper Mary Jo Ballator's back patio watching rare birds, many of which never make it much farther north than right here. Stay in the cute little cottage, and you'll be able to catch all the bird activity at sunrise and sunset. By the way, the casita is built from straw bales and consequently is very energy efficient.

5255 Spring Rd., Hereford, AZ 85615-9029. ✆ **520/378-0773.** www.ashcanyonbandb.com. 1 unit. $135 double ($125 if staying 2 or more nights). Rates include full breakfast. No credit cards. *In room:* Kitchen, fridge, coffeemaker, hair dryer.

Casa de San Pedro ★ Built with bird-watching tour groups in mind, this modern inn is set on the west side of the San Pedro River on 10 acres of land. While the setting doesn't have the historical character of the San Pedro River Inn (see below), it is much more up-to-date, with large, comfortable hotel-style guest rooms. Built in the territorial style around a courtyard garden, the inn has a large common room where birders gather to swap tales of the day's sightings. The inn also offers birding, cultural, and history tours. This is by far the most upscale inn in the region, and my favorite.

8933 S. Yell Lane, Hereford, AZ 85615. ✆ **888/257-2050** or 520/366-1300. Fax 520/366-0701. www.bedandbirds.com. 10 units. $149–$175 double. Rates include full breakfast. AE, DISC, MC, V. No children under 12. **Amenities:** Outdoor pool; Jacuzzi; concierge; business center; guest laundry. *In room:* A/C, hair dryer, high-speed Internet access, Wi-Fi, free local calls.

Ramsey Canyon Inn Bed & Breakfast ★ Adjacent to the Nature Conservancy's Ramsey Canyon Preserve, this inn is the most convenient choice in the area for avid birders to see the canyon's famous hummingbirds. The property straddles Ramsey Creek, with guest rooms in the main house and apartments reached by a footbridge over the creek. A large country breakfast is served in the morning. Book early.

29 Ramsey Canyon Dr., Hereford, AZ 85615. ✆ **520/378-3010.** www.ramseycanyoninn.com. 9 units. $130–$150 double; $150–$225 suite. Room rates include full breakfast (except in suites). MC, V. No children under 16 in inn, but children over 12 accepted in suites. *In room:* No phone.

CAMPGROUNDS

There are two Coronado National Forest campgrounds—14-site **Reef Townsite** and 8-site **Ramsey Vista**—up winding Carr Canyon Road south of Sierra Vista off Arizona 92. Both charge $10 per night. For information, contact the Coronado National Forest Sierra Vista Ranger District, 5990 S. Hwy. 92, Hereford, AZ 85615 (✆ **520/378-0311;** www.fs.fed.us/r3/coronado).

WHERE TO DINE

Sierra Vista supports quite a number of good Asian restaurants, with an emphasis on Chinese, Japanese, and Korean cuisine.

Adobe Southwestern Cuisine ★★ SOUTHWESTERN The fact that Bisbee residents are willing to drive to Sierra Vista to eat dinner is a sure sign that the food at this southwestern restaurant is some of the best in the region. Rivaling Cafe Roka (see below) in creativity, Adobe specializes in south-of-the-border flavors. There's adobo-rubbed pork tenderloin with chipotle-spiced sweet potatoes and bourbon-pecan glaze, chile-crusted rack of lamb with prickly-pear sauce, and halibut encrusted with fresh cilantro and coriander seeds. To start things off, try the scallop-and-mango ceviche. You'll find this restaurant near the turnoff for Ramsey Canyon.

5043 S. Hwy. 92. ✆ **520/378-2762.** Reservations recommended. Main courses $16–$26. AE, DISC, MC, V. Wed–Mon 5–9pm.

The Mesquite Tree STEAKHOUSE This casual steakhouse south of town (and not far from the mouth of Ramsey Canyon) has long been a favorite of locals. It's funky and dark, and the prices can't be beat. Although you can get chicken and fish dishes done in a variety of traditional Continental styles, most people come here for the steaks. Try the Vargas rib-eye, which is smothered with green chiles, jack cheese, and enchilada sauce—a real border-country original. When the weather is warm, try to get a seat on the patio.

S. Ariz. 92 and Carr Canyon Rd. ✆ **520/378-2758.** Reservations recommended. Main courses $9–$22. AE, DISC, MC, V. Tues–Sat 5–9pm; Sun 5–8pm.

The Outside Inn ★ STEAKHOUSE/SEAFOOD/ITALIAN Much more formal than the nearby Mesquite Tree, The Outside Inn has long been Sierra Vista's top special-occasion restaurant. Housed in a cottagelike building south of town and just north of the turnoff for Ramsey Canyon, The Outside Inn may not be in the most picturesque of surroundings, but the food is definitely among the best you'll find in the area. In the main dining room or out on the patio, you can enjoy such fare as blackened mahimahi or crab-stuffed giant Guaymas shrimp.

4907 S. Ariz. 92. ✆ **520/378-4645.** Reservations recommended. Main courses $8–$12 lunch, $16–$34 dinner. AE, MC, V. Mon–Fri 11am–1:30pm and 5–9pm; Sat 5–9pm.

Tanuki Sushi Bar & Garden JAPANESE Of all the many Asian restaurants in Sierra Vista, this is one of my favorites. Take a glance around at the signed plates on the walls, and you'll see that other visitors, including actor Tom Selleck, like the food here, too. I like to get the sushi, but there are plenty of traditional hot Japanese dishes available as well.

1221 E. Fry Blvd. ✆ **520/459-6853.** Main courses $8–$21. AE, MC, V. Mon–Thurs 11am–2:30pm and 5–9pm; Fri–Sat 11am–2:30pm and 5–9:30pm.

6 Tombstone ★

70 miles SE of Tucson; 181 miles SE of Phoenix; 24 miles N of Bisbee

All it took was a brief blaze of gunfire more than 125 years ago to seal the fate of this former silver-mining boomtown. It was on these very streets, outside a livery stable known as the O.K. Corral, that Wyatt Earp, his brothers Virgil and Morgan, and their friend Doc Holliday took on the outlaws Ike Clanton and Frank and Tom McLaury on October 26, 1881. Today, Tombstone, "the town too tough to die," is one of Arizona's most popular attractions, but I'll leave it up to you to decide whether it deserves its reputation (either as a tough town or as a legitimate tourist attraction).

Tombstone was named by Ed Schieffelin, a silver prospector who ventured into this area at a time when the region's Apaches were fighting to preserve their way of life. Schieffelin was warned that all he would find here was his own tombstone, so when he discovered silver, he named the strike Tombstone. Within a few years, the town of Tombstone was larger than San Francisco, and between 1880 and 1887, an estimated $37 million worth of silver was mined here. Such wealth created a sturdy little town, and as the Cochise County seat of the time, Tombstone boasted a number of imposing buildings, including the county courthouse, which is now a state park. In 1887, an underground river flooded the silver mines, and despite attempts to pump the water out, the mines were never reopened. With the demise of the mines, the boom came to an end and the population rapidly dwindled.

Today, Tombstone's historic district consists of both original buildings that went up after a fire in 1882 destroyed much of the town and newer structures built in keeping with the architectural styles of the late 19th century. Most house souvenir shops and restaurants, which should give you some indication that this place is a classic tourist trap, but kids (and adults raised on Louis L'Amour and John Wayne) love it, especially when the famous shootout is reenacted.

ESSENTIALS

GETTING THERE From Tucson, take I-10 E to Benson and then Arizona 80 S to Tombstone. From Sierra Vista, take Arizona 90 north to Arizona 82, heading east.

VISITOR INFORMATION The **Tombstone Chamber of Commerce** (✆ **888/457-3929** or 520/457-3929; www.tombstone.org) operates a visitor center at the corner of Allen and Fourth streets.

SPECIAL EVENTS Tombstone's biggest annual celebrations are **Ed Schieffelin Territorial Days,** in mid-March; **Wyatt Earp Days,** in late May; and **Helldorado Days,** on the third weekend in October. The latter celebrates the famous gunfight at the O.K. Corral and includes countless shootouts in the streets, mock hangings, a parade, and contests.

GUNSLINGERS & SALOONS: IN SEARCH OF THE WILD WEST

As portrayed in novels, movies, and TV shows, the shootout has come to epitomize the Wild West, and nowhere is this great American phenomenon more glorified than in Tombstone, where the star attraction is the famous **O.K. Corral,** 308 E. Allen St. (✆ **520/457-3456;** www.ok-corral.com), site of a 30-second gun battle that has taken on mythic proportions. Inside the corral, you'll find not only displays on the shootout, but also an exhibit on Tombstone prostitutes and another focusing on local photographer C. S. Fly, who ran the boardinghouse where Doc Holliday was staying. Next door is **Tombstone's Historama,** a kitschy multimedia affair that rehashes the well-known history of Tombstone's "bad old days" and has a recorded narration by Vincent Price. The O.K. Corral and Tombstone's Historama are open daily from 9am to 5pm, and admission is $5.50; for $7.50, you can visit both attractions and take in a shootout reenactment almost on the very site of the original gunfight.

If you aren't able to catch one of the staged shootouts at the O.K. Corral (daily at 2pm), don't despair—there are plenty of other shootouts staged in Tombstone. In fact, all over Arizona there are regular reenactments of gunfights, with the sheriff in his white hat always triumphing over the bad guys in black hats. However, nowhere else in the state are there as many modern-day gunslingers entertaining so many people with their blazing six-guns as in Tombstone. Shootouts occur fairly regularly around town between noon and 4pm. Expect to pay $4 for any of these shows. For a little fun and games, try to catch the Tombstone Cowboys shootout at **Helldorado,** Fourth and Toughnut streets (© **520/457-9035;** www.helldoradotown.com). These shootouts, which are staged two to three times a day, are more hysterical than historical.

When the smoke cleared in 1881, three men lay dead. They were later carted off to the **Boot Hill Graveyard** (© **520/457-3300**) on the north edge of town. The graves of Clanton and the McLaury brothers, as well as those of others who died in gunfights or by hanging, are well marked. Entertaining epitaphs grace the grave markers; among the most famous is that of Lester Moore—"Here lies Lester Moore, 4 slugs from a 44, No Les, no more." The cemetery is open to the public Monday through Thursday from 9am to 5pm and Friday through Sunday from 9am to 6pm; admission is by suggested $2 donation. Enter through a gift shop on Arizona 80.

When the residents of Tombstone weren't shooting each other in the streets, they were likely to be found in the saloons and bawdy houses that lined Allen Street. Most famous was the **Bird Cage Theatre,** Allen and Sixth Streets (© **520/457-3421**), so named for the cagelike cribs (box seats) suspended from the ceiling. These velvet-draped cages were used by prostitutes to ply their trade. For old Tombstone atmosphere, this place is hard to beat. Admission is $8 for adults, $7.50 for seniors, $6 for children 8 to 18, or $22 for a family; the theater is open daily from 8am to 6pm.

For a cold beer, Tombstone has a couple of very lively saloons. The **Crystal Palace Saloon,** at Allen and Fifth streets (© **520/457-3611;** www.crystalpalacesaloon.com), was built in 1879 and has been completely restored. This is one of the favorite hangouts of the town's costumed actors and other would-be cowboys and cowgirls. **Big Nose Kate's,** 417 E. Allen St. (© **520/457-3107;** www.bignosekate.com), is an equally entertaining spot full of Wild West character and characters.

Tombstone has long been a tourist town, and its streets are lined with souvenir shops selling wind chimes, Beanie Babies, and other less-than-wild souvenirs. There are also several small museums scattered around town. At the **Rose Tree Inn Museum,** at Fourth and Toughnut streets (© **520/457-3326**), you can see the world's largest rose tree. Inside are antique furnishings from Tombstone's heyday in the 1880s. The museum is open daily from 9am to 5pm (closed Thanksgiving and Christmas). Admission is $3 (free for children under 14).

Tombstone Courthouse State Park, at 223 Toughnut St. (© **520/457-3311;** www.azstateparks.com), is the most imposing building in town and provides a much less sensationalized version of local history. Built in 1882, the courthouse is now a state historic park and museum containing artifacts, photos, and newspaper clippings that chronicle Tombstone's lively past. In the courtyard, you can still see the gallows that once ended the lives of outlaws. The courthouse is open daily from 8am to 5pm (closed on Christmas); the entrance fee is $4 ($3 between Memorial Day and Labor Day) and children under 14 are free.

At the **Tombstone Epitaph Museum,** Fifth Street between Allen and Fremont streets (✆ **520/457-2211;** www.tombstone-epitaph.com), you can inspect the office of the town's old newspaper and learn about John Clum, the original editor of the paper. The museum is open daily from 9:30am to 5pm; admission is free.

A must-stop is the **Tombstone Western Heritage Museum,** Arizona 80 and Sixth Street (✆ **520/457-3800;** www.thetombstonemuseum.com), a privately owned museum that is filled with Tombstone artifacts. Included in this impressive collection are artifacts that once belonged to Wyatt and Virgil Earp, rare photos of the Earps and the outlaws of Tombstone, and all kinds of original documents that date to the days of the shootout at the O.K. Corral. The museum is open Monday, Tuesday, and Thursday through Saturday from 9am to 6pm and Sunday from 12:30 to 6pm; admission is $5 for adults and $3 for children 12 to 18 ($13 for families).

It just wouldn't be right to leave town without spending some time in the saddle like any good cowpoke, lawman, or outlaw should. So, get in touch with **Blue Sky Ranches/Chiricahua Trail Rides** (✆ **520/824-1660** or 818/726-5430; www.bluesky ranches.com), which leads horseback rides from Tombstone. Trail rides start at $30 for a 1-hour ride and go up to $115 for an all-day ride.

WHERE TO STAY

Best Western Lookout Lodge This comfortable motel is a mile north of town overlooking the Dragoon Mountains. Stone walls, porcelain doorknobs, Mexican tiles in the bathrooms, and old-fashioned "gas" lamps give the spacious guest rooms an Old West feel. Ask for a room with a view of the mountains.

781 N. Hwy. 80, Tombstone, AZ 85638. ✆ **877/652-6772** or 520/457-2223. Fax 520/457-3870. www.bestwestern tombstone.com. 40 units. $75–$120 double. Children under 12 stay free in parent's room. AE, DC, DISC, MC, V. Pets accepted ($20 per night). **Amenities:** Restaurant; lounge; seasonal outdoor pool. *In room:* A/C, TV, dataport, fridge, coffeemaker, hair dryer, iron, high-speed Internet access, Wi-Fi, free local calls.

Holiday Inn Express ★ On the northern outskirts of Tombstone, right next door to the older Best Western, this is the newest and most reliable hotel in Tombstone. The decor draws on a bit of Southwestern and Spanish colonial styling, but basically this is just a modern motel.

580 W. Randolph Way, Tombstone, AZ 85638. ✆ **888/465-4329** or 520/457-9507. Fax 520/457-9506. www.hi express.com. 60 units. $75–$125 double. Rates include continental breakfast. Children under 18 stay free in parent's room. AE, DISC, MC, V. **Amenities:** Outdoor pool; Jacuzzi; concierge; coin-op laundry. *In room:* A/C, TV, dataport, coffeemaker, hair dryer, iron, high-speed Internet access, free local calls.

Tombstone Boarding House Housed in two whitewashed 1880s adobe buildings with green trim, this inn is in a quiet residential neighborhood only 2 blocks from busy Allen Street. The main house was originally the home of Tombstone's first bank manager. Guest rooms are in an old boardinghouse. Accommodations are comfortable and clean, with country decor. Hardwood floors and antiques lend a period feel.

108 N. Fourth St. (P. O. Box 1700), Tombstone, AZ 85638. ✆ **877/225-1319** or 520/457-3716. www.tombstone boardinghouse.com. 5 units. $89–$109 double. Rates include full breakfast. DISC, MC, V. Pets accepted ($10 per night). **Amenities:** Restaurant (Continental). *In room:* No phone.

WHERE TO DINE

Big Nose Kate's Saloon SANDWICHES Okay, so the food here isn't all that memorable, but the atmosphere sure is. Big Nose Kate's dates back to 1880 and is primarily a saloon. As such, it stays packed with visitors who have come to revel in Tombstone's outlaw past. So, while you sip your beer, why not order a sandwich and call it lunch? You might even catch some live country music.

417 E. Allen St. ✆ **520/457-3107.** www.bignosekate.com. Reservations not accepted. Sandwiches $6.50–$8. AE, MC, V. Mon–Fri 11am–8pm; Sat–Sun 9am–8pm.

The Lamplight Room ★ CONTINENTAL Located a few blocks off busy Allen Street, this restaurant serves the best food in Tombstone. The Lamplight Room is in the living room of an old 1880s home, which also lends this place more character than that of any of the other restaurants in town. The menu is short and includes such dishes as chicken *cordon bleu* and roasted pork loin. On Friday and Saturday nights, there's live classical guitar music.

At the Tombstone Boarding House, 108 N. Fourth St. ✆ **520/457-3716.** Reservations recommended. Main courses $6–$17. DISC, MC, V. Mon–Sat 11:30am–8pm; Sun 11:30am–7pm.

7 Bisbee ★★

94 miles SE of Tucson; 205 miles SE of Phoenix; 24 miles NW of Douglas

Arizona has a wealth of ghost towns that boomed on mining profits and then quickly went bust when the mines played out, but none is as impressive as Bisbee, which is built into the steep slopes of Tombstone Canyon on the south side of the Mule Mountains. Between 1880 and 1975, Bisbee's mines produced more than $6 billion worth of metals. When the Phelps Dodge Company shut down its copper mines here, Bisbee nearly went the way of other abandoned mining towns, but because it's the Cochise County seat, it was saved from disappearing into the desert dust.

Bisbee's glory days date from 100 years ago, and because the town stopped growing in the early part of the 20th century, it is now one of the best-preserved historic towns in the Southwest. Old brick buildings line narrow winding streets, and miners' shacks sprawl across the hillsides above downtown. Television and movie producers discovered these well-preserved streets years ago, and since then, Bisbee has doubled as New York, Spain, Greece, Italy, and, of course, the Old West.

The rumor of silver in "them thar hills" is what first attracted prospectors in 1877, and within a few years the diggings attracted the interest of some San Francisco investors, among them Judge DeWitt Bisbee, for whom the town is named. However, it was copper and other less-than-precious metals that would make Bisbee's fortune. With the help of outside financing, large-scale mining operations were begun in 1881 by the Phelps Dodge Company. By 1910, the population had climbed to 25,000, and Bisbee was the largest city between New Orleans and San Francisco. The town boasted that it was the liveliest spot between El Paso and San Francisco—and the presence of nearly 50 saloons and bordellos along Brewery Gulch backed up that claim.

Tucked into a narrow valley surrounded by red hills, Bisbee today has a funky cosmopolitan air. Many artists call the town home, and aging hippies and other urban refugees have for many years been dropping out of the rat race to restore Bisbee's old buildings and open small inns, restaurants, and galleries. Between the rough edges left over from its mining days and this new fringe-culture atmosphere, Bisbee is one of Arizona's most interesting towns. However, be aware that Bisbee is not for everyone. It appeals mostly to young, hip travelers who don't expect much from their accommodations and who like to stay up late partying. The rumble of motorcycles is a constant on Bisbee's streets, especially on weekends.

ESSENTIALS

GETTING THERE Bisbee is on Arizona 80, which begins at I-10 in the town of Benson, 45 miles east of Tucson.

VISITOR INFORMATION Contact the **Bisbee Visitor Center,** 2 Copper Queen Plaza (✆ **866/2-BISBEE** or 520/432-3554; www.discoverbisbee.com).

SPECIAL EVENTS Bisbee puts on **coaster races** (similar to a soap-box derby) on the Fourth of July; **Brewery Gulch Daze,** a celebration of Bisbee's bawdy past, in September; and a **Fiber Arts Festival** and the **Bisbee Stair Climb 1000** in October.

EXPLORING THE TOWN

At the Bisbee Visitor Center, in the middle of town, pick up walking-tour brochures that guide you past the most important buildings and sites. On the second floor of the **Copper Queen Library,** 6 Main St. (✆ **520/432-4232**), some great old photographs give a good idea of what the town looked like in the past century.

Don't miss the **Bisbee Mining and Historical Museum** ★, 5 Copper Queen Plaza (✆ **520/432-7071;** www.bisbeemuseum.org), housed in the 1897 Copper Queen Consolidated Mining Company office building. This small but comprehensive museum features exhibits on the history of Bisbee. It's open daily from 10am to 4pm; admission is $7.50 for adults, $6.50 for seniors, and $3 children 16 and under.

For another look at early life in Bisbee, visit the **Muheim Heritage House,** 207 Youngblood Hill (✆ **520/432-7698**), which is reached by walking up Brewery Gulch. The house was built between 1902 and 1915 and has an unusual semicircular porch. The interior is decorated with period furniture. It's open Friday through Tuesday from 10am to 4pm; admission is by $4 suggested donation for adults.

O.K. Street, which parallels Brewery Gulch but is high on the hill on the southern edge of town, is a good place to walk for views of Bisbee. At the top of O.K. Street, there's a path that takes you up to a hill above town for an even better panorama of Bisbee's jumble of old buildings. Atop this hill are numerous small, colorfully painted shrines built into the rocks and filled with candles, plastic flowers, and pictures of the Virgin Mary. It's a steep climb on a rocky, very uneven path, but the views and the fascinating little shrines make it worth the effort.

Mining made this town what it is, so you should be sure to head underground on a tour to find out what it was like to be a miner here in Bisbee. **Queen Mine Tours** ★ (✆ **866/432-2071** or 520/432-2071; www.queenminetour.com) takes visitors down into one of the town's old copper mines. Tours are offered daily between 9am and 3:30pm and cost $12 for adults and $5 for children 4 to 15. The ticket office and mine are just south of the Old Bisbee business district at the Arizona 80 interchange.

For an exploration of some of the steeper and narrower streets of Bisbee, take a 90-minute tour ($35) of old Bisbee with **Lavender Jeep Tours** (✆ **520/432-5369**). Several other tours are also available. For a walk on the dark side, sign up for the **Old Bisbee Ghost Tour** (✆ **520/432-3308;** www.oldbisbeeghosttour.com). These 90-minute tours are offered Friday through Sunday nights at 7pm (and occasionally at 9pm as well) and cost $12 for adults and $7 for children under 12.

Bisbee has lots of interesting stores and galleries, and shopping is the main recreational activity here. To get a look at some of the quality jewelry created from minerals mined in the area, stop by **Czar Jewelry,** 13 Main St. (✆ **520/432-3027**). Another good place to shop for jewelry is **Bisbee Blue,** at the Lavender Pit View Point on Arizona 80 (✆ **520/432-5511**), an exclusive dealer of the famous Bisbee Blue turquoise.

A Golfer's Nightmare

Beware the Bogeyman on tiny Naco, Arizona's, **Turquoise Valley Golf & RV Park,** 1794 W. Newell St. (✆ **520/432-3091;** www.turquoisevalley.com). This little public course dates to 1908, is the oldest golf course in Arizona, and boasts the only par-6 hole west of the Mississippi. The hole, called the rattler, stretches for 747 yards and is every golfer's nightmare. A round of golf here will run you only $25, plus $15 for a golf cart.

Turquoise is associated with copper mines, and Bisbee's mines once produced some of the most famous turquoise in the country.

If it's art you're after, check out some of the local galleries. At the **Johnson Gallery,** 28 Main St. (✆ **520/432-2126**), you'll find an outstanding selection of Native American crafts, including Navajo rugs and jewelry, Hopi kachinas and pottery, and lots of Zuni fetishes. **Bisbee Clay,** 30 Main St. (✆ **520/432-1916**), has beautiful pottery, both functional and decorative, in unusual designs and colors. For fine contemporary crafts that will fit in a suitcase, visit **Twist,** 51 Main St. (✆ **520/432-3046**).

To protect your face from the burning rays of the sun (and make a fashion statement), visit **Optimo Custom Hat Works,** 47 Main St. (✆ **888/FINE-HAT** or 520/432-4544; www.optimohatworks.com), which sells and custom-fits Panama straw hats as well as felt hats. (By the way, Panama hats actually come from Ecuador.)

WHERE TO STAY

MODERATE

Copper City Inn ★ *Finds* This inn is operated by Fred Miller, who has been the bartender at Bisbee's Cafe Roka for more than a decade. The inn boasts the best and most attractive rooms in Bisbee these days, which has made it my new favorite place to stay in town. One room is done up with French antiques, while the other room has a modern Art Deco styling and is dedicated to early-20th-century hotel designer Mary Jane Colter. The suite has modern mission-style furnishings, tile floors, and a full kitchen. All the rooms have balconies overlooking Bisbee, and there is a pleasant deck at the back of the inn. Whichever room you reserve, you'll receive a complimentary bottle of wine upon check-in. Unlike most inns, the Copper City Inn is a "self-service" sort of place; when you make your reservation, you'll be given the key code for the door of your suite and allowed to check yourself in.

99 Main St., Bisbee, AZ 85603. ✆ **520/432-1418** or 520/456-4254. www.coppercityinn.com. 3 units. $110 double; $135 suite. AE, DC, DISC, MC, V. *In room:* TV/DVD, fridge, coffeemaker, hair dryer, Wi-Fi, no phone.

Letson Loft Hotel ★★ Located up a flight of stairs, the Letson Loft Hotel feels a bit like an old Italian villa and has the prettiest rooms in town. High ceilings, old wood floors, Asian antiques, and plush beds with great linens all add up to comforts and class rarely seen in this funky town. Book one of the front rooms and you'll have a front row seat for watching the Main Street action through bay windows. If you're a light sleeper, ask for a room at the back of the hotel or avail yourself of the bedside earplugs; Bisbee can be a bit noisy at times. One of my favorite rooms has a huge skylight and another has a claw-foot tub. There's even a suite with a kitchen.

26 Main St. (P.O. Box 623), Bisbee, AZ 85603. ✆ **877/432-3210** or 520/432-3210. www.letsonlofthotel.com. 8 units. $110–$145 double; $135–$165 suite. Rates include continental breakfast. AE, DISC, MC, V. No children under 12. **Amenities:** Concierge; business center; massage. *In room:* A/C, TV/DVD, hair dryer, iron, Wi-Fi.

INEXPENSIVE

Bisbee Grand Hotel ★ The Bisbee Grand Hotel is the sort of place you'd expect Wyatt Earp and his wife to have patronized—classy, but a little rough around the edges. At street level is a historic saloon with a pressed-tin ceiling and an 1880s bar; upstairs you'll find small, though attractively decorated, guest rooms. The Oriental Suite features an incredibly ornate Chinese wedding bed, claw-foot tub, and skylight, and the Victorian Suite has a red-velvet canopy bed. All units have private bathrooms, but some are across the hall and not in the room itself.

61 Main St., Bisbee, AZ 85603. ✆ **800/421-1909** or 520/432-5900. www.bisbeegrandhotel.net. 13 units. $79–$175 double. Rates include breakfast. DISC, MC, V. **Amenities:** Saloon. *In room:* A/C, Wi-Fi, no phone.

Canyon Rose Suites ★ *Value* Located on the second floor of a commercial building just off Bisbee's main street, this property offers spacious suites with full kitchens, which makes it a good bet for longer stays. All units have hardwood floors and high ceilings, and the works by local artists and the mix of contemporary and rustic furnishings give the place plenty of Bisbee character. Constructed on a steep, narrow street, the building housing this lodging has an unusual covered sidewalk, making it one of the more distinctive commercial buildings in town.

27 Subway at Shearer St. (P.O. Box 1915), Bisbee, AZ 85603. ✆ **866/296-7673** or 520/432-5098. www.canyonrose.com. 7 units. $89–$220 double. Children under 12 stay free in parent's room. AE, MC, V. **Amenities:** Access to nearby health club; guest laundry. *In room:* A/C, TV/DVD, kitchen, fridge, coffeemaker, hair dryer, iron, Wi-Fi, free local calls.

Copper Queen Hotel Built in 1902 by the Copper Queen Mining Company and right at the center of town, this is Bisbee's grande dame. The atmosphere is casual yet quite authentic. Behind the check-in desk, there's an old oak roll-top desk and a safe that has been here for years. Spacious halls lead to guest rooms furnished with antiques but that vary considerably in size (the smallest being quite cramped). The hotel has been undergoing renovations for several years; be sure to ask for one of the renovated units, which are up-to-date and attractively furnished. The restaurant serves decent food, and out front is a terrace for alfresco dining. And what would a mining-town hotel be without its saloon?

11 Howell Ave. (P.O. Drawer CQ), Bisbee, AZ 85603. ✆ **520/432-2216.** Fax 520/432-3819. www.copperqueen.com. 52 units. $87–$177 double. Children under 17 stay free in parent's room. AE, MC, V. **Amenities:** Restaurant (American); lounge; small outdoor pool. *In room:* A/C, TV.

Shady Dell RV Park *Finds* Yes, this really is an RV park, but you'll find neither shade nor dell at the Shady Dell's roadside location just south of the Lavender Pit mine. What you will find are nine vintage trailers, a 1947 Airporter bus done in retro-Tiki style, and a 1947 Chris Craft yacht. All have been lovingly restored. Although the trailers don't have their own private bathrooms (a bathhouse is in the middle of the RV park), they do have all kinds of vintage decor and furnishings—even tapes and records of period music and radio shows. In the trailers that have vintage TVs, there are VCRs and videotapes of old movies. After numerous write-ups in national publications, the Shady Dell has become so famous that reservations need to be made far in advance. **Dot's Diner** (see "Where to Dine," below), a 1957 vintage diner, is also on-site.

1 Old Douglas Rd., Bisbee, AZ 85603. ✆ **520/432-3567.** www.theshadydell.com. 11 units. $45–$145 per trailer (for 1–2 people). MC, V. No children under 10. **Amenities:** Restaurant; coin-op laundry. *In room:* A/C, kitchen, fridge, coffeemaker, no phone.

WHERE TO DINE

Café Cornucopia, 14 Main St. (© **520/432-4820**), offers fresh juices, smoothies, and sandwiches. It's open Thursday through Monday from 10am to 5pm. For good coffee and a mining theme, check out the **Bisbee Coffee Co.,** Copper Queen Plaza, Main Street (© **520/432-7879**). For gourmet picnic supplies, peruse the shelves of the **High Desert Market,** 203 Tombstone Canyon Rd. (© **520/432-6775**), which has organic produce, imported cheeses, wine, and other assorted goodies for a great picnic.

Bisbee Breakfast Club ★ *Finds* AMERICAN Located in the Lowell district on the far side of the Lavender Pit from old Bisbee, this huge diner is a locals' favorite. Big breakfasts (served all day) are the specialty here, and the cinnamon rolls are legendary around town. At lunch, try the coffee-charred breast of chicken salad; it'll really wake up your taste buds. The owners, Pat and Heather Grimm, are the couple who originally put Bisbee's diminutive Dot's Diner on the map.

75A Erie St. © **520/432-5885.** www.bisbeebreakfastclub.com. Main courses $4–$7. AE, MC, V. Thurs–Mon 7am–3pm.

Cafe Roka ★★ CONTEMPORARY Wow! The food at Cafe Roka is reason enough to visit Bisbee. Casual and hip, this place is a real find in such an out-of-the-way town and offers good value as well as delicious and imaginatively prepared food. Meals include salad, soup, sorbet intermezzo, and entree. The grilled salmon with a Gorgonzola crust and artichoke-and-portobello lasagna are two of my favorites. Flourless chocolate cake with raspberry sauce is an exquisite ending. Local artists display their works, and on some evenings jazz musicians perform.

35 Main St. © **520/432-5153.** www.caferoka.com. Reservations highly recommended. Main courses $14–$24. AE, MC, V. Summer Fri–Sat 5–9pm; spring and fall Wed–Sat 5–9pm; winter Thurs–Sat 5–9pm.

Dot's Diner ★ *Finds* AMERICAN At Dot's Diner, an original 1957 Valentine diner, you can take a step back into the Eisenhower years. This tiny diner has barely a half-dozen stools at the counter, which overlooks the kitchen and soda fountain area. As in the old days, meals are simple—filling breakfasts, basic sandwiches, fresh house-made burgers, and foot-long hot dogs. However, there are daily specials that may include grits so good they could call them polenta and charge twice as much for them.

At Shady Dell RV Resort, 1 Old Douglas Rd. © **520/432-1112.** www.theshadydell.com. Reservations not accepted. Main courses $5–$6.25. No credit cards. Wed–Sun 7am–3pm.

BISBEE AFTER DARK

For more than a century, Bisbee's Brewery Gulch has been known for its many bars. Although there aren't nearly as many drinking establishments today as there were 100 years ago, a few dive bars remain especially popular with the weekend Harley-riding crowd from Tucson. My favorite nightspot, however, is a slightly less rowdy place called the **Hot Licks Barbecue & Blues Saloon,** 37 O.K. St. (© **520/432-7200;** www.hotlicksbbq.com), which overlooks Brewery Gulch from high above town. This bar, in a restored historic building, has live music several nights a week and serves a limited menu of barbecue and the like. For something a bit more cultured, check the calendar at the **Old Bisbee Repertory Theatre,** 94 Main St. (© **520/432-9064;** www.bisbeerep.com), a dinner theater that also does high teas.

8 Exploring the Rest of Cochise County ★

Willcox: 81 miles E of Tucson; 192 miles SE of Phoenix; 74 miles N of Douglas

Although the towns of Bisbee, Tombstone, and Sierra Vista all lie within Cochise County, much of the county is taken up by the vast Sulphur Springs Valley, which is bounded by several mountain ranges. It is across this wide-open landscape that Apache chiefs Cochise and Geronimo once rode. Gazing out across this country today, it is easy to understand why the Apaches fought so hard to keep white settlers out.

The Apaches first moved into this region of southern Arizona sometime in the early 16th century. They pursued a hunting-and-gathering lifestyle that was supplemented by raiding neighboring tribes for food and other booty. When the Spanish arrived in the area, the Apaches acquired horses and became even more efficient raiders. They attacked Spanish, Mexican, and eventually American settlers, and despite repeated attempts to convince them to give up their hostile way of life, the Apaches refused to change. Not long after the Gadsden Purchase of 1848 made Arizona U.S. soil, more people than ever began settling in the region. The new settlers immediately became the object of Apache raids, and eventually the U.S. Army was called in to put an end to the attacks; by the mid-1880s, the army was embroiled in a war with Cochise, Geronimo, and the Chiricahua Apaches.

Although the Chiricahua and Dragoon mountains, which flank the Sulphur Springs Valley on the east and west, respectively, are relatively unknown outside the region, they offer some of the Southwest's most spectacular scenery. Massive boulders litter the mountainsides, creating fascinating landscapes. The Chiricahua Mountains are also a favorite destination of bird-watchers, for it is here that the colorfully plumed elegant trogon reaches the northern limit of its range.

In the southern part of this region lies the town of Douglas, an important gateway to Mexico. Unless you're heading to Mexico, though, there aren't many reasons to visit. But if you do find yourself passing through, be sure to stop in at the historic Gadsden Hotel (see "Where to Stay," below); the Slaughter Ranch is also well worth a visit.

ESSENTIALS

GETTING THERE Willcox is on I-10, with Arizona 186 heading southeast toward Chiricahua National Monument.

VISITOR INFORMATION The **Willcox Chamber of Commerce and Agriculture,** 1500 N. Circle I Rd. (✆ **800/200-2272** or 520/384-2272; www.willcoxchamber.com), can provide information.

SPECIAL EVENTS **Wings Over Willcox** (✆ **800/200-2272;** www.wingsoverwillcox.com), a festival celebrating the annual return to the area of more than 30,000 sandhill cranes, takes place in January.

WILLCOX

Railroad Avenue in downtown Willcox is slowly developing into something of a little historic district. Here you'll find the Rex Allen Museum, plus the restored **Southern Pacific Willcox Train Depot,** 101 S. Railroad Ave., a redwood depot built in 1880. Inside the old depot is a small display of historical Willcox photos. Also worth checking out is the **Willcox Commercial,** 180 N. Railroad Ave. (✆ **520/384-2448**), a general store that has been around since the days of Geronimo.

Rex Allen Arizona Cowboy Museum If you grew up in the days of singing cowboys, then you're probably familiar with Willcox's favorite hometown star: Rex Allen, who made the song "Streets of Laredo" famous. Here at the small museum dedicated to him, you'll find plenty of Allen memorabilia, as well as a Cowboy Hall of Fame exhibit. The town celebrates Rex Allen Days every October.

150 N. Railroad Ave. ✆ **520/384-4583.** www.rexallenmuseum.org. Admission $2 per person, $3 per couple, $5 per family. Daily 10am–4pm. Closed New Year's Day, Thanksgiving, and Christmas.

SOUTHWEST OF WILLCOX

SCENIC LANDSCAPES

While Chiricahua National Monument claims the most spectacular scenery in this corner of the state, there are a couple of areas southwest of Willcox in the Dragoon Mountains that are almost as impressive. The first of these, **Texas Canyon,** lies right along I-10 between Benson and Willcox, and can be enjoyed from the comfort of a speeding car. Huge boulders are scattered across this rolling desert landscape.

South of the community of Dragoon, which is now known for its pistachio farms, lies a much less accessible area of the Dragoon Mountains known as **Cochise Stronghold** ★ (www.cochisestronghold.com). During the Apache uprisings of the late 19th century, the Apache leader Cochise used this rugged section of the Dragoon Mountains as his hide-out and managed to elude capture for years. The granite boulders and pine forests made it impossible for the army to track him and his followers. Cochise eventually died and was buried at an unknown spot somewhere within the area. This rugged jumble of giant boulders is reached by a rough gravel road, at the end of which you'll find a campground, a picnic area, and hiking trails. For a short, easy walk, follow the .4-mile Nature Trail. For a longer and more strenuous hike, head up the Cochise Trail. The Stronghold Divide makes a good destination for a 6-mile round-trip hike. For more information, contact the **Coronado National Forest Douglas Ranger District,** 1192 W. Saddleview Rd., Douglas (✆ **520/364-3468;** www.fs.fed.us/r3/coronado).

A MEMORABLE MUSEUM IN AN UNLIKELY LOCALE

Amerind Foundation Museum ★★ It may be out of the way and difficult to find, but this museum is well worth seeking out. Established in 1937, the Amerind Foundation is dedicated to the study, preservation, and interpretation of prehistoric and historical Indian cultures. To that end, the foundation has compiled the nation's finest private collection of archaeological artifacts and contemporary pieces. There are exhibits on the dances and religious ceremonies of the major Southwestern tribes and cases full of archaeological artifacts amassed from the numerous Amerind Foundation excavations over the years. Fascinating ethnology exhibits include amazingly intricate beadwork from the Plains tribes, old Zuni fetishes, Pima willow baskets, old kachina dolls, 100 years of Southwestern tribal pottery, and Navajo weavings. The art gallery displays works by 19th- and 20th-century American artists, such as Frederic Remington, whose paintings focused on the West. The small museum store has a surprisingly good selection of books and Native American crafts.

2100 N. Amerind Rd., Dragoon. ✆ **520/586-3666.** www.amerind.org. Admission $5 adults, $4 seniors, $3 college students and children 12–18, free for children under 12. Tues–Sun 10am–4pm. Closed major holidays. Located 64 miles east of Tucson between Benson and Willcox; take the Dragoon Rd. exit (Exit 318) from I-10 and continue 1 mile east.

EAST OF WILLCOX

In the town of Bowie, the **Fort Bowie Vineyard,** 156 N. Jefferson St. (✆ **888/299-5951** or 520/847-2593; www.fortbowievineyards.net), has a tasting room (open Mon–Sat 8:30am–4pm and Sun 10am–3pm) and sells some very drinkable, inexpensive wines. It also produces an unusual pecan-flavored sparkling wine and sells locally grown pecans, pistachios, walnuts, and peaches.

If you'd like to explore the Chiricahua Mountains from the back of a horse, **Blue Sky Ranches/Chiricahua Trail Rides** (✆ **520/824-1660** or 818/726-5430; www.blueskyranches.com) offers trail rides of anything from 1 hour ($30) to all day ($115). A 4-hour ride in Chiricahua National Monument costs $120.

Chiricahua National Monument ★★ Sea Captain, China Boy, Duck on a Rock, Punch and Judy—these may not seem like appropriate names for landscape features, but this is no ordinary landscape. These gravity-defying rock formations—called "the land of the standing-up rocks" by the Apache and the "wonderland of rocks" by the pioneers—are the equal of any of Arizona's many amazing rocky landmarks. Rank upon rank of monolithic giants seem to have been turned to stone as they marched across the forested Chiricahua Mountains. Some of these rocks, including Big Balanced Rock and Pinnacle Balanced Rock, seem ready to come crashing down at any moment. Formed about 25 million years ago by a massive volcanic eruption, these rhyolite badlands were once the stronghold of renegade Apaches. If you look closely at Cochise Head peak, you can even see the famous chief's profile. If you're in good physical condition, don't miss the chance to hike the 7.5-mile round-trip **Heart of Rocks Trail** ★★, which can be accessed from the visitor center or the Echo Canyon or Massai Point parking areas. This trail leads through the most spectacular scenery in the monument. A shorter loop is also possible. Within the monument are a visitor center, a campground, a picnic area, miles of hiking trails, and a scenic drive with views of many of the most unusual rock formations.

Ariz. 186, 36 miles southeast of Willcox. ✆ **520/824-3560.** www.nps.gov/chir. Admission $5 adults. Visitor center daily 8am–4:30pm. Closed Christmas.

Fort Bowie National Historic Site ★ The Butterfield Stage, which carried mail, passengers, and freight across the Southwest in the mid-1800s, followed a route that climbed up and over Apache Pass, in the heart of the Chiricahua Mountains' Apache territory. Near the mile-high pass, Fort Bowie was established in 1862 to ensure the passage of the slow-moving stage as it traversed this difficult region. The fort was also used to protect the water source for cavalry going east to fight the Confederate army in New Mexico. Later, it was from Fort Bowie that federal troops battled Geronimo until the Apache chief finally surrendered in 1886. Today, little more than Fort Bowie's crumbling adobe walls remain, but the hike along the old stage route to the ruins conjures up the ghosts of Geronimo and the Indian Wars.

3203 S. Old Fort Bowie Rd. (off Ariz. 186). ✆ **520/847-2500.** www.nps.gov/fobo. Free admission. Visitor center daily 8am–4:30pm; grounds daily dawn–dusk. Closed Christmas. From Willcox, drive southeast on Ariz. 186; after about 20 miles, watch for signs; it's another 8 miles up a dirt road to the trail head. Alternatively, drive east from Willcox to Bowie and go 13 miles south on Apache Pass Rd. From the trail head, it's a 1.5-mile hike to the fort.

DOUGLAS & ENVIRONS

The town of Douglas abounds in old buildings, and although not many are restored, they hint at the diverse character of this community. Just across the border from Douglas is Agua Prieta, in Sonora, Mexico, where Pancho Villa lost his first battle. In Agua Prieta, whitewashed adobe buildings, old churches, and sunny plazas provide a contrast to Douglas. At the **Douglas Chamber of Commerce Visitor Center,** 345 E. 16th St. (✆ **888/315-9999** or 520/364-2477), pick up a map to the town's historic buildings, as well as a rough map of Agua Prieta.

Slaughter Ranch Museum ★ *Finds* Down a dusty gravel road outside Douglas lies a little-known Southwestern landmark: the Slaughter Ranch. If you're old enough, you may remember a Walt Disney TV show called *Texas John Slaughter.* This was his spread. In 1884, former Texas Ranger John Slaughter bought the San Bernardino Valley and turned it into one of the finest cattle ranches in the West. Slaughter later went on to become the sheriff of Cochise County and helped rid the region of the unsavory characters who had flocked to the many mining towns of this remote part of the state. Today, the ranch is a National Historic Landmark and has been restored to its late-19th-century appearance. Surrounding the ranch buildings are wide lawns and a large pond that together attract a variety of birds, making this one of Arizona's best winter birding spots. For the-way-it-was tranquility, this old ranch can't be beat.

6153 Geronimo Trail, about 14 miles east of Douglas. ✆ **520/558-2474.** www.slaughterranch.com. Admission $5 adults, free for children under 14. Wed–Sun 10am–3pm. Closed Christmas and New Year's Day. From Douglas, go east on 15th St., which runs into Geronimo Trail; continue east 14 miles.

BIRDING HOT SPOTS

At the **Willcox Chamber of Commerce,** 1500 N. Circle I Rd. (✆ **800/200-2272** or 520/384-2272; www.willcoxchamber.com), you can pick up several birding maps and checklists for the region.

To the east of Chiricahua National Monument, on the far side of the Chiricahuas, lies **Cave Creek Canyon** ★, one of the most important bird-watching spots in the United States. It's here that the colorful elegant trogon reaches the northern limit of its range. Other rare birds that have been spotted here include sulfur-bellied flycatchers and Lucy's, Virginia's, and black-throated gray warblers. Stop by the visitor center for information on the best birding spots in the area. Cave Creek Canyon is just outside the community of Portal; in summer, it can be reached from the national monument by driving over the Chiricahuas on graded gravel roads. In winter, you'll likely have to drive around the mountains, which entails going south to Douglas and then 60 miles north to Portal or north to I-10, and then south 35 miles to Portal.

Cochise Lakes ★ (actually, the Willcox sewage ponds) are another great bird-watching spot. Birders can see a wide variety of waterfowl, including avocets and ibises. To find the ponds, head south out of Willcox on Arizona 186, turn right onto Rex Allen, Jr., Drive at the sign for the Twin Lakes golf course, and go past the golf course.

Between October and March, as many as 30,000 sandhill cranes gather in the Sulphur Springs Valley south of Willcox, and in January, the town holds the **Wings Over Willcox** festival, a celebration of these majestic birds. There are a couple of good places in the area to see sandhill cranes during the winter. Southwest of Willcox on U.S. 191 near the Apache Station electricity-generating plant and the community of Cochise, you'll find the **Apache Station Wildlife Viewing Area.** About 60 miles south of Willcox, off U.S. 191 near the town of Elfrida, is the **Whitewater Draw Wildlife Area.** To reach this latter area, go south from Elfrida on Central Highway, turn right on Davis Road, and in another 2½ miles, turn left on Coffman Road and continue 2 miles. The last 2 miles are on a dirt road that should be avoided after rainfall. The Sulphur Springs Valley is also well known for its large wintering population of raptors, including ferruginous hawks and prairie falcons.

Near Douglas, the **Slaughter Ranch,** which has a large pond, and the adjacent **San Bernardino National Wildlife Refuge,** are good birding spots in both summer and winter. (See the description of the Slaughter Ranch Museum, above, for directions.)

North of Willcox, at the end of a 30-mile gravel road, lies the **Muleshoe Ranch Cooperative Management Area** (✆ **520/507-5229;** www.muleshoelodging.org), a Nature Conservancy preserve that contains five perennial streams. These streams support endangered aquatic life as well as riparian zones that attract a large number of bird species. To get here, take Exit 340 off I-10 and go south; turn right on Bisbee Avenue and then right again onto Airport Road. After 15 miles, watch for a fork in the road and take the right fork. If the road is dry, it is usually navigable by passenger car. In May and from September to February, the headquarters, which includes the visitor center, is open Thursday through Monday from 8am to 5pm (Mar–Apr open daily and June–Aug open only Sat and Sun). Between September and May, there are guided 1-mile hikes on Saturdays at 8am. Overnight accommodations in casitas ($100–$170 double) are available by reservation (2-night minimum Sept–May, 3-night minimum on holidays).

WHERE TO STAY

IN & NEAR WILLCOX

Cochise Stronghold B&B ★ *Finds* Set on 15 acres of private land within Coronado National Forest's Cochise Stronghold area, this remote and beautiful B&B is one of my favorites in the state. The inn is an energy-efficient, passive solar home with two housekeeping suites. It makes a superb base for hikes amid the area's fascinating rock formations and for excursions farther afield in Cochise County. Owners John and Nancy Yates are a great source of information both on solar-home design and on the preservation of desert. In-room breakfast options include Southwestern dishes such as mesquite-cornmeal pancakes that are made with flour produced by grinding mesquite-bean pods. For a more adventurous experience, there are also a tipi and a yurt.

2126 W. Windancer Trail (P.O. Box 232), Pearce, AZ 85625. ✆ **877/426-4141** or 520/826-4141. www.cochisestronghold bb.com. $179–$209 double; $99 tipi; $119 yurt. Rates include full breakfast. 2-night minimum stay. AE, DISC, MC, V. **Amenities:** Jacuzzi; massage. *In room (but not in tipi):* A/C, TV/VCR, kitchenette, fridge, coffeemaker, microwave, free local calls.

IN DOUGLAS

Gadsden Hotel Built in 1907, the Gadsden bills itself as "the last of the grand hotels," and its listing on the National Register of Historic Places backs up that claim. The marble lobby, though dark, is a classic. Vaulted stained-glass skylights run the length of the ceiling, and above the landing of the Italian marble stairway is a genuine Tiffany window. Although the carpets in the halls are well worn and rooms aren't always spotless, many units have been renovated and refurnished. The bathrooms are, however, a bit worse for the wear. The lounge is a popular local hangout, with more than 200 cattle brands painted on the walls.

1046 G Ave., Douglas, AZ 85607. ✆ **520/364-4481.** Fax 520/364-4005. www.hotelgadsden.com. 160 units. $60–$80 double; $100–$150 suite. AE, DC, MC, V. **Amenities:** Restaurant (American/Mexican); lounge. *In room:* A/C, TV.

IN PORTAL

Portal Peak Lodge, Portal Store & Cafe This motel-like lodge, located behind the general store/cafe in the hamlet of Portal, has fairly modern guest rooms that face one another across a wooden deck. Meals are available in the adjacent cafe. If you're seeking predictable accommodations in a remote location, you'll find them here.

2358 Rock House Rd. (P.O. Box 16282), Portal, AZ 85632. ✆ **520/558-2223.** Fax 520/558-2473. www.portalpeak lodge.com. 16 units. $75–$85 double. AE, DISC, MC, V. **Amenities:** Restaurant (American). *In room:* A/C, TV, coffeemaker, no phone.

Southwestern Research Station, The American Museum of Natural History ★ *Finds* Located far up in Cave Creek Canyon, this is a field research station that takes guests when the accommodations are not filled by scientists doing research. As such, it is the best place in the area for serious bird-watchers, who will find the company of researchers a fascinating addition to a visit. Guests stay in simply furnished cabins scattered around the research center. Spring and fall are the easiest times to get reservations and the best times for bird-watching.

P.O. Box 16553, Portal, AZ 85632. ✆ **520/558-2396.** Fax 520/558-2018. www.research.amnh.org/swrs. 12 units. Mar–Oct $150 double (rate includes all meals); Nov–Feb $60–$80 double (no meals provided). Children under 4 stay free in parent's room. DISC, MC, V. **Amenities:** Dining room; outdoor pool; volleyball court; guest laundry. *In room:* No phone.

AREA GUEST RANCHES

Grapevine Canyon Ranch ★ Located about 35 miles southwest of Willcox in the foothills of the Dragoon Mountains adjacent to Cochise Stronghold, this guest ranch can be either a quiet hideaway where you can enjoy the natural setting, or a place to experience traditional ranch life—horseback riding, rounding up cattle, mending fences. The landscape of mesquite and yucca conjures up images of the high chaparral, and a variety of rides are offered, with an emphasis on those for the experienced. If you don't care to go horseback riding, sightseeing excursions can be arranged. The small cabins (with shower-only bathrooms) and larger casitas are set under groves of manzanita and oak trees; you can view wildlife and the night sky from the decks.

P.O. Box 302, Pearce, AZ 85625. ✆ **800/245-9202** or 520/826-3185. Fax 520/826-3636. www.grapevinecanyonranch.com. 12 units. $296–$416 double. Rates include all meals. 3-night minimum stay. Various 1-week packages available. DISC, MC, V. No children under 12. **Amenities:** Dining room; lounge; outdoor pool; Jacuzzi; guest laundry; horseback riding. *In room:* A/C, minibar, coffeemaker, hair dryer, no phone.

Price Canyon Ranch ★ Despite the address listed below, this ranch is in Arizona, although just barely. Price Canyon is located northeast of Douglas off U.S. 80 and down a 7½-mile dirt road. Can you say remote? If you're looking to get away from it all and do some cowboying (or cowgirling), this is your best bet in the area. The ranch guest rooms have all been recently renovated and now have a luxurious, modern rancho-deluxe feel with the sort of furnishings you might expect to find in Scottsdale or Tucson. Set in the southern foothills of the Chiricahua Mountains, Price Canyon Ranch is a mix of grasslands and forests that provides loads of great horseback-riding opportunities. Whether you just want to head out on an easy trail ride or join the ranch cowboys checking on the herd and riding fences, you've got plenty of options here, and at certain times of year, guests can even help with cattle drives.

P.O. Box 39, Rodeo, NM 88056. ✆ **800/727-0065** or 520/558-2383. www.pricecanyon.com. 10 units. $400 double ($175 per night for children under 13). All rates plus 15% gratuity. Rates include all meals and horseback riding. 2-night minimum (3-night minimum Oct and May). AE, DC, DISC, MC, V. **Amenities:** Dining room; outdoor pool; Jacuzzi; game room; horseback riding. *In room:* A/C, fridge, coffeemaker, hair dryer, no phone.

Sunglow Guest Ranch ★★ *Value* Located in the western foothills of the Chiricahua Mountains roughly 40 miles southeast of Willcox, this remote ranch is surrounded by Coronado National Forest and is one of the most idyllic spots in the state. Rising behind a small lake are the peaks of the Chiricahuas. There's great bird-watching both on the ranch and in the nearby hills, and guests can use the ranch's mountain bikes. The guest rooms are quite large, and decor includes rustic Mexican furnishings. More than half the units have wood-burning fireplaces. This guest ranch is different from others around the state, in that it doesn't offer horseback riding, but there is a stable just down the road that will bring its horses to the ranch. There's a beautiful little dining hall/cafe built in classic Western-ranch style that serves some of the best food available in this corner of the state.

14066 S. Sunglow Rd., Pearce, AZ 85625. ✆ **866/786-4569** or 520/824-3334. www.sunglowranch.com. 9 units. $250–$350 double. Rates include breakfast and dinner. Children 5 and under stay free in parent's room. AE, DC, DISC, MC, V. Pets accepted ($25 per night). **Amenities:** Dining room; bikes. *In room:* Fridge, coffeemaker, microwave, no phone.

CAMPGROUNDS

A 22-site campground charges $12 per night at **Chiricahua National Monument** (described above), on Arizona 186 (✆ **520/824-3560**). Along the road to Portal not far from the national monument, there are several small national forest campgrounds. Some are free and some charge $10 for a site. At **Cochise Stronghold,** 35 miles southwest of Willcox off U.S. 191, a 10-site campground charges $10 per night. For information on the national forest campgrounds, contact the Coronado National Forest Douglas Ranger District, 1192 W. Saddleview Rd., Douglas (✆ **520/364-3468;** www.fs.fed.us/r3/coronado). Reservations are not accepted for these campgrounds.

WHERE TO DINE

IN WILLCOX

Right across the parking lot from the Willcox Chamber of Commerce (off I-10 at Exit 340), you'll find **Stout's Cider Mill** ★, 1510 N. Circle I Rd. (✆ **520/384-3696;** www.cidermill.com), which makes delicious concoctions with apples. You can get cider, cider floats, "cidersicles," apple cake, and the biggest (and contender for the best) apple pie in the world. Open daily from 9am to 5pm.

Rodney's *Finds* BARBECUE Willcox doesn't have much in the way of good restaurants, but if you're a fan of barbecue, you'll want to schedule a stop at Rodney's. This hole-in-the-wall near the Rex Allen Museum is so nondescript that you can easily miss it. Inside, you'll find Rodney Brown, beaming with personality and dishing up lip-smackin' barbecued pork sandwiches and plates of ribs, shrimp, and catfish. If you're really hungry, try the gumbo. Be sure to ask Rodney about the park across the street, which he has looked after for years.

118 N. Railroad Ave. No phone. www.rodneysfood.com. Main courses $3–$9.50. No credit cards. Tues–Sun 11am–8pm.

NORTH TOWARD PHOENIX: THE SAFFORD AREA & MOUNT GRAHAM

Roughly 50 miles north of Willcox, off U.S. 191 in a unit of Coronado National Forest, rise the Pinaleño Mountains and 10,717-foot **Mount Graham,** a favorite summer vacation spot for desert dwellers. Here you'll find campgrounds, hiking trails, and an astronomical observatory (see the box "Starry, Starry Nights," earlier in this chapter). This observatory, funded partly by the University of Arizona and partly by the Vatican, was built despite concerns that the mountaintop was the last remaining habitat of 400 endangered Mount Graham red squirrels.

To the northwest of Mount Graham, at the end of a 45-mile gravel road, is the **Aravaipa Canyon Wilderness,** through which flows the perennial Aravaipa Creek. This scenic canyon is bordered on both ends by the Nature Conservancy's **Aravaipa Canyon Preserve.** Together these natural areas protect Arizona's healthiest population of native desert fishes, as well as cougars, desert bighorn sheep, bobcats, and 200 species of birds. Permits, which are required for hiking in the canyon, can be requested from the **Bureau of Land Management,** Safford Field Office, 711 14th Ave., Safford, AZ 85546 (✆ **928/348-4400;** www.az.blm.gov/sfo/index.htm), 13 weeks in advance of your visit (spring and fall are the most difficult times to get reservations).

Not far from the turnoff for Mount Graham and just south of Safford, you'll find **Roper Lake State Park** (✆ **928/428-6760;** www.azstateparks.com), which has a hot spring, a campground, rustic rental cabins ($35 per night), and a lake with a swimming beach. The day-use fee is $5 per car ($3 between Memorial Day and Labor Day); camping costs $10 to $20. There's good bird-watching here and at nearby Dankworth Pond (where you'll find a nature trail and an outdoor exhibit on the Native American cultures that used this site). The state park is off U.S. 191, about 6 miles south of Safford; the Dankworth Pond site is another 3 miles farther south.

In this same area is the **Kachina Mineral Springs Spa,** 1155 W. Cactus Rd. (✆ **928/428-7212**), 6 miles south of Safford. Visitors can soak in hot mineral waters, enjoy a sweat wrap, and get a massage. A soak costs $10; treatments range from $25 for a 40-minute soak and sweat wrap to $90 for a soak, sweat wrap, foot reflexology, sinus treatment, and 1-hour massage. Just around the corner is **Essence of Tranquility,** 6074 S. Lebanon Loop (✆ **877/895-6810** or 928/428-9312; www.geocities.com/essenceoftranquility), which offers similar services. Use of tubs is $5 per person for 1 hour; 1-hour massages go for $50.

Just south of Safford off U.S. 191, you'll find **Eastern Arizona College's Discovery Park Campus,** 1651 W. Discovery Park Blvd. (✆ **928/428-6260;** www.discoverypark.com), an interesting stop for both kids and adults. This science park includes the Gov Aker Observatory, which is home to the world's largest camera obscura (a dark room inside of which views of the outdoors can be seen projected on a wall). The observatory also has a 20-inch telescope that is available for public use and a space-flight simulator ride that is one of the park's top attractions. A marsh offers good birding opportunities. The park is open Saturday from 4 to 10pm; admission is free.

Twenty miles northeast of Safford off U.S. 70, you'll come to the **Gila Box Riparian National Conservation Area,** a popular hiking area on BLM land. As at Aravaipa Canyon, this area preserves the landscape around a perennial stream, in this case the upper reaches of the Gila River. There is no fee to hike the area.

For more information on the Safford area, contact the **Graham County Chamber of Commerce,** 1111 Thatcher Blvd., Safford (✆ **888/837-1841** or 928/428-2511; www.graham-chamber.com); or the **Bureau of Land Management,** Safford Field Office, 711 14th Ave., Safford (✆ **928/348-4400;** www.az.blm.gov/sfo/index.htm).

11

Arizona's "West Coast"

I bet you thought the West Coast was over there by Los Angeles. But Arizona also has a "west coast," or at least that's how Arizonans see it. However, Arizona's west coast is formed not by the Pacific Ocean, but by the Colorado River.

Separating Arizona from California and Nevada are 340 miles of Colorado River waters, most of which are impounded in three huge reservoirs—Lake Mead, Lake Mohave, and Lake Havasu—that provide the water and electricity to such sprawling Southwest boomtowns as Phoenix and Las Vegas. It is because of all this water that the region has come to be known as Arizona's West Coast, and it is to the waters of this inland "coast" that boaters, water-skiers, and anglers head throughout the year.

In some ways, Arizona's West Coast is superior to California's Pacific coastline. Although there aren't many waves on this stretch of the Colorado River, both the weather and the water are warmer than California's. Watersports of all types are extremely popular, and the fishing is some of the best in the country. Due to convolutions in the landscape, Lake Havasu, Lake Mohave, and Lake Mead also offer thousands of miles of shoreline.

While the Colorado River has always been the lifeblood of this rugged region, it was not water that first attracted settlers. A hundred years ago, prospectors ventured into this sun-baked landscape hoping to find gold in the mountains flanking the Colorado River. Some actually hit pay dirt, and mining towns sprang up overnight, only to be abandoned a few years later when the gold ran out. Today, Oatman (see chapter 6) is the most famous of these mining boomtowns, but it has too many people and wild burros to be called a ghost town.

People are still venturing into this region in hopes of striking it rich, but now they head across the river from Bullhead City, Arizona, to the casinos in Laughlin, Nevada, where a miniature version of Las Vegas has grown up on the banks of the Colorado.

Laughlin and Bullhead City aren't the only towns in this area with an abundance of waterfront accommodations. As with any warm coastline, Arizona's West Coast is lined with lakefront resorts, hotels, RV parks, and campgrounds. For the most part, it's a destination for desert residents, so you won't find any hotels or resorts even remotely as upscale or expensive as those in Phoenix, Tucson, or Sedona. You will, however, see plenty of houseboats for rent. These floating vacation homes are immensely popular with families and groups. With a houseboat, you can get away from the crowds, dropping anchor and kicking back when you find a remote cove, the best fishing, or the most spectacular views. You can even houseboat to London Bridge, which is no longer falling down, but rather bridges a backwater of Lake Havasu and is now one of Arizona's biggest tourist attractions.

Western Arizona

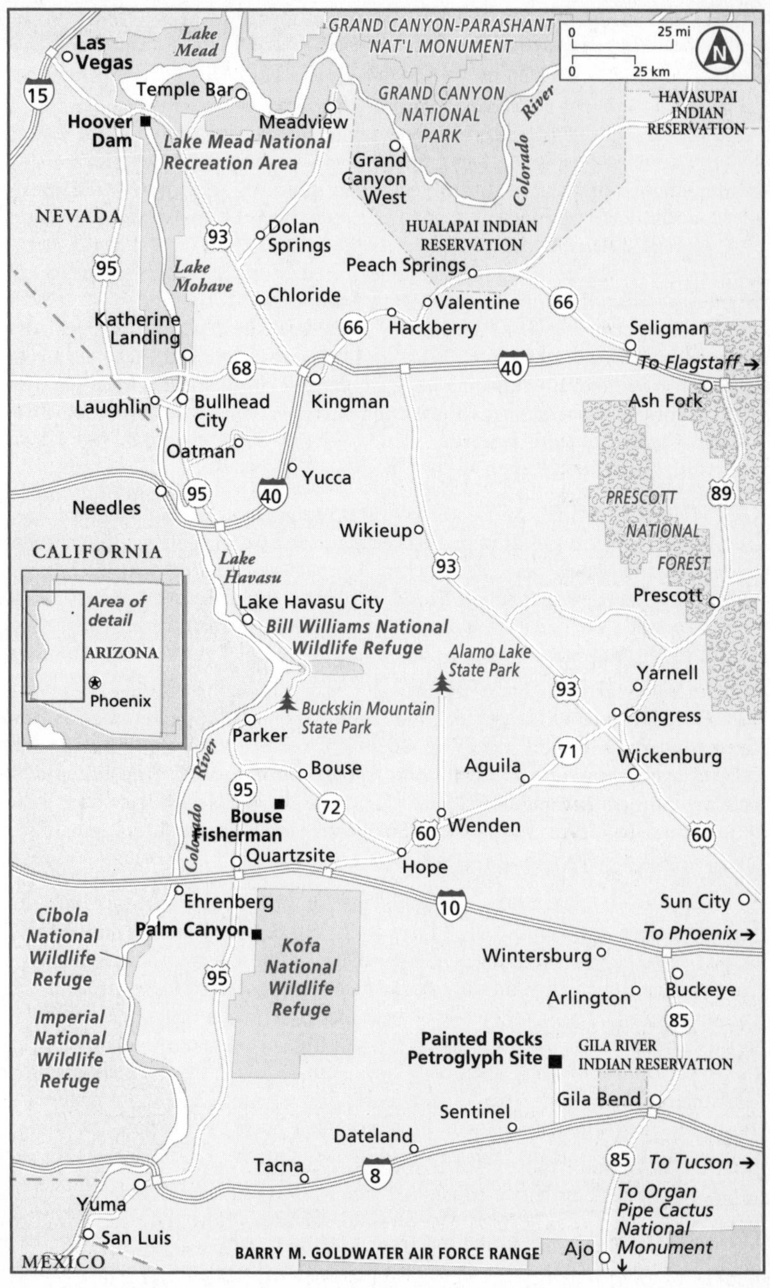

1 Lake Mead National Recreation Area

70 miles NW of Kingman; 256 miles NW of Phoenix; 30 miles SE of Las Vegas, NV

Lake Mead National Recreation Area straddles the border between Arizona and Nevada, and, with its two reservoirs and scenic, free-flowing stretch of the Colorado River, is a vast watersports playground. Throughout the year, anglers fish for striped bass, rainbow trout, channel catfish, and other sport fish, while during the hot summer months, Lake Mead and Lake Mohave attract tens of thousands of water-skiers and personal watercraft riders. Due to its proximity to Las Vegas and the fact that there are more facilities on the Nevada side of Lake Mead, the recreation area tends to be more popular with Nevadans than with Arizonans.

The larger reservoir, Lake Mead, was created by the Hoover Dam, which was constructed between 1931 and 1935. Hoover Dam was the first major dam on the Colorado River, and by supplying huge amounts of electricity and water to Arizona and California, it set the stage for the phenomenal growth the region experienced in the latter half of the 20th century.

ESSENTIALS

GETTING THERE U.S. 93, which runs between Las Vegas and Kingman, crosses over Hoover Dam, and traffic backups at the dam have in the past been absolutely horrendous. However, now that trucks are prohibited from crossing the dam, the traffic jams have lessened somewhat. Several small secondary roads lead to various marinas on the lake. There are also many miles of unpaved roads within the recreation area. If you have a high-clearance or four-wheel-drive vehicle, these roads can take you to some of the least visited shores of the two lakes.

VISITOR INFORMATION For information, contact the **Lake Mead National Recreation Area,** 601 Nevada Way, Boulder City, NV 89005 (✆ **702/293-8906;** www.nps.gov/lame), or stop by the **Alan Bible Visitor Center** (✆ **702/293-8990**), between Hoover Dam and Boulder City. The visitor center is open daily from 8:30am to 4:30pm (closed New Year's Day, Thanksgiving, and Christmas).

DAM, LAKE & RIVER TOURS

Standing 726 feet tall, from bedrock to the roadway atop it, and tapering from a thickness of 660 feet at its base to only 45 feet at the top, **Hoover Dam** (✆ **866/730-9097** or 702/494-2517; www.usbr.gov/lc/hooverdam) is the tallest concrete dam in the Western Hemisphere. Behind this massive dam lie the waters of **Lake Mead,** which at 110 miles long and with a shoreline of more than 550 miles is the largest artificial lake in the United States. To learn about the construction of Hoover Dam, stop in at the visitor center, which is open daily from 9am to 5pm (closed Thanksgiving and Christmas). Guided tours cost $11 for adults, $9 for seniors, and $6 for children 7 to 16. Parking is $7. Including a tour, it takes about 2 hours to visit the dam.

If you'd like to tour the lake, call **Lake Mead Cruises** (✆ **702/293-6180;** www. lakemeadcruises.com) to book passage on the *Desert Princess* or *Desert Princess Too* paddle-wheeler. These cruises leave from Lake Mead Cruises Landing, off Lakeshore Drive on the Nevada side of Hoover Dam. Day tours, which go to the dam, last 1½ hours and cost $22 for adults and $10 for children 2 to 11. Other options include dinner cruises ($46 for adults, $25 for children), brunch cruises ($37 for adults, $18 for children), and weekend dinner-and-dancing cruises ($58).

One of the most interesting ways to see remote parts of Lake Mohave is by sea kayak. **Desert River Outfitters** (© **888/KAYAK-33;** www.desertriveroutfitters.com) will rent you a boat and shuttle you and your gear to and from put-ins and take-outs. The trip through Black Canyon ($55 per person with a four-person minimum) starts at the base of Hoover Dam and is the most interesting route. (***Note:*** This trip requires advance planning because a permit is necessary.) You can also paddle past the casinos in Laughlin ($25), through the Topock Gorge ($45), or around Lake Mohave ($35). Raft trips through Black Canyon are offered by **Black Canyon River Adventures** (© **800/455-3490;** www.blackcanyonadventures.com). The 1-day rafting trips, on big motorized rafts, are an easy float through a scenic canyon and cost $83 for adults, $80 for children ages 13 to 15, and $51 for children ages 5 to 12. If you're not a paddler, this is a great way to see this stretch of river, definitely a highlight of a visit the state. This company also has a marina where it rents a variety of motorboats.

OUTDOOR PURSUITS

As you would expect, swimming, fishing, water-skiing, sailing, windsurfing, and powerboating are the most popular activities in Lake Mead National Recreation Area. On Arizona shores, there are swimming beaches at Lake Mohave's Katherine Landing (outside Bullhead City) and Lake Mead's Temple Bar (north of Kingman off U.S. 93). Picnic areas can be found at these two areas, as well as at Willow Beach on Lake Mohave and at more than half a dozen spots on the Nevada side of Lake Mead.

Fishing for monster striped bass (up to 50 lb.) is one of the most popular activities on Lake Mead, and while Lake Mohave's striped bass may not reach these awesome proportions, fish in the 25-pound range are not uncommon. Largemouth bass and even rainbow trout are plentiful in the national recreation area's waters due to the diversity of habitats. Try for big rainbows in the cold waters that flow out from Hoover Dam through Black Canyon and into Lake Mohave. To fish from shore, you'll need a license from either Arizona or Nevada (depending on which shore you're fishing from). To fish from a boat, you'll need a license from one state and a special-use stamp from the other. Most Lake Mead marinas sell both licenses and stamps.

The season for striped bass starts around the beginning of April, when the water begins to warm up. If you don't have your own boat, try fishing from the shore of Lake Mohave near Davis Dam, where the water is deep. Anchovy pieces work well as bait, but put some shot on your line to get it down to the depths where the fish are feeding. You can get bait, tackle, licenses, and fishing tips at the **Lake Mohave Resort and Marina,** 2690 E. Katherine Spur Rd. (© **928/754-3245**), at Katherine Landing.

In Arizona, marinas can be found at Katherine Landing on Lake Mohave (just outside Bullhead City), near the north end of Lake Mohave at Willow Beach (best access for trout angling), and at Temple Bar on Lake Mead. There's also a boat ramp at South Cove, north of the community of Meadview at the east end of Lake Mead. This latter boat ramp is the closest to the Grand Canyon end of Lake Mead. On the Nevada side of Lake Mohave, there's a marina at Cottonwood Cove, and on the Nevada side of Lake Mead, you'll find marinas at Boulder Beach, Las Vegas Bay, Callville Bay, and Echo Bay. These marinas offer motels, restaurants, general stores, campgrounds, and boat rentals. At **Temple Bar Resort & Marina** (© **800/255-5561** or 928/767-3211), you can rent speedboats for $250 to $350 per day. At **Lake Mohave Resort** (© **800/752-9669** or 928/754-3245), you can rent ski boats, fishing boats, and patio boats for between $90 and $260 per day. Personal watercraft go for $285 per day at either location.

Despite the area's decidedly watery orientation, there's quite a bit of mountainous desert here that's home to bighorn sheep, roadrunners, and other wildlife. This land was also once home to several indigenous tribes, and petroglyphs scratched into rocks are reminders of the people who lived here before the first settlers arrived. The best place to see petroglyphs is Grapevine Canyon, due west of Laughlin, Nevada, in the southwest corner of the National Recreation Area. To reach Grapevine Canyon, take Nevada 163 west from Laughlin to milepost 13 and turn right on the marked dirt road. From the highway, it's about 2 miles to the turnoff for the parking area. From the trail head, it's less than a quarter-mile to the petroglyph-covered jumble of rocks at the mouth of Grapevine Canyon. Covering the boulders are thousands of cryptic symbols, as well as ancient illustrations of bighorn sheep. To see these petroglyphs, you'll have to do a lot of scrambling, so wear sturdy shoes (preferably hiking boots).

For information on other hikes, contact **Lake Mead National Recreation Area** (✆ **702/293-8906** or 702/293-8990; www.nps.gov/lame).

WHERE TO STAY

HOUSEBOATS

Seven Crown Resorts ★ *Kids* Why pay extra for a lake-view room when you can rent a houseboat that always has a 360-degree water view? There's no better way to explore Lake Mead than on one of these floating vacation homes. You can cruise for miles, tie up at a deserted cove, and enjoy a wilderness adventure with all the comforts of home. Houseboats come complete with full kitchens, air-conditioning, and space to sleep up to 13 people. Bear in mind that the scenery here on Lake Mead isn't nearly as spectacular as that on Lake Powell, Arizona's other major houseboating lake.

P.O. Box 16247, Irvine, CA 92623-6247. ✆ **800/752-9669.** www.sevencrown.com. $1,250–$4,250 per week. DISC, MC, V. Pets accepted. *In room:* A/C, kitchen, fridge, coffeemaker, microwave, no phone.

MOTELS

Lake Mohave Resort *Kids* Just up Lake Mohave from Davis Dam and only a few minutes outside Bullhead City, the Lake Mohave Resort is an older motel, but the huge rooms are good for families. Most have some sort of view of the lake, which is across the road, and some have kitchenettes. Also across the road are the resort's nautical-theme restaurant and lounge, which overlook the marina. The resort also has a convenience store and a bait-and-tackle store.

Katherine Landing, 2690 E. Katherine Spur Rd., Bullhead City, AZ 86429. ✆ **800/752-9669** or 928/754-3245. www.sevencrown.com. 51 units. Mid-Apr to early Sept $95–$125 double, $250 suite; early Sept to mid-Apr $60–$90 double, $250 suite. Children 5 and under stay free in parent's room. DISC, MC, V. Pets accepted ($50 deposit plus $10 per pet per night). **Amenities:** Restaurant; lounge; boat and personal watercraft rentals. *In room:* A/C, TV.

Temple Bar Resort Although basically just a motel, the Temple Bar Resort has a wonderfully remote setting that will have you thinking you're on vacation in Baja, California. With a beach right in front, great fishing nearby, and 40 miles of prime skiing waters extending from the resort, this place makes a good budget getaway for anyone into watersports. A restaurant and lounge overlook the lake. The resort offers ski rentals, powerboat rentals, and a convenience store.

Temple Bar, AZ 86443. ✆ **800/255-5561** or 928/767-3211. www.templebarlakemead.com. 18 units. Apr–Oct $85–$125 double; Nov–Mar $70–$100 double. Children 5 and under stay free in parent's room. AE, DISC, MC, V. Pets accepted ($50 deposit plus $10 per pet per night). **Amenities:** Restaurant; lounge; boat and personal watercraft rentals. *In room:* A/C, TV.

CAMPGROUNDS

In Arizona, there are campgrounds at Katherine Landing on Lake Mohave and at Temple Bar on Lake Mead. These campgrounds have been heavily planted with trees, so they provide shade during the hot, but popular, summer months. In Nevada, you'll find campgrounds at Cottonwood Cove on Lake Mohave and at Boulder Beach, Las Vegas Bay, Callville Bay, and Echo Bay on Lake Mead. Campsites at all campgrounds are $10 per night. For more information, contact **Lake Mead National Recreation Area** (© **702/293-8906** or 702/293-8990; www.nps.gov/lame).

2 Bullhead City & Laughlin, Nevada

30 miles W of Kingman; 60 miles N of Lake Havasu City; 216 miles NW of Phoenix

You may find it difficult at first to understand why anyone would ever want to live in Bullhead City. This is one of the hottest places in North America, with temperatures regularly topping 120°F (49°C) in summer. However, to understand this town's attraction, you need only gaze across the Colorado River at the gambling mecca of Laughlin, Nevada, where the slot machines are always in action and the gaming tables are nearly as hot as the air outside. Laughlin is the southernmost town in Nevada and, before the advent of Indian casinos, was the closest place to Phoenix to do any gambling. The 10 large casino hotels across the river in Nevada still make Bullhead City one of Arizona's busiest little towns.

Laughlin is a perfect miniature Las Vegas. High-rise hotels loom above the desert like glass mesas, miles of neon lights turn night into day, and acres of asphalt are always covered with cars and RVs as hordes of hopeful gamblers go searching for Lady Luck. Cheap rooms and meals lure people into spending on the slot machines what they save on a bed and dinner. It's a formula that works well. Why else would anyone endure the heat of this remote desert? Actually, most visitors come here only in the winter, when the weather is just about perfect.

ESSENTIALS

GETTING THERE From Phoenix, take U.S. 60, which becomes U.S. 93, northwest to I-40. From Kingman, take Arizona 68 W to Bullhead City.

Sun Country Airlines (© **800/359-6786;** www.suncountry.com) flies into Bullhead City from a handful of cities in the Midwest and West. However, Las Vegas has better airline connections. Shuttle-bus service between Laughlin and the Las Vegas McCarran Airport is operated by **Tri-State Super Shuttle** (© **800/801-8687** or 928/704-9000; www.tristatesupershuttle.com), which charges $45 to $55 one-way and $80 to $90 round-trip.

VISITOR INFORMATION For information on Bullhead City and Laughlin, contact the **Bullhead Area Chamber of Commerce,** 1251 Hwy. 95, Bullhead City (© **800/987-7457** or 928/754-4121; www.bullheadchamber.com). In Laughlin, stop by the **Laughlin Visitors Information Center,** 1555 Casino Dr. (© **800/452-8445** or 702/298-3321; www.visitlaughlin.com).

GETTING AROUND For car rentals, contact **Avis** (© **800/331-1212** or 928/754-4686), **Enterprise** (© **800/261-7331** or 928/754-2700), or **Hertz** (© **800/654-3131** or 928/754-4111). The **Southern Nevada Transit Coalition** (© **702/298-4435;** www.sntc.net) provides public bus service in Laughlin. The fare is $1.50 for adults and 75¢ for seniors. Ferries also that shuttle to and from parking lots on the Arizona side of the river and water taxis that go from casino to casino.

CASINOS & OTHER INDOOR PURSUITS

The casinos of Laughlin, Nevada, just across the Colorado River from Bullhead City, Arizona, are known for having liberal slots—that is, the slot machines pay off frequently. Consequently, Laughlin is a very popular weekend destination for Phoenicians and other Arizonans. In addition to the slot machines, there's keno, blackjack, poker, craps, off-track betting, and sports betting. All of the hotels in Laughlin offer live entertainment of some sort, including an occasional headliner, but gambling is still the main event after dark.

If you'd like to learn more about the history of this area, visit the **Colorado River Museum,** 355 Hwy. 95, Bullhead City (✆ **928/754-3399**), a half-mile north of the Laughlin Bridge. It's open Tuesday through Saturday from 10am to 4pm and Sunday 1 to 4pm (closed June–Aug). Admission is $2 for adults and $1 for seniors.

BOAT TOURS

If you'd like to see a bit of the Colorado River, daily paddle-wheeler cruises are available through **Laughlin River Tours** (✆ **800/228-9825** or 702/298-1047; www.laughlinrivertours.com) at the **Aquarius Casino Resort** and the **Edgewater Hotel & Casino** (see "Where to Stay," below). These cruises cost $12 for adults and $6 for children 4 to 12; dinner cruises ($35) are also available. At **Don Laughlin's Riverside Resort Hotel & Casino** (✆ **702/298-2535** or 928/763-7070), you can take a tour on the 65-foot USS *Riverside* to Davis Dam. These excursions last 80 minutes and cost $10 for adults and $6 for children ages 3 to 12.

If you'd rather look at natural surroundings than casino towers, consider booking a 6-hour jet-boat tour to the London Bridge with **London Bridge Jet Boat Tours** (✆ **888/505-3545** or 702/298-5498; www.jetboattour.com). On the way, the boat passes through scenic Topock Gorge. These powerful boats cruise at up to 40 mph and make the 58-mile one-way trip in 2 hours. Tours cost $52 for adults, $47 for seniors, and $32 for children ages 12 and under.

OUTDOOR PURSUITS

Desert River Outfitters, 2649 U.S. 95, Suite 23, Bullhead City (✆ **888/KAYAK-33;** www.desertriveroutfitters.com), will rent you a boat and shuttle you and your gear to and from put-ins and take-outs. The least expensive trip is down the Colorado River past the casinos in Laughlin ($25 per person).

For information on fishing in nearby Lake Mohave, see the section on Lake Mead National Recreation Area, above. If you'd rather just feed the fish, seek out the carp that hang out at the dock behind the Edgewater Hotel & Casino. There are machines dispensing carp chow so you can feed these piscine vacuums.

In Laughlin, golfers can play a round at the **Mojave Resort Golf Club,** 9905 Aha Macav Pkwy. (✆ **702/535-4653;** www.mojaveresortgolfclub.com), adjacent to the Avi Resort & Casino. Carved out of dense thickets of desert vegetation, this course has wide, user-friendly fairways and charges greens fees of $74 to $109 during the cooler months (lower rates for guests of Avi Resort & Casino). In Bullhead City, try the **Desert Lakes Golf Course,** 5835 Desert Lakes Dr. (✆ **928/768-1000**), 15 miles south of town off Arizona 95. Greens fees range from $75 to $85 in the cooler months. Rates after 1 or 2pm are usually lower at these courses.

Bird-watching is excellent in **Havasu National Wildlife Refuge** (✆ **760/326-3853;** http://southwest.fws.gov/refuges/arizona/havasu/index.html), a wintering area for many species of waterfowl. However, much of this refuge lies within the scenic Topock Gorge and is accessible only by boat. The most accessible birding areas are along the marshes in the vicinity of the communities of Golden Shores and Topock, which are both north of the I-40 bridge over the Colorado. Topock Gorge, one of the most scenic stretches of the lower Colorado River, is a 15-mile stretch of river bordered by multicolored cliffs.

WHERE TO STAY

IN LAUGHLIN, NEVADA

Laughlin, Nevada, currently has 10 huge hotel-and-casino complexes, eight of which are on the west bank of the Colorado River (the 9th is across the street from the river, and the 10th is on the river but several miles south of town). All offer cheap rooms (usually under $30 on weeknights) to lure potential gamblers. In addition to huge casinos with hundreds of slot machines and every sort of gaming table, these hotels have several restaurants (with ridiculously low prices in at least one restaurant, which usually has long lines), bars and lounges (usually with live country or pop music nightly), swimming pools, video arcades, ferry service to parking lots on the Arizona side of the river, valet parking, room service, car-rental desks, airport shuttles, gift shops, and gaming classes. The only real difference between most of these places is the theme each has adopted for its decor.

Should you wish to stay at one of these hotels, here's the information you'll need:

- **Aquarius Casino Resort,** 1900 S. Casino Dr., Laughlin, NV 89029 (✆ 888/662-5825 or 702/298-5111; www.aquariuscasinoresort.com)
- **Avi Resort & Casino,** 10000 Aha Macav Pkwy., Laughlin, NV 89029 (✆ 800/284-2946 or 702/535-5555; www.avicasino.com)
- **Colorado Belle Hotel & Casino,** 2100 S. Casino Dr., Laughlin, NV 89029 (✆ 877/460-0777 or 702/298-4000; www.coloradobelle.com)
- **Edgewater Hotel & Casino,** 2020 S. Casino Dr., Laughlin, NV 89029 (✆ 800/677-4837 or 702/298-2453; www.edgewater-casino.com)
- **Golden Nugget Laughlin,** 2300 S. Casino Dr., Laughlin, NV 89028 (✆ 800/955-7278 or 702/298-7111; www.gnlaughlin.com)
- **Harrah's Laughlin,** 2900 S. Casino Dr., Laughlin, NV 89029 (✆ 800/HARRAHS or 702/298-4600; www.harrahs.com)
- **Pioneer Hotel & Gambling Hall,** 2200 S. Casino Dr., Laughlin, NV 89029 (✆ 800/634-3469 or 702/298-2442; www.pioneerlaughlin.com)
- **Ramada Express,** 2121 S. Casino Dr., Laughlin, NV 89029 (✆ 800/243-6846 or 702/298-4200; www.ramadaexpress.com)
- **River Palms Resort & Casino,** 2700 Casino Dr., Laughlin, NV 89029 (✆ 800/835-7904 or 702/298-2242; www.river-palms.com)
- **Riverside Resort Hotel & Casino,** 1650 S. Casino Dr., Laughlin, NV 89029 (✆ 800/227-3849, 702/298-2535 or 928/763-7070; www.riversideresort.com)

WHERE TO DINE

The dozens of inexpensive casino-hotel restaurants are usually the top choice of visitors to Laughlin and Bullhead City. Cheap steaks, prime rib, and all-you-can-eat buffets are the specialties of these places.

3 Lake Havasu & the London Bridge

60 miles S of Bullhead City; 150 miles S of Las Vegas, NV; 200 miles NW of Phoenix

"London Bridge is falling down, falling down, falling down." Well, not anymore it isn't. There once was a time when the London Bridge really was falling down, but that was before Robert McCulloch, founder of Lake Havasu City, hit upon the brilliant idea of buying the bridge and having it shipped to his undertouristed little planned community in the Arizona desert. That was more than 35 years ago, and today the London Bridge is still standing and still attracting tourists by the millions. An unlikely place for a bit of British heritage, true, but the London Bridge has turned Lake Havasu City into one of Arizona's most popular tourist destinations.

Lake Havasu was formed in 1938 by the building of the Parker Dam, but it wasn't until 1963 that McCulloch founded the town of Lake Havasu City. In the town's early years, not too many people spent time in this remote corner of the desert, where summer temperatures are often more than 110°F (43°C). Despite its name, Lake Havasu City at the time was little more than an expanse of desert with a few mobile homes on it. It was then that McCulloch began looking for ways to attract more people to his little "city" on the lake. His solution proved to be a stroke of genius.

Today, Lake Havasu City attracts an odd mix of visitors. In winter, the town is filled with retirees, and you'll rarely see anyone under the age of 60. On weekends, during the summer, and over spring break, however, Lake Havasu City is popular with Arizona college students. In fact, the city has become something of a Fort Lauderdale or Cancún in the desert, and many businesses now cater primarily to young partiers. Expect a lot of noise if you're here on a weekend or a holiday. Summers bring out the water-ski and personal-watercraft crowds.

ESSENTIALS

GETTING THERE From Phoenix, take I-10 W to Arizona 95 N. From Las Vegas, take U.S. 95 S to I-40 E to Arizona 95 S.

US Airways (✆ **800/428-4322**) has regular flights to Lake Havasu City from Phoenix. The **Havasu/Vegas Express** (✆ **800/459-4884** or 928/453-4884; www.havasuvegasexpress.com) operates a shuttle van between Lake Havasu City and Las Vegas. Fares are $55 one-way and $95 round-trip ($51 and $86 for seniors).

VISITOR INFORMATION Contact the **Lake Havasu Convention & Visitors Bureau,** English Village, 314 London Bridge Rd., (✆ **800/242-8278** or 928/453-3444; golakehavasu.com), which is at the foot of the London Bridge.

GETTING AROUND For car rentals, try **Avis** (✆ **800/331-1212** or 928/764-3001), **Enterprise** (✆ **800/261-7331** or 928/453-0033), or **Hertz** (✆ **800/654-3131** or 928/764-3994).

LONDON BRIDGE

Back in the mid-1960s, when London Bridge was indeed falling down—or, more correctly, sinking—into the Thames River due to heavy car and truck traffic, the British government decided to sell the bridge. Robert McCulloch and his partner paid nearly $2.5 million for the famous bridge; had it shipped 10,000 miles to Long Beach, California; and then trucked it to Lake Havasu City. Reconstruction of the bridge began in 1968, and the grand reopening was held in 1971. Oddly enough, the 900-foot-long bridge was not built over water; it just connected desert to more desert on a peninsula jutting into Lake Havasu. It wasn't until after the bridge was rebuilt that a mile-long channel was dredged through the base of the peninsula, thus creating an island offshore from Lake Havasu City.

Although the bridge that now stands in Arizona is not very old by British standards, the London Bridge has a long history. The first bridge over the Thames River in London was probably a wooden bridge built by the Romans in A.D. 43. In 1176, the first stone bridge over the Thames was built. They just don't build 'em like that one anymore—it lasted for more than 600 years but was eventually replaced in 1824 by the bridge that now stands in Lake Havasu City.

At the base of the bridge sits **English Village,** which is done up in proper English style and has a few shops and casual restaurants and Lake Havasu's main visitor center. There is also a waterfront promenade, along which you'll find several cruise boats and boat-rental docks.

Unfortunately, the London Bridge is not very impressive as bridges go, and the tacky commercialization of its surroundings makes it something of a letdown for many visitors. On top of that, over the years the jolly olde England styling that once predominated around here has been supplanted by a Mexican beach-bar aesthetic designed to appeal to partying college students on spring break. Lately, however, Lake Havasu City has been going a bit upscale with a few stylish bars and restaurants.

LAND, LAKE & RIVER TOURS

Several companies offer different types of boat tours on Lake Havasu. **Bluewater Jetboat Tours** (© **888/855-7171** or 928/855-7171; www.coloradoriverjetboattours.com) runs jet-boat tours that leave from the London Bridge and spend 2½ hours cruising up the Colorado River to the Topock Gorge, a scenic area 25 miles from Lake Havasu City. The cost is $38 for adults, $35 for seniors, and $20 for children 5 to 12. You can also go out on the ***Dixie Belle*** (© **928/453-6776** or 928/855-0888), a small replica paddle-wheel riverboat or the even smaller ***Kontiki.*** Cruises are $15 for adults and $8 for children 5 to 12. The *Kontiki* goes to Copper Canyon, the narrow cliff-ringed cove that is the destination for college-age partiers during spring break.

To explore the desert surrounding Lake Havasu City, arrange an off-road adventure in a six-wheel-drive Pinzgauer truck with **Outback Off-Road Adventures** (© **928/680-6151;** www.outbackadventures.us), which charges $65 to $80 for a half-day tour and $165 for a full-day tour.

WATERSPORTS

While the London Bridge is what made Lake Havasu City, these days watersports on 45-mile-long Lake Havasu are the area's real draw. Whether you want to go for a swim, take a leisurely pedal-boat ride, try parasailing, or spend the day water-skiing, there are plenty of places to get wet. Lake Havasu is also known as the Jet Ski Capital of the World, so don't expect much peace and quiet when you're out on the water.

London Bridge Beach is the best in-town beach, located in a county park behind the Island Inn, off West McCulloch Boulevard. This park has a sandy beach, lots of palm trees, and views of both the London Bridge and the distant desert mountains. There are also picnic tables and a snack bar. Just south of the London Bridge on the "mainland" side, you'll find the large **Rotary Community Park,** which is connected to the bridge by a paved waterside path. Adjacent to the park is the **Lake Havasu Aquatic Center,** 100 Park Ave. (© **928/453-2687**), which has an indoor pool, 254-foot water slide, and lots of other facilities. There are more beaches at **Lake Havasu State Park** (© **928/855-2784;** www.azstateparks.com/Parks/parkhtml/havasu.html), 2 miles north of the London Bridge; and at **Cattail Cove State Park** (© **928/855-1223**), 15 miles south of Lake Havasu City. Lake Havasu State Park also has 20 miles of shoreline to the south of Lake Havasu City, but there are no roads to this shoreline. If you have your own boat, you'll find lots of secluded little beaches. Both state parks charge a $9 day-use fee.

Moments Canoeing the Colorado

Paddling down a desert river is an unusual and unforgettable experience: rocks and cacti on the banks and cool water beneath your boat. If you're interested in a scenic canoe tour, there are a couple of outfitters in the area. Both provide boats, paddles, life jackets, maps, and shuttles to put-in and take-out points, but usually no guide. **Western Arizona Canoe and Kayak Outfitters** (✆ **888/881-5038** or 928/715-6414; www.azwacko.com) offers self-guided kayak or canoe trips through the beautiful and rugged Topock Gorge, where you can see ancient petroglyphs and possibly bighorn sheep. Trips take 5 to 6 hours, and the cost is $45 per person, which includes the use of a kayak or canoe, paddles, life jackets, dry bags, coolers, and, most important, the shuttle service to the put-in point and back from the take-out point. **Jerkwater Canoe & Kayak Company** (✆ **800/421-7803** or 928/768-7753; www.jerkwater.com) offers a similar Topock Gorge excursion and also arranges other canoe and kayak trips of varying lengths. Jerkwater's Topock Gorge self-guided 5- to 6-hour trip is $40 per person if you opt for a canoe or $55 per person if you opt for a kayak. There is a two-person minimum. Another popular trip is through Black Canyon, but advance planning (6 months–1 year) is required to get the necessary permit. It's easier to get a permit for Black Canyon midweek than on a weekend. Some trips include additional overnight campground or bunkhouse bed-and-breakfast fees.

The cheapest way to get out on the water in Lake Havasu also involves the greatest expenditure of energy. At the **Adventure Center,** in English Village (✆ **928/453-4386**), you can rent pedal boats for $20 an hour. You can also go for a ride on the **London Bridge Gondola** (✆ **928/486-1891;** www.londonbridgegondola.com); the gondolier even sings in Italian as you cruise beneath the London Bridge. Ride prices range from $15 to $35. If kayaking or canoeing is more your style, contact **Western Arizona Canoe and Kayak Outfitter** (✆ **888/881-5038** or 928/715-6414; www.azwacko.com), which charges $25 to $35 per day for canoes and kayaks.

If you didn't bring your own boat, you can rent one from **Fun Time Boat Rentals,** 1685 Industrial Blvd. (✆ **800/680-1003** or 928/680-1003; www.funtimerentals.com). Pontoon boats and ski boats equipped with water skis or knee boards both rent for $300 per day.

If your main reason for getting out on the water is to catch fish, you'll likely come away from Lake Havasu with plenty of fish stories to tell. Striped bass, also known as stripers, are the favorite quarry of anglers here. These fish have been known to weigh in at more than 60 pounds in these waters, so be sure to bring the heavy tackle. Largemouth bass in the 2- to 4-pound range are also fairly common, and giant channel catfish of up to 35 pounds have been caught in Topock Marsh. The best fishing starts in spring, when the water begins to warm up, but there is also good winter fishing.

Seeing the Light

Lighthouses may seem as out of place in the desert as the London Bridge, but there are now 12 lighthouses along the shores of Lake Havasu. The lights are replicas of famous navigation beacons from around the country and are roughly ⅓ the size of the originals. The lighthouses were built by the **Lake Havasu Lighthouse Club** (www.lh-lighthouseclub.org), and several of the lighthouses can be seen in the parks flanking the London Bridge.

GOLF

Lake Havasu City has three courses, all of which are open to the public. Panoramic views are to be had from each of the courses here, and there's enough variety to accommodate golfers of any skill level.

London Bridge Golf Club, 2400 Club House Dr. (✆ **928/855-2719;** www.americangolf.com), with two 18-hole courses, is the area's premier course. High-season greens fees (with cart) top out at $75 on the West Course and $65 on the East Course. The **Havasu Island Golf Course,** 1040 McCulloch Blvd. (✆ **928/855-5585**), is a 4,012-yard, par-61 executive course with lots of water hazards. Greens fees are $25 if you walk and $35 if you ride. The 9-hole **Bridgewater Links,** 1477 Queens Bay Rd. (✆ **928/855-4777;** www.londonbridgeresort.com), at the London Bridge Resort, is the most accessible and easiest of the area courses. Greens fees for 9 holes are $18 if you walk and $24 if you ride.

Golfers won't want to miss the **Emerald Canyon Golf Course** ★, 7351 Riverside Dr., Parker (✆ **928/667-3366;** www.emeraldcanyongolf.com), about 30 miles south of Lake Havasu City. This municipal course is the most spectacular in the region and plays through rugged canyons and past red-rock cliffs, from which there are views of the Colorado River. One hole even has you hitting your ball off a cliff to a green 200 feet below! Expect to pay $35 to $55 for greens fees in the cooler months. Also in Parker is the golf course at the **Havasu Springs Resort,** 2581 Ariz. 95 (✆ **928/667-3361**), which some people claim is the hardest little 9-hole, par-3 course in the state. It's atop a rocky outcropping with steep drop-offs all around. If you aren't staying here, greens fees are only $10 for 9 holes and $15 for 18 holes.

WHERE TO STAY

Agave Inn ★★ *Finds* Located at the foot of the London Bridge, this surprisingly stylish boutique hotel is by far the hippest hotel between Scottsdale and Las Vegas. Guest rooms are reminiscent of those at W hotels, although here you get much more room at a much lower price. Rooms are large and have balconies, and most overlook the bridge or the water. Platform beds, stylish lamps, and a sort of Scandinavian modern aesthetic make this the most distinctive hotel on this side of the state. Room no. 305, a corner room, has a great view of the bridge and is my favorite in the hotel. One caveat: the open-air bar directly across the channels plays loud music until 2am on warm nights (especially during spring break).

1420 McCulloch Blvd N., Lake Havasu City, AZ 86403. ✆ **866/854-2833** or 928/854-2833. Fax 928/854-1130. www.agaveinn.com. 23 units. $119–$429 suite. Children under 18 stay free in parent's room. AE, DISC, MC, V. **Amenities:** Exercise room; concierge; massage; dry cleaning. *In room:* A/C, TV/DVD, dataport, coffeemaker, hair dryer, iron, microwave, high-speed Internet access, Wi-Fi, free local calls.

London Bridge Resort ★ Merry Olde England was once the theme at this time-share resort, and Tudor half-timbers are jumbled up with towers, ramparts, and crenellations. However, England has given way to the Tropics and the desert as the resort strives to please its young, partying clientele (who tend to make a lot of noise and leave the hotel looking much the worse for wear). Although the bridge is just out the hotel's back door, and a replica of Britain's gold State Coach is inside the lobby, guests are more interested in the three pools and the tropical-theme outdoor nightclub. The one- and two-bedroom units are spacious, comfortable, and attractive, and those on the ground floor have double whirlpool tubs.

1477 Queens Bay, Lake Havasu City, AZ 86403. ✆ **866/331-9231** or 928/855-0888. Fax 928/855-5404. www.londonbridgeresort.com. 122 units. $179–$259 1-bedroom condo. AE, MC, V. **Amenities:** Restaurant (American); 2 lounges; 3 pools; 9-hole executive golf course; tennis court; exercise room; spa; Jacuzzi; babysitting; coin-op laundry. *In room:* A/C, TV/VCR, dataport, kitchen, coffeemaker, hair dryer, iron, high-speed Internet access.

CAMPGROUNDS

There are two state park campgrounds in the Lake Havasu City area. **Lake Havasu State Park** (✆ **928/855-2784**) is 2 miles north of the London Bridge on London Bridge Road, while **Cattail Cove State Park** (✆ **928/855-1223**) is 15 miles south of Lake Havasu City off Arizona 95. The former campground charges $14 to $25 per night per vehicle, while the latter charges $19 to $25 per site. Reservations are not accepted. In addition to sites in these campgrounds, there are boat-in campsites within Lake Havasu and Cattail Cove state parks.

WHERE TO DINE

For a decent latte or cappuccino, stop by **Kelly's Coffee & Fudge,** 1420 McCulloch Blvd. (✆ **928/680-4454**), which is located underneath the London Bridge on the same side as the Agave Inn and Shugrue's restaurant.

Cha-Bones AMERICAN Move over Scottsdale, Lake Havasu City is gettin' hip and crowdin' your turf. Well, sort of. This very stylish little restaurant a few blocks north of the London Bridge could hold its own in the big city, at least as far as the decor goes. The menu, on the other hand, sticks to familiar mesquite-grilled steaks, barbecued ribs, build-your-own burgers, and a few designer pizzas. Granted, the menu doesn't break any new ground, but the setting is so unlike anything else in Lake Havasu City that this is my new favorite restaurant in town. During happy hour (weekdays 3–6pm), appetizers are half price.

112 London Bridge Rd. ✆ **928/854-5554.** Main courses $7–$12 lunch, $10–$37 dinner. AE, DISC, MC, V. Sun–Thurs 11am–9pm; Fri–Sat 11am–10pm.

Javelina Cantina MEXICAN Located at the foot of the London Bridge on the island side, this large, modern Mexican restaurant is affiliated with Shugrue's on the other side of the street. As at Shugrue's, there is a great view of the bridge. In this case, it is from a large patio area that is kept heated during the cooler winter months. The bar has an excellent selection of tequilas, and margaritas are a specialty here. Accompany your libations with tortilla soup, fish tacos, or a salad made with blackened scallops, papaya, pecans, and blue cheese.

1420 McCulloch Blvd. ✆ **928/855-8226.** www.javelinacantina.com. Reservations not accepted. Main courses $7.50–$16. AE, DISC, MC, V. Sun–Thurs 11am–8:30 or 9pm; Fri–Sat 11am–10 or 11pm.

Mudshark Brewing Company ★ SOUTHWESTERN/INTERNATIONAL At this big, boisterous brewpub a few blocks south of the London Bridge, you'll find excellent brews that go especially well with the pizzas, pastas, and other more substantial dishes on the menu. There's a movie theater right next door, which makes this a good spot for a night out.

210 Swanson Ave. ✆ **928/453-2981.** www.mudsharkbrewing.com. Reservations not necessary. Main courses $7.50–$20. AE, MC, V. Daily 11am–10 or 10:30pm.

Shugrue's *Kids* STEAKHOUSE/SEAFOOD Just across the London Bridge from the English Village shopping complex, Shugrue's seems to be popular as much for its view of the bridge as for its food. Offerings include seafood, prime rib, burgers, sandwiches, and pastas. It's a favorite of vacationing retirees and families, especially for its inexpensive sunset dinners, which are served Sunday through Thursday from 5 to 6:30pm. The adjacent affiliated Barley Brothers Brewpub has the same good view of the bridge and serves a menu appeals to a younger clientele.

At the Island Mall, 1425 McCulloch Blvd. ✆ **928/453-1400.** www.shugrues.com. Reservations recommended. Main courses $7–$12 lunch, $11–$25 dinner. AE, DC, DISC, MC, V. Sun–Thurs 11am–3pm and 4:30–9pm; Fri–Sat 11am–3pm and 4:30–10pm.

LAKE HAVASU CITY AFTER DARK

With themed dance nights each week, the **Red Room,** 1519 Queens Bay Rd. (✆ **928/505-7226**), is just about the hottest and swankiest place in Lake Havasu City. Lake Havasu City also has two brewpubs. I prefer Mudshark Brewing Company (see above), but if you want a brew with a view of the London Bridge, head to **Barley Brothers Brewery & Grill,** 1425 McCulloch Blvd. (✆ **928/505-7837;** www.barley-brothers.com). If you're staying at the Agave Inn and have eaten at Cha-Bones, then you'll want to do your drinking at the swanky **Martini Bay,** 1477 Queens Bay (✆ **928/855-0888,** ext. 4400; www.londonbridgeresort.com), at the London Bridge Resort. You can also do some gambling across Lake Havasu at the **Havasu Landing Resort and Casino** (✆ **800/307-3610** or 760/858-4593; www.havasulanding.com), which is located in California and is operated by the Chemehuevi Indian Tribe. A ferry operates from the Island Mall beside the London Bridge.

EN ROUTE TO YUMA

THE PARKER AREA

About 16 miles south of Lake Havasu City stands the **Parker Dam,** which is said to be the deepest dam in the world because 73% of its 320-foot height is below the riverbed. Beginning just above the dam and stretching south to the town of Parker is one of the most beautiful stretches of the lower Colorado River. Just before you reach the dam, you'll come to the **Bill Williams National Wildlife Refuge** (✆ **928/667-4144;** http://southwest.fws.gov/refuges/arizona/billwill.html), which preserves the lower reaches of the Bill Williams River. This refuge offers some of the best bird-watching in western Arizona. Keep your eyes open for vermilion flycatchers, Yuma clapper rails, soras, Swainson's hawks, and white-faced ibises.

Continuing south, you'll reach a dam overlook and the Take-Off Point boat launch, where you can do some fishing from shore. Below the dam, the river becomes narrow and red-rock canyon walls close in. Although this narrow gorge is lined with mobile-home parks, the most beautiful sections have been preserved in two units of **Buckskin Mountain State Park** (✆ **928/667-3231** or 928/667-3386 for the River Island unit; www.pr.state.az.us). Both units—Buckskin Mountain and River Island—have campgrounds ($19–$25 for campsites or cabanas at Buckskin; $14–$25 for campsites at River Island), and a few of the campsites can be reserved. There are also day-use areas that include river beaches and hiking trails leading into the Buckskin Mountains. The day-use fee is $8 per vehicle at either park. In this area you'll also find the spectacular Emerald Canyon Golf Course (see "Golf," above, for details).

On the north side of Parker, keep an eye out for **Lemon Tree Nursery,** 500 Riverside Dr. (✆ **928/669-8002**), which sells fresh local citrus fruit in season.

Where to Stay

Blue Water Resort and Casino ★★ Located 37 miles south of Lake Havasu City, this riverside casino resort is western Arizona's most impressive hotel. Even if you aren't interested in spending your time at the slot machines, you'll find something here that appeals to you. There's a marina, a mile of riverfront land, a miniature golf course, a theater for live entertainment, and a big indoor pool complex (with water slide) that's designed to resemble ancient ruins. Guest rooms are all close to the water, which means nice river views but also traffic noise from the ski boats. Furnishings are standard motel modern.

11300 Resort Dr., Parker, AZ 85344. ✆ **888/243-3360.** www.bluewaterfun.com. 200 units. $45–$125 double; $96–$170 suite. AE, DISC, MC, V. **Amenities:** 3 restaurants; snack bars; 2 lounges; 4 pools; miniature golf; exercise room; Jacuzzi; video arcade; room service; casino; movie theater; marina. *In room:* A/C, TV, dataport, coffeemaker, hair dryer.

THE QUARTZSITE AREA

For much of the year, the community of **Quartzsite** is little more than a few truck stops at an interstate off-ramp. But the population explodes with the annual influx of winter visitors (also known as snowbirds), and from early January to mid-February it's the site of numerous gem-and-mineral shows that attract more than a million rock hounds. Among these shows is the **Quartzsite Pow Wow,** which is held in late January and is one of the largest gem-and-mineral shows in the country. During the winter months, Quartzsite sprouts thousands of vendor stalls, as flea markets and the like are erected along the town's main streets. A variety of interesting food makes it a good place to stop for lunch or dinner. For more information, contact the **Quartzsite Chamber of Commerce,** 100 E. Main St., Quartzsite (✆ **928/927-5600;** www.quartzsitechamber.org).

For information on parking your RV in the desert outside Quartzsite, contact the **Bureau of Land Management,** Yuma Field Office, 2555 E. Gila Ridge Rd., Yuma (✆ **928/317-3200;** www.az.blm.gov/yfo/index.htm). Alternatively, you can get information and camping permits at the Long-Term Visitor Area entrance stations just south of Quartzsite on U.S. 95. The season here runs from September 15 to April 15, with permits going for $140 for the season and $30 for 14 consecutive days.

There are only three places in Arizona where palm trees grow wild, and if you'd like to visit one of these spots, watch for the Palm Canyon turnoff 18 miles south of Quartzsite. Palm Canyon lies within the boundaries of the **Kofa National Wildlife Refuge,** which was formed primarily to protect the desert bighorn sheep that live here in the rugged Kofa Mountains. The palms are 9 miles off U.S. 95 in a narrow canyon a short walk from the end of the well-graded gravel road, and although there are fewer than 100 palm trees, the hike to see them provides an opportunity to experience these mountains up close. Keep your eyes peeled for desert bighorn sheep. Incidentally, the Kofa Mountains took their name from the King of Arizona Mine. For maps and more information, contact the Kofa National Wildlife Refuge, 356 W. First St., Yuma (✆ **928/783-7861;** www.fws.gov/southwest/refuges/arizona/kofa.html).

The mountains of this region were once pockmarked with mines. To get an idea of what life was like in the mining boomtowns, make a detour to **Castle Dome City Mines Museum** (✆ **928/920-3062**), a reconstructed mining town in the middle of the desert. To find this place, turn east at the Castle Dome turnoff near milepost 55 and continue another 10 miles (only the first mile or so is paved). The museum/ghost town is open Tuesday through Sunday from 10am to 5pm, and admission is $5 for adults. There are guided tours ($5) on Wednesday at 10am.

4 Yuma ★

180 miles SW of Phoenix; 240 miles W of Tucson; 180 miles E of San Diego, CA

According to the *Guinness Book of World Records,* Yuma is the sunniest place on Earth. Of the possible 4,456 hours of daylight each year, the sun shines in Yuma for roughly 4,050 hours, or about 90% of the time. Combine all that sunshine with the warmest winter weather in the country, and you've got a destination guaranteed to attract sun worshippers and other refugees from colder climes. In fact, each winter, tens of thousands of snowbirds (retired winter visitors) drive their RVs to Yuma from as far away as Canada. However, by late spring, all those RVers head north to escape the steadily rising temperatures, and by high summer, Yuma starts posting furnacelike high temperatures that make this one of the hottest cities in the country.

Way back in the middle of the 19th century, long before RVers discovered Yuma, this was one of the most important towns in the region, known as the Rome of the Southwest because all roads led to Yuma Crossing—the shallow spot along the Colorado River where this town was founded. Despite its location in the middle of the desert, Yuma became a busy port town during the 1850s as shallow-draft steamboats traveled up the Colorado River from the Gulf of California. Later, when the railroad pushed westward into California in the 1870s, it passed through Yuma. Today, it is I-8, which connects San Diego with Tucson and Phoenix, that brings travelers to Yuma and across the Colorado River.

However, despite having more than a dozen golf courses and two important historic sites, Yuma constantly struggles to attract visitors (blame it on the lure of San Diego, which is just a few hours away). In the hopes of luring more travelers off the interstate, Yuma has in recent years upgraded and restored some of its downtown historic buildings, expanded its historic sites, and restored its natural setting on the Colorado River. There is even a visual arts center downtown that rivals any gallery in Scottsdale, and an adjacent historic movie theater has been restored to its former glory and now serves as a performing arts center.

ESSENTIALS

GETTING THERE Yuma is on I-8, which runs from San Diego, California, to Casa Grande, Arizona. **Amtrak** (✆ **800/872-7245**) runs passenger service to Yuma on its Sunset Limited route, which runs between Los Angeles and Orlando. The station is at 281 Gila Street.

The Yuma International Airport, 2191 32nd St., is served from Phoenix by **US Airways** (✆ **800/428-4322**) and from Los Angeles by **United Express** (✆ **800/864-8331**).

VISITOR INFORMATION Contact the **Yuma Convention and Visitors Bureau,** 377 S. Main St. (✆ **800/293-0071** or 928/783-0071; www.visityuma.com). November through April, the visitor center is open Monday through Friday from 9am to

6pm, Saturday from 9am to 4pm, and Sunday from 10am to 1pm. May through October, the visitor center is open Monday through Friday from 9am to 5pm and Saturday from 9am to 2pm.

GETTING AROUND Rental cars are available from **Avis** (✆ **800/331-1212** or 928/726-5737), **Budget** (✆ **800/527-0700** or 928/344-1822), **Enterprise** (✆ **800/261-7331** or 928/344-5444), and **Hertz** (✆ **800/654-3131** or 928/726-5160).

SPECIAL EVENTS The Yuma area is a major producer of lettuce, and celebrates this during **Yuma Lettuce Days** (www.yumalettucedays.com) in late January. **Yuma Crossing River Daze,** in mid-February, features historical reenactments, tours of historic sites, and an arts-and-crafts festival.

HISTORIC SITES

Arizona Historical Society Sanguinetti House Museum If you'd like to find out more about pioneer life in Yuma, stop by this territorial-period home, which is full of historical photographs and artifacts, and surrounded by lush gardens and aviaries containing exotic birds. Adjacent to the museum is The Garden Cafe, a wonderful alfresco breakfast and lunch spot (see "Where to Dine," below).

240 S. Madison Ave. ✆ **928/782-1841**. www.arizonahistoricalsociety.org. Admission $3 adults, $2 seniors and students 12–18, free for children under 12; free 1st Sat of each month. Tues–Sat 10am–4pm.

Yuma Quartermaster Depot State Historic Park ★ In 1865, Yuma Crossing, the narrow spot on the Colorado River where the town of Yuma sprang up, became the site of the military's Quartermaster Depot. Yuma was a busy river port during this time, and after supplies shipped from California were unloaded, they went to military posts throughout the region. When the railroad arrived in Yuma in 1877, the Quartermaster Depot lost its importance, and by 1883, the depot was closed. Today, the depot's large wooden buildings have been restored, and although they're set back from the current channel of the Colorado River, it's easy to imagine being stationed at this hot and dusty outpost in the days before air-conditioning. Exhibits tell the story of those who lived and worked at Yuma Crossing.

201 N. Fourth Ave. (at the Colorado River). ✆ **928/329-0471**. www.pr.state.az.us. Admission $3 adults, free for children under 14. Daily 9am–5pm. Closed Christmas.

Yuma Territorial Prison State Historic Park ★ If you've ever wondered where they really locked up the bad guys in the Wild West, check out this fortresslike prison on a bluff above the Colorado River. This prison opened for business in 1876 and, despite the thick stone walls and iron bars, was considered a model penal institution in its day. It even had its own electricity-generating plant and ventilation system. The prison museum has some interesting displays, including photos of many of the men and women who were incarcerated here.

1 Prison Hill Rd. ✆ **928/783-4771**. www.pr.state.az.us. Admission $4 adults, free for children under 14. Daily 8am–5pm. Closed Christmas.

DOWNTOWN YUMA

While Yuma may not seem at first like the sort of place to expect to see cutting-edge contemporary art, that's just what you sometimes encounter at the **Yuma Art Center/Yuma Fine Arts Museum,** 254 S. Main St. (✆ **928/329-6607;** www.yumafinearts.com), which is next door to the Historic Yuma Theatre and is a gorgeous gallery that could hold its own in Scottsdale. The **Yuma Symposium** (✆ **928/782-1934;** www.yumasymposium.org), held here each year in February, brings in talented artists from all over the country. Don't leave town without stopping by to see what's on view. The center is open Tuesday through Saturday from 10am to 5pm (Fri until 7pm) and Sunday from 1 to 5pm. Admission is by suggested $3 donation.

Historic downtown Yuma isn't exactly a bustling place, and it doesn't exactly abound in historical flavor. Funky and inexpensive crafts and antiques shops occupy an occasional storefront, and down a landscaped alleyway off Main Street (at 224 Main St., across from Lutes Casino), there's a potpourri of small tourist-oriented stores. Just off Main Street, you'll also find two pottery studios/galleries: **Tomkins Pottery,** 78 W. Second St. (✆ **928/782-1934;** www.claystuff.com), and **Colorado River Pottery,** 67 W. Second St. (✆ **888/410-2689** or 928/343-0413; www.coloradoriverpottery.com).

Within just a couple of blocks of downtown, you can play in the sand or go for a stroll along the Colorado River at **Colorado River Crossing Beach Park.** The park is at the north end of Madison Avenue.

DATES & DESERT TOURING

Date palms, which are among the most ancient of cultivated tree crops, flourish in the heat of the Arizona desert. Here in Yuma, you'll find **Ehrlich's Date Garden,** 868 Ave. B (✆ **928/783-4778**), which sells nearly a dozen varieties of organically grown dates, as well as organic oranges. Prices are incredibly low. The old-fashioned fruit stand is open Monday through Friday from 9am to 5pm (but closed early May–Sept).

While you're in a Middle Eastern mood (or if you've got the kids with you), consider spending some time at the **Saihati Camel Farm,** 15672 S. Ave. 1E (✆ **928/627-7511**), which is on the east side of Yuma at the corner of County 16th Road (call for directions). Here at the farm you can get to know the resident camels and the other 20 species of exotic animals here. The farm is open Monday through Saturday from 9am to 5pm, and admission is $3 (seniors are $2.50); children under 4 are free.

The Colorado River has been the lifeblood of the Southwestern desert for centuries, and today there's a wealth of history along its banks. **Yuma River Tours** (✆ **928/783-4400;** www.yumarivertours.com) operates narrated jet-boat tours from Yuma to the **Imperial National Wildlife Refuge** (see below) and a 48-mile trip upriver to Draper. Along the way, you'll learn about the homesteaders, boatmen, Native Americans, and miners who once relied on the Colorado River. Tours cost $38 to $75. This company also does more low-key boat tours in a paddle-wheeler. Three-hour tours are $38 ($45 with lunch), and 2-hour sunset dinner cruises are $49.

If you're a bird-watcher, an angler, or a canoeist, you'll want to spend some time along the Colorado River north of Yuma. Here you'll find the Imperial and Cibola national wildlife refuges, which preserve marshes and shallow lakes alongside the river. Plenty of bird species, good fishing and canoeing, and several campgrounds make it a popular area. For more information, contact the **Imperial National Wildlife Refuge** (✆ **928/783-3371;** www.fws.gov/southwest/refuges/arizona/imperial.html) or the **Cibola National Wildlife Refuge** (✆ **928/857-3253;** www.fws.gov/southwest/refuges/cibolanwr/index.html).

One of the best ways to explore the Imperial National Wildlife Refuge is by canoe. You can rent one from **Martinez Lake Resort** (✆ **800/876-7004;** www.martinezlake.com) for $18 a day and paddle around Martinez Lake. Multiday canoe trips are offered by **Yuma River Tours** (✆ **928/783-4400;** www.yumarivertours.com) along this stretch of the lower Colorado, which features rugged, colorful mountains and quiet backwater areas.

Bird-watchers will want to head out to **Betty's Kitchen Wildlife and Interpretive Area** ($5 day-use fee per vehicle) and the adjacent **Mittry Lake Wildlife Area.** To get there, take U.S. 95 east out of town, turn north on Avenue 7E, and continue 9 miles, at which point the road turns to gravel. Turn left in a quarter of a mile to reach Betty's Kitchen; continue straight to reach Mittry Lake. Fall and spring migrations are some of the best times of year for birding at these spots; many waterfowl winter in the area as well. For information on Betty's Kitchen and Mittry Lake, contact the **Bureau of Land Management,** Yuma Field Office, 2555 E. Gila Ridge Rd., Yuma (✆ **928/317-3200;** www.az.blm.gov/yfo/index.htm).

GOLF

While Yuma's golf courses are not nearly as impressive as those in Phoenix and Tucson, there are plenty of them, and you can't beat the winter climate. The **Mesa del Sol Golf Club,** 12213 Calle del Cid (✆ **928/342-1283;** www.mesadelsolgolf.com), off I-8 at the Fortuna Road exit, is the most challenging local course open to the public. Greens fees range from $36 to $45 during the cooler months. On the other hand, the **Desert Hills Municipal Golf Course,** 1245 W. Desert Hills Dr. (✆ **928/344-4653;** www.deserthillsgc.com), has been rated one of the best municipal courses in the state. Greens fees range from $24 to $46 during the cooler months.

WHERE TO STAY

MODERATE

Best Western Coronado Motor Hotel ★ With its red-tile roofs, whitewashed walls, and archways, this mission-revival building on the edge of downtown is the picture of a mid-20th-century motel—but rooms are as up-to-date as you would expect from a major chain. The convenient location puts you within walking distance of several good restaurants, Yuma Quartermaster Depot State Historic Park, the Arizona Historical Society Sanguinetti House Museum, and the Yuma Valley Railway.

233 Fourth Ave., Yuma, AZ 85364. ✆ **877/234-5567** or 928/783-4453. Fax 928/782-7487. www.bwcoronado.com. 86 units. $79–$150 double; $99–$175 suite. Rates include full breakfast. Children 12 and under stay free in parent's room. AE, DC, DISC, MC, V. Pets accepted. **Amenities:** Restaurant (American); lounge; 2 outdoor pools; Jacuzzi; coin-op laundry. *In room:* A/C, TV, dataport, fridge, hair dryer, iron, safe, free local calls.

Best Western InnSuites Hotel & Suites Located just off I-8, this modern hotel offers an attractive setting and spacious accommodations at reasonable rates. Although not all the rooms are full suites, all are quite large and have loads of amenities and nice decorative touches. The pool, though small, is in a pleasant courtyard.

1450 Castle Dome Ave., Yuma, AZ 85365. ✆ **800/922-2034** or 928/783-8341. Fax 928/783-1349. www.bestwestern.com. 166 units. $80–$142 double. Rates include full breakfast and evening social hour. Children under 18 stay free in parent's room. AE, DC, DISC, MC, V. Pets accepted ($25 fee). **Amenities:** Outdoor pool; 2 tennis courts; exercise room; Jacuzzi; business center; coin-op laundry; laundry service; dry cleaning. *In room:* A/C, TV, dataport, fridge, coffeemaker, hair dryer, iron, microwave, high-speed Internet access, free local calls.

La Fuente Inn & Suites Conveniently just off the interstate, this appealing hotel is done in Spanish colonial style with red-tile roof, pink-stucco walls, and a fountain out front, and the theme continues in the lobby, which has rustic furnishings and a tile floor. French doors open onto the pool terrace and a large courtyard, around which the guest rooms are arranged. Standard units feature modern motel furnishings, while the well-designed suites offer much more space. The Spanish styling and pleasant courtyard pool area set this place apart from other off-ramp hotels in Yuma.

1513 E. 16th St., Yuma, AZ 85365. ✆ **800/841-1814** or 928/329-1814. www.lafuenteinn.com. 96 units. Jan–Apr $110–$159 double; May–Dec $83–$139 double. Rates include continental breakfast and evening happy hour. Children 12 and under stay free in parent's room. AE, DC, DISC, MC, V. **Amenities:** Pool; exercise room; access to nearby health club; Jacuzzi; courtesy airport shuttle; coin-op laundry. *In room:* A/C, TV/VCR, dataport, fridge, coffeemaker, hair dryer, iron, microwave, high-speed Internet access.

WHERE TO DINE

You can stock up on all sorts of gourmet goodies, including wine, bread, pastries, chocolate truffles, and imported cheeses, at **Anthony's Uptown Food & Deli,** 2100 S. Fourth Ave. (✆ **928/782-DELI**). This large deli also sells soups, salads, sandwiches, and a variety of prepared foods such as meatloaf, lasagna, and even leg of lamb.

The Garden Cafe ★★ BREAKFAST/SANDWICHES/SALADS In back of the Arizona Historical Society Sanguinetti House Museum is Yuma's favorite breakfast and lunch spot. Set amid quiet terraced gardens and large aviaries full of singing birds, The Garden Cafe provides a welcome respite from Yuma's heat. On the hottest days, misters spray the air with a gentle fog that keeps the gardens cool. There's also an indoor dining area. The menu consists of various delicious sandwiches, daily special quiches, salads, and rich desserts. Pancakes with lingonberry sauce are a breakfast specialty. On Sunday, there's a brunch buffet. This place is a favorite with retirees.

250 Madison Ave. ✆ **928/783-1491.** Reservations not accepted. Main courses $7–$12. AE, MC, V. Tues–Fri 9am–2:30pm; Sat–Sun 8am–2:30pm. Closed late May to early Oct.

Lutes Casino *Kids* BURGERS/SANDWICHES Lutes, in business since the 1920s, is a dark and cavernous restaurant known for serving the best hamburgers in town and for having the strangest decor, too. You don't need to see a menu—just walk in and ask for a special, or *especial* (this is a bilingual joint). What you'll get is a cheeseburger/hot dog combo. Then cover your special with Lutes' own secret-recipe hot sauce to make it truly special. You won't find any slot machines or poker tables at Lutes Casino anymore—just a few very serious domino players.

221 S. Main St. ✆ **928/782-2192.** Reservations not accepted. Sandwiches and burgers $2.25–$6. No credit cards. Mon–Thurs 10am–8pm; Fri–Sat 10am–9pm; Sun 10am–6pm.

River City Grill ★★ INTERNATIONAL With its hip, big-city decor and colorful exterior paint job, this restaurant is a novelty in Yuma, and the lines out the door testify to the fact that the town really appreciates such a dining experience. Although you can get a steak or a burger, seafood dominates the menu, and sushi is served every night except Wednesday. The crab-and-salmon cakes with spicy Thai peanut sauce are a must for a starter. Flavor combinations range all over the globe: Vietnamese spring rolls, Mediterranean salad, seafood gumbo, and jerk chicken. The owners of this restaurant also operate **Ciao Bella,** 2255 S. Fourth Ave. (✆ **928/783-3900**), an upscale Italian restaurant.

600 W. Third St. ✆ **928/782-7988.** www.rivercitygrillyuma.com. Reservations highly recommended. Main courses $8–$12 lunch, $14–$26 dinner. AE, DISC, MC, V. Mon–Fri 11am–2pm and 5–10pm; Sat–Sun 5–10pm.

YUMA AFTER DARK

In most small towns across Arizona, you'll find an old downtown movie theater. Most of them are boarded up and abandoned. Not so with Yuma's old theater. The renovated and updated **Historic Yuma Theatre,** 254 S. Main St. (✆ **928/373-5202;** www.ci.yuma.az.us/parksandrec), is now host to live theater productions and touring musical groups. Originally opened in 1912, the theater has been restored to the way it looked in the 1930s, when it sported a distinctive Art Deco decor.

Looking for something else to do after dark in Yuma? You can try your luck at the **Paradise Casinos,** 450 Quechan Dr. (© **888/777-IWIN;** www.paradise-casinos.com), across the Colorado River on the Quechan Indian Reservation, or at the **Cocopah Casino,** 15318 S. Ave. B, Somerton (© **800/23-SLOTS;** www.wincocopahcasino.com), 15 minutes south of Yuma.

EAST TOWARD TUCSON

It's a long stretch of desert from Yuma east to Tucson, and there's not much to break up the monotony of the drive. However, keep an eye out for Exit 67, the Dateland exit. Although **Dateland Palms** (© **928/454-2772;** www.dateland.com) is little more than a gift shop and diner, it is well known for its thick and creamy date shakes (on a hot afternoon, nothing tastes better).

The next exit to watch for is Exit 102 (Painted Rock Dam Rd.). Getting off at this exit will lead you north to an impressive collection of petroglyphs at the Bureau of Land Management's **Painted Rocks Petroglyph Site.** To find this ancient rock art, drive north on Painted Rock Dam Road for 11 miles to a left turn onto dirt Rocky Point Road. Continue another ½ mile to the parking area. There is a $2 day-use fee here. For more information, contact the BLM Phoenix Field Office, 21605 N. 7th Ave. (© **623/580-5500;** www.az.blm.gov/pfo/paint.htm).

WEST TOWARD SAN DIEGO

West of Yuma, I-8 heads out across the California desert toward San Diego, soon passing through barren, windswept sand dunes that Hollywood has long used to represent the Sahara. This region may seem like it's a long way from anywhere, but if you pull off the freeway 9 miles west of Yuma at the Sidewinder Road exit, you'll find yourself in the "town" of **Felicity** (© **760/572-0100;** www.felicityusa.com), which, according to town founder Jacques-Andres Istel, is the center of the world. Actually, it was a dragon in a fairy tale that claimed that Felicity was the center of the world, and who's going to argue with a dragon? The fact that Istel wrote the fairy tale shouldn't matter. Make a pilgrimage to this unusual attraction, and you can stand inside a pyramid at the "exact" center of the world. As an added bonus, you can admire Istel's monument to the history of French aviation and marvel at his granite remembrance walls. The Official Center of the World is open for tours from Thanksgiving to Easter.

Appendix: Arizona in Depth

Despite the searing summer temperatures, the desolate deserts, and the lack of water, people have been drawn to Arizona for hundreds of years. In the 16th century, the Spanish came looking for gold but settled for saving souls. In the 19th century, despite frightful tales of spiny cactus forests, ranchers drove their cattle into the region and discovered that a few corners of the state actually had lush grasslands. At the same time, sidetracked forty-niners were scouring the hills for gold (and found more than the Spanish did). However, boomtowns—both cattle and mining—soon went bust. Despite occasional big strikes, mining didn't prove itself until the early 20th century, and even then, the mother lode was neither gold nor silver, but copper, which Arizona has in such abundance that it is known as the Copper State.

In the 1920s and 1930s, Arizona struck a new source of gold—sunshine. The railroads had made travel to the state easy, and word of the mild winter climate spread to colder corners of the nation. Among the first "vacationers" were people suffering from tuberculosis. These "lungers," as they were known, rested and recuperated in the dry desert air. It didn't take long for the perfectly healthy to realize that they, too, could avail themselves of Arizona's sunshine, and wintering in the desert soon became fashionable with wealthy Northerners.

Today, it's still the golden sun that lures people to Arizona, and Scottsdale, Phoenix, Tucson, and Sedona are home to some of the most luxurious and expensive resorts in the country. Then there are those who come to Arizona on vacation and decide to make the move permanent. In the past half-century, the state has seen a massive influx of retirees, many of whom have found the few pockets of Arizona where the climate is absolutely perfect—not too hot, not too cold, and with plenty of sunshine.

While the weather is a big draw, it's the Grand Canyon that attracts the most visitors to Arizona. However, the state has plenty of other natural wonders, as well. The largest meteorite crater, the Painted Desert, the spectacular red-rock country of Sedona, the sandstone buttes of Monument Valley, and "forests" of saguaro cacti are just a few examples.

The human hand has also left its mark on Arizona. More than 1,000 years ago, the Ancestral Puebloan (formerly called Anasazi), Sinagua, and Hohokam tribes built villages on mesas, in valleys, and in the steep cliff walls of deep canyons. In more recent years, much larger structures have risen in canyons across the state. The Hoover and Glen Canyon dams on the Colorado River are among the largest dams in the country and have created the nation's largest and most spectacular reservoirs, although at the expense of the rich riparian areas that once thrived in the now flooded desert canyons. Today, these reservoirs are among the state's most popular destinations.

Just as compelling as Arizona's sunshine, resorts, and reservoirs are the tall tales of the state's fascinating history. This is the Wild West, the land of cowboys and Indians, of prospectors and ghost towns, coyotes and rattlesnakes. Scratch the glossy surface of modern, urbanized Arizona, and you'll strike real gold—the story of the American West.

1 Arizona Today

Combining aspects of Native American, Hispanic, and European cultures, Arizona is one of the most culturally diverse states in the country. While the wealthy residents of Scottsdale raise Arabian horses as investments, the Navajos of the Four Corners region ride hardworking horses to herd sheep, which they still raise for sustenance and wool. Vacationers on Lake Powell water-ski through flooded canyons while cowboys in the southeast corner of the state still ride the range.

Although Arizonans are today more likely to drive Mustangs and Thunderbirds than to ride pintos and appaloosas, cowboy boots, cowboy hats, blue jeans, and bola ties are acceptable attire at almost any function in the state. Horses are still used on ranches, but most are kept simply for recreational or investment purposes. In Scottsdale, once one of the nation's centers of Arabian-horse breeding, horse auctions attract a well-heeled (read: lizard-skin-booted) crowd, and horses sell for tens of thousands of dollars. Even the state's dude ranches, which now call themselves "guest ranches," have changed their image, and many are as likely to offer nature hikes and massages as horseback riding.

A long legacy of movies being filmed here has further blurred the line between the real West and the Hollywood West. More city slickers wander the streets of the Old Tucson movie set and videotape shootouts at the O.K. Corral than ever saddle up and ride herd on a cattle drive. Even dinner has been raised to a cowboy entertainment form at Arizona's many Wild West steakhouses, where families are entertained by cowboy bands, staged gunfights, hayrides, and sing-alongs.

For Arizona's Indians, those were days of hardship and misery, and today the state's many tribes continue to strive for the sort of economic well-being enjoyed by the state's non-native population. Traditional ways still survive, but tribes are struggling to preserve their unique cultures—languages, religious beliefs, ceremonies, livelihoods, and architecture.

Arizona is home to the largest Indian reservation in the country—the Navajo nation—as well as nearly two dozen smaller reservations. As elsewhere in the United States, poverty, unemployment, and alcoholism are major problems on Arizona reservations. However, several of the state's tribes have, through their arts and crafts, managed to both preserve some of their traditional culture and share it with non-natives.

Lately, however, many non-natives have been visiting reservations not out of an interest in learning about another culture, but to gamble. Throughout the state, casinos have opened on reservation land, and despite the controversies surrounding such enterprises, many native peoples are finally seeing some income on their once-impoverished reservations.

Many of the people who visit these new casinos are retirees, who are among the fastest-growing segment of Arizona's population. The state's mild winter climate has attracted thousands of retirees over the past few decades. Many of these winter residents, known as snowbirds, park their RVs outside such spots as Yuma and Quartzsite. Others have come to stay, settling in retirement communities such as Sun City and Green Valley.

This graying of the population, combined with strong ranching and mining industries, has made Arizona one of the most conservative states. Although by today's standards Barry Goldwater could almost be considered a liberal, his conservative politics were so much a part of the Arizona mindset that the state kept him in the Senate for 30 years.

Arizona's environmental politics have been somewhat contentious in recent years. Although many people think of the desert as a wasteland in need of transformation, others see it as a fragile ecosystem that has been endangered by the encroachment of civilization. Saguaro cacti throughout the state are protected by law, but the deserts they grow in are not.

In many parts of the Tucson metropolitan area, houses have been built right up to the edge of national forest lands. The consequences of creating such a stark line between wild and developed lands came to the forefront of the news in 2004, when mountain lions moved into the popular Sabino Canyon recreation area and were even seen on the grounds of a public school. The presence of the big cats caused the immediate closure of Sabino Canyon and other nearby trails into the national forest. Today when you visit Sabino Canyon, you'll be warned repeatedly about the presence of mountain lions in the area.

At the north end of the state, remote Grand Canyon National Park is suffering from its own popularity. With roughly four million visitors a year, the park now sees summer traffic jams and parking problems that can make a visit an exercise in patience. To alleviate congestion and air pollution, the national park uses alternative-fuel buses to transport visitors around the South Rim and Grand Canyon Village, and in 2007 added extra lanes at the park's most popular entrance.

Efforts at preserving the state's environment make it clear that Arizonans value the outdoors, but a ski boat in every driveway doesn't mean the arts are ignored. Phoenix and Tucson have become centers for the visual and performing arts. The two cities share an opera company and a ballet company, and the Valley of the Sun is home to a number of symphony orchestras and theater companies.

The arts, though, are often overshadowed by the Phoenix area's obsession with professional sports. Downtown Phoenix has positioned itself as the state's primary sports and entertainment mecca, with Chase Field, the US Airways Center, and numerous sports bars and nightclubs. However, it isn't just downtown Phoenix that is big on professional sports. The city of Glendale, west of Phoenix, is now home to both Glendale Arena, where the NHL's Phoenix Coyotes play professional hockey, and University of Phoenix Stadium, where the NFL's Arizona Cardinals now play football.

Suburban sprawl has long been a fact of life in the Phoenix area, but there are signs that even Phoenicians are tiring of the metro area's never-ending expansion. Inner-city Phoenix neighborhoods are beginning to be rediscovered, and old homes are finally being restored. There are even hip new loft-style condominiums being built near downtown Phoenix, and a trendy, urban art scene has begun to flourish in long-abandoned commercial and industrial neighborhoods in downtown Phoenix.

The new urban vibe that is taking hold in the Phoenix metro area is most evident in the Old Town Scottsdale area, which is now home to the ultra-hip Hotel Valley Ho and is getting a W Hotel as well. Scottsdale also now has one of the hottest nightlife scenes between New York and Los Angeles, and high-style bars and clubs attempt to outdo each other with their daring interior decors.

It isn't just in Phoenix that Arizona style is changing. Chic hotels have opened in Sedona and even Lake Havasu City. Prescott, a classic small-town-America sort of place, even has a great little jazz club. What's a cowboy to do?

Today the New West and the Old West are coming to grips in Arizona. Hopis still perform their age-old dances atop their mesas, while in Phoenix and Tucson, fashionistas dance to the latest techno beats. Grizzled wranglers lead tourists on horseback rides across open range, and ranchers find they have something in common with environmentalists—preserving Arizona's ranch lands. All these people share something else: a love of sunshine, which, of course, Arizona has in abundance.

2 History 101

EARLY HISTORY Arizona is the site of North America's oldest cultures and one of the two longest continuously inhabited settlements in the United States—the Hopi village of Oraibi, which has had inhabitants for roughly 1,000 years. However, the region's human habitation dates back more than 11,000 years, to the time when paleo-Indians known as the Clovis people inhabited southeastern Arizona. Stone tools and arrowheads of the type credited to the Clovis have been found in southeastern Arizona, and a mammoth-kill site has become an important source of information about these people, who were among the earliest inhabitants of North America.

Few records exist of the next 9,000 years of Arizona's pre-history, but by about A.D. 200, wandering bands of hunter-gatherers took up residence in Canyon de Chelly in the northern part of the state. Today these early Arizonans are known as the Ancestral Puebloans. The earliest Ancestral Puebloan period, stretching from A.D. 200 to 700, is defined as the Basket Maker period due to the large numbers of baskets that have been found in ruins from this time. During the Basket Maker period, the Ancestral Puebloans gave up hunting and gathering and took up agriculture, growing corn, beans, squash, and cotton on the canyon floors in northeastern Arizona.

Between 700 and 1300, during what is called the Pueblo period, the Ancestral Puebloans began building multistory pueblos and cliff dwellings. However, despite decades of research, it is still not clear why the Ancestral Puebloans began living in niches and caves high on the cliff walls of the region's canyons. It may have been to conserve farmland as their population grew and required larger harvests, or for protection from flash floods or attacks by hostile neighbors. Whatever the reason, the Ancestral Puebloan cliff dwellings were all abandoned by 1300. It's unclear why the villages were abandoned, but a study of tree rings indicates that the region experienced a severe drought between 1276 and 1299, which suggests the Ancestral Puebloans left in search of more fertile farmland. Keet Seel and Betatakin, at Navajo National Monument, as well as the many ruins in Canyon de Chelly, are Arizona's best-preserved Ancestral Puebloan sites.

During the Ancestral Puebloan Basket Maker period, the Sinagua culture began to develop in the fertile plateau northeast of present-day Flagstaff and southward into the Verde River valley. The Sinagua, whose name is Spanish for "without water," built their stone pueblos primarily on hills and mesas such as those at Tuzigoot near Clarkdale and Wupatki near Flagstaff. They also built cliff dwellings at places such as Walnut Canyon and Montezuma Castle. By the mid–13th century, Wupatki had been abandoned, and by the early 15th century, Walnut Canyon and pueblos in the lower Verde Valley region had also been deserted.

By A.D. 450, the Hohokam culture, from which the Sinagua most likely learned irrigation, had begun to farm the Gila and Salt river valleys between Phoenix and Casa Grande. Over a period of 1,000 years, they constructed a 600-mile network of irrigation canals, some of which can still be seen today. However, because the Hohokam built their homes of earth, few Hohokam ruins remain. One exception is the Casa Grande ruin, a massive earth-walled structure that has been well preserved. Despite the lack of pueblo ruins, the desert is filled with signs of the

Hohokams' time here. Numerous petroglyph (rock art) sites are a lasting reminder of the people who first made the desert flourish. By the 1450s, the Hohokam had abandoned their villages. Today many archaeologists believe that the irrigation of desert soil for hundreds of years may have left a thick crust of alkali in farm fields, which would have made further farming impossible. The disappearance of the Hohokam is commemorated in the tribe's name, which, in the language of today's Tohono O'odham people, means "the people who have vanished."

HISPANIC HERITAGE The first Europeans to visit the region may have been a motley crew of shipwrecked Spaniards, among whom was a black man named Estévan de Dorantes. This unfortunate group spent 8 years wandering the Southwest, and when they arrived back in Spanish territory, they told a fantastic story of seven cities so rich that the inhabitants even decorated their doorways with jewels. No one is sure whether they actually passed through Arizona, but in 1539 their story convinced the viceroy of New Spain (Mexico) to send out an expedition, led by Father Marcos de Niza and Estévan de Dorantes into the region. Father de Niza's report of finding the fabled Seven Cities of Cíbola inspired Don Francisco Vásquez de Coronado to set off in search of wealth in 1540. Instead of fabulously wealthy cities, however, Coronado found only pueblos of stone and mud. A subordinate expedition led by Garcia Lopez de Cárdenas stumbled upon the Grand Canyon, while another group of Coronado's men, led by Don Pedro de Tovar, visited the Hopi mesas.

In the 150 years that followed, only a handful of Spaniards visited Arizona. In the 1580s and 1600s, Antonio de Espejo and Juan de Oñate explored northern and central Arizona and found indications that there were mineral riches in the region. In the 1670s, the Franciscans founded several missions among the Hopi pueblos, but the Pueblo Revolt of 1680 obliterated this small Spanish presence.

In 1687, Father Eusebio Francisco Kino, a German-educated Italian Jesuit, began establishing missions in the Sonoran Desert region of northern New Spain. In 1691, he visited the Pima village of Tumacácori. Father Kino taught the inhabitants European farming techniques, planted fruit trees, and gave the natives cattle, sheep, and goats to raise. However, it was not until 1751, in response to a Pima rebellion, that the permanent mission of Tumacácori and the nearby presidio (military post) of Tubac were built. Together these two Spanish outposts became the first permanent European settlements in what is today Arizona.

In 1775, a group of settlers led by Juan Bautista de Anza set out from Tubac to find an overland route to California, and in 1776, this group founded the city of San Francisco. That same year, the Tubac presidio was moved to Tucson. As early as 1692, Father Kino had visited the Tucson area and by 1700 had laid out the foundations for the first church at the mission of San Xavier del Bac. However, it was not until some time around 1783 that construction of the present church, known as the White Dove of the Desert, began.

In 1821, Mexico won its independence from Spain, and Tucson, with only 65 inhabitants, became part of Mexico. Mexico at that time extended all the way to Northern California, but in 1848, most of this land, except for a small section of southern Arizona that included Tucson, became U.S. territory in the wake of the Mexican-American War. Five years later, in 1853, Mexico sold the remainder of what is today southern Arizona to the United States in a transaction known as the Gadsden Purchase.

INDIAN CONFLICTS At the time the Spanish arrived in Arizona, the tribes living in the southern lowland deserts were peaceful farmers, but in the mountains of the east lived the Apache, a hunting-and-gathering tribe that frequently raided neighboring tribes. In the north, the Navajo, relatively recent immigrants to the region, fought over land with the neighboring Ute and Hopi (who were also fighting among themselves).

Coronado's expedition through Arizona and into New Mexico and Kansas was to seek gold. To that end he attacked one pueblo, killed the inhabitants of another, and forced still others to abandon their villages. Spanish-Indian relations were never to improve, and the Spanish were forced to occupy their new lands with a strong military presence. Around 1600, 300 Spanish settlers moved into the Four Corners region, which at the time supported a large population of Navajo. The Spanish raided Navajo villages to take slaves, and angry Navajo responded by stealing Spanish horses and cattle.

For several decades in the mid-1600s, missionaries were tolerated in the Hopi pueblos, but the Pueblo tribes revolted in 1680, killing the missionaries and destroying the missions. Encroachment by farmers and miners moving into the Santa Cruz Valley in the south caused the Pima people to stage a similar uprising in 1751, at Tubac. This revolt led to the establishment of the presidio at Tubac that same year. When the military garrison moved to Tucson, Tubac was quickly abandoned because of frequent raids by Apaches. In 1781, the Yuman tribe, whose land at the confluence of the Colorado and Gila rivers had become a Spanish settlement, staged a similar uprising that wiped out the settlement at Yuma.

By the time Arizona became part of the United States, it was the Navajo and the Apache who were proving most resistant to white settlers. In 1864, the U.S. Army, under the leadership of Col. Kit Carson, forced the Navajo to surrender by destroying their winter food supplies. The survivors were forced to walk to an internment camp in New Mexico; the Navajo refer to this as The Long Walk. Within 5 years they were returned to their land now a reservation.

The Apache resisted white settlement 20 years longer than the Navajo did. Skillful guerrilla fighters, the Apache, under the leadership of Geronimo and Cochise, attacked settlers, forts, and towns despite the presence of U.S. Army troops sent to protect the settlers. Geronimo and Cochise were the leaders of the last resistant bands of rebellious Apaches. Cochise eventually died in his Chiricahua Mountains homeland, while Geronimo was finally forced to surrender in 1886. Geronimo and many of his followers were subsequently relocated to Florida by the U.S. government. Open conflicts between whites and Indians finally came to an end.

TERRITORIAL DAYS In 1846, the United States went to war with Mexico, which at the time extended all the way to Northern California and included parts of Colorado, Wyoming, and New Mexico. When the war ended, the United States claimed almost all the land extending from Texas to Northern California. This newly acquired land, called the New Mexico Territory, had its capital at Santa Fe. The land south of the Gila River, which included Tucson, was still part of Mexico, but when surveys determined that this land was the best route for a railroad from southern Mississippi to Southern California, the U.S. government negotiated the Gadsden Purchase. In 1853, this land purchase established the current Arizona-Mexico border.

When the California gold rush began in 1849, many hopeful miners from the east crossed Arizona en route to the gold fields, and some stayed to seek riches in Arizona. However, despite the ever-increasing numbers of settlers, Congress refused to create a separate Arizona Territory. When the Civil War broke out,

Arizonans, angered by Congress's inaction on their request to become a separate territory, sided with the Confederacy, and in 1862, Arizona was proclaimed the Confederate Territory of Arizona. Although Union troops easily defeated the Confederate troops who had occupied Tucson, this dissension convinced Congress, in 1863, to create the Arizona Territory.

The capital of the new territory was temporarily established at Fort Whipple near Prescott, but later the same year was moved to Prescott itself. In 1867 the capital moved again, this time to Tucson. Ten years later, Prescott again became the capital, which it remained for another 12 years before the seat of government finally moved to Phoenix, which has remained Arizona's capital to this day.

During this period, mining flourished, and although small amounts of gold and silver were discovered, copper became the source of Arizona's economic wealth. With each mineral strike, a new mining town would boom, and when the ore ran out, the town would be abandoned. These towns were infamous for their gambling halls, bordellos, saloons, and shootouts. Tombstone and Bisbee became the largest towns in the state and were known as the wildest towns between New Orleans and San Francisco.

In 1867, farmers in the newly founded town of Phoenix began irrigating their fields using canals that had been dug centuries earlier by the Hohokam. In the 1870s, ranching became another important source of revenue in the territory, particularly in the southeastern and northwestern parts of the state. In the 1880s, the railroads finally arrived, and life in Arizona changed drastically. Suddenly the region's mineral resources and cattle were accessible to the East.

STATEHOOD & THE 20TH CENTURY By the beginning of the 20th century, Arizonans were trying to convince Congress to make the territory a state. Congress balked, but finally in 1910 allowed the territorial government to draw up a state constitution. Territorial legislators were progressive thinkers, and the draft of Arizona's state constitution included clauses for the recall of elected officials. President William Howard Taft vetoed the bill that would have made Arizona a state because he opposed the recall of judges. Arizona politicians removed the clause, and on February 14, 1912, Arizona became the 48th state. One of the new state legislature's first acts was to reinstate the clause providing for the recall of judges.

Much of Washington's opposition to Arizona's statehood had been based on the belief that Arizona could never support economic development. This belief was changed in 1911 by one of the most important events in state history—the completion of the Salt River's Roosevelt Dam (later to be renamed the Theodore Roosevelt Dam). The dam provided irrigation water to the Phoenix area and tamed the violent floods of the river. The introduction of water to the heart of Arizona's desert enabled large-scale agriculture and industry. More dams were built throughout Arizona, and, in 1936, the Hoover Dam on the Colorado River became the largest concrete dam in the Western Hemisphere. This dam also created the largest man-made reservoir in North America. Arizona's dams would eventually provide not only water and electricity but also the state's most popular recreation areas.

Despite labor problems, copper mining increased throughout the 1920s and 1930s, and with the onset of World War II, the mines boomed as military munitions manufacturing increased the demand for copper. However, within a few years after the war, many mines were shut down. Today, Arizona is littered with old mining ghost towns that boomed and then went bust. A few towns, such as Jerome, Bisbee, and Chloride, managed to hang on after the mines shut down and were eventually rediscovered by artists, writers, and retirees. Bisbee and Jerome are now major tourist attractions known for their many art galleries.

World War II created a demand for beef, leather, and cotton (which became the state's most important crop). Arizona's clear desert skies also provided ideal conditions for training pilots, and several military bases were established in the state. Phoenix's population doubled and after the war, many veterans returned with their families. However, it would take the invention of air-conditioning to truly open up the desert to major population growth.

During the postwar years, Arizona attracted a number of large manufacturing industries and moved away from its agricultural economic base. Today, electronics manufacturing, aerospace engineering, and other high-tech industries provide employment for thousands of Arizonans. The largest economic segment, however, is now the service industries, with tourism playing a crucial role.

Even by the 1920s, Arizona had become a winter destination for the wealthy, and the Grand Canyon, declared a national park in 1919, was luring visitors even when you had to get there by stagecoach. The clear, dry air also attracted people suffering from allergies and lung ailments, and Arizona became known as a healthful place. With Hollywood Westerns enjoying immense popularity, dude ranches began to spring up across the state. Eventually the rustic guest ranches of the 1930s gave way to luxurious golf resorts. Today, Scottsdale, Phoenix, and Tucson boast dozens of luxury resorts. In addition, tens of thousands of retirees from as far north as Canada make Arizona their winter home and play a substantial role in the state's economy.

Continued population growth throughout the 20th century resulted in an ever-increasing demand for water. Yet, despite the damming of nearly all of Arizona's rivers, the state still suffered from insufficient water supplies in the south-central population centers of Phoenix and Tucson. It took the construction of the controversial and expensive Central Arizona Project (CAP) aqueduct to carry water from the Colorado River over mountains and deserts, and deliver it where it was wanted. Construction on the CAP began in 1974, and in 1985 water from the project finally began irrigating fields near Phoenix. In 1992, the CAP reached Tucson. However, recent years of drought in the Southwest have left Phoenix, Tucson, and Las Vegas once again pondering where they will come up with the water to fuel future growth.

By the 1960s, Arizona had become an urban state with all the attendant problems. The once-healthful air of Phoenix now rivals that of Los Angeles with smog. Allergy sufferers are plagued by pollen from the nondesert plants that have been introduced to make this desert region look more inviting. However, the state's economy is still growing. High-tech companies continue to locate within Arizona, and the steady influx of both retirees and Californians is giving the state new energy and ideas. And, of course, the sun is still shining, even in January and February, when much of the country is locked in a deep freeze. As long as winters in Arizona continue to be sunny and warm, the state will continue to boom.

Index

AAA (American Automobile Association), 58
The Abyss, 224
Accommodations, 56–58
best, 15–19
Active vacations, 8, 48–55
A Day in the West (Sedona), 196
Agua Fria National Monument, 165
Aguirre Lake, 396
Airport Mesa, 190, 191
Airport Mesa Trail, 197–198
Airport security, 31
Air tours. *See* Scenic flights
Air travel, 29–32, 34, 55
Alpine, 318
Alvadora (Phoenix), 146
Amado, 397–398, 400
American Automobile Association (AAA), 58
American Express, 58
Phoenix, 84
America the Beautiful-National Park and Federal Recreational Lands Pass
Access Pass, 1, 40
Senior Pass, 1, 41
Amerind Foundation Museum (Dragoon), 14, 423
Amitabha Stupa (Sedona), 2, 195
A Mountain (Sentinel Peak), 362
Ancestral Puebloans (Anasazi), 213, 220, 223, 268–269, 272, 288, 289, 292, 454
Angel & Vilma Delgadillo's Route 66 Gift Shop & Visitor's Center (Seligman), 265
Angel's Window Overlook, 240
Antelope Canyon, 9, 300–301
Antelope Canyon Navajo Tribal Park, 300–301
Antelope House Overlook, 288
Antigua de Mexico (Tucson), 383
Apache Cultural Center & Museum (Fort Apache), 311–312
Apache Indians, 183, 311, 314, 395, 411, 414, 422, 456
Apache Lake, 163
Apache Station Wildlife Viewing Area, 425
Apache Trail, 10, 162–164
Aravaipa Canyon Preserve, 428–429
The Arboretum at Flagstaff, 246, 248
Archaeological tours, 47–48
Arcosanti, 48, 165
Area codes, 58
Arivaca Cienega, 396
Arivaca Creek, 396
Arizona 179, 2
Arizona Biltmore Golf & Country Club (Phoenix), 138
Arizona Biltmore Resort & Spa (Phoenix), 95, 130
Spa, 146–147
Arizona Capitol Museum (Phoenix), 127
Arizona Cowboy College (Scottsdale), 53
Arizona Cowboy Poets' Gathering (Prescott), 28
Arizona Diamondbacks (Phoenix), 143
Arizona Doll & Toy Museum (Phoenix), 134
Arizona Folklore Preserve (near Sierra Vista), 408
Arizona Historical Society Downtown Museum (Tucson), 363, 369
Arizona Historical Society Museum in Papago Park (Tempe), 127
Arizona Historical Society Pioneer Museum (Flagstaff), 248
Arizona Historical Society Sanguinetti House Museum (Yuma), 446
Arizona Historical Society Tucson Main Museum, 363–364
Arizona Jewish Theatre Co. (Phoenix), 162
Arizona Mills (Tempe), 153
Arizona Mining & Mineral Museum (Phoenix), 129
Arizona Museum for Youth (Mesa), 134
Arizona Opera Company (Phoenix), 161
Arizona Opera Company (Tucson), 389
Arizona Renaissance Festival, 26
Arizona Science Center (Phoenix), 128
Arizona Snowbowl (Flagstaff), 245
Arizona–Sonora Desert Museum (Tucson), 5, 12, 357
Arizona State Fair (Phoenix), 28
Arizona State Museum (Tucson), 364
Arizona State University Art Museum at Nelson Fine Arts Center (Tempe), 126
Arizona Theatre Company (ATC; Tucson), 389
Arizona Vineyards Winery (near Nogales), 401
Art galleries
Bisbee, 419
Cottonwood, 186
Flagstaff, 246
Jerome, 182
Patagonia, 404
Phoenix area, 147–149
Prescott, 176
Sedona, 199, 200
Tubac, 396
Tucson, 380–381
Wickenburg, 168
Winslow, 272

Art One (Scottsdale), 148
Arts and crafts. *See also* Native Americans, arts and crafts
Bisbee, 419
Tucson, 381
Yuma, 446, 447
ASARCO Mineral Discovery Center (Sahuarita), 373
Astronomer's Inn (Benson), 399
Astronomy. *See* Stargazing
ASU Karsten Golf Course (Tempe), 139
ATMs (automated teller machines), 34–35
Auto racing, 143

Bacavi, 275
Backpacking, 52–53
Grand Canyon, 227–228
Bajada Loop Drive (Tucson), 374
Baldy, Mount, 314
Ballet Arizona (Phoenix), 161
Barrett-Jackson Collector Car Auction (Scottsdale), 26
Barrio Histórico District (Tucson), 326
Baseball, 143–144, 377–378
Basketball, 144
The Bead Museum (Glendale), 129
Bell Rock, 190, 191
Bell Rock Pathway, 197
Benson, 407–408, 412
Bentley Projects (Phoenix), 148
Besh-Ba-Gowah Archaeological Park, 15, 163
Betatakin, 9, 293
Betty's Kitchen Wildlife and Interpretive Area (Yuma), 448
Big Lake, 315
Big Nose Kate's (Tombstone), 415
Big Springs Environmental Study Area, 311
Big Surf (Tempe), 142
Biking and mountain biking, 48–49
Phoenix area, 136–137
Prescott area, 175
Sedona, 8, 198
Sunrise Park, 314
Tucson, 373–374
Williams Valley, 319
Bill Williams National Wildlife Refuge, 443
Biltmore Fashion Park (Phoenix), 151–152
Biosphere 2 (Tucson), 365
Bird Cage Theatre (Tombstone), 415
Bird-watching, 8, 28, 49
best spots for, 11–12
Bill Williams National Wildlife Refuge, 443
Dead Horse Ranch State Park, 184
Garden Canyon, 409
Hassayampa River Preserve, 170
Havasu National Wildlife Refuge, 436–437
Holy Trinity Monastery (St. David), 411
Las Cienegas National Conservation Area, 403
Patagonia Lake State Park, 404
Patagonia–Sonoita Creek Preserve, 403
Sierra Vista and San Pedro Valley area, 407, 409, 411
Sonoita Creek State Natural Area, 404
Tucson, 374
Willcox area, 425–426
Yuma, 448
Bisbee, 417–421
Bisbee Mining and Historical Museum, 418
Bischoff's at the Park (Scottsdale), 152
Blue Mesa, 282
Blue Range Primitive Area, 319
Blue Sage Gallery (Scottsdale), 152
Boating (boat rentals). *See also* Canoeing; Kayaking; Rafting and float trips; White-water rafting
Bullhead City, 436
Lake Havasu, 439, 440
Sunrise Lake, 315
Boat tours and cruises
Canyon Lake, 163
Glen Canyon National Recreation Area, 299–300
Lake Havasu, 439
Lake Mead, 432
Laughlin, Nevada, 436
Yuma, 447
Bonelli House (Kingman), 266
Boot Hill Graveyard (Tombstone), 415
The Borgata of Scottsdale, 152
The Boulders Resort & Golden Door Spa (Carefree), 132
el Pedregal Shops & Dining at, 152, 161
golf courses, 50, 137
spa, 145
Boyce Thompson Arboretum (near Superior), 5, 163–164
Boynton Canyon, 190, 191, 197
Boynton Canyon Trail, 191
Bright Angel Point, 240
Bright Angel Trail, 223–224, 226, 228
Bucket shops, 30–31
Buckskin Mountain State Park, 443–444
Buenos Aires National Wildlife Refuge, 11, 396–397
Bullhead City, 435–437
Burton Barr Library (Phoenix), 130
Business hours, 58
Butler Canyon Trail, 314
Butterfly Lodge Museum (near Greer), 315

Calendar of events, 25–29
Camelback Golf Club (Phoenix), 138
Camelback Mountain, 8, 140
Cameron Trading Post, 232, 280
Campgrounds
Buckskin Mountain and River Island, 443
Buenos Aires National Wildlife Refuge, 397
Canyon de Chelly, 292
Coronado National Forest, 413
Grand Canyon, 228, 236–237, 244
Greer, 316
Lake Havasu City area, 442
Lake Mead area, 435
Lake Powell, 305
Lyman Lake State Park, 318
Monument Valley Navajo Tribal Park, 297
Payson area, 309
Pinetop-Lakeside area, 313
Quartzsite, 444
Springerville-Eagar and Clifton-Morenci areas, 320
near Willcox, 428
near Williams, 258
Canoeing, 49, 52, 175, 440, 447
Canyon de Chelly National Monument, 10, 15, 287–292
Canyon Lake, 163

Cape Royal, 240
Capitol Butte, 191
Carefree, 82–83, 132. *See also* Phoenix area
  accommodations, 93–95
  restaurants, 110–111
Carnegie Library (Tucson), 372
Carr Canyon, 409
Car rentals, 33
  for disabled travelers, 40
Car travel, 33, 55. *See also* Scenic drives
Casa Grande Ruins National Monument, 15, 164
Casa Malpais Visitor Center and Museum (Springerville), 317
Casinos, 162, 308, 312, 390, 436, 450
Castle Dome City Mines Museum, 445
Castles & Coasters (Phoenix), 134
Catalina Highway, 357
Catalina State Park, 376
Cathedral Rock, 190, 191, 193
Cathedral Rock Trail, 197
Cathedral Wash Trail, 303
Cattail Cove State Park, 439, 442
Cave Creek, 82–83, 132. *See also* Phoenix area
  accommodations, 93–95
  restaurants, 110–111
Cave Creek Canyon, 12, 425
Cave Creek Museum, 132
Celebration of Fine Art (Scottsdale), 148
Celebrity Theatre (Phoenix), 159
Cellphones, 44
Center for Creative Photography (Tucson), 362
Center for Meteorite Studies (Phoenix), 129
Central Arizona, 21, 166–211
Centre for Well Being (Scottsdale), 146
Ceramics Research Center (Tempe), 126
Cervini Haas Gallery (Scottsdale), 148
Chandler, 82
  restaurants, 118
Chapel of the Holy Cross (Sedona), 194
Chapel of the Holy Dove (near Flagstaff), 246
Chiaroscuro (Scottsdale), 148
Chiricahua Mountains, 424
Chiricahua National Monument, 424
Chloride, 267
Chloride murals, 267
Cinco de Mayo, 27
Cliff Castle Casino (Camp Verde), 186
Cliff dwellings
  Betatakin, 9
  Canyon de Chelly, 288
  Montezuma Castle National Monument, 184–185
  Navajo National Monument, 292, 293
  Tonto National Monument, 15, 163
  Walnut Canyon National Monument, 250
Clifton, 319
Climate, 24–25
Cochise Cowboy Poetry & Music Gathering (Sierra Vista), 26
Cochise Lakes, 12, 425
Cochise Stronghold, 423
COFCO Chinese Cultural Center, 115
Coffee Pot Rock (Rooster Rock), 191
Colossal Cave Mountain Park (Tucson), 357
Conley Museum of the West (Tucson), 363
Consolidators, 30–31
Consulates, 59–60
Copper Queen Library (Bisbee), 418
Corbett House (Tucson), 369–370
Coronado National Memorial, 410
Coronado Trail, 318–320
Cosanti (Paradise Valley), 130
Cottonwood, 186
Courthouse Butte, 191
Courthouse Plaza (Prescott), 173
Cowboy Artists of America Annual Sale & Exhibition (Phoenix), 28–29
Coyote Buttes, 241
CrackerJax Family Fun & Sports Park (Scottsdale), 134
Credit cards, 35
  lost or stolen, 60–61
Crescent Moon Recreation Area, 192–193
Cricket Pavilion (Phoenix), 160
Cross-country skiing, Williams Valley Winter Recreation Area, 319
Crystal Forest, 282
Crystal Palace Saloon (Tombstone), 415
Culture Quest Scottsdale, 125
Currency, 58
Customs regulations, 58–59

Dates, 447, 450
Davis Dominguez Gallery (Tucson), 380
Daylight saving time, 62
Dead Horse Ranch State Park, 184
De Anza Trail, 397
Debit cards, 35
Deep vein thrombosis, 38
Deer Valley Rock Art Center, 124
De Grazia Gallery in the Sun (Tucson), 362
Desert Botanical Garden (Phoenix), 5, 124, 160
Desert Caballeros Western Museum (Wickenburg), 13, 168
Desert View, 219
Desert View Drive, 219–222
Desert View Watchtower, 219–220
Devil's Bridge Trail, 197
Devine, Andy, 263
Dinnerware Contemporary Art Gallery (Tucson), 380
Dinosaurs, 129, 280, 317, 368
Disabilities, travelers with, 39–40
Dodge Theatre (Phoenix), 159
Douglas, 424–425
Dove Valley Ranch Golf Club (Cave Creek), 139
Drinking laws, 59
Dude ranches. *See* Guest ranches

Eagar, 316–318
Eagle Head Rock, 191
Eagle Trail, 319–320
Eastern Arizona College's Discovery Park Campus (near Safford), 429
Eastern Arizona's high country, 22, 306–320
East Fork Trail, 314
East Rim, 241
Echo Canyon Recreation Area, 140
Echo Canyon Vineyard & Winery (Page Springs), 2, 195

Economy class syndrome, 38
Ecotourism, 42–43
Ed Schieffelin Territorial Days (Tombstone), 27
Ehrlich's Date Garden (Yuma), 447
El Capitan, 297
El Cortijo (Tucson), 380
Elden Pueblo, 251
Electricity, 59
Elks Opera House (Prescott), 180
El Presidio Gallery (Tucson), 380
El Presidio Historic District (Tucson), 326, 379
El Presidio Park/Plaza de las Armas (Tucson), 370
El Tiradito (Tucson), 356, 372
Embassies, 59–60
Emergencies, 60
English Village (Lake Havasu), 439
Entry requirements, 23–24
Environmental Operations Park (Sierra Vista), 409–410
Escorted tours, 46–47
Escudilla Mountain, 319
Etherton Gallery (Tucson), 372, 380
Etter General Store (Wickenburg), 168
Explore Navajo Interactive Museum (Tuba City), 3, 278

F

Face Rock Overlook, 289
Fairbank, 411
Families with children, 42
  best experiences for, 12–13
  best vacations for, 13
  Phoenix area attractions, 133–135
  suggested itinerary, 69–70
Famous Sam's (Tucson), 387
Faust Gallery (Scottsdale), 152–153
Fax machines, 62
FBR Open Golf Tournament (Scottsdale), 26
Felicity, 450
Festival of Lights (Sedona), 29, 189
Festival of the West (Chandler), 27
Festivals and special events, 25–29
Fiesta Bowl Parade (Phoenix area), 29
Fighter Combat International (Mesa), 135
Finger Rock Trail, 376
Fish House (Tucson), 370
Fishing, 52
  Greer Lakes, 314–315
  Lake Havasu, 440
  Lake Mead National Recreation Area, 433
  Lake Powell, 302
  Lees Ferry, 240–241
  Patagonia Lake State Park, 403–404
Flagstaff, 244–255
Flandrau Science Center & Planetarium (Tucson), 366
The Flattops, 282
Football, 144, 378
Foothills Mall (Tucson), 383
Forest Road 300, 308–309
Fort Bowie National Historic Site, 424
Fort Bowie Vineyard (Bowie), 423–424
Fort Huachuca Historical Museum, 408–409
Fort Lowell Museum (Tucson), 364
Fort McDowell Casino (Fountain Hills), 162
Fort Verde State Historic Park, 184
Fort Whipple Museum (Prescott), 173–174
Fossil Creek Road, 309
Fountain Hills fountain (near Scottsdale), 134
Four Corners Monument Navajo Tribal Park, 297–298
The Four Corners Region, 21–22, 268–305
Four-wheel tours. *See* Jeep, four-wheel-drive and off-road tours
Fox Theatre (Tucson), 388–389
Frommers.com, 43
Frontier Street (Wickenburg), 168
Frontier Town (Cave Creek), 132

G

Gadsden-Pacific Division Toy Train Operating Museum (Tucson), 368
Gallery West (Tucson), 380, 384
Garcia Little Red Schoolhouse (Wickenburg), 168
Garden Canyon, 409
Gaslight Theatre (Tucson), 389–390
Gasoline, 60
Gay and lesbian travelers, 40–41
  Phoenix area, 158–159
  Tucson, 388
Ghost towns, 266–267
Giant Logs self-guided trail, 281
Gila Box Riparian National Conservation Area, 429
Gilbert, restaurants, 118
Gilbert Ortega Gallery & Museum (Phoenix), 153
Glen Canyon Dam, 299
Glen Canyon National Recreation Area, 48, 299–300
Glendale, 82
Glider rides, 135
Globe, 163
Gold Canyon Golf Resort (near Phoenix), 10, 100–101, 138
Goldfield Ghost Town, 13, 132, 162
Goldfield Superstition Museum, 132
Gold King Mine (Jerome), 181
Gold Nugget Art Gallery (Wickenburg), 168
Gold Rush Days (Wickenburg), 167
Golf, 8, 50–52
  best courses, 10–11
  Bisbee, 419
  Bullhead City and Laughlin, Nevada, 436
  Gold Canyon, 164
  Lake Havasu City, 441
  Lake Powell, 303
  Phoenix area, 137–140, 144, 151
  Pinetop-Lakeside, 311
  Prescott, 176
  Sedona, 198–199
  Tubac, 397
  Tucson, 374–375, 378
  Wickenburg, 170–171
  Yuma, 448
Golf n' Stuff (Tucson), 368
Goodyear Balloon & Air Spectacular (Litchfield Park), 28
Goulding's Museum & Trading Post (Monument Valley), 296
Grady Gammage Auditorium (Tempe), 159
Graham, Mount, 428

Grand Canyon, 21, 212–244
East Rim, 241
North Rim, 239–244
South Rim, 213–238
accessibility, 217–218
accommodations, 232–237
activities outside the canyon, 232
backpacking, 227–228
climate, 218
Desert View Drive, 219–222
fees, 218
getting around, 217
Grand Canyon Village and vicinity, 222–223
Hermit Road, 223–225
hiking, 225–227
interpretive programs, 230
organized tours, 224, 228–230
orientation, 216
parking, 218–219
rafting, 231–232
restaurants, 237–238
safety, 219
traveling to, 214, 216
visitor information, 216
special-interest trips, 47
Grand Canyon Caverns, 261, 265
Grand Canyon Field Institute, 230
Grand Canyon Music Festival, 28, 218
Grand Canyon National Park, 3
Grand Canyon-Parashant National Monument, 242
Grand Canyon Railway, 12, 229, 256
Grand Canyon Village, 222–223
Grand Canyon West, 258–261
Grand Falls, 249
Grandview Point, 220, 222
Grandview Trail, 227
Granite Dells, 175
Granite Mountain Wilderness, 175
Grasshopper Point, 194
Greer, 313–316
Greyhound racing, 145, 378
Guest ranches (dude ranches), 13, 14
Tucson, 341–342
Wickenburg, 171–172
Willcox area, 427–428
Guild Indian Fair and Market (Phoenix), 124

Hackberry Store & Old Route 66 Visitor Center, 265
Hall of Flame Firefighting Museum (Phoenix), 129–130
Hannagan Meadows, 319
Hano, 274
Hantavirus, 38
Harvey, Fred, and the Harvey Girls, 290
Hassayampa River Preserve, 170
Havasu, Lake, 437–443
Havasu Canyon, 258–262
Havasu National Wildlife Refuge, 436–437
Havasupai tribe, 259, 260
Hawley Lake, 311
Health concerns, 37–39
Health insurance, 37
Heard Museum (Phoenix), 13, 124–125, 153
Heard Museum Guild Indian Fair and Market (Phoenix), 26–27
Heard Museum North (Scottsdale), 2, 124–125
Heard Museum West (Surprise), 125
Heart of Rocks Trail, 9, 424
Helicopter tours. *See* Scenic flights
Helldorado (Tombstone), 415
Helldorado Days (Tombstone), 28
Herberger Theater Center (Phoenix), 160, 161
Hereford, 410, 412–413
Hermit Road (Grand Canyon), 223–225
Hermit's Rest, 225
Hermit Trail, 226–227
Hieroglyphic Canyon, 2, 121, 124
Highline Trail, 308
Hikes and nature walks, 8, 48, 52–53. *See also specific trails*
best, 8–9
Blue Range Primitive Area, 319–320
Canyon de Chelly, 291
de Anza Trail, 397
Flagstaff, 245–246
Gila Box Riparian National Conservation Area, 429
Grand Canyon
North Rim, 240
South Rim, 225–227
Hannagan Meadows, 319
Havasu Canyon, 259, 260
Huachuca Mountains west of Sierra Vista, 412
Mogollon Rim, 308
Oak Creek Canyon, 194
Petrified Forest, 281
Phoenix area, 140
Prescott area, 175
Sedona, 197
Tucson area, 375–376
Historic Heritage Square (Phoenix), 128
Historic Route 66 Museum (Kingman), 265, 266
Historic Yuma Theatre, 449
History of Arizona, 454–458
Hockey, 145
Holbrook, 281, 283–284
Holidays, 60
Holy Trinity Monastery (St. David), 411
Homolovi Ruins State Park, 272
Hoover Dam, 432
Hopi Cultural Center (Second Mesa), 275
Hopi Festival of Arts and Culture (Flagstaff), 28
Hopi House Gift Store and Art Gallery (Grand Canyon Village), 223
Hopi Indians, 220, 223, 268–269, 273–280
Hopi Point, 224
Hopi Reservation (Hopiland), 273–280
accommodations, 277, 280
exploring, 275–276
shopping, 276–280
villages, 274–275
Hopkins, Mount, 399
Horseback riding, 8, 53
Canyon de Chelly, 291
Fort Huachuca, 412
Grand Canyon North Rim, 240
Monument Valley Navajo Tribal Park, 295
Oatman, 266
Patagonia/Sonoita area, 404
Phoenix area, 132, 142
Pinetop-Lakeside, 310
Prescott area, 175
Sedona, 198
Tombstone, 416
Tonto Natural Bridge State Park, 308
Tucson area, 376–377
Horse racing, 145, 378
Horseshoe Lake, 311

Hot-air ballooning, 28, 53–54, 135, 197, 377
Hotel Congress (Tucson), 372–373
Hotevilla, 275
Houseboats, 13, 54, 304, 434
House Rock Ranch, 241
Huachuca Mountains, 407, 409, 410, 412
Hualapai Mountain Park, 266
Hubbell Trading Post National Historic Site, 284–286
Huhugam Heritage Center (Chandler), 125
Hummingbirds, 374, 410
Humphreys Peak Trail, 246
Hunt's Tomb (Phoenix), 131

Immigration and customs clearance, 31–32
The Immortal Gunfighters (Chloride), 267
Imperial National Wildlife Refuge, 447
Independence Day, 28
Insurance, 36–37
The International Wildlife Museum (Tucson), 366
Internet access, 45
Invisible Theatre (Tucson), 389
Itineraries, suggested, 64–75

Jacques Marsh, 311
Jail Trail, 186
Jail Tree (Wickenburg), 168
Jane Hamilton Fine Art (Tucson), 380
Jasper Forest Overlook, 282
Jeep, four-wheel-drive and off-road tours
- Canyon de Chelly, 290
- Grand Canyon, 230
- Lake Havasu, 439
- Phoenix area, 136
- Sedona, 190, 196
- Tucson, 373
- Wickenburg, 170

Jerome, 180–183
Jerome Historical Society's Mine Museum, 181
Jerome State Historic Park, 181
Jewelry. *See also* Native Americans, arts, crafts and jewelry
- Bisbee, 418–419
- Jerome, 182
- Phoenix area, 151
- Sedona, 200
- Tucson, 383

John C. Hill Antique Indian Art (Scottsdale), 153
John Wesley Powell Memorial Museum (Page), 303–304
Juan Bautista de Anza National Historic Trail, 397
Julius Kruttschnidt House (Tucson), 370
Junction Overlook, 289

Kachina Mineral Springs Spa (near Safford), 429
Kachinas (kachina dolls), 124, 153, 199, 223, 246, 248, 273, 276–278, 283, 384, 419, 423
Kaibab National Forest, 48–49, 230, 237
- campgrounds, 244, 258

Kartchner Caverns State Park, 408
Kayaking, 49, 52, 175, 301–302, 433, 440
Keet Seel, 293
Kendrick Park Watchable Wildlife Trail, 246
Kerr Cultural Center (Scottsdale), 160
Kierland Commons (Scottsdale), 152
Kierland Golf Club (Scottsdale), 139
Kingman, 262–267
Kinishba Ruins, 312
Kitt Peak National Observatory, 399
Kofa National Wildlife Refuge, 444
Kolb Studio (Grand Canyon), 223
Kykotsmovi, 275

La Casa Cordova (Tucson), 369
La Fiesta de los Vaqueros (Tucson), 26
Lake Havasu City, 438, 439, 441–443
Lake Havasu State Park, 439, 442
Lake Mead National Recreation Area, 432–435
Lake Powell, 298–305
La Placita Village (Tucson), 370
La Posada (Winslow), 272
Las Cienegas National Conservation Area, 403
Laughlin, Nevada, 435–437
Ledge Ruin Overlook, 288
Lees Ferry, 240–241
Legacy Golf Resort (Phoenix), 139
Legal aid, 60
Lemmon, Mount, 10
Lighthouses, Lake Havasu, 441
Linda Vista Trail, 376
Lipan Point, 220
Lisa Sette Gallery (Scottsdale), 148
Little House Museum (between Eagar and Greer), 317
Little Painted Desert, 272
Llama hikes, 308
London Bridge (Lake Havasu City), 438–439
London Bridge Beach (Lake Havasu City), 439
London Bridge Gondola (Lake Havasu City), 440
Lookout Studio (Grand Canyon), 223
Lost and found, 60–61
Lost Dutchman State Park, 162
Lost-luggage insurance, 37
Lowell Observatory (Flagstaff), 248
Luna Lake, 319
Lyman Lake State Park, 317–318

McCormick-Stillman Railroad Park (Scottsdale), 134–135
McDowell Sonoran Preserve (Scottsdale), 2, 141
Madera Canyon National Forest Recreation Area, 11, 374
Mail, 61
Maricopa Point, 223
Mark Sublette Medicine Man Gallery (Tucson), 380–381, 384
Massacre Cave Overlook, 289
Mather Point, 222
Mead, Lake, 432
Medical insurance, 37
Medical requirements for entry, 24
Medicine Man Gallery Foothills (Tucson), 380
Mesa Amphitheater, 160
Mesa and the East Valley, 82. *See also* Phoenix area
- accommodations, 100–102
- restaurants, 117–118

Mesa Arts Center, 160
Mesa Contemporary Arts, 126

Mesa Golfland Sunsplash, 142
Mesa Southwest Museum, 129
Mescal (Benson), 408
Meteor Crater (near Winslow), 271
Mining and mines
- Arizona Mining & Mineral Museum (Phoenix), 129
- ASARCO Mineral Discovery Center (Sahuarita), 373
- Bisbee, 418
- Castle Dome City Mines Museum, 445
- Clifton and Morenci, 319
- ghost towns (near Kingman), 266
- Jerome, 181
- Kingman area, 263
- Wickenburg, 168, 170

Mishongnovi, 274
Mission San Xavier del Bac (Tucson), 361
Mittry Lake Wildlife Area (Yuma), 448
Moenkopi, 275
Mogollon Rim, 193, 306–307
Mogollon Rim Interpretive Trail, 310
Mohave, Lake, 430, 432–436
Mohave Museum of History and Arts (Kingman), 263
Mohave Point, 224
Money matters, 34–36
Montezuma Castle National Monument, 15, 184–185
Montezuma Well, 185
Monument Valley Navajo Tribal Park, 10, 14, 293–298
Moran Point, 220
Morenci, 319
Mother and Child Rock, 191
Mountain biking. *See* Biking and mountain biking
Mount Graham International Observatory (near Safford), 399
Mount Lemmon Recreation Area, 376
Movies on the Square (Flagstaff), 255
Muheim Heritage House (Bisbee), 418
Mule rides, Grand Canyon, 228–229
Muleshoe Ranch Cooperative Management Area, 426
Mummy Cave Overlook, 288
Murray Springs Clovis Site, 411
Museum Club (Flagstaff), 255
Museum of Northern Arizona (Flagstaff), 14, 248
Museum of Rim Country Archaeology (Payson), 308
Museums, best, 13–14
My Sister's Closet (Phoenix), 153
Mystery Castle (Phoenix), 130
Mystic Trail, 197

N

National Geographic Visitor Center (Tusayan), 232
Native Americans (Indians). *See also* Cliff dwellings; Rock art; Ruins and archaelogical sites; *And specific tribes, reservations, and sights*
- arts, crafts and jewelry
  - Bisbee, 419
  - Canyon de Chelly, 291
  - Flagstaff, 246
  - Holbrook, 283
  - Hopi Reservation, 276–277
  - near Page, 303
  - Phoenix area, 124–126, 152–153
  - Prescott, 173, 176
  - primer on, 278–279
  - Sedona, 199, 200
  - Tuba City, 277–279
  - Tucson, 380, 384
  - Window Rock, 285–286
- Flagstaff, 248
- Phoenix area attractions, 124–126, 128
- Prescott, 174
- Roper Lake State Park, 429
- Santa Cruz Valley, 395
- Sedona, 196
- special events and festivals, 26–29
- suggested itinerary, 71–74
- tours, 48

Native Trails (Scottsdale), 125
Natural environment, best places to commune with, 5
Navajo Arts and Crafts Enterprise (Window Rock), 286
Navajo Bridge, 240
Navajo Festival of Arts and Culture (Flagstaff), 28
Navajo Indian Reservation (Navajo Nation), 269–270. *See also* Antelope Canyon; Canyon de Chelly National Monument; Monument Valley Navajo Tribal Park; Window Rock
Navajo Indians, 3, 270. *See also* Native Americans; Navajo Indian Reservation; *and specific sights and attractions*
- Canyon de Chelly National Monument, 287–291
- dancing, in Tusayan, 232
- silver work, 278

Navajo Museum, Library & Visitor's Center (Window Rock), 285
Navajo National Monument, 15, 292–293
Navajo Nation Fair (Window Rock), 28, 284
Navajo Nation Zoo & Botanical Park (Window Rock), 285
Navajo Point, 220
Navajo rugs, 152, 153, 199, 279, 286, 408
Navajo Village Heritage Center (near Page), 303
Newspaper Rock, 282
Newspapers and magazines, 61
Nogales, 400–402
Northern Arizona, 21
- en route to, 165

North Kaibab Trail, 240
North Mountain Park (Phoenix), 141
North Scottsdale. *See also* Phoenix area
- accommodations, 93–95
- restaurants, 110–111

O

Oak Creek Canyon, 10, 193–194
Oak Creek Canyon Vista, 193
Oak Creek Vineyards and Winery (Page Springs), 2, 195
Oatman, 265, 266
Observatories. *See* Stargazing
Ocotillo Golf Club (Chandler), 139
O.K. Corral (Tombstone), 12–13, 414
O.K. Street (Bisbee), 418
Old Jerome High School, 182
Old Territorial Shop (Scottsdale), 153
Old Town Artisans (Tucson), 369, 381
Old Trails Highway, 257
Old Trails Museum (Winslow), 272
Old Tucson Studios, 12, 14, 361

Old West Museum (Holbrook), 283
Omni Tucson National Golf Resort and Spa, 375
O'odham Tash (Casa Grande), 26
Oraibi, 274–275, 277
Organ Pipe Cactus National Monument, 5, 392
Orphan Mine (Grand Canyon), 224
The Orpheum Theater (Flagstaff), 255
Orpheum Theatre (Phoenix), 159
Ostrich Festival (Chandler), 27
Out of Africa Wildlife Park, 185
Overland Gallery of Fine Art (Scottsdale), 148
Owl's Club Mansion (Tucson), 370

P

Package tours, 45–46
Page, 298–300, 302–305
Page Springs Vineyards & Cellars, 2, 195
Painted Desert, 280–283
Painted Rocks Petroglyph Site, 450
Palatki Heritage Site, 191–192
Papago Park (Phoenix), 140
Parada del Sol Parade and Rodeo (Scottsdale), 27
Paria Canyon, 303
Parker Dam, 443
Passports, 23–24, 61–62
Patagonia, 11, 402–407
Patagonia Lake State Park, 403–404
Patagonia–Sonoita Creek Preserve, 403
Paton's Birder's Haven (Patagonia), 403
Payson, 306–310
Peavine Trail, 175
Penske Racing Museum (Scottsdale), 130
Peralta Trail, 8–9, 141
Petrified Forest National Park, 280–283
Petroglyphs. *See* Rock art
Petrol, 60
Philabaum Contemporary Art Glass (Tucson), 381
Phippen Museum (Prescott), 14, 174
Phippen Western Art Show and Sale (Prescott), 27
Phoenician Golf Club, 138
Phoenix area, 21, 76–165. *See also* Carefree; Cave Creek; Glendale; Mesa; North Phoenix; Paradise Valley; Scottsdale; South Phoenix; Tempe
- accommodations, 85–102
- airport. *See* Sky Harbor International Airport
- arriving in, 77
- central Phoenix and the Camelback Corridor (Biltmore District), 82
  - accommodations, 95–97
  - restaurants, 111–114
- doctors and dentists, 84
- downtown Phoenix, 79, 82
  - accommodations, 99–100
  - restaurants, 114–116
- finding an address in, 79
- getting around, 83–84
- Internet access, 85
- layout of, 78–79
- neighborhoods, 79, 82
- newspapers and magazines, 85
- nightlife, 154–162
- organized tours and excursions, 135–136
- outdoor pursuits, 136–143
- performing arts, 159–162
- post offices, 85
- restaurants, 102–121
- safety, 85
- shopping, 147–154
- sights and attractions, 121–136
- spas, 145–147
- spectator sports, 143–145
- street maps, 79
- taxes, 85
- visitor information, 78
- weather, 25, 85
- what's new in, 1–2

Phoenix Art Museum, 2, 13, 126–127
Phoenix Greyhound Park, 145
Phoenix International Raceway, 143
Phoenix Museum of History, 128
Phoenix Symphony, 161
Phoenix Theatre, 161–162
Phoenix Waterworld Safari, 142
Phoenix Zoo, 133
Picacho Peak State Park, 9, 164–165, 377
Pictographs. *See* Rock art
Piestewa Peak (Squaw Peak), 77, 140
Pima Air & Space Museum (Tucson), 366
Pima Canyon Trail, 376
Pima County Courthouse (Tucson), 370
Pima Point, 225
Pine, 309
Pine-Strawberry Museum, 309
Pinetop-Lakeside, 310–313
Pinnacle Peak Park (Phoenix), 141
Pipe Spring National Monument, 241–242
Plaza Palomino (Tucson), 383
Point Imperial, 240
Polacca, 274
Pole Knoll trail system, 314
Police, 62
Powell, John Wesley, 213–214, 224
Powell, Lake, 298–305
Powell Point, 224
Prescott, 172–180
Prescott Brewing Company, 180
Prescott Frontier Days/World's Oldest Rodeo, 27
Prescott National Forest, 174
Presidio Santa Cruz de Terrenate, 411
Primitive Arts Gallery (Tucson), 380
Pueblo Grande Museum and Archaeological Park (Phoenix), 125–126
Pueblo Grande Museum Indian Market (Phoenix), 29, 125
Puerco Pueblo, 282

Q

Quartzsite, 444
Quartzsite Pow Wow, 444

R

Rafting and float trips, 302, 433. *See also* Whitewater rafting
Rainbow Bridge National Monument, 300
Rainbow Forest Museum, 281
Rainbow Lake, 311
Ramsey Canyon Preserve, 11, 410
Rancho Mañana Golf Club (Cave Creek), 139
Rattlesnakes, 38
Rawhide at Wild Horse Pass (Phoenix), 13, 132–133
Red Mountain., 246
Red-rock country, 189–193

Red Rock Healing Arts Center (Sedona), 195
Red Rock State Park, 193
Regions of Arizona, 21–22
Reid Park Zoo (Tucson), 367
Reneé Cushman Art Collection (Springerville), 317
Respiratory illnesses, 38–39
Restaurants, best, 19–20
Restrooms, 63
Revive (Phoenix), 146
Rex Allen Arizona Cowboy Museum (Willcox), 422–423
Rillito Park Race Track (Tucson), 378
Rillito River Park path (Tucson), 373
Rim Country Museum (Payson), 308
Rim Trail (Grand Canyon), 226
Rimview Trail, 303
Riordan Mansion State Historic Park (Flagstaff), 248–249
Riva Yares Gallery (Scottsdale), 148
River Reservoir, 314
River Trading Post (Scottsdale), 153
River Trail, 303
Roberts Gallery (Carefree), 148
Robson's Arizona Mining World (Wickenburg), 168, 170
Rock art (petroglyphs and pictographs), 2, 242, 267, 275, 295
- Deer Valley Rock Art Center, 124
- Garden Canyon, 409
- Homolovi Ruins State Park, 272
- Painted Rocks Petroglyph Site, 450
- Petrified Forest National Park, 282
- Rock Art Ranch (near Holbrook), 283
- V Bar V Heritage Site, 193

Rock Art Ranch, 283
Rodeos, 14, 26–28
- Navajo Reservation, 284
- Payson, 307
- Phoenix area, 145
- Prescott, 173
- Tucson Rodeo Parade Museum, 365

Rolling Hills Golf Course (Tempe), 139–140
Romero House (Tucson), 369
Romero Pools, 376
Rooster Rock (Coffee Pot Rock), 191
Roper Lake State Park, 429
Rose Tree Inn Museum (Tombstone), 415
Route 66, 246, 256–257, 263–265, 272
Route 66 Fun Run (Kingman area), 27, 265
Roy P. Drachman Agua Caliente Park (Tucson), 374
Ruby, 397
Ruby Road, 397
Ruins and archaelogical sites. ***See also*** **Cliff dwellings;** ***and specific sites***
- Agua Fria National Monument, 165
- Besh-Ba-Gowah Archaeological Park, 163
- best places to see, 15
- Canyon de Chelly, 288–289
- Casa Grande Ruins National Monument, 164
- Casa Malpais Visitor Center and Museum (Springerville), 317
- Elden Pueblo, 251
- Homolovi Ruins State Park, 272
- Kinishba Ruins, 312
- Navajo National Monument, 293
- Palatki Heritage Site, 191–192
- Shoofly Village, 308
- tours, 47–48
- Tuzigoot National Monument, 185–186
- Wupatki National Monument, 250

S

Sabino Canyon Recreation Area (Tucson), 360, 373, 374, 376, 377
Safety, 39
Saguaro National Park, 5, 360–361, 375, 377
Sahuarita, 396
Saihati Camel Farm (Yuma), 447
St. Augustine Cathedral (Tucson), 372
St. Michaels Historical Museum (Window Rock), 285
St. Philip's Plaza (Tucson), 383
San Bernardino National Wildlife Refuge, 425
Sanders Galleries (Tucson), 380
San Pedro House, 411
San Pedro Riparian National Conservation Area, 11–12, 411
San Pedro Valley, 407–413
Santa Cruz River Park path (Tucson), 373
Santa Fe train station (Wickenburg), 167
Scenic drives
- best, 10
- Catalina Highway, 357
- Fossil Creek Road, 309
- Mogollon Rim, 308–309
- Monument Valley, 294
- Pinal Pioneer Parkway, 164
- Ruby Road, 397

Scenic flights
- Glen Canyon, 300
- Grand Canyon, 230
- Grand Canyon West, 260
- Phoenix area, 136
- Sedona, 196

Schnebly Hill Road, 190
Schoolhouse Museum and Store (Fairbank), 411
Scorpions, 38
Scottsdale, 82. ***See also*** **North Scottsdale; Phoenix area**
- accommodations, 88–93
- restaurants, 103–110

Scottsdale Arabian Horse Show, 26
Scottsdale Arts Festival, 27
Scottsdale Center for the Arts, 160
Scottsdale Desert Stages Theatre, 162
Scottsdale Fashion Square, 152
Scottsdale Mall, 125, 126
Scottsdale Museum of Contemporary Art, 13, 127
Scottsdale Waterfront, 151
Scuba diving, Lake Powell, 303
Sears-Kay Ruins (near Cave Creek), 121
Seasons, 24–25
Sedona, 2–3, 187–211
- accommodations, 200–207
- exploring, 189–197
- getting around, 188
- nightlife, 211
- organized tours, 195–197
- outdoor pursuits, 197–199
- restaurants, 207–211
- shopping, 199–200
- special events, 188–189
- traveling to, 188
- visitor information, 188

Sedona Arts Center, 194

Sedona Arts Festival, 28
Sedona Heritage Museum, 194
Sedona International Film Festival, 26, 188–189
Sedona Jazz on the Rocks, 28, 189
Seligman, 257, 265
Senior travel, 41
Sentinel Peak (A Mountain), 362
Settlers West Galleries (Tucson), 380
Seven Falls Trail, 9, 376
Sharlot Hall Museum (Prescott), 174
Shemer Art Center and Museum (Phoenix), 127
Shipping your luggage, 32
Shoofly Village, 308
The Shops Gainey Village (Scottsdale), 152
Show Low Lake, 311
Show Up Now Pass (Phoenix), 121
Shrine of St. Joseph of the Mountains (Yarnell), 172
Shungopavi, 274
Sichomovi, 274
Sidewalk Egg-Frying Challenge (Oatman), 28
Sierra Vista, 407–413
Signal Hill (Tucson), 360
Sinagua people, 184, 191
Elden Pueblo, 251
Tuzigoot National Monument, 185
Walnut Canyon National Monument, 250
Wupatki National Monument, 250
Singing Wind Bookshop (Benson), 407
Sipaulovi, 274
Sipe White Mountain Wildlife Area, 318
Skiing, 54, 245, 314, 377
Sky Harbor International Airport (Phoenix), 77, 78
accommodations near, 99–102
restaurants near, 114–116
SkyWalk (Grand Canyon West), 3, 260–261
Slaughter Ranch (near Douglas), 425
Slaughter Ranch Museum (near Douglas), 425
Slide Rock State Park, 193–194
Sliding House Overlook, 289
Smithsonian Institution Fred Lawrence Whipple Observatory (Mount Hopkins), 399
The Smoki Museum (Prescott), 174
Snake Dance, 274, 276
Snake Gulch, 242
Snow Cap Drive-In (Seligman), 265
Sonoita, 402–407
Sonoita Creek State Natural Area, 404
Sosa-Carillo-Frémont House Museum (Tucson), 364, 372
Southeastern Arizona, suggested itinerary, 70–71
Southeastern Arizona Bird Observatory (near Bisbee), 409
Southern Arizona, 22, 391–429
Southern Arizona Transportation Museum (Tucson), 364–365, 373
Southern Pacific Willcox Train Depot, 422
South Kaibab Trail, 9, 226
South Mountain Park/Preserve, 140
South Phoenix. *See also* Phoenix area
accommodations, 99–100
restaurants, 114–116
Southwest Wings Birding and Nature Festival (Bisbee), 28
Southwest Wings Birding Festival (Sierra Vista), 409
Spas
Phoenix area, 145–147
near Safford, 429
Sedona, 194–195
Tucson, 340–341, 378–379
Special events and festivals, 25–29
Special-interest trips, 47–48
Spencer Trail, 303
Spider Rock Overlook, 289–290
Spirit Mountain Ranch (near Flagstaff), 246
Springerville, 316–318
Springerville Volcanic Field, 316
Squaw Peak (Piestewa Peak), 77, 140
Stagebrush Theatre (Scottsdale), 162
Stargazing (observatories), 12, 399
Eastern Arizona College's Discovery Park Campus (near Safford), 429
Flandrau Science Center & Planetarium (Tucson), 366
Lowell Observatory (Flagstaff), 248
Mount Graham, 428
Sedona, 196
Stellar Vision Astronomy Shop (Tucson), 382
Steele Indian School Park (Phoenix), 133
Steinfeld House (Tucson), 370
Stevens House (Tucson), 370
Stonecreek Golf Club (near Scottsdale), 139
Strawberry, 309
Strawberry Schoolhouse, 309
Sunrise Park Resort, 314
Sunset Crater Volcano National Monument, 249
Sustainable tourism/ecotourism, 42–43
Sweetwater Wetland (Tucson), 374
Swimming
Lake Havasu City, 439
Lake Mead National Recreation Area, 433
Lake Powell, 302–303
Sycamore Creek, 186
Symphony Hall (Phoenix), 159

Taliesin West (Scottsdale), 130–131
Tanner Trail, 227
Taxes, 62
The Teepees, 282
Telegraph and telex services, 62
Telephones, 44
Tempe, 82. *See also* Phoenix area
accommodations, 100–102
restaurants, 117–118
Tempe Town Lake, 133
Temple of Music and Art (Tucson), 372, 388
Tennis, 8, 54, 142, 377
Territorial Days (Prescott), 173
Texas Canyon, 423
Theodore Roosevelt Dam., 163
Therapy on the Rocks (Sedona), 194–195
Three Golden Chiefs, 191
Thumb Butte, 174–175
Time zones, 62
Tipping, 62–63
Titan Missile Museum (Tucson), 366–367
Tlaquepaque (Sedona), 199
Tohono Chul Museum Shops (Tucson), 382–383
Tohono Chul Park (Tucson), 5, 367
Toilets, 63

Tombstone, 14, 414–417
Tombstone Courthouse State Park, 415–416
Tombstone Epitaph Museum, 416
Tombstone's Historama, 414–415
Tombstone Western Heritage Museum, 416
Tonto National Monument, 15, 163
Tonto Natural Bridge State Park, 307–308
Topock Gorge, 440
Tostitos Fiesta Bowl Football Classic (Glendale), 25
Tournament Players Club (TPC) of Scottsdale, 138
Trail Dust Town (Tucson), 368
Trailview Overlook, 223
Train travel and railways, 33–34, 55–56
- Grand Canyon Railway, 12, 229, 256
- McCormick-Stillman Railroad Park (Scottsdale), 134–135
- Southern Pacific Willcox Train Depot, 422
- Verde Canyon Railroad, 183–184

Traveler's checks, 35–36
Travel insurance, 36–37
T Rex Museum (Tucson), 368
Trip-cancellation insurance, 36–37
Troon North Golf Club (Scottsdale), 138
Tsegi Overlook, 289
Tubac, 394–400
Tubac Center of the Arts, 395
Tubac Festival of the Arts, 26
Tuba City, 276–280
Tuba City Trading Post, 277
Tubac Presidio State Historic Park, 395
Tubing, 143
Tucson, 22, 321–390
- accommodations, 3, 329–342
- arriving in, 322–323
- emergencies, 328
- en route to, 164–165
- finding an address in, 323
- gay and lesbian bars and clubs, 388
- getting around, 327–328
- guest ranches, 341–342
- history of, 321
- for kids, 367–368
- layout of, 323
- neighborhoods, 326
- nightlife, 385–390
- organized tours, 373
- outdoor pursuits, 373–377
- parks, gardens and zoos, 367
- performing arts, 388–390
- restaurants, 3–4, 342–355
- safety, 329
- shopping, 379–385
- sights and attractions, 356–373
- spas, 340–341, 378–379
- spectator sports, 377–378
- street maps, 323, 326
- taxes, 329
- visitor information, 323
- walking tour, 368–373
- what's new in, 3–4

Tucson Botanical Gardens, 367
Tucson Children's Museum, 368
Tucson Convention Center (TCC), 372
- Music Hall, 388

Tucson Gem and Mineral Show, 26
Tucson Greyhound Park, 378
Tucson International Mariachi Conference, 27
Tucson Mall, 383
Tucson Mountain Park, 376
Tucson Museum of Art & Historic Block, 362–363, 369
Tucson Museum of Art Shop, 381
Tucson Presidio, 369
Tucson Rodeo Parade Museum, 365
Tucson Symphony Orchestra, 389
Tumacácori National Historical Park, 395
Tunnel Overlook, 289
Tunnel Reservoir, 314
Turf Paradise (Phoenix), 145
Tusayan
- accommodations, 235–236
- activities, 232
- restaurants, 238

Tusayan Museum (Grand Canyon), 220
Tuzigoot National Monument, 185
Twin Nuns, 191

UN Center/UNICEF (Tucson), 383
University of Arizona Centennial Hall (Tucson), 388
University of Arizona College of Fine Arts School of Music and Dance (Tucson), 389
The University of Arizona Museum of Art (Tucson), 363
University of Arizona Museum of Art (Tucson), 14
U.S. Army Military Intelligence Museum (Fort Huachuca), 409

Valley fever, 38–39
V Bar V Heritage Site, 193
Vegetarian travel, 42
Ventana Canyon Trail, 376
Verde Canyon Railroad, 183–184
The Verde Valley, 183–187
Verkamps Curios (Grand Canyon Village), 223
Vermilion Cliffs, 241
Visas, 23–24, 63
Visitor information, 22–23
Voice over Internet protocol (VoIP), 44–45
Vortexes, Sedona, 12, 190
Vultee Arch Trail, 197
The Vulture Mine (Wickenburg), 170

Waila Festival (Tucson), 27
Wa:k Pow Wow (Tucson), 27
Walhalla Overlook, 240
Walnut Canyon National Monument, 250
Walpi, 274, 275
Walpi Village, 12
Waterfall Trail, 141
Water parks, Phoenix area, 142
Watersports. *See also specific sports*
- Lake Havasu, 439–440
- Lake Powell, 301–302

Watson Lake, 175
Watson Lake Park, 175
Watson Woods Riparian Preserve, 175
We-Ko-Pa Golf Club (Fort McDowell), 138–139
Welcome Back Buzzards (Superior), 27
Wells Fargo History Museum (Phoenix), 128
Western Arizona, 22, 430–450

Western culture and history. *See also specific museums and other attractions*
- best places to discover, 14
- Bisbee, 418
- Fort Verde State Historic Park, 184
- ghost towns, 266–267
- Holbrook, 283
- Imperial National Wildlife Refuge, 447
- Phoenix area, 128
  - Wild West theme towns, 131–133
- Prescott, 173–174, 179–180
- Slaughter Ranch Museum (near Douglas), 425
- special events and festivals, 27–29
- Tombstone, 414–416
- Tucson, 363–365
- Wickenburg, 168, 170
- Willcox, 422–423
- Yuma, 446

Western wear and gear, 153–154, 384–385, 401
West Fork of Oak Creek, 9, 194
West Fork Trail (near Greer), 314
WestWorld of Scottsdale, 145
Whiskey Row (Prescott), 179
White House Overlook, 289
White House Ruins Trail, 9, 289
White Mountains Trail system, 310
White Tank Mountain Regional Park (Waddell), 141
Whitewater Draw Wildlife Area, 425
White-water rafting, 54–55
- Grand Canyon, 8, 231–232, 261
- Phoenix area, 142–143
- Pinetop-Lakeside, 311

Wickenburg, 167–172
The Wigwam Golf Resort & Spa (near Phoenix), 10, 102, 137
Wigwam Motel (Holbrook), 264
Wildcat Trail, 9, 295
Wilde Meyer Gallery (Scottsdale), 149
Wildflowers, 124, 164, 377
Wildlife. *See also* **Bird-watching; Zoos**
- Aravaipa Canyon Wilderness, 428–429
- Buenos Aires National Wildlife Refuge, 11, 396–397
- Eagle Trail, 319–320
- The International Wildlife Museum (Tucson), 366
- Kendrick Park Watchable Wildlife Trail, 246
- Kofa National Wildlife Refuge, 444
- Lake Mead National Recreation Area, 434
- Out of Africa Wildlife Park, 185
- Ramsey Canyon Preserve, 410
- safety concerns, 38
- Sipe White Mountain Wildlife Area, 318
- Whitewater Draw Wildlife Area, 425

Wild Roses of Chloride, 267
Willcox and environs, 422–428
Williams, 255–258
Williams Valley Winter Recreation Area, 319
Willow Creek Park, 175
Willow Stream–The Spa at the Fairmont Scottsdale Princess, 145–146
Window Rock Tribal Park, 284–286
Wineries and vineyards, 2
- Arizona Vineyards Winery (near Nogales), 401
- Fort Bowie Vineyard (Bowie), 423–424
- Granite Creek Vineyards (Chino Valley), 176
- Patagonia/Sonoita area, 404

Wings over Willcox, 25–26, 425
Winslow, 271–273
Winter, 25
- suggested itinerary, 74–75

Wishing Well (Wickenburg), 168
Woodland Lake, 311
Woodland Lake Park, 310
World Championship Hoop Dance Contest (Phoenix), 26
World's Oldest Continuous Rodeo, 28
Wright, Frank Lloyd, 130–131, 159
Wrigley Mansion (Phoenix), 131
Wukoki Ruin, 250
Wupatki National Monument, 15, 250
Wyatt Earp Days (Tombstone), 27

X Diamond Ranch (between Eagar and Greer), 318

Yaki Point, 222
Yarnell, 172
Yavapai Observation Station, 222
Yavapai Point, 222
Young, 312
Yuma, 445–450
Yuma Art Center/Yuma Fine Arts Museum, 446
Yuma Quartermaster Depot State Historic Park, 446
Yuma Symposium, 446–447
Yuma Territorial Prison State Historic Park, 446

Zócalo (Tucson), 383–384
Zoos
- Navajo Nation Zoo & Botanical Park (Window Rock), 285
- Phoenix, 133
- Tucson, 367

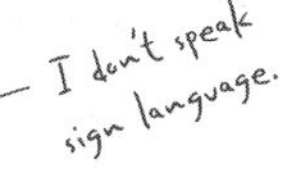

A hotel can close for all kinds of reasons.

Our Guarantee ensures that if your hotel's undergoing construction, we'll let you know in advance. In fact, we cover your entire travel experience. See www.travelocity.com/guarantee for details.

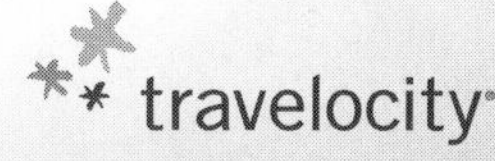

There's a parking lot where my ocean view should be.

À la place de la vue sur l'océan, me voilà avec une vue sur un parking.

Anstatt Meerblick habe ich Sicht auf einen Parkplatz.

Al posto della vista sull'oceano c'è un parcheggio.

No tengo vista al mar porque hay un parque de estacionamiento.

Há um parque de estacionamento onde deveria estar a minha vista do ocea

Ett parkeringsområde har byggts på den plats där min utsikt över oceanen borde vara.

Er ligt een parkeerterrein waar mijn zee-uitzicht zou moeten zijn.

نالك موقف للسيارات مكان ما وجب ان يكون المنظر الخلاب المطل على المحيط .

眼前に広がる紺碧の海・・・じゃない。窓の外は駐車場

停车场的位置应该是我的海景所在。

©2007 Travelocity.com LP CST# 2056372-50.

I'm fluent in pig latin.

Hotel mishaps aren't bound by geography.

Neither is our Guarantee. It covers your entire travel experience, including the price. So if you don't get the ocean view you booked, we'll work with our travel partners to make it right, right away. See www.travelocity.com/guarantee for details.

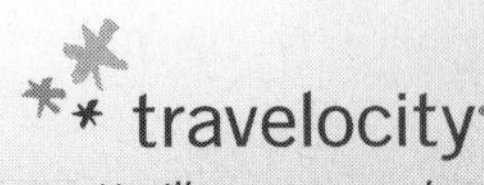